To Canon + Joan
from

Dahn Batchelor.

Life and Times of
DAHN A. BATCHELOR

WHISTLING IN THE FACE OF ROBBERS

Volume I:
The Childhood Years
1933—1944

iUniverse, Inc.
Bloomington

Life and Times of Dahn A. Batchelor
Whistling in the Face of Robbers

Copyright © 2012 by Dahn A. Batchelor

All rights reserved. No part of this book may be used or reproduced by any means, graphic, electronic, or mechanical, including photocopying, recording, taping or by any information storage retrieval system without the written permission of the publisher except in the case of brief quotations embodied in critical articles and reviews.

iUniverse books may be ordered through booksellers or by contacting:

iUniverse
1663 Liberty Drive
Bloomington, IN 47403

www.iuniverse.com
1-800-Authors (1-800-288-4677)

Because of the dynamic nature of the Internet, any web addresses or links contained in this book may have changed since publication and may no longer be valid. The views expressed in this work are solely those of the author and do not necessarily reflect the views of the publisher, and the publisher hereby disclaims any responsibility for them.

Any people depicted in stock imagery provided by Thinkstock are models, and such images are being used for illustrative purposes only.

Certain stock imagery © Thinkstock.

ISBN: 978-1-4620-2815-3 (sc)
ISBN: 978-1-4620-2817-7 (hc)
ISBN: 978-1-4620-2816-0 (e)

Printed in the United States of America

iUniverse rev. date: 01/16/2012

Introduction

I have known Dahn for many years and I am always impressed anew with the tireless manner in which he grasps his talents and stretches them as far as they will go, wasting none. Most of us let our gifts slip through our fingers in self-indulgent pursuits but Dahn has always seemed to recognize his ability, and therefore responsibility, to fully develop his own varied and considerable talents and then use them to help others. His life has indeed been interesting, because he made it so. His autobiography is a generous sharing of his experience, rather than any sort of conceit. It is simply part of his philosophy that no part of a life should go to waste, not even the telling of the tale. And in the end, you will find that Dahn has chosen to present to us in his autobiography, not simply his own story, but the story of the centuries in which he lived. His life has been well lived and his story well told.

Jack Hope *barrister & solicitor*

Preface

It was the Roman satirist, Juvenal (c.60—c.140) who said that 'if you are poor, you will whistle in the face of robbers.' All through my childhood years, I was so poor, I was always whistling. It's ironic when one thinks about it. My great maternal grandfather was one of the richest men in Canada and I could have been born with a golden spoon in my mouth, but because my mother was date raped (resulting in me being conceived at that time) and subsequently ran away from home, and because she was too proud to return to the security of her family, my life as a child began in a two-room shack in a field with no water or electricity, with my crib being the bottom drawer of an old beat-up dresser. It was from these humble beginnings, that I eventually had to make my own way into the world. The only thing I had going for me from my humble beginnings was the gradual development of a creative mind.

A creative life is a meaningful one. However, Bob Sharpe, emeritus professor of philosophy at the University of Wales, has stated: "Actions within a life have meaning—life does not. Most human lives are meaningless in that they have no overriding purpose. It does not follow that they have no value or significance. Indeed, they may achieve more and do less harm than those who are devoted to some grand plan." *unquote*. The vast majority of human beings have no grand plan other than reaching their goals of acquiring their basic needs of warmth, shelter, clothing, food, sex, love and of course, happiness and seeking to acquire those needs in themselves is not wrong.

Life without purpose can be meaningless, of that there is no doubt. The late Princess Leila Pahlavi, formerly of Iran, said it rather well when she said and I quote; "The most important thing is to find yourself, to find a reason for existing, to find a direction in life, a goal." *unquote*. Unfortunately, despite her great wealth and education, she found no purpose in life and sank into bouts of depression and eating disorders and died an early death on June 17, 2001 at the age of 31. Adrienne Clarkson, the Governor General of Canada when appearing before the graduates of the University of Toronto on June 19, 2001 said in her address: "Mediocrity is safe, very easy and therefore, to be avoided at all costs. The purpose of life, it seems to me, is to leave no one and nothing indifferent. It means taking risks, going down paths that are not approved. It means the possibility of loneliness and isolation. It means, in sum, all that is opposite to mediocrity." She later said; "....if the moral stance you take is that you can change things, that you can effect things, that you do not have to accept the immediate and expedient way, (then) only with this stance can you even vaguely hope to make a difference." *unquote*.

I will paraphrase Rick Warren from his book, *The Purpose Driven Life* in which he said in part; "Our unspoken life metaphor influences our lives more than we realize. It determines our expectations, our values, our relationships, our goals and our priorities. For instance, if we think life is a party, our primary value in life will be having fun. If we see it as a race, we will value speed and we will probably be in a hurry all of the time. If we view life as a marathon, we will value endurance. If we see it as a battle or a game, winning will be very important to us." *unquote*

As I grew older, I gradually realized that if life is simply being an on-going party, then it isn't as much fun as living one's life as one grand scavenger hunt.

As I see it, all our lives are influenced by these aspects of life, some more than others. It's simply a human trait in all of us. But with some, it goes to the extreme.

Although the majority of the world's population is satisfied in acquiring basic needs and settling for these needs alone, many of us at some time or another, have had desires of one sort or another to achieve some grand purpose in life beyond acquiring our basic needs. Many of us are or have been devoted to some 'grand plan' and for this reason, we sometimes wish to bring about a change for the better in the status quo that will have a beneficial effect on the lives of others and in the process of doing this, we make a name for ourselves. As fate would have it, many of us have been fortunate enough to have left our works and our names behind us to play a role in and be part of history and in that sense, have a desirable effect on the future of our fellow human beings.

But as the years went by and I grew older, I realized that having an IQ of 122 was no guarantee of success. There are many Phi Beta Kappas who wear the key and that is the only real thing they ever accomplished. Social scientists have established that having a high IQ coupled with a good upbringing and going to the right schools and choosing a lucrative career matters little. There are however five aspects in our lives that brings our goals to the fore. They are fate, competence on-the-job, ambition, hard work and sacrifice.

A great many persons aspiring to leave their mark have had wretched childhoods and often lived mundane lives until some incident in their lives changed their own directions in life. There is no doubt in my mind that fate plays an enormous role in our lives although it would appear that some people seem to have all the luck. But having a lot of luck is not a sign that one should rely upon. During the American Civil War, General George Armstrong Custer had almost a dozen horses shot from under him and he emerged from the war with hardly a scratch. Then along came the battle of the Little Big Horn.

Fate being as fickle as it is, my life could have been mundane and insignificant to anyone other than my immediate family, friends and co-workers but when I saw the opportunities that fate was giving me, I ran along side of fate like a person wanting to hitch a ride on a passing train and I let it take me wherever it was going. I grabbed that proverbial brass ring on that train and it has taken me around the world and into the lives of many millions of my fellow human beings and possibly indirectly, even yours too.

Many people choose to make their mark, beginning in their childhoods and despite their hardships and sometimes handicaps in life; they somehow manage to do just that. My own existence comprises of a wretched childhood, hardship, hard work and sacrifice and admittedly, sometimes laziness to boot and on occasion, outright stupidity on my part but thanks to fate and the other attributes I spoke of, I have been able to etch my mark on the tablets of history.

My story is that of an ordinary human being and like everyone else, I have my own failings, idiosyncrasies, talents, desires and aspirations. But as fate would have it, I just happen to be on some occasions, given the opportunity to do something special at the right places and at the right times and that's what has made my existence have some significance on the lives of so many of my fellow human beings.

If by reading my story, it inspires you to grab that brass ring as the train of fate moves along side of you so that you too can serve your fellow human beings, then my having been here will definitely have an effect on your life also as well as those to whom you would serve and inspire.

There is something I want to add in my preface that I feel should not be left out. I have done something in this book that very few of my fellow autobiographers have done, if any—that is to write about our times. I think it is important that those of us who have written our memoirs, to take on the responsibility of telling our readers what it was really like to live in our era and what occurred when we were alive. If we don't do this, then the writing of history will be left to those who were born long after the events we write about took place and long after those of us who were there during those events, have passed on. There is a responsibility on us to correct any errors being promulgated.

For example, there are some who maintain that the slaughter of almost six million Jews by the Germans is fiction when in reality, it is a fact and the Japanese for many years refused to put in their school text books anything relating to the atrocities committed by the Japanese from 1937 to 1945. Often statements of leaders of nations bring about these errors also.

In September 2001, Tony Blair, the prime minister of Great Britain while visiting President George W. Bush in the White House said to the president; "My father's generation went through the experience of the Second World War when Britain was under attack through the days of the Blitz. There was one nation and one people that stood side by side with us at that time, and that nation was America and that people was the American people, who stand side by side with us now." *unquote.*

The prime minister was historically wrong. In my September 21, 2001 letter to him, I wrote in part; "Anthony Eden, the newly appointed Dominions Secretary wrote the Canadian government on September 6th, 1939; 'It is hoped that Canada would exert her full national effort as in the last war, even to the extent of the eventual dispatch of an expeditionary force.' On the following day, Prime Minister King told the House of Commons; 'We stand for the defence of Canada. We stand for the co-operation of this country at the side of Great Britain and if this house will not support us in that policy, it will have to find some other government to assume the responsibilities of the present.' On the 10th of September 1939, Canada cabled a text of a declaration of war against Germany to Vincent Massey, the Canadian High Commissioner in London. It was Canada that stood side by side with Great Britain during the Blitz. Ninety-seven Canadian airmen flew along side the airmen of the Royal Air Force when fighting the oncoming German bombers and forty-seven of them died in the air battles. The German bombing of England ended in June of 1941. The United States didn't enter the war until five months later when Germany declared war against the United States in December 1941." *unquote*

Without appearing to being too facetious, I am compelled to add that a study in 2002 showed that only three percent of the people in the U.K. could name three continents and only 15 percent could name all seven. If Blair got the same education these people did, then I can readily forgive him for his gaffe. George W. Bush made a similar gaffe while visiting Tokyo on February 18, 2002. He said to the Japanese officials; "My trip to Asia begins here in Japan for an important reason. It begins here because for a century and a half now, America and Japan have formed one of the great and enduring alliances of modern times. From that alliance has come an era of peace in the Pacific." *unquote*

Obviously this man forgot about America's war with Japan between December 1941 and August 1945. There was no era of peace in the Pacific during those years and certainly no great and enduring alliance between the United States and Japan during those war years.

In all likelihood, both Prime Minister Blair and President Bush knew the real truth of their gaffes and were simply stroking, so to speak, their hosts.

Arnold Schwarzenegger, the former governor of California who was born in Austria made a terrible blunder when he addressed the Republican convention in New York in September 2004. He said that he remembered seeing Soviet tanks in the streets in the province of Styria in Austria after the Second World War.

That was not possible because he was born in 1947 and by that time, the Soviets were gone and the British occupied that province. He probably made that statement to forward the old communist threat for Bush's election campaign on the latter's fight against terrorism.

The danger of leaders in various nations making false statements publicly is that many people will believe what these people of power are saying and it is these kinds of mistaken beliefs where the errors in history are formulated.

Another example of a historical error came about on December 10, 2001. An article was published in the *Law Times* in which one of its writers wrote, "….it strikes me that before the two world wars, they interned Japanese people and they interned the German people."

unquote.

In actual fact, neither the Japanese nor the Germans were interned before either of the two great wars in the Twentieth Century had begun. Germans were interned after the First World War began and it was only after the Second World War had begun that the internment of the Germans and Japanese took place.

Here is another example of a historical error. On December 27, 2001, the narrator of a television history program describing the attack on Pearl Harbour, said, "The war with Japan ended with one plane and one bomb." *unquote.*

During that moment in his broadcast, he was speaking of the atomic bomb dropped on Hiroshima from the American bomber, *Anola Gay*. In actual fact, the war with Japan ended after a second plane dropped a second atomic bomb on the Japanese city of Nagasaki three days after the first bomb had been dropped on Hiroshima. It was because of the dropping of the second bomb, that the emperor of Japan, Hirohito was able to convince the diehards in the Japanese military to surrender.

Sometimes, a caption under a picture in a newspaper can be misleading. As an example, in November 2010, the *Toronto Sun* printed a picture of a wooden bench that was used to seat some of the major Nazi war criminals that were tried by the International Military Tribunal at Nuremberg. In the caption under the picture it stated in part; "The dock where Nazis including Herman Goering and Martin Bormann stood to answer charges of crimes against humanity 65 years ago goes on display for the first time today in a special exhibition." *unquote*

Martin Bormann was the private secretary to Hitler and as such, he had considerable influence over Hitler in many ways. The International Military Tribunal at Nuremberg tried Bormann in absentia in October 1946 and sentenced him to death. He actually died on a street in Berlin by ingesting cyanide on May 1st, 1945 while trying to flee Soviet soldiers in Berlin. That being the case, he couldn't have stood in the dock to face his accusers. Anyone reading that caption would believe that he was actually alive in October 1946 and present during the Nuremberg trials—eighteen months after he died.

Atlas Editions, a Quebec firm that prints very detailed atlases that are put in binders with commentaries on the back side of each atlas stated in the atlas titled, *The Great Lakes of Africa* the following erroneous statement with respect to events taking place after colonial days had passed. "Some of these events were widely published as was the massacre of Hutis by Tutsis in 1994." That statement was a terrible blunder and did an injustice to the Tutsis. In actual fact, the assassination of president Habyarimana in April 1994 set off a violent reaction, resulting in the Hutus' conducting mass killings of Tutsis and pro-peace Hutus. Primarily responsible were two Hutu militias associated with political parties: the Interahamwe and the Impuzamugambi. The Hutu Power group known as the Akazu directed the genocide. As many as 800,000 Tutsis and pro-peace Hutus were murdered enmasse by the Hutus. The publishers of Atlas Edition later acknowledged to me that they had made a mistake.

It's scandalous indeed to think that so many Canadians know so little about the Twentieth Century. For example, a study in 2002 showed that only 31 percent of Canadians knew anything about the Dieppe Landing in the shores of Northern France during the Second World War in which over 1000 Canadians needlessly died in the battle. And worse yet, when the late Pierre Trudeau, a long-time prime minister of Canada (1968 - 1976 and 1980 - 1984) died in September 2000, many of the high school students didn't even know who he was and yet most knew who General Armstrong Custer of the Battle of the Big Horn was.

Lord William Rees-Mogg in his book *The Great Reckoning* said in part about what was taught in the United States with respect to history. "Surveys of students suggest that they have little or no grasp of the past. They cannot say in what half century the Civil War was fought much less recognize more subtle patterns in history. What Madonna (female singer) said about her latest boyfriend or girlfriend is much more known than what Winston Churchill (prime minister of Great Britain) said about Hitler during World War II. Madonna has had far more press than Churchill, who is a largely unknown figure for those who came of age in the last two decades of the Twentieth Century. (1980-2000) When world historic figures are forgotten a generation after their death, it is a clear hint that popular culture has discounted history almost to the vanishing point." *unquote*

These examples explain why I feel that we as autobiographers should include in our memoirs, not only the particulars of our own lives, but also the particulars of the local, national and world events that encompassed us and became part of our lives. If we don't do this, then those who come after us after we are all gone; will not have the advantage of having been here when we were here while those authors in the future are writing the history of our times.

Writing one's memoirs is an adventure even though it is an enormous task. At first, it is enjoyable and entertaining to nostalgically go back into one's own past; then the book becomes one's mistress, and later, one's master. But finally, it becomes a tyrant with demands that seem impossible to meet.

It has taken me many years to search for the historical facts in books and on the Internet that I have included in my memoirs but I have done this because I want my readers to fully understand what it was really like to be alive during the years of the Great Depression and the wars that followed it and to learn of the discoveries and new appearances and life in general in the remaining two thirds of the Twentieth Century and partway into the Twenty-first Century in which I was still alive at the time of this writing. This book is not only a book of my memoirs but also a history book that explains in some considerable detail what was really going on around the world during my lifetime. From my observations, very few if any autobiographers have chosen to write about their times in their memoirs.

In order to be accurate, I have found much of the historical information I needed for the creation of this book from various books and internet sources. I strongly urge you to obtain a good atlas so that you can have some idea as to where all the places I have described in this book can be located. It will make it easier for you to see where the events I will be describing to you really took place in the world.

Writing my memoirs that covers the last two-thirds of the Twentieth Century and part of the Twenty-first Century and which includes the historical events encompassing my life is much too vast to include in one book so I have divided my memoirs into three series; my childhood years, my early adulthood and my later years. The first series is titled, *Whistling in the Face of Robbers*, the second series is titled, *Patience: The snail will reach the ark* and the third series is titled, *Rising from the Ashes*. This first volume of the first series covers a time frame beginning in January 1933 and finishing in June 1944.

I hope you enjoy reading this first volume of my first series of my memoirs. Think of it as a trip back in time as you not only promenade with me through my own life but also in the collective lives of millions of others whose lives were equally affected in one way or another by the events of history that encompassed us all.

Dahn Alexander Batchelor

Chapter One

It was during the early morning hours on one of the last few days of August 1951 that my heart stopped. I was naked and had been strung up by my heels and later by my wrists. I had been tortured for ten hours non-stop and suffered from excruciating pain every moment. All the time I was being tortured and screaming in agony, I was alternately begging God to let me die and cursing him for letting me be born. At the end of the tenth hour, my heart finally stopped. My torturers cut me down from the beam in the ceiling, resuscitated me, dressed me and then after driving me through a deep forest, they dumped my unconscious body into a small creek to die and then drove away. As fate would have it, cursing God for letting me be born was pointless because I was born anyway and as you have fathomed by now, I didn't die in the creek.

The year 1933 was the year of my birth. It was not the best of times and it certainly wasn't the worst of times but those people who were still alive at the arrival of the century that was to follow and remembered what life was like in 1933, would have attested that 1933 was to them like Queen Elizabeth II pronounced the year 1992 for herself, as being; *Annus Horribilis*. I suppose everyone has some year in their lives that was particularly bad for them but in 1933, that year was particularly bad for everyone, unless of course they were very wealthy; of which the vast majority of us were not.

Like every year, great events occurred, some bad, some good but for the majority of the people in Canada and the United States in 1933, life for every one of us was just one difficult struggle after another to survive without losing everything we had in the process.

It was in January 1933, the month I was conceived, that the worst thing that could have occurred that year, did occur. It was an event that would have a direct effect on millions upon millions of people in Europe and North Africa in the near future. Adolf Hitler, one of history's most infamous and cruel dictators, came into power in Germany that year. As a result, over 50 million people died in the conflagration in Europe that was to ensue.

On January 30th, Hitler was appointed the Chancellor of Germany by President Hindenberg. The aging president had knuckled under the pressure he was subjected to by Hitler and his cronies. Several days after the November 1932 elections, the Reichstag (parliament) rejected the program of the incumbent Chancellor, Franz von Papen, for a 'government of national concentration.' In response, von Papen resigned. Hitler then asked President Paul von Hindenburg to appoint him chancellor, but the president refused, knowing that Hitler would use the office to obtain dictatorial power for himself. In early December, he appointed the Minister of Defense, Kurt von Schleicher, to the premiership, but he too resigned less than two months later. Hindenburg had no other choice but to choose Hitler who had been the recommendation of the Conservatives, who themselves thought they could manipulate him for their own purposes. I think he was a bit afraid of Hitler since it appeared that Hitler had an enormous power base.

It was during one evening while Hindenburg was standing at the window of the Chancellery, the 'brown shirts' (Hitler's followers) marched in front of Hindenburg's window by the thousands carrying torches and flags. There weren't that many actually in the parade. Hitler had cleverly arranged to have them walk around several blocks and keep returning to the street which the Chancellery was located. After watching the parade for more than an hour, the chancellor must have felt very intimidated in not tired from standing up so long at one time.

The new era in Germany started out modestly since only three of the 11 ministers in Hitler's government were Nazis; Hitler, William Frick, minister of the interior and Goering, minister for Prussia. Hitler swiftly took over all mechanisms of governance and functions of state, making Nazi Germany a totalitarian dictatorship.

In February of 1933, the month after I was conceived, Mayor Cermak of Chicago traveled to Miami, Florida to meet with President-elect Franklin Roosevelt. They arrived together on Wednesday, February 15th and sat together in one of the cars in the parade. The parade car moved slowly down the street as Roosevelt and Cermak smiled and waved at the people lining the streets. The car stopped and Roosevelt gave a speech while sitting at the back of the car. A man named Guiseppe Zangara pushed through the crowd. He fired five shots at the President-elect. The bullets hit four people and Mayor Cermak. The mayor fell out of the car and called out "The President, get him away!" But Roosevelt ordered his car to stop and further ordered that Mayor Cermak was to be put in the car with him. Roosevelt held Cermak all the way to the hospital. Mayor Anton J. Cermak died three weeks later, on Wednesday, on March 8th, 1933. His body was taken back to Chicago and buried in the Bohemian National Cemetery.

Guiseppe Zangara was tried, convicted, sentenced and executed in the electric chair on Tuesday, March 21st, 1933 only 35 days after Mayor Cermak was fatally shot. That was probably the shortest period in the United States between the murder of a victim and the legal execution of his assailant. Nowadays, the waiting period can go on for many decades.

At midnight on January 16th, 1920, one of the personal habits and customs of most Americans suddenly came to a halt in the United States. The *Eighteenth Amendment* was put into effect and all importing, exporting, transporting, selling, and manufacturing of intoxicating liquor was put to an end. Shortly following the enactment of the *Eighteenth Amendment,* the *National Prohibition Act,* or the *Volstead Act,* as it was called because of its author, Andrew J. Volstead, was put into effect. This determined intoxicating liquor as anything having an alcoholic content of anything more than 0.5 percent; omitting alcohol used for medicinal and sacramental purposes. This act also set up guidelines for enforcement. Prohibition was meant to reduce the consumption of alcohol, seen by some as the devil's advocate, and thereby reduce crime, poverty, death rates, and improve the economy and the quality of life. National prohibition of alcohol—the 'noble experiment' was undertaken for the purpose of reducing crime and corruption, solve social problems, reduce the tax burden created by prisons and poorhouses, and improve health and hygiene in America. This was of course to no avail. The inclusion of the Prohibition amendment of the 1920s was ineffective because it was unenforceable, it caused the explosive growth of crime, and it increased the amount of alcohol consumption in the United States and Canada. Much of the alcohol was illegally shipped into the USA from Canada and much of it was made by moon shiners in the forests of most of the states. However, in February 1933, prohibition in the USA came to an end.

On March 11th, 1918 the Canadian federal government called for Prohibition making the production, importation and sale and consumption illegal. Prohibition in Canada was a part of the *War Measures Act* because with so many young Canadian men dying in the war over-seas, the members of parliament didn't think it was ethical that people in Canada should continue partying and enjoying life back home. In addition, the country needed a unified home front with social discipline and industrial alcohol was needed for the war effort and grain was needed more for food production than for alcoholic beverages. Canada's distilleries turned to producing industrial alcohol. After the war was over, most of the members of Parliament wanted Prohibition to continue however the Canadian Senate had a sober second thought (now there is a play on words) about it but their thoughts didn't actually change anything.

Prohibition however continued on the provincial level (except for Quebec) and many taverns and stores remained closed. It really was a farce. All the loopholes were exploited again and again. People could still get liquor via mail from other provinces like Quebec or Saskatchewan.

Samuel and Harry Bronfman formed the Canada Pure Drug Company to market their 'medicinal alcohol' that was considered legal at that time. The drug store became a popular place. So popular in fact that in Ontario during 1923 and 1924, as many as 810,000 prescriptions for the 'medicinal alcohol' were written which in effect gives you an idea of the medical profession's complicity in all of this. Moonshine production increased in the rural areas which found its way into the mouths of their friends and neighbours. In 1919 a federal report revealed that in the first ten months of that year, 85 stills were seized across Canada whereas only 24 had been seized during the previous year. Incidentally, the term 'moonshine' was derived from the fact that much of the work creating the illegal liquor was done at night when the moonshiners did their work only by the light of the moon.

In the 1920s the creation of liquor control boards brought a slow but gradual end to Prohibition. It was obvious that if the politicians wanted to get elected, they had to move in the direction of their constituents who wanted an end to any form of prohibition, so they readily went along with the idea of having liquor control boards having direct control over the sale of liquor to the public.

In Ontario during 1927, the province opened the first liquor store in Toronto and thus, it ended the 11th year of prohibition in that province. Ontario did successfully withhold the withdrawal of Prohibition within several municipalities in the Toronto area for many years but national Prohibition was over in a heartbeat. With this new control in place, temperance advocates moved on to other social problems facing the country such as women's suffrage (their right to vote).

On February 10th, 1933, the New York City based Postal Telegraph Company introduced the first singing telegram. I never witnessed a singing telegram until sometime in 1970 when a woman brought such a telegram into a police station in Toronto and began singing the message to the police officer the telegram was directed to. On the 17th,

Newsweek came into being. On February 25th, the Americans launched their first custom-made aircraft carrier, *USS Ranger*.

On Monday, the 27th of February, the Reichstag (Germany's parliament building in Berlin) was empty as it had been in recess since December 1931. At around 8:30 in the evening, one of the caretakers patrolled the building and found nothing unusual. At 8:50 a postman was passing the entrance to the session chamber and he too noticed nothing unusual. But at 9:05 a student saw a man carrying a burning torch on the first floor. By 9:14 the fire alarm was received by the local fire station and the firemen were in the building by 9:24 but by then, fires were breaking out everywhere. At 9:27 there was a huge explosion and the great chamber was enveloped by flames. In the rear of the building a half naked Dutchman, Marinus van der Lubbe was discovered and arrested. He claimed to have set fire to the building as some form of protest. Hitler and Goering (head of the Gestapo) arrived on the scene. Goering at once accused the communists. The next day the ageing President under duress by Hitler, signed a decree which allowed the Nazis to suspend the freedom of speech which they use to ban virtually the entire opposition press. Communists were arrested wholesale.

The German authorities retained the services of Harry Sodermann, the chief of the Stockholm Criminal Investigation Department to investigate the cause of the fire. In his report, he put the blame entirely on Goering. Sodermann was immediately hustled out of Germany. Soon after the Second World War, evidence surfaced that Goering and his henchmen may have been responsible for setting fire to the Reichstag. The motive was clear enough; blame the communists. Some people however now generally believed that the Communists and Goering's henchmen had nothing to do with the burning of the Reichstag and that it was solely the action of the Dutchman. Who was Lubbe the naked Dutchman found on the scene and what happened to him after he was caught? Lubbe had decided he wanted to live in the Soviet Union rather than in Holland (The Netherlands) but was unable to raise enough money for his train fare. However, in 1933 he moved to Germany where he immediately began protesting against the new government headed by Adolf Hitler. Obviously the man was a bit demented, considering the danger of publicly protesting against Hitler while living in Nazi Germany, an act that was extremely risky at best.

When they police arrived at the Reichstag fire and found Lubbe on the premises, they arrested him and the Gestapo (secret police) began torturing him. As said earlier, he confessed to starting the Reichstag fire however he denied that he was part of a Communist conspiracy. Herman Goering refused to believe him and he ordered the arrest of several leaders of the German Communist Party. As well as Lubbe, the German police charged four communists with setting fire to the Reichstag. This included Ernst Torgler, the chairman of the Communist Party and Georgi Dimitrov of the Soviet Comintern. They were completely innocent but that matter little to Goering as he was all for getting rid of the Communists in any way he could.

Marinus van der Lubbe was tried and found guilty of setting the Reichstag Fire and was executed on the 10th of January 1934 by decapitation with a guillotine. He wasn't the first or the last to be guillotined by the Nazis. Over 20,000 people would eventually be executed in this manner by the Nazis. Other accused persons however were found not guilty which angered Hitler to no end. At this stage of his career, he didn't have complete control of the courts so there was nothing he could really do about the verdicts. In the year 2000, my wife and I visited the Reichstag. It is a very beautiful building inside.

On Saturday, March 4th, 1933, Franklin D. Roosevelt was inaugurated as the president of the United States. It was during his inaugural speech that he made that famous comment, "The only thing we have to fear, is fear itself." He made that statement in context with his address in which he outlined an aggressive policy to deal with the economic emergency. As soon as he became president, he appointed Frances Perkins as the Secretary of Labour. She was the first woman in the USA to be appointed to a cabinet post. Richard Bennett, a Conservative and who by 1933 was still indecisive and ineffectual, was the Prime Minister of Canada. His great deeds would come about two years later.

In the years preceding World War II and the Hollocaust, (the extermination of millions of Jews) a Nazi concentration camp was built in the city of Dachau. Construction of the camp was completed by March 20th, 1933. Although many Jews and prisoners of war later died there nonetheless from the horrible living conditions, it was a concentration camp and not an extermination camp such as Auschwitz and several others which were to be built later. Herman Goering was the man who conceived the idea of concentration camps in Germany although Great Britain created them during the Boer War in South Africa although I think the conditions in the ones in South Africa weren't as bad as the ones in Germany.

On March 23rd, Hitler was given total control of German legislation. He was by now, almost an absolute dictator whose future actions would have an effect on the lives of everyone in Europe, many in Africa and everyone in the Western Hemisphere to some degree, no matter how remote.

Everyone has a community they call home and a great many people consider their home the place where they were born. I was born in the City of Toronto, the capital of the province of Ontario and the largest city in Canada. This city and environs have been my home for most of my life.

The western and centre parts of the city gradually slope upwards from Lake Ontario to the northern part of the city whereas the eastern part of the city begins at the top of the 350-foot (100-metre) bluffs overlooking the lake. Over the years, Toronto developed an incredible network of recreational and park facilities. Walkers, joggers, cyclists and hikers can follow over 56 miles (90 km) of paved trails and many more hundreds of miles of unpaved trails. There are many locations in many of the parks for family picnics and group events. Anyone who has flown over the city or gone up to the Observation Deck near the top of the CN Tower, the deck being as high as 1,465 feet (447 metres) from the street when looking over the city, will think that they are looking over a vast forest. Every street except those downtown for the most part is tree-lined with shade trees.

The city is on the north shore of Lake Ontario, a lake that is one of the largest lakes in the world. It has 712 miles (1,146 km) of shoreline. It is 193 miles (311 kilometres) in length and its breadth is 53 miles (85 kilometres). The southeastern shores of the lake are in the State of New York.

Toronto is blessed with a series of beautiful islands in its harbour. The Toronto Islands were not originally islands but actually a series of continuously moving sand-bars, or littoral (shore) drift deposits, originating from the Scarborough Bluffs and carried westward by Lake Ontario currents. By the early 1800s, the longest of these bars extended nearly 5.6 miles (9 km) south-west from Woodbine Avenue, through Ashbridge's Bay and the marshes of the lower Don River, forming a natural harbour between the lake and the mainland. The island's sandy beaches and the island's paved pathways that meander through expansive lawns bordered by flowers and thousands of trees makes the island park a haven for 1,225,000 visitors each year who visit this 230 hectare (568 acre) park after alighting from the ferry after a 10-minute ferry trip from downtown Toronto. All of the islands are connected with one another by arched foot bridges.

Truly one of the most beautiful sights to be seen is the sun setting over western Toronto from the islands in the harbour. The distant buildings silhouetted in black against the golden sun and the gold sparkling waters shimmering between the island and the mainland with the trees of the island silhouetted in black truly is a feast for the eyes.

By the turn of the Twenty-first century, Toronto was and still is a cosmopolitan city and has developed into one of the world's most multicultural and diverse cities in the world with it being home to more than 80 ethnic communities from Africa, Asia, the islands of the South Pacific, South America and Europe. Toronto by the turn of the Twentieth First century had become the home of four professional sports teams and the third largest English-speaking theatre district in the world, behind New York and London. It boasts of a world renowned concert hall (which I once performed in as a solo pianist) and a highly respected symphony orchestra. Toronto is also the business centre of Canada with skyscrapers exceeding 70 floors.

The city cares for its own citizens and everyone for the most part are conscious of the rights of others. All its citizens (including those that are landed immigrants) have free medical and hospital coverage, the people are concerned for the homeless and care for them when possible and for the most part, no one in the city needs to go to bed hungry. In the winter months, many citizens roam the streets looking for homeless people and providing them with sleeping bags, warm clothing and food. Those who visit the city and even those who live in it praise it for its many attributes.

In the year I was born however, the city was vastly different then than it was by the end of the Twentieth Century. Most of the people were terribly poor, jobs were difficult to get and anyone who wasn't a white Anglo-Saxon protestant suffered terrible abuses heaped upon them that are no longer acceptable in any decent community. Thousands upon thousands of unemployed, including children, were homeless and roaming the streets looking for handouts. The police tortured their suspects, the courts were a farce, the jails were archaic and strapping the butts of unruly inmates was the norm. There were no such things as human rights and simply put, the well-to-do for the most part, didn't give a damn about the vast majority of those less fortunate. Both the air and the water in the city of Toronto were often polluted and even living in the surrounding towns, Scarborough, East York, North York, York, Etobicoke, New Toronto, Port Credit and Streetsville (later all incorporated into the city of Toronto) didn't make breathing its air and drinking its water brought in from the lake, acceptable by any standards.

The widespread prosperity of the 1920s ended abruptly with the stock market crash in October 1929 that brought about the great economic depression that followed. The depression threatened people's jobs, savings, and even their homes and farms. At the depths of the depression, over one-quarter of the American and Canadian workforce was out of work. For many in the United States and Canada, these were hard times. The economic troubles of the 1930s were worldwide. Economic instability led to political instability in many parts of the world. Political chaos, in turn, gave rise to dictatorial regimes such as that of Adolf Hitler in Germany and the militarists in Japan. (Totalitarian regimes in the Soviet Union and Italy predated the depression) These regimes pushed the world ever-closer to war in the 1930s. It was the longest and most severe economic depression ever experienced by the Western world. It began in the U.S. with the New York Stock Market Crash of 1929 and lasted until 1939 when I was six years of age. By late 1932 stock values had dropped to about 20% of their previous value. Between the years of 1929 and 1939, the world saw one of the most devastating periods of hardship, poverty, and governmental instability in modern world history. With the start of the Great Depression, governments from around the world were thrown into almost ten years of turmoil. The depression did not come to an end for most of these nations until World War II began in 1939.

It was unfortunate indeed that in order for the depression to come to an end, a world war had to begin. That makes sense when you consider that once the war began, employment was on the rise because so many factories were building war machines etc. They needed manpower to function fully to meet the demands of war.

By 1933, as many as 11,000 of the U.S.'s 25,000 banks had failed. Millions of depositors lost their savings because of the bank failures. In those days, governments didn't insure the bank accounts of its depositors. This led to much-reduced levels of demand and hence of production, resulting in high unemployment (by 1932, 25-30% compared with 9.1 % in the US in 2011). Since the U.S. was the major creditor and financier of postwar Europe, the U.S. financial collapse led to collapses of other economies, especially those of Germany, France and Britain. Nations sought to protect domestic production by imposing tariffs and quotas, reducing the value of international trade by more than half by 1932.

The Great Depression had grown worse and had spread a pall of fear and desperation around the world. Soup kitchens flourished all over North America where millions in the United States and Canada lined up to get their daily meal. Those who had some money would go to a cafe where a cup of soup was reduced to pouring ketchup into a cup of hot water for those who couldn't afford soup with their meal. Millions of unemployed and dispossessed crossed Canada and the USA in box cars like lemmings, all looking for work. It was common to see the homeless begging at the doorsteps of farmers for an hour's work so that they could have something to eat.

The farmers and their families weren't that better off and many of them abandoned their farms to seek employment somewhere else. The farmers, whose farms they were forced to abandon, congregated in the cities in the hopes of finding employment there. In 1931, over a quarter of a million farmers, homeowners and small businessmen lost their farms, homes and businesses in North America. Others, from small towns and villages, singly, in pairs and in groups of a dozen or more, crossed the country in box cars in faint hopes that the next large town or city offered more hope than the last one did. Thousands upon thousands of homeless people could be seen hitchhiking across the country with their suitcases with no hope other than getting something to eat in exchange for pushing a wheelbarrow or digging a ditch for a few hours. Millions of men and women and also boys and girls who were left to fend for themselves, drifted in and out of cities in search of a job or a home in the faint hope that another family would care for them.

Near every freight yard, there were hobo jungles where weary vagrants congregated to exchange intelligence about travel conditions, such as which trains to avoid because of the 'bulls', (railroad cops) where they could scrounge a free bed or in which town they could get a free meal or a few day's work. The railroads gradually became tolerant towards these railroad hobos because there really wasn't much that they could do to stem the millions of free riders as the numbers far exceeded the 'bulls' who patrolled the yards with axe handles and beat vagrants out of the boxcars.

The average family had no more that $20 on hand at any one time but that money was a lot of money then. It was equivalent to $256.31 American and $334.48 Canadian in 1999. It would pay the rent for a small flat over a store for one month, or pay for a dinette set or pay the wages for a live-in maid for a month; if anyone but the rich could afford a maid. For most employable men, the wage was one dollar a day. That comes to $12.82 American and $16.73 Canadian in 1999. Interns in the hospitals weren't paid anything accept their room and board. In 1933, nine out of ten farmers didn't even have electricity. I remember living on a farm during the summer of 1941 and there was no electricity on that farm then either. Breakfast was 25 cents. (That is equivalent to $3.20 American and $4.18 Canadian in 1999. Lunch was 40 cents and that is equivalent to $6.41 American and $8.36 Canadian. A four course dinner cost 50 cents. That is $7.69 in American money and $10.03 in Canadian money in 1999. Oddly enough, these were almost the same prices in Winnipeg in the mid 1950s. Airfares from Chicago to Los Angeles return on the other hand were $207 American. If you wanted to take an 'around-the-world-cruise' visiting 14 countries for 85 days, it would cost you $749.00 American which in 1999 money would be equivalent to $9,598.72 American and $12,526.33 Canadian. In 1999, I got to spend an all inclusive week (airfare included) in a large hotel in Cuba for the same price of $749 Canadian.) If you wanted to purchase a Kodak Brownie camera for your trip, it would cost you $2.50 American which in 1999 would be $32.04 American and $41.81 Canadian.

Housewives saved near-microscopic and sometimes inedible portions of leftovers to mix in the next meal. They patched clothes, mended socks, relined winter coats with old blankets and steamed off unused one-cent stamps from their incoming mail for their outgoing mail.

Many families in the rural areas of North America were so poor, they lacked indoor privies and even used newspapers and sometimes leaves and twigs (hence the phrase—the dirty end of the stick) for use as toilet paper when they had to go into the outhouses to relieve themselves. Alas, the pages of department store catalogues didn't do the trick, as they were too stiff and hard. Use of the Sears catalog for this purpose declined in the 1930's due to the fact that they started printing on glossy, clay-coated paper. Many people complained to Sears about this glossy paper. Can you imagine writing a letter to Sears: "Dear Sir, I want to register a complaint about your new glossy catalog paper. It is no longer soft and absorbent and as such, it is difficult to use as toilet paper."

Wage earners had to support their families of six to eight on ten dollars a month. Many of them had lived their entire lives without electricity and few of them had wandered more than ten miles from their homes, a great many never having seen a small town, let alone seen a large city.

Anyone who lived through the thirties, could easily understand why that decade was called the 'Dirty Thirties' but of course, I was too young to remember the consequences of being poor; such as sleeping in the bottom drawer of a cheap dresser in a two-roomed shack with no electricity or water of which I did during the years 1933 and 1934.

The people in the United States think they had it bad in May of 2011 with their unemployment figures being 9.1 %. The year 1933 was the worst year of the depression with unemployment being so bad, it resulted in one out of every four (25%) adults being unemployed. The physical signs of distress were everywhere. Clusters of men and women, some with their small children in hand, were begging on the streets for handouts or waiting endlessly at the food relief stations for a small amount of food that would last them through the day. A proud family breadwinner, who had never begged for a thing in his life, would find himself standing in a long line to get the 'Pogey'. (a term which was used in parts of Canada during the Great Depression to mean government relief—similar to welfare.) Soup kitchens flourished all over Toronto for the single unemployed who had no money at all in their pockets. Factories were closed along with many stores because of forced bankruptcies or because the landlords evicted them. Many a proud father, brother or son was seen with stooped shoulders, standing on street corners with hands outstretched, begging for a dime or even a five-cent piece that would get them a cup of coffee. Bing Crosby's hit, *Brother, can you spare a dime?* from the musical, *Americana* was not only the song of the times; it was also the sign of the times. The St. Lawrence Hall on King Street East in Toronto, once the local focal point for wealth and splendor, where famous artists like Jenny Lind once sang, had been transformed into a large dormitory for the homeless. Even the smallest of houses were crammed with the evicted and unemployed who moved in with relatives. Relatives from out of town who found a place to sleep in a home slept on living-room couches, sometimes three or four to a bed or on mattresses placed in the kitchens. In some communities, as many as 15 percent of the homes were sheltering 'extra' family members.

The problems of the Great Depression affected virtually every group of Americans and Canadians. No group was harder hit than African Americans however. As the economy struggled through the 1930s, jobs grew even scarcer. Competition between whites and blacks brought added hostility. By 1933, approximately half of black Americans were out of work in the United States. In some Northern cities, whites called for blacks to be fired from any jobs as long as there were whites out of work. Racial violence again became more common, especially in the Southern states.

Lynching is the extrajudicial execution carried out by a mob, often by hanging, but also by burning at the stake and shooting, in order to punish an alleged transgressor, or to intimidate, control, or otherwise manipulate a population of people, however large or small. It is related to other means of social control that arise in communities, such as, riding the rail, (tied to a pole and carried out of town) and tarring and feathering. Lynchings were more frequent in times of social and economic tension, and often were means by the politically dominant population to oppress social challengers.

Mobs of unruly citizens thought of lynching as a form of

punishment for presumed criminal offenses, performed by self-appointed commissions, mobs, or vigilantes who without due process of law, took the law into their own hands. This occurred in the United States before the American Civil War and afterwards, from southern states to western frontier settlements.

Violence in the United States against African Americans, especially in the South, rose in the aftermath of the American Civil War, after slavery had been abolished and when recently freed black men were given the right to vote. Violence rose even more at the end of the century, after southern white Democrats regained political power in the South in the 1870s. Nearly 5,000 African Americans were lynched in the United States between 1860 and 1890. Despite the foregoing, not all lynchings in the United States were targeted against African Americans. Between 1882 and 1968, the Tuskegee Institute recorded 1,297 lynchings of whites as well as the 3446 lynchings of African Americans during that period of time. There were 28 lynchings in 1933 in the United States in which two whites and 24 blacks were lynched by mobs.

For many African Americans growing up in the South in the 19th and 20th centuries, the threat of lynching was commonplace. In the South, an estimated two or three blacks were lynched each week in the late 19th and early 20th centuries. The number of lynchings of blacks by white mobs increased from eight in 1932 to 28 in 1933, 15 in 1934, and 20 in 1935. The number of lynchings finally dropped to two in 1939 as economic conditions improved for whites.

Homicides totaling 1,937 were the reasons that people were lynched, followed by 255 for felonious assault. There were also 912 lynchings for rape, 288 for attempted rape, 232 for robbery and theft, and (get this one) 85 blacks were lynched for supposedly insulting a white person.

Lynch mobs enforced the racist social order through beatings, cutting off fingers and/or genitals, burning down houses, and/or destroying the crops of African/Americans. Murder was a common form of lynch mob justice. Most lynchings terminated with a hanging but prior to the final act, victims were sometimes tortured prior to being killed by such methods as beating, burning, stabbing, sexual mutilation and eye-gouging. Photographs of these events frequently show the perpetrators laughing and smiling. Next to hanging, the most common methods of killing were burning alive, shooting, and beating the victims to death.

Often victims were lynched by a small group of white vigilantes late at night. Sometimes however, lynchings became mass spectacles with a circus atmosphere. Children often attended these public lynchings, which anti-lynching advocates saw as a form of indoctrination. A large lynching might be announced beforehand in the newspaper, and there were cases in which a lynching was started early so that a newspaper reporter could make his deadline. It was common for postcards to be sold depicting lynchings, typically allowing a newspaper photographer to make some extra money. These postcards became popular enough to be a real embarrassment to the government, and the postmaster officially banned them in 1908. However, the lynching postcards continued to exist through the 1930's.

Many lynchings were carried out with full participation by law enforcement and government officials. Police would on occasion arrest and detain a lynching victim and then release him into a location where a lynch mob could easily, and quietly, complete their deed. Fewer than 1% of lynch mob participants were ever convicted. Trial juries in the southeastern United States were typically all-white, and would not vote to convict lynchers and often coroner's juries never let the matter get past the inquest. In a typical 1892 example in Port Jervis, New York, a policeman tried to stop the lynching of a black man who, it was revealed after his death, had been wrongfully accused of assaulting a white woman. The mob responded by putting the noose around the officer's own neck as a way of scaring him off. At the coroner's inquest, the officer identified eight people who had participated in the lynching, including the former chief of police, but the coroner's jury found that the murder had been carried out 'by person or persons unknown.'

Not all racially motivated lynchings in the United States took place in the South. A black woman in a northern state was lynched because she tried to prevent the lynching of her son. One incident which occurred in Duluth, Minnesota on June 15, 1920, was when three young African-American travelers were dragged from their jail cells (where they were confined after being accused of raping a white woman) and lynched by a mob believed to number more than one thousand.

By the 1930s, the rate of lynchings was reduced to ten per year in southern U.S. states. In 1946, a mob of white men shot and killed two young black men and two young black women near Moore's Ford Bridge in Walton County, Georgia. The savagery of this lynching shocked the nation, and was a key factor that led President Truman to make civil rights a priority.

In 1964, three civil rights workers were lynched by white racists in Neshoba County, Mississippi. Michael Schwerner (24), Andrew Goodman (20) of New York, and James Chaney (22) from Meridian, Mississippi, members of the Congress of Racial Equality (CORE), were dedicated to non-violent direct action against racial discrimination. They disappeared in June of that year while investigating the arson of a black church being used as a 'Freedom School'. Their bodies were found six weeks later in a partially constructed dam near Philadelphia, Mississippi. Many years later in 2005, eighty-year-old Edgar Ray Killen was convicted of manslaughter for the killings, and sentenced to 60 years in prison. His tentative release date is April 2, 2033 if he is released because of good conduct in prison. He will be 108 years of age then. I think it is safe to say that he will die in prison.

On June 13, 2005, the United States Senate formally apologized for its failure in previous decades to enact a federal anti-lynching law, all of which fell victim to filibusters by powerful Southern senators. This tells you something about the character of some senators who live in the Southern states. The following statistics for the period from 1882 to 1951 are; 88% of victims were black, and 10% were white. 59% of the lynchings occurred in the Southern states of Kentucky, North

Carolina, South Carolina, Tennessee, Arkansas, Louisiana, Mississippi, Alabama, Georgia, and Florida. Lynching was not uncommon in the west and Midwest, but was virtually nonexistent in the northeast.

For most of the history of the United States, lynching was rarely prosecuted, and when it was, it was under state murder statutes. In one extraordinary example in 1907-1909, the Supreme Court tried its only lynching case in history, 203 U.S. 563 (*U.S. v. Sheriff Shipp*). Shipp was found guilty of criminal contempt for lynching Ed Johnson in Chattanooga.

Starting in 1909, over 200 bills were introduced to make lynching a federal crime, but they failed to pass. During the Roosevelt administration, the Civil Rights Section of the Justice Department tried, but failed, to prosecute lynchers under Reconstruction-era civil rights laws. The first successful federal prosecution of a lyncher for a civil rights violation was in 1946, and by that time, the era of lynchings as a common occurrence was over.

Many states now have specific anti-lynching statues. California, for example, the participation of a lynching which is punishable by 2-4 years in prison, is defined as 'the taking by means of a riot of any person from the lawful custody of any peace officer,' with the crime of 'riot' defined as two or more people using violence or the threat of violence. A lyncher could thus be prosecuted for several crimes arising from the same action, e.g., riot, lynching, and murder. Some states, South Carolina for example, require premeditation. Although lynching in the historic sense is virtually nonexistent today, the lynching statutes are sometimes used in cases where several people try to wrest a suspect from the hands of police in order to help him escape, as alleged in a July 9th, 2005 violent attack on a police officer in San Francisco.

Using such a statute for that purpose is wrong in my opinion.

In the Nineteenth Century, few people lived to see 70 years and practically no one lived for 80 years. Of course, that is much more years of life than the Anglo-Saxons back in the Early Middle Ages (400 to 1000 A.D) lived. Rarely did anyone live past 45 years of age in those times. The average life span of anyone living in North America in 1933 was only 59 years. It reached 72 in 2000. In some of the major industrialized countries, it is now about 80 years, with the bulk of this increase having come in the past 150 years.

In some of the African countries, the average life span is less than 40 years. Now that heart bypass operations are reducing the number of deaths by heart attacks, the life span in Westernized nations will increase dramatically.

In 1933, the Douglas DC-1 which carried 12 passengers and flew 150 miles (241 km) per hour was introduced. That same year, Eatons, the large department store in Toronto, Canada, brought in a television set and entertained its customers with a variety show and magic show shown on the small screen in which the performers were being televised in a nearby room.

As an interesting aside, in September 7th, 1927, Philo T. Farnsworth demonstrated for the first time that it was possible to transmit an 'electrical image' without the use of any mechanical contrivances whatsoever. In one of the first triumphs of relativistic science, Farnsworth replaced the spinning disks and mirrors with the electron itself, an object so small and light that it could be deflected back and forth within a vacuum tube tens of thousands of times per second. In essence television as we know it today; was born six years before my own birth.

The song, *Whose Afraid of the Big Bad Wolf* came out as a popular hit. The German dictator, Hitler loved that song. It was sung in the Walt Disney cartoon, *Three Little Pigs*. The song, *Easter Parade* was a popular hit also. For first time appearances, 1933 gave us blood banks, Campbell's cream of mushroom and also chicken noodle soups, Ritz crackers, a drive-in theater, singing telegrams, walkie-talkies and margarine made from soybeans.

That year, it cost eight cents to mail a letter and only one cent to mail a post card. A four-course dinner in a restaurant cost 60 cents, and you could have breakfast for as low as 25 cents. I would be remiss if I didn't mention that even in 1956, in Winnipeg; you could have breakfast for as low as 25 cents and for that price, you got ham and eggs along with two slices of toast and coffee. A four-course dinner cost only $1.75. At the time of this writing, (2011) breakfast could cost five to six dollars and a four-course dinner could cost as much as twenty dollars. A Kodak Brownie camera could be purchased for as low as $2.50. The average cost of new house was $5,750.00. The average cost for renting a house was $18.00 per month. The cost of a gallon of gas was 10 cents. A loaf of bread cost 7 cents. A pound of hamburger meat cost 11 cents. A can of Campbells Vegetable Soup cost 10 cents. You could buy a new Plymouth 6-cylinder car for $445.00. But at the same time, you have to keep in mind that the average laborer's wage was only $20.00 per week which came out to $1,040 a year less income taxes.

The chocolate chip cookie was created as was the board game, Monopoly. The first ever drive-in theatre was established in the State of New Jersey. Many years later while I was a private investigator conducting an investigation in that state, I went to that drive-in to see a movie one evening.

Some very famous people (besides myself naturally) were born that year. They were; Joan Collins, TV personality, May 23rd, Larry King, TV personality, November 19th, Yoko Ono, wife of John Lennon, one of the Beatles, February 18th, Roman Polanski, movie director and later a fugitive, August 18th, Michael Caine, actor, March 14th, Marty Feldman, bug-eyed comedian, July 8th, Jayne Mansfield, actress, April 19th, the Kray twins, later gangsters in England, October 24th and Willie Nelson, singer, April 30th.

On November 30th 1934, it was finally established that the bones discovered in an urn in the Bloody Tower in the Tower of London were actually those of Edward V, age 14 and his younger brother, the Duke of York, age 12 who were allegedly murdered on the instructions of their uncle, King Henry III.

Chapter Two

At 9:15 on the morning of Friday, October 27th, 1933, I was born in St. Michael's Hospital in downtown Toronto. The hospital was built in 1892 and has always been operated by a Catholic order called the *Sisters of St. Josephs*. It was originally a boarding house for working women but it became a hospital in response to an earlier diphtheria epidemic.

My mother had to pay the hospital $35 for her 10-day stay in the hospital and a dollar a day for my stay in the hospital. In 1933, $35 would be equivalent to $343 Canadian at the end of 1999. I have no idea where she got that kind of money at the time of my birth. In the year 2007 in the Northeastern part of the United States, a five-day stay in a hospital would cost the patient as much as $55,448 and that isn't counting the services of the doctors. In 1999, when I was in two hospitals in the City of Toronto for two months because of problems with my heart, it would have cost me $332,688 and that also didn't factor in the costs of the doctors who operated on my heart and the MIR and other tests given to me. However, because I am a resident of the province of Ontario, it didn't cost me a cent. I did however pay a small token payment for the use of the phone and television in my room.

The nurses were very concerned about the condition of my mother at this time because my mother had been in labour for 72 hours which was much too long for a woman to be in labour and they still couldn't reach her doctor at the critical moment as he was out golfing somewhere. For this reason, they wanted to do the delivery themselves. In those days, doctors weren't on hand in any case in the hospitals as they are these days.

My mother was twenty-one and a half years of age and still single then. She was a petite woman and it was obvious to the nurses on duty in the hospital that my birth was going to be a difficult one for her. The awkwardness of my birth was on every one's minds, even on the minds of the other patients in the hospital and no doubt on my own also. Yes. Fetuses have minds before they are born and they are aware of their surroundings.

It was the policy in those days that in Catholic hospitals, if a pregnant woman was in danger dying or losing her child, and it came to choosing who of the two was to survive; the woman or her about-to-be born baby, the woman was expected to give up her life in place of her baby, the reason being that the un-baptized baby would go to Purgatory in the afterlife and remain there forever if it died before it was born. To prevent this, the pregnant woman would die and the baby would then be removed from its dead mother's uterus and resuscitated if at all possible and baptized immediately after its resuscitation. As an interesting aside, the Roman Catholic Church no longer promotes the idea of the existence of Purgatory so all those maternal sacrifices in the past were for naught.

However, the problem facing the staff in St. Michael's was that my mother was not a Catholic and this policy didn't apply to non-Catholics. This meant that the alternative measure could and might very well be taken, a measure taken in non-Catholic hospitals—that being that the live baby's head would be crushed so that the then dead baby could be removed from its mother's uterus, thereby saving the mother's life.

The hierarchy in the hospital asked the staff who in turn passed the request on to their patients, to pray for the protestant mother and her about-to-be-born baby. This request was also passed onto St. Michael's Cathedral across the street and the Catholic school up the street.

At 9:15 that morning, the hospital and the school almost came to a standstill with so many people praying for my mother and me at that moment. Through the assistance of forceps and a cesarean, I was born weighing seven pounds, seven ounces and screaming and kicking while joining the rest of the people in the delivery room.

As I mentioned earlier, in those days, mothers and their newborns were kept in the hospital for ten days. My mother wanted to breast feed me but she was unable to and by a rather sad coincidence, the woman in the bed next to her had lost her baby during its birth so she had the need and the desire to breast feed me. This situation was beneficial to both women although I think they might have asked me for my views on the subject since I was to be the direct beneficiary of the much needed mother's milk.

This raises another interesting rhetorical question. It is said that breast feeding a baby develops a bond between the baby and its mother. I am forced to wonder if after being breast fed by the other woman, which woman did I developed the immediate bond with? The question is academic of course as there was a bond between my mother and me that only children and their mothers can develop over the years.

What is equally amazing is that the officials and nurses in the hospital were very sympathetic towards my mother since they knew or suspected that she was about to give birth to me while she was out of wedlock. In those days, women having children born out of wedlock were looked down on in the same manner that people in the 1980s looked down on people suffering from AIDS. Rumor had it at that time that when my mother first looked at me; her first born, she cried out in anguish, "They've taken away my baby and left me the stork!" Of course this was only rumor you understand which was probably spread by my enemies at the time.

When it was time for us to leave the hospital, my mother and my father (Louis Vincent Batchelor) the man who raped my mother while on a date) took me to their home in Scarborough, a suburb of Toronto

They had previously found a two-room shack on a small plot of land in a farmer's field in what was then, the town of Scarborough. Their farm animals comprised of chickens, a cat and a dog. The two rooms consisted of a bedroom that had a small bed in it and a dresser and a smaller room with a table and stove along with two chairs in it. There was no water piped into the shack hence there was no sink or toilet or a bathtub. My mother had to walk a hundred feet (33 meters) to the road where a tap came out of a pipe and where she would fill up a bucket with water. The toilet was an outhouse at the back of the shack. There was also no electricity either. It was a far cry from the beautiful house my mother had lived in before she met my father and another she later ended up living in after she married my second step-father many years later when she and he built their ultra-modern house at a beach on the northern end of the Island of Oahu in Hawaii.

My father disappeared again claiming he was looking for work in Toronto, which was a lie as he was living with a girlfriend so my mother eked out a meager living selling eggs laid by her chickens. In August 2001, almost 68 years later, I spoke with my 76-year-old cousin Alan Banfield whose father; Harry Banfield was a brother to Alex Banfield, my grandfather. While my wife and I visited Alan in his summer home in Jackson's Point in Ontario, he told me that after I was born, his father learned where my mother and I were living in Scarborough and he remembered (when Harry was eleven years old) he and his father bringing food hampers to our shack because they knew that my mother and I were starving. My mother insisted that they not tell her parents where she and I were living. They kept their word.

For some time even after I was born, my mother and I were still dirt poor to the extent that I didn't even have a crib to sleep in so she placed me in the bottom drawer of her dresser as soon as I was brought home after my birth. One night, shortly after my birth, my father kicked the drawer shut because I kept crying and keeping him awake but my mother was awake when that happened so she opened up the drawer again. My crying hadn't stopped of course. My father had enough. He was rarely ever home anyway (he was gallivanting about with his girlfriends and alternately shacking up with each of them) so again he left my mother to fend for herself and me. My mother later told me that as a baby, I was always crying or screaming and it was quite unnerving for her because she didn't know if there was something wrong with me and she couldn't go back to the hospital to find out because she had no means of transportation. There were no buses or streetcars in Scarborough then and a taxi would have been beyond her means and obviously out of the question.

When Christmas arrived in 1933, my father returned home and he and my mother drove to her parent's home to deliver a Christmas gift. While my father sat in his car and held me in his arms, with the engine of the car still running, my mother ran across the street, opened the door to the stairway at the side of the house leading to the upper floor of the duplex where my grandparents lived (on Avenue Road, just south of Eglinton) and placed the small package on the steps. Then she bolted across the street, got into my father's car and grabbed me from my father's arms and my father drove us back home to our shack in Scarborough.

Chapter Three

My maternal grandmother was in some ways, a mean woman who eventually drove my mother from her home with her continuous nitpicking, especially when it became obvious to her that my mother was pregnant out of wedlock. On one occasion, she cooked and ate one of my mother's favourite pigeons. It was strange behaviour for a woman who unselfishly sacrificed herself in the service of her church.

My maternal grandfather whose full name was Alex Woods Banfield was born on August 3rd, 1878 in Quebec City. He enrolled for a brief time at the *Toronto Bible College* (now called the *Ontario Bible College*) and in 1901; he was one of four young pioneer missionaries who had been chosen by the *Africa Industrial Mission* to go to Africa that year to preach the gospel. He was the smallest and frailest and the one that everyone presumed would be the first to perish. He survived in Africa for twenty-five years. One of the other three missionaries perished and the other two were too sick to remain in Africa so they returned home. West Africa at that time was known as the 'white man's grave', a reputation it repeatedly earned.

I have had an opportunity to read my grandfather's book, *Life among the Nupe Tribe in West Africa* before I donated one of my two copies to the rare book section of the Royal Ontario Museum in Toronto. After reading it, I began to appreciate the sacrifices he and later my grandmother made when they served in Nigeria. There were no hotels or cars in Nigeria then. Everyone walked, rode a horse or rode in a horse-drawn cart or traveled by canoe or steamboat.

My grandfather (who was single at this time) left Canada on September 17th 1901 and he along with the three other missionaries in that pioneer party (one from Michigan, another from New York and the third from Hamilton, Ontario) who were sponsored by the *Africa Industrial Mission* (the forerunner of the *Sudan Interior Mission*), individually took a train to New York, then all together, they sailed to Liverpool, England. They left Liverpool on October 30th 1901 (thirty-two years before I was born) on the Royal Mail Steamer *Bornu*, and headed southward to Africa. After thirteen days at sea, they arrived at Sierra Leone and after spending only six hours there, they re-boarded their ship and sailed to Nigeria.

On the morning of November 18th, they arrived at the mouth of the Niger River. It was from there that they boarded a British government-operated steamboat with a paddle wheel at the stern and spent the next six days going up the Niger River to a town that was at the convergence of the Niger River and the Benue River that ran westward into the Niger River. The town they stopped at was called Lokoja. In 1859 a British trading and missionary settlement was founded in Lokoja. From 1867 to 1869 a British consulate was maintained there.

In 1900, Lokoja served as the staging point for the British conquest of Northern Nigeria (then called Soudan which was the French name for Sudan) and became the temporary capital of the protectorate of Northern Nigeria. But when my grandfather was there, Lokoja was a small city of 20,000 inhabitants populating it. The city only had five grass huts for travelers to rest in. Nowadays, the city has many fine hotels in it. In 1987 the population was 45,600. It had approximately the same population as the Canadian cities; Fredericton, New Brunswick or Bellville, Ontario did that same year.

Lokoja is currently the trade and distribution center for an agricultural (chiefly cotton) region and has food-processing industries. Iron ore deposits serve the nearby Ajaokuta mill.

During the several months my grandfather stayed in Lokoja, he suffered continuously from attacks of malaria and black water fever. He made trips into the hinterland so that he could find a place where he would be welcome by the natives and where he could build his mission station. The area he headed into was where the people spoke the Bassa dialect. At one point, he and the other missionaries were attacked by natives but they managed to escape with their lives. Finally on the 15th of March 1902, they left Lokoja and headed further westward up the Niger River.

Three days later, while going up the Niger River, my grandfather saw the town of Pategi on the top of a small hill in the distance south of him. It is located three miles south of the south shore of the Niger River and almost across the spot where the Kaduna River heading southward runs into the Niger River. Pategi being on a small hill, it follows that the word patigi means 'small hill'. Over the years, the name of the town changed from Petigi to Pategi. Later it became known as the 'White Man's City' meaning a city made by the white man. Its population was 10,000 by the time my grandfather arrived. In 2010, the population was a little over 28,000. It was there that my grandfather and his other fellow missionaries decided to build their base station of the *African Industrial Mission*. Their aim was to establish a mission among the 60 million people in Northern Nigeria of what was then commonly known as the Soudan, the area south of the Sahara between the nations east of Nigeria and the Nile River. It is now spelled as Sudan but it is not to be confused with the nation east of Nigeria that runs along the Nile River.

Most of the inhabitants of the area my grandfather decided to remain at are Muslim Nupe people. Trying to turn Muslim natives into Christians would turn out to be an impossible task for my grandfather. The main language in that area is Nupe. The Nupe people live in the heart of Nigeria, spread over the low basin formed by the two rivers, Niger and Kaduna.

After my grandfather and their native assistants embarked from their canoes, it took sixty bearers to carry all of their belongings to Pategi. One of the bearers carried atop of his head, my grandparent's wood stove which weighed four hundred pounds. (181 kg) As they moved in closer to the town, they discovered that for the most part, it comprised of mud huts with straw or grass roofs. Like all other towns in Africa at that time, it was governed by an African king. My grandfather and the others introduced themselves to the king and the king invited them to build their mission on a vacant farm outside the town. My grandfather was pleased with the prospect of being that far from the town as the town, like most of the other towns in Nigeria in that era were extremely filthy places to live and the stench of human waste and rotting garbage was overwhelming to anyone who hadn't spent a lifetime living with it.

The king ordered the building of four grass-roofed huts for the missionaries to be used for their living quarters and those of their native staff. The huts were made of straw mats secured to upright poles connected to the roofs which were comprised of straw. The floors were made by sprinkling gravel and water on a mud base and then beating the floors with a small pounder until they were as solid as hard clay. Three of the houses were built to live in and the fourth was used to cook their meals in. Their furniture comprise of boxes, four cots, a small table and folding chairs. The temperature during all the days of the year fluctuated between 90 and 108 degrees Farenheight (32—43 Celsius) in the shade and at night, the gnats bit them continuously despite the netting around their cots. This in my opinion was really roughing it. That kind of sacrifice is daunting, of that, there can be no doubt.

Pategi grew quite quickly while my grandfather was there because it was well known that slaves who escaped and arrived in Pategi would be considered free thereafter if they continued to reside there. But many of them came with diseases, running sores and open ulcers and they presumed that the white man had knowledge of medicine and for this purpose; they would come to my grandfather for help. He was not a doctor but he knew how to dress wounds and use simple medicines to keep the wounds from becoming too infected. Those suffering from leprosy, tuberculosis and sleeping sickness were beyond any help he could give them of course.

In his book, my grandfather mentioned how goods and services were bought in Northern Nigeria. British currency had just been introduced in Nigeria but most of the people didn't know about its existence at that time. He said salt was the most commonly used currency. Cowery shells were commonly used also but he said that if you carried a thousand Canadian dollars worth of them with you as you traded with the natives, you would need a thousand bearers to carry them since they were so bulky. This being as it was, salt was the most preferable of all currencies in Northern Nigeria. A fifty-six pound bag of salt cost him $1.50 in Canadian money at that time. For that kind of currency in salt, one could hire a native labourer for a week.

My grandfather settled down among the Nupe tribe. The Nupe are an ethnic group located primarily near the confluence of the Niger and Kaduna rivers in west-central Nigeria in the Middle Belt and northern Nigeria in Niger and Kwara States. He immersed himself into the study of the Nupe language. This was extremely difficult for him because very few of the people there understood English. For two years, he lived, prayed, thought and dreamed in Nupe because he realized that unless he learned the Nupe language which was the prominent language in the upper regions of Nigeria, his work would be seriously curtailed. He arranged for natives who could speak English to teach him their language. About a year later, my grandfather was very conversant with the Nupe language.

Of course, preaching the gospel to the natives in Northern Nigeria was the main purpose of his mission. In 1903, he was appointed Superintendant of the Soudan Industrial Mission. Also in 1903, he translated the Gospel of St. John into Nupe. My grandfather used it in his services in the church he and the others had built from grass. Naturally the grass church didn't have a bell so he called them to his service by blowing the cornet he brought with him from Toronto. When he was younger, he was a member of the Queen's Own Rifles Band.

My grandfather then returned to Canada in 1905 for a furlough as he was suffering from poor health and it was wearing him down. He suffered from four attacks of African black water fever. Despite the condition of his health, he began lecturing around Canada and the United States. It was during this time that he was ordained and had married my grandmother, Althea Priest who at one time had ministered at the Toronto East mission. They honeymooned throughout Ontario, Michigan, Indiana, Ohio and Pennsylvania where he told churchgoers about his experiences in Nigeria. It was that same year that he published his book, *Life among the Nupe Tribe of West Africa.*

He then returned to Nigeria with my grandmother. The *Mennonite Brethren in Christ* (MBC) had established a mission society for Nigeria in 1905, and appointed my grandfather as its first superintendent. However, he really wanted to go further north in order to establish an area in which the *MBC*, now the *Evangelical Missionary Church (Canada)* and the *Missionary Church* (US) could work. To do this, he and my grandmother traveled five hundred miles (804 km) up the Niger River to the town of Shonga which is 70 kilometres (44 miles) along the Niger River and west of Petagi. It is in the central western part of Nigeria. The population of Shonga at that time was 5,000. It was about the same at the beginning of the year 2000. Under his leadership, the mission became the first headquarters station for what was to develop into the *United Missionary Society.*

He also built his home in Shonga. The porch steps of the house he built can still be seen today. He built all of this by hand.

When my grandfather had previously returned to Toronto for a few months leave in 1905, he purchased a printing machine, dismantled it and later took it to Nigeria with him. Apparently, he was quite adept at handling anything mechanical. He set up his printing press (later called *The Niger Press*), and then he printed a great number of books on his hand press. In spite of great difficulties, he eventually translated the whole Bible into Nupe, which was printed in England by the *British and Foreign Bible Society* but all his other books were printed on his own press. Among these is the Nupe hymnbook, used by Nupe churches to this day. He printed a Nupe grammar, and two dictionaries, one from English to Nupe and the other from Nupe to English. The dictionary, which when studied by thousands of businessmen in England (after it was published in London, England and elsewhere) made it possible for them to communicate with the Nupe people and subsequently trade with them thus bringing considerable more commerce to that part of Nigeria. I was surprised in 2008 to discover that the book is still in print and is sold on *Amazon*. It is the only Nupe/English dictionary in the world. He also translated the English school books in Nigeria into the Nupe language so that the children of Nigeria could go to schools and be educated in their own language. Of course, he wasn't the first missionary to do this. The founders of the Armenian Church were the apostles Thaddeus and Bartholomew but they and all missionaries after them up to the Fourth Century could only preach by word of mouth because up to then, Armenia didn't have an alphabet. It was then, that the Armenian monk, Mesrop Mashtots invented the Armenian alphabet.

Among many other books he wrote and printed in Nupe was a book popular among the Nupe, simply called *Old Testament Stories*.

As mission superintendent, Banfield gave direction to the development of UMS work and welcomed numbers of new missionaries who engaged in evangelism among other tribes as well as among the Nupe. The strongest opposition to the work of the mission in Petagi and the surrounding Nupe area came from fanatical Muslims who gave my grandparents a great deal of trouble. However, the respect my grandfather had among the people of Shonga is indicated by the name they gave him–"the *White Nupe*."

In 1905 my grandfather began publishing his Scriptures in Nupe, notwithstanding the fact that he had no previous training on how to operate the press. Once he learned how to operate the press, he trained others how to operate it and the *Niger Press* became one of the great Christian publishing houses in Africa. He translated all four Gospels into the Nupe dialect in 1908. In 1912, he completed the translation of the Acts of the *New Testament* and by 1914; he had translated the entire *New Testament* into Nupe. It was later put on permanent display at the *Banfield Memorial Church* in Toronto—now called the *Wellspring Worship Centre* (The congregation has been affiliated with the *Mennonite Brethren in Christ Church* (1897-1947), the United Missionary Church (1947-1969), the *Missionary Church* (1969-1993), and the *Evangelical Missionary Church of Canada*, Canada East District (1993). When the church was called the *Banfield Memorial Church*, my wife and I were married in that church on May 29th 1976.

While my grandparents were in Nigeria during my grandfather's second visit, they had a daughter, Althea but in 1912, my grandparents decided to return to Canada with their first daughter, so that my grandmother could give birth to their second daughter (my mother whose birth was imminent) in a hospital rather than in Nigeria where hospitals in that area were unknown.

My grandmother was a frugal woman and could go without if it served a greater purpose in life then live a life of luxury with no purpose. It was that frugalness that invariably saved her life, her family and of course, my mother's life which later made it possible for my brother and I to be born and our children to be born and my grandchildren's children to be born *ad infinitum*.

In April of 1912, my grandparents and my aunt arrived in Liverpool and my grandparents were told by the church organization that sponsored them as missionaries that they could take one of two ships to New York. The trip would be paid for by the church organization. The first ship was a very large British ship and very luxurious to boot. The second was a Belgium ship, which was much smaller and less luxurious as far as passenger liners were concerned. Being frugal, my grandmother said that she would rather take the Belgium ship. Further, the fact that that ship left for New York a week earlier prompted her to choose that ship. The choice she made is one of those strange quirks in life that makes us all wonder if fate has a hand in what we are and what we do and more importantly, what is waiting for us in the future.

The British ship was the *Titanic* which sank on the night of April

12th 1912 with the loss of the lives of 1,500 passengers and crew. I can just see it now—my grandmother being asked to get into the lifeboat and her refusing to do so, claiming that there are many others more worthy. Frugal and a nitpicker that she was, she was still a selfless woman and she would have invariably stayed on board with my grandfather as she never would have left him alone on the sinking ship and the both of them would have gone down with the ship, carrying my unborn mother who was born three weeks later on May 4th 1912 and finished off any chance of my mother and I and my brother and our children and their children etc, ever coming into this world. I will tell you more on the sinking of the *Titanic* later in Volume Two of my memoirs and how it indirectly affected my own future and subsequently the lives of millions of children world-wide.

According to the Mennonite records of the *Mennonite Brethren of Christ Church* in Pennsylvania, my grandparents were in Nigeria in October 1912 so I have to presume from that information that they returned to Africa sometime after my mother was born in Toronto.

In 1915, while my grandparents were again on furlough in Toronto, my grandfather was given the appointment as Secretary for West Africa (Nigeria) of the *British and Foreign Bible Society of London* and for the next 15 years he held that position while he and my grandmother served again in Nigeria as missionaries. He was also the first superintendent of the *United Missionary Church of Africa* while he was there.

With native help, they built a fairly large and reasonably comfortable home in Shonga. It was built on forty-eight cement pillars to protect the house from being destroyed by the white wood-eating ants. It had originally been built in Canada for him and shipped piece by piece to West Africa and then rebuilt. They also built twelve mud houses for their native staff. The cook house was separate from their home because if a fire took place in the cooking area, (as was quite common then) the entire place would be lost so they chose to keep it thirty feet (nine metres) away from the main building. Also, they didn't want the heat from their wood-burning stove to add to the already stifling heat in their home from the sweltering sun. The mission compound took up an acre and was surrounded by a wire fence. It was built right in the middle of the town of Shonga amongst all the smells of that small city as sewage facilities at that time still didn't exist then in Shonga.

As the years progressed while my grandparents were living and preaching in Shonga, they tried to 'save' thousands of natives but they were unsuccessful since the Nupe in that part of Africa had converted to Islam at the end of the eighteenth century and trying to convert Muslims to Christianity is as fruitless as trying to unscramble an egg. From what I learned later, he didn't convert one Nupe native into Christianity in all the years he was there.

I learned from my mother about an interesting incident in my grandparent's lives while they were there. When my uncle was a small child, the natives likened him as Jesus when the latter was a small child. When my uncle became very ill, my grandfather asked the natives to pray for him by repeating various *New Testament* passages in unison. My grandfather could by then communicate with them in their Nupe language as he had become by then, an accomplished linguist in their language. Apparently praying the Christian way didn't work. Then the natives prayed to Allah and recited passages from the *Koran*. My uncle got well again. I think that can be attributed to the power of collective prayers no matter what religious text they were using.

Although my uncle Frank and my aunt Althea spent their early years in Africa (my mother was later jealous of that fact since she was never taken to Nigeria by her parents) my grandparents wisely concluded that their children could not be educated in Nigeria so they left my aunt and uncle in Canada to live with foster parents. My mother was already living with a family (H.S. Hillmans) in West Toronto, my aunt Althea later lived with my great maternal grandmother (Priest) in East Toronto and my uncle Frank went to live with a Mennonite family (Rev. C.N. Good) in the City of Berlin, west of Toronto, later renamed Kitchener after the British general after World War I began. This was the lot of missionary children in those days being shuffled around while their parents served their church in faraway places. Reverend Good of the Mennonite Church arranged for my grandfather to be a guest lecturer at various Mennonite churches around eastern and mid-United States and Canada.

In 1930, several years prior to my own birth, my grandparents retired and returned to Toronto where they spent a good part of the rest of their lives. My grandfather in his final years suffered from a stroke. He died on November 22nd, 1949 at the age of seventy-one. I remember my mother telling me when I was sixteen years old that he had just died and reminded me that he had been extremely ill having suffered from a stroke years earlier that had paralyzed him and left him unable to speak and that his death was God's mercy to a man who spent so many years in the service of God.

My grandmother lived on for another seventeen years after my grandfather passed away. She moved from their beautiful home in Toronto where she had been living alone to a rest home in St. Catharines in Ontario to be near my Uncle Frank and his family who also lived in that city. I visited her at the rest home a couple of months before she died in her nineties on June 23rd, 1966. Both are buried in the Mount Pleasant Cemetery in Toronto in the large Banfield plot, less than 100 steps from the burial plot of George Howard Ferguson who was the premier of Ontario between 1923 and 1930. They are all in good company.

Chapter Four

I'm going to take you to a time prior to my grandparent's deaths. After my grandparents returned to Toronto permanently, my mother and her brother Frank lived with them at 962A Avenue Road. Due to the fact that my mother was gradually becoming more obviously pregnant and coupled with my grandmother's meanness and nit-picking, my mother decided in June of 1933 that she had to leave their home before her mother realized that her suspicions were true—my mother really was pregnant and out of wedlock at that.

By a stroke of good fortune, there was a woman who was a friend of my grandparents and she had a large house at the edge of the Scarborough Bluffs and she had converted part of it into a restaurant. She offered to hire my mother on as a waitress and my father on as a caretaker. My mother told her parents that she was going to take the job. Her parents were pleased, probably because my mother and her mother were always arguing with each other in any case.

My father picked up my mother in his new car, which he had purchased with the money my mother gave him from her inheritance from her maternal grandfather and he drove her to the house at the Scarborough Bluffs. I remember seeing the restaurant when I was six when my grandmother took us there one day. I was excited walking along the edge of the bluff. My grandmother was extremely upset. She didn't want me falling down the cliff.

The owner of the restaurant gave my parents a single room to live in while they were there. Perhaps she thought that they were married.

It must have later become apparent to this woman that my mother and father were not married. My mother and my father left the following month. It was then that they moved into the two-roomed shack in Scarborough.

When my birth was becoming imminent, my father's mother convinced my father that my mother should leave the two-room shack and return to my father's mother's small flat in Toronto so my father took her to his mother's flat. My mother slept on a day-couch in the living room. A few days later, she went into labour and a taxi was called and the driver took my mother to St. Michael's Hospital on Bond Street in Toronto. As said earlier, after I was born, my father took my mother and I back to their two-roomed shack in the middle of what was then primarily farmland.

Almost immediately upon assuming the Chancellorship of Germany, Hitler began promulgating legal actions against Germany's Jews. In 1933, he proclaimed a one-day boycott against Jewish shops, a law was passed against kosher butchering and Jewish children began experiencing restrictions they had to undergo in Germany's public schools. Hitler's dislike of the Jews goes back prior to his ascension in power. In a speech delivered by Hitler in Salzburg, Austria on the 7th of August 1920 in a NSDAP meeting, he said in part; "......and here is one thing that perhaps distinguishes us from you (Austrians) as far as our programme is concerned, although it is very much in the spirit of things: our attitude to the Jewish problem."

He then said, "For us, this is not a problem you can turn a blind eye to one to be solved by small concessions. For us, it is a problem of whether our nation can ever recover its health, whether the Jewish spirit can ever really be eradicated. Don't be misled into thinking you can fight a disease without killing the carrier, without destroying the bacillus. Don't think you can fight racial tuberculosis without taking care to rid the nation of the carrier of that racial tuberculosis. This Jewish contamination will not subside, this poisoning of the nation will not end, until the carrier himself, the Jew, has been banished from our midst." *unquote*   On March 15th, 1934, Hitler declared the existence of the 'Third Reich' and five days later he opened his first concentration camp for political rivals. On August 29th it was officially confirmed that Hitler was sending Jews to concentration camps and on November 10th, the Nazi pogrom, *Kristallnacht (The Night of the Broken Glass)* went in effect on the instructions of Goebbels, the Nazi propaganda minister. The resultant orgy against the Jews brought about the complete destruction of 815 shops, 171 homes, and 76 synagogues and the arrest and detention of 20,000 Jews in the newly created concentration camps.

When in Hitler's life did he begin to hate Jews? It seems that when he moved to Vienna as a teenager in 1905, he was not an anti-Semite. At least, that is what he wrote in the opening chapters of his book, *Mein Kampf (My Struggle)*. If anything, he was indifferent to them. He wrote in part; "In the Jew, I still saw a man who was (merely) of a different religion and therefore on grounds of human tolerance, I was against the idea that he should be attacked because he had a different faith." *unquote*

However, his attitude changed when he was observing Jews in Vienna. He saw them as being distinct in their dress and habits than the Europeanized Jews in the city of Linz in Austria. He claimed that the Jews in Vienna smelled bad and seemed to be un-Germanic in their appearance. In time, he became convinced that all Jews were foul and diseased which was really a metaphor for their effect on culture and politics. In his book he said, "Here was a pestilence, a moral pestilence with which the public was being infected. It was worse than the black plague." *unquote*

In those words, we can see from his recollections of his teenage life, his three delusions that subsequently had an enormous effect on the lives of millions of European Jews. The first was that the theories with respect to fighting germs could be applied to whole societies as well as individuals, the second being that Jews were a deadly pathogen and third, that he had been ordained by fate to save human civilization be exterminating this pathogen. It was his decision to embrace his third delusion that made him a malignant human being in European history. This delusional triumvirate—ignorance, hate and megalomania was the substance of his calling card; which all mass murderers and evil prophets present to society. This is typical of all mentally sick humans who target Jews, homosexuals, Muslims, blacks etc., because they believe that these people are human contaminants. Even when they begin killing people, they expect the world to thank them for their campaign in removing these so-called diseases from humankind. That's what makes them insane. Hitler was insane even though as a leader, he was brilliant, at least up until the last year of his life. Anyone that can lead a nation like he did has to be brilliant but as history has shown us, brilliant mass murderers in the past were also extremely evil also.

I strongly suspect that when the Devil and Hitler met, the Devil asked for tips from Hitler on how to be really evil.

It is unfortunate indeed that even in North America during these times and even much later, Jews were barred from hotels and social clubs, thereby forcing them to close ranks and be a people isolated from the rest of the people in the communities they lived in. I remember when I was booking into a hotel in Vancouver, British Columbia in 1953; the clerk asked me if I was of the Jewish faith. If I said that I was, I wouldn't have been given a room for the night. I would have had a better chance of getting a room in that hotel if I said I was an atheist. The only people treated worse were the blacks in the United States. More on that later in other volumes of my memoirs.

On August 16th, during a softball game at Toronto's Christie Pits, (a large park) a huge swastika flag was suddenly unfurled to shouts of "Heil Hitler!" This provoked outrage among the Jewish baseball players and spectators and a four-hour riot occurred which sent many to the hospitals as a direct result the riot which was the culmination of a summer of conflict between residents of the Kew Beach area and Jewish visitors at the beach area. On August 17th, the mayor of Toronto ordered that those wearing armbands with the German swastika on them would be arrested and charged as troublemakers.

In Canada, a great event occurred. The Dionne quintuplets were born on May 28th 1934. They were the miracle babies of their time. It was a bright story in the depth of the Depression. Their births were announced all over the world. But their story is tragic; their lives were like living in a circus. The five sisters, Annette, Cecile, Yvonne, Marie and Emilie, were born from a single egg in 1934. The public seemed to adore them. But, they were abused by the world and also (they later claimed) by their father. As babies, the quints were taken from their parents by the Ontario government and made wards of the state. Although their health was fine, they lived at a hospital that became a tourist Mecca called 'Quintland.' Between 1934 and 1943, about 3 million people visited Quintland, a low, modern building with a garden and a high fence near the village of Corbeil, in northern Ontario. The government and nearby businesses made an estimated half-billion dollars off the tourists. The sisters were the nation's biggest tourist attraction. The attraction was bigger than the Niagara Falls. Three died before I finished this part of my book--Emilie (August 6th 1954 at age 20, of accidental suffocation during an epileptic seizure at her convent), Marie (February 27, 1970, age 35, of an apparent blood clot of the brain in Montreal), and Yvonne (June 23, 2001, age 67, of cancer).

There were some other interesting arrivals that year. Sophia Loren, Shirley MacLain and Woody Allen, all to later star in movies in Hollywood, Ralph Nader, the consumer advocate, and Carl Sagent, the space scientist, were also born that year. Unfortunately in 1934, some notables died such as composers, Fredrick Delius, Edward Elgar and Gustav Holst, scientist, Marie Curie and Canadian actress, Marie Dressler.

The year 1934 wasn't any better as far as the Depression was concerned. Hitler was more powerful, Stalin brought about the starvation of millions in the Soviet Union through his collective farming plan. The liner, *Morro Castle* burned off a beach in New Jersey, killing 130.

Colonel Roscoe Turner flew from Los Angeles to New York in 15 hours, 37 minutes. The journey back to California took 18 hours,

42 minutes. To celebrate his achievements, Turner decided to set yet another record, this time across three countries. In July, he flew nonstop from Vancouver, Canada, to Auga Caliente, Mexico, in a record 9 hours, 14 minutes.

Cigarette smoking was not at this time considered dangerous to one's health and Camels Cigarettes put out an ad of a pretty woman in which the caption said; "For Digestion's Sake—Smoke Camels." Even doctors were displayed on bill boards telling everyone that cigarettes were good for smoker's health. It certainly was good for the cigarette manufacturers but it was quite a while before it was realized that millions of people were dying from lung cancer as a result of them smoking cigarettes that the ads said was good for the smokers and non-smokers alike.

The first Bob Hope radio show premiered and a new phrase came into existence, it being; "The wheel of fortune goes round and round and where she stops, nobody knows."

The movie, *It Happened One Night* won five Oscars—best picture, best director; Frank Capra, best actress; Claudette Colbert to name three.

As a bit of irony, Clark Gable was at odds with MGM so he went to Columbia and won an Oscar as best actor in the aforementioned movie. The most popular Hollywood stars were, Will Rogers, Clark Gable, Janet Gaynor, Wallace Beery, Joan Crawford, (which wouldn't have happened if anyone knew then how she was mistreating her adopted daughter) Bing Crosby,(who also mistreated his children) Shirley Temple (child star) and Marie Dressler—although she had died earlier in the year.

The songs, *Tumbling Tumbleweeds* and *Blue Moon* were hits that year and Serge Rachmaninoff performed for the first time his great piano piece, *Rhapsody on a Theme of Paganini*. As an aside, I played a selection from that piece at a concert 31 years later in Toronto.

Up to now, the six-day week was prevalent but because of the shortage of work, companies began providing their employees with work for five days only. Sad isn't it. Sure it is. The year 1934 was the turning point in the great depression in the United States and Canada with unemployment decreasing to 22%.

The average cost of a new car was $600 American (1999—$7,460.00 American) which was almost as much as the average income was for a worker for a year. A Studebaker truck cost $625.00 Average cost of a new house was $5,970.00. The rent for house was $20.00 per month, the cost of a gallon of gas was 10 cents. A loaf of Bread cost 8 cents, a pound of hamburger meat cost 12 cents and an Arrow Men's Shirt cost $2.50. Average wages per year was $1,600.00

Near their hide-out in Black Lake, Louisiana; FBI men ambushed bank robbers, Bonnie Parker and Clyde Barrow on May 23rd and sprayed their vehicle with hundreds of bullets and killed them. The State of Oklahoma experienced a ravaging drought with temperatures reaching 117 degrees in the summer of 1934. After 2 years of near drought conditions, which caused further crop failure, many farms went bankrupt with more land turning from fertile soil to dust.

In this same year, the Charles Lindbergh baby kidnapper, Bruno Hauptmann was arrested and charged with kidnapping and murder. Many people including me believe that he was framed for a crime he didn't commit. I later wrote a large article about that case in my blog.

It was this year that the federal prison, Alcatraz, situated on the little island in the San Francisco Bay, was opened up as an American federal prison. American gangsters, Dillinger, "Baby Face" Nelson, "Pretty Boy" Floyd, Bonnie Parker and Clyde Barrows were never sentenced to the "Rock as they were all shot dead instead. I visited Alcatraz in 1990. It was a tourist area then as the prison had been closed many years earlier.

Even though Josef Stalin, the dictator of the Soviet Union had complete control over the Soviet Union, he still felt that many people were against him. In a great purge, Stalin went after and killed anyone that proposed any kind of threat to him. In the end, almost 800,000 people were executed as a result of his paranoia. From the mid 1930s he began using show trials as public events where the accused had to follow a script, nearly always ending in a guilty verdict. He was expelling great numbers from the party and arresting people arbitrarily. Fear became one of the main weapons Stalin used against the Soviet people. No one was safe in Russia. Stalin was also responsible for the starvation of Ukrainians who were dying at a rate of 2,500 per day in which its peak was in 1933.

The Hays Office, under pressure from the *Catholic Legion of Decency*, prescribed a code for motion pictures—no long kisses, no double beds in any of the scenes, no naked babies shown or exposure of breasts and if a couple was to be shown on a bed, a man's both feet had to be touching the floor. I remember watching movies when there were implied scenes that the men and women would be making out. The music built up while the cameras were aimed at windows with birds in the distance. We had to imagine what the birds were seeing when they were looking in the window. Further there was to be no suggestion of seduction or living together while unmarried. To the Latin, sex is an hors d'oeuvre, to the Anglo Saxon, it is a barbecue but to those twirps in the Hays Office and in the *Catholic Legion of Decency*, sex was a smorgasbord of sin. To them, having sex was a Cardinal sin and being naked was evil incarnate. What were they? Nuns? It's amazing what the following 65 years of morality changes did considering what was later determined as appropriate in film by the end of the Twentieth Century. Nowadays the cameras are filming what is really going on in the beds. In November 2010, I saw a movie being shown on TV that showed a naked man straddling a naked woman lying face down and clearly having sex with her. Admittedly, I didn't see his penis but I guess that day will eventually come about as it has in pornographic movies. In the television series called *ROME*, a man is standing in a room and his huge penis was seen by the viewers up close. Believe it or not, the Sears & Roebuck catalog began advertising contraceptive devices in 1939.

After movie heart throb, Clark Gable removed his shirt and revealed his naked chest in the movie, *It Happened One Night*, the male underwear business slumped.

Droughts occur throughout North America, and in any given year, at least one region was experiencing drought conditions. The major drought of the 20th Century, in terms of duration and spatial extent, has been considered to be the 1930s Dust Bowl drought which lasted up to 7 years in some areas of the Great Plains.

The 1930s Dust Bowl drought, memorialized in John Steinbeck's novel, *The Grapes of Wrath*, was so severe, widespread, and lengthy that it resulted in a mass migration of millions of people from the Great Plains to the western U.S. in search of jobs and better living conditions. As much as 300 million tons of top soil was blown away, much of it out to sea. It forced farmers off the land in states like Colorado, New Mexico, Texas, Kansas and Oklahoma. The drought came in three waves, 1934, 1936, and 1939-40, but some regions of the High Plains experienced drought conditions for as many as eight years. The 'dust bowl' effect was caused by sustained drought conditions compounded by years of poor land management practices that left topsoil susceptible to the forces of the wind. The soil, depleted of moisture, was lifted by the wind into great clouds of dust and sand which were so thick, they concealed the sun for several days at a time. They were referred to as 'black blizzards'.

There were good things that happened in 1934 including many first-time appearances. They included the electric organ, talking books for the blind, laundromats, hi fi records, the launching of *SS Queen Mary*, intravenous anaesthesia became widely used, and Irene and Frederic Curie discovered the first radioactive material by bombarding aluminum with alpha particles which created a radioactive phosphorus.

And then came comic books such as *Donald Duck*, *Lil Abner*, *Flash Gordon*, and *Jungle Jim*. They weren't in colour for quite a few years and then only for a year or so before the illustrations were returned to black and white again because of the Second World War. The colour returned after the war ended. The comics business's last good year was 1993, when the industry reported gross revenues of close to $1-billion (U.S.). This was at a time when collectibles were king; when a mint-condition premiere edition of a 12-cent comic from the 1950s or 1960s could fetch $3,000 on the resale market when speculators would buy 12 copies of one issue and put 11 in storage in anticipation of a future windfall; when comic publishers would sometimes spin off six or seven titles from one character and print five or six different covers for the same issue. The poor suckers who bought them didn't realize that they had been had until they got home and compared them with the ones they purchased a month or so previous. I can't help but wonder if that's where the phrase, "You can't tell a book from its cover." came from.

Marvel Comics finally decided to abandon the Comics Code Authority. The code is a self-policing mechanism that the American industry created in 1954 to counter charges in Frank Wertham's influential book, *Seduction of the Innocent*. Wertham, a psychologist who had the ear of Congress and President Dwight Eisenhower, argued that comics propagated communism, juvenile delinquency, premarital sex and disrespect of authority. The Comics Code was once the primary way distributors gained access to newsstands, confectioneries and drug and department stores while easing parental concerns about the comic-book 'menace'. The Comics Code in this current era is pretty much an anachronism.

Contrary to the belief of some, the Comics Code Authority does not run to dozens of pages or involve detailed rules and regulations governing every kind of human and superhuman behaviour. It totals about 1,800 words that are organized into two overarching categories (Code for Editorial Matter; Code for Advertising Matter). Here are some of its edicts:

"In every instance good shall triumph over evil and the criminal punished for his misdeeds—scenes of excessive violence shall be prohibited. Scenes of brutal torture, excessive and unnecessary gunplay, physical agony, gory and gruesome crimes was to be eliminated—scenes dealing with, or instruments associated with walking dead, torture, vampires and vampirism, ghouls, cannibalism and werewolfism were prohibited. Further, it dictated that all characters shall be depicted in dress reasonably acceptable to society. Seduction and rape was never to be shown or suggested; females were to be drawn realistically without exaggeration of any physical qualities. Advertising for the sale of knives, concealable weapons or realistic gun facsimiles was prohibited." *unquote*

The Comics Code Authority has been such a whipping boy for publishers, comic fans and freedom-of-expression advocates for so long that it's a bit of a surprise to discover that its current incarnation (the year 2000) was just an operation of one person (a woman) alone functioning with a budget on such a shoestring that couldn't even afford a Web site. Working from a small office on the 17th floor headquarters of the Comics Magazine Association of America in Manhattan, Heidi Koenig perused about 100 comic titles a month in their pre-published form, looking for, variously, scenes of nudity, drug use and religion-bashing, as well as word balloons with curses and obscenities. If she spotted something questionable, for example on Page 8, middle-deck, far-right panel, she phoned the publisher.

The Code was voluntary and existed primarily to protect younger readers and guide the 15 per cent of the market that were not specialty stores. There were no fines or bans. If a publisher felt strongly about a particular story line that transgressed the Code in some way, he could still publish the work, albeit with the realization that some distributors and shops might not carry it since its cover would be minus the Comics Code seal.

In Canada, parliament passed a law prohibiting certain kinds of stories that could be printed in comic books. Section 163(1)(b) of the *Criminal Code of Canada* (2008) makes it an offence to publish or distribute a crime comic, and section 163(8) which makes it an offence to publish or distribute anything where the content is the undue exploitation of sex or of sex and violence and any of the following, crime, horror, cruelty and violence, the punishment being as much as two years in prison. In essence what that means that even if someone has in his possession one of the originals of such a comic book that is in mint condition and could be worth $3000 or more on the open market, the moment he attempts to sell it, he could be sent to prison, albeit not likely.

However, it is conceivable that that aspect of the law may be an anachronism because parliament has created a defense in ss. 163.1 (3) of the Code which should be liberally construed as they further the values protected by the guarantee of free expression. The defense of 'artistic merit' can be established objectively and can be interpreted as including any expression that may reasonably be viewed as art. This defense could apply to material that serves an 'educational, scientific or medical purpose'. This refers to the purpose the material, viewed objectively, may serve, not the purpose for which the possessor actually holds it. Parliament has made available a 'public good' defense. As with the medical, educational or scientific purpose defenses, the defense of public good can be liberally construed. In other words, is it conceivable that a crime comic which depicts the likes of the notorious gangster, Al Capone spending the last years of his life before he succumbed to syphilis a few years after his release from Alcatraz is a good example.

In the fall of 2001, Marvel replaced the Code with its own ratings system, using categories such as; 'All Ages, Marvel PG, Marvel PG Plus, Parental Advisory/Explicit Content' that, unsurprisingly is not unlike the classifications adopted by movie ratings boards.

A more recent issue of one of their comic books was a 24-page non-stop profanity-laced gorefest. Half of it is taken up with hand-to-hand combat between Nick Fury and a one-time Cold War nemesis, Colonel. Gagarin. Noses and ears are chewed; groins are grabbed; heads are stomped on by men wearing hobnailed boots. Finally, Fury puts an end to it all by sticking a hunter's knife in Gagarin's abdomen, yanking out his entrails and strangling the man to death, using his intestines as a garrotte. The original comic was a kind of balancing act. On the one hand, it was a relatively authentic portrayal of a tight-knit group of soldiers who talked tough and acted Macho; on the other hand, it respected the Comics Code by 'not using dirty words' or revelling in violence. It certainly wouldn't pass muster under the old code but it passed their censors under the Parental Advisory/Explicit Content aspect of their own code. As a child, I certainly didn't see anything like that and even when I was reading comics at our navy base at Cornwallis, Nova Scotia in 1951, there weren't any comics like that for sale at the base's store.

Some of the comic book industry's most enduring comics included *Superman, Batman, Green Lantern, Wonder Woman* and the *Justice League of America* which abided by the old code. Later movies were made about the first three characters. My favourites were the comic books under the heading *Classics* in which great novels were the substance of those comic books.

At the same time, the Wal-Mart's of this world, with their relentless demand for super-profits, have by and large forsaken the sale of comics, realizing that the rack that once featured *Archie* and *Flash Gordon* generates greater revenue when it displays tennis shoes or porcelain figurines. Nowadays, the characters in the comics will sometimes say "shit" and "ass". Although I haven't seen the word 'fuck' in any comic book but if it was used, similarly like kids in school use it daily, it's not that onerous. I believe that the comics industry is eventually going by the way of the dodo bird as it's has slowly been replaced by cartoons on television.

Now back to 1934. I will compare the 1934 costs of various items with the 1999 costs in American money. Elgin 17-jewel watch, $35.00—$435.15; Barbizon Plaza Hotel room for one month, $68.00—$845.43; Dinner at Rosoff's in New York City, 75 cents—$9.32; Movie, 35 cents—$4.35; ticket for the Metropolitan Opera, $4.00—$49.73; fifty tulip bulbs, $2.19—$27.23.

The Jews in Germany were still suffering under the auspices of Nazism. By 1935, the *Nuremberg Laws* deprived Jews of German citizenship. By 1936, Jews were prohibited from participation in parliamentary elections and signs reading 'Jews Not Welcome' appeared in many German cities. In the first half of 1938, numerous laws were passed restricting Jewish economic activity and occupational opportunities. In July, 1938, a law was passed (effective January 1st,

1939) requiring all Jews to carry identification cards. On October 28th, 1939, as many as 17,000 Jews of Polish citizenship, many of whom had been living in Germany for decades, were arrested and relocated across the Polish border. The Polish government refused to admit them so they were interned in 'relocation camps' on the Polish frontier. This was the prelude to what was going to be far worse for Jews in Europe.

This was the year that Prohibition was repealed after 17 years of Ontarians and most every other adult North American slaking their thirst on nothing stronger than fruit juice. On December 5th, the State of Utah became the 36th state to repeal Prohibition. Twelve states were still prohibiting the sale of alcohol at that time however. In the City of Toronto, there were some districts that were still referred to as dry areas as late as the 1990s.

It was the year that Hollywood made the first *King Kong* movie, and Charles Laughton starred in the first movie version of *Mutiny on the Bounty*.

Bank robberies in the United States resulted in bankers being shot and killed, George 'Machine-Gun' Kelly collected a ransom of $200,000 when he kidnapped oilman Charles Urschel. That would be two million dollars in 1999 money. Two kidnapers in San Jose, California didn't fare so well after they were arrested and placed in the local jail after kidnapping and then drowning their hostage. They were seized by the townspeople and taken to a lamp post nearby and lynched. The governor of California praised the townspeople for the 'good job' and recommended that every state learn from it.

As I have said earlier, I might have been born with a gold spoon in my mouth if my grandfather had chosen another lifestyle. My grandfather could have chosen to be rich since he and his five brothers and two sisters each inherited a great deal of money from their father. Of course, that raises the interesting question of whether or not I would have been born. Since I can't really answer that question, I guess I have to settle for whom my mother ended up being raped by prior to my birth. In any case, my great maternal grandmother was

Elizabeth Johnston.

My great maternal grandfather, William Henry Banfield was born in Toronto in 1842 but moved to the United States as a young man and years later, he returned to Toronto to make his fortune. He initially lived on Parliament Street and opened a small shop behind his house where he worked as a small manufacturer of metal goods. By the time World War I had come about, he had thriving businesses under way. One of them was the manufacturing of munitions for the Canadian armed forces, another was the making of metal mailboxes for apartment buildings and the third was the making of cream can lids for Neilsons Milk. His fourth business was the manufacturing of electrical panels and electrical switches. His businesses made him extremely rich and he and my great grandmother, Elizabeth Jane Johnston hobnobbed with the Eaton family, which was one of the richest families in Canada. He died at the age of 83 in 1925, eight years before my birth. My great grandparents had six children—four boys and two girls. In order of their births, they were; Rebecca, Edwin, Alex (my grandfather) William, Annie and two other sons, both called Harry. Uhh?

Because my maternal grandparents were missionaries in Africa, they later arranged for my late Uncle Frank who was four years younger than my mother, (and who was born in Nigeria) to stay at a boarding school in Oshawa and for my mother and her older sister Althea (the latter also born in Nigeria) to stay at the 'Ontario Ladies College' boarding school for girls in Whitby. Strangely enough, my mother's younger brother (Frank) was a twelve-year-old when my mother and he first met. When she visited him at his boarding school in Oshawa and told him that she was one of his two older sisters, he denied having any sisters. Up until then, he didn't know he had any siblings at all. Why my grandparents kept that information from him is beyond my understanding especially since he saw his older sister in Africa when they were both there with my grandparents.

As an interesting aside, the famous ventriloquist, Edgar Bergen who had a very popular radio show in the 1940s called *Edgar Bergen and Charlie McCarthy*, used to sit his two life-sized dummies (Charlie and Mortimer Snerd) at the kitchen table and for years, he would talk to them and they would talk to him and his young daughter Candice. (born in 1946) To her, they would appear to be alive and she thought that they really were her older brothers. Edgar never told her otherwise because he actually thought they were his sons. He only recovered from his mental illness when his radio show ended. It's ironic when you think about it. His shows probably wouldn't have been as funny as they were if he really knew that he was sharing the stage with dummies instead of two boys he never had.

To appreciate the circumstances leading to my birth, I have to take you back to the time before my mother met my father. About 1931 or 1932, my Aunt Althea had left the boarding school in Whitby and was going to McGill University in Montreal so at that time, only my mother and my Uncle Frank were still attending the boarding schools. Later when my mother moved to Parkside Drive in Toronto which is across from High Park, to live with an aunt, my mother met my father, Louis Vincent Batchelor (born on October 1st, 1907) through another of her aunts, Eva Priest. Eva lived in a large three-story house somewhere on Carleton Street between Yonge and Sherbourne Streets in Toronto. There were three flats on the main floor and in the larger flat at the rear of the house, lived my father-to-be, Louis and his brother Leslie and their mother who was in her 50s and her father. Her husband (my paternal grandfather) and she were divorced. Prior to his retirement, he had been a mining promoter. They were all originally from Hendon, England. My father and Leslie were only staying at the flat sporadically. When Eva saw my father about the house, she would ask my father to play the piano for her in her flat as she was quite taken by his performances on the keyboard as was everyone else when they heard him, albeit, he played by ear.

I learned (through the Archives in Ottawa) that my father had gone to Grove Prep in Lakeview, Ontario between 1919 and 1921, St. Clements College in Toronto in the 1921/1922 school year, Grammar School in the 1922/1923 school year in England and St. Andrews

College in Toronto for two years between 1923 and 1925. During those latter years, he studied Chemistry, Physics, French, German, Geometry, Algebra, Metaphysics, and Advanced Psychology.

I also learned that my father had worked in the Northern Central Mines as a machine operator between 1926 and 1929. My father was working full time as a mechanic for Toronto United Garages when he met my mother but he quit in 1934 after having an argument with his boss.

One day my mother was visiting her Aunt Eva (my mother was 19 years of age at that time) when her aunt said to my mother, "Oh, there is this nice man living in the back with his mother and brother and he plays the piano so beautifully." My mother responded with, "Why don't you ask him to come over?" That evening, Eva invited my father over to her flat, telling him that she had a pretty niece visiting her whom he might like to meet. I can say this unabashedly after having looked at pictures of my mother when she was in her early twenties; she was a very beautiful woman. He went over to Eva's flat and played the piano for my mother and Eva and they sang as he played. My mother later told me that she thought that my father was very handsome at the time. I have a picture of him sent to me by the Archives when he joined the RCAF during the Second World War. He looked like "Oil Can Harry" in the cartoon, *Popeye the Sailor Man* with his thin mustache and his black hair combed straight back. In any case, that's how my mother and father met. A few months after that, my great grandfather on my father's side, (Ernest Batchelor) died. He was close to eighty at that time. I never did learn the date or place where my paternal grandfather died.

My father also worked part-time as a life guard at a pool at the Mineral Baths Swimming Pool on the north side of Bloor Street West, a block north east end of High Park. In one of those odd coincidences in life, I applied for a job as a lifeguard at that very swimming pool in the summer of 1959 and when I gave the owner my name, he asked, "Was your father's name, Lou?" When I told him that it was, he invited me to his home which was on the hill north of the pool and he opened up a scrapbook and showed me a picture of my dad holding my mother over his head at the edge of the pool. My father weighed 170 pounds and my mother weighed only 90 pounds so he had no difficulty holding her over his head with one hand. Needless to say, I was quite amazed that the owner of the pool remembered my father and mother that far back. Notwithstanding those past links, I didn't get the job. He simply didn't need any more lifeguards. The pool and his property were later purchased by the city as the Bloor/Danforth subway line was going to run straight through it—which it did and still does.

My maternal grandparents didn't like my father so my grandfather forbade my mother to see my father. As my mother later rhetorically asked me, "Who obeys their parents under those circumstances?" and since she didn't, my mother and father dated on the sly.

My mother's older sister, Althea got a scholarship to study for her doctorate in English at McGill University in Montreal and she asked my mother to stay with her in Montreal as her roommate. Mom agreed and she got a job at the large Eatons department store in Montreal because they wanted English-speaking ladies to serve the English-speaking customers at the store.

One day when my mother and aunt were in their room, Althea told my mother that she felt a draft. My mother then wrote a letter to my father telling him that she had felt as if he had been in the room. My father wrote her back two days later and in his letter he asked her why she and Althea didn't speak to him when he called out their names in his dream. He described what they were doing and believe it or not, his description was accurate. Althea was at her desk reading a book and Mom was also reading a book with half closed eyes when Althea told Mom that she felt the draft. I have no idea how my father could have dreamed so accurately something that was actually happening in another city. Something similar to that happened years later between my mother and father during the war, which is even more amazing, but I will get to that later. As an interesting aside, one night in July 2000, I dreamed that I was getting dressed to attend my wife's funeral. When I got up, my wife told me that she was going to attend a funeral later that day. I really believe that people who are intimately close with one another can and do unwittingly communicate with one another by thought waves. If not, what other explanation can there be?

When my mother eventually returned to Toronto, she learned that my father had got a job in Huntsville, Ontario and by coincidence, my mother, and her parents and siblings went to a religious retreat on the Lake of Bays near Huntsville. Since my mother didn't know where in Huntsville my father was, they spent the summer months apart. I guess their thought waves weren't in sync at that point in their lives. While she was in Toronto, she learned that my father had also returned to Toronto so they began going out with each other again.

Althea meanwhile went to the University of British Columbia on a scholarship. She was studying English Literature. While she was there, she met Harold Fullerton (who was raised in Vancouver, B.C.,) and one day in the following summer, they were married.

My mother was 20 years old at this time and my father was 25. They were still seeing each other and she often visited him at his mother's new residence.

Around the end of January, 1933, my father who was by now 26 years old at this time, asked my mother who was still 20 years of age at this time, to have sex with him but my mother, because of her upbringing, didn't feel that it was right, at least not until they were married. He forced himself on her to the extent that my mother fell victim to what we would call today, a date rape.

Acquaintance rape is the least reported type of rape. 1 in 12 males responded that they committed sexual acts which meet the legal definition of rape. The average age when a rape incident occurred is 18.5 years old for both men and women; perpetrator and victim. Acquaintance rape survivors tend to take longer to recover than survivors of stranger rape because it is a violation of trust with an acquaintance being a major factor. A woman's risk of being raped by an acquaintance is four times greater than being raped by a stranger. In a 1994 study surveying more than 6,000 students at 32 colleges and universities in the U.S., 84% knew their attacker, and 57% of the rapes happened on dates. 13.3% of college women indicated that they had been forced to have sex in a dating situation. The majority of the victims were between 15 and 25 years of age. These figures only apply to those victims who reported the rapes. Of those who were raped, 30% contemplated suicide in the weeks after the incident.

One of the reasons why rape victims in the 1930s and beyond didn't report being raped to the police is because in those days, many police officers were prone to not believing the victim's account of the rape. According to the FBI Uniform Crime Reports, less than 5% of all reported rapes are false reports; the same percentage as for all other felonies. Despite this low percentage, this could account for the disbelief on the part of many of the investigating police officers. The women knew this or at least suspected this and for this reason, they chose to remain silent just as my mother did. Of those who were raped, nearly 50% told no one about the incident—ever. I only learned of the rape of my mother by my father in the 1980s when she sent me a tape recording of her life with him.

I was conceived as a direct result of my father raping my mother. I would have preferred to have been conceived under better circumstances but that is life. Obviously, had my father not raped my mother when he did, I may never have existed, or at least into what I developed into being what I am now for whatever that is worth. The inevitable but most challenging question comes to the fore. If my father hadn't raped my mother, would I have ever been born as a result of another sexual union or would I have died in stillbirth or if I had been conceived later as a result of a loving sex act, would I have been born a girl instead of a boy or born mentally retarded or with my IQ of 122? If my mother looked upon abortion as many women do nowadays, would I have been aborted? Would I have ever been born? I think I will abandon these rhetorical questions and accept what happened and settle for what I am.

On May 4th, 1933, the day my mother turned 21 and was approximately four months pregnant with me, she inherited a sum of money ($3,000) left to her by her grandfather. In 2009 dollars, it would be equivalent to $310,000 dollars. She spent almost all of the money on my father I suppose in hopes of keeping him. By then, she had become aware that she was pregnant. After my father raped my mother, my father rarely visited her but when June of that year rolled by, she approached my father and told him that she was carrying his child and she wanted him to marry her. Nowadays, pregnant girls and women aren't that willing to marry the single men who impregnate them, least of all the men who date rape them but in those days, girls and women who were pregnant out of wedlock would be shunned and as bad as my father was, she felt that marrying him was the better of two evils. It was then that she learned from my father that he couldn't marry her because he was already married (although he was separated) and that he had a young son. He seemed to have his way with women. I didn't learn until many years later when my Aunt Althea accidentally blurted it out that my father had married another woman prior to him meeting my mother. In 1963, I talked with a dentist in Toronto who told me that his father had the same full name as my father. We concluded from our talk together that we were probably half-brothers.

When my maternal great grandfather died, he left each of his seven children a sizable inheritance so my grandfather and grandmother fared reasonably well before they went to Nigeria in 1905 and after they returned to Canada in the early 1930s, they could afford to purchase the second floor of their beautiful two-family home where they had lived for many years prior to my birth. Notwithstanding the year we lived with my grandparents, most of my childhood was generally in some state of wretched poverty. As I said in the preface of my autobiography, it was Juvenal, the Roman writer who said that when you are poor, you can whistle in the face of robbers, hence the title of my first volume which depicts my childhood. I was so poor; I was always whistling—even to myself.

It was about eight months after my birth (around June 1934) that my maternal grandfather finally found out that his youngest daughter was not only living out of wedlock with the married man that he warned her against, but also that she had a baby with him the year before. I never learned how my grandmother reacted when she heard the news, but I suppose it would be akin to a man learning that his football-playing son is gay. They learned of this *blot* in their lives when a newspaper reporter discovered that the eminent Alex Banfield's younger daughter had a child out of wedlock and was still living in sin. He tried to blackmail my grandfather by promising not write about my mother's 'sin' if my grandfather gave him money. My grandfather tossed him out of the house and the reporter published the story in a Toronto newspaper.

Soon after that newspaper article was published, my mother was looking out the window and suddenly she saw her parents walking across the grass towards the shack where we lived in Scarborough. My mother wasn't sure she wanted to open the door but when she did, her mother kissed her and asked, "Where's the baby?" When she grabbed me in her arms, she remarked how beautiful I was; something I have always maintained that I was then and even to this day. My grandfather was more reserved and really didn't show any signs of affection towards my mother or me. He asked, "Why didn't you let us know?" My mother didn't know what to say in response since she had purposely attempted to remain hidden from her parents. When anyone visited my mother, she hid me inside the small closet so no one would know that she had a child out of wedlock. How I kept quiet while in the dark closet must have been a miracle. Perhaps I was gagged.

My mother's parents suggested that my mother and I move back to Toronto with them since my father was seldom around to care for us. My mother didn't really want to live with her parents because of her mother's constant nagging so she declined their offer. She remained in the small shack on the farm and waited until my father returned and he found us a flat on MacPherson Street in Toronto. He wanted a flat that was close to his own mother's residence. Notwithstanding that, his mother never invited my mother or me over for a visit, not even on Christmas. To say that the relationship between my father and my mother's parents was close at this juncture in their relationship would be a misuse of the word, 'close'. They did however give my father and mother money to assist them in supporting the three of us, not that it improved our lot that much. Naturally, I don't remember any of this as I only had three things that occupied my thoughts at this time—eating, sleeping and being hugged—or so I have been told.

Not long after this time in my life, my father deserted us again so my mother's parents again invited my mother and me to live with them in their home at 962A Avenue Road. Needless to say that since I was eighteen months old at this time, I didn't really understand and appreciate the significance of living in such a beautiful home surrounded by such fine furnishings, including, African spears, swords, knives and shields hanging on all the walls along with other African brick-a-brack and the lion's skin and head on the floor of the living room. We lived there for at least a year. As an interesting aside; all that African paraphernalia is now in the Royal Ontario Museum in Toronto with the exception of certain items given to family members. I have an 18-inch ivory African crocodile in my study that is well over a century old at the time of this writing. I also have a cut-glass sugar bowl and creamer that are also from Africa and well over a century old.

My father, who was not living with us at this time, got himself a job as a collector of debts this year and the following year with Able Shoe Company.

TWA (Transcontinental & Western Air) had reduced the flying time from coast to coast to 18 hours including refueling stops in between the coasts.

In Germany, the four million brown shirted Nazi SA (Sturmabteilung) storm troopers, included many members who actually believed in the 'socialism' of National Socialism and wanted to become a true revolutionary army in place of the regular German Army. But as far as the regular Army High Command and its conservative supporters were concerned, this potential storm trooper army represented a threat to centuries old German military traditions and the privileges of rank. Adolf Hitler had been promising the generals for years that he would restore their former military glory and break the shackles of the *Treaty of Versailles* which limited the Army to 100,000 men and prevented modernization. Adolf Hitler recognized the fact that the behavior of the SA was a problem that now threatened his own political survival and the entire future of the Nazi movement. The SA's anti-capitalist, anti-tradition sentiments often expressed by SA leaders and echoed by the restless masses of storm troopers also caused considerable concern to big industry leaders who had helped put Hitler in power. Hitler had promised them he would put down the trade union movement and Marxists, which he did. However, now his own storm troopers with their talk of a 'second revolution' were sounding more and more like Marxists themselves. (the first revolution having been the Nazi seizure of power in early 1933).

The SA was headed by Ernst Röhm, a battle scarred, aggressive, highly ambitious street brawler who had been with Hitler from the very beginning. Röhm and the SA had been very instrumental in Hitler's rise to power by violently seizing control of the streets and crushing Hitler's political opponents.

However, by early 1934, a year after Hitler came to power, the SA's use as a violent, intimidating, revolutionary force had invariably come to an end. Hitler now needed the support of the regular Army generals and the big industry leaders to rebuild Germany after the Great Depression re-arm the military and ultimately accomplish his long range goal of seizing more living space for the German people. There was no longer a need, as far as he was concerned, with a group of unruly armed men like the SA existing in Germany.

Further, the average German also feared and disliked the SA brown shirts with their arrogant, gangster-like behavior. The SA thugs extorted money from local shop owners, showed off by driving around in fancy news cars, often got drunk, beat up and even murdered innocent civilians so Hitler knew that he would have the support of the citizenry if he could remove the SA from their midst.

Sometime near the end of February 1934, Hitler held a meeting attended by SA and regular Army leaders including Röhm and

German Defense Minister General Werner von Blomberg. At this meeting Hitler informed Röhm that the SA would not be a military force in Germany but would be limited to certain political functions. In Hitler's presence, Röhm gave in and even signed an agreement with Blomberg to this effect.

Obviously Röhm was not happy with this change in his status and that of the SA so he soon let it be known he had no intention of keeping to the agreement. In April he even boldly held a press conference and proclaimed, "The SA is the National Socialist Revolution!"

Within the SA at this time was a highly disciplined organization known as the SS (Shutzstaffel) which had been formed in 1925 as Hitler's personal body guard. SS chief Heinrich Himmler along with his second-in-command, Reinhard Heydrich, and Hermann Goering, began plotting against Röhm by prodding Hitler into action against his old comrade, hoping to gain favour with Hitler from Röhm's downfall.

On June 4th, Hitler and Röhm had a five-hour private meeting lasting until midnight. A few days later Röhm announced he was taking a 'personal illness' vacation and the whole SA would go on leave for the month of July. Röhm also convened a conference of top SA leaders for June 30th at a resort town near Munich which Hitler promised to attend to sort out the differences between them.

On June 17th, Vice Chancellor Franz von Papen, who had helped Hitler become Chancellor, stunned everyone by making a speech criticizing the rowdy, anti-intellectual behavior of the SA and denouncing Nazi excesses such as strict press censorship. Papen also focused on the possibility of a 'second revolution' by Röhm and the SA and urged Hitler to put a stop to it. Papen asked. "Have we experienced an anti-Marxist revolution in order to put through a Marxist program?" His speech drastically increased the tension between German Army leaders and SA leaders and further jeopardized Hitler's position. But for the moment Hitler hesitated to move against his old comrade Röhm. I cannot fathom why he was so hesitant at this stage of his career.

A few days later however, on June 21st, Hitler went to see President Paul von Hindenburg at his country estate. Hindenburg was in failing health and was confined to a wheelchair. Hitler met with the Old Gentleman (as Hitler often called him) and Defense Minister Blomberg and was stiffly informed that the SA problem must be solved or the president would simply declare martial law and let the German Army run the country, effectively ending the Nazi regime. Now Hitler knew he had to act fast because the Army would jump at the chance to boot Hitler out of power.

Meanwhile, Himmler and Heydrich spread false rumors that Röhm and the SA were planning a violent takeover of power (putsch).

On June 25th, the German Army was placed on alert, leaves canceled and the troops confined to the barracks. An agreement had been secretly worked out between Himmler and Army generals ensuring cooperation between the SS and the Army during the coming action against the SA. The Army would provide weapons and any necessary support, but would remain in the barracks and let the SS handle the matter on their own.

On Thursday, June 28th, Hitler, Geöring, and Goebbels attended the wedding of Gauleiter Josef Terboven in Essen. Hitler was informed by phone that he faced the possibility of a putsch by Röhm's forces and also faced the possibility of a revolt by influential conservative non-Nazis who wanted Hindenburg to declare martial law and throw Hitler and his government out of office. Hitler then sent Göering back to Berlin to get ready to put down the SA and also the conservative government leaders there. The SS was put on full alert. On Friday, June 29th, Hitler made a scheduled inspection tour of a labor service camp and then went to a hotel near Bonn for the night. He was informed by Himmler that evening by phone that SA troops in Munich knew about the coming action and had taken to the streets. Hitler decided to fly to Munich with intentions of putting down the SA rebellion and confronting Röhm and top SA leaders who were gathered at the resort town of Bad Wiessee near Munich.

After Hitler arrived in Munich near the dawn of Saturday, June

30th, he first ordered the arrest of the SA men who were inside Munich Nazi headquarters, then he proceeded to the Ministry of the Interior building where he confronted the top SA man in Munich after his arrest, even tearing off his insignia in a fit of rage. His next destination was to go where Röhm was staying. A column of troops in cars containing Hitler, Rudolf Hess and others, sped off toward Röhm and his men.

At this point, the story is often told (partly created by the Nazis) of Hitler arriving at the resort hotel about 6:30 a.m. and rushing inside with a pistol to arrest Röhm and other SA leaders. However it is more likely the hotel was first secured by the SS before Hitler went anywhere near it. Hitler then entered the hotel, confronted Röhm and the others and sent them to Stadelheim prison outside Munich to be later shot by the SS.

An exception was made in the case of Edmund Heines, an SA leader who had been found in bed with a young man. When told of this, Hitler ordered the immediate execution of both men at the hotel. They were immediately taken outside and shot.

A number of the SA leaders, including Röhm, were homosexuals. Prior to the purge, Hitler for the most part ignored their behavior because of their usefulness to him during his rise to power. However, their usefulness and Hitler's tolerance had now come to an abrupt end. Later, their homosexual conduct would be partly used as an excuse for the murders he was bringing about.

Saturday morning at about 10 a.m. a phone call was placed from Hitler in Munich to Göering in Berlin with the prearranged code word 'Kolibri' meaning 'hummingbird' that unleashed a wave of murderous violence in Berlin and over 20 other cities in Germany.

SS execution squads along with Göering's private police force roared through the streets hunting down SA leaders and anyone on the prepared list of political enemies (known as the *Reich List of Unwanted Persons*).

Included on the list: Gustav von Kahr, who had opposed Hitler during the *Beer Hall Putsch* of 1923 was found hacked to death in a swamp near Dachau; Father Bernhard Stempfle, who had taken some of the dictation for Hitler's book *Mein Kampf* and knew too much about Hitler was shot and killed; Kurt von Schleicher, former Chancellor of Germany and master of political intrigue, who had helped topple democracy in Germany and put Hitler in power was shot and killed along with his wife; Gregor Strasser, one of the original members of the Nazi Party and formerly next in importance to Hitler; Berlin SA leader Karl Ernst, who was involved in torching the Reichstag building in February, 1933; Vice-Chancellor Papen's press secretary; and Catholic leader Dr. Erich Klausener were also murdered.

That Saturday evening, Hitler flew back to Berlin and was met at the airport by Himmler and Göering in a scene later described by Hans Gisevius, a Gestapo official, present. He wrote; "On his way to the fleet of cars, which stood several hundred yards away, Hitler stopped to converse with Göering and Himmler. From one of his pockets Himmler took out a long, tattered list. Hitler read it through, while Göering and Himmler whispered incessantly into his ear. We could see Hitler's finger moving slowly down the sheet of paper. Now and then it paused for a moment at one of the names. At such times the two conspirators whispered even more excitedly. Suddenly Hitler tossed his head. There was so much violent emotion, so much anger in the gesture, that everybody noticed it. Finally they moved on, Hitler in the lead, followed by Göering and Himmler. Hitler was still walking with the same sluggish tread. By contrast, the two blood drenched scoundrels at his side seemed all the more lively." *unquote*

As for Ernst Röhm; on Hitler's orders, he had been given a pistol containing a single bullet to commit suicide, but he refused to do it, saying "If I am to be killed let Adolf do it himself." Two SS officers, one of whom was Theodore Eicke, commander of the Totenkopf (Death's Head) guards at Dachau, entered Röhm's cell after waiting fifteen minutes for Rohm to do himself in but when it was apparent that he wasn't going to shoot himself, Eicke shot Rohm point blank in his chest. Reportedly, Röhm's last words were "Mein Führer, mein Führer!" In his mind, he was probably asking himself, "Why are you doing this to me?"

On Sunday evening, July 1st, while some of the murders were still going on, Hitler gave a tea party in the garden of the Chancellery for cabinet members and their families in order to give the appearance that things were getting back to normal.

By 4 a.m., Monday, July 2nd, the bloody purge had ended. The exact number of murders is unknown since all Gestapo documents relating to the purge were eventually burned. Estimates vary widely from 200 or 250, to as high as 1,000 or more. Less than half of those murdered were actually SA officers. Obviously, that was because of personal vendettas.

Not everything went according to plan however. A man named Willi Schmidt was at home playing the cello. Four SS men rang the doorbell, entered and took him away, leaving his wife and three young children behind. They had mistaken Dr. Willi Schmidt, music critic for a Munich newspaper, for another Willi Schmidt who was on the list. Dr. Schmidt was assassinated and his body later returned to his family in a sealed coffin with orders from the Gestapo that it should not be opened. One can assume that the man had been also shot in the face and disfigured by the slashing and the Gestapo didn't want that fact to become public. This incident reminds me of the 13-year-old boy in Syria in 2011 who was grabbed by Syrian police at a protest and tortured to death and his body was returned to his parents with orders not make it public about the condition of his body. They made the sight of the body public by putting the image of the tortured boy in Facebook. The picture of the boy with the burn and slash marks all over his body was flashed around the world.

On July 13th, Hitler gave a long speech to the Nazi controlled Reichstag (parliament which was held in another building) in which he announced seventy four people had been shot and he justified the murders by saying in part;

"If anyone reproaches me and asks why I did not resort to the regular courts of justice, then all I can say is this: In this hour I was responsible for the fate of the German people, and thereby I became the supreme judge of the German people. It was no secret that this time the revolution would have to be bloody; when we spoke of it, we called it *The Night of the Long Knives*. Everyone must know for all future time that if he raises his hand to strike the State, then certain death is his lot." *unquote* I doubt that he had the state in mind when he made that pronouncement. He really meant that anyone who went against his wishes would die. This became very apparent to everyone by the end of the war.

By proclaiming himself the supreme judge of the German people, Hitler in effect had placed himself above the law, making his word the law and thus he had instilled a permanent sense of fear in the German people.

The German Army generals, by condoning the unprecedented events of the *Night of the Long Knives*, effectively cast their lot with Hitler and began the long journey with him that would eventually lead them to the brink of world conquest and for two of them, later to the gallows as war criminals after the war.

A few weeks after the purge, Hitler rewarded the SS for its role by raising the SS to independent status as an organization that was no longer part of the SA. The leader of the SS, Reichsführer Heinrich Himmler was now answerable directly to Hitler and no one else. Reinhard Heydrich, as Himmler's deputy was promoted to the rank of SS Gruppenführer (Lieutenant-General). The only rank higher would be that of a marshal of the army which of course would be academic for him as he was not in the army.

From this time on, the SA brownshirts would be diminished and all would disappear eventually as its members were inducted into the regular Army after Hitler re-introduced military conscription in 1935. The SS organization under Himmler and Heydrich would greatly expand and become Hitler's instrument of mass murder and terror throughout Europe.

On May 1st, 1934, Engelbert Dollfuss, the fascist chancellor of Austria proclaimed a new constitution, that provided for a state organization through professional corporations or syndicates similar to those in Fascist Italy. During his administration, Dollfuss had balanced the Austrian budget, reduced unemployment by 54,000, the savings banks were now above their pre-crisis level of 2,000,000,000 schillings; the tills of the National Bank were filling up fast, and note circulation had been cut back by almost 30 percent. The currency had become healthy enough to withstand the effects of all the Western devaluation measures of 1933, and the nation's adverse trade balance had been reduced from 25 to 19 percent of the total. The overall index of industrial output jumped from 78 to 88 from October of 1932 to October of 1933.

Despite the improvement in the economy, the opposition by German and Austrian Nazis to his regime intensified and acts of murder, terror and sabotage became so rampant that the death penalty in Austria was reinstituted and detention camps established. All that was to no avail because Hitler would send in two more agent provocateurs for every one the Austrians took out.

The situation came to a head on July 25th, 1934 when a detachment of Austrian Nazi Storm Troopers invaded the Chancellery building which housed the government offices. They shot President Dollfuss then let him lay bleeding to death for four hours and refused to allow him any medical assistance. He died a martyr's death.

The Nazis who were holed up in the chancellery, repeatedly called for help from the Austrian Storm Troops and SS, but their help never came. When it became apparent to them that no help was forthcoming, they negotiated a surrender. The surrender terms agreed upon were that they would be taken to the German/Austrian border and be released. The forces outside the Chancellery were unaware that Dollfus had been murdered by the traitors when they agreed to the armistice. At 5:30 Kurt von Schuschnigg and his forces took the Chancellery back. Then they realized that the president had been murdered. The Austrian Nazi traitors would have been escorted to the German border and released as promised had they not murdered Dollfuss. Austrian citizens tried to lynch the assassins but were unsuccessful. The captured Austrian traitors were tried, convicted and put to death and Schuschnigg became the new Chancellor of Austria.

Mussolini upon hearing of the attempted coup called up his army and sent them to the Brenner Pass and the Corinthian border. German intelligence became alarmed when they found out that the Italian army was being issued battle ammunition. Mussolini didn't just confine himself to the military sphere; he had received the British and French Ambassadors to discuss common diplomatic action in the crisis.

Dollfuss by dying as a martyr did more to unite his nation than anything he did or could have done while he was alive. Over one million of his countrymen attended his funeral. As a London paper wrote on July 30th, 1934 "By his death, Dr. Dollfuss has proved that a German culture really exists that is worth saving. The murdered Chancellor might have hoped for greater help from Britain while he was alive. But he could not have wished for a better epitaph once he was dead." *unquote*

Despite the fact that Hindenburg was now lapsing in and out of senility;(now called Alzheimer's Disease) he was persuaded to run for re-election in 1932, as the only candidate who could defeat Adolf Hitler. Hindenburg defeated Hitler for the Presidency, but Hitler staged an electoral comeback, with his Nazi party wining the majority of the seats in the Reichstag. Hindenburg stayed on as President after appointing Hitler to become Chancellor of Germany in 1933 and Hindenburg remained in office until his death on August 2nd, 1934 at his home in Newdeck, East Prussia (part of Poland) exactly two months short of his eighty-seventh birthday. He would be Germany's last President until after World War II.

Following Hindenburg's death, Hitler merged the offices of President and Chancellor into the new office of Fuhrer (leader) and Chancellor (*Führer und Reichskanzler*) making him Germany's Head of State and Head of Government. He had already presumed to be the head of the judiciary after the 'Night of the Long Knives' so in effect, he was an absolute ruler of Germany, answerable to no one, not even the courts.

While enroute to New York from Cuba carrying American vacationers, the ocean liner *Morro Castle* caught fire off the coast of

New Jersey near Asbury Park. The ship eventually washed up on the beach and stayed there for some time before being removed from the beach directly behind Convention Hall in March, 1935. Over 150,000 people watched from the shore as the ship burned and 130 passengers died. The ship was towed to the Union Shipbuilding Yard in Baltimore, Maryland where she was completely scrapped.

The inquiry afterwards heard of panic stricken passengers unable to board lifeboats because the boats were not properly stowed in their davits. Fire hydrants on deck had been capped to prevent their leaking onto the deck and causing passenger falls. Reports indicated that the crew had allegedly abandoned their obligation to the passengers and fled the ship in the few accessible lifeboats on the ship. No evacuation drill had been conducted during the voyage and the results of the inquiry led to legislation that required ships to be built with fire resistant materials and that crews be better trained in handling emergency situations. From then on, all ocean-going passenger ships were to conduct at least one evacuation drill during any trip. Generally, one and only drill takes place within an hour or so after the ship heads out to sea. Attendance on the boat deck is mandatory however because I am partially disabled, my wife explained to the officer on the deck of the cruise ship we were supposed to report to that I couldn't attend as I can't remain standing for more than ten minutes at any time. The officer then asked my wife to give me all the particulars as to where we are to go in case of an emergency. She actually showed me where we were to go.

The Kingdom of Serbs, Croats and Slovenes was renamed the Kingdom of Yugoslavia in 1929. It was ruled by King Alexander Karageorgevic. On October 9th 1934, the king was assassinated during a state visit to Marseilles, France by an exiled Macedonian named Vlada Gheorghieff, a member of the Macedonian Revolutionary Organization. The French Foreign Minister, Louis Barthgou was also shot while riding in the same car and he died a few hours later. Their assassin, Gheorghieff was attacked on the spot by French police and he died of his wounds that evening. This was the first assassination to be captured on a motion picture film.

Chapter Five

In 1935, the economic recovery was looking a little better than the year I was born. A new car in 1935 sold for anywhere from $500 to $1000. In 1999 money, $500 American money would be $6,080.29. A thousand dollar car would be twice as much. A used 1932 Pontiac could be had for as little as $325 USD which in 1999 money would be $3,952.19. A used 1932 Ford, would be $275 USD which would be in 1999 money, $3,344.16 and a 1928 Buick for as little as $68 USD and in 1999 money, would be $826.92. A three-piece business suit could be bought for $17.85 USD and in 1999 money, that would be $217.07 USD and a brass bed and mattress could be bought for $21.45 USD which in 1999 would be $260.54 USD with as little as $3.00 American down which in 1999 would be $36.48 USD. That may not seem like much by today's standards but considering the fact that the average weekly income was between six and twelve dollars, which in 1999 would be $72.96 USD. It was still a lot of money to pay out and many simply didn't have any money left after wage earners paid their rent and bought their food. Mind you, food wasn't that expensive—at least not by today's standards. Prime sirloin beef sold for 25 cents USD which in 1999 would be $3.04 USD a pound. Ten pounds of sugar could be bought for 46 cents US which would be $5.59 US. Tea and coffee were both 35 American cents a pound which in 1999 would be $4.26 USD—$5.56 Canadian). A young man could take his girl to a movie in a cab, and later treat themselves to a dish of ice cream for less than 50 American cents all told which in in 1999 would be $6.08 USD.

If the breadwinner had a steady job, he could rent a six-room house for $15 USD a month or a ten-room house for $50 USD a month. For an American with a large family who was earning only $6 a week, he would only have $24 a month in which to support himself and his family in which $15 would be spent on housing, leaving $9 for food and clothing and that is if taxes weren't deducted from his pay cheque. It was extremely difficult for a great many families, especially large families to live on such meager earnings in this era. One could see why the kids practically wore rags to school and went to school hungry and why the prospects of owing a car were slim indeed. One out of every two households in the United States was on some form of relief. At the other extreme, William Randolph Hearst, the newspaper magnate and Mae West, the movie star were the highest paid persons in the United States.

It was that year that the first China Clipper, an enormous four-engine sea plane, crossed the Pacific to its destination in Manila; the first of a fleet of such planes owned by Pan Am that was to open the Trans-Pacific air mail and passenger service. Pan Am folded 57 years later because of a fatal blunder involving their lack of security. More on that in a later volume. On November 11th, 1935, two men ascended in a gondola of the then largest balloon in the world to a height of 72,395 feet (13.7 miles—22 kilometres).

The radio shows, *Fibber McGee* and *Molly*, *Dick Tracy* and *Flash Gordon* premiered that year. As an interesting aside, the man who played Flash Gordon, a futuristic science fiction character, was none other than Gale Gordon of the later sitcoms who performed in the radio and later TV show, *Our Miss Brooks* as the high school principal and in *Beverly Hillbillies* as the bank president.

The Hollywood top box-office stars were, Shirley Temple, Will Rogers, Clark Gable, Fred Estaire and Ginger Rogers, Joan Crawford, Claudette Colbert, Dick Powell, Wallace Beery, Joe E. Brown and James Cagney. The best picture was *Mutiny on the Bounty* (filmed the previous year) with Charles Laughton playing, 'Captain Bligh'.

The hit songs were, *Begin the Beguin*, *I've Got Plenty of Nuthin*, *Red*

Sails in the Sunset, and *Summertime* from the musical, *Porgy and Bess*.

The first wearable hearing aid was made, and an aircraft-detecting device was created. It was called, radar which played an enormous role during the Second World War that was to follow in 1939.

Bingo was now being played in movie theatres and branched into halls all over the USA and Canada. The board game, Monopoly hit the market and in that year, as many as 7,355,000 Monopoly sets were sold before the year was out. And for a first appearance, a car that exceeded 300 m.p.h. (482 km per hour), beer in cans, Richter scale for earthquakes, ReaLemon, Jolly Green Giant, and the creation of the Gallop Poll also came into existence.

It was in 1935 that the 'send a dime' chain letters flooded the post offices of the USA and Canada. Millions of people, both in the USA and Canada got worked up over it. If was a daffy idea but no one got hurt by it and no one made a killing with it. It worked like this. You would receive a letter in the mail with six names and address on it. You were urged to send a dime to the person whose name was at the top of the list. Then you crossed off his name and placed yours at the bottom and then sent five copies to your friends. Through five such progressions, (provided no one broke the chain) your name would reach the top and you would be eventually rewarded with 15,625 dimes—$1,565.50 on a ten-cent investment. Mathematically, it was sound, even if it was preposterous to believe that the chain letters would go on for ever. Millions of people did such as clerks, labourers, housewives, kids, government officials, pensioners—everybody. The scheme ballooned into a national mania that was clogging up the post offices with millions of pieces of mail, disrupting classrooms and, businesses. Millions of dimes had to be created to meet the demand, and the post offices had to hire more staff. Soon the con men got into the act and in Springfield, Missouri; the city came to a standstill when the chain letter pitchmen offered guaranteed notarized chain letters anywhere from $1 to $5. The madness finally came to an end in June, about three months after it began. Finally everyone agreed it was silly but it was fun while it lasted except for the exhausted mailmen. This whole idea sounds like the beginnings of the Pyramid schemes. As a matter of interest, it was this scheme that later prompted the *March of Dimes* to fight polio.

The world's second largest reflector telescope (at that time) comprising of a 74-inch Pyrex disc, was completed on May 7th, 1935 and still sits on a hill in Richmond Hill, Ontario. Years later it was dwarfed by many larger telescopes and because of the night lights of nearby Toronto and Richmond Hill interfering with its purpose, it was later used only for studying the sun. My wife and I visited the telescope one night in the 1970s.

The Americans brought in the *Social Security Act* for old age pensioners and their pensions were based on a percentage of their earnings before they turned 65. Canada brought in a similar pension called the *Canada Pension Plan* many years later. On June 10th, two reformed alcoholics organized *Alcoholics Anonymous* in New York City.

On September 8th, a dentist, Carl Weise who had a grudge against the governor, Huey Long, a powerful demagogue who was the governor of Louisiana, shot him in the corridor of the state capital building in Baton Rouge. The governor's bodyguards opened fire on the dentist and fired 62 bullets into him, killing him. Huey Long died two days later.

There were still some lynchings going on in the southern states, most of the victims being black. Six deputies were escorting Stacy (a black man) to Dade County jail in Miami on the 19th of July 1935, when he was taken by a white mob and hanged by the side of the home of Marion Jones, the woman who had made the original complaint against him. The New York Times later revealed that "subsequent investigation revealed that Stacy, a homeless tenant farmer, had gone to the house to ask for food; the woman became frightened and screamed when she saw Stacy's face."

The vigilantes had hanged an innocent man.

When Hitler marched into the Rhineland in March 1935 and seized it from the control of the British and French, Great Britain and France stood by and did nothing. It was learned much later that if Great Britain and France had done more than merely protested, the German army would have retreated. In fact Hitler later admitted; "The forty-eight hours after the march into the Rhineland were the most nerve-wracking in my life. If the French had then marched into the Rhineland, we would have had to withdraw with our tail between our legs, for the military resources at our disposal would have been wholly inadequate for even a moderate resistance." *unquote*

Hitler had counted on the British and the French doing nothing and that is what they did. The Allies missed the greatest opportunity to stop Hitler before he progressed any further in his ambition for conquests and they blew it by sitting idly by. I think it is safe to say that millions of lives would not have been lost later if the Allies stepped in and stopped Hitler when he marched into the Rhineland.

King George V was born on June 3rd, 1865, the second son of Edward VII and Alexandra. His early education was somewhat insignificant as compared to that of the heir apparent, his older brother Albert. George chose the career of professional naval officer and served competently until Albert died in 1892, upon which George assumed the role of the heir apparent. He was knock-kneed, had bright blue eyes, golden brown hair, a full mustache and beard and had a sturdy build. He married Mary of Teck (affectionately called May) in 1893; who bore him four sons and one daughter. George ascended the throne in the midst of a constitutional crisis: the budget controversy of 1910. Tories in the House of Lords were at odds with Liberals in the Commons pushing for social reforms. When George agreed to create enough Liberal peerages to pass the measure the Lords capitulated and gave up the power of absolute veto, resolving the problem officially with passage of the Parliament Bill in 1911.

The outbreak of the First World War created problems for the royal family because of its German background. Owing to strong anti-German feeling in Britain, it was decided to change the name of the royal family from Saxe-Coburg-Gotha to Windsor. I believe that the name Windsor was chosen because the royal family spent much of their time in the castle in the small community near London called Windsor. Windsor Castle is named after the town. To stress his support for the British, the king and queen made several visits to the front lines in France and Belgium. On one visit to France in 1915 he fell off his horse and broke his pelvis causing him life-long pain as a direct result.

The relationship between England and the rest of the Empire underwent several changes. An independent Irish Parliament was established in 1918 after the Sinn Fein uprising in 1916. The *Government of Ireland Act* (1920) divided Ireland along religious lines. Canada, Australia, New Zealand and South Africa having come to the aid of the empire, demanded the right of self-governance after the First, World War resulting in the creation of the British Commonwealth of Nations by the Statute of Westminster in 1931. India was accorded some degree of self-determination with the *Government of India Act* in 1935. Canada would no longer be referred to as the Dominion of Canada. It would simple be called Canada after that. I remember when I was in grade school being given Dominion of Canada maps to study from.

As a matter of interest, the word Canada is derived from the Huron-Iraquois word, *kanada* which means village or settlement. I suppose when the first settlers arrived at the shores of the world's second largest country, Indian villages and settlements (kanadas) was all there was. When Jacques Cartier was nearing Ile d' Anticosti, two Indian youths he was bringing back to France with him referred to the settlement as "kanada" and from then on; the name, Canada stuck.

The worldwide depression of 1929-1931 deeply affected England, prompting the king to persuade the heads of the three political parties, (Labour, Conservative and Liberal) to unite into a coalition government. By the end of the 1920's, George and the Windsors were but one of a few royal families who still retained their status in Europe.

The nature of the monarchy evolved through the influence of George. In contrast to his grandmother and father—Victoria's ambition to exert political influence in the tradition of Elizabeth I and Edward VII's aspirations to manipulate the destiny of nations—King George's royal perspective was considerably more humble. He strove to embody those qualities, which the nation saw as their greatest strengths: diligence, dignity and duty. The monarchy transformed from an institution of constitutional legality to the bulwark of traditional values and customs (particularly those concerning the family). Robert Lacey describes King George as such: "As his official biographer I felt compelled to admit, King George V was distinguished by no exercise of social gifts, by no personal magnetism, by no intellectual powers. He was neither a wit nor a brilliant raconteur, neither well-read nor well-educated, and he made no great contribution to enlightened social conversations. He lacked intellectual curiosity and only late in life acquired some measure of artistic taste.' He was, in other words, exactly like most of his subjects; mundane. He discovered a new job for modern kings and queens to do and that is; representation." *unquote*

I hardly think that he was really a nice man to be around. He was ill-tempered, fanatically punctual, and a harsh disciplinarian which may explain why his second son (later to be King George VI) was so shy and stuttered, an infliction which remained with him most of his life. George V was however extremely close to his mother (Alexandra of Denmark) who pampered him. He was scared of his father (Edward VII). His meanness became more apparent when in 1917; he made the controversial decision to deny political asylum to the Tsar Nicholas II and his family after the Bolshevik Revolution. People where shocked by George's unwillingness to protect his cousin but his advisers argued that it was important for the king to distance himself from the autocratic Russian royal family. Some people later questioned this decision when it became known that the Bolsheviks had executed Tsar Nicholas, his wife and their five children by shooting all of them to death in a cellar in Yekaterinburg, Siberia on the night of July 16th, 1917.

I remember seeing engravings and pictures of George V with his mustache and full beard on our Canadian coins and postage stamps.

Of course, when he died, the new issues of the coins and stamps bore the face of George VI but I saw the coins of George V around for many years after his demise until they finally disappeared into collector's hands or were melted down by the mint in Ottawa. In 2010, a firm was advertising the sale of silver one dollar Canadian coins with the image George V on them. These coins were printed that year.

He died the year following his silver jubilee after a series of debilitating attacks of bronchitis on January 20th 1936. He died under most unusual circumstances. He was very close to death on the night of January 20th and it was doubtful that he would survive the night. It is strongly suspected that on the night of his death, he died from an overdose of morphine injected into him to hasten his death so that the newspapers could publish his death in the morning news that had to go to press almost immediately. Canada didn't get that news as soon as he died because the telegraph cable from London to Halifax wasn't completed until some considerable time later. I was just two years and three months old when King George V died.

The Duke of Windsor, then Prince of Wales, was proclaimed King Edward VIII, sovereign of Great Britain and Emperor of India, on the death of his father, George V. Strangely enough, there were no British or Canadian coins officially issued bearing the name or portrait of Edward VIII. The reason for this was probably because he hadn't actually yet been crowned as the king in Westminster Abby as is the custom in Britain. However, British West Africa and East Africa countries issued coins dated 1936 bearing his name, but with no portrait. Official dies and pattern coins for Edward were produced in 1937 but the gold Double Florins were never issued for circulation, and to this day, remain as very rare collectors items.

Before succeeding to the throne, Edward had been an extraordinarily popular Prince of Wales. He spent nearly ten years constantly traveling throughout the Empire to great personal acclaim and to the advantage of the British crown. In Britain he was known for his presence at the front throughout the First World War, and had won a reputation for sincere concern about the deprived conditions in which many people in Britain were living. He was also known to be modern, stylish and an enthusiastic sportsman. He was widely acclaimed as a 'decent fellow'.

He had not yet been formally crowned when he chose to abdicate his throne in order to marry the American divorcee, Wallis Simpson. For many, this was the single most romantic gesture of our time. For others it was felt to be an act of betrayal.

The prince had met Wallis Simpson at a hunting weekend at Melton Mowbray in January 1931. She was part of the American expatriate community, a society girl from Baltimore in the USA, with a divorce in her past. Edward had previously visited the United States and was a fan of the American way of life. Mrs. Simpson quickly became part of Edward's favoured circle and was soon his intimate confidante. While the prince was shamefully cutting back on the wages he was paying his staff, he spent almost a third of his wealth on Mrs. Simpson. He constantly bought her jewels and diamonds and they traveled together extensively all around Europe.

By common consent, the British press of the time did not gossip about the royal family but the overseas press was free to talk about their love affair. In 1936 when Mrs. Simpson joined the King on a cruise in the Adriatic, the relationship became widely known abroad and a crisis began to develop. In 1936 she started the process of divorcing her second husband, Ernest Simpson. The British government became concerned about the relationship. Under English law, the King could marry whomever he chose, as long as Parliament approved. Since the bride he had in mind was about to be twice divorced, and was a foreigner and a commoner to boot, approval was not a foregone conclusion, especially since the King of England was also the head of the Church of England that prohibited anyone marrying a divorcee.

The Prime Minister, Stanley Baldwin, consulted across the political spectrum before informing Edward that Parliament and the Empire would not countenance Edward's marriage to Mrs. Simpson. When Wallis Simpson heard this, she fled abroad. Edward refused to abandon her, nor would he continue with the relationship without formalizing it. As soon as the situation became known in Britain, public opinion was shown to be against Wallis Simpson as a consort. Edward would not compromise by accepting the suggestion of a morganatic marriage to her—that is where she would not be a queen but merely a consort. That foolish decision was to invariably lead to his downfall.

It was Gustave Flaubert (1821-1880), French novelist who said, "Stupidity is something unshakable; nothing attacks it without breaking itself against it; it is of the nature of granite, hard and resistant." *unquote*

Despite the intervention of his friend Winston Churchill and others as mediators on his behalf, there was nothing that could be done for him. The instrument of abdication was signed on the 11th of December 1936. Edward then spoke to the nation on BBC Radio explaining to his listeners, "I have found it impossible to carry the heavy burden of responsibility and to discharge my duties as King as I should wish to do, without the help and support of the woman I love." *unquote*

Wallis Simpson listening in her hide-away in Cannes; hid her face as she heard it. That night, after saying farewell to his family, the ex-monarch (hence to be thereafter known as the Duke of Windsor) was driven to Portsmouth from where he embarked on a ship bound for France and what turned out to be a life of exile. Later he was estranged from his immediate family in England and his homeland.

A great many people in England and the commonwealth countries felt betrayed by Edward's abdication. George Bernard Shaw (1856-1950), Anglo-Irish playwright said it best, "Self-sacrifice enables us to sacrifice other people without blushing." *unquote*

Prior to Edward's speech, Ernest Simpson, the former husband of Wallis Warfield Simpson who was to marry Edward VIII, spoke of his divorce from the lady, when he paraphrased the American Revolutionary spy, Nathan Hale who was about to be hanged by the British. "I regret that I have but one wife to lay down for my country." *unquote*

The Duke of Windsor met with his brother who was now the king and he told his brother that he needed $25,000 English pounds a year to support himself and his wife because he had no money of his own and the king agreed to put him on the Civil List along with the other members of the royal family who would be supported by the government. However, later the prime minister met with the king and informed him that the duke had over a million English pounds of his own. Upon hearing that, the king immediately removed him from the Civil List.

The duke then arranged to have an intermediary meet with the king for the purpose of permitting the duchess to be referred to as Her Highness. The Queen was aghast at the suggestion and persuaded her husband to refuse the request. After the war, the duke met with the king and repeated the same request personally and his request was refused again. From that moment on, the two brothers were estranged and never met face to face again while they were both alive.

The Duke and Duchess were married at the Chateau de Cande in June 1937. It was a quiet wedding with very few people attending. After that, they divided their time between Paris and the South of France, waiting for the call to return to Britain; a call that never came. One of the reasons was because the Duke had been friends with Hitler and had visited Hitler in an attempt to smooth relations between Germany and Great Britain. He had even previously arranged to invite Von Ribbentrop, Hitler's foreign minister (later hanged in 1946 for war crimes) to visit England but during that visit, the British were rather cool to Von Ribbontrop to say the very least.

At the outbreak of the Second World War, the Duke came back to Britain offering to take on a worthwhile wartime job. He was neither received with courtesy or enthusiasm by his family or the government. Queen Elizabeth (the late Queen Mother) never forgave him for saddling her husband (King George VI) with the task of being the monarch. She and her husband had been quite happy being a duke and duchess without taking on the additional burden of being the monarch.

The Duke of Windsor was nevertheless appointed as liaison officer in Northern France but this post came to an abrupt end in the face of the German advance. Still unwelcome in England, he was appointed Governor General of the Bahamas; a ceremonial post with little authority but he and the Duchess filled this role with some success for the duration of the war by making useful trips to the United States and using his friendship with Franklin Roosevelt to draw in America as an ally in the war in Europe.

At the end of the war in 1945, the Duke and Duchess returned to their chateau in France. In 1952, they realized that acceptance of the Duchess by the Royal family was never going to happen so instead of returning to England; they bought the only property they ever really wanted, a Mill just outside Paris. The following year they leased from the City of Paris, the Villa in Neuilly, which was to be their main home. They spent the next five years restoring and decorating their two houses. The Duchess made the villa a palace in miniature for her ex-king. They lived in great comfort and style and were known as excellent hosts, making all their many friends, French, British and American, feel enormously welcome. Their year was broken by trips abroad. There was duck shooting in Florida and visits to New York in the winter, and trips to England and southern Europe at other fixed times in the year.

They maintained this way of life until just before the Duke's death on May 28th 1972. There was a lot of bad blood between the Queen, now the Queen mother, and the duchess because the duke had taken much of the family jewels with him when he abdicated and not only gave it to the duchess but spent a great deal of his own money buying her more jewels. In fact he spent so much money buying her jewels; he had to lay off many of his long-time staff who were quite upset at being laid off in order that the duchess could get more jewels. The Duke and Duchess continued to be excluded from the British royal circle and, in fact, the only time the Duchess entertained Queen Elizabeth II, (the new queen) was when she was alone with her husband, Edward dying in a room upstairs. To the end, it rankled with the Duke that his wife was denied the title of 'Her Royal Highness' which he believed was hers by right as his wife. The Duchess lived on at the Villa in increasing ill health for another fourteen years before she died on April 24th, 1986. I don't know what happened to the jewels but you can be sure they weren't returned to the Royal Family.

What wasn't known by the general public until 65 years after the Duke's abdication was that the Duchess had another lover while she was going out with the Prince of Wales. His name was Guy Trundle. Trundle was born in 1899 in York, the son of a Church of England priest. As a teenager toward the end of World War I, he joined the Royal Air Force, flew in Greece in the 1920s and became a Wing Commander. By the early 1930s, he was a car mechanic and salesman in London and had married Melosine Cary-Barnard, daughter of a retired army officer. In 1937 the couple had a daughter, Pamela, who died in infancy. He was also the lover of a woman who would eventually marry a British king. In secret papers released by the government on January 30, 2003 after more than 65 years, police named Trundle as the paramour of Wallis Simpson.

Detectives said Simpson was having an affair with Trundle in 1935, while she was still married to her second husband, Ernest Simpson, and was developing a relationship with the future king, then the Prince of Wales. A police report dated the July 3rd, 1935, named him as Guy Marcus Trundle, an engineer and salesman for the Ford Motor Company. The report describes Trundle as "a very charming adventurer, very good looking, well bred and an excellent dancer." He is said to have boasted that every woman falls for him. The report said that Trundle, "meets Mrs. Simpson quite openly at informal social gatherings as a personal friend, but secret meetings are made by appointment when intimate relations take place." *unquote* Trundle had admitted receiving money and gifts from Simpson. The revelation that Simpson 'was two-timing the Prince of Wales' raised new questions during the abdication crisis. The (police) Special Branch knew about it, the Home Office knew about it. Why didn't the prime minister and the king know about it? Had the Prince of Wales known, it may have ended the abdication crisis with him ending his relationship with Wallis Simpson. Trundle, who died in 1958, seems to have kept the romance a secret which is more than some of the suitors of the royalty in England were able to do years later.

I suppose this is as a good a place as any in my book to describe the late Queen Mother who was the wife of King George VI, and who was the mother of Queen Elizabeth II.

She was born the Honourable Elizabeth Angela Marguerite Bowes-Lyon on the 4th of August 1900 (daughter of Lord Glamis, later 14th Earl of Strathmore and Kinghorne) and spent her early childhood at St Paul's Waldenbury in Hertfordshire, north of the capital. This was the country home of her parents. The Bowes-Lyon family is descended from the Royal House of Scotland. One of the Queen Mother's 14th-Century ancestors became Thane of Glamis, home of Macbeth 300 years before and for this reason, Glamis Castle is the family seat.

From her childhood days, she and her older sisters had been friendly with the children of King George V and Queen Mary. Occasionally members of the Royal family stayed at Glamis Castle. In 1922 Lady Elizabeth acted as one of the bridesmaids at the wedding of their daughter, Princess Mary. In January 1923, the month she became betrothed to the Duke of York after she turned down his two previous proposals. He was King George V and Queen Mary's second son. They were married on the 26th of April 1923 in Westminster Abbey.

They had two children, Princess Elizabeth, born on the 21st of April 1926 at the Strathmores' London home at 17 Bruton Street, and Princess Margaret, born on the 21st of August, 1930 at Glamis Castle. When her eldest daughter Elizabeth became the Queen, her mother became the Queen Mother.

The Queen Mother died at 3.15 p.m. (10.15 a.m. ET) on March 30th 2002 at the age of 101 at the Royal Lodge in Windsor with her daughter Queen Elizabeth II, the current British monarch, at her bedside. I watched the funeral procession on TV as it was heading to Windsor Castle from London.

Chapter Six

My parents continued to live on and off in a common-law relationship although I am not sure one could say my parents were living in any real relationship since my father was always disappearing for months on end.

We moved out of the shack in Scarborough sometime in 1934 and lived at 23 MacPherson Street, just west of Yonge Street in Toronto. Then around 1935 we moved to 153 Hallam Street which was (and still is at the time of this writing) a two storey house that is approximately 12 feet wide.

It was around this time that my younger brother, Dale was conceived. He was born on Sunday, March 1st, 1936 (at that time my brother was named Gail until he demanded to be called Dale when he was ten or eleven years old). He was born at the Women's College Hospital on College Street, the same hospital my mother was born in. That hospital developed from the Women's Medical College which opened in 1883 because women at that time were barred from medical training. It was the only place in Toronto (and probably in Canada also) where women could get treatment from unlicensed women physicians.

Dale had the same father as I but he was conceived as a result of consensual sex with my mother this time who then married my father just before the birth of my brother. My father had previously got his divorce from his first wife and when it was obvious to my maternal grandfather that my mother was pregnant again as a result of having sex with my father, my grandfather demanded that my father marry my mother, which he did.

My father was by now employed with Sealtest Shoe Company as a collector of its accounts. Later, he quit that job and got a job at H. Rose Jewelers as a credit investigator and he held that job until 1938. As one of those strange quirks in life, I got a job in that same firm when I was in my thirties as a collector of bad accounts but was fired a week later for a reason the owner never disclosed to me.

By now, we were living in a house at 517 Concord Avenue, just south of Dupont Street and while we were there, my mother was on welfare. Prior to the birth of my younger brother, she told the welfare officials that she was a single mother with one child. Considering the fact that my father was hardly ever around and didn't pay her any support for herself or me, I guess she really didn't lie to them—at least not in spirit.

Sometime during that same year that my brother was born, I remember one thing and that was watching my father drive away from our garage in a black motorcycle (which my mother bought for him out of her own money) when we lived at 153 Hallam Street prior to us moving two blocks east from that house into the house at 517 Concord Street that was a short distance south of Hallam. It was a larger two-story house than the one we lived in on Hallam. I was around three years old, going on four when we moved there. I know that we were there in July 1937 because I saw a photo of me at that house which has that date on the back of the photo. I also remember accompanying my mother to the Women's College Hospital when my brother was taken there earlier for some reason or another.

There were only three things I remember about living on Concord Street. The first was my first nightmare; the second was falling off of my tricycle and seriously cutting the tip of my right middle finger. To this day, I still have the scar on that finger. The third was being taken to the hospital because I had swallowed the small base of a metal toy soldier. My mother thought that the base was made of lead. The doctor told her that if it was lead, they would have to open up my stomach before the lead was further digested into my body. If they didn't remove the lead in time, I would suffer permanent brain damage. My mother took a taxi home and got another metal soldier and brought it to the hospital. As luck would have it, the base was not made of lead; hence the scalpel was not used on my body that day. I had to wait another sixty-three years before the doctors would get to use a scalpel to open me up, this time for my open-heart bypass surgery in 1999.

On May 13th, 1931, the International Olympic Committee, headed by Count Henri Baillet-Latour of Belgium, awarded the 1936 Summer Olympics to Berlin. The choice signaled Germany's return to the world community after defeat in World War I.

For two weeks in August 1936, Adolf Hitler's Nazi dictatorship camouflaged its racist, militaristic character while hosting the Summer Olympics. Soft-pedaling its anti-Semitic agenda and its plans for territorial expansion, Hitler's aim was to exploit the Games in order to bedazzle many foreign spectators and journalists with an image of a peaceful, tolerant Germany.

The Olympics were a perfect arena for the Nazi propaganda machine, which was unsurpassed at staging elaborate public spectacles and rallies. Choreographed pageantry, record-breaking athletic feats, and warm German hospitality made the 1936 Olympic Games memorable for both athletes and spectators.

In August 1936 Olympic flags and swastikas bedecked the monuments and houses of a festive, crowded Berlin. Most tourists were unaware that the Nazi regime had temporarily removed anti-Jewish signs. Neither would tourists have known of the 'Gypsy clean up' ordered by the German Ministry of Interior in which the Berlin Police arrested all Gypsies prior to the Games. On July 16th, 1936, some 800 Gypsies were arrested and interned under police guard in a special Gypsy camp in the Berlin suburb of Marzahn. Also in preparation for the arrival of Olympic spectators, Nazi officials ordered that foreign visitors should not be subjected to the criminal dictates of the Nazi anti-homosexual laws.

On August 1st, 1936, Hitler opened the 11th Olympiad. Musical fanfares directed by the famous composer Richard Strauss announced the dictator's arrival to the largely German crowd. Hundreds of athletes in opening day regalia marched into the stadium, team by team in the alphabetical order of the nations they represented. Inaugurating a new Olympic ritual; was a lone runner arrived bearing a torch carried by relay from the site of the ancient Games in Olympia, Greece.

The Olympic torch was lit by the rays of the sun at Olympia in Greece and carried by 3,000 relay runners to the main stadium in the German capital. It is a tradition that has continued since then at every subsequent Olympic Games.

Eighteen black athletes represented the United States in the 1936 Olympics. African/American athletes won 14 medals; nearly one-fourth of the 56 medals awarded the U.S. team in all events, and dominated the popular track and field events. Many American journalists hailed the victories of Jesse Owens and other blacks as a blow to the Nazi myth of Aryan supremacy. The continuing social and economic discrimination the black medalists faced upon returning home underscored the irony of their victory in racist Germany.

The *Baltimore Afro-American* (August 8, 1936) and other newspapers spread the story that Hitler refused to shake Jesse Owens's hand or congratulate other black medalists. In fact, during the very first day of Olympic competition, when Owens did not compete, Olympic protocol officers implored Hitler to receive either all the medal winners or none, and the Fuhrer chose to receive none of them. Whether he did this to avoid shaking hands with 'non-Aryans' is unclear. Privately, the Minister of Propaganda, Goebbels called the victories by blacks "a disgrace." Ignoring censors' orders to avoid offending foreign guests with racist commentaries, the radical Nazi newspaper *Der Angriff* (*The Attack*) wrote on August 6th: "If the American team had not brought along black auxiliaries, one would have regarded the Yankees as the biggest disappointment of the Games." When one thinks of it, blacks have traditionally played a very large role in sports.

Thirteen Jews or persons of Jewish descent won medals in the

Nazi Olympics, including six Hungarians.

Foreign press correspondents and technical support staffers were given access to over 300 microphones, 200 amplifiers and over 20 wireless transmitter vans. The latest German wireless transmission and television technology from such giants as Siemens and Telefunken was put on display. Over 150,000 Germans followed the Olympic Games via television at 21 television centers in Germany. When television started its regular broadcasting service in Germany on the 22nd of March 1935, the National Socialists (Nazis) celebrated the new technology as proof of German superiority. Geobbels actively encouraged the development of German television for the very fact of propaganda, hence the public viewing rooms were constructed and the people's television sets were being designed and built so that the Germans could see special Nazi events. German radio reporters were made available to the news and press organizations of nations which did not have the resources to send their people to Berlin.

Meanwhile in Spain, the death of Calvo Sotelo, the prime minister of Spain had the effect of accelerating a military coup in July 1936 that had meanwhile been under preparation for a long time. For some time, the conspirators had been awaiting General Franco's decision to begin the uprising. On July 18th it spread to other garrisons in metropolitan Spain and the following day Franco took command of the army in Morocco. The rising was successful in Seville under the command of General Queipo de Llano, the Balearic Islands under the command of General Goded, the Canary Islands, and Old Castile on the mainland.

Santiago Casares Quiroga of the Left Republican Party resigned from the post of Prime Minister of the Republic of Spain. President Manuel Azana then asked Diego Martinez Barrio who was a member of the Republican Union Party, to form a moderate government that could negotiate with the rebels. When Barrio was unable to form a government that enjoyed any real support, he resigned. Professor Jose Giral of the Republican Party; replaced him and ordered that arms be distributed to the workers.

General Francisco Franco flew from Tenerife to Tetuan to take over command of the Army of Africa on the 20th of July 1936. Prime Minister Giral appealed to the French Socialist Government whose Prime Minister was Leon Blum for arms supplies. General Francisco Franco then sent emissaries to Hitler and Mussolini to ask for military aid and technical assistance in which the two dictators readily agreed to honour his request.

The nominal leader of the 'Uprising', General Jose Sanjurjo, was killed when the aircraft bringing him from Portugal to Burgos crashed on take-off. It is suspected that he had too much baggage with him that resulted in his plane being overloaded.

Nowadays, he would have paid dearly for that access baggage.

When it became apparent that the 'Uprising' in Madrid had failed, the Nationalist supporters in the town of Toledo, which is 40 miles (64 km) to the southwest of Madrid, the capital of Spain, occupied the Military Academy in the Alcazar fortress, between July 20th and September 27th. The garrison was mainly drawn from the local Guardia Civil and Falange, and was commanded by the Commandant of the Academy, Colonel Jose Moscardo. For two months the defenders held out against the Republican Militia units besieging them. Franco had to divert an army to relieve the nationalists, which in turn gave Madrid enough time to put up the barricades and delay Republican control until the end of the war. But the siege became a symbol of the Franco regime and it was embellished and made into a legend. Even the National newspaper changed its name to Alcazar in its honour.

No trip to Toledo is complete without a trip to the Alcazar (castle) and the views of the surrounding Castilean plain are sensational from its windows. The four-cornered Renaissance *Alcazar de Toledo* is the pride of Spain. Originally built by the powerful king, Charles V, it served as a military garrison in a conservative town for hundreds of years but its great moment of fame came in the 20th century.

King Charles V also built a magnificent palace in Grenada inside the fortification of the *Alhambra* which my wife and I had the pleasure of visiting in November 2007.'

When I visited Toledo in 1974, I observed that the Alcazar was visible from most places in Toledo but I found it to be a real challenge to locate it due to the narrow twisting streets. Once I arrived at it and walked up the horse ramp, now used by jeeps and military vehicles, I paid a small fee to go inside. I entered it and was fascinated by the replicated building. Explosives by the Republicans had destroyed the original structure during its siege. The Alcazar was damaged so severely by the siege that it was finally torn down and rebuilt. It is still owned by the military and contains the Ejerito (Army) museum. I wandered around the rooms and seen models and photos of the Alcazar after the siege and a photo of Franco greeting Colonel Moscardo amongst the rubble.

Upstairs was a room left in exactly the same state as it was on the last day of the siege. The ceiling was shredded and the walls were peppered and along one wall on a table was the famous telephone used by Colonel Moscardo. At one point during the siege, the Nationalists had captured Moscardo's son and they phoned Moscardo and told him that if he didn't surrender, they would shoot his son. The colonel asked to speak to his son on the phone. He told his 16-year-old son that he couldn't surrender and concluded with; "I love you, son. Commend your soul to God and die like a patriot." His son replied, "That I can do." He was not shot at that time but about a month later, he was shot in reprisal for an air raid. Troops from the Army of Africa, led by Colonel Jose Varela, stormed Toledo and came to the rescue of its defenders. The raising of the siege of the Alcazar did much to enhance General Franco's reputation.

General Franco was immediately proclaimed Commander-in-Chief (Generalissimo—a title he would hold until his death) and Head of State in Burgos.

A large part of Spain's gold reserve (which remained in Republican controlled Spain after the uprising) was transferred on the 25th of October to Russia. This was to pay for Russian 'aid'. Four days later, Russian tanks and aircraft appeared in the front-line for the first time and shortly after that, German and Italian bombers began a series of raids on Madrid in the hope of destroying civilian resistance. Soon after that, Russian fighter aircraft appeared for the first time in the skies over Madrid. This city was the first European city to be bombed from the air.

Because they expected Madrid to fall at any moment to the Nationalists, the Republican Government moved to Valencia on November 6th. A Defense Junta, under the leadership of General Jose Miaja, was established to organize the last-ditch defense of Madrid.

From November 8th to the 23rd, the battle for Madrid was in earnest. The Nationalists were now poised to make an all-out attack on Madrid in the hope of capturing the Spanish capital and thus ending the war. General Emilio Mola led the forces at their disposal and the majority of them were units of the Army of Africa. Mola ordered Colonel Jose Varela to attack the northwest flank of Madrid's defenses and by 16th of November; Varela's troops had forced a bridgehead over the River Manzanares. By the 23rd of November both sides were exhausted by the fighting and began digging in. Varela had failed to achieve the desired break-through. Although the Nationalists held the areas to the North and West of the city, it was obvious that all further frontal attacks upon Madrid would be costly and likely to fail.

On the 15th of November, the German Condor Legion went into action for the first time. Their air attacks were made in support of further Nationalist attempts to capture Madrid and on the 18th, Italy and Germany recognized General Franco's government.

Jose Antonio Primo de Rivera (the leader of the Falange), who had been stranded in Republican Spain at the time of the uprising, was captured by the Republicans and executed on the 20th of November in Alicante.

On the 6th of December, Nationalist aircraft bombed Barcelona. They probably bombed the fortress on the hill overlooking the city but I saw no evidence of it when I visited the fortress in 1974 and again in 2006. By the end of 1936, things did not look well in Spain for either side and especially for the unarmed civilians.

On the 13th of December, Italian General Jose Varela launched an offensive towards the Corunna Road, which runs 25 miles to the North of Ethiopia, a landlocked country of eastern Africa situated on the Horn of Africa. Ethiopia is bordered on the north by Eritrea, on the east by Djibouti and Somalia, on the south by Kenya, and on the west by The Sudan.

Under the Ethiopian ruler, Menilek II, Ethiopia expanded to its present size. A railway was constructed between Addis Ababa (the capital) and Djibouti, and the capital was modernized with new schools and hospitals. Coffee exports led Ethiopia to relative economic prosperity in the 1920s. In the 1920s, there was tension with Italy and Great Britain, as each tried to extend its influence in Ethiopia. Ras Tafari was given additional powers by the empress in 1928, and on her death in 1930 he was crowned emperor as Haile Selassie I. He expanded modernization projects in the 1930s.

Mussolini was determined to establish an Italian empire and to avenge the defeat at Adwa. A border clash at Welwel in SE Ethiopia along the border with Italian Somaliland on December 5th of 1934, increased tension and on October 3rd, 1935, Italy invaded Ethiopia. The League of Nations (which Ethiopia had joined in 1923) called for mild economic sanctions against Italy but that had little effect and an attempt by the British and French governments to arrange a settlement by giving Italy much of Ethiopia failed also. The Italians quickly defeated the Ethiopians and in May, 1936, Addis Ababa was captured and Haile Selassie fled the country. On June 1st, 1936, the king of Italy was also made emperor of Ethiopia. The Italians occupied most of the country until 1941; two years after the Second World War had begun.

There were enormous dust storms denuding large portions of the farmlands of Kansas, Oklahoma, Colorado, Nebraska and both states of North and South Dakota. In fact, a Colorado farmland survey indicated that half of the 6000 farmhouses in one area alone had been abandoned. Many of the farmers from Oklahoma (called Okies) moved to California and did well in their farming ventures in that state.

The top soil was drawn up 3000 metres (almost 2 miles) into the air and the high winds blew the dust eastward towards the Atlantic. It blew over New York City for three days with such thickness that the city was enveloped in darkness. The lights of the city had to be turned on midday.

The worst heat wave in Canada took place in July 1936 between the 5th and 17th. It was said that someone one actually fried an egg on the City Hall steps. That would be impossible. To fry an egg, the surface of the pan must be at least 158 Farenheight (70 Celsius). It only reached a scorching 41 Celsius for three days in Toronto. Mind you, the surface of a dark painted car would make such a feat possible. The heat wave in Toronto claimed 220 lives in the city out of 1,180 deaths nationwide. It was the worst weather disaster of a non-marine nature in Canadian history. It was like we were living in a furnace. Nevertheless, it wasn't as hot in Toronto as it was in Austin Texas. In that city, the temperature rose to 145 F (62.7 Celsius) Now that is hot.

Many people of Toronto took blankets and mattresses, and camped out all night on the Sunnyside, Cherry, Simcoe and Kew beaches because those were the only cool places in the city. Some climbed onto roofs, hoping to catch a breeze. I remember doing that twice in my life; the first time in Winnipeg and the second time in Toronto. One woman took refuge in a cemetery, using a cool tombstone as a pillow. Others beat the heat by staying in their cellars or spending nights in parks.

Many sidewalks and roadways in Toronto cracked and buckled under the blasting heat; city workers had to sand streets to increase traction because the asphalt would melt and cars would skid and crash. Horses carrying milk and bread dropped dead in the streets. People collapsed in factory sweatshops. Some employers shut down operations and sent workers home. In the country, crops scorched and in the Niagara peninsula, fruit baked on fruit trees.

Many of the victims were sent to the Toronto morgue during the heat wave. One could smell the morgue blocks away despite the ice blocks used to retard decomposition. There were so many deaths, the coroner couldn't keep up. A funeral director, who usually dealt with four calls a day, handled more than 25 funerals in 48 hours.

The heat in 1936 didn't have the humidity that Toronto has today, because the heat wave began in the prairies, plus it carried less smog and haze but it was hotter and probably harder on residents than the August 2001 heat wave because people had fewer means to cool off then, like air conditioning to cope with it. It must be remembered that air-conditioning in homes was something in the future at that time and not that many families could afford electric fans and most of the farms in Ontario didn't even have electricity to operate electric fans in any case. We had no fan in our house then so I suffered like everyone else did in our house and from what my mother told me, I cried much of the time. Hey! It was too damn hot not to cry. What did you expect from me? I was a baby then. Babies cry for the simplest reasons. I know. My wife and I had two of them and they cried for the simplest of reasons.

The sweltering temperatures prompted men to swim without their bathing tops; which was considered immodest at the time. The city also allowed ice delivery on Sunday, which struck many foolish citizens as being sacrilegious despite the necessity.

An article in the July 9th edition of the *Daily Star* (later called the *Toronto Star*) said 5,000 electric fans were sold that week and ice plants had to increase their staff by 50 per cent to meet demands. Most people would go into department stores such as Simpson's and Eatons. A couple of theatres on Yonge Street had a form of air conditioning, so people went to the movies just to get cool. People even reversed the flow of their vacuum cleaners to get some kind of air circulation. I remember one night in the 1970s during a heat wave, I was so hot, I placed a fan next to the freezer in my fridge just to get cool air blowing onto my face.

Dry ice was used to reduce the temperatures in hospital wards. The nurses put a tub of ice cubes at the end of the hall to keep their patients cool. They couldn't keep the beds dry so they often changed the sheets but within five minutes the sheets were soaked again with the sweat from their patient's bodies.

In 1936, one could buy a four-piece bedroom suite for $179 USD which in 1999 would be $2,145.42 USD and a living room suite sold for $129 USD which in 1999 which would be $1,546.15 USD.

It was during this year that the first helicopter flight was made. It was built by Heinrich Focke. The first jet-powered plane flew in the German skies that year also. The Douglas twin-engine DC-3, which carried 21 passengers and was able to cross 1,500 miles (2413 km) of the USA non-stop in 15 hours, began production. The planes were built with heated cabins, and in that year, hot meals were served on board the planes. On July 30th, Canada's first national airline—Trans-Canada Airlines, which was part of Canadian National Railways, flew one of its planes across Canada, from Montreal to Vancouver (4,025 kilometers) with five brief stopovers for refueling. The total time was 18 hours; a real accomplishment in those days. In 2005, my wife and I flew from Toronto to Hong Kong in less time with only one stopover (Aaska) for refueling. In 1936, only registered nurses were hired as stewardess with Trans-Canada Airlines and unlike their American contemporaries, they only served boxed lunches to their passengers.

Bell Labs invented a voice recognition machine. Co-axial cable connected New York to Philadelphia.

According to *Life* magazine, (which was its first edition) one out of ten Americans were tattooed. The *National Geographic News* stated in April 2000 that 15% of Americans were tattooed (or approximately 40 million people) *Esquire Magazine* estimated in March 2002 that one in eight Americans was tattooed.

This was the year that people really took a keen interest in photography owing to technical advances like the exposure meter and the creation of the 35 mm camera. I remember my mother using a camera that had a very small peephole in it with very small lenses. The 35 mm cameras were too expensive at that time for her to invest in one. The black and white pictures came out pretty good. A sleeper berth from Newark, New Jersey to Los Angeles, California cost only $150.00 American (1999—$1,787.94 American) and a bus ride on most streets cost anywhere from 5 to 10 cents American.

Margaret Mitchell's novel, *Gone With The Wind* sold 1 million copies in one six month period. It's ironic when you think about it. Seven publishers turned her down because the novel was too long. A drunk driver who had many previous convictions for drunk driving later drove into her as she was walking across an intersection and killed her. He got forty years in prison for that drunken stupidity.

First appearances included, newspapers microfilming previous issues, Penguin books, the Ford Foundation, Chunky Peanut Butter, florescent tubes and for the women, Tampex. Also discovered in this year were sulfa drugs, the first artificial heart, Vitamin E and Vitamin B. Rudyard Kipling, the famed writer died in England in 1936.

In that year, you could buy a 1936 Plymouth sedan for $510.00 with 6% interest and with no down payment. An electric shaver costs $16.50. A tour of India and twenty of its cities with a personal servant would cost you $369.00. You and another person could stay at the famous Waldorf Astoria Hotel in New York City in a room with a private bathroom for as little as $8.00 as night. You could also sail from New York to Hamburg, Germany on one of the United States passenger liners first class in a cabin with a private bathroom for as little as $133.00.

On the 15th of May, Largo Caballero resigned as Prime Minister of Spain. After the resignation of Largo Caballero, Dr Juan Negrin (a Socialist) became Prime Minister on May 17th. The new Government was dominated by now by Communists. On the last day of May, the Republicans began an offensive to capture Segovia. Three Republican Divisions, under the command of General Domingo Moriones, broke through the Nationalist front-line at San Ildefonso and captured La Granja. Nationalist troops, led by General Jose Varela, were detached from the Madrid front and used to mount a counter-attack that stopped any further Republican advance.

On the 15th of August, a new political police force, the SIM (Servicio Investigacion Militar), was formed in Republican Spain. It was controlled by the Communists and contained many Russian 'advisers'

During the Spanish Civil War at Paracuellos del Jarama, at least four thousand suspected right-wingers, both military and civilians, including many women, were executed and then buried in common graves by the Spanish Republican soldiers and militiamen during the Battle of Madrid (November 8–9, 1936). It is disputed whether Santiago Carrillo, the Communist leader in Madrid, ordered these executions or not, albeit they were committed under his authority. Paracuellos del Jarama is a small town in the urban area of Madrid, Spain. It is located northeast from Madrid and very close to the Barajas International Airport.

Brother Joseph, who lived in Montreal, Canada and who died in January 1937, was credited with spiritual powers which resulted in hundreds of inflicted being healed; or so they claimed. It was he who inspired the building of the famous St. Joseph's Oratory in Montreal. This imposing domed Renaissance-style basilica perched on Montreal's Mount Royal can hold 16,000 persons. The Vatican in 2010 expressed its wish to make him a saint.

Armand Bombardier, a Montrealer, patented his Ski-doo snowmobile, the first in the world. I remember seeing a movie film in the late 30s taken by my grandfather of one of Bombardier's snowmobiles going up a ski hill. It certainly didn't look like the snowmobiles of today, which were first put on the market in November 1959, but it was a fascinating thing to see. By the year 2000, Bombardier was building huge airliners and trains.

That was the also first year that sliced bread came to Vancouver. I can't remember if we had sliced bread in Toronto when I lived there but I think I first experienced it sometime in the late forties in Vancouver. Prior to that, the use of the bread knife was the only way you could have sliced bread.

The first practicable electron microscope was created at the University of Toronto although simpler versions were created several years earlier. Bell Labs invented the first electrical digital calculator. NBC sent a mobile TV truck onto New York streets. The photocopier was invented that year.

Alberta raised its minimum wage to 33 cents an hour or $15 a week which was $173.72 USD in 1999 for a 40-hour week. It was worse in British Columbia in 1951 because when I got my first full-time job in Vancouver in the summer of 1951, I was only paid $15 a week and I worked five and a half days for a 44 hour week.

Two Toronto newspapers, the *Globe* and the *Mail* merged and the two called themselves *The Globe and Mail*. Vancouver, B.C., had its first CBC radio broadcast in February of that year.

Hollywood actress, Jane Fonda was born, as was English actor, Edward Fox and Hollywood star, Dustin Hoffman. The Disney movie, *Snow White and the Seven Dwarfs* was the first feature-length movie ever shown. What was remarkable about this movie was that it was also the first full-length movie produced in colour.

Child actress Shirley Temple still led the top box office stars. She queried about her future when she asked at the age of eight and at the height of her career, "Suppose I'm not so cute when I grow up as I am now?" The question was academic. She married in 1950, became a popular TV personality between 1951 and 1961. She has served the United States under four presidents: Richard Nixon appointed her United States Representative to the United Nations in 1969, for Gerald Ford, she was Ambassador to the Republic of Ghana and later the first female White House Chief of Protocol, for Ronald Reagan, she served as a foreign affairs officer with the State Department, and for George H. W. Bush, he appointed her Ambassador to Czechoslovakia. In 1988 she published her best-selling autobiography.

Shirley Temple's popularity was followed by Clark Gable, Robert Taylor, Bing Crosby, William Powell, Fred Astaire, Ginger Rogers and Gary Cooper. The song *Whistle While You Work* from the movie *Snow White and the Seven Dwarfs* was a hit, as was *The Lady is a Tramp* from the musical *Babes in Arms* and the song, *Thanks for the Memories* which was also a hit, and later became Bob Hope's theme song. The best book sellers were *Gone With the Wind* and *Of Mice and Men*; just to name a couple.

Strange things happened that year. For example, programs for the

NBC symphony concert were made of satin so that the concert goers didn't disturb the conductor, Toscanini with their constant rattling of their programs. It is a good thing that they don't permit food to be brought into concert halls nowadays for the same reason. *Sun Chips America* has disposable potato chip bags that crackle and pop with such intensity; if they were being opened during a concert as a quiet section of a symphony was being played, the audience would think that there were handguns being fired in the auditorium and in the panic, scamper out of the building in a mad rush in order not to be hit in the crossfire. Hugo Black, a former member of the Ku Klux Klan was appointed as a member of the Supreme Court of the United States. He joined the Ku Klux Klan shortly after, thinking it necessary for his political career. Running for the Senate as the "people's" candidate, Black believed he needed the votes of Klan members. Black would near the end of his life, admit that joining the Klan was a mistake, but said, "I would have joined any group if it helped get me votes. "He actually was a very good judge in that court. As soon as Black was appointed to the Court, he advocated judicial restraint and worked to move the Court away from interposing itself in social and economic matters. Black vigorously defended the 'plain meaning' of the Constitution, rooted in the ideas of its era and emphasized the supremacy of the legislature. As far as Black was concerned, he felt that the role of the Supreme Court was limited and constitutionally prescribed. He died on the 25th of September 1971.

In 1937, the average salary earned for an entire year was $1,250 which in American USD in 1999 was $9,715. A factory worker would make $1,376, a teacher, $1,367, a doctor, $4,285 and a lawyer, $4,885. A double cocktail would be 25 cents, a cashmere dress, $12.95, a woman's woolen coat, $95, and a leopard fur coat, $119. In that year, the exchange rate between Canadian money and American money was the same.

There were also a number of other firsts that year such as shopping carts and trampolines. Coaxial cable for television was used to hook up the stations between New York and Philadelphia.

In January 1937, the 25 millionth Ford car was driven off the assembly lines in Michigan, and Howard Hughes flew his plane from Los Angeles to New York in just over seven hours. In this same month, over a million persons in the United States were made homeless because of flooding. In February, a Du Dupont chemist created nylon—material which later replaced the silk in stockings for women. In March of that year, the Golden Gate Bridge in San Francisco, then the largest suspension bridge in the world, was opened and on the day of the opening, 200,000 pedestrians crossed it.

Leaving New York City and sailing to Hamburg, Germany return cost only $190.00 with meals included and your own stateroom. Of course you could go by freighter and with meals and a luxurious cabin, it would cost you only $60.00 one way. If you took a train from New York City to Miami, it would take just over 27 hours.

The English government decided to order 40 million gas masks to be issued to its citizens in case of another war. Everyone in England carried gas masks with them during the Second World War that followed two years later but they weren't needed. Both Hitler and Churchill realized the horror that would ensue if poisonous gas was used. Churchill later admitted after the war that if the Germans had landed on British soil, he may very well have used poisonous gas against them.

Chapter Seven

During the year of 1937, terrible atrocities against helpless human beings in China occurred. The Japanese army routed Chinese soldiers during their war against China. In August 1937, Japanese warplanes bombed the Chinese city of Shanghai. On October 14th, 1937, Canadians, plus millions all over the world, were angered when they saw what was to become a famous published photograph in *Life* magazine; a picture of a small baby crying alone in a bombed street in Shanghai after the Japanese bombed the city. They were angered even more when they learned that the Japanese planes bombed a train station in Shanghai in August which resulted in the deaths of 1,500 women and children trying to flee the city on its trains.

Hitler opened another concentration camp called Buchenwald near the town of Weimar (85 km—53 miles) southwest of the City of Leipsig in August. Weimar is a famous German town known for centuries for its cultural life. Goethe, Schiller, Franz Liszt, and Bach lived in Weimar. Goethe used to climb the Ettersberg and sit and work under a beech tree. It was this place which was chosen by the Nazis to establish the concentration camp of Buchenwald. Up to the end of the war years, hundreds of thousands of Jews were systematically slaughtered in that camp. Although Hitler opened 50 concentration camps after he became Chancellor of Germany in 1933, Buchenwald was at that time, to become one of the largest concentration camps in Germany.

The commandant, SS colonel, Karl Koch invited his small children to shoot prisoners paraded in front of them and his wife Ilse, who was called the 'Bitch of Buchenwald' was permitted to select which prisoners with tattoos were to be killed so that their skins could be made into lampshades. After the war, she was sentenced to life imprisonment and later her sentence was commuted to four years but she was rearrested and again sentenced again to life imprisonment by German authorities. She later went insane and committed suicide in 1967 while serving her sentence in the Aichack Prison. Her husband Karl however died earlier. He was accused by the Nazis of 'excesses' and fraud and given the option of serving at the 'Russian Front' or death by firing squad. The former option was a virtual sentence of death in any case since such persons were deliberately set out on 'no-return' missions. The SS leader in the district in which Buchenwald was located decided nevertheless to execute the ex-commandant by firing squad and he did just that.

From July 1937 to March 1945, 238,980 prisoners from 30 countries passed through Buchenwald. 43,045 of these were killed, died from brutal conditions, or didn't survive forced evacuations. On April 11, 1945, the underground took control of the camp and 21,000 surviving inmates were liberated.

MacKenzie King, the prime minister of Canada was the worst of the lot. He could have helped in stopping some of that but instead he turned a blind eye to this anti-Semitic abuse. When the European Jews were desperate to get out of Nazi-controlled countries, he told his underlings that he was worried that the infusion of more Jews in Canada would pollute Canada's bloodstream. Give me a break. I wonder if he read that in his tea leaves. What a psycho-ceramic (crackpot) that man was.

In 1932, this nut case attended a séance conducted by Etta Wriedt, a medium from Detroit. From then on, he was convinced he had spoken to loved ones who had passed on. By 1933, he had progressed to 'table rapping'. He also experimented with 'numerology and reading tea leaves. He even made decisions after ascertaining which way the wind blew. He later said that the spirits rarely instructed him; they merely confirmed his own views. When he returned from a visit in Europe, he told some of his friends that he communicated with the spirits of Leonardo da Vinci, Louis Pasteur and even Philip, the Apostle. And it was in this politician's hands; that Canada was to be in during the war years. Can you believe it? Canadians voted him into the office of prime minister of Canada. Would he have been elected if they knew how crazy he really was?

In the State of Kansas, it was learned that during 1937, as many as 62 of the 148 girls lodged in the girl's reformatory had been sterilized and in one instance, it was because the girl had a bad temper. In looking back, I wonder what I would have done had I known in 1980 about this shameful incident in American history while I was preparing my speech for my address before a United Nations crime conference being held in Caracas on the subject of abuses of children in American reformatories. Would I have included it? Probably not since the American delegation ended up complaining that the abuses I did speak about were five years old at that time and I anticipated that complaint coming forth at the end of my address even before I gave it. However, I did come up with a great ending for that speech which moved even the American delegates. I said in part; "If what is happening to these unfortunate children in some of these institutions is called justice, then justice is going under an assumed name."

In September, Hitler held his biggest rally yet in Nuremberg with 600,000 soldiers parading in front of him.

Oswald Mosley was born in 1896. Educated at Winchester and Sandhurst he fought with the 16th Lancers on the Western Front during the First World War. He later transferred to the Royal Flying Corps but was invalided out of the war after a plane crash in 1916.

When Tamsay MacDonald formed his Labour Government after the 1929 General Election, he appointed Mosley as Chancellor of the Duchy of Lancaster. In 1930, Mosley proposed a programme that he believed would help deal with the growing unemployment in Britain. It was based on the ideas of Maynard Keynes stimulating foreign trade, directing industrial policy, and using public funds to promote industrial expansion. When MacDonald and his cabinet rejected these proposals, Mosley resigned from his post.

The following year Oswald Mosley founded the New Party, but in the 1931 General Election, none of the New Party's candidates were elected. In January 1932 Mosley met Mussolini in Italy. Mosley was impressed by Mussolini's achievements and when he returned to England, he disbanded the New Party and replaced it with the British Union of Fascists.

In October, Oswald had stones thrown at him by some of the people in a crowd of 10,000 who didn't like his views. One of the funniest stories to come out of this period of time was when Mosley hired a large hall to give a speech. The hall was packed with hundreds of people. The lights were dimmed and a spotlight shone down onto Mosley who was standing alone at center stage. There wasn't a sound to be heard. Mosley's right arm was thrust upward in a Nazi salute. Suddenly a voice from the back of the large hall called out, "Yes, Mosley. You can leave the room to go to the loo." (toilet) The remark brought the entire place down. The laughter continued on for several minutes and Mosley realizing that there wasn't anything he could say that could best that remark, walked off stage, humiliated. It is said that from then on, he was a nonentity. Later, he was interned until the end of the war. He died in 1980.

Ironically, if Hitler has succeeded in his planned invitation of Britain, some say that he might have initially chosen Mosley to be his lackey in running Britain.

Prior to Japanese military activities in Manchuria, the population of Nanking had been approximately 250,000, but this number had grown to about one million by late 1937. With Beijing under siege, Nanking had been made the capital of China, accounting for some of this increase; but the greater portion had come from refugees who had fled to the city from the dangerous northern countryside. In the autumn of 1937, Japanese war planes began bombing Nanking, concentrating their efforts on the downtown areas, which were most densely populated by civilians.

As Nanking came under attack, the capital was again moved, this time to Chungking. Knowing that Japanese troops were en route toward the city, the people panicked and tried to flee. On the 9th of December 1937, Japanese ground forces reached Nanking, where they were met with minimal resistance from overwhelmed and fatigued Chinese military units. By December 13th, with Japanese troops attacking the city from all angles, the Chinese forces were routed. Fearing the consequences of surrender to the Japanese, Chinese military men donned civilian clothing and retreated into the city. It was on this day that the six-week stretch of atrocities against the civilian population of Nanking began.

Known historically as the *Rape of Nanking*, the first few weeks of barbaric rampage by Japanese troops were the grisliest. Tens of thousands of Chinese men, women, and children perished as they desperately attempted to flee across the Yangtze River by swimming or using makeshift flotation devices, while Japanese soldiers fired upon them and launched grenades at the scurrying masses. On the city streets, soldiers who claimed to be searching for hidden members of the Chinese army were in reality shooting and bayoneting civilians at will. They also set fire to many buildings, looted homes and robbed citizens of their few possessions.

The Chinese soldiers had been abandoned by their senior officers and left to fend for themselves in Nanking. When they surrendered, it was on the understanding that they would be treated as prisoners of war by the Japanese invaders. Thousands of Chinese soldiers who had surrendered to the Japanese were then rounded up and marched to the banks of the Yangtze River where they were all machine-gunned to death.

In the early weeks, there were mass murders with deaths numbering in the thousands. Civilians and suspected soldiers were rounded up and shot until their dead bodies piled atop one another, after which Japanese soldiers haphazardly bayoneted the mounds of dead bodies to make sure to kill any who had survived the shootings. On other occasions, crowds of Chinese people were assembled to be doused with gasoline and torched alive. Frequently, Japanese soldiers eagerly tossed grenades into such crowds.

Nanking of course was certainly not the only Chinese city that suffered at the hands of the invading Japanese forces. Soochow, Wuhsi, Shanghai, Hangchow, many other cities, and countless towns and villages were all savaged as well; but it was at Nanking that this brutality reached its nadir.

The crimes committed on many of the victims boggles the mind. Soldiers would go out in groups of ten or more and hunt down their victims. Any victim would do. The Japanese officers were well aware of the horrors being performed by their men, but took no measures to stop them. Their behaviour, especially the attacks on women, was considered an outlet for their animal urges; a boost to the morale of the soldiers.

In another effort to boost morale and make sport out of murder, the soldiers held contests to see who could rack up the most kills. The most pronounced example of this was a competition between two sub-lieutenants, Toshiaki Mukai and Takeshi Noda, who decided to compete with one another to see who would get one hundred kills first. They had to extend this goal because it was unclear which one had committed his hundredth murder first, and then they eventually lost count. They had perfected their decapitations of their victims with their swords to such an extent; they could cut through the necks of their victims and stop within a fraction of an inch so that only the skin around the area of the throat prevented the victim's head from falling to the ground. The victim being in a kneeling position would then automatically topple into the ditch because of the weight of his head resting on his chest pulling him over.

It is for the crimes against the women of Nanking that this tragedy is most notorious. Over the six weeks of the massacre, in addition to the murder of about 300 000 civilians and Chinese POW prisoners, the Japanese troops raped over 80, 000 women, most of who were later murdered.

Women of all ages (including children as young as seven and

elderly women in their seventies) were violated, many of them being gang-raped or attacked on multiple occasions. Some women were held captive so that they could be repeatedly abused. Rapes were committed in broad daylight, in front of spouses, children or other family members, and with appalling frequency. The soldiers' usual practice, officially condoned by high-ranking officials so as to 'avoid difficulties later', was to murder the women when they were finished with them. This was most often done by cutting off their breasts and/or disemboweling them by slicing through their abdomens with bayonets. Senior officers were not only aware of these acts, but they also participated in them as well.

These men made games of torturing their captives and finding new and cruel ways to kill them. They would throw babies into the air and bayonet them when they fell towards them. They would suspend other victims from meat hooks with the hooks inserted through their victim's tongues so that the full weight of their bodies were suspended by their tongues.

Particularly disturbing is that the Japanese perpetrators derived great pleasure from these heinous crimes, while their superiors condoned and even supported them. One outstandingly revolting account is of several soldiers who, after raping and killing a pregnant woman, presented her fetus on a bayonet to their commanding officer, who responded with laughter. There were innumerable gruesome occurrences like this one; acts of cruelty seemingly beyond human capacity but commonplace, in the massacre of Nanking.

In the following six weeks, the Nanking Red Cross units buried around 43,000 bodies. Between December 1937 and March 1938 at least 369,366 Chinese civilians and prisoners of war were slaughtered by the invading Japanese troops.

Foreigners (including a Nazi official) in Nanking had set up a 'safety zone' in which civilians would be safe from the marauding Japanese troops, but the willingness of the Japanese to comply was quite limited. The foreign leaders stated that there were no Chinese soldiers in their refuges, but still the Japanese often came to round up and execute young men whom they claimed to be members of the Chinese defense forces. Although foreigners in the area were generally unharmed, Chinese women were raped and buildings were looted within these areas designated for asylum, acts which the foreigners made known outside of China. Were it not for their reports, much less would be known in the West today about the Japanese massacre of the Chinese victims in Nanking.

Once the international community became aware of some of the atrocities that were taking place in Nanking, Tokyo started to restrain its troops and limit their savagery. The butchering of the citizens of Nanking eventually petered out by the end of January 1938, at which time the Japanese army began to request the assistance of foreign support groups in Nanking to clear away the thousands of corpses that littered the streets. The details of the massacre would later be officially revealed in the Tokyo War Crimes Trials which were held from 1946 to 1948, after the Allies had defeated Japan in the Second World War.

Twenty-eight men, including former foreign ministers and high-ranking military officials, were tried in Tokyo by an international jury for their part in the leadership behind the Nanking Massacre. It became clear that Tokyo had known about the atrocities and ignored them, considering them at the time as wartime policies. Of the twenty-eight men, two died during the trials, one broke down and was admitted to a mental institution, and the remaining twenty-five were all found guilty on one or more charges. All were sentenced in 1948 either to death by hanging or life imprisonment, but by 1956 every one of them had been paroled with the exception of General Iwane Matsui who was the man in charge of the troops in Nanking at the time of the massacre. After the Second World War, he was found guilty of a war crime unrelated to Nanking and sentenced to death. The Americans hanged him in 1948.

August 14th, 1937, during the Japanese invasion of China, the Japanese battleship Isuma was tied up at the dock in Shanghai. In an attempt to sink the Isuma, Chinese planes bombed the harbour but mistakenly the bombs hit a crowded department store and other adjacent buildings killing over 1,900 people.

The Nazi dirigible, *Hindenburg* was the largest airship in the world which carried 98 people and had 50 private cabins. The *Hindenburg* was an aircraft known as a zeppelin or dirigible. It was 803.8 feet (244 meters) in length, 135 feet (41 meters) in diameter, and took 7 million cubic feet (1.982 million cubic meters) of hydrogen gas to fill it. The hydrogen gas was in cells throughout the airship. In May 1936, the *Hindenburg* broke the trans-Atlantic speed record of only 61 and one-half hours to travel from Germany to Lakehurst, New Jersey.

On May 6th 1937, however, while coming in for a landing at Lakehurst, it suddenly burst into flames. Sixty seconds later, nothing was left of the dirigible but molten and twisted metal. Despite the destruction, out of 97 on board, 64 escaped alive, including 44 of the crew of 61 and 20 of the 36 passengers. Two of the 20 passengers, however, were seriously injured. Twenty-six bodies were recovered, of which nine were never identified.

In 1937, another disaster occurred. The town of New London in the State of Texas was an oil well community. The public school there was heated with natural gas. (At that time natural gas was odourless and colourless.) One day in March, there was a gas leak from a pipe in the school boiler room which began filling up the school rooms with the undetectable gas. Triggered by a spark in the wood shop, the whole school exploded.

Everyone in the community rushed to the rescue. Men started digging through the rubble as the women prepared food and aid for the rescue workers. As the digging went on they found what they were looking for—the bodies of their children. Over 300 children and their teachers where killed. One news reporter's estimate at the time was 425 children killed. With the loss of so many children, no one took an actual count of how many died from the explosion. Only 300 bodies were recovered, some having been blown to pieces. Those that weren't blown apart were buried somewhere in the debris.

The bodies where taken to the American Legion post where a

temporary morgue was set up for identification. In some instances, all the children of various families where lost and everyone in the community had lost someone in the explosion.

As a direct result of this devastating catastrophe, the United States Government passed a law that the chemical, 'Mercaptan' was to be put into natural gas to give it an identifying smell.

I almost had a disaster of my own in 1937 albeit on a much smaller scale. I was four years old that year and one day my mother had taken me downtown on the Queen Street streetcar from our home in Parkdale. In those days, we could get off the streetcar near the rear of the car. My mother got off first and then she held her hand out to assist me in getting off. The steps were deep for a four-year-old and naturally I was afraid that I would fall so I hesitated. She reached towards me and gently pulled me towards her. I began to fall forward and just as she grabbed my other hand, the doors of the streetcar closed with my two feet wedged behind them. No matter how hard my mother pulled, she couldn't pull me free.

When the streetcar began to move forward, she began to scream for help. The driver didn't hear her because of the street noise outside the streetcar. My mother began to run alongside the streetcar holding me by my hands. By now, I knew I was in serious trouble. Even as a four-year-old, I knew that eventually my mother would not be able to keep up and once she lost her grip on my hands, I would be dangling from the doors and my face would be dragged along the street. Needless to say, I too was screaming out of sheer terror.

Suddenly I saw a crowd of people running towards us from the sidewalk. Some of them tried to get the motorman's attention but he thought they merely wanted him to stop so that they could get on. He didn't stop for them. Others were running alongside of my mother while grabbing my arms. Within seconds, a man got behind the streetcar and pulled on the rope at the back of the streetcar that was connected to the trolley boom that in turn was connected to the overhead wires. As soon as he pulled the trolley boom downwards, the streetcar slowed to a halt. Those holding onto my arms pulled some more and my feet finally came free from the doors. The operator of the streetcar approached my mother and apologized. He said he didn't know that the closing doors had caught my feet. After that, I was always wary about exiting streetcars. When I do, (which is rare nowadays) I always have a firm grip on the railing leading down to the doors.

By the end of 1937, The American Medical Association recognized that birth control advice was a concern to them. A *Fortune Magazine* poll stated that as many as 50% of all college men and 25% of all college women had premarital sexual relations.

Spinach growers erected a statute of *Popeye*; the cartoon character that was so popular with kids. He was supposed to get his powers by eating spinach. It makes me wonder if they were the people who dreamed up the concept of that cartoon. Marijuana was so popular then so the US federal government passed a law called *The Marijuana Taxation Act* that made it illegal to import, sell or possess Marijuana and fixed heavy penalties for anyone caught doing so.

Because sound in movies came into vogue, some of the silent movie comedians such as Buster Keaton, Harold Lloyd and Langdon were no longer acting in movies anymore since their voices sounded so silly. There were some really fine movies made that year such as *The Life of Emile Zola, Captain Courageous, The Good Earth, Lost Horizon,* and *A star is Born*. These movies are still shown on TV. Top box office stars included, Shirley Temple, Clark Gable, Robert Taylor, Bing Crosby, William Powel, Fred Astaire, Ginger Rogers, Gary Cooper and Myrna Loy.

Great songs came out that year also which included; *Harbor Lights, Whistle While Your Work,* from the cartoon movie, *Snow White, The Lady is a Tramp, Thanks for the Memory,* and *In the Still of the Night.*

John D Rockefeller died and left an estate of one billion dollars. In 2009, that would be equivalent to $64,400,000,000. Maurice Ravel, the famous composer of symphony music and George Gershwin, the famous composer of *Rhapsody in Blue* also died that year.

First appearing was the National Cancer Institute, trampolines, skywriting at night, Spam, franchising (Howard Johnson Hotels)

Chapter Eight

In 1938, Hitler promoted himself to be the head of the German Armed Forces. One is forced to ask, "How can a former corporal fully understand the complexities of warfare? The answer is, "He can't." And as history shows, he couldn't. However, now being in charge of the armed forces, he was in a position to concentrate on taking over his former homeland, Austria. 'Anschluss' is a specific German term designating the incorporation of Austria into Germany. The Austrian Social Democrats first advocated Anschluss. The 1919 peace treaty of St. Germain prohibited Anschluss as a measure to prevent Austria being taken over by German interests. After Hitler's rise to power, he renewed his desire to do just that.

German intrigues in Austria had continued since 1936 through the agency of Arthur Seyss-Inquart's Nazi movement. When Papen, now ambassador to Vienna, reported on February 5th 1938, that the Schuschnigg regime showed signs of weakness, Hitler invited Schuschnigg, the Austrian Chancellor to a meeting at Berchtesgaden on the 12th. That was where Hitler's mountain residence, the Berghof, was located in the German Alps high above the town of Berchtesgaden.

In the course of an intimidating tirade, Schuschnigg, nevertheless insisted that Austria remain free, independent from Germany and continue being a Christian and united nation free from the overtures of Hitler. That really didn't hold Hitler back. Hitler demanded that Nazis be included in the Vienna government. After Schuschnigg's humiliating capitulation to Hitler, the German dictator was determined to reassert national independence through a plebiscite to be held on March 13th. He scheduled a plebiscite for that day through which Austrians might express their will. But his plans were moot as they were effectively negated by the German invasion and annexation of Austria. (Anschluss)

On March 14th, Hitler drove into Austria in a fleet of cars, preceded by forty tanks. When he arrived in Vienna in his personal car, he simply took the country over. Within days, as many as 60,000 Austrians were arrested including the country's ex-chancellor. Hitler claimed that he was doing this at the behest of the German people living in Austria. That being as it was, there was no fighting as such. The Austrian Chancellor, Kurt Schuschnigg was bullied by Hitler to capitulate when Hitler massed troops at the Austrian border and capitulate, the Austrian Chancellor did. It was the first easiest takeover Hitler had undertaken. While in Vienna, he proclaimed; "What we are experiencing at this moment is being experienced also by all other German People. Whatever happens, the German Reich as it stands today shall never be broken by anyone again and shall never be torn apart." *unquote* Little did Hitler or anyone else for that matter know at that moment that the German Reich would be torn apart exactly seven years and three weeks later.

Hitler hurriedly issued directives to the military, and when Schuschnigg was induced to resign, Seyss-Inquart simply appointed himself chancellor and invited German troops to intervene. A last-minute Italian proposal inviting Britain to make colonial concessions in return for Italian support of Austria met only indignant resignation and Anthony Eden's ignored complaints about Italy's troops in Spain. A French plea for Italian firmness, in turn, provoked Ciano, the Italian foreign minister (Mussolini's son-in-law) to ask, "Do they expect to rebuild Stresa in an hour with Hannibal at the gates?" Still, Hitler waited nervously on the evening of March 11th until he was informed that Mussolini would take no action in support of Austria. Hitler replied with effusive thanks and promises of eternal amity. He was sincere. In the night-time invasion, 70 percent of the vehicles sent into Austria by the unprepared Wehrmacht broke down on the road to Vienna, but despite that, they met no resistance

Adolf Hitler occupied Austria on March 11th, 1938, and, to popular approval, annexed it as the province of Ostmark. Austrians cheered deliriously on the 13th, when Hitler declared Austria a province of the Reich.

Schuschnigg had been forced to resign on that same day. After the invasion, he was arrested by the Germans, kept in solitary confinement and eventually interned in various concentration camps. He was liberated in May 1945 by the advancing American Army. After World War II, Schuschnigg emigrated to the United States, where he worked as a professor of political science at Saint Louis University from 1948 to 1967 after which he returned to Austria where he wrote *Im Kampf Gegen Hitler* (*In the Struggle with Hitler*) (1969) and *The Brutal Takeover* (1971). He died in Mutters, near Innsbruck, Austria on November 18th, 1977 at the age of 80.

Arthur Seyss-Inquart didn't fare as well. He previously served in the Austro-Hungarian army during World War I and was seriously wounded. Returning to Vienna after the war, he became a lawyer there in 1921. He also became a fervent advocate of a political union of Austria with Germany, and he cultivated close ties with the Austrian Nazi Party. A leader of the moderate 'legal' faction of the Austrian Nazis, Seyss-Inquart was appointed to the Austrian Staatsrat (federal council of state) in June 1937 in order for him to bring the Nazis into line with the government. In February 1938, in response to German pressure, he was named minister of interior and security, a prelude to his replacement of Kurt von Schuschnigg as chancellor on March 11th, 1938, the eve of Anschluss. Long a proponent of German-Austrian unification, he openly welcomed the incorporation of Austria into Germany that followed in the same month after the invasion by German troops.

Subsequently he served as Reichsstatthalter (governor) of the new Austrian provincial administration until April 30th, 1939. He was later appointed deputy governor in Poland and eventually Reichskommissar (commissioner) of the occupied Netherlands. Following the defeat of Germany in World War II, he was tried and convicted of war crimes at Nüremberg as a war criminal and on October 16th 1946, at the age of 54, he ended up strangling at the end of a hangman's rope attached to one of three gallows built in the gymnasium attached to the Spandau prison which is located in a suburb of the western part of Berlin.

The Spanish civil war was still ongoing. On the 7th of February 1938, Nationalist cavalry attacked the Republican forces to the North of the Teruel and forced them to retreat and by the 17th of February, Moroccan troops led by General Juan Yague had crossed the River Alfambra. Three days later the Nationalists had almost surrounded the city and the Republican armies were forced to retreat along the Valencia road to the south-east. On the 6th of March, the modern Nationalist cruiser *Baleares*, which was escorting a convoy of merchant ships off the Mediterranean coast near Cartagena, was sunk by torpedoes launched by Republican destroyers.

On September 21st, Dr. Negrin announced, in a speech to the League of Nations, (the forerunner of the United Nations) that the International Brigades were withdrawing from the fighting. On the 15th of November, the International Brigades paraded through Barcelona before they were disbanded. Many of these men from those brigades were Canadians who simply wanted to fight in a war. Many members of the brigades unfortunately didn't return to Canada alive. I have mixed feelings about that Brigade. I think they were very foolish to fight in a war that really wasn't their war to begin with. Being killed or severely wounded is a very high price to stick one's nose in where it really doesn't belong. This is not to imply that we shouldn't intervene in every situation. But the International Brigade simply comprised of men who simply wanted to fight in any war with the exception of the Spaniards who were returning to Spain to participate in the war that was going on against their own families and friends. They were no different than the blacks who lived in Chad, Niger and Mali who accepted the invitation of Libya's leader in 2010 to fight the revolutionaries who eventually overthrew their Libyan dictator.

Having cut the Republic into two, the Nationalists now launched an offensive against Catalonia. The attack on the forces defending the Republican front-line was made by six Nationalist armies on a front that stretched from the Pyrenees to South of the River Ebro. It proved too much for the already exhausted Republicans. They retreated towards Barcelona and once Borjas Blancas was captured on 4th January, the retreat became a rout. Tarragona surrendered on the 14th of January 1939, and by the 24th of January, the Nationalists were within three miles of Barcelona. At this point the Government, led by Juan Negrin, fled to Gerona which is 53 miles (85.5 km) northeast of Barcelona as the crow flies.

The Republican troops in Barcelona continued to maintain a token resistance until the 26th of January 1939 when the city finally surrendered.

The 4,200 foot (1,280 metres) Golden Gate Suspension Bridge in San Francisco was completed and became the largest suspension bridge in the world at that time. The strapless gown made its debut also. I suspect that to many women, the suspensions of their gowns were more fascinating than the suspension of the Golden Gate Bridge. The Akashi-Kaikyo Bridge, also known as the Pearl Bridge, has the longest central span of any suspension bridge, at 1,991 metres (6,532 ft). It is located in Japan and was completed in 1998. The bridge links the city of Kobe on the mainland of Honshū to Iwaya on Awaji Island by crossing the busy Akashi Strait. It carries part of the Honshū-Shikoku Highway. There are also other suspension bridges longer than the Golden Gate Bridge, such as the Tsing Ma Bridge in Hong Kong. It is 1,377metres in length. The bridge was named after two of the islands at its ends, namely Tsing Yi and Ma Wan. It has two decks and carries both road and rail traffic, which also makes it the largest suspension bridge of this type. The bridge has a main span of 1,377 metres (4,518 ft) and a height of 206 metres (676 ft). The span is the largest of all bridges in the world carrying rail traffic. My wife and I crossed that bridge many times when we flew in and out of Hong Kong. The minimum wage in the United States was set at 24 cents an hour and laws were created in the USA that anyone who worked more than 44 hours a week was to be paid time and a half. That didn't help the 10 million people who were still unemployed as the depression worsened. Fortunately, child labour was finally abolished in the USA during that year.

Jerry Siegel, an American, together with Canadian-born boyhood friend, Joe Shuster, created the comic strip, *Superman*. It later became very popular in the form of comic books bringing millions of dollars to its publishers. Often, people who have opportunities to benefit from great ideas, lose out because of their own stupidity. What follows is from an editor at United Features with respect to publishing *Superman*: "It's an immature piece of work, attractive because of its freshness and naiveté, but this is likely to wear off after the feature runs for a while.' That's about as dumb as the man who was given the opportunity to manage the Beatles singing group and turned them down by saying that no one wants to hear another guitar-playing group.

Orson Welles, later to be a famous movie star, wrote and stared in a radio show called *War of the Worlds*. After the October 30th 1938 Halloween-eve broadcast of his nationwide radio show *The War of the Worlds* based on a novel by H.G. Welles (no relation) also entitled *The War of the Worlds*, all hell broke loose.

What everyone heard on the radio was a series of very realistic-sounding news announcements interrupting a program apparently devoted to popular music with the news that landings on planet Earth were being done by hostile Martians armed to the teeth with deadly 'Ray Guns' in Grover's Mills, a small town in New Jersey.

Grover's Mill is an unincorporated area within West Windsor Township, New Jersey where it was depicted as ground zero for a Martian invasion, on October 30th of that year. They even have a small monument dedicated to that radio show.

During its broadcast it made many local New Jerseyites hysterical (especially those in Grover's Mill) and as some ran to their closets to find firearms, others went crazy looking for improvised weapons such as pitchforks to defend themselves with. There were minor street-riots and traffic-jams in the more populous, surrounding areas. As other New Jerseyites sought ways of getting out of the imperiled cities of New Jersey and to immediate safety, others in neighboring states also racked their brains, considering methods, whether by train or plane, Model T or roller-skates, and skate-board or by horse and buggy if necessary so that they too could at least put a few extra miles between themselves and the invaders. As hitchhikers appeared up and down the East Coast, thronging many roadsides, the panic kept spreading until officials of 'The Blue Network' went on the air a few hours afterwards to make an announcement explaining that its listeners had been the unwitting victims of an unintended hoax and that the radio show *The War of the Worlds* was just one more in a series of highly effective radio programs presented by Orson Welles in his weekly radio series called 'Mercury Theatre' and that had all listeners tuned in at the start of the program when an announcement was made clearly stating to their audiences that Welles' program was fictional, there would have been no reason to panic.

The powers that be in Washington, D.C., were nevertheless especially angry considering the fact that at first, they too weren't sure that the radio show was a hoax.

As a result of that broadcast, Orson Welles was reprimanded by practically everybody connected with radio-broadcasting, from the Executive-in-Chief of 'The Blue Network' on down to the Manager of the station in whose studios the program had originated, with some furious citizens even quaintly suggesting that the Manager of the Station on which the broadcast had originated and Welles himself should be immediately taken out and shot.

Orson Welles apologized (albeit rather laconically) to his radio public, the public at large, the United States in general and the authorities specifically in Grovers Mills for scaring them with his radio show. I doubt that he was really sorry. It made him renowned after that and he went on to produce and direct and star in great movies; *Citizen Kane* being one of them.

A similar show was broadcasted on television in the latter 1970s or early 1980s. (I can't remember which) The movie was played as if it was a news account of an actual event taking place. The story line was that terrorists had conducted an act of terrorism for the release of some of their fellow terrorists. What heightened the story was that the terrorists also had an atomic bomb with them on a small tug boat across the river from a large city and if they detonated it, the entire city across the river would be completely destroyed.

Whenever there was a station break, an announcer would remind its viewers that what they were watching was a movie and not a newscast. I knew in advance what was coming with this show because I read something in the newspaper earlier about it when it made references to Welles' radio show, *The War of the Worlds*.

My wife, Ayako was sitting next to me and whenever a station break came, I turned down the sound so that she wouldn't hear the announcement that said that we were really watching a movie and not an ongoing news event. When the part of the show when the nuclear bomb was detonated, she was absolutely aghast at what she just saw, as no doubt were millions of others who believed that what they were watching was a real newscast. Of course, the people in the city that supposedly had been killed and incinerated by an atom bomb must have been quite puzzled as they continued to watch on their TVs how the explosion that supposedly completely destroyed their city with them in it, had killed and incinerated them all.

It was a nasty thing to pull on my wife but oh my, it really was fun looking at the expression on her face when she saw what she believed was the complete destruction of a large city by a nuclear blast.

As a promotional strategy, airlines in 1938 were offering wives free passage with their husbands because it was believed that women were more afraid of flying then men were. A funny thing happened that year. A flyer called Corrigan sought a permit to fly across the Atlantic to Dublin, Ireland and was refused the permit. He did however get a permit to fly to California. He took off and shortly thereafter, he reversed his direction and flew across the Atlantic to Dublin. Later when asked to explain, he replied, "Sorry, I flew the wrong way." Sure he did. From then on, he was referred to as Wrong-Way Corrigan.

This was the year the Biro brothers invented the ballpoint pen. One could buy corduroy overalls for $1.95 USD which in 1999 would cost 23.04 USD. A matching jacket would cost $3.95 USD which in 1999 would cost $46.67 USD. Children's shoes $3 USD which in 1999 cost $35.40 USD. A Chenile bedspread cost $3.95 USD which in 1999 would cost 46.67 USD. Custom venetian blinds cost per square foot, 39 cents USD and in 1999 it would cost $4.61 USD. Lace net curtains sold for $1.79 USD a pair whereas in 1999, it cost 21.19 USD. Movie cameras in colour could be purchased for as little as $55.00 USD. In 1999, it would cost $2,380.00 in 1999.

The United States guaranteed its savings bonds by guaranteeing its purchasers that in ten years; the purchasers would reap 33% of what they originally invested.

The January 1938 edition of the *National Geographic Magazine* showed a picture of the Hungarian Royal Crown which is locked in a walk-in vault guarded by three armed soldiers. It is guarded 24 hours a day every day of the year and one of the soldiers is required to keep his eyes on the crown via a small opening in the vault at all times he is on watch. Strangely enough, no one has worn the crown in centuries.

The Americans built large flying boats that had four 3600-power engines that made it possible for the aircraft to fly thirty passengers and seven crew members from San Francisco to Honolulu non-stop. Lincoln-Zephyr automobiles that year had 12 cylinders. That would really give you a smooth ride.

Every once in a while, we hear the blatherings of politicians and the Prime Minister of Great Britain was no exception to the rule. The following is the wording of the printed statement that Neville Chamberlain waved as he stepped off the plane on 30th September, 1938 after the Munich Conference with Hitler had ended the day before: "We, the German Fuehrer and Chancellor, and the British Prime Minister, have had a further meeting today and are agreed in recognizing that the question of Anglo-German relations is of the first importance for our two countries and for Europe. We regard the agreement signed last night and the Anglo-German Naval Agreement as symbolic of the desire of our two peoples never to go to war with one another again. We are resolved that the method of consultation shall be the method adopted to deal with any other questions that may concern our two countries, and we are determined to continue our efforts to remove possible sources of difference, and thus to contribute to assure the peace of Europe." *unquote*

Chamberlain later read the above statement in front of 10 Downing Street and said: "My good friends. For the second time in our history, a British Prime Minister has returned from Germany bringing peace with honour. I believe it is peace for our time. Go home and get a nice quiet sleep." *unquote*

We all know now of course that the written agreement between himself and Hitler, which he proudly waved in the air when he got off the plane wasn't worth the paper it was written on. Hitler marched into Czechoslovakia the following year. So much for honour and political blather.

My mother moved us to 251 Symington Avenue in Toronto. It is a small building at the northeast corner of Symington and Antler Street. On the main floor was a small store with our residence on the floor above the store. I rarely saw my father before or after my fifth birthday (but he did show up for my fifth birthday) and I learned many years later that he still rarely ever came home. He would be away five and six months at a time. He claimed that he had been looking for work out of town. If he was looking for work, how did he support himself all those months? Where he went, I have no idea but my mother presumed that he had been living with another woman somewhere in Toronto and no doubt being supported by that woman also. He certainly didn't send any support money to my mother.

My brother was only one year old when we moved to Symington Avenue so my mother had to tie a rope around his waist and tie the other end to the top of the stairs on the north side of the building. He had just enough room to reach the far edge of the sidewalk and no more. My mother says that I used to hold him back when he tried to reach the top of the stairs, by pulling on the rope from the bottom of the stairs. That's nasty but, hey, I was only a five-year-old kid then.

My mother also told me that while we lived on that street, I fed my brother a worm. I can't imagine a charming sweet young boy like me doing something that dastardly to a baby brother—can you? My mother must be mistaken. In any case, my mother called the doctor when she learned that I had fed my brother a worm but the doctor assured her that lots of kids eat worms and nothing bad comes of it. This is not an endorsement that you should feed your kids worms. I don't even think that fish like worms. I know. Whenever I tried to catch fish with a worm on the hook, they just swam right by without as much as a second glance.

Certainly, the German soldiers who were ordered by two of their officers to eat worms on a field exercise in 1992 didn't like eating the worms they were ordered to eat. One threw up and other ran around in circles while gagging on the worm. The two officers were demoted. I on the other hand, was spanked.

Why am I writing about worms? I just thought this gross subject might titillate my readers. No? Then let's move on.

I later learned many years later that my father during that year was employed at H. Rose Jewelers as a collector of accounts but later in the year, he quit because his expenses were too high. I guess that means he was underpaid. Maybe his girlfriend wasn't supporting him anymore.

For my mother, life with my father at this time in our lives was terrible; that is when he showed up and moved in with us again. He was a very selfish man. He blamed my mother for bearing him two boys in the first place and considering the fact that I was conceived as a result of him raping my mother, his blaming my mother for his own misdeed brought his attitude towards her to an all-time low.

When my mother would get up early in the morning to feed me and my brother, my father would yell at her to forget us and make him his breakfast first even though he didn't go to work. Sometimes my mother would get up before dawn and wake my brother and I up and tell us to be very quiet. She would give my brother his bottle and she would feed me cereal. Sometimes my father would wake up while she was feeding my brother and I, and my father would yell at my mother, "Me first! I told you, I come first!" One day his yelling "Me first—" infuriated my mother so much, she threw an egg at him. She missed. His fist didn't and she ended up with a split lip. She walked over to the phone, which was being paid for by her parents, and she called the police. She had barely walked away from the phone when the police arrived. Two burly cops entered the flat when she opened the door. They took one look at her bleeding mouth and torn nightgown and one of them asked my father, "Have you been beating your wife?" He responded with, "Have you ever been married?" The cop said, "That's got nothing whatever to do with it." My father replied, "It certainly has. My wife thinks her children are more important to her than I am." Considering how he was mistreating her, his statement was par for the course for him. They asked my mother if she wanted him arrested but she told them that she didn't want to press charges but she warned my father that if he beats her again, she would call the police and lay a charge of assault against him. Notwithstanding her warning, he continued to push her around and on one occasion, she fell backwards and her head banged against the edge of the bathtub and she was knocked unconscious. She didn't call the police—she merely continued to endure his abuse—like so many millions of abused wives both before and after her.

    Two burly cops coming to one's door brings to mind an event that took place in Toronto around 1964. Two women whom I knew were living in a dingy room on Church Street in Toronto. It was Christmas Eve and the carols and other Christmas songs were being sung on the radio, the white snow was gently falling to the ground and the owner of their rooming house was ordering them and one of the girl's three-week-old baby to vacate the premises immediately because they were a week behind in their rent. It seems that their welfare cheques hadn't arrived on time. One of the women managed to reach me on the phone so I arrived at their room an hour later. I tried to reason with the owner but he refused to budge. I called the police department and spoke to an officer who owed me a favour. He told me to leave everything to him. About half an hour later, two burly, I mean BURLY, cops showed up and they asked the owner, who was in his fifties as to why he was throwing the two young women and the three-week-old baby out into the street on that cold, snowy Christmas Eve. He blurted out. "Because they didn't pay their rent on time. They got to get out now!" I didn't get to see it but I sure got to hear it. THUMP, SMASH, CRASH, "Ohhh" BANG, BUMP "Ohhh" etc. A few minutes later, the cops knocked on the girl's door and said, "The owner says to tell you that you can stay here as long as you like. Merry Christmas to you all." Yes, it was a merry Christmas for all. I felt good, the girls felt good, the cops felt good and the owner, well I don't think he was feeling too good that night—and all the next day judging by the way he was limping about. Who said that cops aren't all heart?

During 1938, I developed tuberculosis in my lungs like thousands of other kids in Canada at that time. My mother took me up University Avenue (it was a beautiful residential street in 1938 with three-story homes on both sides of the street with maple trees on the boulevards) until we reached College street and then we walked east on College to the Children's Hospital which was at 67 College Street. It was a 320-bed hospital and was also called the Victoria Hospital for Sick Children. The hospital later moved to 555 University Avenue in 1951. In any case, I remember being laid down on a table and the huge X-ray machine above me being lowered towards me. My mother later said that it took five nurses to hold me down. I can still see that monster coming down from the ceiling to devour me. In any case, the X-ray negative showed that I had a spot of TB in my left lung.

The doctors suspected that I caught it from another person since TB in the lungs is highly contagious. In Ontario alone that year, 1,327 people died of gradual and slow asphyxiation after their lungs were slowly eaten away by the tubercle bacillus. It's a horrible way to die. Milk had been pasteurized in Toronto from 1915 onward so I didn't get it from milk being processed in Toronto. Bovine tuberculosis was prevalent in the rest of Ontario since the pasteurization of milk didn't become mandatory in the rest of Ontario until 1938. There was no such thing as homogenized milk in the 1930s. The cream always went to the top. The lower part was bluish. In wintertime the milk froze and pushed the round cardboard lids out of the glass bottles. In the summertime, the milk was still cool because there was ice in the milk wagon to keep the milk cool.

Tuberculosis is an airborne disease. When a non-infected person is in contact with a person suffering from TB, only then does the non infected person get the infection. These TB germs come from a TB patient, whose sputum contain germs and are spread in the air by coughing, spitting, talking and sneezing, thereby releasing microscopic particles into the air at 90 km an hour which are then inhaled by the persons nearby. These particles, also called droplet nuclei, contain live tubercle bacteria. Once infected by TB, most people remain healthy and develop only latent infection. People with latent infection are neither sick nor infectious. However, they do have the potential to become sick and infectious with active TB.

In the year 1999, as many as a third of the world's population suffered from some form of TB. As many as 8,640 persons died every day from it. That amounts to 3,153,600 a year. Of that amount of deaths from TB, 2,053,000 were men, 1,000,000 were women and 100,000 were children. One percent of the people who die in Canada, die from TB. The World Health Organization predicted that by the year 2020, as many as 1 billion people will be suffering from TB. In Canada, at least 2000 cases are reported each year with 63% of the victims being foreigners and of which 50% of those victims were refugees.

In the early years of the last century, indigent adults who had TB in Toronto were sent to the West Park Hospital (then called the Toronto Free Hospital for the Consumptive Poor; it opened in 1904) in the Weston Road and Jane Street area in Weston, Ontario, now a suburb of Toronto.

In my case, they decided that because the tubercle bacilli were sitting down to feast on the lower portion of my left lung, I should be sent to the *Imperial Order of Daughters of the Empire Preventorium* which was located in Weston. The *IODE Preventorium* in Weston was the first institution of its kind in North America, established for the treatment of children who had been exposed to, but not yet contracted tuberculosis. Of course by the time I was there, the patients were children who were already suffering from TB. The buildings were finally torn down in 1952.

This was to be the first time that I had to live away from my mother. I was not happy with the prospects of leaving my mother at all and judging from my crying; everyone within a city block was probably also aware that I was not happy with those prospects.

The thing that stands out in my memory about the Preventorium's main two-story building was the requirement that we sleep outside on a wide screened porch (no glass windows) every night of the year, be it raining or snowing and irrespective of the temperatures being ninety degrees above or ten below freezing Fahrenheight. It was the belief of the doctors that plenty of fresh air and sunlight was what we needed and plenty of air is what we got. We were also required to spend a great deal of time out in the sun because it was the belief then (and a valid one) that the ultraviolet rays from the sun helped cure TB patients. It must have worked because less than a year later, I was cured notwithstanding the fact that in those days, there was no effective medicine to combat TB. That didn't really come about until the introduction of the antibiotic 'streptomycin' years later.

Every night during the winter months, we had to go through the same ritual of first, having our shower inside the building, then getting into our pyjamas and putting on heavy woollen socks to cover our feet, heavy woollen toques that was to cover our heads and ears and woollen mitts to cover our hands and then after the nurses filled up the large wool-covered crockery-like 'pigs' with hot water which were to warm our feet, we took them with us (the 'pigs' that is) and climbed into our beds. The fresh air may have done something for our tubercle lungs but it sure didn't do anything for our toes and fingertips and especially our noses that were to be kept outside the blankets so that we could breathe in all that fine fresh air. It was ironic when you think of it however, that a small factory next door had a square-shaped brick smoke stack that emitted smoke and soot occasionally that mingled with all that fine fresh air that we inhaled every night. No wonder the X-ray couldn't find signs of TB in my lungs the following year—the TB was probably hidden behind all that soot that I had breathed in while sleeping outside next to the belching smokestack. Who knows, it may have been the belching smoke and soot that cured me of my TB.

One night, sparks came out of the smokestack and fell around the base of the Preventorium's main building. The outside wall at the rear of the building caught fire and I remember after the staff herded us outside, one of them sent me back into the building to get my shoes. When I reached my bed, flames were licking up the outside walls. I feared that cranky nurse more than the flames so I ran to my bed on the veranda at the back of the building, grabbed my shoes and ran stocking-footed out of the building again. The building was saved without too much damage so later that night, we returned to the building (I, still in my stocking feet) and to our beds and after much yakking to each other about the 'great fire', and screams from the cranky nurse to be "QUIET!" we finally went to sleep.

We were constantly doing calisthenics, such as swinging Indian clubs about our heads. Those clubs were heavy for a five-year-old, I assure you. Obviously, the hospital felt that our treatment should include rigorous exercise when inhaling all that fine fresh air. One song I remember being taught to sing while swinging the clubs was that old favourite, *Early One Morning*.

I missed my mother terribly and she did come on occasion to visit me and I really looked forward to her visits but unfortunately I never really got to see her that much when she came. While she would be talking to the doctor, it was my grandmother that would spend the hour or so with me, telling me how to behave—an experience that was not on the top of the list of things that I looked forward to in those days—my grandmother's visit, that is.

I remember on one occasion, I began coughing quite bad and a male nurse carried me in his arms to the first building I had been in for several months when I arrived at the Preventorium. It turned out that my lungs weren't being eaten away at this time, I was just suffering from an itchy throat, or something like that. Within a week or so, I was sent back to the building I had been taken from. This time, I had to walk back on my own two feet. Well, I really wasn't expecting the free ride on the return trip anyway.

It was this year that I saw my first cartoon in colour. All the kids and most of the staff oohed and aahed when we saw it because for the most part, the cartoons we had been shown in the past—like everyone else in North America, were in black and white as were the Laurel and Hardy silent films shown to us.

It was while I was at the Preventorium that I learned to tie one of my shoelaces. A week later, I learned to tie the other one. Up to then, I had tried everything else to keep my shoes on but nothing had worked. I was finally sent home sometime in early 1939.

As an interesting aside, in 1959 I applied for a job at the young offender's reform school in Brampton, Ontario and the superintendent and his wife took me to lunch in that city. About half an hour into our lunch, the wife said to me, "Where you ever in the Preventorium in Toronto in the 1930s?" Apparently she was a nurse in that institution and she remembered me. I must have been very good or very bad for her to remember me twenty years later.

Meanwhile, my father had got a job in 1938 with Imperial Oil as a mechanic around this time. He was a shift boss. It turned out that this is what he liked doing best; being a mechanic working with engines. Later he was to work on the engines of Lancaster bombers while serving in the Royal Canadian Air Force during the Second World War.

The major news event of May and June of 1939 was the Royal Visit; the first visit ever to Canada by a reigning Monarch. King

George VI and Queen Elizabeth arrived by ship in Quebec City and forty-three days after a coast to coast tour of Canada, they sailed for home from Halifax. City-by-city, local broadcasters gave 'live' coverage of the Royal couple's visit to their communities.

I first saw King George VI and Queen Elizabeth (years later, the late Queen Mother) and the two princesses, Elizabeth (years later the Queen) and Margaret when they were driven up Parkside Drive in Toronto, a street that borders High Park, when my mother took us to see them from the verandah of the home of one of her aunts. The king was on the east side of the car when it was being driven north on Parkside. The waving of his right hand was sort of constrained but the queen who was sitting next to him on his left, waved quite enthusiastically to the crowds on her side of the street.

My mother decided to go somewhere for the summer (I don't know where) and she made arrangements for my brother and me to spend the summer on a small farm on the east side of Highway 50, a few kilometers south of Bolton, a small community north west of Toronto. I don't remember much of my experiences on that farm as I was only five years old then going on six.

When I was at the farm, King George VI and his family were traveling across Canada so when the farmer learned that the royal train was going to be passing somewhere near the farm, he decided to take his family, my brother and me to watch the train carrying the royal family. We pulled up near a spot where the train tracks crossed the road and he subsequently parked his car on the side of the road. There was a fairly large crowd near the junction of the road and tracks so he took my brother and me up the tracks about fifty or so metres from the crowd. As the train slowly approached us, the farmer placed me onto his shoulders and stood about two meters (six feet) from the tracks. It was a 30-metre train passenger car which was painted green with yellow letters painted on it. It had seven windows on each side of it with a platform at the rear of it. It was the last car in the train. It had been built by the Canadian National Railway in 1924 for wealthy customers and CNR executives.

Together we waited for the great moment when we would see the royal couple standing on the rear platform of the royal car. As the royal couple was abreast of us on the platform and heading back inside the car, I waved and cried out, "Hello." I expected that the train would stop and when it didn't, I yelled out, "Goodbye." The king and queen turned towards me and began laughing and then they waved back at me. This tells you something about their royal majesties. They were the kind of people who would take time to acknowledge the greetings of a five-year-old.

As another interesting aside, when their eldest daughter, Queen Elizabeth II and her consort, Prince Phillip crossed Canada in 1951; they too stood on that same rear platform of the train car her parents stood on in 1939. I wasn't near the tracks at that time however.

For many years, I wondered where that farm was but no one in my family knew, not even my mother. Sometime in the mid-1980s, I was a process server and I often drove north on Highway 50 on my way to Bolton to serve court papers in Bolton. One day, coming back, it suddenly hit me. I had been passing the farm for years and didn't realize that until that particular day. What made it stand out in my mind was that there was a very small graveyard across the highway. I should point out however, that Highway 50 wasn't a paved highway in 1939. It was just a dusty dirt road.

I went to the small farmhouse and spoke to the owners. I told them that back in 1939, my brother and I lived in the farmhouse. I asked them if the shed next to them was used for storing blocks of ice covered by sawdust. They said it was. I asked them if when walking into the barn, one would pass the pigsty on one's right that was just inside the barn. They said that too was true. I had finally found the first farm my brother and I had lived in during the summer of 1939. The couple I had spoken to were two generations younger of the actual farmer and his wife that ran the farm when we were there. A year later, after the farm was vacant, I walked into the house but recognized nothing. When I stood in the field and faced a similar sunset I had faced in 1939, it confirmed my belief that I had been on that farm so many years earlier.

When we moved to Symington Avenue from Concord Avenue, (which was only a few blocks away) I used to go to a dump just a block east of Symington and running south a block and running right up against the railroad tracks to the east of it where my friends and I would play hide and go seek. There were large empty oil tanks strewn throughout the dump. The dump was finally replaced with a park called the Campbell Avenue Playground. My mother told me to stop playing in the dump as it was getting my clothes filthy. That was because we played inside the oil tanks. There was also a small lane behind our house and I used to play with the other kids in the lane and the open garages that back onto it. I remember one day watching a man in the middle of the intersection handing out streetcar tickets to all of us kids milling around him. Of course I didn't know what they were then but I always had my hand out for something or other, not counting the times I later had to hold it out for the strap. Later that evening, my mother gave me a couple of pennies for each of the tickets. I guess it was a buyer's market then.

When school started in September of 1939, I was still five years old so I was put in kindergarten at Perth Avenue Elementary School at Perth and Buskin Avenues even though I would be six years old two months later. I remember that day clearly. My mother took me to school with my brother tagging along but we were late. The halls were empty and the principal came out of this office and said to my mother. "Why are you three children not in your classes?" He was really shocked when my mother told him that she was the mother and I and my brother were the children. Later in the year, I was moved up to grade one but I had missed so much of grade one because of having been in kindergarten the first part of the school year, I was later returned to kindergarten before June of 1940. My first failure in life; not counting the many times I attempted to tie my shoelaces. Actually I was glad I had been sent back to kindergarten. The teacher there was much nicer in kindergarten than the crabby grouch in grade one.

Chapter Nine

After being betrayed by England and France, Czechoslovakia was marched into in March 1939 by the German Army and it too succumbed to Hitler's tyranny. Once again Hitler would make use of national self-determination to confuse the issue, as 3,000,000 German-speaking Czechs that inhabited the Czech borderlands in the Sudeten Mountains were organized by another Nazi henchman, Konrad Henlein. On February 20th, before the Anschluss, Hitler had denounced the Czechs for their alleged persecution of their German minority and on April 21st he ordered Field Marshall Keitel to prepare for the invasion of Czechoslovakia by October even if the French were to intervene.

British Prime Minister Chamberlain was intent on appeasing Hitler but this meant that he intended to 'educate' him to seek redress of grievances through negotiation and not by not force. Chamberlain issued a stern warning to Germany while pressuring President Edvard Benes of Czechoslovakia to compromise with Henlein. Germany, however, had instructed Henlein to display obstinacy so as to prevent an agreement. In August, a very concerned British Cabinet dispatched the elderly Lord Walter Runciman to mediate, but Henlein rejected the program of concessions he had previously arranged with Benes. As the prospect of war increased, the British appeasers grew more frantic.

The French Cabinet of Édouard Daladier and Georges-Étienne Bonnet agreed, after the latter's frantic pleas to Roosevelt failed to shake American isolation. This failure on Roosevelt gave Hitler confidence in his ultimate goal of seizing Czechoslovakia. The Czechs, however, resisted handing over their border fortifications to Hitler until September 21st, when the British and French made it clear that they would not fight for the Sudetenland. Chamberlain flew to Bad Godesberg the next day only to be met with a new demand that the entire Sudetenland be ceded to Germany within a week. The Czechs, fully mobilized as of the 23rd, refused, and Chamberlain returned home in a snit: "How horrible, fantastic, incredible it is that we should be digging trenches and trying on gas masks here because of a quarrel in a far-away country between people of whom we know nothing." *unquote* His views on isolationism were no different that those of Roosevelt. But his sorrowful address to Parliament was interrupted by the news that Mussolini had proposed a conference to settle the crisis peacefully. Hitler agreed, having seen how little enthusiasm there was in Germany for war and on the advice of Göering, Joseph Goebbels, and Hitler's generals. Chamberlain and Daladier, elated, flew to Munich on September 29th.

The Munich Conference ended on the 30th in a compromise prearranged between Hitler and Mussolini. The Czechs were to evacuate all regions indicated by an international commission (which was dominated by the Germans) by October 10th and were given no recourse since the agreement was final. Poland took the opportunity to grab the Teschen district (now called Gieszyn) immediately east of Czechoslovakia disputed since 1920. Czechoslovakia was no longer a viable state, and Benes resigned the presidency in despair. In return, Hitler promised no more territorial demands in Europe. That's akin to a child promising never to be bad again while he still has his hand in the cookie jar. Hitler also promised to have consultations with Britain in case of any future threat to peace. Chamberlain, needless to say, was ecstatic. Chamberlain was the kind of man who if he had lived in this century, anyone could have successfully sold that gullible politician the window washing concession of the World Trade Towers in New York even after he saw the first one crumbling to the ground on September 11th 2001.

One is forced to ask rhetorically as to why the Western powers abandoned Czechoslovakia, which, by means of its geographic position in Europe, democracy, military potential (more than 30 divisions and the Skoda arms works), and commitment to collective security, could rightly be called the keystone of interwar Europe? There is no question that the Munich settlement was extremely popular, probably because Hitler assured the conferees that he would no longer expand his grasp for more territories in Europe. Chamberlain returned to London claiming "peace in our time" and was greeted by applauding throngs. So was Daladier in France. Of course, they didn't know it at the time that both men had been duped. The relief nevertheless was short lived because in Germany, Hitler swore he would allow no more meddling by "English governesses" to cheat him of his war. Aside from the Czechs, who wept openly in the streets, Churchill spoke for a growing minority when he observed that the British Empire had just suffered its worst military defeat and in the process, had not fired a shot in its defence.

Could Czechoslovakia have been defended? Possibly. The Munich Accord (Agreement) could be considered as a necessary evil to buy time for Britain to rearm. However, the British air defenses were unready, France's defenses scarcely existed, and the strength of the Luftwaffe, so recently discounted by the British Cabinet, was now built up. The French and Czech armies still outnumbered the German armies, but the situation was far actually worse because the French intelligence erroneously magnified German strength, while the French army had no plans for invading Germany in support of the Czechs. The Munich participants to the Accord were criticized for ignoring the U.S.S.R., which had claimed readiness to honour its alliance with Prague. The U.S.S.R., however, would hardly confront Germany unless the Western powers were already engaged, and the ways open to them were few without transit rights across Poland. The West discounted Soviet military effectiveness in light of Stalin's 1937 purge of his entire officer corps down to battalion level which was an enormous big mistake on the part of the Soviet dictator, Stalin that was to haunt him later. The Soviets were also distracted by division-scale fighting that broke out with Japanese forces on the Manchurian border in July-August 1938. At best, a few squadrons of Soviet planes might have been sent to Prague however that wasn't going to come about in any case.

The moral cause of liberating the Sudeten Germans was ludicrous in view of the nature of the Nazi regime and was far outweighed by the moral lapse of deserting the brave and determined Czechs. French Ambassador André François-Poncet, upon reading the Munich Accord, exclaimed, "Thus does France treat her only allies who had remained faithful to her." That betrayal, in turn, seemed more than outweighed by the moral cause of preventing another war. As it turned out, the war was delayed only a year and whatever the military realities of 1938 versus them in 1939, the appeasement policy was an exercise in self-delusion.

Hitler obviously had no intention of honouring the Munich Accord. That became obvious when in October, the Nazis encouraged the Slovak and Ruthene minorities in Czechoslovakia to set up autonomous governments and then in November, he gave Hungary back the 4,600 square miles north of the Danube taken from it in 1919. On March 13th, 1939, Gestapo officers carried the Slovak leader Monsignor Jozef Tiso off to Berlin and deposited him in the presence of the Fuehrer, who demanded that the Slovaks declare their independence at once. Tiso returned to Bratislava to inform the Slovak Diet (parliament) that the only alternative to becoming a Nazi protectorate was by a German invasion. The Slovaks complied with Hitler's demands. All that remained to the new president in Prague, Emil Hácha, was the core region of Bohemia and Moravia. It was time, said Hácha with heavy sarcasm, "to consult our friends in Germany." There Hitler subjected the elderly, broken-spirited man to a tirade that brought tears, a fainting spell, and finally a signature on a 'request' that Bohemia and Moravia be incorporated into the Reich. The next day, (March 16th) German units occupied Prague, and from that moment until after the war, Czechoslovakia, a country of slightly over 14 million, ceased to exist as a nation.

Three thousand two hundred and eighty one feet above Berchtesgaden, (a small German town in the Bavarian Alps that is 74 miles—120 km southeast of Munich as the crow flies) a lawyer named Winter from Hamburg built the Bavarian style house called Haus Wachenfeld. (the maiden name of his wife which was Wachenfeld). He leased the house to Hitler in 1928 for 100 marks per month. When Hitler finally bought the property after becoming Chancellor, it was shown on picture postcards as *The little cottage of the People's Chancellor*. The architect Alois Delgado was called in to rebuild and enlarge the house which was then renamed the *Berghof*. Costing around thirty million Reich marks, the work employed 3,000 workers who completed the project in 390 days. It was a bizarre blend of the grandiose and the mundane. Its huge windows provided panoramic views of the surrounding peaks, but its kitsch architecture was suburban, and although the decor was lavish, the overall effect was more bourgeois than palatial.

In the vicinity of Hitler's chalet, houses were built for Göering, Goebbels (Hitler's propaganda chief) and Bormann, (Hitler's personal assistant who wielded a great deal of authority). A special road was constructed from Berchtesgaden to the *Berghof*. On April 25th, 1945, a force of 318 RAF Lancaster bombers unloaded a total of 1,232 tons of bombs on the area scoring three direct hits on one wing of the *Berghof* and damaging nearly all the other buildings nearby. Then the vandals, looters and souvenir hunters from the American armed forces moved in to ransack the place. Even the badly damaged carpets were cut up into strips and carried away as souvenirs. Shortly before the American troops arrived on May 4th, the SS set fire to the house with gasoline. At 5.05 pm on 30th of April, 1952, the ruins of the *Berghof* were blown sky high on orders of the Bavarian government. The former site is now a level sports field and golf course. Although the *Berghof* may have had historical value to it, it existence was an insult to democracy that the Bavarian government didn't want it around to remind them of Hitler's Nazism.

The *Eagle's Nest* was a masterpiece of construction and was built on the tiny summit of the 6,017 foot wooded Kehlstein Mountain high above Berchtesgaden. Officially known as the *Kehlsteinhaus*, the hexagon shaped building was built as a conference and entertainment center for visiting diplomats at the request of Martin Bormann and presented to Hitler on his 50th birthday. Francois Poncet, the French ambassador coined the name *Eagle's Nest* after a visit there in 1938. It was never known as the *Teahouse* but today it gets confused with the actual teahouse Hitler used situated not far from his residence, the *Berghof*. Hitler disliked the *Eagle's Nest* from the very beginning and visited the *Eagle's Nest* only thirteen times before the war but never visited it during the war.

Hitler's *Berghof* lifestyle was similarly contradictory. He received Lloyd George and Mussolini there, plus the recently abdicated Edward VIII who later wrote in his letter to Hitler; "Thank you for the lovely hours that we spent with you." When he used the word, 'we' he was referring to his new wife, the former Wallis Simpson and himself. A year later, Prime Minister Neville Chamberlain went there to sign away Czechoslovakia.

Yet between affairs of state, Hitler's *Berghof* days were a monotony of tedious meals and boring movies. This dull, empty routine was captured with unwitting accuracy by Eva Braun's (Hitler's lover and later his wife) home movies. Guests who craved an invitation often couldn't wait to leave. That's because Hitler would stay up all night talking to them until sleepness over took him. They certainly didn't let sleepness overtake them while Hitler was talking.

It was however the place where Nazi VIPs could toady to Hitler like they never could in busy Berlin. They confiscated dozens of farms, hotels and private houses to clear the area; their owners being forced to leave. Hermann Goering, who enjoyed hunting, built a house just around the corner from Hitler. Martin Bormann, whose sycophancy knew no bounds, built his house between Goering's and Hitler's.

In Spain, the civil war was finally coming to an end. On February 28th, 1939, Manuel Azana resigned from the post of President of the Republic. The failure of Dr. Negrin's Communist Government to sue for peace resulted in a civil-war-within-a-civil-war on the streets of Madrid. The National Defense Council, led by Colonel Casado, triumphed in the struggle for control of the Republic and tried to negotiate peace terms with General Franco. In the meantime Dr, Negrin, his Cabinet and his Russian advisers flew out of Madrid to safety on March 12th.

On March 28th, the Nationalist army entered Madrid and the following day, hostilities ceased. A couple days later, General Franco announced to the world that the Spanish Civil War was over.

There were atrocities during the Spanish Civil War, but they were nearly all committed by the Fascist troops led by Franco. There were also atrocities committed by individuals and some of the anarchist militias, which the Republican government struggled to end, not promote.

In East Andalusia, lorries manned by the CNT (Confederación Nacional del Trabajo—National Confederation of Labour, terrorist group) drove into villages and ordered mayors to hand over their fascists. The mayors often said that they had all fled but the terrorists would often hear from informers which of the better off people were still there, arrest them and shoot them in the nearest ravine. In the vast majority of cases, the murderers were of the rank and file of the 'Right'. Often members of the working class would be killed by their own acquaintances for hypocrisy, for having kow-towed too often to their social superiors. Some were shot simply for untruthfulness. In Altea, near Alicante, for example, a cafe proprietor was killed with a hatchet by an anarchist for having overcharged for stamps and for the glass of wine that buyers of stamps were forced to purchase while waiting. It's not likely that the townspeople wept over that gouger's demise however.

Hundreds of churches and convents were burned or put to secular uses. The priests, nuns, bishops and even an archbishop were murdered. There was a definite plan to eradicate the Catholic Church in Spain. As many as 1,215 monks, nuns, and priests died in the province of Barcelona alone. Thousands of members of the clergy and religious orders as well as of the propertied classes were killed, but others, fearing arrest or execution, fled abroad, including many prominent liberal or moderate Republicans.

The torture of many victims by the Nationalists included severe beatings, the breaking of bones, one by one, the rape of women and young girls in the presence of their family members and the application of candles, red hot irons, and electrical currents to the bodies of both men and women. Sometimes this torture was so extreme and humiliating that individuals chose to commit suicide which was a rare occurrence considering the Spanish culture.

Although the tactic of torture was viewed as being valuable in attaining information about the enemy's military strategies, the individuals tortured were more often than not simply accused of having aided the Republic in some manner, no matter how slight. They were people that would have no information whatsoever as to the military strategies of the Republic. The purpose of using torture on women, children, old men, schoolteachers and a variety of other individuals who had no military value at all, is obviously clear. It was merely for pure enjoyment. Torture to many who apply it is a sexual turn-on for them. Therefore, it should not be puzzling as to why such extreme methods of torture were practiced when there was no military purpose involved. The use of rape is a very questionable tactic also when said to be performed solely in the pursuit of victory. Obviously, it too was a sexual turn-on for the rapists who were thugs first and soldiers fighting for a cause, second.

Some of the abuses heaped on individual victims was for sport only and not in the name of vengeance or punishment. There is a story of a man forced to fight as if he were a bull in the bullring at Bajadoz. The bright-tasseled banderillas (small flags) had been jabbed into his shoulders; he had been forced to charge madly at the waving red flags of the capoteadores (bullfighter's cape); the mounted picador (mounted bullfighter) had jabbed his long pole with a knife on the end into the victim's side; and finally, amid the yells of the Falangist mob and the cries of other Nationalist spectators, the matador (standing bullfighter) had driven the death-sword between the heaving shoulder blades of the man and thusly into his heart, a man whose only so-called offence was that he had been elected to the Republican Cortes of the province.

In one Nationalist prison, it was discovered that the prison was so crowded that inmates could barley move. A jail with a normal capacity for 600 men was holding approximately 6,000. Many of the prisoners were chosen to be executed by lottery with not even the slightest thought of them being given a trial. They were taken outside, made to dig their own graves, and then shot. The randomness in which prisoners were selected to be killed is comparable with that of the Nazi labor camps of World War II, which were also notorious for their excessive violence. The horrible conditions and constant fear that were a normal part of life in a Nationalist prison seem too extreme for the simple purpose of attaining victory.

There were a great many summary executions in Spain during its civil war conducted by both sides. The Republicans executed 72,344 and the Nationalists executed 35,021 however, after the war, the Nationalists executed another 22,641.

The explanation given by Franco and his supporters for the excesses in executions was that the 'State of War' called for violence which was simply in response to the Republic's terror, that it was necessary to gain support and that it was the victim's fault. But despite that rational, most of the victims were innocent of any wrongdoing so it does not even begin to justify the brutality. The only explanation is that the Nationalist terror was a planned, systematic method for effecting large-scale reprisals. The Francoist terror did not serve a strictly military purpose, rather it's reason was to destroy any potential opposition, be the victims guilty or, as it was too often, completely innocent.

The Spanish Civil War brought a great deal of death (over 1,200,000 died) to its nation but that figure was to later pale with the coming of the Second World War in Europe that was just looming ahead.

In May, 1939, twelve years after Lindenberg flew across the Atlantic, Pan Am flew its first cross Atlantic plane to the Azores, opening up a scheduled service to Europe. The plane was a flying boat which would take off and later land in water.

Italy and Germany signed a pact and later were referred to as the Axis powers.

As many as 22,000 American Nazis held a rally in New York. They were members of the German/American Bund. (Federation).

Canada along with other free nations around the world turned away the Jews sailing on the Liner *St. Louis* that was carrying 907 Jewish refugees fleeing from Germany. A truly disreputable Canadian and a disgrace to what Canada stands for today, Ernest Lapointe, who was at that time, the finance minister for Canada, ordered that the liner could not dock in Canada. The liner finally returned to Germany with its passengers. Nearly all of them later died in Nazi concentration camps.

Ontario still had that silly Statute called the *Female Refuges Act*. It was enacted in 1897 and repealed in 1964. Under the Act, a woman between 16 and 35 who was found to be unmarried, unemployed and incorrigible or leading an otherwise idle life could be arrested and made to work at an industrial institution (Belmont Home) where she would be forced to live and if she didn't tow the line there, she could be sent to the Mercer Reformatory for Women on King Street West in Toronto.

To give my readers an idea of how this silly and most unjust law was enforced, I will tell the story of Velma Demerson. She was 18 and living with a man who was Chinese. She even had his baby. One day in 1939, the police arrived at their door and arrested her. Velma was taken to 'Women's Court' at City Hall. Years later, (1963) I represented women in that court. A social worker questioned Velma. She made three strategic mistakes. When she was asked how many men she had slept with, she tried to protect her man from accusations of seducing her, by falsely saying that she slept with two men. And then, thinking that impending motherhood might save her, she blurted out that she was pregnant. The social worker immediately slammed her file shut and left the room. Taken before Judge Robert Browne, Velma, in her innocence, made one final error. "Just let me out and I'll marry him!" she begged.

She didn't know that 'promiscuity', being 'illegitimately' pregnant, and consorting willingly with a Chinese man, were all grounds for imprisonment under the *Female Refuges Act* of 1897. Indeed, anyone at all could charge a woman aged 16 to 35 with being 'dissolute' under the *Act*, and she could be packed off to serve years as a laundress or seamstress in a church-run 'refuge' or reformatory.

In less than an hour, with no trial, lawyer or due process, Velma was remanded one week for sentencing. She spent the week sleeping on a bench in the Don Jail. Brought back to court, she was told by Browne that she was to serve one year of incarceration in the Belmont Home for 'incorrigibility'

The Belmont Home, now a swanky retirement residence in midtown Toronto, was then an 'industrial refuge' for incorrigible girls, and it was run as a commercial laundry by a Protestant church. But only six weeks after Velma's arrival, the money-losing laundry was shut down and the 47 young women inmates were transferred, many of them weeping in terror, to the notorious Mercer Reformatory on King Street in Toronto. She was eventually released and she and her man were married, a marriage which only lasted a couple of years. Their son later drowned himself when he was 26 years old. The government of Canada finally compensated her in the year 2002 for the wrong it had done to her.

In 1963, I met and assisted a young woman, Diane Maguire (now deceased) who was one of the last women to be arrested and placed in jail for being pregnant out of wedlock except in her case, after she was released, they returned her baby girl to her but the baby died accidentally when Dianne rolled over her one night while sleeping while in a drunken stupor.

The 1939, the Americans were very concerned about Canada's rather skimpy armed forces. They knew that if the Germans attacked

Canada and got a foothold in Canada, the Americans would be facing German armed forces to its north. On August 26th, 1939, Roosevelt phoned the prime minister of Canada, MacKenzie King to meet with him the next day at Ogdensberg, New York, (the president's retreat) to discuss their mutual concerns. King actually considered himself as being the matchmaker between Roosevelt and Churchill but in 1941 when Roosevelt and Churchill met off Argentia, Newfoundland, Prime Minister King wasn't invited. What did he expect? Canada's armed forces were too miniscule at that time for anything he had to offer to be meaningful.

As the summer of 1939 moved on and tension grew between Germany and her neighbours, additional measures of preparation for war were undertaken in Canada. Prime Minister Chamberlain of Great Britain had told his House of Commons; "We find ourselves confronted with the imminent peril of war." *unquote* Most Canadians felt the same way. But Canada was not really prepared for war. She only had 4,261 of all ranks in her regular Army albeit the Non-Permanent Active Militia comprised of slightly over 51,000 men. Canadian Prime Minister Mackenzie King had been more concerned about the defense of Canada than sending an expeditionary force to Europe or the Far East. In fact, in a private address to members of his party in Parliament on January 20th, 1937, he gave an indication of the considerations which controlled Canada's defense policy. He said in part: "We are not concerned with aggression. We are concerned with the defense of Canada. The possibility of conflict with the United States is eliminated from our mind. There is nothing here for an expeditionary force, only for the defense of Canada against those who would wantonly assail us or violate our neutrality." *unquote*

In my opinion, the prime minister was wrong not to concern himself about Hitler's aggression. I realize that I have the advantage of hindsight when I make that statement. It was that same lack of concern that kept the Americans out of the war initially. Had the Americans been concerned earlier, millions of lives could have been saved because the war would have ended earlier. However, neither they nor the Canadians were prepared at this time to go to war with Germany but both leaders of these two countries knew for some time what was going on in Europe and had they been sufficiently concerned with the aggression of Hitler when the latter grabbed Czechoslovakia for himself. If they made their concerns known to Hitler then, as a consequence, he may not have been so willing to march into Poland later. Bernard Shaw said it best in 1897 in his book, *The Devil's Disciple*, when he said; "The worst sin towards our fellow creatures is not to hate them, but to be indifferent to them: that's the essence of inhumanity."

Canada was not prepared defensively to ward off an armed attack. In fact, there was no doubt in anyone's mind at that time that had Germany or Japan, or even Italy decided to invade Canada, they would have been successful. The Germans would not have had planes bombing Canada since none of their planes could reach Canada and they didn't have aircraft carriers, but they could have bombarded Halifax or Sidney with her battleships and the Japanese could have bombarded Victoria and Vancouver with her battleships and aircraft coming in off her aircraft carriers. The Japanese and German troop ships would then have landed thousands of troops in those cities and Canada then would have undergone a slow and painful war that she would have lost unless the Americans came to its aid; which they probably would have if for no other reason than to protect their northern border. But this means that Canada would have been an enormous bloody battleground between the Americans and the two Axis powers for years.

Much emphasis by the Canadian authorities at that time was laid on coastal defense and in Canada, there were, as there still are, only two major naval bases—the Halifax base (*HMC Stadacona*) on the east coast and the Esquimalt base (*HMC Naden*) on the west coast and most of the efforts with reference to the defense of these two coasts were directed towards the Pacific coast. Strangely enough, there were no officers in Canada qualified to advise the Canadian War Office as to how the coastal areas were to be protected so the British loaned a

Major Treat to the Canadian War Office for the purpose of advising the Canadians how to guard its coastal areas. It was finally decided not to fortify every coastal town as the cost would be prohibitive. It was concluded however that if there was an attack on a port such as Victoria on Vancouver Island or Vancouver on the mainland, or Halifax, it would comprise of a bombardment raid by a battleship, by air with a maximum of twelve ship-based aircraft and by land, a force of enemy soldiers. Despite the fact that no forces ever attacked Canada during the almost six years of fighting in World War II, this prospect didn't seem so ludicrous at the time. It certainly is a good thing that no enemy battleships arrived at our coasts in these prewar years. Canada only had three re-lined naval 9.2 inch (23.3 centimetre-guns as shore batteries in place and they would have been blown into smithereens in the first hours of the war.

On August 27th, all Military Districts in Canada had reported that civilian guards had been placed at most of the venerable points, such as railway stations, canals, railway bridges, R.C.A.F. airfields etc. The Royal Canadian Navy and the Royal Canadian Air Force were also moving units into the Atlantic coastal area.

By the end of the summer of 1939, the complete plans for the mobilization of a Mobile Force of two divisions and ancillary troops, and of Special Forces for local defense and internal security duties were completed. However, because so little had been done to set up an armament industry in Canada, the peak of war production would not be reached until 1943. This was in line of Winston Churchill's line of thought when he said; "Munitions production on a nation-wide plan is a four-year task. The first year yields nothing, the second, very little, the third a lot and the fourth, a flood."

Reich Marshall Goering was given a similar task to fulfill in Germany. Hitler must have also concluded that it would take Germany four years to complete its task.

Shortly after Germany had concluded its pact with the Soviet Union on August 23rd, the Canadian Cabinet by Order in Council, declared a *State of Apprehended War*, thus enabling the armed forces to go onto a war footing. That German/Soviet *Non Aggression Pact* signed on August 23rd was a real coup for Hitler. All his territorial intentions up to now were directed towards the north, the west and the south. He wanted no problems from the Soviets in the east. The agreement between the two countries were, amongst other things, that neither country would attack the other and if either country was attacked by a third, neither of the two partners of the Pact would go to the aid of that third country. This left Hitler with a free hand to attack Poland knowing that if Britain and France went to Poland's aid and declared war on Germany, Hitler wouldn't have to worry about the Soviet bear biting him at his rear. Of course the Soviets might bite him in his ear because when he later invaded Poland, the Soviets had the same designs against Poland as Hitler did.

After his success at Munich that led to the takeover of Czechoslovakia in 1938, Hitler believed that Britain and France would not interfere in Europe as long as Germany headed east towards the Soviet Union. He therefore began to make plans for his next step. Poland was his obvious choice as it was in the east and included areas of land taken from Germany by the *Treaty of Versailles*. Hitler began to make speeches demanding the return of Danzig, and German access to East Prussia through Poland. Danzig (now called Gdańsk) is Poland's principal seaport on the Baltic Sea. Gdańsk is situated at the mouth of the Motława River and is connected to the Leniwka, a branch in the delta of the nearby Vistula River, whose waterway system supplies 60% of the area of Poland and connects Gdańsk to the national capital in Warsaw. This gives the city a unique advantage as the centre of Poland's sea trade.

Hitler's previous lies about not wanting to expand into other countries brings to mind something that was said by the war criminal Charles Taylor (formerly of New York City) who as the president of Liberia was addressing his nation on August 11th, 2003 just before he was flying to Nigeria in exile. He told the story of three cows and a lion. One cow was black, another was red and the third was white. The lion told the three cows that he wouldn't eat them. But soon he was telling the red and white cows that they shouldn't concern themselves about the black cow and they agreed and when they did, the lion ate the black cow. Soon after the lion got hungry again, the lion went to the white cow and told it that it shouldn't concern itself with the red cow and the lion promised that the red cow would be the last cow it would eat. The white cow acquiesced and the lion ate the red cow. But it wasn't that much later when the lion began eying the white cow. And shortly thereafter, the lion ate the unsuspecting white cow.

Taylor was obviously referring to the United States as being the lion, Afghanistan as being the black cow, Iraq being the red cow and Liberia being the white cow. In actual fact, The United States invaded Afghanistan and Iraq as liberators and used its influence to oust Taylor from Liberia (which it did) whereas Hitler marched into Austria and Czechoslovakia and invaded Poland as their conqueror.

Hitler knew that he still needed Mussolini's approval (if not his material support) and decided that the best way to invade Poland was on the pretext that Poland had in fact invaded Germany. It was called *Operation Himmler.* This was to be done by arranging for SS men outfitted in Polish uniforms shooting drugged concentration camp inmates in German border guard's uniforms at the radio station at Gleiwitz next to the German/Polish border so that it would appear as if Polish soldiers had shot German border guards as a prelude to a Polish invasion of Germany. It is beyond me as to how Hitler presumed that the rest of the world would believe such a fabrication. But then when you consider the fact that Chamberlain had knuckled under at Munich, and Austria and Czechoslovakia were now in his hands and that Mussolini would keep still and that Stalin and he had agreed about dividing Poland between them, Hitler had every reason to not concern himself as to what anyone had to say about his invasion of Poland. Nevertheless, he decided to use the phony pretext just in case there was some flak facing him in the future. Hitler knew that the falsehood of *Operation Himmler* was highly transparent but while he lectured his senior staff the week before, he told them, "The victor will not be asked whether he told the truth." Perhaps not but a lot of people asked themselves that question.

Unbeknown to either President Roosevelt or Prime Minister King, on August 26th, a week earlier than the main attack on Poland in the middle of the night on September 1st, Hitler ordered several German Army units into Poland but Mussolini told him he wouldn't support him if he attacked Poland so Hitler ordered his soldiers back out of Poland before the Polish government knew that they had been there. However, on September 1st, in the early hours of the morning, he pounced on Poland and 800,000 German soldiers, supported by Stuka dive bombers, attacked Poland. Naturally the German invasion came without warning or an official declaration of war. Supported by Stuka dive bombers, they made rapid progress through the Polish countryside. Warsaw was bombed as were the airfields of the Polish Air Force. The Poles were brave but they were undermanned and simply didn't have the materiel or the manpower to hold back such a blitzkrieg. They only had a handful of tanks and a dozen cavalry brigades to fight nine German armoured divisions. When Hitler marched into Poland, he was 50 years of age by then.

This was the beginning of the Second World War. France declared war on Germany the next day and Britain followed suit the day after that. On the 10th of September, Canada declared war against Germany after parliament debated the subject for three days. Only three MPs dissented. The United States on the other hand continued to remain neutral and sat on the proverbial fence watching from afar in the belief that the war would never be visited upon them. That belief was later shattered in December 1941.

Chapter Ten

I remember the day when Canada unofficially declared war on Germany. I say 'unofficially' because the signature of King George VI wasn't signed on the official declaration of war until later to make it official. We were still living above the store at 251 Symington Avenue in Toronto and I had just finished my lunch and was returning to school. I had no sooner walked to the front of the store from the side entrance of our home when I saw thousands of postcard-size pieces of paper falling from the sky. The planes that flew over Toronto that had been dumping the paper over the city were long gone. On each sheet of paper, was a notice that Canada was at war with Germany. I ran all over the place grabbing paper as it fell in front of me. I was late for school and after my teacher admonished me, she looked at the text on one of the many papers I had given to her and she was astounded at what she read. It must be pointed out that not everyone had radios then and newspapers were not sold at stores or brought to our homes. If you wanted to read a newspaper, you had to go to a newspaper vendor who could only be found at a major intersection which could me three or four blocks away. The announcement from the sky was the quickest way to bring the news of the Canadian declaration of war on Germany to us. If anyone dropped leaflets from the sky nowadays, they would be charged with littering.

With Britain declaring war on Germany, this created a problem for Prime Minister Mackenzie King for although he wasn't an isolationist, he didn't want to drag Canada into another war like Canada had been drawn into the First World War. But Canada was a member of the British Commonwealth, so there was a moral duty, if not a legal one, to come to the aid of her mother country. As a monarchist and a sentimental Anglophile, he was drawn towards the inevitability of a war with Germany. There was only one possibility he could foresee that would keep Canada out of the war and that was if Chamberlain assured him that Britain didn't need assistance from Canada. That assurance obviously wasn't forthcoming when Anthony Eden, the newly appointed Dominions Secretary entreated on September 6th for Canada to send to England an expeditionary force.

In 1939, Canada was still a British Colony. The official name of Canada was the 'Dominion of Canada'. When Britain declared war, Canada was officially at war as well. But on September 9th, it was learned that two Canadian women were on the unarmed ocean liner, *SS Athenia* which had been sunk 250 miles (402 km) Northwest of Ireland by a German U-boat with a loss of 112 passengers six days earlier. (more on the fate of the captain of the U-Boat later) One of my aunts (related to my mother's sister's husband's family) was one of those women that sailed on that ship and when she was in the lifeboat that was lowered, a wave caused it to capsize and her foot was jammed under a seat and as a result, she always walked with a limp. Previously on September 4th, Hitler had ordered that under no circumstances were attacks to be made on passenger ships, even in convoy, regardless of its nationality.

On September 10th, Canada declared war on Germany independently. Prime Minister William Lyon McKenzie said in the House of Commons;

"For months, indeed for years, the shadow of impending conflict in Europe has been ever present. Through these troubled years, no stone has been left unturned, no road unexplored in the patient search for peace. Unhappily for the world, Herr Hitler and the Nazi regime in Germany have persisted in their attempt to extend their control over other peoples and countries, and to pursue their aggressive design in wanton disregard of all treaty obligations, and peaceful methods of adjusting international disputes. They have had to resort increasingly to agencies of deception, terrorism and violence. It is this reliance upon force, this lust for conquest, this determination to dominate throughout the world, which is the real cause of the war that today threatens the freedom of mankind.

"This morning, the King (of England) speaking to his peoples at home and across the seas, appealed to all to make their own, the cause of freedom, which Britain again has taken up. Canada has already answered that call. On Friday the government, speaking on behalf of the Canadian people, announced that in the event of the United Kingdom becoming engaged in war in the effort to resist aggression, they would, as soon as parliament meets, seek its authority for effective co-operation by Canada at the side of Britain.

"In what manner and to what extent Canada may most effectively be able to co-operate in the common cause is, as I have stated, something which parliament itself will have to decide. All I need to add to the moment is that Canada, as a free nation of the British Commonwealth, is bringing her co-operation voluntarily. Our effort will be voluntary.

"The people of Canada will, I know, face the days of stress and strain which lies ahead with calm resolute and courage. There is no home in Canada, no family, and no individual whose fortunes and freedom are not bound up in the present struggle. I appeal to my fellow Canadians to unite in a national effort to save from destruction all that makes life itself worth living, and to preserve for future generations those liberties and institutions which others have bequeathed to us."
unquote

The special war session of Parliament lasted three days and all except three members of the House approved of declaring war with Germany.

On the following day, Prime Minister King told the House of Commons, "We stand for the defense of Canada. We stand for the co-operation of this country at the side of Great Britain and if this house will not support us in that policy, it will have to find some other government to assume the responsibilities of the present." *unquote*

On the 10th of September, 1939, Canada cabled a text of the declaration of war against Germany to Vincent Massey, the Canadian High Commissioner in London. There was a problem however in the manner in which the declaration of war was made official. When the Prime Minister of Canada cabled the declaration of war to Vincent Massey and the High Commissioner took it to King George IV for his signature to ratify it, the declaration didn't have Mackenzie King's signature on it. King George signed it nevertheless but asked that the original with Mackenzie King's signature be sent to him as soon as possible. It arrived on November 27th and King George signed the original on that date, albeit it had been backdated to the 10th. Now Canada was 'officially' at war with Germany.

At this time in Canadian history, there were a little over 11 million Canadians and about 8 million over the age of eighteen—many of them unemployed men who then rushed to the nearest armoury in their city or town to enlist.

The act of aggression on the part of Hitler against Poland was to unleash a war of global consequences that would bring about the deaths of 55 million combatants and innocent civilians of which 3.5 million were Germans and which the war dead included 43,000 members of the Canadian armed forces.

Before Hitler had attacked Poland, Canada took some war precautions, limited as they were. Militia call-outs from the reserves guarded key points. Two destroyers headed south from Esquimalt to the Panama Canal. Their destination was Halifax. Aged RCAF aircraft flew to Halifax also. After war was declared, four destroyers and the only RCAF squadron that had modern aircraft headed to England. A number of obsolete tanks that had been dug out of the Texas sand for the purpose of being used as scrap iron suddenly had a new use. They were to be part of a single army tank brigade being formed in Canada.

At the outbreak of World War II, the Canadian Navy was in a sorry state of affairs; its entire strength consisting of a mere 13 ships and some 3,500 personnel including naval reserves. After initiating a rapid expansion program, the Navy by the end of the war would be the third largest in the world with over 373 warships. This does not mean 373 battleships. The Canadian navy comprised mainly of destroyers, frigates and corvettes with two cruisers (the *Ontario* and the *Quebec*) and one small aircraft carrier. (the *Bonaventure*) and many mines sweepers. The Canadian navy also had 100,000 sailors serving in her ships. Of course, those figures pale compared to the American and British navies which had over 1,900 and 1,200 warships respectively. The majority of the Canadian Navy was to be engaged in what has become known as the 'Battle of the Atlantic'. Fighting off German U-boats to protect the convoys of ships which were so vital to the survival of Britain, the role of the Canadian Navy in World War II was of the utmost importance and its significance in the achievement of victory for the allies which cannot be exaggerated. The cost of victory was however to be a high one with 24 ships lost and the deaths of 2,024 Canadian navy sailors.

The Canadian Parliament passed the *National Resources Mobilization Act* which gave the government unfettered power to control manpower however it was for home defense only. When Mayor Houde of Montreal denounced national registration, he was immediately arrested and tried and interned for the duration of the war. So were hundreds of Nazi, Fascist and Communist supporters.

Canada was not industrially or as said earlier, militarily ready to go to war. The prewar army comprised of only 4,000 men buttressed by a militia of 51,418 volunteers who were only partly trained. For example, many of the men who volunteered for the armed services as soon as war was declared weren't even given uniforms, and many had to sleep on mattresses on floors and without bedding at that. There weren't enough rifles to hand out to the new inductees. There were only 16 light tanks in Canada, 23 anti-tank rifles, 4 two-pounder anti-tank guns and 4 modern anti-aircraft guns. The navy was pitifully small and the air force was almost non existent. And with this, Canada was going to fight one of the largest and most powerful armed forces in the world, albeit, alongside Great Britain and France. Those first weeks of Canada's preparation for war were like a comic opera without the music.

At the outbreak of war, around 70,000 Germans and Austrians were living in Britain. Most were refugees from the Nazis and considered 'safe'. Others, about 11,000, were restricted in their movements around the country and ordered to report to their local police daily and to obey an 8:00 p.m. to 8:00 a.m. curfew. Some 230 from the eastern counties of England and Scotland were interned in special camps set up throughout the country and remained there until the end of the war.

The first RAF raid in the war nearly ended in disaster. The day after war was declared; RAF bombers attacked the German naval ports of Wilhelmshaven and Brunsbuttel. Ten bombers returned to base after failing to find the target. Seven were shot down by German anti-aircraft batteries. Three planes prepared to attack British warships in the North Sea until they discovered their mistake then they flew home. Eight bombers found their target and attacked the battleship *Scheer* and the cruiser *Emden*, where one of the Blenheim bombers crashed on the ships' deck.

Hitler knew that if he could stop the flow of food, men and materiel originating in Canada from reaching Great Britain, he could bring Great Britain to its knees so he ordered a number of German submarines to sink the freighters and tankers in the Atlantic to stop the flow. Ironically, he later concentrated a great many more submarines in Norway and the Mediterranean instead of concentrating on the Atlantic and this decision was one which invariably contributed greatly to his downfall. The Royal Air Force of Great Britain protected the convoys for 400 miles (643 km) westward from Great Britain and the Royal Canadian Air Force protected the convoys for similar distances eastward but in between these two ranges, was an area in which the convoys were on their own. It was this area that was called the 'Black Pit' that the German submarines concentrated their submarine into wolf packs. Upon reaching the 'Black Pit' the merchant ships would fan out in all directions on their own so as to make it more difficult for the U-boats to catch them all together and then later when they were within the protective range of Canada or Great Britain, depending on the direction they were headed, they would meet at a secret rendezvous and regroup.

The Canadian navy by this time only had six destroyers, five minesweepers and four thousand men in its regular and volunteer reserve establishments so some of these craft would be used to assist in the protection of the convoys. In 1939, the natural harbour of Halifax, already the nation's principle naval base on the east coast, and the nearby Bedford Basin were the scenes of enormous shipping activity in which hundreds of merchant ships from all over the world congregated for the eastward voyage across the North Atlantic. Canada's destroyers at that time accompanied the merchant ships eastward towards the 'Black Pit' for a couple of days each trip before returning back to Canada to ready themselves for the next convoy. By the end of September, despite the efforts of Great Britain to protect the convoys arriving or leaving the approaches of Great Britain, as many as forty merchant ships had been sunk.

There was a greater danger facing the merchant men than just the attacks from the U-boats. Germany had a number of battleships and cruisers capable of remaining at sea for long periods of time and these ships waiting in the 'Black Pit' for their prey to approach them, could sink a merchant ship with just one shell fired from one of their great guns. Great Britain, realizing this threat, ordered a number of her capital ships to North Atlantic duty. It was a common sight for people on the coast of Nova Scotia and Newfoundland to look eastward and see a large British battleship in the distance, waiting to accompany the merchant ships across the Atlantic.

On September 11th, as many as 158,000 British soldiers were sent to France to bolster the French forces but they were seriously short of equipment. The British and French soldiers then sat in France and twiddled their thumbs while Germany smashed its way through Poland. So much for Britain's and France's commitment to stand along side of Poland in her hour of need.

At this particular period in history, very few people knew that Germany and the Soviet Union had signed an agreement which in effect, divided Poland in two; the Germans getting the western half and the Soviets, the eastern half. In essence, what this meant was that the Germans would get the industrial part of Poland and the Soviets, the agricultural areas and its oil.

On September 17th, the Soviets invaded Poland from the east and because the Polish army was concentrating most of its efforts in the west, fighting the Germans, the Soviets entered Poland with very little difficulty. The Germans bombed Warsaw mercilessly until not one building remained standing fully intact. Many thousands of civilians died in the bombing of that city. When British composer, Richard Addinsell wrote his famous piano piece, the Warsaw Concerto in 1941 for the movie, *Dangerous Moonlight*, he had the bombing of Warsaw in mind. When I used to play that piece at concerts, I had the bombing of Warsaw in mind. In fact whenever I pounded any piece on the piano, my listeners probably had the bombing of Warsaw in mind also.

After the war, it was learned that the Soviets had committed a terrible massacre of Polish officers they had captured during their invasion of eastern Poland. In 1939, during the Russian invasion, 14,500 Polish officers were captured and interned in three POW camps in the Soviet Union. The next time the world heard of these prisoners was a news broadcast on April 13th, 1943, from Radio Berlin. It stated that the German Army had discovered mass graves at Katyn, 18 kilometres north-west of Smolensk, near the village of Gneizdovo and containing the bodies of Polish officers. Eight graves were opened and 4,253 bodies exhumed. All were dressed in Polish uniforms, with badges of rank and medals intact. No watches or rings were found on the corpses.

It was established that the bodies were of Polish officers from the camp at Kozielsk, situated in the grounds of a former Monastery, near Orel. Two other camps, at Starobielsk (3,910 men) and at Ostashkov (6,500 men) were closed in the first days of April, 1940. From evidence obtained after the war, all prisoners of Kozielsk camp were shot by

Stalin's NKVD. The officers had their hands wired together behind their backs and their heavy coats were then brought up from behind them and put over their heads. They were then individually led to the edges of deep pits dug in the forest. From there, they were each shot in the back of their necks next to the base of their skulls where the bullet would smash through the cerebellum; that part of the brain located in the posterior part of the skull situated immediately behind the brainstem, bringing about instantaneous death. Their lifeless bodies were then pushed into the pits by each of their executioners.

As an interesting aside, the Russians executed condemned prisoners in the same way up until 1996. Boris Yeltsin signed a decree commuting the death sentence for all of the convicts on Russia's death row. Yeltsin issued the decree after the presidential commission for pardons reviewed the cases of all 716 convicts on death row and recommended that they be given either life sentences or 25-year prison terms. Russia has not executed anyone since that year. The regulations of the Council of Europe prohibit it from doing so at any time in future. Despite that, the death penalty in Russia still remains in their criminal code.

In Russia, the manner in which they executed condemned prisoners was as follows. They took them to a cell in which the floor was slightly slanted toward a drain in the center of the cell. The executioner tilted the condemned man's head slightly forward and then fired the bullet into the base of the condemned's skull. The condemned was dead before he fell to the floor. It was later learned that Lavrenti Beria, who was the head of the Soviet Union's security apparatus when the Soviets marched into Eastern Poland in 1939, and in that capacity, he headed the Soviet security troops in Poland and was directly responsible for the murder of all those Polish officers, finally got his just deserts when he too was executed on the 23rd of December 1953 in the same manner by the order of Soviet leader Nikita Khrushchev.

On April 13th 1990, fifty years after the massacre, the USSR for the first time admitted its responsibility for the murders. The whole controversy was finally laid to rest when President Boris Yeltsin handed over the secret files on Katyn to the Polish president, Lech Walesa, on October 14th 1992. In May 1992, in a forest near Kharkov, a Russian private investigation team discovered a mass grave containing 3,891 bodies of Polish officers from the camp at Starobielsk in the Ukraine. In June of that year, Soviet authorities discovered 30 mass graves at Miednoje, one hundred miles north-west of Moscow. They contained the remains of 6,287 Polish prisoners from the Ostashkov island camp on Lake Seliguer. Before the massacre, 245 officers from Kozielsk, 79 from Starobielsk and 124 from the camp at Ostashkor, were transferred, for no apparent reason, to a camp at Pavlishchev Bor, a hundred miles north-west of the Kozielsk camp. These 448 officers proved to be the only survivors of the Katyn massacre. In other parts of the Katyn Forest, other graves were discovered containing the bodies of Russian political prisoners who were executed in pre-war days by the NKVD. It seems that the Katyn Forest was the main execution site for Stalin's secret police. The city of Toronto, Ontario has a memorial of the massacre at the corner of King Street and Roncesvalles Avenue. Other cities round the world have memorials relating to that massacre. It wasn't until 2010 when Russian government officially admitted that Stalin had personally ordered the massacre of the Polish officers.

By the 27th of September 1939, Poland had succumbed to the ravages of the two aggressors and gave up the fight. Then the Poles really began to suffer at the hand of the Nazis. Many captured Polish soldiers were taken to ditches along the roadsides and machine-gunned to death. Thousands of citizens were rounded up to be shot. In one instance, a young girl tried to say farewell to her father who was being led away to be shot and she was shot on the spot for her impertinence. Anyone who insulted Hitler or the Third Reich was summarily executed. Perhaps the Nazis were getting revenge for their own losses. Germany's casualties in her war with Poland were 10,572 killed, 30,322 wounded and 3,400 missing. Poland on the other hand had lost 60,000 soldiers and 25,000 civilians, most of the latter who died during the bombing of Warsaw.

No sooner had the Germans overrun western part of Poland; the

Nazi terror was close behind the invading army. The SS Death's Head Division which offered no tactical contribution towards the invasion began terrorizing the civilian population. The hunt for Jews was increasing by the day. In the town of Bydgoszcz, eight hundred persons whose names were on an SS list were hunted down, arrested and shot. Can you believe it? The first victims shot were Boy Scouts, ages twelve to sixteen. A priest who was administering the Last Sacraments was shot while kneeling over a victim who had just been shot.

Great Britain was now having blackouts every night. Every home and office had to have heavy curtains drawn across their windows at night. Often, one could hear the voices of the 'blackout wardens' patrolling the streets at night with their loud voices yelling; "Put out that bloody light." All curbs and trees near the curbs had to be painted white and anyone walking across a street at night really took their life in hand if he or she didn't wear white clothing.

In Britain, gas masks were handed out to everyone and even children going to school were required to carry them at all times. It later turned out that the Germans didn't use gas during the war so carrying the gas masks was purely academic.

Since there was an order that all theatres and cinemas were to be closed at 6 p.m., most people stayed home and listened to the radio. Television wasn't vogue in Britain at that time or anywhere else for that matter other than in Germany.

Chapter Eleven

Toronto had a blackout one night soon after the war started. My father was driving us in the area of the lakeshore at the time. Suddenly all the street lights and the lights in the houses and buildings went out. But the motorists kept their lights on. If Toronto was approached by enemy aircraft, the airmen would have no difficulty in seeing the layout of Toronto below them with the streets lit up by the headlights of the thousands of cars on the street. That is why in England, all car headlights were covered except for a thin horizontal slit across the face of the headlights. The thin light from the headlights couldn't be seen from the air. Vancouver was having blackouts all the time, not that they were needed since there wasn't much chance that there would be a Japanese invasion and obviously, there would be no invasion of Vancouver by the Germans.

    I would be remiss if I didn't mention that Toronto had two more blackouts, one in 1965 and the other in 2003 but they were unrelated to any war.

    Sometime during the autumn months of 1939, while playing in our back yard, I saw a small tin and opened it. What I saw inside looked like sugar flakes of some sort. Not knowing any better, I put the flakes in my mouth to eat them. I had swallowed a handful of caustic soda (Lye) and nearly died from suffocation when my throat began to swell up as a direct result of that foolishness. Strangely enough, the Lye didn't begin to burn at first. In about a minute later however, while I was playing across the street with two friends, my face suddenly began to feel as if it was on fire. I ran across the street and was nearly hit by a car. I ran screaming into my house and told my mother of the pain I was enduring. Then my throat began to really hurt. Soon she realized what had happened when the woman downstairs in the store discovered the open can of Lye in the back yard. The doctor was called and he told my mother and the woman downstairs to make me vomit the Lye up and to pour lemon juice down my throat. There I was, with the two women taking turns thrusting their fingers down my mouth and while I was gagging, they were pouring lemon juice down my throat. I didn't throw up but the lemon juice did the trick. I would have liked the lemon juice better had they been kind enough to put a little sugar into it and let me drink it out of a straw instead of prying my mouth and clenched teeth open and pouring the sour lemon juice down my throat. Nevertheless, I was damn lucky the caustic soda didn't kill me. For example, in November 2000, a woman in Philadelphia, USA, had some liquid Lye hurled in her face and as she later explained, it was like someone had thrown fire in her face. When she arrived at the hospital, she lost consciousness and nearly died.

Unfortunately, the searing of my throat by the caustic acid had done its irreversible damage. My voice remained soprano for many years to follow. The up side was that it made my voice improve as a soprano when I later sang in church and I could reach an octave above Middle A. I sang soprano until I was 15 and then I sang alto in another church until I was nearly eighteen years old.

Poland's pain made Britain's pain appear as if it was being tickled by the stroke of a feather. Hans Frank, a Nazi lawyer who was appointed to the position of Governor-General of occupied Poland, maintained a cruel and brutal regime from his headquarters at Wawel Castle in Krakow. Under his orders, all Jewish males between 14 and 60 were to work as slaves. Despite the German need for slaves, thousands of Polish citizens continued to be rounded up and shot. Thousands more were starving to death without any hope of aid coming from the German authorities. Another example of German brutality occurred in December 1939. Two German officers were killed in a brawl in a bar in the city of Wawer, Poland. As a result, the Germans exacted a vengeance against the Poles. As many as 107 men and boys were rounded up at random and shot to death.

The V for Victory sign was the idea of a Belgian refugee in London, Victor De Laveleye. In a short-wave broadcast from London, he urged his countrymen to paint or chalk the letter V on all public places as a sign of confidence in ultimate victory. This was included in all BBC foreign language programs and later supported by the two-finger V sign of the British Prime Minister, Winston Churchill. The BBC's contribution to the motto of victory for the allies was the opening passage of Beethoven's *Fifth Symphony* which in relation to the Morse Code was dot dot dot dash which represents the letter V for victory. Despite the significance of the BBC playing the first bar of that symphony with the announcer saying, "This is the BBC" in its broadcasts to the rest of Europe. The *Ninth Symphony* of Beethoven was performed repeatedly under the Nazi flag in the context of the celebration of the Third Reich.

On October 16th 1939, German JU 88s flying from the island of Sylt, attacked naval ships in the harbour at Rosyth, Scotland. About to enter dry dock for repairs was the battleship *HMS Hood*, but the pilots had strict orders not to attack the warship. A personal order from Hitler stated "Should the Hood already be in dock, no attack is to be made. I won't have a single civilian killed." *unquote*. I think that is strange considering the fact that he was later quite indifferent to millions of civilians being killed during the war. After the raid, in which the 9,100 ton cruiser *HMS Southampton* was damaged, Spitfires from RAF Turnhouse near Edinburgh attacked the departing JUs. One was shot down, hitting the sea off Port Seton. This was the first enemy plane to be brought down by RAF Fighter Command.

Britain 'bombed' Berlin on October 1st with leaflets. The leaflets told the German populace (in German naturally) that they were forced to go to war on hunger rations while Himmler (a top Nazi) was secreting large sums of money out of Germany. Within a month, 31 million leaflets had been dropped on Germany. Another 39 million were finally pulped because the British government felt the scheme wasn't working. The reminder to the Germans about their rations however would really hit home to them because at the time the leaflets were dropped on Germany, the German citizens were already undergoing a reduction of foodstuffs. For example, each German's weekly allotment of foodstuffs was, as an example, less than a quarter pound of butter, less than half a pound of meat and the milk was powdered. Housewives stood in long lines hours on end to get that and other staples which were also in short supply. As to the bit about Himmler, it did infuriate the Germans to think he had secreted that much money out of Germany (which he hadn't) when it was against the law for any German to take more that ten marks out of the country, an offence that was punishable by death.

By the middle of November, there was a real fear in Britain and Canada that there were German spies and fifth columnists everywhere. In Britain as many as 6,000 men and women were detained, most of them until the end of the war because of suspicions by the authorities that they were spies or traitors. Canada had the *Emergency Measures Act* to fall on in support of their actions to arrest suspected spies and traitors but the arrest of Canadians and aliens at this juncture of the war was nothing compared to what was obviously happening in Britain and what was happening in Europe which was far worse. For example, on November 30th, the Gestapo in Prague, the capital of Czechoslovakia, chose nine university students who had protested in the streets and executed them by machine gun fire.

Stalin, the dictator of the Soviet Union had delayed attacking Finland for some considerable time and like Hitler, he wanted his invasion to appear as if it was a response to an earlier attack on the part of the Finns against Russia. He realized that Finland would not acquiesce to his demands for Finish territory so he accused the Finns of shooting at Soviet soldiers in the area of Leningrad (which of course was an outright lie) so then on November 30th, as retaliation for the alleged shooting, he invaded Finland, concentrating his attacking force on the Karelian Isthmus. When Finland mobilized its armed forces, it only had 150 thousand men who were also short of materiel and ammunition. Russia put 800 thousand men into the fight with its neighbour. By the middle of December, the Finns had shown the world, and also the Soviets, that they were a hardy kind of people and that they could withstand the onslaught of the Russian soldiers and tanks. At this time in the Russo/Finnish war, it appeared that the Finns were getting the better hand of the Russians.

Germany had a pocket battleship called the *Graf Spee* which had six 11-inch (280 mm) guns on her. Even before the war had broken out, this ship had been sent to the South Atlantic to sink Allied ships as soon as the war began. When December 2nd came about, the *Graf Spee* was sighted in the waters off South America in the area of the River Plate and the British Admiralty decided to send two battleships to do battle with her. Until those ships arrived, three British cruisers, *Ajax*, *Archilles* and *Exeter* harried the *Graf Spee* with hit and run tactics. Finally, Captain Langsdorf of the *Graf Spee* took his battleship into the shelter of the harbour of Montevideo, Uruguay which was neutral rather than try and fight his way southward with the British ships dogging him. Of course he could only remain there for four days otherwise he, his men and their ship would be interned for the rest of the war and that being as it was, Captain Langsdorf headed back into the estuary before the four days were up.

He was certainly faced with a problem. He knew that if he headed towards the North Atlantic, he would be facing British battleships heading southward from the North Atlantic and if he headed south, he would eventually run out of oil if he tried to circumvent the globe trying to get back to Germany the round-about way. He decided that he had no other choice but to scuttle his ship. Huge crowds had gathered on the waterfront of Montevideo that Sunday evening, December 17th to watch what was expected to be a great sea battle in their front yard, so to speak. After the crew of the *Graf Spee* abandoned her (to be later interned) the battleship blew up. Great columns of fire shot skyward, lighting up the faces of all those on the shore. For the next four days, the ship burned and finally sank in the shallow waters of the River Plate, only a few miles from the Montevideo harbour. A few days later, Captain Langsdorf, while alone in a small hotel room in Buenos Aires, wrapped himself within an Imperial Flag of Germany (as an insult to Hitler) and shot himself. He probably shot himself rather than face a court martial in Germany for failing to fight the British cruisers waiting for him in the River Plate. Although he had been given permission to scuttle the ship by Admiral Raeder, it was learned later that Hitler was nevertheless furious.

In 1953, I saw the masts of the *Graf Spee* while I was serving on board *HMCS Ontario*, a Canadian cruiser while we were on the River de la Plata sailing to Buenos Aires in Argentina. Years later, the masts were removed because they caused a danger to the many ships sailing in that very wide river.

When the *Graf Spee* was hunting down British merchant ships in the South Atlantic, the battleship's supply ship, the *Atmark* was putting the survivors of the sunken ships in its hold for the purpose of eventually taking them to prisoner-of-war camps in Germany. The *Atmark* headed towards the Arctic so as to throw off any scent the British might pick up. When the ship reached the shores of Norway and was later heading southward along the Norwegian coast, she was stopped by Norwegian authorities and searched. And believe it or not, the Norwegians couldn't find one prisoner aboard—not one of the 299 men captured earlier in the year and notwithstanding the fact that the prisoners were hammering and whistling SOS signals during the search. None of the Norwegians thought it odd that the fire hoses were in use (against the prisoners to keep them quiet) when there was no fire and that the winch was in use (to drown out the noise of the prisoners) when nothing was being brought aboard or being taken off the ship.

The British warship, *Cossack* which was nearby suspected that the *Atmark* had their countrymen in their hold so they ran along side of it. Then a boarding party took over the ship which resulted in the loss of four German crewmen. The boarding party rescued the merchant seamen. Of course, the action of the British in attacking a German vessel in the neutral waters of Norway was a no no. But to paraphrase Clarke Gable in his final scene of *Gone With The Wind*, the British response to the protestations of the Norwegians at this time was, not unlike that of Clarke Gable, "Frankly, my dear, I don't give a damn." The Norwegians were well aware what happened to those countries who stood up to the Germans; they were crushed. That's why they ignored the fact that there were British prisoners in the hold of the *Atmark*. They were probably of the mind that if you make a prisoner of your tongue, your body may go free. That didn't apply much longer however since Hitler had his eyes on Norway's body also.

As many as 7,400 Canadian soldiers sailed to England on five ocean liners. The officers got the suites. Mind you, the men didn't do so badly. Many shared the first class cabins. The Division landed in Liverpool. Their commander, Major-General McNaughton must have felt good having a large suite to himself on that trip. When he made the trip in 1914, he was cramped in a hammock for 28 days at night. Mind you that's not much to complain about. I was cramped in a hammock when I was sleeping on board Canadian warships many months at a time during the early 1950s.

The phony war was going nowhere. In the latter part of October, the French and British with their combined 110 divisions at the border with Germany were doing nothing. And the irony of this is that in September, the German army facing them had only enough ammunition for three days. Further, they didn't have one tank at the western front and the Luftwaffe was in the east. Alas, hindsight comes at the wrong time. If the British and French had known of the circumstances the Germans had found themselves in, they could have attacked and pushed the German army that they were facing right into the middle of Germany. Instead, the British and French paused, refreshed, and sang songs. It was small wonder everyone was calling it the 'phony war', a term coined by Senator William Borah of the United States.

The mistakes the British and French made were colossal. The

French believed that the Germans couldn't get past the heavy fortifications along France's eastern border with Germany. The British also believed that the building of defense works along the Franco-Belgium border would protect France from any onslaught of Germans who might try to enter France from Belgium. They didn't take into consideration the problem that could occur if the Germans parachuted into France behind the fortifications. And naturally, the French guns were entrenched and facing Germany only. They weren't much help when the Germans later parachuted behind the fortifications and attacked the French forces from the rear.

On October 14th, the British suffered a great loss. As many as 833 sailors were lost when a German submarine (U-boat U-47) sank the battleship, *Royal Oak* with her eight 15-inch guns while at anchor. Only three of her crew survived. The U-boat managed to slip into the seemingly impenetrable defenses of Scapa Flow, the great British naval base in the Shetlands and fire four torpedoes into the massive battleship and then slip out of Scappa Flow, again undetected while the *Royal Oak* was sinking under the waves. As a result of the sinking of that great battleship, all British warships were put to sea. Britain was beginning to feel the pain albeit the pain they were suffering was but a pin-prick of what was to follow.

Chapter Twelve

The year of 1939 was not a good year for most people and certainly not for Jews or for that mater Europeans and the Chinese in general but for those of us in Canada and the United States, it wasn't such a bad year especially for the children as the year really wasn't any different then than it was in the previous years. As children we didn't really understand the significance of the Great Depression.

It wasn't until 1940 that all of us began to feel to some extent, the pain of war. To some, the pain was excruciating, to others, numbing, and to others still, just a slight throbbing but to all of us, the pain was there. That was because there were many things we had to do without. The twenties were the 'roaring twenties' then came the 'dirty thirties' and now the world was facing the 'fighting forties'.

It was during 1939 that Al Capone was finally released from Alcatraz but it was apparent to everyone that he was suffering from his third stage of syphilis. No more gangster roles for him. He was just sitting at home in Florida with his dying rotting brain.

During 1939, there were 704,000 motor vehicles in Ontario alone compared to 8,016,875 in 2006 in Ontario 67 years later. There were 682 motorists killed in Ontario in 1939 compared to 769 killed in Ontario in 2006. It must be kept in mind however that the cars in the 1930's were not as secure inside as they are nowadays and of course no one wore seat belts then because seat-belts were not installed in cars in those days. The 2006 fatality rate per 10,000 licensed drivers (0.87) and the rate per 100 million kilometers driven (0.59) is lower than what occurred in 1939 when you consider that 682 motorists killed out of 704,000 motor vehicles on the road far exceeds 769 motorists killed out of 8,016,875 motor vehicles on the road in 2006.

In 1939, ninety-per cent of urban dwellers had flush toilets but only 13 percent of rural dwellers had them. When I lived on the two farms, we didn't have rolls of toilet paper on hand. We used old newspapers and/or the Sears catalog which had became popular in rural Canada. People simply hung it up on a nail and had a free supply of hundreds of pages of absorbent, uncoated paper.

The record for swallowing live gold fish was 210. Some of these idiots were also swallowing live beetles and eating live white mice and phonograph records. I should add however that there was a TV program on in the summer of 2001 in which contestants ate live crickets. If they had refused, they would have lost the opportunity to win $50,000 so I can see them doing that for that purpose. Sometime in the middle of the 20th Century, an American bet another man $10,000 that he couldn't eat his car. Over a period of several years, the car eater ground the car into sand-like particles, mixed it with his food and ate his entire car. When he went to collect, the man who was to pay him off didn't have the money. Imagine taking on that kind of bet without some assurance that he would be paid off. That's stupidity. To paraphrase Dr. Thomas Fuller (1732) "He that makes himself an ass must not take it ill if men ride him.

The world learned of a creepy act of stupidity when the newspapers published the story that the world famous black opera singer, Marian Anderson who had performed before 75,000 concert goers in front of the Lincoln Memorial in Washington, had to stay with friends overnight because none of the hotels would put her up since they didn't cater to blacks. From stupidity to the intelligent, it was with sadness that psychiatrists worldwide learned that Sigmund Freud, the father of psychoanalysis died on September 25th of that year.

Some good things happened in 1939 however. Nylon yarn was commercially manufactured and as a result, nylon stockings came into vogue. Later in the year, nylon stockings unfortunately were to virtually disappear. The nylon was to be used for the making of parachutes. The Packard was the first automobile to have air conditioning. The electric slicing knife was sold and transatlantic airmail services came into being, only to end up being curtailed because of the war. The drug, sulfanilamide was created which would fight many forms of coccal infection such as strep throat.

Hollywood brought out some good movies, such as *Gone With The Wind* (3 Oscars) and *Pinocchio*, produced by Walt Disney which won an academy award for its title song, *Wish Upon A Star*, plus other famous movie classics such as *Goodbye Mr. Chips*, *Mr. Smith goes to Washington* and *Stagecoach*. The 1939 MGM Technicolor film version of the novel, *The Wonderful Wizard of Oz* was shown for the first time in 1939. It starred 14-year-old Judy Garland as Dorothy. I never got to see that movie until some time in the mid 1950s. In 1939, *The Hunchback of Notre Dame*, was also produced that year. Mickey Rooney was still the top star followed by Tyrone Power, Spencer Tracy, Clarke Gable, Shirley Temple, Betty Davis, Alice Faye, Errol Flynn and James Cagney; in that order. Hollywood temporarily lifted its code on decency and permitted Clark Gable in his final scene in *Gone With The Wind* to say, "Frankly my dear, I don't give a damn." That cost the studio $5,000. (worth $322,000 US in 2009) The irony is that the phrase isn't profane if the word 'damn' is spelled the way it was supposed to be spelled. It comes from the phrase, 'tinker's dam' which is a Dutch phrase. The 'dam' was a small plug that the tinker used and was worth next to nothing. The proper phrase is, "I don't give a tinker's dam." If Clark Gable had used that phrase, it wouldn't have been considered profane. In any case, his statement was a far cry from the use of profanity heard in today's movies such as, "Frankly asshole, I don't give a shit."

The average wage was 62 cents an hour which came out to $26 a week (women only made $15 a week. That came to 30 cents an hour and that was what I was getting in 1951 as a teenager when I first went to work) In 1939, one could go to a good restaurant for dinner and a show to boot for as little as $1.00 or $2.50 at most. A mincemeat pie cost 35 cents and a glass coffee maker could be purchased for a mere $2.99. Still, by British or European standards, Canadians were unbelievably well off. Clothing and most foods at this time were not rationed. By the time 1939 came to a close, Canada's population was 11,267,000 compared to 34,300,000 in 2010.

DDT (from its scientific name, dichlorodiphenyltrichloroethane) is one of the most well-known synthetic pesticides. First synthesized in 1874, DDT's insecticidal properties were not fully discovered until 1939 and it was used with great success in the second half of World War II to control malaria and typhus among civilians and troops but years later, it became outlawed in many countries resulting in millions of deaths from malaria. More on that in another volume of my memoirs.

When 1940 rolled in, the war between Finland and Russia was not going well for the Russians by the winter of that year. By January 5th, the Russians were on the defensive and by the 8th, church bells in Helsinki were pealed to ring in the Finnish victories. The Russians were simply not prepared for the cold; many of them freezing to death at their battle stations. By the time the 20th came about, all of Europe was held in an icy grip. There was snow as far south as Spain and Portugal. In Norway, the mercury in the thermometers froze and on the Danube in Hungary, as many as 1,200 ships were stuck fast in the ice. The Thames River in England was frozen for eight miles (13 km) and much of England was buried in deep snow. The war had in effect, come to a standstill.

Stories were beginning to come out of Poland about Nazi atrocities. There were stories of the Germans having shot 5,000 Poles in the city of Pozan alone. Many thousands more were being held in makeshift concentration camps. Public executions, forced labour, looting and hostage taking was commonplace. The two million Jews and gypsies in Nazi-occupied Poland suffered the most from the German persecution. And the thing the Poles feared most was happening——100,000 German families were migrating to German-occupied Poland to grab the homes left empty by the thousands of Polish families shipped by the Germans to the Nazi concentration camps in Poland.

By the time February arrived, the war in Finland had escalated again. The Russians had lobbed 300,000 artillery shells onto Finnish positions in one day alone. On top of that, the Russians had assembled as many as 1,500 aircraft for the offensive. The Allies had pledged support for the Finns by providing an Anglo-French expedition of three or four divisions but the promise didn't materialize in time and by the middle of February, the Russian forces had passed through the Karelian Isthmus of Finland, that appendage that protrudes southward from Finland proper.

Despite Hitler's promises to the contrary, he had every intention of invading Western Europe and by the time of the last week of February, he had his plans formulated. He intended to mount a massive Panzer drive through the wooded area of the Ardennes of Belgium to get at Belgium and France. If successful, his forces would then sweep through the French countryside southwest from Belgium towards Paris and the channel coast, thereby cutting off the British forces and bypassing the Maginot line of defense. Of course, it wouldn't take much brain power on anyone's part to conclude that the German's way to France's belly would be down Belgium's gullet.

It's incredible when you think of it. The Maginot Line was defensible, in fact, almost impossible to breach from the front. When it was built along France's border with Germany, it stretched from Switzerland to just below the Ardennes in Belgium, it cost half a billion dollars. (probably twenty times that by today's standards) It consisted of an elaborate chain of underground forts, some as much as six levels deep, each containing living quarters, kitchens, ammunition dumps, telephone systems, miniature railways linking the forts, power stations, water reserves, all with bombproof above ground casements. The two-story buildings above ground were indestructible. Their concrete roofs were eight feet thick. The stupidity of building such a defensive line is no different than spending thousands of dollars reinforcing your front door and at the same time, having no lock on your back door. Obviously the 'geniuses' who thought up that idea didn't realize that a chain is only as strong as its weakest link. In this case, history was to show that Belgium was France's weakest link and Hitler knew that fact when he decided to forgo the task of trying to break through the French chain at their mutual borders. It invariably ended up as a half billion dollar blunder (not counting the millions providing for the thousands of men who manned the Maginot Line) that cost France her freedom for the years to come.

By the 23rd of February, the Russian successes in Finland were such that she could make demands upon the Finns. The Russians wanted the entire Karelian Isthmus, including Vipuri, the second largest city in Finland and the naval base at Hango which the Finns regarded as a key to their country, a key which could unlock the security protecting Finland.

From 146 Canadian cities, towns and villages, the airmen sailed to England to join their comrades who had gone before them to fight in that seething cauldron of fire in European skies.

Propaganda has always had its place in warfare and the Second World War was no exception. The Germans had their Lord Haw-Haw (William Joyce) an Irishman born in the United States who possessed a British Passport. The Japanese later had their "Tokyo Rose' an American of Japanese ancestry.

Lord Haw-Haw always started his radio show with; "Gairmanee calling." It was the British who gave him his title of Lord Haw-Haw. One out of every six Britons (6 million) used to listen to his show at nine at night after listening to the BBC News. At the end of the war, it was his highly distinctive and readily recognizable voice that resulted in his capture in a German forest by the Allies and his eventual trial for treason and his subsequent hanging on January 3rd, 1946. It was his British passport that did him in. He maintained that he was Irish and therefore couldn't be tried for treason. But the court concluded that since he entered Germany on a British passport, he was subjected to the British laws of treason. Ironically, of all the passports he chose to acquire under false pretences, it was the British passport that resulted in him being hanged as a traitor.

Tokyo Rose fared better. Her real name was Iva D'Aquino, born to Japanese American parents in 1916. She went to Japan before Japan bombed Pearl Harbour and used her sweet seductive voice to enrage the American GIs by telling them that their sweethearts were going out with the 'cowards' at home. Of course, she, not unlike Lord Haw Haw, was looked upon as a sick joke and after the war; she was tried for treason, sentenced to ten years imprisonment and fined $10,000 (equivalent to $653,000 in 2009). After her release, she subsequently moved to Chicago and disappeared forever from public life. She died on September 26th 2006 at the age of 90.

The Finns found it difficult to forgive the Swedes for refusing to permit the Allies to cross Sweden to assist the Finns. Because of the decision of Sweden to remain neutral, it turned out that the promised 1,000 Canadian soldiers were not shipped to Finland to fight the Russians. As a result of the war with Russia, the Finns lost 15,700 soldiers and citizens with their fight with the Russians.

On March 18th 1940, under a leaden sky with snow whipping down from the Alps, two of Europe's most powerful men met at a railway station at the Austrian border. Mussolini, (Il Duce, meaning, 'The Leader') the dictator of Italy and Hitler (Der Fuerher also meaning, 'The Leader') the dictator of Germany spent two hours in the saloon car of Mussolini's train discussing Italy's support in case of war with the west. Mussolini gave Hitler his promise to support him should Hitler call on him. Mussolini was a ludicrous and comic figure at the time when Hitler and Mussolini were meeting at Brennero but he was a powerful dictator just the same. Mussolini was 57 years of age. He was at the high point of his life. Hitler was six years younger then. He was at a higher point in his life than Mussolini was then.

As a child, Mussolini was a bully and when he turned eighteen, he was five feet, six inches in height and not really a big man in stature. If he took off his outer garments to anyone, they would have observed that his shoulders were quite narrow, his chest were like that of an arching pigeon and his arms and legs were quite spindly. It was his big head that made him appear larger than he really was. His low brow, wide mouth, jutting jaw and piercing black eyes made him look quite fearsome. Like Napoleon, it was said that his piercing eyes could strike fear into anyone who looked into them.

Even though he was married, he went after anyone in skirts and most of the women he went after, with the exception of Clara Petacci, his mistress during the Second World War, were not beautiful. But then, he wasn't handsome either. He once raped an American woman newspaper reporter on the top of his desk because she hinted during the interview that he might be impotent. He had an illegitimate child with another woman and he abandoned the child and its mother to a life of miserable existence although he finally 'rescued' the mother in 1937 by sending her to a mental hospital.

To give you an idea of the kind of showman he was, you have to look to his debate with a pastor in Lausane, Switzerland. He bought a cheap pocket watch and brought it out just as he was about to debate with the pastor on the existence of God. He yelled for the large crowd to hear. "It is now 3:30 P.M. If God exists, I give him five minutes to strike me dead." *unquote* Naturally he wasn't struck dead although an American tried that enduring cheap trick once while standing on the prow of a canoe on a lake during a thunderstorm. Anyone who knows that lightening comes from the ground and shoots upwards to the clouds wouldn't have done that trick in an open space like a lake during a thunderstorm. A million volts shot out of the American's outstretched arms towards the clouds above him and the American was no more. Mussolini pulled that stunt when there were no thunder clouds nearby so nothing happened to him. In fact, when five minutes passed, he snapped his watch closed and the hundreds who watched his performance called out in unison, "Duce! Duce! Duce!" (Pronounced, DOO-chay) Even if there were no thunder clouds in sight, he still could have been struck by lightening.

He was eventually to become a member of the Socialist Party and that's when his real power began. He easily swayed the other members and soon was to become their leader. His power extended through the First World War and right through most of the Second World War;

that is until near the end of World War II, he was seized and executed by patriots and then strung up by his heels at a service station in Milan where an enraged crowd spit on him and one woman fired a pistol bullet into his inert body. (more on this later in Volume Two of this two-part series, *WHISTLING IN THE FACE OF ROBBERS*)

Despite his pomposity, there were things that could be said for Mussolini such as him getting the trains to run on time. They were even running on time for the most part when I was in Italy in 1974. I know; I nearly missed one because as to be expected in Italy, even at that time in history, it left the Venice train station on time in October 1974 when I was there. It left on time when I and my wife Ayako caught it again in Venice in April 2000. They didn't always arrive on time but they did leave on time. He also fixed the exchange rate of the lira and drained the Pontine marshes to produce as much as 200,000 new acres of farmland. He had great ships built which sailed the world's seas. For the most part, the Italians in their prewar history lived reasonably well. He was nevertheless a bully and this became apparent when he invaded Ethiopia in 1935 and when he sent troops to fight in Spain in 1936 and later invaded Albania in 1939.

And then, the greatest mistake of his life was made by him when he signed a pact with Hitler. It's ironic when you think of it. Mussolini was originally far more powerful than Hitler in the early thirties. He had earned the respect of Roosevelt and other leaders around the world. If fact, Hitler once wrote Mussolini for an autographed photo of the man of steel but his request was returned with the words "Refused" scrawled across Hitler's letter. But by the beginning of the forties, when Mussolini and Hitler were to later meet at Munich to discuss armistice terms between Germany and France, Mussolini was basking in Hitler's glory for Hitler was by then, far more powerful than Mussolini.

MacKenzie King (the prime minister of Canada) despite his unpopularity in some circles won the election on March 29th 1940 in a record poll. Of course, it was of considerable help to his election when he previously stated that he wanted to limit the number of Canadians serving overseas until the war industry in Canada was increased. Killing two birds with one stone; that's what I call it. Limitation on Canadians getting killed in an overseas war and an increase in the workforce because of the need for an enhanced war industry would pass muster at any time. Canadians weren't willing to chance it by electing someone else who might reverse those two pre-election promises.

One would think that Chamberlain had learned his lesson from his 1938 folly but that was not to be. Again he underestimated Hitler. Two years later when addressing a Conservative Party meeting on April 5th, 1940, he wanted to ensure the attendees that Hitler wasn't going to do any more harm. Knowing what we know now, his remarks hinge on the ludicrous. He said in part; "One thing is for certain, Hitler has missed the bus. It was natural then to expect that the enemy would take advantage of his initial superiority to make an endeavor to overwhelm us and France before we had time to make good our deficiencies. Is it not extraordinary that no such attempt was made? Whatever the reason, Hitler has very little margin of strength still to call upon." *unquote*

Did Antonio Machado in 1943 have someone like Chamberlain in mind when he said in his book, *Juan de Mairena*; "To see things as they are, the eyes must be open; to see things as other than they are, they must open even wider; to see things as better than they really are, they must be open to the full." *unquote*

I can't help but wonder if Chamberlain suffered from myasthenia gravis, an infliction caused by a defective nerve transmission which prevents its victims from opening their eyes. He would have been better off if he suffered from lock jaw. He was either badly informed about the true status of Hitler's willingness to proceed even further or alternatively, his statement was pure bravado hinged on pure bunko. The bus Chamberlain claimed Hitler had just missed had in fact just left with Hitler driving it. Four days after Chamberlain's ridiculous speech, German forces attacked Norway, Denmark, and what was then called Holland and is now called, The Netherlands. The early morning attacks took the Allies by surprise which is, in itself a surprise since the Allies had plenty of forewarning that something like that was about to happen. Germany couldn't keep an invasion like that totally secret especially with all those German radio transmissions being intercepted.

The attack on Norway was undertaken during the early hours of April 9th. It was led by the German battle cruiser called the *Blucher* followed by the pocket battleship *Lutzow* both of which were heading northward up the long Oslo Fjord towards Oslo, Norway's capital city. It was the intentions of the Germans to shell Oslo prior to an air attack on the Norway's Kjeller airfield nearby. There is a fascinating story that has been told and retold about this first day's attack on Norway involving the *Blucher* that bears retelling again.

Part way up the fjord is the old Oscarborg naval fortress. The fortress wasn't manned by active sailors and for all intents and purposes, it was unmanned. An old retired naval officer who lived nearby saw the oncoming lights of the German warships which were heading up the fjord towards the old fort so he rowed a small boat from the mainland to the fort to fight the Germans.

When he arrived, he discovered that the sailors were running around not knowing what to do. It seems that there were two old naval guns at the fort which hadn't been fired for many years. In fact they were mere museum pieces but they were very large museum pieces. He rallied the young officers to man the two antique guns. As the *Blucher* leisurely moved in the darkness to within five hundred feet of the muzzles of these two large guns; affectionately called *Moses* and *Aaron*. *Moses* belched and its very heavy and very explosive shell hit the ship's bridge and the bridge with the bodies of its bridge crew and their captain, along with the German general in charge of the invasion, and the hierarchy of the Gestapo, were blown right off the ship and into the water in minute pieces of flesh. *Aaron* followed suit and when its shell slammed into the *Blucher*, the ship shuddered and began sinking. Over a thousand Germans fought death in the icy waters or succumbed to the burning oil or were simply blown to bits. Their journey up the Fjord was their last. Even the German negotiators who were to negotiate a surrender with King Haakon VII were no more. Fortunately for the citizens of Oslo, the unknown retired naval officer had the sense to activate two old relics of the First World War. Had he not done that act, Oslo could have been shelled into oblivion. As to the fate of the *Lutzow*, it hightailed it out of the Fjord to fight another day. As an interesting aside, the *Lutzow* was formerly called the *Deutschland* but Hitler ordered it renamed because if the ship sank, it might be construed as a bad omen for Germany.

King Haakon VII agreed with his cabinet that there was no way his armed forces could successfully fight off the German invasion so he and his family and the members of parliament and their families, along with twenty-three trucks laden with Norway's gold, slipped out of Oslo, sought temporary sanctuary inland. By the time the Germans entered Oslo, the city had in effect been abandoned by the Norweigian authorities and the stunned citizens stood on the streets and wept as the Germans goose-stepped their way into the city streets.

When I think of Chamberlain's statement about Hitler missing his bus, I think of the drivers of three buses in Norway shortly after the Germans invaded that country. A detachment of German soldiers arrived in a Norwegian town shortly after the invasion. The officer in command ordered three local bus drivers to drive the 300 soldiers to another town. The three bus drivers asked if they could write their families first and permission was granted. The three men wrote the same message. It said; "If we are forced to make this trip, you will not see us again, ever."

The soldiers climbed into the buses and the drivers headed towards their next destination. Part way down the road there was a sharp turn in which all vehicles had to slow down lest they break through the barrier at the bend and drop to the bottom of the canyon far below. As the first bus driver neared the bend, he gunned his engine, and his bus, along with himself and his German passengers crashed through the barrier and went over the edge of the canyon to their deaths. The soldiers in the second and third buses saw what had happened to the first bus load of their companions as their own buses were rushing towards the bend but they couldn't stop their drivers from killing them either and so they too went over the edge of the deep canyon and plummeted to their deaths far below.

This story brings to mind the statement of Ernest Renan in which he said, "As soon as sacrifice becomes a duty and necessity to the man, I see no limit to the horizons before me." *unquote* I suppose for the immediate families of the martyrs, that wouldn't necessarily apply but for the rest of the Norwegians who resisted the Germans throughout the war, it certainly did.

The *Gage Canadian Dictionary* (of which I helped compile their first edition) defines the word 'quisling' as 'a person who collaborates with his country's enemies' and the term is coined from the name of Norway's worst German collaborator, Vidkun Quisling. He had been an ex-Army officer who rose to the rank of major in the Norwegian Army. He founded the fascist National Unity Party in 1933 and in 1939; he visited Hitler and exacted a promise from Hitler for financial support for his party. He persuaded Hitler to invade Norway and he further promised Hitler that his party would support Hitler if he did invade Norway. When the Germans marched into Oslo on the 9th of March, Quisling seized his opportunity to seize complete power in Norway which for all intents and purposes had been at that moment, abandoned by its king, parliament and the armed forces—or at least so it appeared at that crucial moment. He seized the radio station in Oslo and broadcasted a statement to all the citizens of Norway. He said about his seizing power, "By virtue of circumstances and of the national aims of our movement (National Unity Party) we are the only ones that can do this and thereby save the country from the desperate situation brought about by the party politicians." *unquote*

This did not go well with the Norwegians who always suspected that Quisling was a German lap dog anyway and that coupled with the fact that King Haakon VII was advocating resistance to the German forces, the Germans soon realized that Quisling could not rule Norway as the self-appointed prime minister, especially since none of his own party were even elected to parliament, and for these reasons, they removed him from office albeit he was given some limited powers later.

At the end of the war, Quisiling was tried by his own people and convicted. While standing on the rampart of Akershus fortress, he claimed he was innocent, his voice being barely audible in the night wind. Vidkun Quisling had been fetched from his cell at 2 o'clock in the morning and was later stood up against the back of the open wooden enclosure which had been erected against the gun tower of the fortress. Wearing plus-fours (baggy trousers cut short just below the knees) and a grey woolen sweater, the condemned man shook the hands of his executioners and when his arms were tied to the stake behind him, he was blindfolded. A piece of white paper was pinned in the area where his heart was so that the ten marksmen could get a better aim at his heart. Everything happened very quickly. Prior to the command to open fire, nothing was heard during the execution ceremony, nothing except Quisling's continued protestations of innocence. Nine bullets penetrated the white paper pinned to his heart. After the lieutenant in charge of the platoon had pulled out his service revolver, he aimed at and delivered the coup de gràce to the temple of the prostrate figure. The police coroner certified Quisling dead at 2:40 on the morning of Wednesday, the 24th of October 1945. At the moment he was walking to the post where he was to be shot, I was just finishing my supper in Wells, British Columbia on Tuesday, October 23rd. I was just four days shy of turning 12 years of age on that day.

After the German invasion, their King tried to flee the Germans so he and his party held up in a small Norwegian village called Nybergsung. From there, he broadcasted messages to his people. The Germans tracked him down and while watching from the forest nearby, he watched the small village disappear from the onslaught of German bombers. Then he and his party marched inland to continue his resistance until June 7th in which on that date, he, his family and his other leaders and their families were rescued by a British ship and taken to London where they would continue leading the Norwegian fight from there.

I am getting ahead of myself so I will return to April 1940. German naval landings took place at five locations along the Norwegian coast. The British, French and Free Polish forces fought the Germans and the sea-saw action continued up until the end of May 1940 when by then, circumstances necessitated them to withdraw and leave Norway in the hands of the German occupying forces.

Alas, even the withdrawal was in part, a disaster. The British Royal Air Force was operating under specific instructions to fly patrols over the vital areas of the evacuation of the Allies from Norway. The British had two kinds of planes in use in the Norwegian campaign— Gladiators and Hurricanes. Orders were given that the Gladiators were to land on the British aircraft carrier *HMS Glorious* and the Hurricanes were to be destroyed. The pilots of the Hurricanes asked for and received permission to also land on a British aircraft carrier. When the Gladiators had landed, they were stored below deck and the deck was cleared for the landing of the Hurricanes.

When the Hurricanes landed on the deck of the aircraft carrier, the ship headed at full speed towards Britain. Unfortunately, the German battle-cruisers Scharnhorst and Gneisenau caught up to the aircraft carrier and its destroyer-escort and began shelling the ships from a distance of 27,000 yards (24.6 km). The aircraft carrier couldn't fight back at that distance and she sank with a loss of all her planes and 1,519 men. Only 39 on board the ship survived.

For six months after the fall of Poland, the Allied armies on the Western Front remained practicably motionless while waiting for the Germans to make their move through Belgium and France.

It was inevitable. On the morning of May 9th, 1940, a surprising number of German tourists on bicycles and in automobiles crossed the German/Luxembourg border and by the time night had fallen, these tourists had brought out their concealed weapons and seized the border crossings and the bridges of that small neutral country which stood in the way of the giant German forces poised for the attack on the west. Soon the panzer tanks began to flow like a flood through the tiny hamlets and villages until all of Luxembourg was inundated by the German forces. Hitler's *Plan Yellow*, the German invasion of the western countries was underway.

At dawn of May 10th, the attack by the German Luftwaffe ended the smug neutrality of the Low Countries—The Netherlands and Belgium. There would be no more fence-sitting on their part as France prepared itself for the inevitable invasion. The Dutch people presumed that they were ready for the invasion. They were so sure of their ability to drown the invading Germans by opening their dikes and flooding the lowlands with the onrushing North Sea that they paid little concern to the warning given to them by Admiral Canaris, the head of the German Naval Intelligence on the night preceding the invasion. As an interesting aside, Canaris hated Hitler and spent much of his time attempting to thwart Hitler's aims and as a result, Canaris suffered terribly for his betrayal just before the end of the war when he was brutally beaten by the Gestapo and then later hanged.

German paratroopers dropped out of the sky in the predawn darkness and headed towards control stations along the dikes and canals. Some of them wore Allied uniforms or the uniforms of Dutch police, postman and railway guards. Assisted by thirty Dutch traitors, they seized the control stations and the unblown bridges. By the time the morning sun had risen, the German forces had neutralized Holland's main defense; that is the flooding of the lowlands.

At 5:00 o'clock in the morning of May 13th, King George VI was awakened by a police sergeant who was his personal bodyguard and was told that Dutch Queen Wilhelmina was on the phone. At first he didn't believe it. He soon learned that it really was her on the phone. King George later wrote in his diary; "She begged me to send aircraft for the defense of Holland. I passed this message on to everyone concerned and went back to bed. It's not often that one is rung up at that hour, and especially by a Queen. But in these days, anything may happen and far worse things too." *unquote*

The German panzers began crossing into Holland and on May 14th, German dive bombers and screeching Stukas began bombing Rotterdam, which was considered an open city at that time. By that,

I mean that the city would surrender rather than fight in order to save the destruction of the city by the enemy. The five-hour bombing of Rotterdam was so thorough that for the most part, the German bombers had leveled the entire city of its 30,000 buildings, which included businesses, factories, homes, churches and schools. None of the buildings standing today in Rotterdam were built before the May 10th bombing of the city. As an interesting side note in history, planning for the reconstruction of Rotterdam began within four days after it was leveled. The Dutch were not that anxious to rebuild the city in the same manner it had been built centuries before so this was their opportunity to rebuild the entire city to meet the modern specifications of concrete, steel and glass although the actual rebuilding didn't take place for the most part until right after the war. That being as it was, it was difficult living in Rotterdam during the war considering the fact that their homes were destroyed. I should add that after the war ended, Berlin was built up with the same purpose in mind.

Some of the German flyers were incensed that the Dutch were shooting parachutists as they were floating to the ground. One of them was shot in the head at close range as soon as he approached a number of civilians and an army patrol with his hands up. One such flyer, Gottfied Leske later wrote, "It's a rotten, beastly business shooting at defenseless parachutists. Typically Dutch. I think it isn't according to international law anyway." *unquote*. What also wasn't according to international law was German flyers such as the likes of Leske straffing innocent civilians such as mothers pushing their baby carriages, and the young and old alike, packed together on the roads while attempting to flee the German attacks on their cities. Typically German—at least as they were then.

The Dutch had fought bravely, but against the overwhelming odds their country was facing, it was pointless to go on. Five days after the invasion of Holland, and the day after the terror bombing of Rotterdam which completely destroyed the city, the Dutch surrendered. The loss of 180 German parachutists killed compared to 980 Dutch killed in the five-day war was nominal for both sides. The Germans spread rumours that as many as 30,000 Dutch citizens had died in the German invasion but that was a scare tactic which had quite an effect on the French who were soon to join in the real fight against the German forces.

There is an interesting footnote to this historic period regarding the invasion of Holland. Just two days before the First World War came to a close in 1918, the German Kaiser (emperor) Wilhelm II was forced to flee from Spa, Belgium to Holland after he and his son, the Crown Prince refused to abdicate. The Kaiser and his son were then interned in Holland and later, they were permitted to remain there notwithstanding the fact that the victorious Allies had requested the extradition of the Kaiser so that he could be tried as a war criminal. No doubt this generosity on the part of the Dutch was because the Dutch were grateful that the Kaiser didn't attack Holland and as such, Holland was able to remain neutral throughout the war and was spared the agony of the outright disastrous war that their neighbour, Belgium was suffering from. The ex-Kaiser spent the rest of his life in a small Dutch town called Doorn which is approximately 60 kilometers southeast of Amsterdam. There he lived in a manor castle surrounded by a forest from 1920 until he died in 1941.

After Hitler came to power, the Kaiser made tentative advances towards the Nazis when they came to power in the hopes that they would find him a niche in the Third Reich. When the Germans in the Second World War were advancing towards Doorn, the British offered to 'rescue' the ex-Kaiser and bring him to England on the understanding that he would not face any trial but he refused their offer. The Germans in turn simply ignored him when they conquered Holland but when the ex-Kaiser died, Hitler did give him a state funeral which is more than the British would have done. It's ironic in one way. Field Marshal Hindenburg was the one who had encouraged the German Kaiser to flee to Holland. Had the ex-Kaiser talked to Hindenburg who, in the early 1930s, was the President of Germany and knowing what Hindenburg knew about Hitler at that time, Hindenburg may have been receptive to bringing the monarchy back as a stabilizing entity in Germany.

The war between Germany and Denmark has to be one of the shortest and least bloodiest of all time. The invasion began at 5 a.m., on April 10th when three troopships sailed into Copenhagen harbour. A lone police officer tried to hold the troops back and was shot dead for his efforts. The city was taken without further bloodshed. Simultaneously, trawlers carrying German troops escorted by German E-boats invaded all the other Danish ports and islands. Other troops came by gliders, trains and ferryboats. All told, there were only 12 deaths in Denmark as a result of the German invasion. There really wasn't anything the Danes could have done to thwart the invasion and that is why they didn't fight the Germans attacking them. Twenty-five hours later, King Christian X officially ordered a ceasefire.

The subsequent occupation placed Germany in an unprecedented legal position. Since Denmark in effect, did not really resist the invasion, Denmark was not officially at war and as such, it was treated to some extent by the Germans as if Denmark was a neutral country. As a result, the German occupying authorities were faced with a Danish coalition government embracing most of the Danish political parties and a parliament operating on democratic principles.

The German justification of the attack on Denmark was that they were protecting their supply of Swedish iron ore from attacks by the British. The Swedish shipped much of their exports from the Swedish port of Goteborg which was across the Kattegat Strait from the northernmost part of Jutland, the mainland of Denmark. The Germans took their ships around the northern tip of Denmark and then headed southward down the Skagerrak Channel and then into the North Sea along the western coastline of Denmark and right into Germany's largest seaport, Hamburg.

I strongly suspect that Hitler was more interested in controlling the sea routes of the Kattegat Strait separating Denmark from Sweden than occupying Denmark. If he controlled Denmark, he could prevent Allied shipping from going into the Baltic Sea by closing off the entry points between Denmark's Zealand Island and neutral Sweden (narrowest point only several miles) and Zealand Island and the Danish mainland (narrowest point approximately 25 miles—40 km).

The German army, under the leadership of General Heinz Guderian, spearheaded across northern France, routing the Allies and forcing them to try and escape France via Dunkirk. Dunkirk lies along the Strait of Dover between Calais and the Belgian frontier, 49 miles (79 km) northwest of Lille by road. Hitler made his first big mistake of the war at this time. He ordered his army which was pursuing the British Expeditionary Force to halt thereby leaving Dunkirk as that last window in the burning house for the Allies to escape from. Hitler probably felt that if he proceeded westward he might have lost much of his tank force to the marshes at the coast. Some of his own generals however felt that he really wanted to assure the British of his peaceful intentions towards them but I doubt this considering the fact that the bombing of London and Conventry could hardly be construed as being peaceful. Of course, stopping the tanks didn't mean that his air force couldn't strafe and bomb the thousands of Allied soldiers trapped on the long beach of Dunkirk and that is what in fact they did.

By May 20th, Churchill had concluded that an evacuation from France was necessary so he ordered the Admiralty to arrange for as many as possible small craft to sail to Dunkirk and rescue the Allied soldiers trapped on the beach.

The first boat away to Dunkirk was an Isle of Man packet steamer called *Mona's Isle,* leaving Dover at 2100hrs (9.00 pm) on May 27th 1940. The journey across the Channel during the hours of darkness was uneventful and she pulled into the harbour at Dunkirk at midnight. The quay was a mass of battle weary troops, many were tired and exhausted; others with bandaged heads, arms and legs were in need of medical attention. 1,420 of them were hoarded onto the *Mona's Isle*, and she left at first light the next morning.

Three routes were allocated to the evacuating vessels. The shortest was Route Z, a distance of 39 miles, which, after leaving Dunkirk followed the French coast as far as No.6 Buoy, then turning

Northwest on a direct line to Dover. The longest of the three was Route Y, a distance of 87 miles that followed the French coast as far as Bray-Dunes then turned northeast until reaching the Kwinte Buoy. Here, after making an almost 270 degree turn sailed in an easterly direction as far as the *North Goodwin Lightship* then headed due south round the Goodwin Sands to Dover. The third, and although the safest from the German shore batteries, was through heavily mined portion of the English Channel. This was Route X, a distance of 55 miles, and ships headed due north out of Dunkirk, through the Ruytingen Pass and onto the *North Goodwin Lightship* before heading due south round the Goodwin Sands to Dover.

Between May and June of 1940, the British Expeditionary Force and other Allied troops, cut off by the Germans, were evacuated from Dunkirk to England by naval vessels and hundreds of civilian boats; small fishing and pleasure boats, some powered by motor or sail, others only by oars, headed across the Channel to ferry the soldiers from the beach to the larger craft further out. Of course, any amphibious evacuation is risky and the Dunkirk evacuation was fraught with danger from both the sea and the air. Strangely enough, the boats only had to contend with the rough sea and not the German navy or air force. Another of Hitler's mistakes.

Many of the Allied soldiers were trapped in the town of Dunkirk when the Germans bombed it. If they weren't burned or crushed to death, they suffocated in the ruins of the cellars. The beach was no picnic either. The constant strafing of the beaches forced the men to scamper about from one spot to another, waiting for the unseen bullets to smash into their bodies. Another German blunder occurred at this time. The bombs would sink into the sand before exploding and the sand would invariably reduce the impact of the explosions. Had the Germans used fragmentation bombs, the effect would have been disastrous for the men on the beach. From the 27th to the 31st of May however, the heavy rain grounded the German planes so there was some respite from the air but three British destroyers and some large passenger ships were sunk. As the final days wore on, the lines of men wading into the water from the beach grew smaller and smaller. At the port, some of the panicking soldiers were shot by their officers lest their panic infect their sturdier comrades.

In all, 350,000 British, French and Belgium Allied soldiers were evacuated to England. It was truly a miracle and the Britons exclaimed it as such but as Churchill quite ably put it when he addressed the Commons; "Wars are not won by evacuations." *unquote*. Churchill was very much aware that in less than three weeks, the Germans had completely routed the British Expeditionary Force and captured all of Holland and Belgium and half of France.

That German conquest of France and the Low Countries was not something Churchill could ignore any longer. It was at this time that he made another of his famous speeches in the Commons when he said; "We shall go on to the end. We shall fight them in France, we shall fight them in the seas and the oceans, we shall fight with growing confidence and growing strength in the air, we shall defend our Island, whatever the cost may be. We shall fight on the beaches, we shall fight on the landing-grounds, we shall fight in the fields and in the streets, we shall fight in the hills; we shall never surrender; and even if, which I do not for a moment believe, this island, or a large part of it were subjugated and starving, then our Empire beyond the seas, armed and guarded by the British Fleet, would carry on the struggle, until in God's good time, the New World, with all its power and might, steps forth to the rescue and the liberation of the old." *unquote*

I can only presume as last night's quarterback) that Churchill was directing that last remark more to the Americans than Canada because he had to know that Canada wasn't really in a position to rescue Great Britain at this juncture of the war.

Meanwhile, on May 26th, 1940 near the small village of Le Paradis around Pas-de-Calais in France, a company of the Royal Norfolk Regiment, trapped in a cowshed, surrendered to the 2nd Infantry Regiment, SS Totenkopf (Death's Head) Division under the command of 28-year-old SS Obersturmfuhrer Fritz Knoechlein. (Within the SS, the rank of Obersturmführer carried a wider range of occupations from staff aide, Gestapo officer, Concentration Camp supervisor, and Waffen-SS Platoon Commander to name but a few. Within both the SS and SA, the rank of Obersturmführer was considered the equivalent of an Oberleutnant in the German Wehrmacht which is equivalent to a first lieutenant in American armies).

Marched to a group of farm buildings, the British soldiers were lined up along side the barn wall. When the 99 prisoners were in position, two machine guns opened fire killing 97 of them. The bodies were then buried in a mass grave on the farm property. Two however managed to escape. Privates Albert Pooley and William O'Callaghan after having hid in a pig-sty for three days and nights; emerged from the slaughter, wounded but alive. When the SS troops moved on, the two wounded soldiers were discovered by Madame Castel of Le Paradis who then cared for them. In 1942, the 97 bodies were exhumed by the French authorities and reburied in the local churchyard. During the war Knoechlein had been awarded three Knight's Crosses. After the war, the massacre was investigated and Knoechlein was tracked down and arrested. He was tried before a War Crimes Court in Hamburg and found guilty and sentenced to death by hanging and on January 28th, 1949, the sentence was carried out.

The day after the Le Paradis massacre, some 80 men of the Royal Warwickshire Regiment, the Cheshire Regiment, and the Royal Artillery, were taken prisoner by the No 7 Company, 2nd Battalion of the SS Leibstandarte. At Esquelbecq, near the town of Wormhoudt, the prisoners were marched into a large barn, and there the massacre began. Stick grenades were lobbed in amongst the defenseless prisoners who died in agony as shrapnel tore into their flesh. When the last grenade had been thrown, the survivors were then ordered outside, there to be mown down under a hail of bullets from automatic weapons. The SS then entered the barn again to finish off the wounded. Fifteen men survived the atrocity, only to give themselves up to other German units to serve out the war as POWs. Unlike the Le Paradis massacre, the victims of Wormhoudt were never avenged, since after the war, no survivor could positively identify any of the SS soldiers involved.

I don't know if the men at Dunkirk around this time of these massacres were aware of what had happened near Pas-de-Calais. If they were, there would have been even greater fear amongst them.

"SAUVE QUI PEUT!" loosely translated means, "Every man for himself." and that was the cry of the French when the Dunkirk evacuation was complete. Hundreds of thousands of civilians fleeing the north front were clogging the roads to Paris. Most were covered with mud from flinging themselves into the ditches to avoid being strafed by the German planes. Old men trundled their equally old wives in wheelbarrows, children shared prams with personal effects as they were pushed along the roads by harried mothers. Horses drew wagons, old cars and shiny new ones shared the road with each other. Military officers blew the horns of their vehicles as they tried to push their way past the civilians clogging the roads but it was to little avail. The mass of people moved slower than a toddler out for walk. Few had relatives in Paris that could care for them so they knew that when they arrived, they would be sleeping on the streets or in the Metro. (subway stations) Into Paris streamed the miserable horde of displaced refugees infecting the already nervous Parisians with their fear.

In the northern part of France, French officers yelled to their men, "Take what you can. Leave nothing for the Germans." Naturally, with orders like that, nothing would hold their men back. Many French soldiers realizing that their 'war' had come to an end began looting and carousing as they escaped southward. Many of the stores were plundered and burned. Soldiers staggered down the streets of small villages and towns, some because of intoxication, others because they overloaded their bodies with plundered booty. Cheese factories were cleaned out. Villages and hamlets were put to the torch. Thus was France served in her dying days by her retreating army, many of her army being nothing but thugs and looters.

With the intensity of an artist painting a miniature painting, Hitler drafted and redrafted the armistice terms at his headquarters at Bruly-de-Peche, a small village just inside the Belgium frontier. Field Marshall Keitel, his Chief of the High Command of the Armed Forces was kept running back and forth like an errand boy from Hitler's headquarters to a little church nearby where Hitler's secretaries were typing up the document. Finally Hitler was satisfied with the terms. France was to be divided in two. The Germans would occupy the northern and the western parts of France and the French Vichy government would occupy the remaining one third of France. Its demarcation line being just north of the city of Vichy) ran southward to the Mediterranean under the leadership of Marshal Petain.

Vichy is located 150 miles (241 km) southeast of Paris and that was to be the capital of the unoccupied part of France which was to be called Vichy France—that is at least until the German troops later completely occupied all of France in November 1942.

The surrender was to take place in the same railroad car in which the Germans had surrendered to the Allies in November 1918. The railroad car stood in a clearing in the forest of Compiegne which was situated 45 miles (72 km) north of Paris. Next to the railroad car was a statue of Marshal Foch who accepted the German surrender in 1918 on behalf of the Allies in the First World War and another statue nearby was of the German Eagle transfixed by a French Sword. On a granite boulder and in gold lettering, were the words, 'Here on the eleventh of November, 1918, succumbed the criminal pride of the German empire—vanquished by the free people it tried to enslave.'

When Hitler arrived on the morning of June 20th, 1940 (he drove in his armoured Mercedes-Benz because fog prevented him from flying) he was greeted by his black-uniformed SS Leibstandarte Adolf Hitler honour guard to the music of a German regimental band playing *Deutschland uber Alles.*

With him was Hess, his second in command; Raeder, Admiral of the German navy; Brauchitsch, Commander in Chief of the German army; and Keitel, Chief of the German Armed Forces. Hitler wore an army cap, a double-breasted field-gray army uniform and gleaming black leather jackboots. Hitler never did appear publicly in a uniform befitting the leader of Germany like others before him and for the most part, he generally wore a simple soldier's uniform. Hitler entered the railway car and sat down, his entourage following suit. The terms of the surrender were read out. Then he rose, gave the Nazi salute, stared intently at each of the French representatives of the armed forces and the civil government, then abruptly turned and strode out. That train car no longer exists. Obviously the French were too proud to let it exist as a reminder of their darkest hour. It was removed from the site after the war and destroyed.

Having achieved what he then considered his greatest moment in life, Hitler could now satisfy a lifelong craving: He would at last, see Paris. It's ironic when one thinks of it. Hitler, both as a young man and later as a powerful leader in Europe, had never visited Paris and that is especially odd when you consider that Paris draws tourists to its bosom like the faithful are drawn to Mecca. He had yearned for years to visit the 'City of Lights' as an artist but the one and only time Hitler ever visited Paris was when he came as a conqueror. He arrived in Paris after dark, two days after France capitulated. Because his visit was unheralded, the normally extreme security precautions were waved. At six the following morning, he was wandering around the Opera House, marveling at its lights (which had been turned on for the occasion) and he amazed many of his entourage as to just how much he really knew about that amazing building.

He later crossed the Place de la Concorde and drove up the Champs Elysées to the Arc de Triumph where an enormous Nazi flag waved over the tomb of the 'Unknown Soldier'. He visited the Invalides, gazing in rapture at the tomb of Napoleon. It had been suggested to him by his advisors that he pay a visit to the Sainte-Chapelle, renown for its beautiful stained glass windows that make up the walls of this church. He was very disappointed when he arrived. All the glass windows had been removed earlier because of the fear that they would be destroyed by German air raids. That was unfortunate for him. It is a beautiful sight to see with the afternoon sun shining through those huge stained glass windows. My wife and I visited it in 2000 and like millions of people who have been inside that incredible chapel; we were amazed at the beauty of the stained glass.

Finally, he was driven to Montemarte, that hill in the center of Paris upon which the beautiful white basilica Sacre-Coeur was built. Morning parishioners rushing up the great steps leading to the basilica pretended to ignore him as they hastened into the building. Alas for Hitler, he didn't really get to appreciate the church's beauty. Had he seen it at night, with the spot lights lighting up the white edifice against the dark blue sky, he would have been overwhelmed as I was one summer evening 24 years later when I stood where he had stood with my back to the city and my eyes facing Sacre-Coeur with the edifice lit up with floodlights.

Hitler stayed in Paris only four hours (I stayed four days in 1974 and three days in 2000) and then he left, never to return. And he missed what most tourists never missed and that was the opportunity to take the three elevators to the top of the Eiffel Tower and look down on the city of Paris. And had he gone up to the top of the Tower, and the need arose, he, like me and thousands of others before and after me, would be expected to pay to use the toilet at the top. This was the only time he ever saw Paris. Incidentally, the man who designed the tower actually lived in the small apartment at the top of the tower. He also didn't take the elevator to the top of the Arc de Triumph and be fascinated by all the streets jutting out in all directions from that edifice.

By the 14th of June 1940, the German Army totally occupied Paris. Paul Reynaud, the French prime minister, now realizing that the German Western Offensive could not be halted, suggested to his ministers that the government should move to its territories it ruled in North Africa. This was opposed by his vice-premier, Henri-Phillipe Petain, and the supreme commander of the armed forces, General Maxime Weygand. They insisted that the government should remain in France and seek an armistice.

Other provisions of the armistice (other than the division of the country) included the surrender of all Jews living in France to the Germans. The French Army was disbanded except for a force of 100,000 men to maintain domestic order. The 1.5 million French soldiers captured by the Germans were to remain prisoners of war. The French government also agreed to stop members of its armed forces from leaving the country and instructed its citizens not to fight against the Germans. Finally, France had to pay the occupation costs of the 300,000 occupying German troops which came to 400 million French francs per day.

Since 100 French francs in June 2011 was worth $65.97 in US currency, multiply that by 400 million per day and then multiply that by 1,460 days that Vichy had to pay this money. Now you have some idea as just how many billions and billions of dollars in US currency that would amount to.

Over the next four years, Marshal Petain led the right-wing government of Vichy France. The famous revolutionary principles of 'Liberty, Equality, Fraternity' were replaced by 'Work, Family, Fatherland'. Prominent figures in the Vichy government included Pierre Laval, Jean-Francois Darlan and Joseph Darnand.

The Vichy government kept troops in Syria during the war. Its position on the Eastern Mediterranean coast made it strategically important for both Britain and Nazi Germany. The Allies also feared that Petain would allow the German Luftwaffe (air force) to establish air bases in Syria.

On the 8th of June 1941, the British Army and Free French forces entered Syria from Iraq and Palestine. After facing tough resistance from the Vichy forces, the Allies captured Damascus on the 17th of June. The armistice between Syria and the Allies was signed on the 12th of July and pro-British regimes were maintained in Syria for the rest of the war.

In January 1943, Joseph Darnand became head of Milice, the secret police in Vichy. Darnand was given the Waffen SS rank of Sturmbannfuehrer (major) and took a personal oath of loyalty to Adolf Hitler.

Darnand expanded the Milice and by 1944 it had over 35,000 members. The organization played an important role in investigating the French Resistance. Like the German Gestapo, the miliciens were willing to use torture to gain information.

After the D-Day landings took place, the French Maquis and other resistance groups emerged to help in the liberation of their country. Petain and his ministers fled to Germany where they established an exiled government at Sigmaringen.

In 1945, the leaders of the Vichy government were arrested, including Laval, Darnand and Petain. Following France's Armistice with Germany in 1940, Laval served twice in the Vichy Regime as head of government, signing orders permitting the deportation of foreign Jews from French soil to the death camps. In January 1943, with German assistance the Vichy government created the *Milice française (French militias)* a paramilitary force to help fight the Maquis. (Frenchmen in the resistance) Laval, who had by then replaced Pétain as Vichy's Prime Minister, was the formal head of the Milice, but its chief of operations, and its real chief, was Secretary of the Interior, and founder of a previous Fascist militia, Joseph Darnand.

Marshal Pétain was tried for treason on the 15th of August 1945 and was convicted and sentenced to death by firing squad. Charles de Gaulle, then President of the Provisional Government of the French Republic; commuted the sentence to life imprisonment on the grounds of his age and his World War I contributions. In prison he soon became totally senile, and required constant nursing care. Pétain at the age of 95, died in prison in 1951.

Joseph Darnand was executed by firing squad on Wednesday, the 10th of October 1945 at the Fort de Châtillon, a week after he was sentenced to death. The fort was built in 1874 as a fortification and was located about 5 kilometres (3.1 mi) south of Paris in the communes of Châtillon-sous-Bagneux and Fontenay-aux-Roses. It was later razed to make way for a nuclear facility. I was living in Wells, B.C. then but I don't really know for sure as to what I was doing when he was executed because I don't know at what time he was executed but if he was executed in the same time of day that Laval was executed, then I was just leaving school and heading home the previous day.

Pierre Laval had been the titular head of the Milice, an SS group of Frenchmen but the actual leader was Secretary General Joseph Darnand. Laval was executed by firing squad on Wednesday, at 12.32 a.m. on October 16th 1946. At that precise moment, I was in Richmond (Lulu Island just south of Vancouver) living on a farm. It was only three in the afternoon on Tuesday in British Columbia when Laval was executed. Our school had burned to the ground so all the students only went to school for half a day at a makeshift school. Since I went to school in the morning, I was free for the rest of the day to play on the farm while Laval was being shot an hour after having failed in a suicide attempt (biting into a suicide pill and being revived). Over the years, the poison's effect had weakened so it wasn't as potent as he had wished. He was wearing his white tie which was his personal symbol.

It is a common misconception that the Vichy regime administered only the unoccupied zone of southern France (incorrectly named 'free zone', *zone libre*, by Vichy), while the Germans directly administered the occupied zone. In fact, the civil jurisdiction of the Vichy government extended over the whole of metropolitan France, except for Alsace-Lorraine, a disputed territory which was placed under German administration (though not formally annexed). French civil servants in Bordeaux, such as Maurice Papon, or Nantes were under the authority of French ministers in Vichy. René Bousquet, head of French police nominated by Vichy, exercized his power directly in Paris through his second, Jean Leguay, who coordinated raids with the Nazis. Some historians claim that the difficulties of communication across the demarcation line between the two zones, and the tendency of the Germans to exercise arbitrary power in the occupied zone, made it difficult for Vichy to assert its authority there. Vichy continued to exercise jurisdiction over most of France until the collapse of the regime following the Allied invasion in June 1944. The Milice meanwhile were still participating in torturing and conducting summary executions and assassinations of résistants and helped round up the Jews in all of France for deportation to the Nazi-operated death camps.

The Nazis stamped their mark upon the French landscape. They made their presence widely felt by being both seen and heard. Their thinly disguised arrogance, their pushy behaviour on the streets and their parades with military bands became intolerable. Even when invisible, they invaded people's minds, even their dreams.

In the beginning, the resistance to the Germans and the Vichy government arose spontaneously among both men and women who were beginning to feel isolated from the rest of the world. Two hours after hearing Petain's radio broadcast on June 17th 1940 ("The fighting must cease"), General Gabriel Cochet, the commander of the French 5th Army-Air Force, called together his men and ordered them to get ready to resist the Nazi horde. And on June 18th, Charles De Gaulle's radio broadcast which has been widely regarded as the first call to resistance said in part, "No matter what happens; the flame of French resistance must not be extinguished and will not be extinguished." *unquote*

An early tract in France was entitled *'Advice to the Occupied'* and contained 33 points, including, 'You do not know their language or you have forgotten it. If one of them addresses you in German, make a sign of ignorance and continue on without remorse'. 'If he questions you in French, you are not obliged to help. He is not a friend'. 'If he asks for a light, extend your cigarette. Never since ancient times has fire been refused, not even to one's most hated enemy.' *unquote*

Gradually the French came to accept the underground propaganda as the only source of truth and reality.

One of the humorous stories went as follows: 'Do you know what happened recently? At nine twenty at night, a Jew killed a German soldier, cut him open and ate his heart' 'Impossible and for three reasons. A German has no heart, Jews don't eat pigs and at nine-twenty, everyone, including the Jews are listening to the BBC.' Exasperated by minor opposition, the Germans stepped up their campaigns against dissidents. They announced that the death penalty would be imposed for any act of sabotage committed against the German army communications in the Occupied Zone. To prove that they were serious, they apprehended a nineteen- year-old boy named Pierre Roche who had cut German telegraph cables in the town of Royan. A French court sentenced him to two years in prison, but three days later a German military court tried him and sentenced him to death by firing squad. This was hardly an isolated case. In the towns of Epinal and Rennes, the Germans shot teenagers who admitted that they had occasionally snipped telephone wires. But this ruthless policy did not have the desired affect. Small acts of sabotage in northern France simply increased.

On October 30th, Marshall Petain met Hitler and a photograph of the two shaking hands created shock and disgust among the French. The resistance, still unnamed as such, became a reflex, a nervous tic so to speak, a refusal to accept German acts of the conqueror and Petainist acts of submission. Winter arrived suddenly in November 1940 and it was brutally cold. In France, Real coffee had disappeared from the stores, cigarettes were in short supply, soap was a precious commodity and there was no meat on Wednesdays, Thursdays and Fridays. All this understandably added to the misery of the French citizens.

The 'Musee' was the oldest and most solid network of undercover workers in Paris. They passed agents and information to the British and had squads of young men in paramilitary training. Boris Vilde's aim was to merge all anti-German groups in the occupied zone. He felt capable of expanding and directing anti-Nazi activities in the North and eventually throughout France. His ultimate aim was to incite the whole people to revolt against the occupation. His newspaper; *The Resistance* was the first instance of the word being employed in its standard sense as a description of the entire movement. Below is an extract from the editorial: "Resist! This is the cry that comes from the hearts of all of you who suffer from our country's disaster. This is the wish of all of you who want to do your duty. But you feel isolated and disarmed. In the chaos of ideas, opinions and systems, you are confused and looking for your duty. Resistance is here to speak to your hearts and minds, to show you what to do. Resistance means above all to act, to be positive, to perform reasonable and useful things. Many of you have tried are discouraged because you think you are powerless. But some have formed themselves into groups, scattered and weak. Patiently, we have searched them out. We have united them." *unquote*

However, the Germans were less patient, and true to their word, they rooted out all dissidents. In January 1942, Vilde and his co-collaborators were executed.

Despite the executions, the resistance went on for years. The men and women of the Resistance had helped to bring France from the acceptance of defeat and the disillusionment of the German conquest to a reawakening of morality, dignity and hope. Members of the 'Chanzy Group', a group of French Resistance Fighters and Francs-Tireurs operated in the 'Centre' region of France. They were fired from their jobs at the French Postal and Telegraph Service because of their communist activities. They had to leave Cognac, their home region, for Orleans where they joined the underground forces. The group's activities only lasted four months before they were all caught and sentenced to death.

On the 22nd of October 1943, the entire group was executed at the firing range in Groues. Just as the firing squad was about to execute them, an Austrian soldier got out of the firing squad and refused to fire. He was put in the firing line with the condemned and executed along side of them. Sadly, no one to this day knows who this anonymous but very brave man was.

During July 16-17, 1942 a total of 12,884 non French Jews were rounded up in Paris for deportation to the death camp at Auschwitz in Poland. For a whole week, 6,900 of them, including 4,051 children, were confined in the huge sports stadium; the Velodrome d'Hiver on the Boulevard de Grenelle. Five days later, the children were separated from their parents and transported to Auschwitz. Without food and little water and only four toilets, the remaining victims were in a deplorable state before being boarded on to trains for Poland. When the Red Army liberated Auschwitz on January 26th, 1945, they found 2,819 inmates still alive but only thirty of the 6,900 non French Jews were alive. Sadly, none of the 4,051 children survived. They were killed in the gas chambers. It is estimated that around 60,000 Jews from 37 countries perished in France under the German occupation. This includes 22,193 French Jews and 14,459 Polish Jews who had fled to France earlier.

Chapter Thirteen

The day Hitler left Paris was my last day of school for that school year. I had been still going to Perth Avenue Elementary School and I had just passed into grade one. I remember all of us kids scrambling out of the school singing, "No more school, no more books, and no more teacher's dirty looks." The original building is gone now of course and replaced with a more modern building.

Since I had previously been sent back to kindergarten when I was six years and a few months old, by the time I was six years and eight months old in June 1940, I had only completed kindergarten when in fact, I should have completed grade one. As recently as 1984, twenty percent of all students between junior kindergarten and grade eight were over-age for the class they were in. That was later reduced to only five percent in the nineties. I have to say that students who fail in school or are sent back a class (I was later sent back again from grade five to grade four) are dealt a critical blow to their self-esteem and it really doesn't do anything to improve their academic performance down the road. Obviously, if this is done in their latter years at school, the students simply become disillusioned and drop out.

My mother was going out of town that summer so she decided to send my brother and me to summer camp for the entire summer and in her wisdom she decided that she would send us to separate camps since (as she later put it to us) oil and water don't mix. My brother went to Camp Pinecrest; (run by the Toronto YMCA on College Street where the Toronto Police Headquarters is now situated) the camp being somewhere near Bala, Ontario on Lake Muskoka about three hours drive north of Toronto. In 1969, I went to that very camp to participate for a two-day conference of Christians and Jews and it was then that I finally saw the camp my brother had been sent to.

My mother sent me to another YMCA camp. It was Camp Sunfish. It was also run by the Toronto YMCA on College Street. The camp was situated somewhere in the Lake Simcoe area but years later, it was later sold and subsequently turned into a subdivision. No one has been able to tell me where the camp was actually located, not even the YMCA in Toronto that ran the camp.

I remember my mother dropping me off at the northwest corner of College Street and Yonge Street where the buses would pick up us kids for the trip to Camp Sunfish. I was crying when she left me there all alone with all these screaming and yelling kids. She hadn't given me any tuck money.

Unlike most camps, Camp Sunfish wasn't located right at the lake. To get to the lake, we had to walk a half kilometer or so. Unlike my brother's camp, Camp Sunfish was more or less on flat terrain, surrounded by beautiful forests and fields.

Right from the beginning, I was treated special but that was simply because I was the only kid that would be spending the entire summer at the camp. The average kid spent two weeks at the camp so I ended up having seniority in the cabin, meaning, I got to stay in the same bed and the new kids were always asking me what camp Sunfish was like.

When I was very young, I like to work. Keep in mind that I was young and foolish in those days. Well, it was decided that I could have an unpaid job at the camp. My job was to guard the garbage fire at the rear of the dining hall where the rubbish was burned during the rest hour right after lunch. One day, when the fire was out, I walked across the cold white embers and was amazed how soft they were to my bare feet. Then I learned a valuable lesson. Don't step into something that looks safe enough on the surface until you have see what is hidden underneath the surface. What was under the cool white soft ashes that particular day was a jagged piece of glass just waiting breathlessly for some fool kid to tramp through the dead rubbish fire. There I was, hobbling towards the director's camp, crying all the way and leaving a bloody trail of my well-needed blood behind me. A counselor ran up to me, took one look at my bleeding foot and carried me across the playing field to the director's cabin. If you think I had a valid reason to cry with that jagged piece of glass sticking out of my instep, you should have heard me when the camp nurse pulled it out and then stitched it without any anesthetic. For about a week after that, I walked around with a pronounced limp. When I say pronounced, I mean, I could have successfully auditioned for the part as Quasimodo in the *Hunchback of Notre Dame*. There is nothing that will elicit more sympathy from adults than when they are watching a crippled, seemingly homeless six-year-old kid hunched over and hobbling around camp with a crutch all by himself. I milked their sympathy for all it was worth but to this day, I still have that scar on my left instep.

One day, my cabin counselor told me to go to my cabin for my afternoon nappy. I reminded him that I had to guard the rubbish fire lest the flames reach out and attack the forest which was very close to the fire. He insisted. He was bigger than I so I followed him back to the cabin. About half an hour later, we all heard the rapid clanging of the dinner bell. It was signaling that there was a fire somewhere. Now, take a guess where you think the fire was. Yes, you're right. You are certainly astute. It was the rubbish fire. It had got out of hand (not that it was in hand in the first place) and some nearby trees had caught fire. The camp director later asked me where I had been during this time. I pointed to my cabin counselor and told the director that "HE told me to return to the cabin." I don't know what was said between them, but 'HE' never bothered me after that but I didn't get to watch over the rubbish fire any more. The director assigned the job to a staff member in the kitchen.

I was the butt of several practical jokes and fell for that old pail-of-water-over-the door trick. One Sunday, just after the late morning swim and after I took off my bathing suit, I discovered to my horror, that the kids in my cabin had hidden my clothes. One of the kids then grabbed my bathing suit which had been lying on my bed, and bolted out of the cabin with it. He ran along the path that led to the main campfire circle deep in the forest. When I got to the campfire circle, he was nowhere to be seen. I was too bashful to return back to the camp naked so I just went into the teepee in the circle and cried. A couple of hours later, I could hear someone approaching the campfire circle. It was my cabin counselor. He had my clothes with him. It seems that he hadn't noticed that I was missing until my Uncle Frank and Aunt Fern (both deceased) had arrived at the camp after lunch. During the rest period, they went to my cabin and asked about me. They were furious when they learned what had happened to me. They gave the director a tongue lashing and threatened to take me out of the camp immediately. He assured them it wouldn't happen again—and it didn't.

I will never forget my first overnight camping trip. We ended up sleeping on a pebble beach. The reason for that was that we weren't allowed to build a campfire anywhere else but on the pebble beach and we were to sleep next to the fire so that the insects wouldn't attack us during the night. I didn't have a sleeping bag so all I had between me and the pebble beach was a blanket. Have you ever slept on a pebble beach when all you have between your soft, delicate skin and those large round pebbles is a blanket? I think the Indian fakirs had a better time of it on their bed of nails for at least, they were used to it. I wasn't.

My favorite group game was 'capture the flag.' There we would be, running through the forest with little coloured balloons fastened to our belts. The 'survivors' would be the kids whose balloons were still intact. One day my balloon burst within the first few minutes when I accidentally leaned against a tree and a twig burst the damn balloon. Was I mad? Is the Pope Catholic? Do doctors practice medicine? I remember another time when I was running through the forest and crying at the same time. I had just previously stooped down to relieve myself and had reached over to a tree to grab some leaves to wipe myself. I didn't know it at the time but I had grabbed a leaf from a poison sumac tree. This tree is generally found in swamps and has attractive leaves but it does not possess the sort of leaves you should choose as toilet paper. They are more poisonous to the touch than poison ivy. Within seconds of wiping myself with this poisonous leaf, the stinging began. When I say stinging, I mean that I can now truly appreciate the sufferings that the victims of the 15th-century Walachian prince, Vlad IV 'the Impaler' had to undergo. What does a young kid whose rear end is inflamed do when sitting in the lake doesn't help? I was too embarrassed and modest to ask the nurse to do anything so I suffered in silence for about two days. However, wiping your ass with poisonous sumac is a great incentive in strengthening your sphincter muscles. Poison oak and poison ivy can also be used as suitable substitutes.

On rainy evenings, the entire camp would sit in the dining hall and be treated to black and white Laurel and Hardy films. The Laurel and Hardy films didn't have sound then but with those two funny comedians, sound was purely academic. We also watched either *Our Gang* or *Little Rascals* and I was mindful of my age in the early 1990s when the little fat kid in the movies (George McFarland who played, 'Spanky' and who was five years my senior) died in July 1993 at age sixty-five.

One of the most moving experiences I ever had was at seven o'clock every evening at that camp. Because Canada was at war, there was a certain patriotic feeling even within our young minds so at seven in the evenings, a counselor with a trumpet played taps as the flag was being lowered down the flag pole which was situated on a little hill in the center of the camp. No matter what we were doing at that time or where we were within the camp, as soon as we heard taps being played, we had to stop talking, face the direction where the flag pole was and stand at attention. One early evening I was very moved as I faced the flag coming down in the distance with the setting sun and red sky behind it while listening to that mournful sound from the trumpet as 'taps' was being played. Everyone was patriotic in those days because the War was not going that well for Canadians and Americans or for that matter, all freedom-loving people in Europe and Asia.

My experience in Camp Sunfish inspired me to want to keep going to camps. Later I went to two boy's camps as a camper and later still, to various boy's camps as a counselor, then as an aquatic director, (I was even the aquatic director of a girl's camp on one occasion) assistant program director, program director and finally as the camp director of three boy's camps in which each one was in British Columbia, Manitoba and Ontario. It was when I accepted the invitation to be the camp director of those three boy's camps that I learned that being the camp director isn't as much fun as I thought. Actually it's the worst job in the camp. It's mostly worry with little or no fun.

Although many Americans were interested in learning about the war in Europe (many purchased maps of Europe for this purpose) the Americans as a nation didn't want to participate in it at all. They had lost thousands upon thousands of men in the First World War and that dampened any incentive they might have had to get involved with another war. Of course, there were a great many Americans whose ancestors and even mothers and fathers immigrated to the United States from Europe so these people had a greater concern about what was going on in Europe but there really wasn't anything they could do about it. If they were able to go back to Europe at this time and fight for their parent's homelands, they would lose their American citizenship. The hope that most Americans had in the war in Europe coming to an end was exceeded only by their hope that the United States would continue remaining neutral. Of course, that would obviously all change on December 7th 1941.

On July 6th, 1940, the Germans created a *Black Book* in which they had listed the names of 2,820 persons to be arrested in the British Isles when the invasion of England was completed. The names included writers such as Virginia Woolfe, Noel Coward, E.M. Forester and H. G. Wells. Naturally the prime minister, Winston Churchill was at the top of the list, followed closely by the Royal family. The Germans also intended to deport all men between the ages of 17 years to 45 years to

Germany to work as slaves. Think about it. The population growth in Britain would come to an almost standstill had the Germans achieved their goal.

On July 11th, the RAF bombed munitions factories in Germany. On July 24th, Italian planes bombed Jerusalem. (The British ruled what was called Palestine then) On August 20th, Winston Churchill gave another of his famous speeches when he was praising the RAF for their fight against the German Luftwaffe. He said in part, "Never in the field of human conflict was so much owed by so many to so few."

Forty-five years later, while I was addressing the Seventh United Nations Congress on the Prevention of Crime and the Treatment of Offenders which was held in Milan, Italy in September 1985, I used almost the same words when I was the last speaker to speak on my earlier 1980 proposed *United Nations Standard Minimum Rules on the Administration of Juvenile Justice.* (of which I am recognized by the UN as the precursor of those Rules) I told the delegates from the 122 nations present at that Milan conference that I would paraphrase Sir Winston Churchill. I said, "Never in the history of juvenile justice will so many owe so much for the efforts of so few." Actually I didn't feel guilty paraphrasing Sir Winston considering the fact that he quoted another who gave the same speech a hundred years earlier.

On August 22, German 35.56 centimeter-guns (14 inch) with a range of 32 kilometers shelled Dover from the French coast. The RAF later bombed the guns that night.

On August 24th, ten German bombers jettisoned their bombs in error while flying over London after bombing some airfields earlier. On August 26th, the RAF made its first bombing raid on Berlin in retaliation for the dropping of the bombs by the German bombers two days earlier.

Looking back at this in hindsight, I have to say these two bombings were two of the biggest blunders in the war. The next day, Germany began bombing London in earnest. That later resulted in a further British retaliation, followed by another German retaliation. It wasn't the original intentions of either side to bomb civilians but as a result of the accidental dropping of the German bombs over London, the citizens on both sides were slaughtered by the subsequent revenge raids. It was a high price for the German's August 24th mistake of unloading their extra bombs over London. I might add that had the British just waited a bit longer to see if there was going to be another air raid on London, they might have learned that there wasn't and as a result, there would haven't been a retaliation raid on Berlin and 23,000 British and two million German civilians would not have subsequently died as a result of the subsequent bombing raids of their cities. I wonder if the German pilots who accidentally dropped their bombs on London lived long enough to suffer from the guilt after realizing that they inadvertently brought about the deaths of 2 million of his own countrymen, not to mention the 23 thousand who died in England.

Of course, there is the persistent belief by many that 'Bomber' Harris; the British Air Chief Marshal intended to bomb the German cities all along as a means of browbeating the Germans into surrendering. He was much criticized during and after the war for his carpet bombing of German cities. Ironically, his carpet bombing of the German cities did in fact assist greatly in demoralizing the Germans, albeit at a very high price in human life.

On September 27th, Japan signed the tripartite pact with Germany and Italy. Now the Axis powers comprised of three belligerents.

Within two weeks of the Soviet occupation of the Baltic states of Estonia, Latvia and Lithuania on August 1st, 1940, almost the entire intelligentsia of these countries had been executed by the KGB. The subsequent German attack on these provinces forced the withdrawal of the Soviet troops and paved the way for Hitler's Einsatzgruppen (mobile death squads) to start their roundup of all resident Jews. About 3,000 had already fled with the retreating Red Army but the 57,000 left behind in Vilna, faced a terrifying future. Einsatzgruppen 'A' operated in the Baltic Provinces under the command of SS Major General Stahlecker who, after five months, reported to Himmler (Document 2273-PS) that 229,052 Jews, men, women and children had been shot. Thousands more were housed in ghettos as they were urgently needed for slave labour. In Duenaburg, on November 9th, 1941, 11,034 Jews were murdered. At Libau, two weeks later, another 2,350 were victims of the SS's bullets. In Lithuania, under the Nazi's, 136,421 Jews were put to death in numerous single actions by Lithuanian mercenaries with the help of the German police squads. In the White Russian Settlement Area, around 41,000 executions had been undertaken by the members of the Einsatzgruppen. In Vilna, around 32,000 Jews (men, women, children and babies) were murdered during the first six months of German occupation.

When Vilna was liberated by the Red Army on July 13th, 1944, a few hundred Jews who had been hiding in the surrounding forests; suddenly appeared in the city square. Altogether, only between three and four thousand Jews, out of the original 57,000 from that area, survived in the concentration camps in Germany.

On August 31st, Hitler gave his orders for *Operation Sealion*, the invasion of England. His plan was to have his army transported across the English Channel in 3,508 vessels. On September 7th, 350 German bombers, protected by as many German fighters, flew over London and bombed the London dockyards and 450 Londoners died in that daylight raid. The British anti-aircraft guns sent up the exploding shells to ward off the enemy planes but the shell fragments ended up raining down on London. Walking on the streets was a deadly experience to many.

The German landing, *Operation Sealion*, was scheduled for the twelfth of September. In reality Hitler was never committed to such an action and no plans had been devised to deal with the British navy. On the seventh of September 1940 the first major German bombing of London took place. The city was turned into a raging inferno and the British government issued the codeword *Cromwell*. It meant simply that a German invasion was imminent and church bells would ring as a call to arms. *Operation Sealion* was cancelled ten days later on the seventeenth of September 1940.

By the end of September, the British had broken the German secret codes and the Americans had broken the Japanese secret codes.

Throughout the remainder of the two theatres of war; European and the Pacific, the Allies generally knew what the Axis plans were in advance as the Axis plans hit the airwaves.

On October 7th, German armies occupied oil-rich Romania and on October 13th, Princess Elizabeth, who was 14 at the time, broadcasted a message to the 13,000 children of London sent to the Dominions and the United States. October 18th, the second evacuation of the half million children in London was underway.

On October 9th, 1940, my father joined the Royal Canadian Air Force in Toronto. On the next day, he was sent to Camp Borden, Ontario for a day and then to St. Thomas, Ontario for his basic training. He stayed there until April of the following year. I don't think my mother was aware of this at this time because this was one of those times when my father had been away for some considerable time previous to him joining up.

With him in the armed forces, the government would deduct $70 from his pay each month an amount that would be sent to my mother for the support of the three of us. But my father originally had other ideas of his own. He told my mother that he had arranged to have half of the deducted money sent to his mother and the other half sent to her. My mother put an end to that plan of his. She complained to Ottawa, and rightfully so and the full deduction went to my mother and his mother had to survive on her own. My mother got $35 a month for her support and another $35 for myself and my brother. Seventy dollars a month (equivalent to $2,170 a month in 2010) was a fair amount of money in those days so when one thinks of it, it was only after my father joined the air force, and was absent for almost three years, that he meaningfully contributed towards his family, albeit grudgingly. This tells you something of the kind of creep my father was.

For almost two years, from late 1940 to late 1942, the island of Malta was mercilessly besieged by the Axis air forces of Italy and Germany. Although no RCAF (Royal Canadian Air Force) squadrons served there during the siege, at least twenty-five percent of Malta's RAF (Royal Air Force) defenders at any one time were Canadians.

In the autumn of 1940, the Canadian liner, owned by Canadian Pacific, the *Empress of Britain* was on trooping mission between England and Suez via the Cape. On her way back, she stopped at Cape Town. Leaving with 643 people on board, no one knew that this was to be her last voyage. On October 26th, (the day before my seventh birthday) when the *Empress of Britain* was off the West Coast of Ireland, she was suddenly attacked by a German long-range Focke-Wulf Condor plane. The ship was set on fire in the attack, and it did not take long before the crew had lost control of the raging blaze. The Captain ordered the ship to be abandoned, leaving a skeleton crew behind in an effort to save the ship. The Polish destroyer *Burza* and the two tugs *Marauder* and *Thames* managed to take the burning vessel in tow, and headed for safe waters. But the German aircraft had reported the ship's position via radio, and soon the German U-boat *U-32* was on the *Empress*' tail. The U-boat stalked its prey for almost 24 hours when on October 28th, she was able to fire three torpedoes against the *Empress of Britain*. One of the torpedoes detonated prematurely, but the other two found their target, and mortally wounded the ship. The *Empress of Britain* went down, the casualties being counted to 49, most of whom had been earlier killed in the air attack. Two days later, the *U-32* was sunk by the Canadian destroyer, *Harvester*.

On Sunday, October 27, 1940, the day of my 7th birthday, French General, Charles de Gaulle, speaking for the Free French Forces from his temporary headquarter in equatorial Africa, called all French men and women everywhere to join the struggle to preserve and defend free French territory and "to attack the enemy wherever it is possible, to mobilize all our military, economic, and moral resources and to make justice reign."

De Gaulle had a long history fighting Germans. He sustained multiple injuries fighting at Verdun in World War I. He escaped German POW camps five times, only to be recaptured each time. At 6 feet, 4 inches tall, it was hard for de Gaulle to remain inconspicuous for any real length of time before being spotted.

At the beginning of World War II, de Gaulle was commander of a tank brigade. He was admired as a courageous leader and was made a brigadier general in May 1940. After the German invasion of France, he became undersecretary of state for defense and war in the Reynaud government, but when Reynaud resigned, and Field Marshal Philippe Petain stepped in, (a virtual puppet of the German occupiers) de Gaulle left for England. On June 18th, de Gaulle took to the radio airwaves to make an appeal to his fellow French not to accept the armistice being sought by Petain, but to continue fighting under his command. "I am France!" he declared. To the loyal people of France, he was France. Ten days later, Britain formally acknowledged de Gaulle as the leader of the 'Free French Forces', which was at first little more than those French troops stationed in England, volunteers from Frenchmen already living in England, and units of the French navy. Another Free French movement had begun in Africa, under the direction of Gen. Henri Giraud. De Gaulle eventually relocated to Africa after tension began to build between himself and the British. Initially, de Gaulle agreed to share power with Giraud in the organization and control of the exiled French forces; that is until Giraud resigned in 1943, unwilling to stand in de Gaulle's shadow or struggle against de Gaulle's deft political maneuvering.

On November 15th, the German bombers bombed the English city of Coventry. As many as 60,000 buildings were damaged or destroyed and 568 people died in the raid, with a loss of only one of the 450 German bombers that set out to destroy that city. The unfortunate irony about the bombing of Coventry is that Churchill knew about the planned attack days in advance and did nothing about it and rightly so. It seems that the British had earlier cracked the German secret code and if the British made any overt attempts at defending Coventry, the Germans would know that their code had been broken and they would change it. The decision to remain 'unaware' of the pending raid on Coventry in the long run saved hundreds of thousands of lives throughout the remainder of the war because the Germans still believed that their secret code was secure. However, many people in Coventry never forgave Churchill for doing nothing to save their city from the bombings even when they finally realized that his inaction was justified and proper.

On December 11th, the British had attacked the Italians in Egypt and had captured 15,000 Italian prisoners. On December 30th, the Germans bombed London with over 22,000 incendiary bombs, destroying a great portion of the southeast part of the city. During the month of December, as many as 3,700 civilians died in that large city.

The war was not looking good for the Allies except in Greece where the Italians had been routed entirely from Greek soil. Hitler had previously warned Mussolini that it was a mistake to attack Greece but Mussolini didn't listen to him. The Greeks have never been a nation to sit still and let conquers simply walk over them.

By the end of 1940, almost the entire world was involved in war. There were battles in Africa, the Baltics and Europe and no sign at all of an end to it. Further, Japan was making inroads deep into China and making threatening noises in Southern Asia that alarmed many of the small countries bordering the western part of the Pacific.

Chapter Fourteen

When my brother and I returned to Toronto from our respective camps in the last days of August 1940, we learned that we were going to live in Parkdale, an area in the southwestern part of Toronto. At that time, and both earlier and for some time later, some of the finest homes in Toronto were in Parkdale, especially those that were south of Queen Street. Unfortunately, in the late fifties and from then on, apartment buildings started getting built in the area, the beautiful three-story homes ended up being converted into rooming houses and they were further renovated into small apartments within the houses. The quality of the people living in them changed and many people living in them were mentally handicapped and also drunks, down and outers, criminals and similar undesirables who gave decent families still living on those streets a difficult time of it. It had been for some time, a neighbourhood rife with poverty, drugs, crime and prostitution and gangs of young thugs. By 2000, this area, once being the home of some of Toronto's wealthiest families, had become one of Toronto's four poorest neighbourhoods.

Our house at 8 Earnbridge Street was not one of those fine homes south of Queen Street but rather one of many houses that are not so nice one finds north of Queen Street. We lived on the main floor and another family lived on the floor above us. The street is two blocks north of Queen Street West and runs east off of Brock Avenue to the railroad tracks. I liked living on this street nevertheless because where the street turned southward, the railroad tracks ran parallel to it and several factories were situated along the eastern side of what is Strickland Avenue. This gave rise to exciting experiences walking on the railway tracks behind the factories.

One of my fondest memories is of the times when I and my brother and our friends used to enter the railroad track area and sneak up to one of the factories on Strickland Avenue and hide in the clouds of steam that blew out of a small pipe extruding from the side of the building. Whenever I am surrounded in steam, my mind invariably goes back to the clouds of steam blasting out of that small pipe from the factory off Strickland Street.

The government was encouraging its citizens to donate their old pots and pans and metal toys and anything else that was made of metal for the war effort. Throughout the city, huge piles of metal objects sprung up and it so happened that there were several huge piles of these metal donations on the other side of the tracks from where we lived.

One day, my brother and I crossed the tracks and we had a field day searching for metal toys. When we returned to the fence we had sneaked through, we were stopped by a police officer. I can still hear his words in my mind. "And what do you two think you are doing?" I replied, "We found some toys on the other side of the tracks." He continued. "And do you know why there is a fence along side of the tracks?" I knew but I played dumb. He continued, "So that little children like you don't get run over by a train." Now, I never would have guessed that. Then he looked at our newly-found goodies under our arms and said, "These toys have been donated by other children for the war effort." I doubted that. They were probably donated by the mothers of the other little children who probably cried when they saw their metal toys being taken away. The cop continued with his barrage. "Now you take those toys right back where you found them." I guess his concern for the war effort superseded his concern for our safety. Well in any case, he had given us permission to cross the tracks and return to the piles of goodies. We spent another hour there and found even better toys and when it was safe to cross the tracks (by that I mean the cop was gone) we crossed the tracks carrying with us our newly found booty.

My mother told me in 1991 that the movie houses got into the public spirit of helping the war effort by offering the kids free admission if we brought old pots and pans to the movie with us. This was happening all over Canada. The movie houses were also accepting metal clothes hangers and giving the children credit for one cent for each hanger. Bring six and we got in to see the movie. My mother gave me an old pot to take to the movie. The manager was pleased and I got in free. The next week, I, on my own initiative, contributed to the war effort. I took another of my mother's pots to the movie. It was a brand new pot. The manager of the movie house was very impressed, whereas my mother was not. She made that very clear to me with her repeated statements that were in unison with her repeated hand slaps on my bare backside.

On the northeast corner of Earnbridge and Brock stood a large chestnut tree. It was still there at the time of this writing sixty years later. When the nuts of the tree ripened in autumn, they fell to the ground. I used to then step on the burrs to crack them open and remove the shiny dark polished wood-like chestnuts. I never ate them and to this day I haven't eaten any although I hear that they taste good. My mother used to run a thread through them and made necklaces out of them. No one wore necklaces out of chestnuts so I guess she did it to humor me.

I had entered grade one (when I should have entered grade two) and was attending the Landsdown Public School which was about four blocks west of my house and two blocks north of Queen Street. One day, while attending that school during the noon hour, I remember watching RCAF fighter planes chasing each other around the sky with smoke tailing behind them. It was quite a show. Because there was always the fear of air raids in the future, we constantly had air raid drills in the school. The entire school lined up along the walls of the main hallway for the drill. The theory was that if Toronto was bombed, it was safer to stand beside the inner walls of the school while the roof came down on us rather than run outside and be killed directly by the falling bombs. No doubt thousands of other kids in Europe stood by the inner walls while the roofs and walls fell on them and crushed them to death.

My mother was working at the time at the 'Palais Royale' (still standing) which is located between Lakeshore Blvd West and the lake and just east of Parkside Drive. The place was a combination restaurant and dance hall where famous dance bands performed such as those of Artie Shaw, Count Basie, Duke Ellington and Benny Goodman, just to name a few.

Originally she was hired during the summer to sell ice cream waffles to the people attending the Sunnyside Amusement Park across the street since ice cream wasn't sold at the park. Her employer was impressed with her work. For this reason, she was hired on as a permanent full-time waitress and because of that, she couldn't look after us during the afternoons and nights of the weekdays so she hired a Dutch woman to care for us. The woman was in her fifties and lived with us. The Dutch nanny shortly thereafter quit and several other women took her place in the firing line. Those women didn't stay long either. My mom said that it was because my brother and I gave them so much trouble. One of them returned for a second round with us but she was KO'd within a week or so and didn't return. I can't believe that my brother and I, the 'sweet wonderful kids' that we were, were so bad that trained nanny's couldn't bear us more than a month or so. It was hard to get good help those days. The war factories were begging for women to work in them so I suppose the nannies had better opportunities there than merely looking after us two 'charming kids'. That's my theory in any case—for what it's worth.

I remember the Christmas tree we had at 8 Earnbridge. It went right to the ceiling and when my brother leaned against it, it went right to the floor. My father came home for Christmas that year. It was one of the few Christmases he shared with us. After Christmas, he left and spent the rest of his Christmas leave with his mother. It was then that my mother noticed that the large diamond ring my father had given her several years earlier (and made from one of the large diamonds that was on my father's mother's bracelet) was missing from her jewelry box. When considering the kind of man my father was, it didn't take my mother long to conclude that the ring was sitting in a pawn shop somewhere downtown or alternatively, had been placed on another woman's finger. And that is how 1940 ended for her and my brother and me.

By the end of 1940, annual salaries were up to $1,299, (I get more than that in federal old age and Canada pensions a month) eggs were 33 cents a dozen, bread was 8 cents a loaf, (in 2003, it was $1.47) butter was 36 cents a pound, bacon was 27 cents a pound, round steak was 36 cents a pound, oranges 29 cents a dozen and coffee was 21 cents a pound. A glass of Coca Cola cost as little as 5 cents. The Canadian dollar in 1999 would have been worth $11.63 in 1940.

In 1940, you could sail on a passenger liner operated by the 'Great White Fleet' from New York to Panama return; all expenses paid for 15 days for as little as $210.00. A nine-day cruise to and around the Alaska Panhandle return cost only $150.00. My wife and I did that same cruise in this century for $900.00 each. You could also sail on the 33,000-ton luxury liner, the SS *Brazil* for 38 days visiting all the major cities along the coast of South America for as little as $360.00.

Gasoline to run your car was 14 to 19 cents a gallon. You could buy a brand new Plymouth 2-door for $649.00 and a 4-door for $699. Now if you were rich and could afford a chauffer to drive you about, you could buy a real fancy car that had a sliding glass panel that separated you from your chauffer and which had separate heating for the passenger part of the car and a two-way radio between you and the chauffer. All of this would cost you $3,895. Hey! If you could afford a chauffer, you could afford this 8-cylinder Buick Townmaster.

Of course, you wouldn't take that car across country so you could take a greyhound bus across the country from New York City to San Francisco for as little as $69.00. You could alternatively take the same trip by train in a Pullman sleeper for as little as $180.00. Of course if you could only afford to take the trip sleeping in a comfortable seat next to the window, it would cost you only $90.00. I remember taking an overnight trip from Toronto to Montreal in a sleeper and it cost me $90.00. Actually, that wasn't bad considering that I also had my own bed, toilet and sink.

In 1940, the largest inner tubes were built for four tires for Admiral Byrd's expedition across the Arctic for his snow cruiser. The diameters of these 12-ply inner tubes were 10 feet (3.04 metres) and each weighed 700 pounds. (317 kilograms) Try pumping air into those tubes by hand. Those tires were as big as the four tires of the BigFoot truck making it the tallest, widest and heaviest pickup in the world. Those tires were originally used on an Alaskan land train that was used by the US Army in the 1950's.

I don't remember much of what happened to me between Christmas of 1939 until the end of June 1940. Little snippets of memories show up occasionally however. For example I remember my father was home on leave in the spring of 1941 and I asked my father's permission for me and my brother to go to Sunnyside with the two boys living next door to us. The Sunnyside Amusement Park was a little over a mile (1.7 km) west of us along Queen Street between the lake and High Park.

Sunnyside was then, what the Midway at the Canadian National Exhibition (CNE) is today, except the rides then were very mundane with the exception of the roller coaster, the Flyer. We didn't have any money with us for the rides but we were given five cents each to buy candy at the Sunnyside Amusement Park.

For anyone who wasn't born before 1956 or lived in Toronto before then, they would not remember the Sunnyside Amusement Park. It was the poor man's Riviera and one of Canada's most popular amusement parks. It ran east and west along the curve at Lakeshore from the CNE to the Humber River with High Park immediately to the north. The amusement park was closed on Sundays but remained open other days until midnight—with the exception of the winter months of course.

The Flyer (a roller coaster) was something to watch when it roared down the steep incline to the bottom. On the day my brother and I and the others went to Sunnyside, we stood at the base of the Flyer waiting for its first run past us. The previous night, it had rained quite heavily and at the bottom of the run, there was a large body of water that hadn't run off. Now the significance of what would happen to that body of water when the Flyer hit it didn't dawn on us as we waited for the Flyer's first run of the day. When that Flyer came down and hit the water, a wave rushed out towards us that would make a tsunami look like a ripple in a bathtub. I have seen some mighty big waves in my day, especially in the Atlantic and the Pacific but believe me; very few ever made an impression on me like the one heading towards us at the bottom of the Flyer. The splash is somewhat similar to that at Wonderland at the Timberwolf Falls when the ride in which people are in a large boat, slide down a ramp and when the bow hits the water, the resulting wave hits the people willing to risk it while standing on the bridge ahead of it.

There were three large merry-go-rounds at the park. They were the finest in all of North America at that time and cost approximately $50,000 each which was a lot of money in those days considering that it was for each of them, equivalent to one and a half million dollars in 2010. You could ride on them all day and not hear the same repertoire of music being played twice. They were later dismantled and one of them was shipped to Disneyland in California.

During the hot summer months, thousands upon thousands of Torontonians flocked to Toronto's 'Coney Island' at Sunnyside to either take in the cool breezes off the lake or swim in the Sunnyside Bathing Pavilion (still standing and active in the summer months to this day). This unique concrete structure which looks like an oversized Roman villa was fortunately saved from the sledge hammer in 1979 when the City Council came to its rescue and restored it. Today, like in the twenties when it was built, and in the early forties and late fifties when I swam in it, it caters to thousands of sun worshippers who won't brave the cold waters of the lake but will swim in the large pool immediately east of the Pavilion.

It was during the spring months that I remember a number of other happenings of no significance to anyone other than myself. The first was how easy it was for us to get free ice cream. There was a dairy just off of Queen Street on the south side just west of the railroad bridge west of Dufferin Street. We would sneak around the back and clean out the remnants of the 'empty' cardboard ice cream tubs just being put out. Yes. We knew the exact time they were put outside. That was better than when we would stand by the ice wagons pulled by horses bringing the ice to the ice boxes in everyone's homes. When the iceman broke up the large chunks of ice with his ice pick, smaller chunks would break off and we kids would scramble to the wagon and grab a piece for ourselves. Then we would suck on the ice until it was all gone or until our hands couldn't bear the cold any longer. Listen, in those days, that's all we could afford—free ice flying through the air as 'the iceman cometh and chippeth away'. The horse-drawn bread wagons and milk wagons would also come every day. The horse-drawn wagons carrying coal came several times a month.

The first time the police were ever called on behalf of my brother and me was when we decided to go for a walk on the upper beams under the railroad bridge crossing Brock Ave which was just south of Florence Street. When we were escorted to our mother, she wasn't pleased. She grounded us for the rest of the day and told us to stop doing dangerous things like that in the future. We promised her that we would never play around the railroad bridge again—and we kept our word. Mind you, we played on the railroad tracks a lot after that but we never played around the railroad bridge again. I believed then and as I do now that keeping one's word is paramount. However, if she told us not to play on the tracks and I promised that we wouldn't, my word would have crumbled like stale cookies when they hit the floor.

There was a kid who lived across the street from our house who was always bullying me. I finally figured out a way to stop him from pestering me. Every school day, I 'loaned' him the cent my mother gave me on each of those days for spending money. In 1999 money, that would be 14 cents Canadian and 11 cents American. Try buying candy these days for that kind of money but in 1941, I could get a couple of gumdrops. Now I know why he always wanted to walk to school with me. I figure that with compound interest on the money he owes me, his debt exceeds my stupidity of giving him a cent every day. I'm sure I could have got him to accept three cents instead of five cents a week if I had persevered enough. In any case, I always made up for the loss on Sundays. My mother gave me ten cents for the Sunday school collection box on behalf of my brother and me. Before we got there, I changed the dime to ten one-cent pieces and gave my brother two cents to drop in the collection box and I donated three cents—because I was bigger, and I kept the extra five one-cent pieces to make up for my loss during the previous week of having to pay that extortionist across the street. In the year 2000, it wasn't uncommon to hear of school kids ripping off other school kids at the point of a gun or knife so nothing has changed except of course, the means of extorting stuff from other kids.

It was one day at the end of the summer that I and my brother were taken to the CNE by a young woman who was our next door neighbour. We didn't have to walk very far since the CNE was and still is and will always be in Parkdale where we lived at that time. Some of Canada's darkest years were later dark years for the CNE. In April 1942, the decision to give the Canadian Government the facilities at Exhibition Park on a rent-free basis was made. A month later it was resolved that the CNE would be discontinued for the duration of the war. Until the end of the war, the CNE was used to house the armed forces. My visit to the CNE in 1940 was my last visit to the CNE for many years.

It was during these years that the Toronto School Board felt that all of us growing kids should have milk so that our bones and teeth would grow. I guess they presumed that our parents were too poor to buy milk for us. They were probably right. So every day at morning recess, we all lined up to get our pint of pasteurized bottled milk. It would have been easier to drink if it was cool but as to be expected, it was warm. Warm milk is for night time, not morning recess. I once had the temerity to ask for chocolate milk. The response from Mr. Slater, the principal of the school, reminds me of Charles Dickens's book, *Oliver Twist* in which Oliver held out his bowl and asked for more. Instead of the principal calling out "MORE?" as the headmaster did in *Oliver Twist*, Slater yelled out, "WHAT?"

One day, while walking to school, I stooped down to pick up what I thought was a cigarette card. In those days, the pictures of hockey or baseball players would be printed on the cards. It turned out to be a ten-dollar bill. (equivalent to $309.00 in 2010) so I guess I had found a real treasure. Just as I picked it up, a woman standing nearby saw me and told me that I should take it to the police station on Queen Street, a couple of blocks away. Yes—I actually did just that. She followed me to make sure I did. The police sergeant on the desk took my name and address down and when I got home from school, my mother told me that a lady had come to the door to thank me for turning the money over to the police. She gave my mother her name and address and said that I could go to her house (a couple of blocks away on Brock Street) and get my reward. When I got there, she gave me a dollar. Considering that it only cost six cents for me to go to a movie and my daily allowance was one cent for candy, a dollar was a lot of money to me. In 2010 money, it would have been $39.90. What I find amazing is that the woman who lost the money actually believed that anyone who found a ten-dollar bill on the street would actually turn it over to the police. I only did it because the other woman who saw me pick it up, told me to do so—and she was bigger than I was. Actually if she hadn't seen me pick it up, I would have taken it home and asked my mother what it was. Up to then, I had never seen a ten-dollar bill before. I thought it was a trading card at first. As an interesting aside, in the year 2001, some kids in London England were trading cards of scantily dressed prostitutes with their phone numbers printed on the back of the cards that had been found it telephone booths. There is a very heavy fine awarded to anyone placing such cards in a public place in London. I strongly suspect that these cards will be increasingly valuable (not unlike cards of sports heroes) as time goes on.

Strangely enough, my brother and I rarely went to the McCormick Playground that was on the east side of Brock Avenue and was a couple of blocks north of our street. The playground covered an area of a square block and had swings in it but most of my friends preferred to play in the immediate area of our houses and of course the railway tracks. After all, which is more fun—playing on the swings in a park or running for our lives along side those huge monster steam engines as they noisily ran along the tracks blowing searing hot steam in every direction?

On October 31st of that year, I experienced my first Halloween outside of my house. My mother took me and my brother around the area and I realized for the first time that it was possible to get things for free—and candy at that. I didn't really understand what was meant by 'trick or treat' but I thought it amazing that when I said those words, candies would appear in the adult's hands like manna from heaven and then drop into the bag I was carrying with me. I fully understood the significance of those words when as a father; I would be handing out the 'manna' to kids dressed up as monsters in our neighbourhood in which some of them really were monsters they pretended to be.

In Canada, because the war needs exceeded luxuries, the federal government exercised its powers via the *War Measures Act* to ban the production of such luxuries such as nylon stockings since nylon was needed for parachutes, cars since the car manufacturers were needed to make jeeps and army trucks, and most importantly at least to us children, metal toys were no longer made since the metal was needed to make tanks, planes and bullets. You can appreciate why I and my brother were willing to risk crossing the railroad tracks to pick out our newly-found toys from that bonanza of metal goodies that reached up to the sky—and beyond.

Chapter Fifteen

The signing of the British Commonwealth Air Training Plan Agreement, (BCATPA) between Canada, the United Kingdom, Australia and New Zealand and signed in Ottawa on December 17th, 1939 was a momentous event. Strategically it was important for three main reasons: it furnished air training fields that were reasonably close to the United Kingdom yet well beyond the reach of enemy aircraft, it provided a uniform system of training and It became the basis for the pooling of Commonwealth air power. Initially, the British hoped and expected that the RAF would be the only operational force that would be one big air force to which Canada and the other Commonwealth countries would contribute manpower much the same as in the First World War. This wish was not completely realized for Prime Minister King demanded that a token number of squadrons (the exact number to be decided later on) be distinctively designated as RCAF. The negotiations almost collapsed over this issue but Canadian Prime Minister King refused to sign the Agreement until the weary British delegates reluctantly gave in.

On April 29th, 1940, No. 1 Initial Training School, accommodated at the Eglinton Hunt Club in Toronto, opened its doors on schedule to the members of the first group of 221 trainees all classified as A.C. II (Aircraftman II) at the very bottom of the rank structure entitled to $1.70 equivalent to $52.60 in 2010) a day plus free room and board. Seventeen of these were washed out in training and the rest went on to become pilots, air observers, wireless operator-air gunners and air gunners. One hundred of them, the envy of their comrades, were selected for pilot training, promoted to the exalted rank of Leading Aircraftman at $2.00 a day (equivalent to $61.90 in 2010) and sent to 15 different flying clubs across Canada for the elementary phase of instruction. Forty-seven who finished their training before the others came together again as No.1 Course at No.1 SFTS at RCAF Station Camp Borden. On the 30th of September, 39 of them received their wings. Two were killed in air accidents and the others ceased training for one reason or another. On graduation about half of the groups were commissioned and the others were promoted to the rank of sergeant.

Proud to be proclaimed as the first class of pilots to graduate from the training plan, the new pilots fully expected to be sent overseas and were naturally disappointed to learn that they were needed in the BCATP as flying instructors, staff pilots or in some other capacity. Such was the experience of the next two or three classes of pilots of which nearly all of whom were plowed back into the training scheme. The first class of pilots to go overseas as a body was a group of 37 Australians who graduated in November 1941 from No.2 SFTS at Uplands, Ottawa.

Before this, however, a class of 37 Canadian observers had already arrived in the United Kingdom. As the first observers to complete their training, they received their wings at Trenton on the 27th of October, 1940 and after a short period of leave; they embarked on the *Duchess of Richmond*. Over half of them went to Bomber Command of the RAF and most of the others to Coastal Command. A year later half of them had been killed in action and by the end of the war, two thirds of them had died for their country. I don't think any of them foresaw their deaths when they originally signed up.

Training continued until March 31st, 1945 when the BCATP came to an end. The total number of graduates was 131,553 which included 49,808 pilots, 29,963 observers and navigators, 14,996 air gunners, 18,496 wireless-operator air gunners, 15,673 air bombers, 1,913 flight engineers and 704 naval air gunners. Of the total 72,835 were members of the RCAF, 42,110 were RAP, 9,606 RAAF and 7,002 RNZAF. It should be noted however, that while the United Kingdom, Australia and New Zealand sent recruits to Canada for training, they also operated training bases of their own. Among the RAF trainees there were large numbers of allied nationals; about 2000 members of the Free French Air Force, 725 Norwegians, 260 Czechoslovakians and slightly smaller numbers of aircrew from Belgium and Holland received their wings at various units of the BCATP. As later proclaimed by President Roosevelt, Canada indeed had become "the aerodrome of democracy."

Rearming the United States meant that it needed to purchase munitions and military supplies from Canada and Canada needed credit. On April 20th, 1941, Prime Minister King met with President Roosevelt at Hyde Park, a small village which is 18 miles (29 km) east of New York City where the president had an estate on the Hudson River away from the White House. An agreement was reached where the economies of Canada and the United States were integrated.

What was unfortunate was that MacKenzie King was originally asked by Great Britain back in 1937 for permission to have British Airmen train in Canada but he refused their request for reasons that have escaped me. Perhaps he made the decision after reading his tea leaves. As a result of that refusal, when Germany began to attack England by air after the war started, the RAF didn't have enough trained airmen and for this reason, they could only train them for six months in Canada since so many of those before them were being killed off by the better trained German airmen who had got their experience in the Spanish Civil War. This just goes to show how stupid some politicians can be.

From the first days of the German battleship, *Bismarck*, the ships projected power. The *Bismarck* would not have a long history though. From the start of the *Bismarck's* active 6-day life, there would be action. The British would concentrate all of their resources in order to stop the mission of Commerce raiding in the Atlantic bestowed on Captain Ernst Lindemann, who would insist that his ship be referred to as 'he' instead of 'she' which is the custom around the world. He said that his decision was based on the fact that the ship was named after the Great Prussian Chancellor Otto Von Bismarck, and for the power that 'he' represented. Admiral Raeder sent out the *Bismarck* on a mission of commerce raiding against the Allies in the spring of 1941. He had seen the efforts of other commerce raiders as successes, even though the *Graf Spee* had been lost despite her brilliant raiding career and the *Scharnhorst* and *Gneisenau* had been damaged with only one good raiding season including the sinking of the British carrier *HMS Glorious*. Admiral Raeder had envisioned having the cruiser *Prinz Eugen* along with the *Scharnhorst* and *Gneisenau* and the Bismarck's brother the *Tirpiz* fighting the British warships at sea.

But this was not to be. The *Scharnhorst* and the *Gneisenau* were in port for repairs. The *Tirpitz* was not ready for sea. Admiral Raeder would make the grievous error of sending the *Bismarck* out with the semi-completed *Prinz Eugen*. This would be the start of a chain of errors that would mean the death of many German sailors along with many British sailors.

The *Bismarck* was to sortie on May 18th, 1941. The British, who were dedicated to the task of sinking it, chose to include all of their Atlantic ships to sink the *Bismark*. The first to get there was the *HMS Prince of Wales* and the battle cruiser *HMS Hood*. The *Hood* could be best described as the pride of the British Fleet. Having sailed around the world many times before the war, the *Hood* was a well known and feared ship in the Royal Navy. This would not help her against the 15-inch shells and accurate fire of the *Bismarck* though. On May 23rd, at six in the morning, the *Hood* was sunk in three minutes after a shell from one of the salvos from the *Bismarck* pierced the thin deck armour of the *Hood* and ignited her magazines. The *Bismark's* shell smashed its way into the *Hood's* aft magazines. It erupted in a massive explosion. The great ship sank with all but three of her large crew of 1,418, an event that shocked the Royal Navy, the British nation and the entire world. The *Prince of Wales* would be heavily damaged also in this battle. In this action though, the *Bismarck* did sustain slight damage.

The mighty German ship was taking on water and leaking fuel.

Instead of taking the *Bismark* along with its victory against the *Hood* to Kiel, a naval port in northern Germany in the Baltic Sea, its home port, the captain of the *Bismarck* decided to make way for the French port of Brest. The British would sortie most of their Atlantic Fleet to sink her, including the battleships *King George V*, *Rodney*, cruisers *Norfolk*, *Suffolk*, *Sheffield*, *Dorsetshire*, along with the carriers *Victorious*, and *Ark Royal*.

The British fleet finally caught up with the *Bismarck* and they launched their attacks. There were two unsuccessful torpedo attacks against the mighty *Bismarck*, (one attack accidentally heading towards the British heavy cruiser *Sheffield*, which she successfully avoided). Incidentally, I once toured that great warship, *Sheffield*. The British launched another torpedo attack, this time being more decisive. One of the *Fairey Swordfish* torpedo bombers successfully fired a torpedo in the rear of the ship, jamming the ship's steering gear. The *Bismarck* then trapped in a 360 degree turn caused by the rudders being jammed at 12 degree right turn, was helpless in the water. Hitler being apprised of the situation, radioed the *Bismark* offering Germany's highest award to anyone who could free the *Bismark's* rudder but alas for the crew of that huge ship, the British closed in and continuously fired upon the *Bismarck* until the *Bismark* sank at 10:47 A.M. on May 27th. The *Bismarck* had 2,876 shells and 12 torpedoes fired at it by British ships throughout the battle. More than 400 of these shells had hit the *Bismark* and along with the scuttling charges set by surviving crew members, this ending the first and only battle of the great German capital ship. After she sank, only nine German sailors out of 2,009 survived its sinking. Another 300 could have been saved by the crew of a British destroyer but regretfully, the latter was scared off by a nearby German submarine, thereby leaving the Germans to drown.

During the week of 22nd to 29th of June 1941, thousands of Ukrainian political prisoners were murdered in their cells by the Soviet secret police, the NKVD (later called the KGB). Soon after the German attack on the Soviet Union, the retreating Soviets had no time to care for their own prisoners locked up in prisons in the Ukraine, so they too were murdered. In some cities the entire prisons were set on fire and the helpless prisoners burned to death. In Lutsk, 2,800 prisoners were murdered. In the city jail of Lviv, as many as 2,400 dead bodies were found by German troops. Some were killed by hand-grenades thrown into their cells however; most were killed by a shot in the neck. Altogether, in the Ukraine, around 10,000 political prisoners were killed in their prisons. It is an ironic fact that many members of the NKVD execution squads in the Ukraine were Jewish.

More than any other city in Europe, 420,000 Jews in which 100,000 were children who lived in Lviv were murdered by the Nazis during the Holocaust. The Nazis also ordered transports of Hungarian and Romanian Jews to Lviv to be slaughtered once the Polish and Ukrainian Jews had been killed. A Ukrainian woman who was a small child during those years said she saw Jews being whipped repeatedly while they walked on their hands and knees for hours before they were shot dead while the Nazis laughed.

The beginning of 1941 was pretty glum for the Allies. The war was spreading across the globe like an out-of-control skin cancer. Hitler had decided to assist Mussolini with the latter's attempt to conquer all the countries bordering the Mediterranean. To begin with, Hitler' Luftwaffe began bombing Malta in January.

Meanwhile atrocities continued to abound everywhere. In Rumania, the Iron Guard slaughtered hundreds of Jews by beating them and then pouring gasoline over them and setting them alight. Others died in fires in the buildings they were trapped in. Fifty were taken to a slaughterhouse, strung up by their heels and after their throats were cut, they died watching their life's blood squirting onto the floor below them. Later, their dead bodies were cut down and beheaded. Thousands of Jews were starving to death in the Warsaw Ghetto—at a rate of 60 to 70 a day. Many were removed from their homes by their families and placed on the sidewalk in hopes that their bodies would be taken away and buried. Often they laid there for days at a time.

Many Jews in ghettos across Eastern Europe tried to organize resistance against the Germans and to arm themselves with smuggled and homemade weapons. Between 1941 and 1943, underground resistance movements formed in about 100 Jewish groups. The most famous attempt by Jews to resist the Germans in armed fighting occurred in the Warsaw ghetto. I am going to jump ahead in my memoir and go directly to the Warsaw Ghetto Uprising.

In the summer of 1942, about 300,000 Jews were deported from Warsaw to the Treblinka extermination camp. When reports of mass murder in the killing center leaked back to the Warsaw ghetto, a surviving group of mostly young people formed an organization called the Z.O.B. (for the Polish name, Zydowska Organizacja Bojowa, which means Jewish Fighting Organization). The Z.O.B., led by 23-year-old Mordecai Anielewicz, issued a proclamation calling for the Jewish people to resist going to the railroad cars. In January 1943, Warsaw ghetto fighters fired upon German troops as they tried to round up another group of ghetto inhabitants for deportation. Fighters used a small supply of weapons that had been smuggled into the ghetto. After a few days, the troops retreated. This small victory inspired the ghetto fighters to prepare for future resistance.

On April 19th, 1943, the Warsaw ghetto uprising began in earnest after German troops and police entered the ghetto to deport its surviving inhabitants. Seven hundred and fifty fighters fought the heavily armed and well-trained Germans. ZOB commander Mordecai Anielewicz led resistance forces in the Warsaw ghetto uprising. In the first days of fighting, Anielewicz commanded the Jewish fighters in street battles with the Germans. On the third day of the uprising, forces under German commander SS General Juergen Stroop began burning the ghetto, building by building, to force the remaining Jews out of hiding. Jewish resistance fighters made sporadic raids from their bunkers, but the Germans systematically reduced the ghetto to rubble. Anielewicz and those with him were killed in an attack on his command bunker, which fell to German forces on May 8th.

On May 16th, 1943, Stroop ordered that the Great Synagogue on

Tlomacki Street was to be destroyed to symbolize German victory. The ghetto itself was in ruins. Stroop reported that he had captured 56,065 Jews and destroyed 631 bunkers. He estimated that his units killed up to 7,000 Jews during the uprising. The Germans had slowly crushed the resistance. Approximately another 7,000 were deported to Treblinka, where they were gassed. The Germans deported virtually all of the remaining Jews to the Poniatowa, Trawniki, and Majdanek concentration camps. His report to Hitler was bound in human skin. Later in 1943, Stroop was appointed SS and political leader of Greece.

In early May 1945, Stroop was captured by American forces in the town of Rottau in Bavaria. Wearing the uniform of an infantry officer, he bore false discharge papers made out to a Wehrmacht Captain of Reserve Josef Straub. He kept to this story for nearly two months before admitting to being Jürgen Stroop on July 2nd 1946. He was then put on trial by the U.S. Military Tribunal at Dachau for the summary executions of Allied airmen downed over Germany in his field of command. On March 21st, 1947, he was sentenced to death by the tribunal. However, that sentence was not carried out; instead, he was extradited to be tried in Poland. On July 23rd, 1951, after a public trial lasting three days, a Polish court sentenced Stroop to death. On Thursday, March 6th, 1952, Stroop was hanged outside the Mokotow prison in Warsaw near the site of the Warsaw Ghetto in front of a large cheering crowd. As was the policy in Poland then, war criminals sentenced to be hanged were dropped less than 12 inches, thus they slowly strangled to death. As he was being hanged in front of a cheering crowd, I was at about that same moment, reporting to the navy base, HMCS *Naden* on Vancouver Island after having had my 30-day's leave in Vancouver. Now back to 1941.

In the spring of that year, Hitler marched on Yugoslavia and Greece and in a frenzy, he ordered 'punishment bombing' of the city of Belgrade, the capital of Yugoslavia. After three days of nonstop bombing, the Luftwaffe leveled the city and killed 17,000 civilians in the process.

On April 5th, the highly respected German soldier, Field Marshal Erwin Rommel (called by the Allies as the 'Desert Fox') launched his African offensive through Lybia on his way to Cairo, Egypt. Within a month, he was already in the western regions of Egypt.

On April 20th, the city of London experienced one of its worst bombing raids. As many as 712 German planes dropped over 153,000 incendiaries and 1,026 tons of high explosive bombs onto the city and in the first week of May, the Luftwaffe dropped bombs on the city of Liverpool causing extensive damage and killing many of its citizens.

At the end of May, the German Luftwaffe flew as far northwest as neutral Dublin and bombed that city in Ireland.

At the beginning of June, 1941, the Germans successfully invaded the island of Crete, forcing the British to flee with about 18,000 men and having to leave another 12,000 behind to be captured by the Germans. As the German parachuters floated down onto the island, they were machine-gunned from below causing some to fall lifeless into the sea, others to fall into trees where they were shot and other's still to fall to the ground and be clubbed and knifed to death. Of the 3,500 German parachutists who dropped out of the planes, few actually survived. It was not a good parachute drop but despite this, the Germans finally overran the island of Crete by other means and by shear numbers alone.

When things were going rather well for Hitler, his second in command, Rudolph Hess, on his own quixotic initiative, flew out of Germany and parachuted into England on a self-imposed mission of peace with the British. One could understand why he had done it of course.

Rudolf Hess had previously been very close to Hitler. They in effect, started the Nazi Party together and when they were arrested after their feeble attempt to take over the country, they were jailed together and Hess became Hitler's personal secretary. In fact, it was Hess that Hitler dictated his book, Mein Kampf. (*My Struggle*) When Hitler was rising to power, he assured Hess that he would always be his second in command. But as the years progressed, Hess found himself being eclipsed by others, such as Goering, who had become the Reich Marshall, Gobbels who was Hitler's propaganda chief, Himmler, who had become the head of the secret police, the Gestapo, Bormann who was the head of the Party Chancellery and private secretary to Adolf Hitler and close confidant and of course, so many others who played a much more important role in the hierarchy of Nazi Germany than Hess ever did. His role was more as a figurehead.

Hess believing that he might serve a more useful purpose to the Reich, suggested one day to Hitler that it might be a good idea if he (Hess) flew to England as a go-between and try to bring about peace between Germany and Britain. Hitler shrugged and said, "It's of no use but if you can, try it." *unquote*. Then no more was said about it. The gesture on the part of Hess was pointless of course. Hess aimed his plane towards the estate of Douglas Hamilton, who by then was also the Duke of Hamilton. He had met Hamilton years previously and respected him, as the Duke was the first person to fly a plane over Mt. Everest.

Hess parachuted out of his plane and landed near the manor of the Duke of Hamilton. Hess had hoped that he could convince Hamilton to act as a go-between for peace negotiations between England and Germany. He never got to meet the duke. Hess was immediately arrested when he landed on the ground by a man with a pitchfork. Hess was quite upset that no one in England was really interested in what he had to say. For all intents and purposes, he was ignored. From May 10, 1941 he was imprisoned in the Tower of London. After the war, he was tried and convicted as a war criminal and sentenced to life in prison. On August 17th 1987, he hanged himself with an electrical chord at the age of 93 in a small shed on the prison grounds of Spandau Prison near the outskirts of Berlin. He had been a prisoner of the Allies for a total of 41 years—much of it as the sole prisoner at the Spandau Prison.

As an interesting aside, the Allies years later were in favour of releasing him but the Soviets didn't agree and since the decision to release him had to be unanimous, he remained as the sole inmate of that prison for years. The motive behind the Soviets decision was that as long as Hess was in Spandau, the Soviets could remain in Berlin. Because of his death, the Soviets had no justifiable reason for remaining in Berlin so they left. After his death, he was buried in a cemetery in Wunsiedel in the family plot but in July 2011, his body was removed along with the headstone because it had become a shrine to neo-Nazis. His remains were cremated and secretly scattered at sea. Now back to 1941 again.

Hitler was furious when he learned what had happened. He even gave orders for Hess to be shot down before he reached the English Channel but it was too late. Hitler's fear was that Hess had been in on all of the major talks between Hitler and his chiefs, and as such, was aware of *Operation Barbarossa* (the planned attack against the Soviet Union) and might spill the beans. As far as I know, Hess never spilled the beans because the invasion of the Soviet Union came as a shock to the Russians and the Allies alike.

It's incredible when you think of it. Hitler had put more on his plate than he could really eat and still he wanted more. He felt that although he and his countrymen were suffering to some degree, he was ready to take on the Soviet Union. The British were more or less holding their own but there wasn't any intentions on the part of the British to attack mainland Europe. The Americans still appeared to be isolationists and Commonwealth countries like Canada, Australia, New Zealand and South Africa were nothing that Hitler had to concern himself about. This is probably why he felt that the only real fronts he had to face would be the North African and Russian fronts.

Fate being fickle as it is, this following story bears retelling. Its significance will become obvious as you read what follows. In 1336, an obscure tribal chieftain, living near the Central Asian city of Samarkland celebrated the birth of his son. He named his son, Timur. Later the boy was crippled by an arrow and because of his limp; he was called Timur the Lame. To the Western world, he is called, Tamurlane. This boy grew up to be one of the most ruthless rulers in history. His empire stretched from the Ganges River in

India to the gates of Europe. Much of Russia was incorporated into his domain. He slaughtered hundreds of thousands of people. After ravaging many of the cities in his path, he built huge pyramids from the heads of his victims—70,000 at Isfahan, 90,000 in Baghdad and 100,000 in Delhi. In Sebsewar, in what was then called Persia (later called Iran) he enclosed 2,000 living people in a tomb and sealed it with brick and mortar. After he died, an inscription was placed on his tomb which stated that should his tomb be opened; a great catastrophe would befall the land.

On June 22nd, Timur's tomb was opened by Russian archeologists. On that same day, Hitler attacked the Soviet Union along the 2,880 kilometre front from the Baltic Sea to the Black Sea with 151 divisions—just over 3 million men. The catastrophe the inscription on Tamerlane's tomb had forecasted resulted in a loss of over six million Soviet civilians alone in the weeks that followed and finally a loss of another 24 million soldiers and civilians during the rest of the war.

The German attack was unexpected. Stalin couldn't believe that Hitler had betrayed him. A Non-Aggression Pact had been earlier signed between Germany and the Soviet Union. It was a one-page document. It read;

"The Government of the German Reich and the Government of the Union of Soviet Socialist Republics, guided by the desire to strengthen the cause of peace between Germany and the Union of Soviet Socialist Republics, and taking as a basis the fundamental regulations of the Neutrality Agreement concluded in April 1926 between Germany and the Union of Soviet Socialist Republics, have reached the following agreement:

"Article I. The two Contracting Parties bind themselves to refrain from any act of force, any aggressive action and any attack on one another, both singly and also jointly with other Powers.

"Article 2. In the event of one of the Contracting Parties becoming the object of warlike action on the part of a third Power, the other Contracting Party shall in no manner support this third Power.

"Article 3. The Governments of the two Contracting Parties shall in future remain continuously in touch with one another, by way of consultation, in order to inform one another on questions touching their joint interests.

"Article 4. Neither of the two Contracting Parties shall participate in any grouping of Powers which is directed directly or indirectly against the other Party.

"Article 5. In the event of disputes or disagreements arising between the Contracting Parties on questions of this or that kind, both Parties would clarify these disputes or disagreements exclusively by means of friendly exchange of opinion or, if necessary, by arbitration committees.

"Article 6. The present Agreement shall be concluded for a period of ten years on the understanding that, in so far as one of the Contracting Parties does not give notice of termination one year before the end of this period, the period of validity of this Agreement shall automatically be regarded as prolonged for a further period of five years.

"Article 7. The present Agreement shall be ratified within the shortest possible time. The instruments of ratification shall be exchanged in Berlin. The Agreement takes effect immediately after it has been signed."

The German foreign minister, Ribbentrop signed for the German Reich Government and the foreign minister of the USSR, Molotov signed it for the Union of Soviet Socialist Republics, their signatures being placed on the document on August 23rd, 1939 a little over a week before Germany attacked Poland. As to expect, Hitler's word wasn't worth the paper it was written on.

Ironically enough, Stalin's own spy (Richard Sorge) in Japan sent him a message by code advising him that Germany was going to attack the Soviet Union on June 22nd but Stalin chose not to believe it. After sulking in his office alone for a week after the attack, Stalin finally emerged on July 3rd and ordered his people to burn their farms, crops and villages in the path of the advancing Germans so that the Germans would face the 'scorched earth' tactics that Napoleon's

Grand Army had faced earlier. The Allies of course were elated with the attack because it meant that Hitler would be confronted with another front; one that would bring some respite to the battle weary Allied soldiers in North Africa. This was unquestionably, Hitler's first major blunder in the war. That statement will become more apparent as you read further in this book.

Despite deep-seated mistrust and hostility between the Soviet Union and the Western democracies, Nazi Germany's invasion of the Soviet Union in June 1941 created an instant alliance between the Soviets and the two greatest powers in what the Soviet leaders had long called the 'imperialist camp': Britain and the United States. Three months after the invasion, the United States extended assistance to the Soviet Union through its *Lend-Lease Act* of March 1941. Before September 1941, trade between the United States and the Soviet Union had been conducted primarily through the Soviet Buying Commission in the United States.

Lend-Lease was the most visible sign of wartime cooperation between the United States and the Soviet Union. About $11 billion (equivalent to $160 billion in 2009) in war materiel was sent to the Soviet Union under that program. Additional assistance came from U.S./Russian War Relief (a private, nonprofit organization) and the Red Cross. About seventy percent of the aid reached the Soviet Union via the Persian Gulf through Iran; the remainder went across the Pacific to Vladivostok and across the North Atlantic to Murmansk. Lend-Lease to the Soviet Union officially ended in September 1945. Joseph Stalin never revealed to his own people the full contributions of Lend-Lease towards their country's survival, but he referred to the program at the 1945 Yalta Conference saying, "Lend-Lease is one of Franklin Roosevelt's most remarkable and vital achievements in the formation of the anti-Hitler alliance." *unquote.* Lend-Lease matériel was welcomed by the Soviet Union, and President Roosevelt attached the highest priority to using it to keep the Soviet Union in the war against Germany.

On July 17th, Reinhardt Heydrick, who was head of the Reich

Chief Security Office under Himmler, had prepared orders for the 'Special Action Groups' (Einsatzgruppen) to begin the murder of all Jews, Gypsies and political leaders in the captured areas of the Soviet Union. The Einsatzgruppen were a special kind of Germany military police who were to conduct the executions. They followed the German army's advance through Eastern Europe and Russia during Operation Barbarossa, exterminating all local Communists and Jews as they went. His orders were followed and the slaughter began in earnest. The SS killers following close behind the advancing German armies, slaughtered hundreds of thousands of Jews and others by hanging them on the multiple gallows festooning the countryside or by shooting them at the edges of the long ditches the victims had been made to dig for themselves. Field Marshal Wilhelm Keitel, chief of the German army's High Command, and recognized by Germans and Allies alike as Hitler's lap dog, ordered the German generals in Russia to cooperate with the EInsatzgruppen and in his own words, "with unprecedented viciousness." This order of his, along with other nefarious orders of his, came back to haunt him at his trial in Nuremberg at the end of the war. He was hanged on October 16th, 1946 in the early hours of the morning in the gymnasium of Spandau Prison just on the western outskirts of Berlin.

By the end of July, Reinhardt Heydrick had received a directive from Reichmarcshall Herman Goering in which the latter ordered; "I commission you to carry out all organizational, material and financial preparations for a total solution for the 'Jewish Question' in the German sphere of influence in Europe." *unquote* The 'Jewish Question' was what to do with European Jewry. That directive later came back to haunt Goering at his trial in Nuremberg also. He too was sentenced to death. The words, 'total solution' later became known as the 'final solution'.

Again, I will jump ahead in my book and deal with the Wannsee Conference just outside of Berlin. At the Wannsee Conference held on the 20th of January 1942, and on further directions of Himmler, Reinhard Heydrich's immediate superior, he chaired a meeting to consider what to do with the large number of inmates in Germany's concentration camps. Heydrich who was the head of Himmler's secret police had invited 14 people to Wannsee, including seven ministers of state, they being: the minister for the Occupied Eastern Territories, the Interior minister, the minister of the Office of the Four-Year Plan, the minister of Justice, the General Government (controlling both central and southern Poland) Minister, the Minister of the Foreign Ministry, the Party Chancellory Minister and the Reich Chancellery Minister. Those in attendance also included, Heinrich Muller (head of the Gestapo), Adolf Eichmann (overseer of the transportation of Jews to the camps) and Roland Friesler, (head of the People's Court) along with four other high ranking SS officers. During the meeting, they enjoyed a small buffet and wine.

What was discussed was the plan to move the Jews from the west to the east where they would be put to work. Any survivors unable to work were to be "dealt with appropriately." That meant that they were to be gassed. The problem of *Mischlinge* (mixed nationality Jews) was also discussed.

Eichmann gave the conference numbers of the Jews living in the occupied territories. This included Nazi occupied territories in Eastern Europe (3,215,500), Germany (131,800), Austria (43,700), France (865,000), Netherlands (160,800), Greece (69,600), Belgium (43,000), Denmark (5,600) and Norway (1,300). He also provided details of the Jews living in countries that the Nazis hoped to have control over during the next few years. This included: the Soviet Union (5,000,000), Hungary (742,000), Romania (342,000), Finland (2,300), Turkey (55,000), Britain (330,000), Switzerland (18,000), Sweden (8,000), Spain (6,000) and Portugal (3,000). Fortunately for the Jews in the last six countries, those coutries were out of reach of Nazi authority so the Nazis had no control over the fate of the Jews in those countries.

At the meeting, it was eventually decided on what became known as the 'Final Solution'. From that date, the extermination of the Jews became a systematically organized operation. It was decided to establish extermination camps in the east that had the capacity to kill large numbers each day including Belzec (15,000), Sobibor (20,000), Treblinka (25,000) and Majdanek (25,000). It has been estimated that between 1942 and 1945 around 18 million Jews were sent to extermination camps. Of these, historians have estimated that between five and eleven million were killed all told. The eleven million figure is in question. Most agree that the number of Jews murdered was closer to 6.5 million.

The Germans intended to slaughter them—men, women, children and babies—and then they proceeded to do just that. By the last day in July, 1941, as many as 10,000 Jews in occupied Soviet Union had been murdered in mass executions. By the end of August, the SS were killing off hundreds of thousands of Jews and other so-called 'undesirables' and the Allies could do nothing to save them at that time even though they were aware of the atrocities to some degree. Churchill couldn't publicly pin Hitler down on the actual figures that were intercepted from radio reports to Germany from the 'action groups' committing the mass executions because to do so, would have compromised one of the best kept secrets of the war—the Allies having access to the German secret code.

Reinhard Heydrick was assassinated by British trained Czech agents on June 4th 1942 at the age of thirty-eight while he was the Protector of Czechoslovakia. Heinrich Muller was last seen in the bunker on the evening of 1st of May 1945, the day after Hitler's suicide. He was never seen again. Adolf Eichmann escaped to Argentina after the war but was later kidnapped by the Israelis and tried and he was later hanged a few minutes before midnight on May 31st 1962, at a prison in Ramla, Israel. His ashes were then dumped in the Mediterranean beyond the territorial waters of Israel. Roland Friesler was killed on February 3rd 1945 when a beam fell on him in his courtroom during an American air raid.

The prime mover behind the expulsion of Berlin's Jews was Albert Speer, Hitler's chief architect who had been given the task of rebuilding Berlin. A close friend of Joseph Goebbels, together in

1941, they planned for the clearance of the Jewish slum areas in the western part of the city. In doing so, Speer could then take control of around 34,000 houses and apartments and start his demolishing and rebuilding programme in Berlin.

The first trainload of these expelled Jews left Berlin on October 18, 1941. There were to be 130 trainloads altogether. On November 30th, a train loaded with 944 Jews left the city bound for Riga in Latvia. Arriving at 9.30 a.m. in Skiatawa, about eight kilometres outside Riga, in zero temperatures and three inches of snow on the ground, they were forced out of the train and shot in deep trenches previously dug in a small forest. Later that day around 4,000 local Jews from Riga itself were transported by trucks to the forest and murdered in the same way at the same spot on the orders of the local SS Commander, Friedrich Jeckeln. By the beginning of 1942, Jeckeln was credited with reducing the Jewish population of Riga from 29,500 to 2,600. This particular massacre was witnessed by Major General Walter Bruns, a German Army bridge building engineer whose testimony is on file at the Public Records Office in London. At the 'Wolf's Lair', Hitler had given instructions to Himmler that the Berlin Jews were not to be liquidated but they were all dead by the time the order finally came through.

On October 5th, 1942, Hermann Graebe, a German engineer and manager of a German construction firm in the Ukraine, and his foreman, inadvertently came upon an Einsatz execution squad killing Jews from the small town of Dubno in the Ukraine. He gave the following eyewitness account to the war crimes trial in Nuremburg:

"My foreman and I went directly to the pits. Nobody bothered us. Now I heard rifle shots in quick succession from behind one of the earth mounds. The people who had got off the trucks—men, women and children of all ages had to undress upon the order of an SS man who carried a riding or dog whip. They had to put down their clothes in fixed places, sorted according to shoes, top clothing and undergarments. I saw heaps of shoes of about 800 to 1000 pairs, great piles of under-linen and clothing. Without screaming or weeping these people undressed, stood around in family groups, kissed each other, said farewells, and waited for a sign from another SS man, who stood near the pit, also with a whip in his hand. During the fifteen minutes I stood near, I heard no complaint or plea for mercy. I watched a family of about eight persons, a man and a woman both of about fifty, with their children of about twenty to twenty-four, and two grown-up daughters about twenty-eight or twenty-nine. An old woman with snow white hair was holding a one year old child in her arms and singing to it and tickling it. The child was cooing with delight. The parents were looking on with tears in their eyes. The father was holding the hand of a boy about ten years old and speaking to him softly; the boy was fighting his tears. The father pointed to the sky, stroked his head and seemed to explain something to him. At that moment the SS man at the pit started shouting something to his comrade. The latter counted off about twenty persons and instructed them to go behind the earth mound. Among them was the family I have just mentioned. I well remember a girl, slim with black hair, who, as she passed me, pointed to herself and said, "twenty-three years old." I walked around the mound and found myself confronted by a tremendous grave. People were closely wedged together and lying on top of each other so that only their heads were visible. Nearly all had blood running over their shoulders from their heads. Some of the people shot were still moving. Some were lifting their arms and turning their heads to show that they were still alive. The pit was nearly two-thirds full. I estimated that it already contained about a thousand people. I looked for the man who did the shooting. He was an SS man, who sat at the edge of the narrow end of the pit, his feet dangling into the pit. He had a Tommy-gun on his knees and was smoking a cigarette. The people, completely naked, went down some steps which were cut in the clay wall of the pit and clambered over the heads of the people lying there to the place to which the SS man directed them. They lay down in front of the dead or wounded people; some caressed those who were still alive and spoke to them in a low voice. Then I heard a series of shots. I looked into the pit and saw that the bodies were twitching or the heads lying already motionless on top of the bodies that lay beneath them. Blood was running from their necks. The next batch was approaching already. They went down into the pit, lined themselves up against the previous victims and were shot." *unquote*

During the occupation of Latvia by Nazi Germany during the summer of 1941, Hubert Cukurs, a famous Latvian aviator became a member the notorious Arajs Kommando, responsible for many of the crimes of the Holocaust in Latvia. Cukurs played a leading role in the atrocities committed in the Riga ghetto. After the war, surviving witnesses reported that Cukurs had been present during the ghetto clearance and fired into the mass of Jewish civilians standing about. Cuckurs also participated in the burning of the Riga synagogues. Cukurs burned the synagogue on Stabu Street, but only after dragging Jews out of the neighboring houses and locking them inside the synagogue before the building was set on fire. Eyewitnesses heard the people who were locked inside screaming for help and saw them breaking the synagogues windows from inside and trying, like living torches, to get outside. Cukurs shot those attempting to escape the flames with his revolver. His crimes not only included the Riga synagogue fire, it also included the drowning of 1,200 Jews in a lake, and participation in the November 30, 1941 murder of 10,600 people in the Rumbula forest near Riga.

After the war, Cukurs escaped to Brazil via France. There, he established a business in São Paulo, flying Republic RC-7 Seabees on panoramic flights. While living in South America he neither hid nor tried to hide his identity.

He was later assassinated on the 23rd of February 1965 by Mossad agents after it was learned that he would not stand trial in Germany for his participation in the Holocaust because of Germany's *Statute of Limitations.* A Mossad agent who had earlier purposely befriended him, cabled Cukurs from Montevideo inviting Cukurs to meet him there. Cukurs was taken by his 'friend' to an empty house in a remote suburb of the city. Once inside the house, Cukurs realized that he was surrounded by assassins and struggled violently to escape but his fight with the five agents was to no avail. He was shot in the head two times with a pistol with a silencer and his body was placed in a large trunk. After the agents fled back to Israel, they contacted the police in Montevideo and told them where they would find his rotting and maggot-infested body. Germany realizing that their *Statute of Limitations* was wrong when it came to war criminals lifted the *Statute* so that other war criminals could still face the music if they were still alive. It is highly unlikely that by the time of this writing (2011) there are many of them still alive.

The Rumbula massacre was the two-day (November 30, 1941 and December 8, 1941) killing of about 25,000 Jews in and on the way to Rumbula forest near Riga, Latvia, during the Holocaust. Save only the Babi Yar massacre in Ukraine, this was the biggest two-day Holocaust atrocity until the operation of the death camps. The first column of people, accompanied by about 50 guards, left the Riga ghetto at 06:00 am. On November 30, 1941, the air temperatures recorded at Riga were -7.5°C at 07:00 hours, -1.1°C at 09:00, and 1.9°C at 9:00 pm. The people could not keep up the pace demanded by the guards, and the column kept stretching out. The guards murdered anyone who fell out of the column or stopped to rest along the 10-kilometer-march route.

The first column of people arrived at Rumbula at about 9:00 am on November 30. The people were ordered to disrobe and deposit their clothing and valuables in designated locations and collection boxes, shoes in one, overcoats in another, and so forth. Luggage was deposited before the Jews entered the forest. They were then marched towards the murder pits. If there were too many people arriving to be readily killed immediately, they were held in the nearby forest until their turn came. As the piles of clothing became huge, members of the Arajs Commando loaded the articles on trucks to be transported back to Riga. The disrobing point was watched carefully by the killers, because it was here that there was a pause in the conveyor-like system, where resistance or rebellion might arise. The people were then marched down the ramps into the pits, in single file ten at time, on top of previously shot victims, many of whom were still alive. Some people wept, others prayed and recited the Torah. Handicapped and elderly people were helped into the pit by other sturdier victims Mothers hung tight to their children.

The shooting continued past sundown into to the twilight, and probably ended at about 5:00 p.m., when darkness fell. The evidence is in conflict about when the shooting ended. One source says the shooting went on well into the night. Their aim may have been worsened by the twilight. The shooters fired from the brink of the smaller pits. For the larger pits, they walked on the bodies among the dead so that they could to shoot victims up close who might still be alive.   Captain Otto Schulz-Du Bois, of the Engineer Reserves of the German Army, was in the area on bridge and road inspection duties, when he heard intermittent but persistent reports of gunfire. Schulz-Du Bois stopped to investigate, and because security was weak, he was able to observe the murders. A few months later he described what he saw to friends in Germany, who in 1980 reported what Schulz-Du Bois had told them. He said that the first thing he came upon was a huge heap of clothes, then men, women, children and elderly people standing in a line and dressed in their underclothing. The head of the line ended in a small forest by a mass gravesite. Those first in line had to leap into the pit and then were killed with a pistol bullet in the head. Six SS men were busy with this grisly chore. The victims maintained a perfect composure. There were no outcries, only light sobbing and crying, and saying soothing words to the children. By the end of the first day about 13,000 people had been shot but not all were dead. Kaufman reported that "the earth still heaved for a long time because of the many half-dead people. The pit itself was still alive; bleeding and writhing bodies were regaining consciousness. Moans and whimpers could be heard well into the night. There were people who had been only slightly wounded, or not hit at all; they crawled out of the pit. Hundreds must have smothered under the weight of human flesh. Sentries were posted at the pits and a unit of Latvian

Schutzmannschaften was sent out to guard the area. The orders were to liquidate all survivors on the spot.

At the end of the war, twenty-four defendants, all members of German mobile killing units, the Einsatzgruppen, were charged with the murder and ill-treatment of POWs and civilians in occupied countries, and with wanton destruction not justified by military necessity.

All twenty-four defendants were found guilty on one or more charge of the charges. Fourteen defendants were sentenced to die, but only four were executed. Why the others weren't executed is a question that is devoid of understanding.

Six of the 15 Einsatzgruppenfuhrer held doctoral degrees; 16 of the 69 Einsatzkommandofuhrer (smaller extermination commando squad) groups also held doctoral degrees. Dr. Franz Alfred Six, the leader of Vorkommando Moskau of Einsatzgruppe B received his doctorate of philosophy in 1936 from the University of Heidelberg. He taught political science at the University of Konigsberg in 1937 and held the chair of foreign political science at the University of Berlin in 1939. He was also the top Jewish expert for the SD (Heydrich's secret police) In 1941 Himmler gave Doctor Franz Six a promotion in writing. "I hereby promote you, effective 9 November 1941 SS Oberfuehrer (somewhere in rank between Brigadier General and Colonel) for outstanding service in the east Einsatz. [Signed H.Himmler]

Doctor Six was sentenced at Nuremberg in 1948 to 20 years in prison, but was released in 1952 even though his Kommando units had killed more than 15,000 people according to the Nuremberg court. Franz Six was also charged with the creation of six Einsatzgruppen to be located in London, Manchester, Birmingham, Bristol, Liverpool and either Edinburgh or Glasgow. These death squads would be charged with the elimination of civilian resistance members and Jews all over Great Britain. After his release from prison, Six was later named head of Porsche advertising after his release. Obviously this is a German insult to the memories of his victims. He died in 1976 in Italy.

Otto Ohlendorf, another Einsatzgruppenfuhrer, held a doctorate in sociology and was a professor at the University of Berlin. Ohlendorf, the leader of Einsatzgruppen D (Crimea) was directly responsible for the deaths of more than 90,000 people. After the war, he was sentenced to death and hanged at the Landsberg Prison in Bavaria on 7th of June 1951.

Paul Blobel was the very heavily-bearded SS commander in Einsatzgruppen C, a mobile killing squad. Blobel commanded Sonderkommando 4a from June 1941 to January 1942 and in that capacity was responsible for the killing of 60,000 people. When Kiev fell to the Germans, his unit organized and carried out the murder of Kiev's Jews at the Babi Yar ravine on September 29-30, 1941. More on that slaughter later. Owing to health reasons brought about mostly by his alcoholism, he was dismissed from his command on January 13th, 1942. Later in the year, he was put in charge of Action 1005, an operation whose goal was to obliterate traces of mass murder.

Blobel was able to convince himself that he was not the lowest person on earth. In the final days of the war, when he knew he faced capture and trial for his crimes, he conjured up a hatred for his drinking partner Eichmann, whom he blamed for his shameful fall from everything that was decent in life. As he lay in the gutter of complete moral irresponsibility, he was determined that he could rise at least an inch or so above Eichmann. With Nazi armies surrendering right and left and isolated units fleeing from the hotly pursuing Allies, Eichmann and Blobel came by chance upon one another in Kaltenbrunner's headquarters in Salzburg. Eichnann advanced eagerly to greet Blobel with plans on how they should pool their resources for a successful escape. Blobel cut him short and went on his way alone and to his eventual capture and his subsequent hanging whereas Eichmann managed to escape to Argentina where he remained for many years before he was apprehended by the Israelis and brought to Israel for trial and execution. Blobel was later sentenced to death by the Americans by their Military Tribunal during his Einsatzgruppen trial. He was hanged at Landsberg Prison on June 8th, 1951.

Landsberg Prison is a penal facility located in the town of

Landsberg am Lech in the southwest of the German state of Bavaria, about 65 kilometres (40 mi) west of Munich. During the occupation of Germany by the Allies after World War II, the US Army designated the prison as *War Criminal Prison No. 1* to hold convicted Nazi war criminals. It was run and guarded by personnel from the United States Military Police (MPs).The first condemned prisoners arrived at Landsberg prison in December 1945. These war criminals had been sentenced to death for crimes against humanity at the Dachau Trials which had begun a month earlier. Between 1945 and 1946, the prison housed a total of 110 prisoners convicted at the Nuremberg trials, a further 1,416 war criminals from the Dachau trials and 18 prisoners convicted in the Shanghai trials. (These were military tribunals conducted by the American forces in Japan between August 1946 and January 1947 to prosecute 23 German officials who had continued to assist the Japanese military in Shanghai after the surrender of Nazi Germany.)

In five and half years, Landsberg prison was used to execute nearly 300 condemned war criminals. Of these, 259 death sentences were conducted by hanging and 29 by firing squad. Executions were carried out expediently. In May 1946, twenty eight former SS guards from Dachau were hanged within a four-day period. Bodies that were not claimed by the families of the condemned; were buried in unmarked grave in the cemetery next to the Spöttingen chapel.

With founding of the Federal Republic of Germany in May 1949 and its abolishment of the death penalty, there were subsequently a number of petitions to close down War Criminal Prison No. 1. On the 31st of January, 1951 the U.S. High Commissioner, John McCloy, agreed to review the sentences from the Nuremberg and Dachau trials. Out of 28 prisoners condemned to death and still waiting for their executions, seven death sentences were confirmed and the other sentences were reduced to terms of imprisonment. The confirmed death sentences included Oswald Pohl, Hans-Theodor Schmidt (adjutant of Buchenwald), and George Schallermair (an SS sergeant at Mühldorf, a Dachau sub-camp). The final executions were conducted on the 7th of June 1951. Incidentally, it was in this prison that Hitler served time when his putsch failed in Munich.

Hitler's siege of Leningrad (later called St. Petersburg after Stalin's death) began on September 8th, 1941 and lasted 900 days. With little food to eat, many starved or were killed by bombs, but the city's determined resistance did hold Nazi troops at bay and helped turn the tide of World War II. This was certainly the most tragic period in the history of this city. It was full of suffering and heroism. For everyone who lives in St. Petersburg the Blokada (the Siege) of Leningrad is an important part of their heritage and for the older generations it brings the memories that they will never forget.

Less than two and a half months after June 22nd, 1941, when the Soviet Union was attacked by Nazi Germany, German troops were already approaching Leningrad. The Red Army was outflanked and on September 8th, 1941 the Germans had fully encircled Leningrad and the siege began. It lasted for 900 days, from September 8th, 1941 till January 27, 1944. The 2,887,000 civilians (including about 400 thousand children) plus troops didn't even consider any German demands for surrender despite the fact that food and fuel stocks were very limited (1-2 months only). All the public transport stopped. By the winter of 1941-42 there was no heating, no water supply, almost no electricity and very little food. Eventually the radio station stopped broadcasting music and news but a ticking clock was placed next to a microphone in the control room and as long as that clock could be heard over the radio, it was a sign that Leningrad hadn't surrendered. In January 1942, in the depths of an unusually cold winter, the lowest food rations in the city were only 125 grams (about 1/4 of a pound) of bread per day. In just two months, January and February, 1942, approximately 200 thousand people died in Leningrad of cold and starvation. As many as 148,000 German shells and bombs struck the city. Notwithstanding all of that, the Soviet war industry still continued to operate inside the city.

A supply route involved crossing the frozen Lake Lagoda. The lake was frozen enough to stop barges bringing in supplies. Ironically, though the weather was extremely cold for the people of Leningrad, it was not cold enough to sufficiently freeze the lake to allow it to cope with the weight of lorries. The ice had to be 200mm thick to cope with the weight of the lorries. It only achieved such a thickness at the end of November, and on November 26th, eight lorries left Leningrad, crossed the lake and returned with 33 tons of food. It was a major achievement - but the city needed 1000 tons of food each day to function. Once the ice had proved reliable and safe, more journeys were made and occasionally this mode of transport brought in 100 tons of food a day.

By the time October 1941 arrived, Russian troop strength had been reduced to 800,000 men, a total of 90 divisions and only 364 aircraft. Hitler on the other hand had 80 divisions (600,000 men) backed by 1,400 aircraft in Army Group Centre alone. The Germans were only 65 miles (104 km) from Moscow and had occupied 600,000 square miles of the Soviet Union. By the time winter had fallen on that part of the world (December 1941) the Germans had got to within 21 miles (40 km) of Moscow. Then Hitler decided not to go farther as he had to outfit his army for the winter months. Since he had earlier believed that he would conquer Moscow before the winter had set in, his army was outfitted with summer wear only. Napoleon made the same mistake. That part of the world can get so cold, the temperatures can drop to 60 degrees farenheight (15.5 Celsius) below zero and even colder when factoring in the wind chill. Sentries who fell asleep, never woke up. German soldiers had to light fires under their tanks for hours to warm up their engines enough to operate. There were 100,000 cases of frostbite in the German ranks and over 2,000 men had limbs amputated as a result. Hitler didn't know it at that time that the Soviets had lost over 4 million men. The remaining Russian soldiers fought with such ferocity, they had recaptured in less than six days in December as many as 400 towns and villages. By the end of 1941, the Center Army Group of the Germans were almost encircled by the Russian soldiers.

By the end of 1942, the city had a population of less than 1 million.

In June 1941, it had been 2.5 million. Though the authorities may have had great difficulty gaining accurate figures for the city's true population, the effect of the siege is clear from these figures. Disease, starvation and those who fled the city may well have accounted for 1.5 million people.

The siege was only lifted after the Germans, as part of their general retreat, withdrew in the face of the advance of the Red Army. Of the half million casualties suffered by the Germans, as many as 125,000 were killed.

Soon after, one of the great ironies of the war occurred. Those who had led the city in its time of need were arrested by the KGB (presumably on the orders of Stalin). Their crime was that they had failed to contact Moscow frequently enough during the siege to ask for support and guidance and that this policy of acting alone like mini-tsars could not be tolerated. Those arrested, after 900 days of being besieged, now had to face life in Stalin's gulags.

Chapter Seventeen

One day in 1941 while I was still living on Earnbridge Street, I did a small task for an employee of a nearby factory. He gave me ten cents. I asked my mother if I could apply for a job at the factory. I was seven years old at that time. My mother told me it was out of the question but said that she would let me wash the dishes if I wanted to. I can't believe that I actually agreed to wash the dishes pro bono—and actually liked doing it. As to be expected, I soon grew out of that foolishness.

It is a known fact that our sense of smell is tied to one's emotions and will bring back memories like nothing else can. The human nose has 10 million olfactory receptor cells in it and these cells are receptive to thousands of different kinds of smells. When the message of a scent reaches the minute nerve cells which operates like an electric switch—on and off (not unlike a binary code in computers) the message goes deep into the brain where the signal searches the brain's memory bank to see if a similar message has been received in the past. If it finds a previous encounter which has been recorded in the memory bank, that information is brought to the fore, almost like reliving the experience again. For example, the smell of bunker oil instantly brings me back to the days when I served on warships when I was in the navy. The smell of perfume brings me back to the days when I lived with a male school teacher and his mother when I put his mother's perfume into flowers I had picked to enhance the scent of the flowers. The smell of waffles takes me to a small cafe a short distance from my mom's apartment in Palm Springs, California. The smell of burning paper brings me to my teenage days when I lived in Vancouver trying to smoke tobacco in rolled newspaper. Don't do it. It tastes like it is—burnt newspaper. Fragrances unfold differently on different people. Further, the temperature of your skin and even your genetic makeup will have an effect on your ability to differentiate various scents. Some unfortunate people are however born with a less powerful sense of smell.

It is the smell of tea that brings me to the backyard of 8 Earnbridge. Somehow, I had gotten a hold of a large square wooden tea box that was lined with silver paper. I don't know what kind of tea had been shipped in the box as there are over 3000 varieties. I used to climb into the box and sit there for hours with the sunlight reflecting off the silver paper into my face. Listen, in those days, what else was there to do? We had no TV, we didn't have a radio, and I could sit in the box and literally escape the world as no sounds of the outside world could be heard from inside the box.

I remember seeing my first zeppelin. We were in the alley behind our house and suddenly one of the neighbourhood boys began yelling. We all looked up and there it was. This huge airship was floating across Toronto and we could hear the sounds of the engines propelling it eastward. In those days, they flew quite low so to us kids, it was very, very big. That zeppelin in our eyes; would make the Goodyear blimp of today look like a wiener in the Harlem Tunnel.

There are two things I enjoy doing and I generally do them both at the same time and that increases my enjoyment. It's eating and reading. For almost all of my life, I have been reading newspapers or books or magazines during my meals. I got into this habit when I was seven years old. I don't know why I had to eat my lunch at a small table next to the window in my bedroom when I lived at Earnbridge but I read from a fairy tale book while I was eating my lunch at that address. Later, as I got older, it was comic books, then school books and later still, magazines and finally, daily newspapers. Well, it's better than the prostitute who indulged in her two favorite activities at the same time—having sex with her tricks (johns) and eating an apple.

My wife has learned to live with this reading/eating idiosyncrasy of mine by simply ignoring me at the table. Mind you, I don't do this when we are having our Easter, Thanksgiving or Christmas dinners or when we have guests over for dinner, so as you can appreciate, I'm not completely addicted to this uncivil habit. However, at times, I have regressed back to my early days of eating my lunch and reading fairy tales—that is, government reports.

My aunt Althea—my mother's sister—had decided to move to Wells, B.C. This small town is 475 miles (764 km) northeast of Vancouver, British Columbia, Canada in the Cariboo Mountains wilderness. Her sister and her sister's husband, Harold Fullerton had moved there the previous year or so. He had been given the job as the principal of all three schools (Elementary, Junior High and Senior High) in that small gold mining town. My mother's sister and my mother got along splendidly as sisters and so my Aunt Althea wrote my mother and asked her to come to Wells to live. When the summer of 1941 had rolled around, my mother decided to accept my aunt's suggestion to visit Wells for the summer to investigate the possibilities of us living there.

Naturally, my mother had to place my brother and me somewhere for the summer so my maternal grandmother came to her rescue. Her family (the Priests in Bath, Ontario) were friends with the Johnston family in that same area and my grandfather had baptized some of the children in the Smith family who were direct descendants from the Johnston family. As it turned out, the Smiths had a large farm on the south shore of Hay Bay in the Bay of Quinty so it was there that I and my brother were to spend our summer of 1941. It was something I wasn't looking forward to since I missed my mother and it appeared to me that I was again being taken away from her or alternatively, she from me.

The farm was and still is located on the peninsula west of Bath (north eastern shore of Lake Ontario) and more or less directly south of Deseronto. The farm is on the southern shore of Hay Bay, on the north side of Concession Road 3 and the farm's northern field, borders

Hay Bay and the bay is about a city block from the farmhouse and barn. Bordering the field and the lake are a number of large trees.

There were four boys on the farm, James, born in 1926, and who died in a car crash in 1992; Jess, born in 1931; Morley, born in 1933, in fact just a week or so before me; and Lyle, born in 1936, who was the same age as my brother. Their sisters who also lived on the farm were; Helen, born in 1928; Edith, born in 1929 and Margarette, born in 1938. With their parents and their grandmother, Mrs. Smith, and my brother and me; there were twelve of us living in that one-story farmhouse.

There was no electricity on the farm, (few farms had electricity then) so everyone congregated in the kitchen after dark to talk or play cards under the light of the Coleman gas lamp. When it was time to go to bed, (eight o'clock for us small ones) I and Morley, (earlier for the wee ones—Dale and Margarette) each of us had a kerosene lamp and that would light our way into our rooms and to light up the bedrooms for anyone wishing to read. I shared the bedroom with Mrs. Smith and my brother slept on a cot somewhere else in the house.

Dairy cows were the mainstay of the farm (as they still are) and in the late afternoon, I, Morley and Jess (my brother and Lyle were too young) would cross the road and walk along narrow dirt road (800 feet—245 meters in length) dividing two of the large fields leading towards the large forest south of the farm and bring the cows home for their milking. To get their attention, we would call out, "Go Boss! Go Boss!" and the cows would come to us and in a single line, follow us down the long dusty road leading towards the barn.

Morley and Lawson Staples, (a boy who lived a mile or so west of the farm) and I who all were of the same age (seven—all three of our birthdays were a few weeks apart) loved to play in the forest and I certainly remember the long thirsty trudge home along that long dusty cow-pied fenced-in dirt road leading from the forest to the farm.

One day when I was with Morley in the forest, he kicked a bee's hive hanging from a low branch of a tree. The average hive has between

20 to 30 thousand bees in it. The bees swarmed out of their hive and chased us down that long dusty road as we ran towards the barn. When I say ran, I really mean RAN. Even when someone isn't allergic to bee's stings, some people will die if they are stung a minimum of a hundred times and it looked like there were more than a thousand bees heading our way. Having been stung once at camp, I didn't want to be stung again. Strangely enough, we didn't get stung, which tells you something about the speed of our flight down that dusty road.

    I remember one of the horses broke loose from the barn and everyone ran for cover in the farmhouse and then we all peered out of the windows as we watched the horse running around the semicircular driveway in front of the house. When the horse had enough, it sauntered back to its stall in the barn. Apparently, several of the horses on that farm had this tendency to bolt but that was the only time I saw one of them do it.

    This didn't alleviate my fear of horses. Considering that I was a small child, these creatures were extremely large and they towered over me. I did two things however to show the boys that I wasn't afraid of horses. The first was to walk under one of the horse's belly. Its belly was higher than I was and to walk under its belly while the horse's feet were pawing the ground did take considerable nerve. I was scared as hell. The second thing I did was to get on the horse's bare back after climbing up a nearby fence and then I clambered on board. At first, it was fun but then I learned to my horror that the horse loved water—I don't mean the water in the trough; I mean the water in the bay. I, on the other hand didn't like water—I don't mean the water in the trough, I mean the water in the bay. There is nothing more frightening for a small boy who can't swim and is afraid of any water above his waist than to be on the bare back of a horse who loves to be in water above its belly. Somehow I survived the ordeal but I didn't get back on the back of a horse until around thirty years later when a girl I knew asked me to take her horse back riding. The horse I rode was called, Gentle Breeze and it answered to that name. I later learned that her nickname was Hurricane and considering the speed that horse would go, I really had no say in the matter. The horse was aptly named. The horse dumped me and I haven't been on the back of a horse since and I might add that I don't walk under the bellies of horses anymore either. What? Do you think I'm stupid?

It was great fun riding on the hay wagon being drawn by the team of horses hitched to it however. Morley and I would jump up and down on the hay as it was piled onto the wagon so that it would be well packed. Then, for the trip back to the farm, we sat atop the hay right in the middle, lest we fall off the edge (it was very high to us seven-year-olds) and we would survey all the land about us as the team was led back to the barn where the hay would then be stacked.

When I was alone, I would play in the bramble bushes behind the house and eat apples that had fallen into them, except those in which worms were crawling in and out of them.

Helen, who was twelve (she seemed much older to me then) hand printed my letters for me that were to go to my mother. I would dictate and she would print. That's the first time in my life I had successfully dictated to any woman. The second time was when a woman at work agreed to let me dictate to her my 1980 speech I was to present to the United Nations as she was typing it. I tried dictating to my wife and one day she told me that I should stop dictating to her. To prove that I was the man in the house, I handed her a pair of my trousers and asked her to get into them. Considering that I was 220 pounds then and she was only 100, it was an easy thing for her to do. Then I said, "As you can see, I am the one who wears the pants in this house." She got out of them and then handed me one of her panties and said, "Try getting into them." I said, "I can't get into them." And she responded with, "And you won't get into my panties until you change your attitude." I changed my attitude real quick.

My maternal grandparents came for my brother and me at the end of the summer. They stayed overnight and the last night that my brother and I were there, my grandfather took all of us to a house several miles away to show us the movies he took while he and my grandmother were in Africa. The house we visited was one of the few that had electricity in that area so the presentation was possible.

Before we left, my grandfather and Mr. Smith had a talk and my grandfather asked for something that could be used by my mother to instill discipline in my brother and me. The other man made him a strap out of a length of an old horse's rein. My mother used it a number of times on us in the years to follow.

I have fond memories of that farm and whenever I smell straw or hay, I invariably think of that farm, notwithstanding the fact that five years later I lived nine months on a farm in Lulu Island, just south of Vancouver. (in which the large city of Richmond is located) I guess the fondest memories we all have are those which got into our minds first.

Forty years later, I decided to try and find the farm on Hay Bay and relive those memories but the problem was that no one in my family knew where the farm was. My mother had never seen it and both of my maternal grandparents were deceased. My Uncle Frank had some idea where it was but he couldn't pinpoint the exact location. He said it was south of Napanee (160 km—100 miles—east of Toronto) on the northeastern shores of Lake Ontario. Actually it is directly south of Deseronto which is a bit west of Napanee. Although the area of Napanee made some sense, I knew that the farm bordered a body of water that was north of Lake Ontario. That meant that either the farm was on a lake or alternatively on a bay. I figured that it was on a bay since anything south of Napanee was the multi-bay peninsula that juts out into Lake Ontario. The peninsula comprises of rolling farmland and forests. This narrowed my search. All I had to do was look for those farms bordering the southern portions of the various bays. The trouble facing me was that it covered a lot of area.

All of Ontario has been stereoscopically photographed so I went to the government buildings in Toronto to study the stereoscopic photographs of the area. I studied the maps and then studied the photographs. All I remembered was a farm house with a semicircular driveway with the road running close to the front of the farm and a body of water behind it and the barn to the east of the farmhouse and field across the road from the farm. Try as much as I could, I couldn't locate it in the stereoscopic pictures. I realized that I would have to go to the peninsula and search for it by car. It was while I and my own family were in Napanee that one of those strange things in my life happened to me. I am speaking of 'coincidences'. This was one of which the chance of it happening even once is so astronomical; it bears retelling. The year was 1981.

My Uncle Frank had told me that he believed that the name of the owner of the farm was a man named Johnston. When I and my family arrived in Napanee and went into the museum (the old jail) I told the curator that I needed to look at the old documents which gave the names of the farmers in the peninsula. I described the farm and told her the year I and my brother had been there and then I told her that the owner of the farm was a man called Johnston.

It was then that the strange coincidental event came about. There was a woman about my age sitting at the long table pouring over some old records and she looked up and said; "The farm you are looking for is owned by the Smith family and it is on Hay Bay." That bay runs into the larger body of water, the Bay of Quinty. It was the one bay I had not looked at earlier through the stereoscopic glasses while peering at the stereoscopic aerial photographs of the area.

I asked her how she knew that and she replied, "When you and your brother lived on that farm in the summer of 1941, my husband who lives down the road from the farm, used to come over and play with you and Morley Smith." I stood there, aghast. It turned out that her husband was Lawson Staples, the seven-year-old boy who lived further west of us down the road. Now I ask you. What are the chances of meeting the wife of an old boyhood friend forty years later at that very precise moment while looking for a farm one had lived on? Twenty minutes later, we would have missed her and perhaps not ever found the farm. In any case, she gave directions on where to look and I took off with great glee in my heart. For at least forty years I had often thought about that farm and now I was going to get visit it again within the hour. It was pretty exciting moment for me as we headed towards the farm.

As we took a side road off of highway 8, and rounded one of the bends. We were now on Concession Road 3. I saw the farm in the distance. It was on our right. We drove up to it and I recognized it right away. I decided not to go to the farmhouse right away because Mrs. Staples told me that Mrs. Smith was living there alone and I didn't want to alarm her by showing up unannounced. However, she told me that Morley and Lyle were living in a large farmhouse we had just passed on our left so I decided to see them first. That house had been divided into two homes to accommodate the families of Morley and Lyle. I went to one of the doors and the man who came to the door turned out to be Morley. I said to him, "I lived on the farm down the road in 1941 with my younger brother. Do you remember me? He asked, "Are you related to Ella Priest?" That was my grandmother's maiden name. I replied, "That was my grandmother." He responded. "Dahn! How are you? We have often spoke of you and your brother and wondered what happened to you both." He then called his brother Lyle and both of their families outside. And then after a few minutes, Mrs. Staples drove by and as she slowed down, she asked, "Was this the right farm?" and I and the other two men replied in unison that it was.

Then the two men and their families and I and my wife and our two daughters drove to the original farmhouse. Mrs. Smith was so excited at seeing me, she was in tears. She remembered my brother and me and showed me a photograph she still had of me and my brother playing in the water of the bay. She invited me and my family back again and a couple of weeks later, we returned and Mrs. Smith put us up and I and my wife slept in a room next to the one I originally slept in 40 years earlier. Mrs. Smith by now was in her eighties and was still the kind woman then as she was when I was a child and it followed that she would make me and my family feel right at home.

There was a big dinner that night as Morley, Lyle, Edith and Helen and their respective families showed up for the reunion. I showed everyone slides of my trips to Europe and Morocco just before dinner. The next day I visited Lawson Staples and his wife and he remembered me. He showed me his magnificent gun collection and later, I and my family visited the museum that his wife was in charge of in the peninsula. Twelve years later, I revisited Lawson and he was in fairly bad shape by then. He was suffering from diabetes, weighed well over 300 pounds, lost both of his legs and was forced to move around in a motorized wheelchair. He wasn't a quitter however. When I saw him in 1993, he was outside working on the repairs of a small motor for one of many electric fans he had been commissioned to repair. He died a few years later.

In 1982, my mother visited us and we all went to see Mrs. Smith on the farm and again Mrs. Smith treated us beautifully. In 1983, I called one of her sons and he suggested that we hold off visiting his mother for a year as she was quite ill and was living with Helen and sometimes with Edith in their homes. In 1984 when I called again, I learned that Mrs. Smith had died in January 1984 and that prior to her death; she had expressed a wish to her sons that I and my family visit her again. Unfortunately I didn't know of her wish and I never saw her again—much to my sorrow and regret.

A Syracuse university made an amazing discovery. Generally when one speaks or writes and prefaces their sentences many times with the pronoun "I" they are the kind of people who think of themselves more than they do others. The university studied the speeches of Hitler, Mussolini and Roosevelt and found that Hitler used that pronoun on the average, once in every 53 words, Mussolini, once in every 83 and Roosevelt, once in every 100. Considering the kind of people they were, the theory had substance.

There were many 'firsts' in 1941—cars with built-in running boards—that is boards not seen after the doors were closed. Tiffany's installed air-conditioning in one of their stores, synthetic rubber was created; stereo music was shown to potential buyers, window burglar alarms were installed and cellophane wrap was sold on the market. Spam was a new kind of processed meat that was sent to England. Cheerios made its first appearance this year as did Quonset Huts.

With the shortage of metal, plastic became common in appliances etc., and silk stockings were rationed.

1 pint of beer cost 5 cents, soft drinks cost 49 cents for a case, 2 pounds of coffee cost 33 cents, a quart of whisky cost $1.59, Veal was 13 cents a pound, shrimp was 15 cents a pound, chicken was 23 cents a pound and a quart of A&P salad dressing cost 25 cents.

Great movies came out this year such as *How Green Was My Valley, Citizen Kane, The Little Foxes, The Maltese Falcon, Sergeant York, Blood and Sand, High Sierra, Meet John Doe* and that great favorite for us kids, *Dumbo*.

New radio shows appeared this year that included, *The Red Skelton Show, Inner Sanctum,* a real spooky show, and *The Thin Man*.

Rosie, the Riveter (named after Rosina Bonavita) was shown on pictures everywhere in North America. It was the emblem showing that women were now working in defence factories.

Pope Pius XII authorized Roman Catholic bishops around the world to allow meat to be eaten on Fridays.

Pan American Airways was advertising that you could travel to 250 cities in 55 countries in their flying boats. In the history of American commercial aviation, the Pan American Airways flying boats occupy an important place. The planes first began carrying mail and then passengers and were part of an ocean-wide network that set a host of aviation records as part of the famous Clipper Ships service. Using these flying boats—a fleet of 25 in total—Pan American became the first airline to cross the Pacific, the first to establish extensive routes in South America, and the first to offer regular airplane commercial service across the North Atlantic. Igor Sikorsky, the Russian genius produced two planes for Pan American, the S-40 and the S-42, which were the first four-engine seaplanes. The former could carry 50 passengers in relative comfort and had a range of nearly 1,000 miles (1,609 kilometers). The S-42 had a range nearly three times the S-40, and was the world's first big luxury airliner.

We moved back to our house at Earnbridge at the end of the

summer and before we went to school that year, my grandmother took my mother, my brother and me to Centre Island across the bay from downtown Toronto. The eight minute trip was quite exciting because we went across the bay in the *Trillium*, a side-wheeler, a boat with paddle wheels on the side of the boat. The *Trillium* was launched in 1910 and I always gravitated to the lower deck when I was on it so that I could look through the small window at one of the side paddlewheels and watch the water swishing around as the paddlewheel turned. I was saddened years later in the 60s, to see that 1,250 passenger ferry languishing in a lagoon at the Toronto Islands. Fortunately, it was later retrieved and given a $1 million dollar facelift and to this day, it still takes passengers for rides around Lake Ontario.

While we were on the island that day, two things happened of consequence. One of the boys on the island was accidentally hit on the side of his head with a softball bat and had to be rushed to the hospital; first by a special boat and then an ambulance. The other occurrence was of a greater magnitude. While we were playing on the island, we suddenly heard a very large bang. One of the planes flying across the bay during the CNE air show, smashed head on into one of the ferry boats. The plane swept the entire top deck of its fore and aft pilot structures etc. There was only one casualty. It was the pilot of the plane. When we were later crossing the harbour on the Trillium, we saw the plane being pulled out of the water by a crane on another vessel. There were other fatalities at the CNE air shows that followed as the years went by, some even more spectacular.

My mother had decided during the summer months that living in that small town (Wells, B.C.) with her older sister (my Aunt Althea) and her husband (my Uncle Harold) would be the best thing for all of us. She was right of course. The town as I said earlier; is in the northern part of the Cariboo Mountains which in themselves are situated in the upper part of the southern interior of British Columbia. It is approximately 120 kilometers (75 miles) west of the Alberta border and southwest of Jasper by approximately 350 kilometers. (217 miles).

When I returned to school in September 1941, I was almost eight years old and I was in grade two instead of grade three. Within a month, my mother, my brother and I were ready for the trip to Wells, British Columbia. We left our house on Earnbridge Street in the latter part of September 1941. The next time I was ever in that house was on July 8th 2001, almost 60 years later. I happened to be driving by that early evening when I notice that construction work was being done in the house. I spoke to the lady who owned the house and she let me look at the inside of the house. Much of the inside had been changed but my room and the room my mother and brother slept in were still the same. The backyard was improved considerably. The woman and her husband had built a beautiful rock garden in it.

Auschwitz was the largest camp complex established by the Germans. It was a complex of camps, including a concentration, extermination, and forced-labor camps. It was located 37 miles west of Krakow, near the prewar German-Polish border town of Oswiecim. At least 1.1 million Jews were killed in Auschwitz. Other victims included 70,000 Poles, 20,000 Roma (Gypsies) and about 15,000 Soviet prisoners of war.

The facilities of Auschwitz I/Main Camp were originally part of a barracks under the Dual Monarchy (later Poland) and were converted into a concentration camp after the war against Poland. After the start of the Russian Campaign, Auschwitz II/Birkenau was rebuilt as a prisoner-of-war camp of the Waffen-SS, to accommodate Russian prisoners-of-war. Later it increasingly served to house Jews, who were deported there from all German-occupied parts of Europe. The arrival of great numbers of people made for severe health-related problems in all the camps.

Every day in all concentration camps, the horrid yell *aufstehen!* (wake up!) accompanied by loud whistles were heard penetrating the barracks long before daybreak when it was still dark outside. The command created general stampede. If a prisoner did not jump to his feet at the first yell, and did not manage to button up the vertically striped greatcoat and tie all rags and tatters with ropes around him lest the wind should tear them off and if he did not have the time to bind his clogs (shoes) with wire lest he should lose them in the snow, once he came out from the barrack to the roll call platform, he had to give up hope as he couldn't do any of these operations with his hands wrapped up in cloth because if he unwrapped them, his hands would freeze.

The prisoners were then ordered to form into columns for the daily roll-call. The command made even the dying men shudder. Often they had to stand in the columns for hours, irrespective of the weather. The roll call was often the one and only event of each day, its major event. There were days when nothing of consequence, beside the roll call, happened. They had one single purpose and that was to form up in rows of fives. That could take as long as four or five hours while the block leaders (kapos) would strike at random with their curbed cudgels if the prisoners were not grouped properly and did not make up the columns in an organized manner. In order to escape the brutes' cudgels, everybody ran towards the already formed lines and wrecked them. The hustle and bustle drove the block leaders angrier as they rushed on the prisoners with mounting rage. After hours of yelling and screaming, while the block leader's cudgels were kept busy at work, the over one thousand prisoners were finally formed into the proper rows. The prisoners were exhausted, hungry, their wounds were bleeding, but they stood at attention waiting for the end of the roll call. Their legs began to sink under them, they grew dizzy but there was no escape. To collapse now, when the lines were made up meant sending the block leaders into a fit of anger. The prisoners were all dressed in vertically striped convict's clothes, wearing clogs on their feet and black caps on their heads. Many were mere skeletons and walking shadows with hollow eyes and sunken cheeks on which sweat mixed with dirt and mud tickled down in black streaks. Some of them had already begun to stagger to their feet. They wouldn't be able to hold out for long. Moans and stifled curses were constantly heard. There were fifteen platforms, stretching on either side of a seven-meter's wide alley between the many buildings that housed the prisoners. There were between 800 and 1,100 prisoners on each platform.

Camp E was waiting for the roll call. And so were the other camps: A, B, C, D, F, bordering one another, separated by a mere barbed-wire fence. And in each camp there were 30 barracks, each with its own platform on which tens of thousand prisoners were standing in the same position. A prisoner once looked sideways when an SS Lieutenant passed by. The prisoner was shot on the spot. A row of fives was not arranged in a perfect line. All of the prisoners in the row were subsequently shot. Food was daily distributed although sometimes that was omitted. Nor were selections made on a daily basis. But the roll call was never left out. From the setting up of the camp and till it was abolished, it was only after roll call that a prisoner could say that he had survived for another day.

The prisoners in camp E of *Birkenau* did not work. They waited to be selected either for the gas chambers or alternatively, sent to another concentration camp in Germany. They did nothing but gaze at the writhes of smoke rising from the crematoria, at the bar bed-wire fences and wait.

Disease was common in the camps. The lice had multiplied to such an extent that typhus was threatening everyone. For this reason all the camps had extensive disinfection and delousing facilities.

Since the end of the First World War, the general fumigant of choice for pest control (lice, bedbugs, fleas, beetles etc.) had been the product Zyklon B (hydrocyanic acid adsorbed onto diatomaceous earth). In Compounds 1a/b of Birkenau, Buildings 5a and 5b each had a wing where one room was reserved for the delousing of clothing with hydrocyanic acid. On the whole, historians today assume that the large cremation facilities in the camps did not serve only the purpose they had originally been intended for, namely the removal of victims of epidemics, which did occur quite frequently despite intensive efforts at disinfection.

After World War II started in 1939, some concentration camps were transformed into sites for carrying out genocide. These camps which were in occupied Poland are sometimes referred to as 'death factories.' These facilities were used for mass extermination, especially that of the Jews. For this purpose, some rooms of the respective cremation facilities were slightly renovated; people were then killed (gassed) there with Zyklon B.

A total of 3.5 million Jews were killed in the gas chambers of the extermination camps, as well as tens of thousands of Gypsies, homosexuals, political prisoners, Jehovah's Witnesses and Soviet prisoners of war. It is estimated that one and a half million men, women and children were murdered there, making it the largest graveyard in human history.

According to eyewitness testimony, there was at that time a 'gas chamber' in Crematorium I of the Main Camp, Auschwitz I. In Birkenau (Auschwitz II), approximately 1.5 miles (2.4 kilometres) away, there are said to have been 4 more 'gas chambers' in Crematoria II through V, as well as two farm houses, located outside the camp itself and renovated for gassing purposes. Auschwitz had been receiving trainloads of Soviet commissars and other POW's who were subject to liquidation. Höess' men (he was the commandant at Auschwitz) had previously shot Russian prisoners at the camps, but on September 3rd, Höess' enterprising subordinate Hauptsturmfuher (Captain) Fritsch thought of an expedient new method based on the camp's own experience at killing off insects in the buildings. The buildings, many of them former Polish army barracks, were full of insects and the camp administration had previously brought in the Hamburg pesticide firm of Tesch and Stabenow to get rid of them. Two experts had fumigated particular buildings with a patented insecticide, Zyklon B, a crystalline form of hydrogen cyanide that turned gaseous when exposed to the air.

On September 3rd, Fritsch decided to experiment with the poison. First he crammed five or six hundred Russians and another 250 sick prisoners from the camp hospital into an underground detention cell. Then the windows were covered with earth. SS men wearing gas masks opened the Zyklon B canisters to remove what looked like blue chalk pellets about the size of peas, and when they hit the air, it creating a cloud of poison gas. After they left, the doors were sealed.

Höess wrote later that death was instantaneous. Perhaps that was what he was told. But he was not present to witness the event; he was away on a business trip. Other sources indicate that even the next day not everyone was dead, and the SS men had to release more insecticide. Eventually all the prisoners died. When Höess returned to Auschwitz, he heard about the successful experiment. On Adolf Eichmann's next visit to Auschwitz, Höess told him about the possibilities of Zyklon B, and, according to Höess, the two decided to use the pesticide for extermination.

SS private Boeck later testified during a war crimes trial; "There was a sign that said, 'to disinfection'. He said 'You see. They are bringing children now'. They opened the door, threw the children in and closed the door. There was a terrible cry. A member of the SS climbed onto the roof. The people went on crying for about ten minutes before the final whimper was heard. Then the prisoners opened the doors. Everything was in disorder and contorted. Heat was given off. The bodies were loaded on a rough wagon and taken to a ditch. The next batch were already undressing in the huts. After that I didn't look at my wife for four weeks." *unquote* The SS guard had poured the Zykon B into vents leading to the gas chamber.

At Birkenau, illusion was the rule. It was not always simple or possible, inasmuch as at least some of the deportees had observed the sign 'Auschwitz' as the train approached the entrance to the camp, or had seen flames belching from the chimneys, or had smelled the strange, sickening odor of the crematoria. Most of them, however, like a group from Salonika, were funneled through the undressing rooms, were told to hang their clothes on hooks and remember the number, and promised food after the shower and work after the food.

These people were told to undress quickly as it was in their own best interest. All gas chambers had a vestry where the victims undressed. To tear the clothes off corpses, which during gassing clang to one another, would have been downright impossible. Therefore each victim had to enter the gas chamber naked. This was true not only for *Birkenau-Auschwitz*, where 2,000 victims entered the gas chambers at a time, but also for the smaller death camps.

The unsuspecting victims, clutching soap and towels, rushed into the gas chambers. Nothing was allowed to disturb this precarious synchronization. When a Jewish inmate had revealed to newly arrived people what was in store for them, he was bodily thrown into the nearby furnace alive by the guards. Only in the case of victims who were brought in from nearby ghettos in Upper Silesia and who had had intimations of Auschwitz was speed alone essential.

The gas chambers were disguised as showers. In Treblinka, 2,500 people could be put to death within an hour. The main killing center however was Auschwitz-Birkennau. It was the largest and harshest Nazi death camp, located in the southwest of Poland. Originally used as a concentration camp in 1940 (after the defeat of Poland), it became a death camp in 1942. The camp included: Auschwitz I (Stammlager); Auschwitz II (Birkenau), the most populated extermination camp; and Auschwitz III, the I.G. Farben labour camp (also known as Monowitz or Buna). As victims arrived by train from all over Europe, they were separated into two lines: men to be used as forced labour; women and children, who were to be killed in the gas chambers that day, or shot to death in a mass grave. As many as 6000 ruthless SS officers worked at Auschwitz.

Auschwitz was liberated by Soviet soldiers on January, 27th, 1945. SS Doctor Kremer made a statement during a hearing held on 18th of July, 1947 about the gas chambers in Auschwitz. He said in part; "I remember I once took part in the gassing of one of these groups of women (from the women's camp in Auschwitz). I cannot say how big the group was. When I got close to the bunker I saw them sitting on the ground. They were still clothed. As they were wearing worn-out camp clothing, they were not left in the undressing hut but made to undress in the open air. I concluded from the behavior of these women that they had no doubt what fate awaited them as they begged and sobbed to the SS men to spare them their lives. However, they were herded into the gas chambers and gassed. As an anatomist I have seen a lot of terrible things: I had had a lot of experience with dead bodies, and yet what I saw that day was like nothing I had ever seen before. Still completely shocked by what I had seen, I wrote on my diary on 5th of September 1942: 'The most dreadful of horrors. Hauptscharfuherer Thilo was right when he said to me today that this is the 'anus mundi', the anal orifice of the world'. I used this image because I could not imagine anything more disgusting and horrific" *unquote*

The following is from the statement of Hans Stark, registrar of new arrivals, in Auschwitz; "At another, later gassing—also in autumn 1941—Grabner ordered me to pour Zykon B into the opening because only one medical orderly had shown up. During a gassing, Zyklon B had to be poured through both openings of the gas-chamber room at the same time. This gassing was also a transport of 200-250 Jews, once again men, women and children. As the Zyklon B—as already mentioned was in granular form, it trickled down over the people as it was being poured in. They then started to cry out terribly for they now knew what was happening to them. I did not look through the opening because it had to be closed as soon as the Zyklon B had been poured in. After a few minutes there was silence. After some time had passed, it may have been ten to fifteen minutes, the gas chamber was opened. The dead lay higgledy-piggedly all over the place. It was a dreadful sight." *unquote*

Hydrocyanic acid was the main ingredient of Zyklon B and is better known as prussic acid which is cyanide based. While some claimed that the gas would need a lot of time to kill, because it would have to spread all over the chamber, that isn't necessarily true since the gas chambers were not that large (those in Krematoria II and III were about 210 square meters), and the Zyklon-B was dropped from four openings (still visible in the ruins of the gas chambers). Nevertheless, death was not very swift. Death was always brought about by suffocation because the Zyklon B had hydrogen cyanide as a main ingredient and when ingested into the lungs, the cyanide slowly suffocated the victims. Cyanide stops oxygen consumption by body tissues. It is hot and bitter when breathed in, produces nausea and a splitting headache. The throat tightens, and the victim gasps for breath, reels, stares wildly without seeing, is seized by convulsions, and falls unconscious. Then, like an expiring balloon, his laboring lungs slowly collapses and his heart and his heart stops beating shortly thereafter. The experience of death by cyanide inhalation could be summed up by the first prisoner to be executed in California's chamber in 1938. His last words as lip-read by a reporter for the *San Francisco Chronicle* were "too slow." Richard Traystman, M.D., Professor of Anesthesiology at Johns Hopkins Medical School, has written: "During this time (several minutes of hypoxia), a person will remain conscious and immediately may suffer extreme pain throughout his arms, shoulders, back and chest. The sensation may be similar to pain felt by a person during a massive heart attack."

Further, the terror of slow asphyxiation qualifies this form of execution as cruel and unusual. I have some idea as to the terror one experiences when slowly being asphyxiated. On several occasions, I suffered from congestive heart failure in which my lungs were saturated with fluid (not unlike pneumonia) and the oxygen was blocked in my lungs. Suffocation is a very scary and horrible way to die.

Prison records at San Quentin Penitentiary in California indicated that average survival time of an executed prisoner was 9.3 minutes, including 1.6 minutes during which the prisoner was reported to be conscious. One prisoner suffered so horribly, he banged his head against the metal pole behind the chair and died as a direct result of the injuries to his head. His death came to my mind when in 1972; I sat in that same metal chair in that same death chamber while visiting the prison system of California at the invitation of the Commissioner of Prisons of that state.

The gas chamber of 'Krema I' was used only for a short time and then it was changed to an air-raid shelter. About 10,000 people were murdered inside it compared to 350,000 and 400,000 in Kremas II and III respectively. If you were to line up 400,000 people who were each a metre (39 inches—a metre) apart, the line would stretch

400 kilometres (248.5 miles). That distance is comparable to driving from San Fransico to Bakersfield. That distance is also comparable to driving west from Ottawa to Buffalo. Standing side by side, they would fill an area that was 2.5 square kilometres (1.6 square miles).

The last time the gas chambers in Auschwitz were used was on October 30th, 1944. During the years they were used, the SS murdered approximately three-quarters of a million Jews in them. Babies, children, old people, the sick and those unable to work were automatically sent to the gas chambers. These were innocent human beings: Jews, Gypsies, homosexuals and Hitler's political opponents—in other words, anyone who did not fit into Hitler's mold of a pure Aryan race.

The SS began evacuating Auschwitz on January 18, 1945. Almost 60,000 prisoners; mostly Jews, were forced on a death march to Wodzislaw. Death marches were forced marches of concentration camp prisoners made over a long distance under heavy guard and extremely harsh conditions. During the forced evacuation of Auschwitz, prisoners were brutally mistreated and many were killed because SS guards shot anyone who fell behind.

On January 27th, 1945, the Soviet army entered Auschwitz and liberated those prisoners who had not been evacuated.

Two German firms, Tesch/Stabenow and Degesch, produced Zyklon B gas after they acquired the patent from Farben. Tesch supplied two tons a month and Degesch three quarters of a ton. The firms that produced the gas already had extensive experience in fumigation. In short, this industry used very powerful gases to exterminate rodents and insects in enclosed spaces and that it later should have become involved in an operation to kill off Jews by the hundreds of thousands had not been brought about by mere accident.

After the war the directors of the firms insisted that they had sold their products for fumigation purposes and did not know they were being used on humans. But the prosecutors found letters from Tesch not only offering to supply the gas crystals but also advising how to use the ventilating and heating equipment. Hoess testified that the

Tesch directors could not help but know of the use for their product because they sold him enough to annihilate two million people. Two of the Tesch partners were sentenced to death in 1946 and hanged. The director of Degesch received five years imprisonment.

Rudolf Franz Höess was born in 1900 and joined the SS in 1933. In 1934 he was attached to the SS at Dachau concentration camp, on August 1, 1938, he was adjutant of the Sachsenhausen concentration camp until his appointment as Kommandant of to the newly-built camp at Auschwitz in early 1940.

In May 1941, Heinrich Himmler told Hoess, "Hitler had given orders for the final solution of the Jewish question. I have chosen the Auschwitz camp for this purpose." Höess subsequently converted Auschwitz into an extermination camp and installed gas chambers and crematoria. Hoess was to become history's greatest mass murderer, the architect and SS Kommandant of the largest killing center ever created—the death camp at Auschwitz, whose name has come to symbolize humanity's ultimate descent into evil.

He admitted being responsible for the death of two and a half million concentration inmates. Despite being responsible for exterminating that many human beings in World War II, he was a mild-mannered, happily married Catholic who enjoyed normal family life with his five children despite their view of the crematoria chimney stacks from his bedroom window. When he had a sexual encounter with an Auschwitz prisoner, he extricated himself by sending her to the gas chamber.

After the war, Höess was hunted down and caught by the British army police sent out to find him. At first he denied being Hoess but after a severe beating, he admitted who he was. He was sent to Poland and put on trial for murder. He was convicted by the Polish Supreme National Tribunal and sentenced to death on April 2nd 1947 and two weeks later, he was hanged in Auschwitz on April 16th, 1947 at the age of 46. The gallows was specifically built for him alone and it was located in the camp where the Gestapo tortured prisoners and his house in the camp could be seen from his gallows.

His death was not an easy one. He only dropped a few inches resulting in him slowly strangling at the end of the rope. While he was slowly strangling to death, there was over a hundred witnesses standing nearby, some of them former inmates of his death camp. No doubt the condemned man heard their cheers as he was slowly dying at the end of his rope.

Four days before he was executed, Höess sent a message to the state prosecutor which included these comments: "My conscience compels me to make the following declaration. In the solitude of my prison cell I have come to the bitter recognition that I have sinned gravely against humanity. As Commandant of Auschwitz, I was responsible for carrying out part of the cruel plans of the 'Third Reich' for human destruction. In so doing I have inflicted terrible wounds on humanity. I caused unspeakable suffering for the Polish people in particular. I am to pay for this with my life. May the Lord God forgive one day what I have done."

On September 8th, the Germans captured the Russian city of Kiev. At the end of the month, it was then that the Germans, under the leadership of Otto Rasch, herded 33,771 naked Jewish men, women and children to a ravine at Babi Yar just outside of Kiev where they were then machine gunned to death.

I have often wondered why that large group of people (and many other similar groups in the years to follow) submitted to being herded like sheep to the slaughterhouse, knowing that the machine gun fire up ahead ringing in their ears was a prelude of what was waiting for them. And equally puzzling is why they would walk to the edge of the ravine after watching those that preceded them being gunned down. There certainly weren't that many armed guards about and if the Jews all bolted in every direction, many would survive, at least temporarily.

I suppose, the key word here is 'temporarily'. As the condemned Jews walked slowly towards their deaths, they were grouped as families. The children wouldn't leave their parents and the parents couldn't abandon their children, and if they all ran away, this is what might have happened. The old, the infirm and the very young would eventually fall behind. If one member of a family fell from a bullet fired from a guard's rifle, the rest of the family would huddle around the victim, only to be shot enmasse within seconds. The victims were all naked so any attempt at sneaking back to their homes were fruitless and there was nowhere else they could flee. The non-Jewish Russians were not sympathetic to Jews so these naked victims would stand out no matter where they fled. In the long run and for the most part, most if not all of them would end up being shot to death anyhow only not as families but as individuals out of sight from their families—alone. I believe that the heads of the families knew this and they felt that it was better to die as a family then live only temporarily and later die alone.

And yet, had they been separated from each other, as was often the practice in the extermination camps, the urge to flee may have been compelling as it was during the Jewish Sonderkommander rebellions when a number of them fled the killing centres at Sobibor and Treblnka in 1943 and Chelno in 1944. And had a small group of the Jews being herded to their deaths at Babi Yar bolted, the entire group may have followed suit without thinking of the inevitable consequences, as following suit would have been instinctive. Throughout history, masses of people have been led to their deaths and submitted meekly to the sword and the bullet. Sadly, it's far too prevalent a human trait to submit meekly to the injustices of our times as it was to those of the past.

The Baltic nations of Estonia, Latvia, and Lithuania, held a very unenviable position in the summer of 1939 prior to the outbreak of World War II. The three nations, which had only recently gained independence at the conclusion of the previous World War, found themselves situated directly between the two nations most likely to plunge them head first into open hostilities—Germany and the Soviet Union. Both of these ambitious nations coveted the territory of the Baltic states in their schemes to acquire land and 'out maneuver' the other, although both countries ultimately had little regard for the actual fate of the three Baltic nations or their people. Hitler, for example, was able to threaten and cajole Lithuania into returning the important port of Memel (Klaipeda) to the Reich prior to the German invasion of Poland. When Germany invaded Poland in September of 1939, the fate of the Baltic nations was sealed. In exchange for the establishment of the German-Soviet non-aggression pact and allowing Germany to invade Poland unhindered by the Soviet Union, Hitler essentially ceded Stalin the right to annex the Baltic States without opposition; all as part of the secret protocols of the Molotov-Ribbentrop Pact. Not that Germany was any sort of friend to the Baltic nations to begin with, but turning a blind eye to Soviet occupation was like throwing them to the dogs. Germany invited Lithuania to join in the invasion of Poland under the pretext of allowing them to 'settle' old border disputes with Poland however the actual German intention was to occupy Lithuania itself under the auspices of providing military support. Lithuania decided against involvement, hoping to avoid such foreign occupation. As it turned out, they were occupied anyway.

Encouraged by the German indifference (and outright betrayal), the Soviets were able to secure rights to establish military bases in the three Baltic nations in 1939, and had begun massing their own armed forces in the areas of Russia adjacent to Latvia and Estonia as early as the summer of 1939. In the summer of 1940, with the powers of Western Europe occupied with the aggression of Germany and the invasion of France, the Soviet Union issued virtually simultaneous ultimatums to the legal governments of the three Baltic nations.

At 11:00 p.m. on night of June 14th, 1940, Lithuania received an ultimatum from the Soviet Union calling for the resignation of the current Lithuanian government. Lithuania was given all of 11 hours to respond, but the deadline was moot anyway since Soviet forces were already gathered on the borders of Lithuania prepared for war. With an invasion imminent, the Lithuanian government resigned in an attempt to forestall the inevitable Soviet occupation. The Soviets then issued further demands early in the afternoon of June 15th, essentially notifying Lithuanian authorities that Soviet armed forces would begin crossing the borders of Lithuania at 3 p.m. that afternoon. Lithuanian independence was all but lost.

By the evening of June 15th, Soviet units were marching into the major Lithuanian cities of Vilna, Kaunas and Kedaini and positioning themselves along the Lithuanian-Latvian border. With Soviet forces now sitting along both the Latvian-Lithuanian and Latvian-Russian borders, Latvia's own continued sovereignty was in great peril. The expected Soviet ultimatum arrived in Latvia on the morning of June 16th. Accusing Latvia of scheming against them, and under the pretence of protecting Soviet troops stationed on the recently established military bases in Latvia, the Soviets demanded that the Latvian government resign and allow the free and unhindered march of Soviet units onto Latvian soil. Latvia could do little to resist. Although it had the largest of the pre-war Baltic armies, it was by no means capable of fighting a two-front war, which is what an open border with Lithuania meant. In attempt to prevent as much bloodshed as possible, the Latvian government instead capitulated to Soviet demands. At 10:00 a.m. on June 17th, Soviet forces rolled across the Lithuanian-Latvian border in the area of Bauske and Dünaburg.

By 12:30 in the afternoon of the same day, troops of the Red Army were marching through the streets of the Latvian capital city of Riga. With both Lithuania and Latvia falling within days of each other to Soviet military and diplomatic pressure, Estonia could not hope to maintain her independence for long. On the same day as Paris fell to the Germans - June 21st, 1940 - the Soviet Union instigated a "communist uprising" in Estonia, supported by Red Army tank units crossing the border from Russia.

Sham elections with no legal basis were held in all three Baltic nations later in the summer of 1940 to validate the Soviet occupation, and on August 3rd, 1940 Lithuania was officially annexed by the Soviet Union. Latvia followed on August 5th, and Estonia on August 6th. For the Baltic States, freedom—which so many had fought and died for at the end of the last Great War—was lost.

Soviet occupation brought rapid change to the three Baltic

nations—the former legal governments were toppled, all private institutions swallowed by the new government and the Soviet communist style applied to everything. Farmlands were taken from their owners and converted to public lands under government (Soviet) control. Any citizen who was thought to be an enemy of the state was arrested or shot out of hand. The Red Army began conscripting troops as well as absorbing elements of the pre-existing Baltic armies, and was able to form a complete native infantry Corps of two Rifle Divisions plus support troops in each of the three nations. Forced conscription in a foreign army and the loss of political and social freedoms were only the beginning of the nightmare that awaited the Baltic peoples. Arrests, deportations, and executions became commonplace, especially among the officers and enlisted personnel of the armies of the Baltic nations, as these were the men who were seen as the biggest threat to Soviet occupation. Sensing the inevitable initiation of hostilities between Germany and the Soviet Union, and perhaps in fear of the potential opposition from the populations they had just recently annexed and brutalized, the Soviets also conducted a massive deportation/extermination operation on the night of June 13/14, 1941—barely a week before the Germans were to invade.

In this one night, literally tens of thousands of so-called 'unreliables' from Estonia, Latvia, and Lithuania were herded aboard trains and deported to Siberia and Northern Russia, from which few, if any, returned. In a scene that would repeat itself innumerable times during the Second World War, entire civilian populations were marked for extermination by the occupation authorities and loaded aboard cattle-cars, and deported to perform slave labour in a prison camp until their deaths spared them from the rigors of slavery. It is estimated that in Latvia alone nearly 15,000 men, women, and children were taken in this one night of terror. In their roughly one-year occupation, the Soviets were estimated to have deported or exterminated a total of 59,700 Estonians, 34,250 Latvians, and 30,500 Lithuanians. The exact figures will certainly never be known. With tens of thousands of their countrymen stolen away in the night, and the horrible yoke of Soviet communism still hanging over them, the people of the Baltic nations now saw only one option left and that was to fight.

It is against the background of this horrific year of Soviet occupation that one can begin to understand the motivation behind the Baltic volunteer movement. Far from being 'pro-Nazi', a great majority of the men who joined the German armed forces did so not to assist Germany in her 'war of annihilation' but instead to seek actual freedom and sovereignty for their beloved homelands from the yoke of the Soviets. Politically naive as it may have been to think that a Nazi Germany would ultimately support Baltic independence efforts, eventual independence was in the hearts and minds of all of the Baltic volunteers and was ultimately the single largest factor in making their determination to fight on the German side. In the Germans they saw an opportunity to finally achieve a sovereignty that they could sustain, that is if Germany conquered the Soviet Union. The Baltic States would no longer be in between the two traditional enemies.

Their hope that Germany would then reward the Baltic nations generously for their assistance was dashed. The reality was that the Germany's own occupational administration did as much as it could to strip the Baltic countries of this pointless optimism. Germany never actually had any real plans for an independent Estonia, Latvia, or Lithuania, at best, these nations were envisioned as simple stooges of the Greater Reich and at worst, they would be stripped of all natural resources (including the able-bodied population) and their properties would be used as frontier properties for ethnic Germans, war veterans and pro-German collaborators from Western Europe. All of that would come in due time however when Germany invaded the Soviet Union on June 22nd, 1941. Previous to that invasion, all that the Baltic people saw was an opportunity to achieve freedom from the Soviets. Correct in their assessment or not, it was an opportunity that most of the Baltic fighters eagerly tried to take advantage of.

On 31st, July 1941, Göering issued the first written order for the extermination of European Jewry. As previously mentioned, on January 20th, Reinhardt Heydrich, met with Eichmann and 12 others at Wannsee, interrupting a celebration to discuss the 'Final Solution' (Endlosung) to the Jewish question. As the war was turning against Germany, Hitler had no way to expel Jews and appears to have decided that if Germany was going to be destroyed, so were Europe's Jews. This action was probably prompted by the Allied declaration in London the previous week, on the 13th of January, that Axis 'war criminals' would be punished. Still, Heydrich had been deporting Jews since October 1941.

Part of the conference minutes read, "Within the framework of the final solution and under appropriate leadership, Jews should be deployed in suitable ways in work groups in the East. Without doubt, the majority of those capable of work and who engage in tasks in the streets will eventually depart through natural wastage. The remainder would, through natural selection, be the most resistant and, therefore, must be treated in an appropriate matter because they would comprise the germ from which a regeneration of Jews would take place.".

Until this meeting, Borkin claims that only Goebbels, Himmler, Göering and Bormann knew about Hitler's extermination plans—Borkin's claim being based on a book by Hilberg, *The Extermination of European Jews.*

After the war was over, American forces used the Villa at Wannsee as an officer's billet. Beginning in 1952, the village of Neukolln had used the villa as a retreat for schoolchildren. In 1987, Berlin's Jewish leader, Heinz Galinski, continued his campaign to make the villa into a Jewish memorial. In 1991, the Berlin city council agreed to comply with Galinski's wishes.

A Jewish family had originally built this lavish villa with its Doric columns, rococo stairway and winter garden in 1914 while Adolf Hitler was fighting on the Somme in the First World War as a corporal. It is located at Wannsee Lake, a suburb in the Southwest part of Berlin. The 4-story, 30,825 square-foot residence with garage and gardener's house, was built on 3.66 acres in 1886. After 1933, Hitler confiscated the villa and converted it into a recuperation home for SS officers.

Around the time that Hitler was planning to exterminate the Jews, it was suggested to him by one of his cronies that history's views on his plans, might not look favorably on him in the future. His response was, "Who remembers the Armenians?" He asked a very poignant question.

The first genocide of the 20th century is one that has gone by largely unnoticed. Still denied by many Turks, the Armenian Genocide of 1915-1916 accounts for the death of one and a half million Armenians in the Ottoman Empire.

The first step in this annihilation was to disarm the Armenians in the army, place them into labor battalions and then kill them. Then, on April 24th, 1915, the Armenian political and intellectual leaders were gathered and killed. Finally, the remaining Armenians were called from their homes, often in a house by house search. Many men were shot immediately or thrown into prison, only to be tortured to death later. The rest of the men, and the women and children were told they would be relocated, and then marched off to concentration camps in the desert between Jerablus and Deir ez-Zor. Here, they would starve and thirst to death in the burning sun. While they were still alive, they were beaten, raped and murdered by unmerciful guards. Many of the surviving Armenians were dispersed all over the world after that so there was no concerted effort on their part to bring to the world's attention of their plight that in anyway compared in the publicity generated after the Second World War about the Holocaust of that war. Of course, Hitler didn't realize when he asked that rhetorical question just how loud the voices of the surviving Jews would be. They were obviously much louder that those of the surviving Armenians.

Chapter Eighteen

I won't ever forget the night in the latter part of September 1941 when we visited my grandparents just before we took the train across Canada to move to Wells, British Columbia. It was a night of sadness. As I said earlier, my grandparents had lived on the second floor of a duplex at the southwest corner of Avenue Road and College View Avenue. The walls and mantles were covered with African spears and shields and African bric-a-brac. On the floor of the living room was the head and skin of a leopard. The dining room was quite large and I can remember big dinners in their house with many dinner guests sitting at the table. My grandfather's study was at the northwest corner of the house in which one day while he was reading, I asked him a rather stupid question, "What are you doing, grandpa?" He replied without looking up, "I'm fishing." That seemed rather odd for such a reply to come from a man whom I highly respected for his ability to move people in his speeches. Then I said, "You don't look like you're fishing, grandpa." He looked up and asked, "What does it look like I'm doing, Danny?" It was obvious to me he was reading, and so I smiled and said, "Fishing". "Then," he responded rather acidly, "Why did you feel it was necessary for you to ask me what I was doing if you already knew?" To this day, I have never asked for an answer to a question in which I already know the answer, except when I was acting for a client in court and I wanted his reply to be on the record.

In any case, back to the last night I ever saw my grandfather alive. He had suffered from a stroke which had left him paralyzed and suffering from aphasia—the inability to be able to speak. However, he could say the word "My, my, my....." to everything asked of him.

I was indeed saddened to see him in such a condition. When my mother leaned over to him to kiss him good bye, he began crying. I knew that he could understand what was going on around him and it must have hurt him deeply to know that his youngest daughter was going to leave him—probably for ever—and he couldn't express in words his love for her or his anguish over seeing her for the last time or even for that matter, even to embrace her. All he could do was cry out the words, "My, my, my......." as his tears ran down his cheeks.

That night, while I was in the upper berth of the sleeper of the train heading northward out of Toronto, I cried to myself for several hours for my grandfather's anguish. Even today, when I think of the suffering he had undergone that night, it brings a lump to my throat. It's incredible when one thinks of it; that a man who had survived the terrors and hardships of Africa in the first, second and part of the third decade of the Twentieth Century, and accomplished as much as he and my grandmother had during their many years in Africa, should end up almost vegetable-like, unable to speak, write, move, or feed himself during the last eight years of his life. It was for this reason, that the members of his church named their church the Banfield Memorial Church while he was still alive. He finally died in his sleep on November 22nd, 1948.

It was a good thing that I witnessed that traumatic episode in my grandfather's bedroom because I learned that it is possible that someone who suffers from a stroke and can't speak can still understand what is being said to them. My mother also suffered from a stroke and when she was ninety in 2003, I thought that if I went to visit her in Olympia, Washington, she wouldn't recognize me either so I didn't visit her. However, remembering that my grandfather was still aware of my mother's presence in his room, I decided to phone her instead. I told the nurse to stay with her and observe my mother while I talked with her on the phone. Fifteen minutes later, I spoke with the nurse and she said that my mother was smiling while I was talking to her.

Three weeks later, she died. I am glad that I made that call.

Back to 1941. My mother, I and my brother were moving to Wells, the small gold mining town near the centre of the Cariboo in the centre of British Columbia so that she could live close to her sister (Althea) and her husband (Harold Fullerton) and their two adopted children, Sharon and Michael.

My father wasn't living with us at that time as he had joined the Royal Canadian Air Force a year after Canada had declared war against Germany and he was still doing his training in Fort MacLeod, Alberta. On April 24th, 1941, my father had been sent to the RCAF training base in Fort Macleod to train as an aero engine mechanic that would later result in him being a flight engineer on Lancaster bombers during the war. The base was near the small city of Fort Macleod which is 48 km (30 miles) west of Lethbridge, Alberta and about 60 miles (96 km) north of the American border. He was later sent overseas to later serve during the war years as a flight engineer on bombers in the near east.

The engines of the trains of today are not as exciting to look at as they were when I first saw them on our way to Wells. The engines were huge behemoths that groaned and hissed as if some monster was inside of them trying to escape. The driving wheels were much taller than I was so that gives you some idea of their size. Whenever our train stopped at a train station, I and many other passengers would walk the length of the platform to stare at the monster that was pulling us towards our destinations.

A steam locomotive was normally controlled from the cab. A crew of at least two people was normally required to operate a steam locomotive. The engineer was responsible for controlling the locomotive's starting, stopping and speed and the fireman was responsible for the fuel for the fire, steam pressure, and water levels in the boiler and storage tanks.

Steam locomotives consumed vast quantities of water because they operated on an open cycle, expelling their steam immediately after a single use rather than recycling it in a closed loop as stationary and marine steam engines do. For this reason, water was a constant logistical problem. The conventional means of watering a locomotive was by refilling its tender or tank from trackside water towers or standpipes that were positioned alongside the tracks at intervals of many miles apart, generally at regular stops. Coal was used as fuel and it was the fireman's job to shovel the coal into the fireboxes. Locomotives used bells and steam whistles from their earliest days. In the United States, India and Canada, bells warned of a train in motion.

Strangely enough, freight trains had cabooses at the rear of the trains so that a man in the caboose could watch for any fires that may have come about by burning cinders coming from the smoke stacks of the locomotives but passenger trains never had cabooses at the end of their trains which seems strange considering the fact that burning cinders could still set fires along the tracks. The inside of the caboose had a toilet, kitchenette and sleeping quarters. I sat in one when I was 14-years-of age when a freight train was heading west towards Nelson B.C., from a boys camp several miles east of that small city.

The introduction of electric locomotives at the turn of the 20th century and later diesel-electric locomotives spelled the beginning of the end for steam locomotives, although that end was long in coming . I can remember seeing steam engines pulling out of the train station in Toronto in the 1960s. Crossing the Spadina Avenue Bridge when a steam locomotive was passing under it was like driving through a black fog.

On our way to Wells, we met my dad at Lethbridge, Alberta and that was the first time I heard him play the piano. I was so impressed, as were many people standing around the grand piano listening to his performance while he was playing the piano in our hotel (the hotel has been long gone since then) that I too wanted to learn to play the piano and play it like he did.

That was the second time in my life, that fate had entered my life and had a direct effect on it. Grabbing that brass ring on that train of fate eventually led me to where I was giving a performance of playing four of my piano compositions on the personal piano that previously belonged to that world renowned classical pianist, the late Glen Gould, fifty four years later on August 15th, 1997 at the Roy Thompson Concert Hall in Toronto, one of the finest concert halls in the world. I also performed on other stages, radio and television.

My brother and I had one room in the hotel and my mother and father had an adjoining room. It was a good thing that my mother didn't have consensual sex with my father because in all likelihood, I would have had another sibling, one that my mother wouldn't have been able to provide for in later years.

My father saw us off on the plane that was to take us to Vancouver, 740 kilometers (460 miles) west of us. It was the last time we were to see him until the spring of 1944. I really didn't feel saddened by our parting because I really hadn't seen much of him up to that point in my life anyway so our parting was more of one acquaintance saying good bye to another.

Our plane was a DC 3 passenger plane with two propellers. It could only carry 20 passengers. It had a wing span of 95 feet (29 metres) The two engines were 1,200 horsepower each and the plane was equipped with retractable landing gear. There were only one aisle with ten passenger seats on one side of it and eleven on the other. That eleventh seat on the other side of the aisle was for the stewardess. I remember getting into the plane by climbing up the steps of a movable platform and then entering a door at the rear of the plane and walking up a fairly steep inclined floor once inside the plane. This was typical of all passenger planes then.

All the time we were in the plane, it was dark outside and the only thing of any consequence that happened on that flight was that my brother had to be administered oxygen. If the plane had to fly above 10,000 feet (3,048 meters) the stewardess (now called flight attendants and there was only one on the plane during those years compared to one for every 18 passengers nowadays) would hand out oxygen masks which could be screwed into the oxygen ports above our seats. If we did fly above 10,000 feet, the masks didn't automatically fall from the area above us. The stewardess would be traipsing down the aisle with her own mask on with an oxygen hose as long as the cabin of the plane following right behind her. I don't know how the passengers would get the oxygen.

The stewardess (as per the law at that time) was a registered nurse so she knew how to administer oxygen. These woman had to be under 32 years of age, weigh less than 110 pounds (50 kilograms) be no taller than five foot three (406 cm) lest the men feel intimidated and they could not wear any jewelry or glasses. Contact lenses hadn't been invented then. I remember on a flight in the 1990s, the flight attendant wore an engagement ring that had a diamond in it that was so large, the light reflecting off of it could be seen at the other end of the cabin.

Up until 1959, the attendants had tranquilizers for the children and cigarettes for the adults. It was a terrifying experience to be sitting in a seat in which the huge propeller to your right or left was whirling at tremendous speeds. The tip of the propellers would be about a foot from the skin of the plane. I had visions of the propeller spinning off and cutting through the cabin like a buzz saw and slicing me into mincemeat. Actually the only time a propeller actually left a propeller shaft was in 1994 when the pilot of a Super Constellation was attempting to land at the Malton Airport (now the Pearson International Airport in Toronto) and accidentally crashed into a farmer's field near Brampton. The propeller beheaded one of the passengers. The only other time I sat that close to a propeller was when I flew from Halifax to Prince Edward Island in the 1980s. It still scared the hell out of me.

We had vomit bags in the back of the seat ahead of us like they do now but in those days, most people had to use them because we were flying fairly low and as such, the plane was subjected to a lot of turbulence especially when we were flying over the Rocky Mountains. It really wasn't any different than riding a roller coaster. When the plane dropped suddenly, I continuously prayed that the plane would crash into a mountain and death would come instantaneously. If they brought passengers their meal (which was a boxed lunch comprising of a sandwich) they couldn't keep it down. I think most sandwiches were regurgitated and ended up in the bag. We didn't have pull-down trays in those days. We would balance everything on the small pillows we were given. If the coffee or other drink tipped over and stained our clothes, no problem, the stewardess would give us a free chit for dry cleaning.

Smoking was permitted and one's eyes smarted with all that tobacco smoke in the air. It was like looking through a blue haze not unlike what used to be seen in a tavern. Of course if the adults ran out of cigarettes, no problem there either. The stewardess always had extras. Of course, no one got served any alcoholic beverage in those days. Anyone caught bringing their own on board was given the same kind of reprimand that someone sneaking a smoke in a plane nowadays would get. And if you boarded a plane sloshed, you were immediately removed from the plane.

There was no speaker system on board so when the captain or co-pilot wanted to make an announcement, he filled out a form (providing he wasn't struggling to keep the plane aloft) and then the stewardess passed it around from one passenger to another. Imagine reading an announcement that the plane is flying 150 miles (241 km) an hour and that you will arrive at your destination in four hours. After reading that message, everyone began reaching for their vomit bag again. Four more hours of that damn gut-wrenching coaster ride would have made even Gravol ineffective. UUGHH! If the passenger compliment of the plane was low, the stewardess would have time to play cards with a passenger or two if the shuffling of the cards while the plane dropped suddenly didn't end up as fifty-two card pickup.

When we arrived in Vancouver, it was around midnight. I stumbled off the plane as if I was drunk. But then so did everyone else. The father of my Uncle Harold picked us up and took us to his home. It was a large home on a hill with a huge front yard. The next morning, while sitting on his front lawn, I saw the mountains of North and West Vancouver in the distance. It was the first mountains I ever saw but since they were many kilometers away, their impact wasn't as great on me as it was two days later when I saw mountains up close.

It was then that I went on my first boat ride on a ship larger than just one of the ferries crossing the Toronto Harbour. The small passenger ship took us up Howe Sound to Squamish, a small town at the head of the Squamish River that is 65 kilometers (40.3 miles) north of Vancouver. The word 'squamish' is a native word for 'strong wind' or 'Mother of the Wind'. As we approached Squamish, (1.6 km one mile from the town) we could see the famous Shannon Falls to our right. It's British Columbia's third highest falls, being 120 meters (393 feet) in height. In 1984, I and my family got a chance to see those falls up close when we were driving on Highway 99 while heading south towards Vancouver. Many people nowadays, take the train to Squamish and catch the ship M.V. *Britannia* back to Vancouver on the return trip. That way they get to enjoy the scenery that Howe Sound has to offer.

The railway line wasn't put in until 1956. Further, there was no Highway 99 running down the coast to Vancouver as there is now so going by boat back in 1941 was the only way people in Vancouver could get to Squamish from the south. Many years later, B.C. Rail built railroad tracks from North Vancouver to Squamish so the train passes through Squamish with tracks running all the way to Prince George. Driving along 99 takes the joy out of going to and from Squamish by ship. The highway is however fittingly called the 'Sea to Sky Highway'. Squamish is at the head of Howe Sound, less than an hour's drive north of Vancouver. Squamish also boasts of being a deep seaport.

After we arrived at Squamish, we immediately got onto the train operated by the then *Pacific Great Eastern Railway*—PEG for short, affectionately called the 'Please Go Easy' which began its run from Squamish and that was to take us northeast partway across B.C. and then north to Quesnel which is situated in the middle of the Cariboo country.

When the PGE (*Pacific Great Eastern*) first came through Lillooet in 1915 it was privately owned. It was acquired by the Province in 1918 and had its name changed to BC Rail Ltd. in 1984. Bringing supplies and communication to isolated people along the line, the train was greatly welcomed. Today the trip from Vancouver into the Cariboo is known far and wide as the most scenic railroad in North America.

The PEG isn't the only railway company that has affectionate names. In England, the *Lancashire and Yorkshire Railway* was called, 'The Languid and Yawning'. The *Midland and Great Northern* became, 'The Muddle and Get Nowhere'. The Americans were not to be outdone when they changed the names of their railways. The *Delaware, Lackawana and Western Railway* became 'The Delay, Linger and Wait'. The *Minneapolis and St. Louis* had three names, 'The Misery and Short Life', 'The Maimed and Still Limping', and 'The Midnight and Still Later'. My favorite is The *Leavenworth, Kansas and Western*, affectionately called by its users, 'Leave Kansas and Walk'. Of course, one can never forget the slowest train in North America which crept along its tracks in Newfoundland. It was part of Canada's national railway, the *Canadian National Railway*. In Newfoundland, it was called, The *Newfie Bullet*. There is a popular joke about the *Newfie Bullet*. It was said that a man was seen sitting on one of the tracks with a loaf of bread in his hands. When asked what he was doing, he replied that he was waiting for the *Newfie Bullet*. When asked why, he replied that he was going to commit suicide by letting the train run over him. When asked why he had the loaf of bread, he replied, 'You don't want me to starve to death waiting for the train, do you?'

All the way north to Quesnel, there were mountains all around us and on occasion, we passed lakes and valleys but for the most part, we were surrounded by high mountains. I was excited as hell as I looked at the ice and snow-covered peaks of the Coast Mountains as the train weaved in between them. The trip took almost an entire day. By the time we arrived at Quesnel, a city of several thousand, it was dark and my Uncle Harold met us at the train station.

He squeezed my brother and me in the back seat of his neighbour's car (since his own car was too small for all of us and our luggage) and put the rest of the luggage in the trunk and then gave us a blanket and pillow each so that we could sleep.

The trip to Wells from the City of Quesnel took three hours. Nowadays the trip can be done in less than an hour. That is because Highway 26 is currently a two-lane winding smooth ribbon of asphalt that runs east from Quesnel to Barkerville in which Wells is just a little under three kilometers west of Barkerville. In 1941 however, and for many years before and after that year, Highway 26 was just an 85 kilometer (53 mile) gravel road which was dotted with pot holes. My uncle must have known where they all were because it seemed like he drove into everyone of them on the road that dark and rainy night. Of course the route is very old, considering the fact that it was built in the middle of the nineteenth century as part of the Cariboo Wagon Road.

There were very few lights on when we finally arrived in the small town of Wells and my uncle took us directly to our three-room house which my mother had previously arranged to rent for $15 a month. It was situated on Dawson Street at the foot of Saunders Avenue. The rent of $15 a month in 1941 money would be equivalent to $732 Canadian in 2009 which is still very cheap for a three-room house that had water and electricity.

The house had a small kitchen with a small table and three chairs. It had a wood stove and a small fridge and a sink with running cold water. (we had our baths in a large wash tub) The living room is where my mother slept on a pullout couch. It also had a small wood stove. The bedroom had a double bed in it and that is where my brother and I slept. We had electricity. Alas, there was no indoor toilet so the outhouse was about fifty feet (15 metres) away. My uncle later built another one in our woodshed which was only twenty-five feet (7.6 meters) away.

The next morning, I got up early to see where we were going to live for the rest of our lives—or so I had been led to believe. With the town being at an elevation of 4,100 feet, Wells is nevertheless surrounded by hills and peaks that offer remnants of a time long past.

The town is in a beautiful valley where moose graze in the meadows. One month later, one of them was standing right at the back door of our house. Its presence scared the hell out of my mother when she opened the door to see what was making the noise.

As I stood in the front yard of our house, I could see that the rear of our house was at the edge of a tiny forest which ended at a large meadow going across a valley to the mountain a third of a mile (half a kilometre) to the north of us. When I looked to my left, (with the back of our house behind me) I saw the continuation of the valley which stretched for a little over a mile to the east of me. The large valley consisted of a very huge meadow and it was always referred to by the people of Wells as 'The Meadows'. Standing at the front door of our house and looking to my right, I could see that we were only a few blocks east of a mountain that gradually raised itself from the valley floor. It was only 1,828 feet (557 meters) in height from the streets of Wells but to a child—that's high. I should add however that in order for a mountain to be classed as a mountain, it must be at least 1,640 feet (500 meters) in height. Anything less than that is merely a hill. When I looked straight ahead, I was looking down Saunders Avenue leading towards the stores near the end of the street. Off in the distance, beyond the end of Saunders Street and across a flat area was 'The Tailings', which was out of sight from our house. South of the 'Tailings' was another mountain called Cow Mountain on which the community ski hill was located.

Wells is divided into two communities, the upper community being next to Island Mountain, (the mountain on the right of our house) and the lower community (South Wells) situated immediately south of the main community at the bottom of a small hill which is also referred to as 'The Tailings' where all the access rock pulled out of the mines was dumped over the years. To get to the 'Tailings', we had to go down that part of Pooley Street which is on a hill leading to 'The Tailings'. To the south and west of the tailings area of Wells and around Island Mountain to our right, and out of sight of our house and about three quarters of a mile (1.2 km) southwest of our house, is the

Jack-O' Clubs Lake, a lake which runs east and west and is almost one and a half miles (2.3 km) in length and a third of a mile (540 metres) in width and according to my mother—bottomless. She lied.

Fred Marshall Wells, a prospector, with the assistance of Dr. Burnett, a true believer and President of the Gold Quartz Mine along with Mr. O.H. Solibakke, a self-proclaimed promoter initiated a series of events that would put this small mining community on the map. During 1926, tunneling had begun on the Gold Quartz Property and by 1933; enough money had been raised to begin construction of the mill. Underground hard rock mining was the life blood of the community called Wells. During the depression years of the 1930's, this small community came into being and thrived on the economic base that this mining created. There were as many as 3,600 people living in Wells in the late 1930s.

There were several hard rock mines in the immediate area, the most notable being the Cariboo Gold Quartz Mine located on the right hand side of the Jack O'Clubs Lake and Island Mountain Mine, on the left, as one approached Wells from the west. In 1939, the 'Quartz' was operating their mill at around 250 tons per day with a total work force of nearly 300 employees. During its years of operation, it produced approximately $30 million dollars worth of gold which, at that time when I was there, gold was only $32.00 per ounce.

The Island Mountain Mine Co. Ltd. began operation in 1933 under the Newmont Mining Corporation of New York, and construction of the mill began in July 1934. It produced steadily at around 80 tons per day with a work force of around 100 employees. Mining continued here under the management of Island Mountain Mines until August 1954 when the property was sold to Cariboo Gold Quartz Co., Ltd.

The town had only been in existence for eight years prior to our arrival but it had grown considerably from Fred Wells' campsite to a thriving community of 3,600 prior to the Second World War and then reduced to 2,500 by the time we arrived in 1941.

Most of the gold still lay deep in the bed rock where men like Billy Barker and Fred Wells found it after hard digging. The original gold lay buried in the ore veins of the hard rock and it was and still is in these twisted, broken faults and veins that were being mined then—the mother lode that so many thousands of miners for over a century searched for and who some found.

I remember being shown a couple of ounces of gold on a tray at the Cow Mountain Mine. I had never seen gold that way before and I asked the assayer how much gold there was in the world. He didn't know but he told me that there was an ounce of it on the scale and it was worth $32 an ounce. By 2011, it was over $1,500 dollars an ounce. Years later, I learned that if it were possible to take all of the gold that had been extracted from the world since the beginning of recorded history and melt it all down and shaped the gold into a block of gold, the block would be about the size of a large house and no more. One can get an idea of just how much that gold would weigh when one realizes that one of the three coffins of Egyptian King Tutankhamen was of pure gold and weighed 2,447 pounds. Of course, gold is malleable—one ounce can be drawn into a thin wire of gold that is 35 miles (56.3 km) in length or beaten into a wafer that is 1/250,000 of an inch in thickness and so thin that light can shine through it and as such, this explains why gold printing on thousands of office doors, covers of books and letterheads can be achieved by using just one ounce of pure gold.

Like thousands before me, I thought pyrite, (iron sulfide) which is called 'Fool's Gold' was real gold so one day I and my brother pulled a small wagon load of our 'treasure' of rocks peppered with pyrite up the hill from the tailings and across town and told our mother that we were rich. She told us that what we had pulled up that hill and across town was a wagon full of old rocks worth about one cent for the entire load. It wasn't until my Uncle Harold visited us the next day (his house was further up Saunders Street) that we learned the real value of our rocks. My mother was wrong. Our treasure was worth about half a cent. I did find however within our load of rocks, a piece of rock about the size of my thumb which was entirely of a silver-like material. I kept it for years like others kept 'pet rocks' in the 1960s.

On September 18th, 1941, during the Soviet army retreat in the direction of Yeletsk, the retreating soldiers came upon a small ravine between Chartsysk and Snizhy stations about sixty kilometres from the city of Staline. The horrible sight that befell their eyes was the dead bodies of many children aged from 14 to 16 years that partly filled the ravine. They were dressed in the black uniform of the F.S.U. Trade and Craft School in Staline. It was discovered that the children were being evacuated from Staline as the German army neared the city. After walking nearly 60 kilometres they became utterly exhausted and had begged for transport. Their guardians promised to send trucks but instead a detachment of Russian political police (NKVD) arrived. Carrying machine-guns, they starting shooting the children in cold blood and throwing the bodies into the ravine. The Soviet soldiers later counted the bodies of 370 slain children.

A picturesque ravine is situated in the Syrets suburb of the city of Kiev. It is about three kilometres miles long, over fifty metres deep and separated from the residential area by a cemetery and a civilian prison. There, on September 29, 1941, the SS (Einsatzgruppe C, with the help of the Ukrainian police) herded the whole Jewish population of Kiev and the surrounding area, into the ravine and systematically began to slaughter all 33,771 victims. They were individually executed with a bullet in the neck. The killing took a whole two days, the bodies then burned in pyres, each containing 2,000 corpses. Later the SS brought in excavators and bulldozers and the ravine was filled in. In early October of that year, Moscow informed the outside world of the discovery of the mass grave. The West, mistrustful of the Russians, dismissed the news as 'products of the Slavic imagination'. During the 778 days of the German occupation of Kiev, many thousands of Russian POWs, Ukrainians and other nationalities, were also killed at Babi Yar. Of a total population of around 900,000, only 180,000 were living in Kiev at the end of the German occupation. In 1976, a 15-metre high memorial was unveiled on the site to commemorate the Russian POWs who were killed there. However, no reference is made to the number of Jewish dead. This tells you something of the minds of the Russians, doesn't it?

During the month of September, 1941, Action Group A, consisting of around eight hundred men, and commanded by SS General Otto Ohlendorf, was operating on the Russian southern front. In the period, 16th to 30th of September, in the area around Nicolaiev, and including the town of Cherson, they rounded up and massacred 35,782 Soviet citizens, mostly Jews. This was the numbers reported to Hitler from the SD office, dated October 2nd, 1942.

I think this is a good time to bring to your attention what a certain religious nut case said about why the Jews were being massacred at this time of the century. The screwball I am talking about was a man called Ovadia Yosef, a rabbi in Jerusalem who was the leader of the Shas Party. Somehow, they let this twerp broadcast his weekly garbage on Israeli radio stations.

He said that those millions of Jews who were slaughtered during the Holocaust by the Nazis were being punished for what they did in their previous lives. Chief Rabbi Israel Meir Lau, a survivor of the holocaust, said that Judaism has a concept of reincarnation and of the righteous Jews dying for sins committed in a previous life but he said that that doesn't explain the Holocaust which has no explanation at all. The reason why the twerp's conclusion makes no sense at all is that there were millions of other people who survived the Holocaust, people who lived in North America for example, and to suggest that if they had a previous life, they didn't sin in it, is preposterous. I strongly suspect that the twerp was speaking as an apologist for Adolf Hitler and was implying that what that demon from Hell had done, was an act of God.

On October 16th, the Romanians and the Germans marched into the Russian city of Odessa only to find it abandoned and burning. This was a replay of what happened when Napoleon marched into Moscow on September 14th, 1812.

On the 28th, in Lithuania, a SS commander called Rauca processed 27,000 Jews by pointing his finger to the right or left. Young children, the old and the sick went to the right—the direction determined who was to become slave labourers and who was to be killed off. He directed 10,000 to his right for immediate execution.

On November 14th, a German submarine sank the British aircraft carrier, *Ark Royal* just off Gibraltar. Only one seaman died in the sinking. The sailors on the British battleship *Barham* weren't so lucky. When that ship was torpedoed and subsequently exploded, 858 of her crew perished. Years later, I worked with a man who was an officer on the *Ark Royal* when it sank.

Chapter Nineteen

Before I describe the particulars of the bombing of Pearl harbour, I want to say something about what prompted the Japanese to even consider such a foolish act. Japan's 1931 invasion of Manchuria and its subsequent full-scale assault in 1937 against China brought expressions of disapproval from the U.S. government. With public opinion strongly isolationist, however, the United States did not act to halt Japanese expansionism. Not until the outbreak of World War II in Europe and the escalation of Japanese aggression did the U.S. response become more forceful.

After World War II started in September 1939, Japan grew angry with the Americans because it was helping China by sending it war supplies. Japan obviously wasn't pleased with this arrangement between those two superpowers because China was the main target of Japanese attacks.

In 1940, Nazi Germany's march into Western Europe opened up opportunities for Japan to consolidate its position in China and penetrate Southeast Asia, thereby advancing the Japanese goal of dominating a 'Greater East Asia Co-Prosperity Sphere.' After the fall of France, the Vichy government accepted (August 1940) Japanese demands that aid through French Indochina to the Chinese resistance be cut off and that Japan be allowed to use air bases in Indochina. In September, Japanese troops moved into northern Indochina, and Japan joined the Axis. Meanwhile, with Britain fighting for its life and the Netherlands under Nazi occupation, Japan called on the British to close the Burma Road to supplies bound for China and pressed the Dutch East Indies for economic and political concessions. In July 1941, Japan occupied southern Indochina—an obvious prelude to further expansion in Southeast Asia, which brought Japan a rich source of rubber, tin, oil, quinine, lumber, foodstuffs, and other vital raw materials.

Prime Minister, Prince Konoe Fumimaro of Japan hoped that the United States would accept Japan's actions, but in September 1940, President Roosevelt imposed an embargo on U.S. exports of scrap iron and steel to Japan. In July 1941 he froze all Japanese assets in the United States. This action virtually ended U.S./Japanese trade, depriving Japan of vital oil imports.

On Sept. 6th, 1941, an imperial conference met in Tokyo to consider the worsening relations with the United States. Emperor Hirohito and Prime Minister Konoe favored a continuation of negotiations in Washington, D.C. The war minister, General Hideki Tojo however, believed that the United States was determined to throttle Japan, that war was inevitable, and that it would be better for Japan to begin the conflict sooner rather than later. Tojo's views had wide support within the Japanese military.

Japan decided to arrange a 'peace' trip to the United States. During this "peace" trip Japan made three demands to the American government. These demands were that the USA stop aiding China, to stay out of Asian affairs, and to begin shipping oil to Japan right away. If this request wasn't acceded too, Japan would attack the U.S.A. President Franklin D. Roosevelt and his government didn't like the threat and ignored Japan's so-called demands and implied threat. At the insistence of the war party, Konoe was given 6 weeks to reach a settlement with the United States and was to insist on a set of minimum demands: immediate cessation of economic sanctions, a free hand for Japan in China, and rights for Japan in Indochina. With no progress occurring in the negotiations, Konoe resigned on October 16th and was replaced by Tojo as Japan's prime minister, whose cabinet decided to wait only until the end of November for a diplomatic breakthrough.

Talks between U.S. Secretary of State, Cordell Hull and Japanese emissaries remained stalled. Meanwhile U.S. cryptographers had broken Japan's major diplomatic code, and American authorities knew that rejection of the minimum demands would mean war. Even so, on November 26th, Hull formally reiterated the U.S. position. Japan, he said, must withdraw from China and Indochina, recognize the Chiang Kai-shek regime in China, renounce territorial expansion, and accept the Open Door policy of equal commercial access to Asia. An imperial conference held in Tokyo on December 1st set the Japanese war machine in motion.

It's the opinion of a great many people and I concur, that if the American government hadn't held a hard-ass attitude towards Japan, the Japanese would not have attacked Pearl Harbour. However, the American government didn't want to let Japan continue invading other countries in the Pacific. Japan was doing what Germany had done earlier and it was obvious to the American officials that someone had to take a stand otherwise Japan would expand its grip across Asia just as Germany had expanded its grip across Europe.

The United States expected the first blow to be in the Philippines or Southeast Asia. Unbeknown to the Americans, Japan had made plans for a devastating aerial strike against the U.S. Pacific Fleet at Pearl Harbor, in the Hawaiian Islands. Subsequently, in late November, a powerful Japanese task force left the Kuril Islands and on December 2nd, it received a coded message issuing the attack order on Pearl Harbour. On December 7th, the Japanese attack force under the command of Admiral Nagumo, consisting of six carriers with 423 planes, was approaching the island of Oahu. (where Honolulu and Pearl Harbour are located) At 6 a.m., the first attack wave of 183 Japanese planes took off from the carriers located 230 miles north of Oahu and headed for the U.S. Pacific Fleet at Pearl Harbor.

Meanwhile at Pearl Harbor at 7:02 a.m., on December 7th, (Sunday) two Army operators at Oahu's northern shore radar station detected the Japanese air attack approaching and contacted a junior officer who disregarded their reports, thinking they were that American B-17 planes which were expected in from the U.S. west coast. When you think about it, that conclusion was rather stupid since those planes would have been spotted earlier coming from the east—and they weren't. The planes were coming in from the west.

Meanwhile, in Washington, D.C., the American State Department was suspicious of an attack by the Japanese somewhere in the Pacific, but the whereabouts of the attack were unknown. They then realized that the time from the messages from Japan sent to its embassy in Washington corresponded with Pearl Harbor time which is six hours behind Washington D.C's time. Washington tried to send a message to Hawaii to warn them of the attack. Unfortunately, it was sent by an ordinary telegram and when it was received in Hawaii, it remained on an officer's desk because he didn't read it and thought it was just another mundane message from Washington. Still unbeknown to the Americans, at 7:15, a second attack wave of 167 planes took off from the Japanese carriers and headed for Pearl Harbor.

Since the Americans had not received the message sent by Washington, the American forces on Hawaii were not on a state on high alert. Senior commanders had concluded, based on available intelligence, that there was no reason to believe an attack was imminent. Aircraft were therefore left parked wingtip to wingtip on airfields, (to thwart any attempt to sabotage them) anti-aircraft guns were unmanned with many ammunition boxes kept locked in accordance with peacetime regulations. There were also no torpedo nets protecting the fleet anchorage. And since it was Sunday morning, many officers and crewmen were ashore.

At 7:53 a.m. the first Japanese assault wave, with 51 Val dive bombers, 40 Kate torpedo bombers, 50 high level bombers and 43 Zero fighters, commenced the attack with flight commander, Mitsuo Fuchida, sounding the battle cry "Tora! Tora! Tora!" (Tiger! Tiger! Tiger!) At that precise moment, I was getting ready for school the morning of the next day (December 8th — Monday).

The Americans were taken completely by surprise. The first attack wave targeted airfields and battleships. The second wave targeted other ships and shipyard facilities. The air raid lasted until 9:45 a.m. Eight battleships were damaged, with five sunk. Three light cruisers, three destroyers and three smaller vessels were lost along with 188 aircraft. The Japanese lost 27 planes and five midget submarines which attempted to penetrate the inner harbor and launch torpedoes.

Escaping damage from the attack were the prime targets, the three U.S. Pacific Fleet aircraft carriers, *Lexington, Enterprise* and *Saratoga* which were not in the port. Also escaping damage are the base fuel tanks. The casualty list included 2,335 servicemen and 68 civilians killed, and 1,178 wounded. Included were 1,177 men aboard the *USS Arizona* battleship killed after a 1,760 pound (800-kilogram) bomb penetrated into the forward magazine causing catastrophic explosions. The color detail was on deck of the battleship *Arizona* in anticipation of raising the flag at the stern at 8:00 am. The *Arizona* came under attack almost immediately, and at about 8:10 received a hit by the Japanese bomb just forward of turret two on the starboard side. Within a few seconds, the forward powder magazines exploded, (50 tons of explosives) gutting the forward part of the ship. The foremast and forward superstructure collapsed forward into the void created by the explosion and turrets one and two, deprived of support, dropped more than 20 feet relative to their normal positions. The explosion ignited furious fires in the forward part of the ship.

The majority of the crew members were either killed by the explosion and fire or were trapped by the rapid sinking of the ship. Many of the survivors displayed remarkable courage in assisting other shipmates to safety. Lieutenant Commander Samuel G. Fuqua was awarded the Congressional Medal of Honor for his role in leading the rescue of other survivors. It was also awarded posthumously to Rear Admiral Isaac Kidd and Captain Franklin Van Valkenburgh who were aboard that gray battleship when she sunk. As many as 1,177 of the crew died on the ship.

After the attack the ship was left resting on the bottom with the deck just awash. In the days and weeks following, efforts were made to recover the bodies of the crew and the ship's records. Eventually further recovery of bodies became fruitless and dangerous and the bodies of at least 900 crewmen remained in the ship. During 1942 salvage work to recover as much of the ship as was practical began. The masts and superstructure were removed for scrap and the two turrets aft were salvaged for use at shore batteries on Hawaii. The forward part of the ship had received the most damage, and only the guns of turret two were removed while turret one was left in place. On December 1st, 1942 the ship was stricken from the registry of U.S. Navy vessels.

In Washington, various delays prevented the Japanese diplomats from presenting their Declaration of War to Secretary of State, Cordell Hull, until 2:30 p.m. (Washington time) just as the first reports of the air raid at Pearl Harbor were being read by Hull.

One of the biggest blunders in the Second World War was done by General Douglas MacArthur who at the time of the bombing of Pearl Harbour was commander in chief of the American armed forces in the Philippines. When he was informed that Pearl Harbour had been bombed by the Japanese, he sat on the edge of his bed for an hour or so and read his bible. Then he ordered his bombers at Clarke Field to patrol the area instead of bombing the Japanese airstrips in Formosa. (now called Taiwan) When noon hour came, he ordered the bombers to return to base and after lunch, while the bomber crews were resting in their barracks; Japanese bombers from Formosa attacked Clarke Field and destroyed the bombers on the ground. Shortly after that fiasco, MacArthur got his fourth star and a medal to boot.

Hours after Pearl Harbor was attacked, General MacArthur prevented air commander General Brereton from bombing Formosa. He further gave three conflicting orders that kept the B-17s at Clark Airfield on the ground most of the morning with orders—bombs up, bombs off, bombs up. The Japanese attack was delayed because of fog. At 11:20, at the same moment that radar at Nichols Field near Manila reported a large mass of enemy planes approaching Clark from 140 miles (225 km) out, MacArthur gave his final bomb-up order.

MacArthur had about one hour to warn Clark and Meba Fields of the coming Japanese air attack and this he did not. Instead he issued 'Field Order Number One: Attack South Formosa at the latest daylight hour that visibility will permit.' This order, time-stamped 11:20 A.M. but delivered at 11:45, is the one that kept the bombers on the ground at the critical moment. The bombers had to bomb up, be serviced and the crews rested for the late afternoon flight. This was the order that lost his air force, given with full and complete knowledge that a large flight of Japanese bombers were coming in.

MacArthur in his autobiography admitted that "at 11:45 a report came in of an overpowering enemy formation closing in on Clark Field." At 11:56 Brereton had to give a full report to MacArthur's Chief of Staff General Sutherland by phone, which kept both Brereton and the single phone line tied up in the critical few moments before the attack (note that Sutherland could have warned Brereton of the radar report but did not). MacArthur could control the teletype and radio but there was a danger that spotters would telephone Clark Field and warn them of the approaching planes.

News of the 'sneak attack' was broadcasted to the American public via radio bulletins, with many popular Sunday afternoon entertainment programs being interrupted. The news sent a shockwave across the nation and results in a tremendous influx of young volunteers into the U.S. armed forces. The attack also united the nation behind the president and effectively ended isolationist sentiments in the country.

During the following months and years of World War II, the destruction of the *Arizona* came to symbolize the reason the U.S. was fighting, as in this poster showing the ship's collapsing foremast silhouetted against the explosion of the ship's magazines.

"Remember Pearl Harbor" became an American theme and the title of the country's most popular war song, but it was the loss of that great ship which seared the minds of navy men. Six months later, when naval Lieutenant Wilmer E. Gallaher turned the nose of his Dauntless dive-bomber down toward the *Akagi* off Midway, the memory of that volcanic eruption of the *Arizona* in Pearl Harbor, which he had witnessed, flashed across his mind. As the *Akagi* blew up, he screamed, "Arizona, I remember you!"

In the years immediately following the end of World War II, the wreck of the *Arizona* was largely ignored. It would cost too much to raise her and the thought of disturbing the final resting places of the doomed men was unthinkable. In fact, the inside of the ship was so torn apart with steel shards everywhere, that it was considered life risking just to enter it. In 1950 the tradition of raising and lowering the colors over the ship daily was started, and momentum gradually began to build toward providing a memorial for the ship and those who died on her. In 1958 legislation was passed authorizing the Navy to erect a memorial and allowing it to accept donations toward that goal. Among the many noteworthy contributions were several generous donations from Hawaii's legislature and a 1961 concert by Elvis Presley. In 1960 construction began and the memorial was dedicated on Memorial Day, 1962. In 1980 a visitor's center on shore was opened and the Navy turned the operation of the memorial over to the National Park Service.

The American aircraft carrier, *USS Enterprise* was 200 miles (322 km) south of Oahu enroute to Pearl Harbor after delivering Marine Corps aircraft to Wake Island. Originally, the *Enterprise* had intended to arrive in Pearl Harbour on December 6th, but weather delayed her. That's what I call pure luck. The aircraft carrier may have been bombed or torpedoed had she been in the area of Pearl Harbour.

The Japanese navy after conducting two strikes on Oahu, and having not located the U.S. carriers, withdrew from the area of Hawaii to avoid being ambushed by American ships that might be in the area. That's what I call shear stupidity. They had time to make a third strike. If they had made it, they would have caused severe damage. For example, during their two attacks, they missed the enormous fuel dump. They neglected to damage other shore-side facilities at the Pearl Harbor Naval Base, including the dry-dock.

The day after the attack on Pearl Harbour, President Roosevelt told a joint session of Congress that December 7th was "a date which will live in infamy." His speech inspired Congress. His speech was as follows:

"Yesterday, December seven 1941, a date which will live in infamy, the United States of America was suddenly and deliberately attacked by naval and air forces of the Empire of Japan. The United States was at peace with that nation and, at the solicitation of Japan, was still in conversation with its Government and its Emperor looking toward the maintenance of peace in the Pacific. Indeed, one hour after Japanese air squadrons had commenced bombing Oahu, the Japanese Ambassador to the United States and his colleague delivered to the Secretary of State a formal reply to a recent American message. While this reply stated that it seemed useless to continue the existing diplomatic negotiations, it contained no threat or hint of war or armed attack.

"It will be recorded that the distance of Hawaii from Japan makes it obvious that the attack was deliberately planned many days or even weeks ago. During the intervening time, the Japanese Government has deliberately sought to deceive the United States by false statements and expressions of hope for continued peace. The attack yesterday on the Hawaiian Islands has caused severe damage to American naval and military forces. Very many American lives have been lost. In addition, American ships have been reported torpedoed on the high seas between San Francisco and Honolulu. Yesterday the Japanese Government also launched an attack against Malaya. Last night Japanese forces attacked Hong Kong. Last night Japanese forces attacked Guam. Last night Japanese forces attacked the Philippine Islands. Last night the Japanese attacked Wake Island. This morning the Japanese attacked Midway Island. Japan has, therefore, undertaken a surprise offensive extending throughout the Pacific area. The facts of yesterday speak for themselves. The people of the United States have already formed their opinions and well understand the implications to the very life and safety of our nation.

"As Commander in Chief of the army and navy, (the US had no air force then. The planes were in the army and the navy at that time) I have directed that all measures be taken for our defense. Always will we remember the character of the onslaught against us. No matter how long it may take us to overcome this premeditated invasion, the American people in their righteous might will win through to absolute victory. I believe I interpret the will of the Congress and of the people when I assert that we will not only defend ourselves to the uttermost but (we) will make very certain that this form of treachery shall never endanger us again. Hostilities exist. There is no blinking at the fact that our people, our territory and our interests are in grave danger. With confidence in our armed forces-with the unbending determination of our people-we will gain the inevitable triumph-so help us God.

"I ask that the Congress declare that since the unprovoked and dastardly attack by Japan on Sunday, December 7, a state of war has existed between the United States and the Japanese Empire." *unquote*

The House of Representatives voted in favour of war with Japan with only one dissenter, she being, Jeanett Rankin, who also voted against the United States participating in World War I. She later said that she felt that a declaration of war, no matter how justified, should never be unanimous.

The resolution put to the members of the Senate was as follows;"Whereas the Imperial Government of Japan has committed unprovoked acts of war against the Government and the people of the United States of America:

"Therefore be it resolved that the State of war between the United states and the Imperial Government of Japan which has thus been thrust upon the United States is hereby formally declared; and the President is hereby authorized and directed to employ the entire naval and military forces of the United States and the resources of the Government to carry on war against the Imperial Government of Japan; and to bring the conflict to a successful termination, all of the resources of the country are hereby pledged by the Congress of the

United States." *unquote*

Germany and Italy declared war on the United States on December 11th. Those were very big mistakes on their parts. In fact it was those decisions that invariably brought the downfall of both those countries and the deaths of both of their leaders.

The Japanese goal was to dominate a 'Greater East Asia Co-Prosperity Sphere.' On December 11th, President Roosevelt sent a message to Congress from the White House. It said; "To the Congress of the United States: On the morning of December 11th the Government of Germany, pursuing its course of world conquest, declared war against the United States. The long known and the long expected has thus taken place. The forces endeavoring to enslave the entire world now are moving toward this hemisphere. Never before has there been a greater challenge to life, liberty, and civilization. Delay invites greater danger. Rapid and united effort by all the peoples of the world who are determined to remain free will insure a world victory of the forces of justice and of righteousness over the forces of savagery and of barbarism. Italy also has declared war against the United States. I therefore request the Congress to recognize a State of war between the United States and Germany and between the United States and Italy." *unquote*

On the 13th of December, the American Senate unanimously passed similar resolutions to the one it passed re the declaration of war on Japan, the resolutions being that a State of War exists between the United States and Germany and Italy.

During the evening of December 7th, 1941, Canada declared war on Japan. Prime Minister King felt that it was necessary to widen the theatre of war. I suppose this decision was due to the fact that the Japanese had already begun their attacks on islands in the Pacific and British colonies. We in Wells were not aware of this decision until the following day however.

In the late evening of December 7th, 1941, the Canadian prime minister announced his Cabinet's decision to declare war on Japan. The King of England approved Canada's declaration of war in the following proclamation issued on December 8th, 1941. "Whereas by and with the advice of our Privy Council for Canada we have signified our approval of the issue of a proclamation in the Canada Gazette declaring that a State of War with Japan exists and has existed in Canada as and from the 7th day of December 1941. Now, therefore, we do hereby declare and proclaim that a State of War with Japan exists and has existed as and from the seventh day of December, 1941. Of all which our loving subjects and all others whom these presents may concern are hereby required to take notice and to govern themselves accordingly." *unquote*

On December 8th, a special session of the British parliament was called and the British parliamentarians and the rest of the British Empire heard Prime Minister Churchill declare war on Japan because of Japan's attack on Malaya. (later called Malasia) Churchill told the commons that the war declaration against Japan was authorized at a noon session of his cabinet. He said; "I spoke to President Roosevelt on the Atlantic telephone Sunday night with a view to arranging the time of our respective declaration. Instructions were sent to our ambassador at Tokyo and a communication was dispatched to the Japanese charge d'affaires at 1 o'clock Monday stating that in view of Japan's wanton acts of unprovoked aggression, the British government informed them that a State of War existed between the two countries. With the full approval of the nation and the empire I pledged the word of Great Britain about a month ago that should the United States be involved in war with Japan, a British declaration would follow within the hour." *unquote*

Most of the families in Wells didn't have radios so there wasn't much news of the war circulating around town other than by word of mouth. On December 7th, rumours of the Japanese attack on Pearl Harbour circulated very quickly however. As the day proceeded, we also learned that Japanese forces had also attacked the Philippines, Malaya, (now called Malaysia) and the islands of Midway and Wake. But it wasn't until around noon December 8th that our entire town, including our school, was buzzing with the news that Japanese planes had attacked Pearl Harbour and the Philippines. Those in Wells who had radios, would stay up after midnight and listen to a rebroadcast of Newscaster Lorne Greene, (later to be a Hollywood actor and star of the Bonanza TV show in the 1960s) reading the ten o'clock (Toronto time) news on CBC radio. His voice was very deep and of course he was always giving us bad news so he was soon thereafter referred to as the 'Voice of Doom'.

Certainly Japan's biggest war-time mistake was made during this time in their history because, in the words of Japan's Admiral Yamamoto, the Japanese admiral who planned the Pearl Harbour attack, when he spoke of the attack on the United States; "We have awakened a sleeping giant." There is no doubt in anyone's minds that when the Americans finally entered the war, everything began to go downhill for the Axis powers. Ironic as it may seem, that Japanese blunder turned out to later be a Godsend to the Japanese people because after the war, the Americans modernized Japan and became it greatest trading partner. It brings to mind that rather humorous movie, *The Mouse that Roared*, in which a small fictional European country declared war on the United States so that the Americans could conquer them also and make it into a modern entity, with the United States as their biggest trading partner.

The Japanese did not wait for the destruction of American air and naval forces to begin landings in the Philippine Archipelago. Hours before the first Japanese plane had taken off to attack targets in the Philippine Islands; three task forces had sailed south from Formosa ports under cover of darkness on the evening of 7th December (Tokyo time). Their destination was the Philippine Islands; two were to land on northern Luzon, and the third was headed for the tiny island of Bataan about 150 miles to the north. The next day another task force left Palau and steamed toward Legaspi, near the southeast tip of Luzon. At the same time, a fifth task force, scheduled to seize Davao, the principal port in Mindanao, was assembling at Palau.

Altogether, the Japanese planned six advance landings: Bataan Island, Aparri, Vigan, Legaspi, Davao, and Jolo Island. All but the last two were on or near Luzon and were designed to provide the Japanese with advance bases from which short-range fighters could attack the fields of the American Far East Air Force and support the main landings to follow. A base at Legaspi, the Japanese believed, would, in addition to providing an airfield, give them control of San Bernardino Strait, between Luzon and Samar, and prevent the Americans from bringing in reinforcements. The landings at Davao and Jolo Island were designed to secure advance bases for a later move southward into the Netherlands Indies. The Japanese also, by landing in Mindanao, to isolate the Philippine Archipelago from Allied bases to the south and to cut the American route of withdrawal and supply.

The forces assigned to these landings were small, even for such limited objectives. But to secure so many detachments for the advance landings, General Homma had had to weaken seriously the two combat divisions Imperial General Headquarters had allotted to him for the Philippine invasion. Not one of the advance landing detachments was strong enough to withstand a determined counterattack; the largest was only about as large as a regiment, and the smallest was hardly stronger than a company. Moreover, the timetable for invasion was a complicated one and could easily be upset by any unexpected event.

The first Japanese invaders on Philippine soil went ashore on Bataan Island in Luzon Strait, midway between Formosa and Luzon, at dawn on the 8th of December. The invasion force, which had left the Formosan ports of Takao and Hozan on the evening of the 7th, consisted of 2 transports escorted by 1 destroyer, 4 torpedo boats, and a large number of other small vessels. Aboard the transports was a naval combat unit of 490 men as well as air corps troops who were to establish an airbase on the island. The combat troops quickly seized the airfield near Basco, and air force troops came ashore to inspect the field. It was found to be barely suitable for fighter and reconnaissance planes, but to require expansion for large-scale operations. The next day, while construction crews worked on the field, planes of the 24th and 50th Fighter Regiments began operations from the Basco base.

When the success of the attack on Clark Field (a direct result of General MacArthur's blunder) became known, the Japanese discontinued work on the Bataan Island field. Such a base was now unnecessary. Early on the morning of the 10th, the men of the 3rd Gunboat Division, part of the Bataan Attack Force, seized Camiguin Island to the south. A seaplane base was immediately established on the island by the naval base force, thus providing the Japanese with an airbase only thirty-five miles north of Aparri.

The Americans did not oppose the Bataan Island landing and seem to have been entirely unaware of it. In fact, General MacArthur reported on the 9th after the Bataan Island landing, that the enemy had not yet landed. It was extremely unlikely that even if USAFFE had been warned of the assault any effort would have been made to meet it. On the morning of the 8th, American planes were being sent aloft to intercept reported enemy flights over Luzon. By the 10th, the Far East Air Force had already been reduced to half strength, and the Japanese had begun to land on the island of Luzon itself.

Luzon is a curiously shaped island. The northern part of the island is about 125 miles wide, (201 km) with only one major indentation along the west coast, at Lingayen Gulf. Mountain ranges extend along the east and west coasts to the central plains just north Manila. The range on the east extends southward to Tayabas Bay. To the west of the central plain are the Zambales Mountains which face the South China Sea across a narrow coastal plain. The southern portion of Luzon is narrow and is irregular in shape, trailing away in a southeasterly direction for 180 miles. (289 km)

North of Manila, the island of Luzon is shaped like a mittened, giant right hand, palm down, with the index finger pointing directly at Formosa. Lingayen Gulf lies between the thumb and the forefinger. From Lingayen south across the top of the hand, like so many veins, are the highways and roads leading to Manila. At the tip of the ring finger lies Aparri, and midway along the forefinger is Vigan. Both were next on the Japanese timetable for invasion.

Before the war, Aparri was a fairly large port with a population of 26,500. Located at the mouth of the Cagayan River and at the head of the Cagayan valley, with formidable mountain ranges to the east, west, and south, Aparri could be reached from the central plains only by way of Balete Pass from the south or by the coastal road around the northern tip of Luzon. The most direct route from Manila to Aparri, along Route 5, through the pass, was 275 miles (442.5 km) long; the more circuitous route along the coast was 100 miles (160.9 km) longer. The Americans could safely assume that any force landing at Aparri would not have Manila as its destination. The Cagayan valley was not the route of invasion.

Vigan, the capital of Ilocos Sur Province, lies on the western shore of Luzon, about 220 miles (354 km) north of Manila on Route 3. To the east lie the Cordillera Mountains separating the Cagayan valley from the narrow coastal plain. About three miles south of Vigan is the mouth of the Abra River, one of the five principal waterways of Luzon. The port for Vigan is Pandan, on the north bank of the river's mouth, linked to the provincial capital by a hard-surface, all-weather road.

Both Aparri and Vigan were in the area defended by General Wainwright's North Luzon Force. With only three Philippine Army divisions, a Philippine Scout cavalry regiment and infantry battalion, one battery of field artillery, and a quartermaster troop, General Wainwright had to defend an area about 625 miles (1,005 km) long and 125 miles (201 km) wide at its widest point. The most he could spare for the entire northern portion of Luzon was one partially trained and equipped Philippine Army division, the 11th, commanded by Col. William E. Brougher. His task was made even more difficult by the absence of headquarters personnel and corps troops necessary to direct and support operations to cover so large an area.

The 11th Division, like the other Philippine Army reserve divisions, had begun to mobilize in September. At the start of the war, its infantry regiments were only at two-thirds their authorized strength of 1,500 men per regiment; its artillery was in the process of mobilization and had not yet joined the division; service elements had joined, but had not yet been organized or trained as units. Transportation was practically nonexistent. The division suffered from a serious shortage of equipment. Individual training, especially in rifle marksmanship, scouting and patrolling, was inadequate. Only one regiment of the division had begun to train in units larger than company or battery size.

The 11th Division, with responsibility for the entire area north of Lingayen Gulf, was spread extremely thin. Most of the division was in position along the gulf as far north as San Fernando, La Union. Beyond that point it maintained only small patrols. One battalion of the division, the 3d Battalion, 12th Infantry, was assigned to defend the entire Cagayan valley. This battalion had its command post at Tuguegarao, with one company (200 men) posted fifty miles to the north, at Aparri, There were no troops at Vigan.

For the landings in north Luzon General Homma organized two forces from the 48th. Division's 2nd Formosa Infantry Regiment. The force which was to land at Aparri numbered approximately 2,000 men. Its main infantry element was the regimental headquarters, the 2nd Battalion, and half of the 1st Battalion. In command was Col. Toru Tanaka, the regimental commander, hence the name 'Tanaka Detachment'. The unit scheduled to take Vigan was known as the 'Kanno Detachment', after the commander of the 3d Battalion, 2d Formosa. It was of approximately the same size and composition as the Tanaka Detachment, and included the rest of the 2nd Formosa—half of the 1st Battalion and the 3rd Battalion.

The Japanese attached a great deal of importance to the success of the Vigan and Aparri landings, and what they lacked in ground troops they made up in naval escort. As a cover force, Vice Admiral Ibo Takahashi personally led a flotilla consisting of two heavy cruisers, the *Ashigara* and *Maya*, one light cruiser, two destroyers, and a converted seaplane tender. He left Mako on the 8th of December with his fleet, and on the morning of the 10th was about 200 miles (321.8 km) west of Vigan.

The transports left Mako on the evening of 7th of December, about the same time as the Bataan Island Attack Force. The 14th Army staff watched them sail with misgivings. The success or failure of these preliminary landings would have a tremendous effect upon the main landings to follow, and the Japanese feared that the Americans might discover and heavily damage, if not destroy, the two detachments.

Careful provision had been made for air support. With the first light of day, planes of the 24th and 50th Fighter Regiments appeared overhead to protect the convoy from air and naval attack. All that day and the next, 5th Air Group planes covered the two convoys. In the early morning hours of the 10th, the convoys had arrived at their anchorages. Not a single American aircraft had been sighted during the entire trip. "It was a miracle," stated the Japanese, "that it (the convoy) wasn't detected by the enemy." Before dawn the Tanaka Detachment was waiting off Aparri; the Kanno Detachment was off Vigan. The wind was strong and the seas high. The next few hours would be the most critical and hazardous of the entire voyage.

In the first light of dawn of the 10th of December, the men of the Tanaka Detachment began to transfer from the transports to the landing craft. Under cover of fighter aircraft from the recently captured field on the Luzon Island, two companies made the trip to shore successfully. But strong northeasterly winds and rough seas threatened to do what the Americans thus far had made no effort to frustrate the landings. The convoy commander therefore decided to land the remaining troops at Gonzaga, over twenty miles to the east, where Cape Engano offered partial protection from the heavy surf. The convoy sailed east along the coast, leaving the two companies at Aparri, and on reaching the new anchorage the rest of the Tanaka Detachment began to debark immediately.

The first report of the landing force, estimated as a regiment in size, reached MacArthur's headquarters late in the day, and aircraft were ordered aloft immediately to attack the landing force. The purpose of the landing was apparently well understood. Lt. Colonel James V. Collier of the G-3 Section noted that the Japanese 'most assuredly' were attempting to seize airfields from which fighters could support Formosa-based bombers. That night, the staff at USAFFE prepared to take the field, and a general plan for establishing an advance headquarters at San Fernando, Pampanga, with a rear echelon in Manila, was discussed.

General Wainwright, the American North Luzon Force commander, first heard of the Aparri landing, this time estimated as a reinforced brigade of 3,000 men, while he was inspecting the beach defenses of the 11th and 21st Divisions at Lingayen Gulf. Believing that the landing was a feint "to pull some of my forces up to that point and weaken the already weak defenses in the Lingayen Gulf region," Wainwright decided not to offer any opposition to the Tanaka Detachment. Since the only route south was down the Cagayan Valley, and since he believed that a battalion at Balete Pass could stop a fairly considerable force, he made no effort to meet the attack. He was certain, he later wrote, that the main Japanese landings would come "in the areas where I had the chief weight of my troops." But he did take the precaution of sending several scout cars of the 26th Cavalry to the Cagayan Valley to provide communication with the 11th Division troops in that area. MacArthur's headquarters in Manila meanwhile issued orders to destroy bridges in the valley and to establish a block at Balete Pass.

The company of the 3rd Battalion, 12th Infantry, located at Aparri on the morning of 10 December was commanded by a young reserve officer, Lt. Alvin C. Hadley. When the two companies of the Tanaka Detachment came ashore at dawn, Lieutenant Hadley reported the landing to battalion headquarters at Tuguegarao and was ordered to attack immediately and drive the enemy into the sea. Estimating the size of the force as considerably larger his was, he prudently withdrew south along Route 5, without firing a shot.

The reaction of the American air forces was more spirited. As the Tanaka Detachment was unloaded at Gonzaga, two B-17s appeared overhead. They had taken off from Clark Field at about 09:30 with orders to attack and sink the naval vessels and transports. The first plane, carrying eight 600-pound (272 kg) bombs, flew over the transport area dropping its bombs. Before being driven off by the Japanese fighter aircraft, the pilot reported a hit on one of the transports. In the second plane was Capt. Colin P. Kelly, Jr., the first war hero and winner of the Distinguished Service Cross. Under orders to attack a Japanese carrier mistakenly supposed to be near Aparri, Captain Kelly had taken off hurriedly in the midst of an air raid with only three 600-pound bombs. When he was unable to find a carrier, Kelly decided to attack what he thought was a large battleship, later erroneously presumed to be the *Haruna*. Of the three bombs, one is believed to have been a direct hit; the other two were near misses. As the B-17 flew away, the ship his bomb hit appeared to have stopped, with black smoke rising in a heavy cloud about it. On return to base, the plane was jumped by two enemy fighters and shot down. He held the plane level so that his crew could bail out but he couldn't bail out himself. Captain Kelly's body was later recovered in the wreckage. It was the first B-17 to be lost in combat in that war. He was also West Point's first graduate to be killed and the first American war hero in that war to be killed.

Captain Kelly had not actually attacked a battleship, and certainly not the *Haruna*. Nor had he sunk any vessel of the Japanese fleet. There were no battleships in Philippine waters at this time; the Haruna was hundreds of miles away supporting the Malayan invasion. Only Admiral Takahashi's cover force, with the heavy cruisers *Ashigara* and *Maya*, was in the vicinity, and it was 200 miles off the west coast of Luzon. Kelly was nowhere near this force, although the Japanese report it was attacked by heavy bombers that day. It is unknown to this day as to what his bomb actually hit.

The air attacks did not seriously hinder the Japanese landing at Gonzaga. Two other attacks against shipping resulted in the reported sinking of a transport. Actually, the Japanese suffered only minor damage; one minesweeper run aground and another heavily damaged.

The Tanaka Detachment was ashore and in Aparri by 13:00 (1:00 pm) when it reported the capture of the airfield. In Aparri, it was joined by the two companies that had landed there earlier. By evening elements of the detachment had penetrated six miles south to occupy the strip at Camalaniugan. Japanese construction troops and air service units moved in immediately and began to extend the airfields, establish depots, and ready the strip for operations. It had not been possible to bring much heavy equipment ashore that day because of the American air attacks, and some supplies, such as drummed oil, had been lost or floated ashore because of the transport crews' anxiety to leave the area.

Early the next morning, the Tanaka Detachment began to march south toward Tuguegarao, along Route 5. Aircraft from the 50th Fighter Regiment and the 16th Light Bombardment Regiment flew over the highway, bombing likely targets. The 3rd Battalion of the 12th Infantry retreated quickly down the Cagayan valley, offering no opposition, and by 05:30 on the 12th of December elements of the Tanaka Detachment had reached Tuguegarao airfield, fifty miles to the south.

Simultaneously with the landing at Aparri, the Kanno Detachment of 2,000 men began to debark at Pandan, near Vigan. An American P-40 pilot flying reconnaissance gave the first warning of the attack at 05:13 of the 10th. Alerted by this message, the Far East Air Force readied five B-17s and escorting P-40s and P-35s to bomb the invaders. By 0600, (6:00 am) the planes were airborne, flying north to the threatened area. The reception of the Kanno Detachment promised to be a warm one.

At Aparri, bad weather and heavy seas upset the landing schedule. Only a small portion of the Japanese force was able to get ashore at Pandan that morning, but these men quickly moved on to seize Vigan by 10:30. Meanwhile the convoy came under attack from American planes and suspended all efforts to land the rest of the force. The five B-17s, each loaded with twenty 100-pound (45.3 kg) demolition bombs, came in for their first run over the target shortly after 06:00. They were covered by P-40s of the 17th Pursuit Squadron. After the B-17s had dropped their bombs, the P-40s dived through the anti aircraft fire to strafe the Japanese ships. The P-35s of the 21st Squadron now arrived on the scene and, despite the lack of armor and leak proof tanks, flew low to strafe the invaders again and again. One of the transports, hit by a B-17 bomb, exploded during the last P-35 run, destroying the squadron commander's plane.

Later in the day, three more heavy bombers attacked the Vigan Attack Force. The first B-17 to arrive over the target dropped its bombs on what was thought to be a carrier, with no observed effect. The second attacked a cruiser unsuccessfully, but managed to score a direct hit on a transport. The last plane had time to load only one of its 600-pound bombs, and the bombardier released it over the water near the transports with no effect on the transports.

Despite the presence of eighteen naval fighters and planes of the Army's 24th Fighter Regiment, the Japanese were unable to fend off the American attack. As a result of the day's action, the enemy lost the transports *Oigawa Maru* and *Takao Maru*, both badly damaged and beached, and one minesweeper was sunk. The Japanese also suffered casualties aboard the destroyer *Murasame* and the light cruiser *Naka*, Rear Admiral Shoji Nishimura's flagship, which was slightly damaged.

The successful attacks of the American planes on the 10th were to be the last coordinated effort of the *Far East Air Force*. On that day, the Japanese attacked Nichols, Nielson, and Cavite, completing the destruction begun two days earlier at Clark. Thereafter the American fighters with few exceptions flew only reconnaissance missions over assigned areas; the 21st and 34th Squadrons covered south Luzon while the 17th and 20th patrolled the northern part of the island.

There was no activity near Vigan during the night of the 10th, but from Lingayen Gulf, 1,200 miles (1,931 km) to the south, came reports of another Japanese landing. Around midnight, several dark shapes were observed approaching the mouth of the Agno River. When confirmation was received, one battery of the 3rd Battalion, 21st Field Artillery (PA), opened fire. "It was like dropping a match in a warehouse of Fourth of July fireworks," wrote the American instructor assigned to the regiment. Instantly Lingayen Gulf was ablaze. As far as the eye could see the flashes of artillery, shell-bursts, tracer machine gun bullets and small arms." According to the American officer in command, thousands of Japanese were killed that night. When morning came, all that was found of the supposed invasion was one life preserver with markings which may have been Japanese characters. The absence of sunken ships did not prevent the 21st Division commander, Brig. General Mateo Capinpin, from reporting to Manila that an attempted hostile landing had been repulsed.

What actually happened that night was that the Japanese had sent one ship into Lingayen Gulf on a reconnaissance mission. The Japanese had no force near Lingayen then and no plan for a landing in the area at that time. Nevertheless, the news of the frustrated enemy landing was reported in the press as a great victory and the 21st Field Artillery was officially credited with repulsing an enemy landing.

Meanwhile, the *Vigan Attack Force*, unable to land troops and supplies in the face of rough seas, had moved four miles to the south. Protected by a squadron of fighters, the Japanese were finally able to put the Kanno Detachment ashore. A small force was immediately dispatched north, along Route 3, to Laoag, the capital of Ilocos Norte Province, fifty miles (80 km) away. By the following evening that town and its airfield had been occupied by Japanese troops.

The Japanese now had a firm foothold in northern Luzon, with planes of the 5th Air Group operating from fields, however inadequate, at Aparri, Vigan, and Laoag. Originally Homma had intended to leave the Tanaka and Kanno Detachments in position, but the American reaction had made it evident that there would be no counterattack. He decided therefore to leave only small garrisons to hold the seized airfields and to send the bulk of the two detachments, forming substantially the 2nd Formosa Regiment, to Lingayen Gulf to meet the main force of the 14th Army when it came ashore. Colonel Tanaka was to march around the north tip of Luzon along Route 3 to Vigan, and there join forces with Kanno. The combined force would then move south along the coastal road to Lingayen Gulf. At the same time Homma sent his chief of staff, General Maeda, to Luzon for a personal inspection and to brief the commanders on the change in plans. Maeda arrived at Aparri on the 14th of December and after talking to Colonel Tanaka placed him in command of both detachments and gave him his new mission.

By the 20th of December, the Tanaka and Kanno Detachments had joined and were ready to move south toward Lingayen Gulf. At 13:00 (1:00 p.m.) that day Colonel Tanaka led his reconstructed regiment (less three companies) out of Vigan, along Route 3. Repairing destroyed bridges along the line of march; forward elements of the regiment reached Bacnotan the next evening. There they made contact with the 11th Division troops, but by a flanking movement to the left (east) were able to force part of the defenders back, while cutting off others who made their way eastward to the mountains. Colonel Tanaka finally reached San Fernando, La Union, on the morning of the 22nd.

Just a few hours earlier the main strength of the 14th Army had begun to land across the beaches at Lingayen Gulf, a short distance to the south. Colonel Tanaka just missed being on the beaches to greet his comrades. The advance landings on northern Luzon, seen in retrospect, accomplished little. The fields seized were poor and by the time they were ready for operations, they were of small value. The detachments that landed did not require close air support, since the Americans didn't offer any determined resistance. The 5th Air Group had planned to operate mainly from Luzon bases by the 17th of December and by the following day had placed a number of Japanese air units on the recently seized fields. But they were not needed. As events turned out, Japanese misgivings were entirely unfounded; the dispersion of force entirely unnecessary. But this was small comfort for the Americans. In General Wainwright's words, "The rat was in the house."

The area held by General Parker's South Luzon Force was ninety miles (144.8 km) at its widest point and stretched from the Rosario-Infanta Line, southeast of Manila, sixty miles to the Atimonan-Padre Burgos line. In this region were five bays, all suitable for landing operations, and two large lakes, Laguna de Bay and Lake Taal. Altogether there were 250 miles (402 km) of possible landing beaches.

The area contained a good network of roads and one railroad which extended from Manila southeast to Daraga. Along the west coast the terrain was rugged, restricting the defenders to the roads. on the east coast, which was mountainous a good part of the way to Atimonan, the terrain presented a formidable obstacle to any military force. Below Atimonan was the Bicol Peninsula, trailing away in a southeasterly direction like the tail of a downcast dog. Near its tip, in Albay Gulf and only one mile from the southern terminus of the Manila Railroad, lay Legaspi, the next Japanese objective.

To defend south Luzon, General Parker had two Philippine Army divisions. On the west was the 41st Division (PA) commanded by Brig. Gen. Vincente Lim, a West point graduate and former deputy chief of staff of the Philippine Army. On the east was Brig. Gen. Albert M. Jones' 51st Division with its northern boundary along the line Pililla-Infanta and its southern boundary at Atimonan-Padre Burgos.

The 51st Division, like Colonel Brougher's 11th Division, was very poorly equipped and imperfectly trained. Presumably all the men had had five and one half months training some time during the past five years, but, said General Parker, "this was never apparent." The enlisted men of the division spoke the Bicolanian dialect, and the majority of the officers, who were from central Luzon, spoke Tagalog, making training even more difficult than it would otherwise have been. One infantry regiment had had thirteen weeks' training, another five weeks, and the last none at all. In the opinion of General Jones, the only troops in his division capable of offering any effective resistance were those of the 52nd Infantry.

For the landing in south Luzon, General Homma had organized a force of approximately 2,500 men from the 16th Division. Led by Maj. General Naoki Kimura, the infantry group commander of the division, this force consisted of infantry group headquarters, the 33rd Infantry (less the 1st Battalion), a battery of the 22nd Field Artillery, and engineer detachments. Accompanying the Kimura Detachment was the Kure 1st Special Naval Landing Force with 575 men.

Two days before General Kimura's men boarded their transports at Palau, Rear Adm. Takeo Takagi sortied from that base with an impressive naval force. By dawn of the 8th, he had reached a point about 120 miles from his destination. The carrier *Ryujo* launched the attack against Davao which the Preston had evaded. Following this strike, Takagi turned northeast and early the next morning, he joined Kimura's transports, which had left Palau at 09:00 the day before. Accompanying the transports was the Legaspi Attack Force; to the rear, en route from Palau, was the 17th Minelayer Division.

By 11:00 of the 11th of December, this combined force of Japanese warships was 135 miles east of San Bernardino Strait. Here the minelayers broke formation. Escorted by two destroyers, one column headed for San Bernardino Strait; another column, accompanied by one light cruiser and two destroyers, turned south for Surigao Strait. By midnight both groups had reached their destinations and had begun laying mines. The U.S. submarine SS-39 on patrol in San Bernardino Strait, was attacked and driven off by two Japanese destroyers without inflicting any damage on the Japanese force. From a point about 100 miles (160 km) offshore, planes of the Ryujo covered the convoy as it moved toward the shores of Albay Gulf. Admiral Takagi's force remained behind to provide distant cover. As the convoy approached the beaches, the Japanese planes shifted operations to the Legaspi area.

The Kimura Detachment began to land at the city of Legaspi early on the morning of the 12th of December. No difficulty was experienced and there was no opposition; the nearest American and Filipino troops were 150 miles (241 km) away. By 09:00 the Japanese were in control of the airfield and the terminus of the Manila Railroad. A few hours later, when he had a firm grip on Legaspi, General Kimura sent advance detachments to the northwest and southeast. The next day the huge cover force returned to Palau to prepare for the next landing.

The initial report of a Japanese landing at Legaspi came from the railroad stationmaster there. The apocryphal story is told that his call was switched from the railroad central to USAFFE headquarters in Manila and the following conversation took place:

STATIONMASTER: "There are four Jap boats in the harbor, Sir, and the Japs are landing. What shall I do?"

USAFFE OFFICER: "Just hang onto the phone and keep reporting."

"STATIONMASTER: "There are about twenty Japs ashore already, sir, and more are coming" A pause. "Now there are about three hundred Japs outside the station, sir, What am I to do?"

USAFFE OFFICER: "Just sit tight."

STATIONMASTER: "Sir, a few of those Japs, with an officer in front, are coming over here."

USAFFE OFFICER: "See what they want."

STATIONMASTER: "Those Japs want me to give them a train to take them to Manila, sir. What do I do now?"

USAFFE OFFICER: "Tell them the next train leaves a week from Sunday. Don't give it to them."

STATIONMASTER, hanging up: "Okay sir."

The subsequent conversation between the Japanese officer and the stationmaster (if it ever took place) was not recorded. It's unknown what happened to the station master but I think I am safe in saying he was probably shot on the spot.

When South Luzon Force headquarters received news of the landing, it considered a proposal to send a strong force south to surprise the Japanese and push them back into the sea. There were many practical difficulties in the way of such an expedition, the most serious of which was how to surprise an enemy who had control of the air and sea. The proposal was soon dropped, but General Jones's 51st Division was ordered to send units south into the Bicol Peninsula to destroy highway and railroad bridges and to evacuate as much railroad rolling stock as possible. Two companies of the 1st Battalion, 52nd Infantry, each with an attached machine gun platoon, were sent south to the outpost on Route 1 and the Manila Railroad, the only two routes north from Legaspi, and a specially trained detachment of the 51st Engineer Battalion was ordered to prepare all bridges for demolition in order to delay the enemy advance.

The first American reaction to the Legaspi landing came on the 12th of December when two fighters struck the Japanese-held airfield, killing three and injuring two men. Two days later, three of a group of six Del Monte-based B-17s, ordered to attack the landing force, reached the area. They attacked a Japanese minesweeper and a transport, thought to be a destroyer, with meager results, and nine naval aircraft based on the Legaspi strip. The unescorted bombers were no match for the Japanese fighters and soon they beat a hasty retreat. Only one of the B-17s was able to make its way back to Del Monte; the others had to crash-land short of their base. The Japanese lost at most, a mere four fighters.

With Legaspi firmly in Japanese hands, the Kimura Detachment moved northwest along Route 1 toward Naga. Ground units first made contact on 17 December when a Japanese patrol ran into a demolition detachment of the 51st Engineer Battalion working on a bridge near Ragay. The engineers managed to destroy the bridge and establish themselves on the near bank of the gorge, whereupon the Japanese patrol withdrew. The next day the Kimura Detachment entered Naga.

Pushing northwest from Naga, rebuilding bridges and repairing roads as they advanced, the Japanese reached Sipoco on the 19th with an estimated force of one battalion of infantry. Patrols were still active near Ragay, and reports reaching the Americans mentioned other Japanese elements moving along Route 1 toward Daet. By this time, the two out posted companies of the 1st Battalion, 52nd Infantry, were at Aloneros and Sumulong, and had thrust strong combat patrols forward. Luzon at this point forms a very narrow neck only seven miles wide, and any force from Legaspi had to pass through one of the two barrios, (small towns) Aloneros on the Manila Railroad or Sumulong on Route 1. The position was an excellent one for the Americans.

On the 21st of December, the American division commander, recently promoted to brigadier general, ordered Lt. Col. Virgil N. Cordero, the regimental commander, to move on Sipoco with

Companies B and C of the 52nd Infantry. At 05:00 the next morning, a Japanese force estimated to be a company attack Company B at Timbuyo, just east of the Negritos Camp along the highway. The Filipino troops, under the command of 1st Lt. Matt Dobrinic, were in a well-organized position, and drove off the Japanese, chasing them down the road for about six miles. They inflicted heavy losses on the enemy, suffering about 15-percent casualties themselves.

On the 23rd of December, General Jones ordered his troops to withdraw from the Bicol Peninsula when a Japanese invasion force appeared off Atimonan. Part of the 1st Battalion, 52nd Infantry, was cut off by the Japanese landing at Atimonan that night, but some of the men made their way back into the American lines. The 51st Division had accomplished its objective. It had delayed the enemy advance and prevented an immediate juncture of the Kimura Detachment with the main elements of the 16th Division soon to land at Lamon Bay.

The Japanese meanwhile were landing in the southern Philippines, in Mindanao and the Sulu Archipelago and those landings were intended primarily to provide bases for the Japanese 16th Army's drive on Borneo. The purpose of the Japanese plans was to prevent American reinforcements from reaching that island from Allied bases to the south and to cut the American route of withdrawal.

Two Japanese landings were scheduled in the south, one at Davao in Mindanao, and another on Jolo Island in the Sulu Archipelago. Two detachments, both under Maj. General Shizuo Sakaguchi, infantry group commander of the 16th Army's 56th Division, were organized for these landings. The first, originally scheduled to capture Davao alone, was led by Lt. Colonel Toshio Miura and consisted of the 1st Battalion of the 16th Division's 33rd Infantry, plus engineer and service elements. To it was later added the Sakaguchi Detachment, composed of the 56th Division's 146th Infantry, an armored unit, and one battalion of divisional artillery. The strength of the entire force was about 5,000 men.

This combined force was under 16th Army control, although the date of departure from Palau was set by 14th Army headquarters in

Formosa. Once Davao was seized, the Miura Detachment was to revert to 14th Army control and the 16th Army's Sakaguchi Detachment was to move on to Jolo Island on its way to Tarakan in Dutch Borneo. For the Jolo Island operation, the Kure 2nd Special Naval Landing Force from Legaspi and a naval airfield maintenance unit were to be added to the Sakaguchi Detachment.

The combined force left Palau at 14:00 on the 17th of December in fourteen transports. Admiral Takagi's force provided naval escort. Direct support was given by a destroyer squadron, while a cruiser squadron and the carrier *Ryujo* constituted a close covering force. That ship was later sunk on August 24th 1942 in the Battle of the Eastern Solomons. On the afternoon of the 19th, from a point about 200 miles (321.8 km) east of Davao, the *Ryujo* launched six planes to attack the radio station at Cape San Augustin, the tip of the eastern arm of Davao Gulf, while the seaplane carrier *Chitose* launched its own planes to reconnoiter over Davao. The transports arrived near the city after midnight on the night of the 19th-20th of December.

At 04:00 in the morning, troops of the Miura Detachment, covered by carrier-based aircraft, began landing in the northern section of Davao while elements of the Sakaguchi Detachment came ashore along the coast southwest of the city. Defending this sector of the island were about 2,000 Philippine Army troops led by Lt. Col. Roger B. Hilsman, commander of the 2nd Battalion, 101st Infantry.

The Miura Detachment was momentarily mistaken for an American naval or marine force when it was first sighted. When a Japanese destroyer began shelling the beaches, this misapprehension was quickly established. The only opposition offered to the landing force came from a machine gun squad which inflicted numerous casualties on the enemy before it was knocked out by a direct hit from a Japanese shell from the destroyer. Thereafter Colonel Miura's men met no further opposition. The casualties suffered made it necessary to commit those elements of the Sakaguchi Detachment which the Japanese were saving for the Jolo Island operation.

By about 10:30 that morning, Colonel Hilsman had pulled his men out of the city along the road leading northwest into the hills, leaving behind three of the eight 2.95-inch (74.9 mm) guns which constituted the artillery of the Visayan-Mindanao Force. The troops remaining in Davao were directed to withdraw also and set up defensive positions along the heights surrounding the city. It's unfortunate that he didn't think to spike the guns before leaving them for the enemy.

The Sakaguchi Detachment apparently met no resistance southwest of the city. Moving northeast along the coastal road, it entered the city and made contact with Colonel Miura's force early in the afternoon. By 15:00 the city and its airfield were occupied. That evening a seaplane base was established south of the city, and the next morning naval shore units began bringing Japanese nationals into Davao.

General Sakaguchi lost no time in dispatching the Jolo Force, consisting of one infantry battalion (minus two companies), with attached artillery, engineer, and communications units, and the Kure 2d Special Naval Landing Force. Its departure was delayed first by the unexpected casualties to the Miura Detachment and then by a B-17 attack. Nine of the bombers had come from Batchelor Field near Darwin, Australia, and they hit the Japanese at sunset of the 22nd. The raid came as a complete surprise to the Japanese. Fortunately, for them, visibility was poor and the Jolo Force suffered only minor damage. The next morning the Japanese convoy set out from Davao, reaching its destination on Christmas Eve.

The first warning of the approaching force reached the 300 Constabulary-troop defenders, at 17:00 (5:00 pm) of the 24th. The landings began three hours later. The Constabulary was able to offer only slight resistance, and by the following morning, the Japanese were in the town of Jolo. From Davao and Jolo the Japanese were in position to launch an attack against Borneo.

By now, the Canadian authorities had realized too late that a month earlier, they had foolishly sent a contingent of Canadian soldiers to Hong Kong to protect that island from any attack from the Japanese when there was little hope that the island fortress could withstand the onslaught of the Japanese forces and that fear was realized on December 25th when Hong Kong capitulated. As many as 290 Canadians were killed and the rest were taken prisoner. Various British Defence studies had already concluded that Hong Kong would be extremely hard to defend in the event of a Japanese attack. To this day, most Canadians think of the decision to send the men to Hong Kong as a colossal blunder on the part of Prime Minister King. One can only presume that his decision was based on his reading of his tea leaves, or the position of the hands on his watch, or whatever psychic phenomenon that moved him. In all likelihood his generals also gave him bad advice for if they knew anything about the risks involved, they would have urged caution. Of the 1,975 men who sailed from Vancouver in November to help man the garrison in Hong Kong, 1,418 survived battle, prison camps and slave labour and all of them bore the marks of having experienced a terrible ordeal.

Winston Churchill and his army chiefs designated Hong Kong an outpost, and initially decided against sending more troops to the colony. In September 1941, however, they reversed their decision and argued that additional reinforcements would provide a military deterrent against the Japanese, and reassure Chinese leader Chiang Kai Shek that Britain was genuinely interested in defending the colony.

The Japanese attack on Hong Kong began shortly after 08:00 on the 8th of December 1941 (Hong Kong local time), less than eight hours after the Attack on Pearl Harbor (because of the day shift that occurs on the international date line between Hawaii and Asia, the Pearl Harbor event is recorded to have occurred on the 7th of December.

British, Canadian and Indian forces, commanded by Major-General Christopher Maltby supported by the Hong Kong Volunteer Defence Corps resisted the Japanese invasion by the Japanese 21st, 23rd and the 38th Regiments, commanded by Lieutenant General Takashi Sakai, but were outnumbered three to one (Japanese, 52,000; Allied, 14,000) and lacked their opponents' recent combat experience.

The evacuation from Kowloon which is just across the harbour from Hong Kong started on the 11th of December under aerial bombardment and artillery barrage. As much as possible, military and harbour facilities were demolished before the withdrawal. By the 13th of December, the Rajputs of the British Indian Army, the last Commonwealth troops on the mainland, had retreated to Hong Kong Island.

Maltby organized the defence of the island, splitting it between an East Brigade and a West Brigade. On the 15th of December, the Japanese began systematic bombardment of the island's North Shore. Two demands for surrender were made on the 13th and the 17th. When these were rejected, Japanese forces crossed the harbour on the evening of the 18th of December and landed on the island's North-East. They suffered only light casualties, although no effective command could be maintained until the dawn came. That night, approximately 20 British gunners were massacred at the Sai Wan Battery after they had surrendered. There was a further massacre of prisoners, this time of medical staff, in the Salesian Mission on Chai Wan Road. In both cases, a few men survived to tell the story.

Fierce fighting continued on Hong Kong Island but the Japanese annihilated the headquarters of West Brigade and could not be forced from the Wong Ne Chong Gap that secured the passage between downtown and the secluded southern parts of the island. From the 20th of December, the island became split in two with the British Commonwealth forces still holding out around the Stanley peninsula and in the West of the island. At the same time, water supplies started to run short as the Japanese captured the island's reservoirs.

On the morning of the 25th of December, Japanese soldiers entered the British field hospital at St. Stephen's College, and tortured and killed a large number of injured soldiers, along with the medical staff—both doctors and nurses.

By the afternoon of the 25th, it was clear that further resistance would be futile and British colonial officials headed by the Governor of Hong Kong, Sir Mark Aitchison Young, surrendered in person at the Japanese headquarters on the third floor of the Peninsula Hong Kong hotel. This was the first occasion on which a British

Crown Colony has surrendered to an invading force. The Hong Kong garrison had held out for 17 days.

What follows is an interesting little tidbit that requires retelling. As we all know, if you throw a stick away from a dog, it will chase after it and bring it back to you. Gander, a dog from New Foundland helped fight the Japanese invaders on three occasions. Gander picked up a thrown Japanese hand grenade and rushed with it back to the enemy, dying in the ensuing explosion, but saving the lives of several wounded Canadian soldiers. After efforts by the Canadian War Museum, the People's Dispensary for Sick Animals awarded Gander the Dickin Medal on October 27, 2000, the first such award since 1949.

General Isogai Rensuke was appointed Governor-General of Japanese-occupied Hong Kong on 20th February 1942 at the recommendation of Prime Minister Hideki Tojo, his former superior officer while serving with the Kwangtung Army. During Isogai's tenure, Hong Kong was subjected to martial law. He based his command post at the Peninsula Hotel in Kowloon. Although Isogai arrived after the worst excesses committed by Japanese troops against civilians during the conquest of Hong Kong, and Isogai's troops (for the most part) were more disciplined than most Japanese forces in mainland China. However the people in Hong Kong suffered much deprivation from food shortages. This ushered in the three years and eight months of Imperial Japanese administration. Japanese soldiers also terrorized the local population by murdering and raping an estimated 10,000 women and looting.

Isogai retired from the post on the 24th of December 1944, and returned to Japan. At the end of the war, he was arrested by the SCAP (Supreme Commander Allied Powers) authorities and extradited to Nanjing, China, where he faced a military tribunal for war crimes committed during the occupation of Hong Kong. He was sentenced to life imprisonment, but released in 1952, and allowed to return to Japan where he died in 1967. It is beyond me how this war criminal was released after only serving five years in prison. He should have been executed.

Guam, a tiny, U.S.-held island only about 1,850 km (1,150 miles) south of Tokyo and within a short distance of the Japanese-mandated Marianas, was unfortified. At dawn on December 7th, 1941, a flight of Japanese bombers struck at the island. Three days later a task force stormed ashore. Without antiaircraft guns or coastal batteries, the small U.S. garrison surrendered. On Wake Island, another U.S. possession, a small marine detachment held off the first Japanese landing attempt on December 11th, 1941, but the Japanese returned in overwhelming force and captured the island on December 23rd. The fall of Guam and Wake Island cut off the U.S. communications line between Hawaii and the Philippines.

In 1942, when I was a nine-year-old child living in Wells, B.C., I saw the movie, *Wake Island* that starred Brian Donlevy, Robert Preston and MacDonald Carey. Hollywood wanted the Americans to have some hope which was badly needed since the war wasn't going that well during that period of time. The movie showed how the Americans heroically fought the Japanese invaders attacking that small island. However, it also showed the Japanese winning the battle.

As Japanese power expanded in the Pacific, the last Allied naval force in the area was dealt a crippling blow. After the disaster at Pearl Harbor, Washington had hoped that help would come from the British Royal Navy in the southwestern Pacific. The new battleship *Prince of Wales* and the battle cruiser *Repulse* were berthed at Singapore. As soon as British vice-admiral Tom Phillips heard of Japanese landings in Malaya, he put to sea with his two capital ships and an escort force but without air cover. Spotted by Japanese planes on December 9th, about 50 miles (80 km) from the coast of Malaya and only about 150 miles (240 km) from Singapore, the two British warships were sunk the next day.

MacArthur said he was going to fight on the "beaches, beaches, beaches," but this plan which is sometimes attributed to MacArthur actually was imposed on him on the 18th of October 1941 by General Marshall. The plan to fight on the beaches was preposterous in October but after the Navy left and the air forces were knocked out on

December 8th, it was suicide to continue the fight to protect Manila. On December 8th, MacArthur told his Chief of Staff General Sutherland they would have to "remove immediately to Bataan." He told the same thing to Quezon four days later. President Quezon also spoke against the plan to fight on the beaches. In the two weeks prior to the main Japanese invasion, MacArthur, knowing that he would have to retreat to Bataan and told this also by General Wainwright and President Quezon, refused to move supplies there. The Orange and Rainbow war plans since 1909 had included plans to move supplies to Bataan that had been changed by Marshall on the 8th of October 1941.

This change of defense to a plan of defending all beaches against superior forces was not just nonsense on its face, but a deliberate sacrifice of all U.S. troops in the Philippines and of the Philippines themselves. Even on its own terms it was no plan at all. It was just used to obliterate the sacrifice of the Philippines. The plan required a very large concentration of U.S. warships to defend the Philippines and Washington had ordered the Pacific fleet south, indicating that there was no plan to defend the beaches. The plan required air superiority which had been lost the first day of the Japanese attack because of MacArthur's blunder. Early on the Japanese invaded both in the north and in the south on December 10th at Apparri and Vigan and December 12th at Legaspi. MacArthur did not even attempt to repel them, proving the that beaches plan really was a farce. That slogan was simply a ruse to prevent the supplying the Bataan forces with what they needed to function. When the Japanese landed at Lingayen, MacArthur abandoned the beaches plan within two days. Some strategy! MacArthur also wouldn't invoke the Orange plan WPO-3 until December 24th after the Japanese had landed in force at nine specific points. He lost 500,000 rounds of artillery ammunition and 3,400,000 gallons of oil and gasoline plus food, clothing and medicines on the beaches. At the single depot at Cabanatuan, he left fifty million bushels of rice, enough to feed all the troops on Bataan for four years. Just 70 miles from Bataan quartermasters found 2000 cases of canned fish but were ordered directly and repeatedly by

MacArthur's headquarters to abandon them or face court-martial. Besides not supplying Bataan, MacArthur went to extraordinary lengths to make sure no food was taken there. He deliberately starved his men. On the 24th of January 1942, Bataan was ordered to send food to the already well-stocked Corregidor which had a six-month supply for 10,000 men. The men on Bataan were starving. This order was to further reduce them to starving rations.

This was the general who got a medal and a raise in rank for this stupidity. In addition to the Philippine Army, Bataan's forces consisted of 11,796 Americans and several regiments of Philippine Scouts who had been part of the United States Army in the Philippines for many years prior to the war. These were magnificent soldiers, well trained, loyal, and dedicated to the war effort. Led by American officers, they repeatedly distinguished themselves in the four months of combat. Adding to the number of military in Bataan were civilians who fled the advancing Japanese. They entered Bataan of their own free will, yet they had to be fed from military supplies.

Forced to feed such a large number of military and civilians, food became an immediate and critical problem to the command. Tons of precious rice were left in the warehouses upon the withdrawal into Bataan and were destroyed by the Japanese. Americans accustomed to "stateside chow" found themselves (mid-January) on half-rations along with the Filipino soldiers. A month later, these rations were cut again (1,000 calories per day) and consisted of rice and fish, or what little meat could be found. Most of the meat came from the horses and mules of the 26th Cavalry, Philippine Scouts, or the Philippine beast of burden, the water buffalo. Occasionally monkeys, snakes, ECT, supplemented the diet. Malaria ran rampant in Bataan, one of the most heavily mosquito-infested areas in the world at that time. Medication to offset the effects of that disease began to disappear early in the campaign.

MacArthur was a great administrator (the proof of that is in the manner in which he administered Japan after the war) but as a tactician, he was outright stupid and a total failure as a general.

On February 23rd 1942, the president of the United States made a radio address to the troops on Bataan which invariably discouraged them. He informed them that they would receive no relief. While Soviet Communists were being rushed billions of dollars of supplies, nothing, not even food, could be spared the soldiers on Bataan. They were left to starve and rot. This is in stark contrast to what happened on Guadalcanal just a few months later. Submarines and fast destroyers supplied American forces and even tankers full of gasoline were sent in and grounded so the troops could be well stocked on Guadalcanal. It would have been easy to break the 'paper blockade', as MacArthur called it, around the Philippines especially since Americans were by now reading the Japanese fleet code and could avoid interception. Not only could submarines have supplied Bataan, (the Asiatic Fleet stationed at Manila had the largest submarine force in the U.S. Navy) but large supply ships could have stood off in the south islands and fast coast-runners could have brought the supplies to Bataan at night. MacArthur wrote, "Since the blockade was lightly held, many medium-sized ships could have been loaded with supplies and dispatched along various routes. It seemed incredible to me that no effort was made to bring in supplies."

Japanese records show that commanding General Homma, who had about half as many troops as MacArthur, was ready to give up: "If only help could have reached the Philippines, even in small form, if only limited reinforcement could have been supplied, the end could not have failed to be a success." (It is incongruous for MacArthur to complain about lack of supplies when he was responsible.) Obviously, since ships were frequently sent out from Corregidor and Bataan in the spring of 1942, MacArthur himself leaving with a flotilla of PT boats on March 11th, ships could have equally well have been sent in. However, saving the 31,095 Americans on Bataan was not going to happen. It was the last thing Roosevelt wanted. Some clue to his thinking was his suggestion to MacArthur of surrendering rather early on in February when he told him, "I authorize you to arrange for the capitulation of the Filipino elements of the defending forces." This discloses intent. This was at a time when President Quezon controlled seventy-five percent of his country, the Japanese really only controlled the cities and the Japanese general was ready to give up. MacArthur did not think it was a good idea to surrender partly because Roosevelt, in typical fashion, had worded his letter so that MacArthur would take the blame.

The Japanese main invasion on December 22nd at Lingayen Gulf consisted of three transport echelons. The first was composed of twenty-seven transports from Takio under the command of Rear Admiral Kensaburo Hara, the second of twenty-eight transports from Mako under Rear Admiral Yoji Nishimura, the third of twenty-one transports from Keeling under Rear Admiral Sueto Hirose. This force of seventy-six transports carried the main part of Lieutenant General Masaharu Homma's 80,000 strong Fourteenth Army. MacArthur correctly predicted the landing site long in advance, probably through decoded JN-25B messages. Homma's transports were surprisingly given no air support or cover whatever.

With perfect timing, Washington ordered all bombers to Australia on December 17th just as the invasion forces embarked. Was it vital that this order was given even though the American bombers could have wreaked havoc on the Japanese invasion force when they were in their vulnerable transports? Further, the Philippine Army greatly outnumbered the Japanese and there was the prospect of strong resistance by them, particularly in light of the marked inferior quality of Japanese artillery and tanks. To give some idea of the devastation that heavy strategic bombers would have caused to the Japanese transports, MacArthur knew that of the twelve transports that approached the Philippines on December 10th (after Clark Field had been wiped out), four were sunk and three damaged. The horrific slaughter American bombers would have wreaked on defenseless transports is almost unimaginable. The Japanese invasion would have been a total debacle.

MacArthur, armed with perfect intelligence of enemy intentions from code breaking, had from December 8th to December 22nd to place his troops in strategic positions. Instead, he misplaced his troops at the head of Lingayen Gulf and left the obvious landing zone of the 120 mile Eastern Shore lightly defended by only Philipino divisions, one of which had no artillery. Fortunately for the Japanese, when they landed, they were unopposed even though the Japanese landing ships foundered horribly in the surf and it took them a long time with extreme difficulty to get their men and especially tanks and artillery ashore. When the Japanese landed, MacArthur demonstrated how hollow and false the 'defend the beaches' joke was and immediately ordered the retreat to Bataan on December 24th.

The destruction of MacArthur's air forces on the ground after nine hours advance warning because of his inaction by failing to bomb Formosa was one of the greatest blunders in the history of warfare and his loss of the Philippines was the greatest defeat of the U.S. Army. It is remarkable how MacArthur escaped any reprimand, kept his command and got his fourth star on December 17th and a Congressional Medal of Honor for 'gallantry and intrepidity' while at Bataan where he spent part of only one day, the 10th of January 1942, doing an inspection. He was awarded the medal after he had already fled and left his troops behind. His ultimate reward was orders of the president to leave the Philippines with his family while his soldiers were subjected to the deadly brutality of the Bataan Death March

The defense of the Philippines cannot be understood in terms of conventional military strategy. In those terms it was one incomprehensible blunder after another, done with due deliberation and afterward shamelessly rewarded. Just as Clauswitz said war is politics by other means, the sacrifice of the Philippines can only be understood in the larger political context. Analysis of local decisions by MacArthur, have missed the point that FDR was actually calling the shots. His motivations, not MacArthur's are at issue. The sacrifice of the 31,095 Americans and 80 thousand Filipino troops with 26 thousand refugees on Bataan is a separate issue from the sacrifice of the Army Air Corps at Clark and Meba.

The bombers were sacrificed, not only to facilitate the loss of the Philippines, but more immediately to trick Hitler into declaring war on the United States and events in the Philippines are analogous to Pearl Harbor which happened the same day. However, Hitler did declare war on December 11th and therefore obviously the sacrifice of Bataan proper springs from other motives. Did the deliberate failure of the Americans to defend the Philippines prompt Hitler to presume that the United States would not be a dangerous adversary?

To understand Roosevelt's strategy we have to ask ourselves a very basic question: Cui bono? "Who benefits?" Who benefited from Japan's temporary ascendancy and the war dragging on? It was obvious that when the Japanese Empire collapsed that there would be a power vacuum in Asia. The ultimate question of the Pacific War was who would fill that vacuum. Who would take China? Did Roosevelt want Russia to fill the vacuum and therefore have to prolong the war so that the Soviet Union could pick up the pieces? Because the Soviet Union had its hands full fighting Germany and could not dominate Asia until the war in Europe was under control, delay in the defeat of Japan was necessary. Bataan perhaps was a pawn in a larger game.

The 'Battling Bastards of Bataan' never understood enough to ask the critical question, "Who was their real enemy?" The orders to fight on all beaches and not supply Bataan were nothing less than the deliberate sacrifice of 31,095 Americans. Bataan obviously was a pawn in a larger game. Their enemy was president Franklin D. Roosevelt coupled with the stupidity of General MacArthur.

Corregidor is a small island in the entrance of the Philippines' Manila Bay. Due to its position in the bay, it had served as a focal point for the naval defenses of the capital city of Manila where 15,000 American and Filipino troops, consisting of anti-aircraft and coastal defenses, along with the Fourth Marine Regiment, recently arrived from China (December 1941), less a detachment stationed on Bataan, as part of a Naval Battalion were entrenched.

There were 23 batteries installed on Corregidor, consisting of 56 coastal guns and mortars. In addition, Corregidor had 13 anti-aircraft artillery batteries with 76 guns (28 3-inch and 48 .50-caliber) and 10

60-inch Sperry searchlights. The longest-range coastal pieces were the two 12-inch (305 mm) guns of Batteries *Hearn* and *Smith*, with a horizontal range of 29,000 yards (27,000 m). Although capable of an all around traverse, these guns, due to their flat trajectories, were not effective for use against targets on Bataan.

During the siege by the Japanese, Corregidor, had ample armor-piercing ammunition but very little of the anti-personnel type, which then was of greatest demand for use against land targets on Bataan. In fact, most of the anti-personnel shells were only for the 12-inch mortars of Batteries *Way* and *Geary*.

Battered by constant shell fire from Bataan and aerial bombardment, with their supplies running out, General Wainwright, successor to MacArthur as commanding officer of the United States forces in the Philippines, decided his situation was hopeless and surrendered Corregidor and the troops in the southern part of the Philippines. With the establishing of a beach head on Corregidor by the Japanese, he avoided a 'bloodbath' that would have most certainly occurred had the Japanese fought their way from the beach to Malinta Tunnel, where most of the defenders of the island had withdrawn as the Americans were greatly outnumbered. Despite the conditions at Corregidor and the impossibility of defending it, MacArthur didn't forgive Wainwrite until after the war when they met on a battleship in Tokyo Bay. The fortress was overwhelmed by Japanese forces and on May 6th 1942. The defender's rations were depleted so the Allied forces were forced to surrender Corregidor to Lt. Gen. Homma Masaharu of the Japanese Imperial Army. The battle for the recapture of Corregidor, between the 16th of February and the 26th of February 1945, was undertaken by American and Filipino liberation forces against the defending Japanese garrison on the island fortress.

Of the 11,796 American soldiers on Bataan on April 3rd, 1942, about 1,500 remained who were wounded or sick in Bataan's two field hospitals after the surrender. Others, relatively few, made their way across the two miles of shark-infested waters to Corregidor, where they were assigned to beach defense. About 9,300 Americans reached

Camp O'Donnell after completing the Death March.

Between 600 and 650 Americans died during the March. Of the 66,000 Filipino troops, Scouts, Constabulary and Philippine Army units, it can be said the approximately 2,500 of them remained in the hospitals of Bataan; about 1,700 of them escaped to Corregidor, (only to be captured when Corregidor fell) and a small number of them remained on Bataan as work details for the Japanese after the surrender.

Those captured on Bataan on or about April 9th, 1942, were in the general area of the town of Mariveles, at the southern tip of the Bataan peninsula. Large fields outside this town were used as staging areas for the thousands of captives, American and Filipino, gathered together.

Mass confusion reigned in these areas and when darkness fell, it became impossible to recognize anyone. In a brief period of time buddies were soon separated and, in many cases, never to see one another again.

Each morning, groups of several hundred would be hustled onto Bataan's only concrete road (National Road) leading north out of the peninsula and began the exodus to prison camp. No design or plans for the group ever materialized. Each sunrise, shouting, shooting, bayoneting, by Japanese, would assemble anyone they could to make up the marching groups.

As a result, individuals generally found themselves among perfect strangers, even if they were fellow Americans. Consequently, a 'dog eat dog, every man for himself" attitude soon prevailed. Few helped one another on the March. Those belonging to the same military unit were fortunate, with their buddies helping when needed. During one group's march, volunteers were sought to carry a stretcher containing a colonel wounded in both legs and unable to walk. Four men offered to help. After hours of carrying the man in a scorching hot sun with no stops and no water, they asked for relief from other marchers. No one offered to pick up the stretcher. Soon, the original four bearers put down the man and went off on their own. The colonel was last seen by the side of the road begging to be carried by anyone. No one assisted him and subsequently a Japanese soldier bayoneted him to death.

After the first day of marching, without food or water, men began to drop out of column. Japanese guards would rush up, shouting commands in Japanese to get back in the group. When that approach failed, shots rang, out killing those who would not or could not rise. Many of those failing to obey the order to march were beheaded by sword wielding-Japanese guards, usually officers and non-coms since they were the ones who carried the swords.

Such actions on the part of the Japanese brought many captives to their feet and they continued the march for awhile longer. As each day and night passed without water, the marchers began to break from their group to run to anything that resembled water. Most often they would hurl themselves into a water puddle alongside of the road and lap up the muddy water; similar to a cat lapping milk from a saucer. Needless to say, the water was not potable and drinking of it soon brought on cramps, diarrhea, and eventually dysentery caused by the numerous flies found in the puddle. Such acts continued for each day of the March, lasting from five to ten days, depending upon where one joined the March, and continued until the marchers reached the town of San Fernando, Pampamga, a distance for most marchers of over 100 kilometers.

Upon reaching San Fernando, the prisoners were forced into railroad boxcars. (40 feet x 8 feet and built in 1918 and used in France during World War I.) With over 100 men in each car, the Japanese then closed the doors on the prisoners. There was no room to sit down or fall down. Men died in the sweltering cars. Upon arriving in the Municipality of Capas in the province of Tarlac, almost four hours later, the men detrained for Camp O'Donnell—another ten kilometer walk.

Official figures estimate that between 44,000 and 50,000 of the Filipinos arrived at O'Donnell after completing the March. Between 12,000 and 18,000 of their number are unaccounted for. What happened to them is unknown, but it is believed that between 5,000 to 10,000 of them lost their lives on the Death March.

The death toll for both Filipinos and Americans, however, did not cease upon reaching O'Donnell. Instead, during the first forty days of that camp's existence, more that 1,500 Americans were to die. At least 25,000 Filipinos died by July 1942 in the same camp. All of the deaths were the direct result of malnutrition on Bataan, disease, and the atrocities committed by the Japanese on the March. Shortly after the last of these prisoners entered O'Donnell (April 24th 1942), Corregidor fell on May 6th.

After two weeks of the famous Japanese 'sun treatment' for prisoners, in the sun-baked areas of Corregidor, these troops were taken across Manila Bay to Manila and then by train to Prison camp Cabanatuan near the city of Cabanatuan, in Northern part of Luzon. The men were in that camp when the Bataan survivors arrived from Camp O'Donnell in June 1942. The extremely high death rate in that camp prompted the Japanese to make such a move, and thereby allowed the American medical personnel to treat the Filipino prisoners remaining behind until their release beginning in July 1942. The condition of the prisoners arriving in Cabanatuan was such as to shock their fellow Americans from Corregidor. In a short period of time, however, they, too, would feel the full effects of Japanese captivity.

It was not however, until June 1942 that the men of Bataan and Corregidor began to share a common experience. During the first nine months of Cabanatuan's existence, when the vast majority of the camp's 3,000 American deaths occurred, most of the deaths were men of Bataan, still suffering from the effects of residing in Bataan, the Death March, and Camp O'Donnell. The text from the Bataan Memorial in the Philippines says; "Sleep my sons, your duty done. For freedom's light has come. Sleep in the silent depths of the sea or in your hallowed bed of sod until you hear at dawn the low clear reveille of God."

By the end of December 1941, Japanese forces penetrated southern Burma from Thailand and took Victoria Point. They drove the small British garrison back into the capital of Burma, Rangoon. (both names later changed to Myanmar and Yangon respectively).

A full account of all massacres of Filipinos by Japanese troops would fill several books. In Manila for example, 800 men women and children were machine-gunned in the grounds of St.Paul's College. In the town of Calamba, 2,500 were shot or bayoneted. 100 were bayoneted and shot inside a church at Ponson. 169 villagers of Matina Pangi (a district of Davao) were rounded up and shot in cold blood. On Palawan Island, 150 American prisoners of war were murdered.

At the War Crimes Trial in Tokyo, document No 2726 consisted of 14,618 pages of sworn affidavits, each describing separate atrocities committed by the invading Japanese troops. The Tribunal listed 72 large scale massacres and 131,028 murders as a bare minimum.

In January, 1942, a company of Australian and Indian soldiers were captured by the Japanese and interned in a large wooden building at Parit Sulong in Malayasia. Late in the afternoon of January 22nd 1942, they were ordered to assemble at the rear of a row of damaged shops nearby. The wounded were carried by those able to walk, the pretext being the promise of medical treatment and food. While waiting at the assembly point, either sitting or lying prone, three machine guns, concealed in the back rooms of the wrecked shops, started their deadly chatter, their concentrated fire chopping flesh and limbs to pieces. A number of prisoners whose bodies showed signs of life, were later bayoneted. In order to dispose of the bodies, which totaled 161, the row of shops was blown up and the debris bulldozed into a heap on top of which the corpses were placed. Sixty gallons of gasoline was splashed on the bodies and then a flaming torch was thrown on the pile. Just before midnight, the debris of the nine shops had burned into a pile of gray ash two feet high and the 161 bodies were totally incinerated.

The perpetrator of this foul crime was Lt-General Takuma Nishimura who later faced trial before an Australian Military Court. Nishimura was previously convicted of massacres in Singapore and sentenced to life imprisonment by a British Military Tribunal on April 2, 1947. After serving four years of his sentence, he was being transferred to Tokyo to serve out the rest of his sentence and while the ship stopped temporarily at Hong Kong, he was seized by the Australian military police and taken to Manus Island where his second trial was held. He was found guilty and hanged on June 11th, 1951.

On the morning of 22/23 of January, 1942, Japanese forces landed on the island of New Britain. Defended by men of the Australian 2/22 Battalion of the 8th Division, AIF, The New Guinea Volunteer Rifles and in of the 2/10 Field Ambulance Unit, they were soon overwhelmed and taken prisoner when the airport at Laha on the Gazelle Peninsular was captured. The first ten taken prisoner were immediately bayoneted to death. The rest, including 60 Dutch and many Ambonese workers were confined in a large house near the airfield. On February 3rd they were taken out one by one and marched to a spot in a grove of coconut trees. There, they were made to kneel at the edge of a large hole, previously dug by the Japanese, and were then blindfolded. They were then beheaded by the sword or stabbed through the chest by a bayonet. Two weeks later, on the 20th of February, another 220 prisoners were killed in the same way at a spot some 140 metres away. Six men survived the massacre, two dying some days later. When the Australian 11th Battalion recaptured the area in April, 1945, a mass grave containing around 150 skeletons was found. The order for the killings was issued by the commander of the Japanese forces, Rear Admiral Hatakeyama. In Australia, the official Government report on the massacre was not released until 47 years later, in 1988. Hatakeyama was captured after the war and arraigned by the Australians, but died before his trial could begin.

The Doolittle bombing raid on Tokyo brought a retaliation against the Chinese people that staggers the imagination. On April 18th, 1942, sixteen twin-engined Mitchell bombers, led by Lt. Col. Jimmy Doolittle, were launched from the aircraft carrier USS Hornet. Their mission was to bomb the Japanese capital, Tokyo and then proceed to friendly airfields in China, 1,200 miles across the East China Sea, to refuel. Some of the planes reached their destination safely but the others ran out of fuel and crashed after their crews had baled out. Sixty four airmen parachuted into the area around

Chekiang. Most were given shelter by the Chinese civilians but eight of the Americans were picked up by Japanese patrols and three were shot after a mock trial for 'crimes against humanity'. The Japanese army then conducted a massive search for the others and in the process whole towns and villages that were suspected of harbouring the Americans, were burned to the ground and every man, woman and child brutality murdered. When the Japanese troops moved out of the area in mid-August of 1942, they left behind a scene of devastation and death that is beyond comprehension. Official Chinese estimates put the death toll at a staggering 250,000.

The Pacific War on the other hand had little impact on Canada. A single Japanese submarine lobbed a few shells at the Estavan Point lighthouse on the west coast of Vancouver Island and fled. The only other time the Pacific side of North America was attacked was via the Japanese balloon bombs carrying incendiaries. More on that in the next volume.

Chapter Twenty

The war with Germany extended right into the St. Lawrence estuary. Once within the St. Lawrence estuary, rampaging over two summers, 1942 and 1944, Nazi U-boats destroyed 23 ships, including four Canadian warships, and killed some 300 people, many of whom were civilian passengers. Deep within what Premier Bouchard would call Quebec territory, in the thick of the Battle of the Atlantic, Hitler's sea-wolves were wreaking deadly havoc and brought about with an almost free rein because domestic defenses were stretched thin by the European war effort.

There are at least two major historic milestones to the so-called Battle of the Gulf of St. Lawrence; so-called because Canadian defenders, though they tried mightily, were unable to disable, sink or capture a single one of the tormenting subs. The Nazi incursions marked the first time since the War of 1812 that a foreign enemy force had cause fatalities on Canadian soil.

It was also the only actual fighting between Allies and Nazis to take place within Canada, even within North America. But because it was such a shocking, alarming, and potentially panic-inducing development, most of what actually happened in the Gulf during the war was kept from the public.

The October 14th, 1942, sinking of the ferry *Caribou*, steaming between Sydney and Port Aux Basques, made the newspapers, since the death toll included five mothers and 10 children, as well as 121 military personnel, including Agnes Wilkie, the only Canadian navy nurse to die due to enemy action at sea.

On the night of May 11/12, Karl Thurmann, captain of *U-553*, piloted his U-boat into the Gulf of St. Lawrence. He had been assigned to *Operation Drumbeat*, Germany's strategic submarine offensive against North America's eastern seaboard. He sighted the *Nicoya*, a British freighter carrying war supplies, sailing outbound from Montréal. He torpedoed it 15 kilometres north of Pointe-à-la-Frégate. Before morning light, he also sank the *Leto*, a Dutch freighter chartered to the British Ministry of War Transport, off Rivière-la-Madeleine. Six merchant seamen died in the first attack and a dozen in the second.

The next day, amidst media accounts of survivors' lifeboats drifting ashore in the Gaspé region, Naval Service Headquarters announced that: "...the first enemy attack upon shipping in the St. Lawrence River took place on 11 May, when a freighter was sunk. Forty-one survivors have been landed from this vessel. The situation regarding shipping in the river is being closely watched, and long prepared plans for its special protection are in operation. Any possible future sinkings in this area will not be made public, in order that information of value to the enemy may be withheld from him."

This development led to a major reinforcement of the Gaspé site and the dispatch of five Bangor minesweepers, three Fairmile launches and an armed yacht, to form the Gulf Escort Force. The latter assumed primary responsibility for escorting Québec-Sydney convoys. Along with the Sydney Force, consisting of two Bangor minesweepers, six Fairmile launches and two armed yachts, they constituted the leading naval forces available for Gulf services.

On the night of May 8/9, 1942, Eastern Air Command picked up a false report of a U-boat sighting from Cape Ray, Newfoundland, and commenced anti-submarine patrols over the Gulf on May 11th, 1942. Before sunset, it received word of the sinking of the *Nicoya*. Air reinforcements were hastily dispatched to a training airfield at Mont-Joli, Quebec. Eventually, 117th (Bomber-Reconnaissance) Squadron, equipped with Canso and Catalina aircraft, was sent to North Sydney, Nova Scotia. Although at half-strength already, 117th Squadron also formed a detachment at Gaspé. Thirteen other squadrons of the Royal Canadian Air Force would eventually join the fray, notable among them 113th (Bomber-Reconnaissance) Squadron of Yarmouth, Nova Scotia. Its Hudson aircraft would be credited with the overwhelming majority of aerial anti-submarine attacks in the Gulf of St. Lawrence by the end of 1944.

During the remainder of the ice-free season, the Canadian navy's modest inland escort force and its air counterparts fought against a canny and highly successful foe that operated with daunting success.

During the deadly summer of 1942, six U-boats, let loose like sharks in a tank of tuna, torpedoed and sank 21 ships in the Gulf and up the river. One, the *Carolus*, was sunk off the ritzy resort town of Metis Beach, a mere couple hours by train from Quebec City.

The majority of the quarry were merchant ships, carrying supplies for the British war effort or construction materials for the Goose Bay air base being built in Labrador. But two warships sank that season as well, the HMCS *Raccoon* on September 7th and the HMCS *Charlottetown*, four days later. Both ships were trying to protect convoys from the U-boat attacks.

Sometime in July 1942, Ernst Vogelsang piloted *U-132* into the Gulf. On July 6th, he sank three ships from the twelve-ship convoy QS-15, the British-registered *Dinaric* and *Hainaut* and the Greek vessel *Anastassios Pateras*. Eventually depth charge runs by HMCS *Drummondville*, commanded by Lieutenant J.P. Fraser, drove the submarine to the bottom, where it hid for twelve hours. Four Curtiss Kittyhawk fighters from 130 Squadron in Mont-Joli, lead by Squadron Leader J.A.J. Chevrier, scrambled to join the attack. Chevrier's aircraft disappeared during the mission, never to be found. On July 20th, Vogelsang added to his tally. He torpedoed the British merchant ship *Frederika Lensen* west of Pointe-à-la-Frégate, killing ten merchant sailors.

The Royal Canadian Air Force threw all it could into the search for the deadly submarines. It rushed more bombers to Mont-Joli. Knowing that the very presence of air cover could deter the U-boats. It even ordered aircraft from the Operational Training Units in Greenwood and Debert, Nova Scotia, and from the General Reconnaissance Schools in Summerside and Charlottetown, Prince Edward Island, into the air. Improved air cover could do little, however, if weather conspired against the defenders. And that is what happened with convoy QS-33. It was enveloped by fog between Cap-Chat and Gaspé and emerged the worst mauled convoy of the Gulf contest.

Ironically, heavy air cover elsewhere drove the U-boats further up the Gulf, west of Pointe-des-Monts, where the St. Lawrence narrows to 50 kilometres in width. There, they intercepted eight merchant ships, escorted by the corvette HMCS *Arrowhead*, the minesweeper HMCS *Truro*, the armed yacht HMCS *Raccoon*, and two Fairmile launches. The convoy was off Cap-Chat shortly after 10 p.m. on September 6, 1942, when U-165 sank the Greek merchant ship *Aeas* with a torpedo, killing two. The *Arrowhead*, the lead escort, turned back and through the glow of starshell, its captain, Commander E.G. Skinner, saw the *Raccoon* zig-zagging in search of the submarine. That was the last time anyone saw the little warship.

A few days earlier near Matane, the *Raccoon* had seen two torpedoes cross its bows at perilously close range, but had escaped unscathed. Now, its luck ran out. At 1:12 a.m. on September 7th, as the convoy passed Rivière-la-Madeleine, two loud explosions rent the night. Ships nearby guessed they were hearing depth charges dropped by the *Raccoon* as it continued to pursue U-165. Only later was it discovered that the sounds were those of a German torpedo ripping through the converted yacht.

HMCS *Raccoon* and its entire crew of 37 were lost in an instant. One of those who perished was Supply Assistant John Shefflin. As his ship was sinking, a train sped through nearby Rivière-la-Madeleine in the Gaspe Peninsula carrying his wife Marguerite and two pre-school children. She had made a spur-of-the-moment decision to move from Toronto to join their family in Eureka, Nova Scotia, so that they could see Shefflin when he took his occasional shore leaves. It would be years before his family discovered just how close together they were, before fate tore them apart forever.

The next day, U-517 attacked the diminished convoy. The sub lay in wait just off Cap-Gaspé, as its prey slowly advanced towards the sub through fog and mist. Within short order, the sub sent three more merchant ships to the bottom. The Battle of the Gulf of St. Lawrence claimed the Greek registered ships *Mount Pindus* and *Mount Taygetus*. Two seamen perished in the first and five in the second. The Oakton, owned by the Gulf and Lake Navigation Co. of Montréal, was the sub's next target. Its torpedo struck its engine room, killing an oiler and two firemen, then sending a cargo of coal destined for Corner Brook, Newfoundland, to the bottom. Lieutenant Bill Grant in Fairmile 083 rescued 17 survivors from the Oakton, along with 61 sailors from the two Greek vessels.

Canadian forces scored no kills in their maddening efforts to protect St. Lawrence shipping from the sea-wolves. But, despite the loss of lives and ships, the U-boats' effectiveness in choking off shipping was limited because the vast majority of goods shipped through the St. Lawrence made it safely to their destination in Great Britain.

My mother got a job in Wells soon after we arrived in September 1941. She hated the job. The owner of one of the stores (MacKenzies) on Saunders Street asked my mother to sit in a small room overlooking the main floor and spy on a particular woman who shopped there every day. The woman was a shoplifter and was the wife of the mill superintendant of one of the mines. My mother quit soon after and actually later became a close friend of the shoplifter for many years.

My mother got another job which she liked. My uncle had appointed her to be the cook for the elementary school. She would prepare the soup and rice pudding for all of us having our lunch at school—which was for practically all of the students in the elementary school which ran along side of Mildred Avenue and fronted on Dawson Street.

I was still in grade two of course and I was put in the one-story elementary school right away. It only had four classrooms. It did have a basement however and on very cold days, we would have our recess in the basement. An additional floor was added after we left Wells. As said earlier, my uncle was the principal of that elementary school and the combined Junior and Senior High School which was across the playing field and east of us. Grades one and two were in one classroom, grades three and four were in another classroom and grades five and six had their own classrooms.

This is a very foolish way to teach kids at school. No matter how hard we tried, it was impossible to ignore what our teacher was teaching the other kids in our classrooms be they behind us or ahead of us. There is a school in Toronto at the time of this writing that is considering having three grades in each classroom. Now that is really stupid.

On one occasion, my uncle decided to strap a number of students of the elementary School on the hands for throwing snowballs on school property. I was accused of doing this also but in this particular instance, I was innocent. He kept the strapping of my hands to the very end and as he told me to hold out my hands, I wailed and cried about my innocence. I guess my uncle couldn't strap his own nephew who wailed and cried so hard about his innocence so he sent me back to my room un-strapped. I walked back to my school room rubbing my hands as if they had been strapped but everyone knew I hadn't been strapped. If I had, everyone in the school would have all heard the strapping noise. It always sounded like loud gun shots in a forest.

My mother had noticed that I seemed to have an ear for picking up tunes when I tried to play them on pianos. She decided that I should take music lessons. My mother paid a Mrs. Berlin, to teach me piano. She was the organist and wife of the Anglican minister of the St. George Anglican Church just off of Pooley Street. She taught me one-hour piano lessons for 50 cents every Saturday morning. Their home was at the bottom end of the bend of the horseshoe-shaped Bowman Crescent and overlooked the Tailings south of the town. They only had to walk a hundred feet to get to their church. Although we didn't have a piano in our house, my uncle solved that problem for me. The school had a piano in it and because he was the principal of the school and I was his nephew, I was probably the only kid in all of North

America who actually carried in his pocket, the key to his school. The piano was in one of the rooms on the main floor.

There I was, night after night, for the next three years, during hot summers when I wanted to play outside, practicing in a hot and stuffy room and during freezing winters when I wanted to get into bed to get warm under the blankets, practicing the piano in a cold room with cold stiff fingers. It was also scary in the winter. Entering the school after dark, with the wind howling outside, with strange sounds coming from everywhere in the building, approaching the piano room armed only with a small flashlight trying to spot with the flashlight any ghosts or bogeymen that may be lurking in the darkness, is not really conducive to wanting to practice on the piano. It didn't help to have the caretaker of the school who lived in a small apartment in the basement deliberately making unusual sounds to add to my fears. To say that all this is conducive to encouraging a young kid to practice at the piano is to say that chicken's have lips. Well this chicken had lips and this chicken's lips trembled every night as it walked through the pitch black hallway of the school with its flashlight waiting for the ghosts or bogeyman or whatever to creep up to it and get it before it could get to the room where the piano was and turn on the lights in the room so that the ghosts and bogeymen would run away.

My mother had a key also, being the school cook so one stormy night she crept up to me and touched my shoulder. I left that piano stool behind me as I shot upward towards the ceiling. This is partly because I was informed a week earlier that a crazy Indian had killed his wife's lover and hacked his body to pieces and distributed his body parts around town a few weeks earlier and by coincidence I happened to be thinking about that incident at that precise moment when my mother decided to sneak up on me and touch my shoulder. Talk about an adrenaline jolt. If adrenaline jolts were electricity, that night I could have lit up the entire town.

I always felt sorry for Mrs. Berlin. She tried to get me to touch the keys lightly but her keys were stiff so I practically had to pound the keys to get them to play. I'm afraid that my pounding stayed with me for many years until I learned the art of 'touch'. Mind you, Franz List had the same problem as I. In fact, he attacked his pianos so violently that the hammers would fly off. Even strings would snap. People would come for miles for one of his performances, if not to hear his music then certainly to watch him almost demolish a piano. The famous pianist and comedian, the late Victor Borge (whom I had the pleasure of personally meeting and performing with) once demolished a piano right in front of his audience. I have never done that purposely but in the 1960s, while giving a performance in a concert on a grand piano, I hit a low chord at the bottom of the piano for the opening chord of the *Theme from Exodus* and the vibrations went down the length of the piano to the piano leg supporting the far end of the piano. The bolt which held the leg to the main frame of the piano, which had been over the years, gradually slipping out of the rotted wood, let go and the far end of the piano, upon receiving that first vibration from my heavy-handed chord, fell heavily to the floor while the strings hummed. Then I walked off the stage with the piano bench under my arms. The laughter that followed immediately after the shock wore off the faces of my audience, was to say the least, loud and long. Fortune smiled upon me that day however as I was able to complete my performance on an upright piano at the foot of the stage—which hadn't been locked. Richard Adinsell composed the *Warsaw Concerto* as background music for a movie depicting the bombing of Warsaw. People have said that when I played the piano and banged down on the keys with fury, they also had the bombing of Warsaw in mind.

It was in the last week of October 1941 that I woke up one morning and observed that the top halves of the mountains had turned white. By the 27th, (my birthday—I had turned eight and I and sixteen million others around the world were celebrating their birthdays that day also) the first snow had arrived in Wells. Until the last week of March, the trees on all the mountains, beginning from October or November, were always covered with snow.

In Toronto, we always had snow in the winter months but in Wells, we had SNOW. During any winter in Wells, as much as four and a half to five meters of snow would fall on the town. Of course, that doesn't break the world record which occurred in Tamarack, California. As much as 73 feet (22.2 meters) blanketing that town in the winter of 1906-7. In any case, in Wells, the snow would pile up to the eaves of the roof and sometimes we had to build a tunnel in the snow to get out the front door to the street. For some reason, we didn't have the same problem with the back door although on occasion, the drifts piled up over that door also. It was a job keeping the snow away from the windows after a real snow storm. The snow drifts would pile up right over the roof in some instances. Fortunately for us, the snow was generally the dry kind so the weight of it didn't bear heavily on the roofs of our houses. Whenever we walked across the snow, we could hear our boots crunching and squeaking across it.

Sometimes we got wet snow so we built snowmen and snow forts. Have you ever seen multilevel, two-story snow forts? In Wells, we built them. When the snow plow piled the snow at the end of Saunders Avenue on the south side of Pooley Street, the snow was two stories high and we built tunnels in the piled snow like ants building a colony. One winter, a number of us kids built a series of snow forts on the raised tennis court on Saunders Avenue. We built tunnels from our main forts to our outer forts and then we bombarded the enemy forts with huge snow balls we had created for the occasion. We placed a wide board over a short log and place the huge snowball on one end and two of us jumped on the other end. It was great fun watching these huge snow balls head upwards and then fall upon the enemy, crashing through the walls of the enemy forts or through the roofs of their tunnels. Then they got the same idea. Within days, all our forts and tunnels were in ruins. Alas—tis the consequences of war.

By the time December 1941 had arrived, I had an idea of what cold really was. In Toronto, we had cold. In Wells, we had COLD. I mean, it would get so cold, as soon as we touched the outside door handle of either the front or back doors, our bare fingers would stick to it. Often I would look at the door knob and wonder what would happen if I did it. I heard of others doing it but I finally came to the conclusion not to do it. I didn't put my tongue on the outside door knob. My brother put his tongue on the outside door handle of our front door however. It took my mother half an hour to get his tongue off the door handle. The ice was so thick on the windows we would have to shave the ice off with a knife in order to see anything outside.

I remember one night in 1944, there was a fire outside of town and my brother and I spent a good half-hour trying to melt a hole through the ice on the glass window with our fingers in order to see out. By the time we succeeded, the fire was out. The temperatures dropped to minus 70 degrees Fahrenheit (38.8 Celsius below freezing in the early hours of some mornings and when it rose to minus 40 degrees Fahrenheit (22 Celsius below freezing) we were required to go to school. If we attempted to go to school when it was colder than that, our noses would bleed. Further, exposed skin freezes at those low temperatures anywhere from within a few seconds to a few minutes. After the sun had been up for a couple of hours, the temperature would rise appreciably so that we were expected to go to school after lunch. Since we rarely had cloudy days in the winter months, other than during blizzards, we were never able to stay home from school an entire day. Fortunately, there was little wind to contend with so we didn't have to deal with a wind/chill factor and because of that, for the most part, the air was dry and there was less risk of frostbite requiring amputation. The entire time I was in Wells, I never heard of anyone there having anything amputated because of frostbite.

One thing I can't remember experiencing in Wells was a blizzard but if the occurred while I was there, they were rare. That could be because there wasn't the wind factor to consider. We could always see our way around during a heavy snow fall because the snow generally just came directly down rather than blow all over the place. My idea of a snow blizzard is what took place in January 2001 in Abag Qi, China. One survivor told of walking 200 meters from his home and realizing that he was hopelessly lost, he walked in a straight line for one and a half days until be blindly walked into the wall of a someone's hut. A woman and her daughter froze to death when they only took several steps from their home to retrieve some firewood. Kids coming home from school froze to death on the way home.

There were two kids in my class who had to walk some considerable distance to school. One of them (a boy) lived about half way up Island Mountain. It was a long walk up the winding road leading to his house. It would take at least an hour for him to walk home and in the winter, that must have been real hell for him since the road up the mountain wasn't plowed. Years later, he and his family moved to Richmond (Lulu Island) where I eventually moved to and he was a neighbour down the road from me. The other kid was a girl called Hannah Randall (now McDonald) and she lived about the same distance from the school except she had to walk along a narrow path that wound its way through the Meadows partway along side of Willow River to her house at the foot of Cornish Mountain on the other side of the valley. I imagine for these two kids, walking home after dark would be a frightening experience for them since grizzly bears and wolves are not uncommon in that area of B.C.

I nearly died that first winter from the cold. My mother told my brother and me that we could use the potty for number one but the potty was not to be used for number two. That meant that we would have to go out to the woodshed and use the outhouse my uncle built in it. If I woke up because I felt the need to go to number two, I would lay in bed arguing with myself as to why I felt that I could wait until it was time to get up for breakfast. When I finally came to the conclusion that my sphincter muscles were not going to wait that long, I then got dressed for the excursion into the blizzard. When I say dressed, I mean like Scott and Byrd dressed for their treks into the Antarctic. If I put any more clothes on, I would have had difficulty getting through the back door. Then there was the long trek. Stomping through a couple of feet of snow in a blizzard to a destination twenty-five feet (7.6 meters) away when your light flickers (a sign that your flashlight's batteries are dying) is a long trek. After struggling with the door of the shed (after finally finding the shed) was a chore because the snow drift always covered it up. I would have to shovel the snow away from it. Then after getting into the shed, I turned to the right and then pulled my pants down, opened the flap of my long johns and sat on the fur-like material on the toilet seat. All toilet seats had to be covered in the winter months. Whoever sat on the bare wood of a toilet seat when it was in any way damp would be stuck there until the spring thaw.

One cold wintry night, I was seated on the toilet in that cold darkened shed and I fell asleep. If my brother hadn't come into the shed ten or fifteen minutes later to use the john, my mother would have had to explain to her friends for the rest of her life how she lost her eldest in the privy. At least, my name would go down in history with such notables as King James I of Scotland, Henry III of France, King Edward of England and of course, the greatest king of all, Elvis Presley—all having died in their privies.

My mother told me years later that as a child in Wells, I was a handful. She said that one day when I was chopping wood, my brother said something that upset me and I chased him into and around the inside of the house with the axe in my hand. I had no intention of hurting him but I intended to scare him and that I did. My brother was sometimes a real pain in the ass and often upset me. My mother on the other hand said that I was often disobedient—not directly disobedient but rather, indirectly disobedient. She was right of course.

As you read what follows, I don't want you to think I have finally turned bonkers on you. What happened to me, really happened. I have no explanation for it other than what I learned years later and even then, I am not sure that what I read really explains it satisfactorily.
If we had a particularly cold night, the surface of the snow that had fallen the previous day would freeze and the depth of the frozen crust would be approximately a half inch. (1.27 cm) The softer snow underneath would be approximately 18 inches to 24 inches deep. (45.7 cm to 60.9 cm) I found that if I tried to walk across the snow the next morning, my feet would smash through the frozen surface and go into the softer snow below it to a depth sometimes reaching above my knees. But on some occasions, as I began to step onto the surface of the snow, I kept saying to myself, "Don't sink. "Don't sink." or words

to that effect. And much to my pleasant surprise, my feet didn't break through the surface. But the moment someone talked to me and I concentrated on their words, my feet broke through the hardened surface of the snow. If I concentrated again on walking on the surface of the snow with a view of not sinking, again my feet wouldn't crash through the hardened surface. This happened many times during the middle of the winters while I was in Wells.

Now I obviously was not lifted off the snow. I would have known that and so would everyone that was around me. But I was the only one of those around me who didn't sink into the snow even though there were others around me who weighed less than I did.

Have you ever tried to sneak up to someone on a floor that creaks and as you gingerly walk across the creaking floor, you are saying to yourself, "Don't creak." If it didn't creak after that, perhaps you were experiencing the same thing I had. But what we did have in common was the desire to be lighter than we really were so that the floor didn't creak and the snow didn't crumble under our individual weights. Our levels of concentration were also extremely intense during these moments.

When I reflect back to my own experiences in Wells, I remember thinking at the time that if I breathed in a great amount of air, I could rise like a balloon. But when I finally exhaled, my feet sank through the surface of the snow. Of course the air in my lungs would have no bearing on any levitation I may have experienced (if any) because the air I would be breathing in would be cold air and balloons require hot air to go up. But it may have simply been my mind's concentration that caused all this to happen and the belief that breathing in air would assist me was simply the medium that further prompted my concentration.

Levitation is a phenomenon of psychokinesis in which objects, people, and animals are lifted into the air and float or fly about without any visible physical means. The phenomenon has been said to have occurred in mediumship, shamanism, trances, mystical rapture, and demonic possession. Some cases of levitation appear to be spontaneous,

while spiritual or magical adepts are said to be able to control it consciously. It is not what you see in a magician's show on a stage. I know their secret and believe me, it isn't levitation. There seems to be several general characteristics about levitation. The duration of the phenomenon may last from a few minutes to hours. Generally it requires a great amount of concentration or being in an advanced State of trance. Physical mediums who have been touched during levitation usually fall back to the surface of what they are levitating above.
Numerous incidents of levitation have been recorded in Christianity and Islam. Among the first was Simon Magus in the first century. Other incidents reported among the Roman Catholic saints include the incident of Joseph of Cupertino (1603-1663), the most famous, who is said to have often levitated through the air. It is reported he often gave a little shriek just before levitating, and on one occasion levitated for as long as two hours.

Saint Teresa of Avila was another well known saint who is reported to have been levitating. She told of experiencing it during states of rapture. One eyewitness, Sister Anne of the Incarnation, said Saint Teresa levitated a foot and a half off the ground for about a half hour.

Saint Teresa wrote of one of her experiences: "It seemed to me, when I tried to make some resistance, as if a great force beneath my feet lifted me up. I know of nothing with which to compare it; but it was much more violent than other spiritual visitations, and I was therefore as one, ground to pieces." Also Saint Teresa observed these levitations frightened her but there was nothing she could do to control them. She did not become unconscious, but saw herself being lifted up.

At the beginning of the twentieth century Gemma Galgani, a Passionist nun, reported levitating during rapture. Incidents also have been reported in the religions of Hinduism and Buddhism. Milarepa, the great thirteenth century yogi of Tibet, is said to have possessed many occult powers such as the ability to walk, rest and sleep during levitating. Such feats were said to be duplicated by the Brahmins and fakirs of India. Similar abilities were reportedly shared by the Ninja of Japan. Within the Eastern traditions levitation is reportedly accomplished through such secret techniques of breathing and visualization. The techniques involve the employment of a universal life force and are called by various names such as: 'prana, ch'I' and 'ki'.

Louis Jacolliot, a nineteenth-century French judge, traveled the East and wrote of his occult experiences. In Occult Sciences in India and among the Ancients, he describes the levitation of a fakir: "Taking an ironwood cane which I had brought from Ceylon, he grabbed the handle and with his eyes fixed upon the ground, he then proceeded about two feet from the ground. His legs were crossed beneath him, and he made no change in his position, which was very like that of those bronze statues of Buddha. For more than twenty minutes I tried to see how he could thus fly in the face and eyes of all known laws of gravity. The stick gave him no visible support, and there was no apparent contact between that and his body, except through his right hand."

In 1906 Clara Germana Cele, a sixteen year-old school girl from South Africa, raised herself up five feet in the air, sometimes vertically and sometimes horizontally in front of many witnesses.

Some physical mediums claimed to have experienced levitations. The most famous is Daniel Douglas Home, who reportedly did it over a forty-year period. In 1868 he was witnessed levitating out of a third-story window, and he floated back into the building through another window. When levitating Home was not always in a trance, but conscious and later described his feelings during the experiences. Once he described "an electrical fullness sensation in his feet. His arms became rigid and were drawn over his head, as though he was grasping an unseen power which was lifting him. He also levitated furniture and other objects.

Italian medium Amedee Zuccarini was photographed levitating with his feet twenty feet above a table.

On January 10th, 2010, I watched on a TV show, Chris Angel literally walk on the surface of Lake Mead in Nevada. I watched him do this (via an underwater camera) which showed that there was nothing under his feet. A bystander actually moved her hand underneath his feet to prove that nothing was supporting him. Further, there was nothing supporting him from above as he walked a hundred feet from the shore. He later levitated again in September 2010. I am mindful that he is an illusionist but is it possible that he really can levitate himself? And didn't Jesus walk on the surface of the Sea of Galilea? Controlled experiments involving levitation are rare. During the 1960s and 1970s researchers reported some success in levitating tables under controlled conditions. The Soviet PK medium Nina Kulagina has been photographed levitating a small object between her hands.

Skeptics of levitation have come up with several theories as to its cause including hallucination, hypnosis, or fraud. These theories are not applicable to all incidents, however. The most likely and acceptable explanation is the Eastern theory of an existence of a force (simply, a universal force) which belongs to another, nonmaterial reality, and manifests itself in the material world.

The technique of 'yogic flying' which consists of low hops while seated in the lotus meditating position has been achieved by advanced practitioners of Transcendental Meditation (TM). This has received worldwide publicity. The technique is claimed to be accomplished by maximizing coherence (orderliness) in brain-wave activity, which enables the brain to tap into the "unified field" of cosmic energy. However, skeptics say yogic flying is accomplished through muscular action.

One thing I am convinced of is that intense thought is put into levitation, no matter how insignificant the levitation or attempt at it may be. If you doubt that, consider how intense you are when you are trying to sneak up to someone when you know that the floor generally creaks and suddenly, it doesn't creak.

I was never able to repeat this strange phenomenon after I left Wells. Obviously, I put on weight after that and whatever powers of levitation I might have had was not enough to stop me from breaking through the surface of the crust of hard snow I was walking on in later years.

It was the powerhouse of the Cariboo Gold Quartz Mine on Cow Mountain that had the big whistle that was blown at noon and at four every week day and in which a year after we moved to Wells, I had the thrill on one occasion of being permitted to pull the lever which blew the whistle at four. It gave me a sense of power to know that when I blew the mine's whistle, almost everyone in Wells either sat down for supper, quit work, began work, set their clocks or watches or did something or other at that precise moment. Now that is definitely a form of control and I sensed it. The man who fired off the Nine O'clock 12-pounder muzzle loader in Stanley Park in Vancouver every night for years really had a sense of control. Thousands of kids all over Vancouver and North and West Vancouver and beyond headed home when they heard the gun being fired. It is no longer used anymore. All the kids nowadays have watches and no doubt cell phones and pagers to boot.

Icicles hanging from the roof eaves were something to see in Wells. They were in many cases, extremely large because, notwithstanding the sun shining almost every day, they didn't melt away and thusly they often reached the snow on the ground and then spread outwards as the melt water ran across the surface at their base. On one occasion, a few of us boys crept under the wooden sidewalk that fronted a number of the stores and the community hall and just as I was crawling on my back out from under the sidewalk beside the north side of the community hall, a very large icicle broke loose from the roof of the shed attached to the building and hurtled downward towards me. Imagine lying face up on the bascule of a guillotine and watching the blade descending. That's how I felt at that precise moment. The 'ice blade' missed me—but just.

Life in Wells was a great experience for me as it was for most if not all of that town's inhabitants. There was no crime, everybody practically knew everyone else and we were never hungry or bored. Of course, that would eventually change for me and my parents and my brother but for a while, we were living in the greatest little town one could ever live in.

In 1941, the movie, *How Green Was My Valley* won the Academy Award for the best picture and Mickey Rooney was the top box office star that year, followed by Clark Gable, Bud Abbot and Lou Costello—the two zany comedians although Errol Flynn and Betty Grable were Hollywood's reigning royalty. The Australian song, *Waltzing Matilda* became a great hit. That song is now and has been for some time, Australia's unofficial national song just as *America* is the unofficial national song for the United States.

With the shortage of certain metals, the use of plastics came into being, and the tin foil that was used for Wrigley's Gum was replaced with cellophane and to give you some idea of how precious metal had become, Lucky Strike cigarettes replaced their green and red bulls eye for a red and white bulls eye because green ink contained metal. Silk stockings became a rationable item and fetched a high price on the black market.

Pope Pius XII ordered the bishops all over the world to authorize Catholics to eat meat on Fridays because of the shortage of fish. It's easy to see why fish had become a rare commodity in British Columbia during the years to follow.

Two sayings became prominent in 1941 and carried on throughout the war—"V for Victory" and "Kilroy was here." The latter was found everywhere, such as walls of buildings, inside the hulls of ships, even on signs posted on the battlefields to come. Legend has it that a man called James Kilroy worked in an American shipyard as an inspector and he painted his famous name on the sides of the ships as it was his way of saying that those parts of the ships had been inspected by him. I saw a war movie in which American marines landed on a Pacific island beach and discovered a sign on the beach saying 'Kilroy was here'. The frogman had planted it there the day before.

The year 1941 saw a number of famous people die. On February 21st, Frederick Banting, the co-discoverer of insulin was killed in a plane crash in Newfoundland. He was the only person who refused to buckle up and he was the only one to be killed. On February 24th,

Canadian writer, Lucy Maud, the author of *Anne and Green Gables* died in Toronto. Two other famous writers died, James Joyce and Virginia Woolf. Jan Paderewski, the famous pianist, composer and former prime minister of Poland also died that year.

The war was looking bad for everyone. The German and the Japanese armed forces were winning the war, or so it appeared to all of us at the end of 1941. The American foot soldier who was risking his life and dying while fighting for his country was only earning $1.65 a day for his service to the people of the United States. The Canadians soldiers weren't faring any better.

I suspected as did everyone else in North America and elsewhere that things were going to get worse because of the war. We in Wells weren't getting much of the information about the war that the people in large cities did since few of us had radios and only a few got newspapers which were at least a week old. But what we were told, frightened us. What news we were getting was for the most part, not encouraging at all. We were pleased that the United States and the Soviet Union had entered the war but by the end of 1941, there was no sign that the Axis powers (Germany, Italy and Japan) were losing the war. In fact, their war efforts appeared to be increasing the number of territories they were invading.

What no one knew at the end of 1941; was that there would be another three years and seven months of warfare, slaughter and terror going on in the world while the Allied nations were fighting the Axis powers before it all came to an end in 1945.

What I didn't know at the end of 1941, was that my life was to take a drastic turn four months after the end of the war; a turn that would bring more misery to me and a life of challenges that I hadn't yet experienced. However, until the arrival of those events in my life, I still had four more years of living in that beautiful town of Wells to enjoy; a town where we had all the food we could eat, a small community that was crime free and every neighbour was a friend. That little town of two and a half thousand souls was the closest I had ever come to being in heaven on earth.

Chapter Twenty-One

After the Japanese Empire attacked Pearl Harbor on December 7, 1941, there was a great deal of panic up and down the Pacific coast of the United States and Canada. The people on the west coasts of those two nations were in a state of hysteria. The Caucasian citizenry and governments alike of both countries believed that Japan was going to extend their Japanese invasions to the mainland of both countries. As a direct result of this hysteria, the Japanese Canadian citizens were mistreated by the Canadian government of the time. For example, effective February 26, 1942, all Canadian citizens of Japanese origin living on the west coast of Canada were to be at their usual place of residence each day before sunset and remain there until after sunrise the next morning. Further, they were not to possess any motor vehicles, boats, cameras, radios or any firearms. Later, all of their homes and contents, 1,200 fishing boats, 1,500 motor vehicles and 700 farms were confiscated and were subsequently sold to Caucasian Canadians at a fraction of their value.

Then the Canadian government passed the "Order in council PC 1486" expanding the power of the Minister of Justice (Louis St. Laurent—later to be prime minister and standing within meters of me while I served on a Canadian warship ten years later) to remove any and all persons from a designated protected zone (100 mile—161 km from the BC coast). This was part of the *War Measures Act*. On March 4, 1942, the BC Security Commission was established and 22,000 Japanese Canadians were given 24 hours to pack, before being incarcerated, interned, and separated from their families. Like the American assembly centers, which housed internees at Santa Anita in California and other race tracks, the Japanese Canadians were initially housed in a temporary facility just as demeaning in Vancouver called Hastings Park Race Track. Families found themselves packed into the stalls where horses had been previously been kept. The Japanese Canadians were then removed from the West Coast of British Columbia. Males between 18 and 45 were forced to work on the highways, railways and sugar beet farms in the interior of Canada, in what can only be called a form of forced slavery while the older men, woman and children were to be placed in interment camps (desolate ghost towns and farms made into small communities) in the interior of British Columbia at Greenwood, Sandon, Kaslo, New Denver, Rosebery, Slocan City, Bay Farm, Popoff, Lemon Creek, and Tashme. As a result, at least initially, families didn't know the whereabouts of other family members.

'Self-supporting' camps were established in Lillooet, Bridge River, Minto City, McGillivray Falls, and Christina Lake. 1,161 internees paid for their relocation and leasing of farms in these desolate areas that provided a less restrictive, less punitive environment. These Japanese Canadians were still considered "enemy aliens" by the government notwithstanding the fact that most of them were Canadian-born citizens.

Some were sent to New Denver in the Kootenays in B.C. and those that had TB were housed in a sanitarium in New Denver. Many years later, I worked in that same building where years after the war; it had become a dormitory where Freedomite children were housed. More on that in another volume of my Memoirs.

About 945 men worked on road construction camps at Blue River, Revelstroke, Hope, Schreiber, Black Spur. Those men who complained of the separation from families (Nisei Mass Evacuation Group) as well as 699 'dissident men' who violated curfew hours were sent to the 'prisoner of war' camps at Angler and Petawawa in Ontario. They were forced to wear shirts with circular, red targets on their backs.

Without their property, assets, or jobs, they were then charged a fee for their internment. As an example of this injustice, consider the fate of Harold Hirose, a Canadian veteran of the First World War. He had owned five acres of Surry farmland (a neighboring area of Vancouver) which was confiscated and sold for $36. He received a check for $15 after deductions for the administrative costs in a transaction which he did not approve. After the war, he subsequently made several appeals to the government to recover the land but these failed.

Unlike the Japanese Americans the Japanese Canadians were not allowed to join the military until after 1945. In spite of their incarceration, the Japanese Canadians nevertheless volunteered to serve in the Canadian Armed Forces.

In 1945 the Canadian government extended the *War Measures Act* which allowed the MacKenzie King government to bring about Canada's version of its 'final solution' which forced 4,000 Japanese Canadian citizens to repatriate to Japan (a country most of the Japanese Canadians had never been to before) or a forced 'dispersal' to eastern or Midwestern Canada. Until 1949 it was illegal for the Japanese Canadians to return to Vancouver or western Canada, despite the fact that the war with Japan had come to an end. For the Japanese Canadians, there were no homes, farms, and other property to return to after their internment. They were forced to start their lives over, with no economic resources, in an estranged and racially repressive environment of the Midwest and Eastern Canada. It was in that year however that they were finally given their voting rights back.

The Japanese Canadians suffered all of this notwithstanding the fact that there was no evidence that any of them were a threat to Canada's security. In 1944, the then prime minister of Canada, Mackenzie King announced, "It is a fact that no person of Japanese race born in Canada has been charged with any act of sabotage or disloyalty during the years of the war." *unquote.*

In 1988, redress for the Japanese Canadians finally came about when Prime Minister Brian Mulroney issued an apology in 1988 to the remaining approximately 11,000 surviving Japanese Canadians who had been incarcerated during the war and were still alive in 1988, for the miscarriage of justice that led to their internment. Yet the $21,000 of redress money that each of the survivors received hardly compensated them for the lost years of incarceration, property confiscated, family separations and disruptions and the invisible psychological scars and memories of racial injustices that remain. For a great many of these unfortunates, the redress and small financial compensation came far too late and for those that were the survivors, far too little. As a comparison to illustrate the injustice of it all, Benoit Proulx of Quebec was awarded $1.6 million dollars in 1987 for the suffering he endured while he was imprisoned for two months for a murder he didn't commit. Ironically, neither the German or Italian Canadians were interned or denied their civil rights during the war. But the reason for that decision was it was Canada that declared war on those two nations whereas Japan initiated the attack on the USA and vicariously on Canada and Great Britain and the Commonwealth countries in the east.

It is often forgotten that for the most part, World War II in the Pacific was a war between colonial powers. The United States did not get involved until military bases on three of its colonial territories—Hawaii, the Philippines, and Guam—were attacked by the Japanese. The British and their dominions were drawn in by the attack on their colonies of Malaya, Singapore, and Hong Kong. And the Dutch declared war on Japan in anticipation of the assault on their colony, the Netherlands East Indies (Indonesia). Before Pearl Harbor, Washington tightened its economic sanctions on Japan when it moved into northern Indochina in September 1940 and southern Indochina in July 1941—that is, when Tokyo encroached on the colonial domains of Vichy France.

The only non-colonies attacked by Japan were Thailand and China. Korea had been annexed by the Japanese in 1910. When Tokyo demanded that Thailand allow Japanese troops permission to use Thai soil for attacks on Burma and Malaya, Bangkok leaders allied with Japan and declared war on the United States and Britain, but they didn't mind the opportunity to regain Thai territory that France and Britain had taken at the beginning of the century and given to their Southeast Asian colonies. China was truly the main victim of Japanese aggression, but that aggression had been going on for ten years before Pearl Harbor with great brutality, though evoking little reaction from Washington and London or any other capital in the world.

Times have certainly changed since the war years. When my wife (also Japanese born) and I visited my mother and stepfather in Hawaii in 1980, the governor of that state was of Japanese origin. A former Governor General of Canada was also of Japanese origin. Born in Hong Kong in 1939, Mme Clarkson came to Canada as a refugee with her family, during the war in 1942. She received her appointment as Governor General of Canada on October 7, 1999. Further, a former president of Perue was of Japanese origin.

The April 18th 1942 air attack on Japan, launched from the aircraft carrier *Hornet* and led by Lieutenant Colonel James H. Doolttle, was the most daring operation yet undertaken by the United States in the Pacific War. Though conceived as a diversion that would also boost American and allied morale, the raid generated strategic benefits that far outweighed its limited goals.

The raid had its roots in a chance observation that it was possible to launch Army twin-engine bombers from an aircraft carrier, making feasible an early air attack on Japan. Appraised of the idea in January 1942, U.S. Fleet commander Admiral Ernest J. King and Air Forces leader General Henry H. Arnold greeted it with enthusiasm. Arnold assigned the technically-astute Doolittle to organize and lead a suitable air group. The modern, but relatively well-tested B-25B 'Mitchell' medium bomber was selected as the delivery vehicle and tests showed that it could fly off a carrier with a useful bomb load and enough fuel to hit Japan and continue on to airfields in China.

Gathering volunteer air crews for an unspecified, but admittedly dangerous mission, Doolittle embarked on a vigorous program of special training for his men and modifications to their planes. The new carrier *Hornet* was sent to the Pacific to undertake the Navy's part of the mission. So secret was the operation that her Commanding Officer, Captain Marc A. Mitscher, had no idea of his ship's upcoming operation until shortly before sixteen B-25s were loaded on her flight deck. On 2 April 1942, the *Hornet* put to sea and headed west across the vast Pacific.

Joined in mid-ocean on 13 April by Vice Admiral William Halsey's flagship *Enterprise*, which would provide air cover during the approach, the *Hornet* steamed toward a planned 18 April afternoon launching point some 400 miles (643 km) from Japan. However, before dawn on 18 April, enemy picket boats were encountered much further east than expected. These were evaded or sunk, but they got off radio warnings, forcing the planes to take off around 8 AM, while still more than 600 (965 km) miles out.

Most of the sixteen B-25s, each with a five-man crew, attacked the Tokyo area, with a few hitting Nagoya. Damage to the intended military targets was modest, and none of the planes reached the Chinese airfields (though all but a few of their crewmen survived). However, the Japanese high command was deeply embarrassed. Three of the eight American airmen they had captured were executed by decapitation. Spurred on by Combined Fleet commander Admiral Isooku Yamamoto, they also resolved to eliminate the risk of any more such raids by the early destruction of America's aircraft carriers, a decision that led them to their disaster at the Battle of Midway a month and a half later.

The spring months in Wells are beautiful and although there are still spots of snow found in the forests and on the mountains, the snow is pretty well gone in the valleys in that area of B.C., by the middle of April. It is cool on some days but it gradually gets warmer as June approaches. Because most of the trees in the Cariboo are coniferous, I really didn't get much opportunity to watch the budding of trees in the spring months. For that matter, I didn't get the opportunity to really enjoy the autumn leaves either. Of course, there were exceptions but they were rare.

In June of 1942, I passed into grade three. The big day in Wells was the July first weekend. Wells had a well developed fair grounds on the flats running adjacent to Highway 26 including a half mile race track, a softball diamond plus other areas for such things as log sawing and log chopping competitions. A nail driving competition was always well attended also.

Of all the sports to draw the largest crowds during the summer months, baseball was the most successful outdoor sport. There was an active league composed of teams from Cariboo Gold Quartz, Island Mountain, Wingdam, and Quesnel, and games were played with Prince George during holiday celebrations. A small fee was charged for the locals to attend the games and sometimes games would be washed out due to the considerable amount of rain that sometimes falls in the Wells area. Willow Creek would overflow and the baseball diamond next to it would be flooded. It would take days before the mud hardened enough to play baseball again. I remember several years later when one baseball game was scheduled and I missed it. I had done something wrong that day that angered my mother so she told me to remain at home. As I lay in my bed with the window open, I could hear the cheers of everyone in town down by the lake as the game was being played. Talk about feeling abandoned. I was probably the only person in town who wasn't watching the game.

The Meadows had (and still does) a large network of trails for both tourists and locals who enjoy hiking in the summer. During the summer it is quite common to see moose and other wildlife on the Meadows.

Summertime in Wells was a great experience for all of us kids also. There was Island Mountain and Cow Mountain to play on, forests to play in, the lake to play at (no one swam in it as it was too rocky) and a narrow river to play in, (Willow River) which wound its way through the Meadows and then through lower Wells to the lake.

I remember one day my brother and I and several of our friends decided that we wanted to go rafting on the river. The trouble was that we didn't have a raft to float on. Then a great idea came to mind.

My mother had taken the storm door off the back door of our house after the snow had gone. It was in the woodshed, but not for long. I and my brother and our friends carted it along Dawson Street, around the bend of the street to the path leading to the small bridge that crossed Willow River. Then we began floating on it up the river. Well, actually, we pushed it some of the way up the river as the river was shallow in many parts and worse yet, going in the wrong direction. We finally reached an impasse—a part of the river that was clogged with logs, bushes and stones. No! We didn't bring the door back home. I thought that the door had been abandoned in the woodshed so we merely abandoned it at the impasse. My mother thought otherwise and was not pleased when she learned what we had done with the door. Remember my earlier observation about the leather strap being handed to my mother so she could use it if the need called for it. Well, that day was one of those days when the need called for it—or so my mother has always maintained.

Not far from Wells (then about an hour's drive east of Wells because of the condition of the roads) is the Bowron Lakes Provincial Park. The park comprises of five lakes in the form of the outer lines of a square. Many canoeists from around the world paddle their way through the 116 km (72 mile) route of the chain of lakes, and when camping, keeping an eye open for grizzly bears. The westernmost lake was the one that everyone in Wells used to visit at one time or another. It was also called Bear Lake. It's about 18 km (11 miles) east of Wells.

When my mother took us there, it was always my uncle that would drive us there in his car with my brother and me sitting in the rumble seat in the back. Unless you have sat in such a seat, you can't imagine what it was like. The trunk had the handle at the top and when it was pulled down, the seat (large enough for two only) would appear. There were no doors to the area of where the seat was so we had to climb over the side and fall into the seat. It was great fun kneeling on the seat and looking backwards as we sped along the dirt road at 10 miles (16 km) an hour. We could only go that speed because there were so many pot-holes in the road, going any faster would cause irreparable damage to the frame of our car, not to mention the cross beams. Unfortunately, sometimes we would end up choking on the dust which flew up into the area of the rumble seat from the front wheels of the car. There were 16,536,075 Model T Ford cars built and the last one was built in 1927 so the one my uncle was driving had to be at least 15 years old when I first saw it. He later sold his car in 1944 to someone in Wells when he and his family moved to Wynndel, British Columbia.

We would stop at a large pond for a rest and my brother and I would clamber onto a floating wharf and try grabbing frogs in the pond. We were unsuccessful. The frogs were obviously quicker than we were.

For two weeks during most of the summers, my mother would rent one of the cottages at the lake for us. I remember one summer however when the roof leaked in the cottage, the owners of the resort put us up in the lodge. It was then, that I first tasted Root Beer. I got the owner of the lodge to punch a hole in the cap with a nail so that when I went to bed, I could prop it onto my pillow, turn my head sideways and suck on the bottle when I was of a mind—which was a good part of the night, until the bottle was empty. It was here that I learned that Root Beer was one of the few drinks that doesn't go bad if you re-open and reseal it repeatedly.

A river ran out of the lake near the lodge and men from the Fisheries Department gathered every day to catch the salmon at the salmon weir and tag them by inserting a needle through their backs and securing each with a button-like tag to them before tossing them back into the river. We were told that these salmon would be swimming to the Pacific Ocean and then later returning back to the Barron Lakes to spawn and die—which was quite a swim considering the fact that they would be swimming almost halfway across British Columbia—twice. As to be expected, the lakes abounded with Rainbow Trout and other trout, those amazing fish, not unlike the salmon, which could even jump/swim up small waterfalls.

One day I picked up a Western rattlesnake near the shore of

the lake and proudly walked with the wiggling snake into the large common room of the lodge to show my mother and her friends. Never have I seen so many people abandon a room as quickly as they did on that day. They moved faster than johns in a cat house during a police raid. When the lodge owner told me what would happen to me if the snake sunk its fangs into me, never have I known anyone abandon a snake as quickly and run away from it as I did on that day. I also moved faster than the johns in a cat house during a police raid.

The lake was rather cold (as was the Jack-O-Clubs Lake in Wells) so we rarely swam in it but nevertheless, it was great fun playing hide and seek in the barn and the forests and around the cottages with my friends.

I remember one summer, my mother sent us out to pick blueberries on the road leading to Bowron Lake. The sides of the roadway were blue with blueberries. I hadn't seen that many blueberries after that until in the late eighties when I took my family through the State of Maine in which at one spot we saw a huge field of wild blueberries stretching for over a mile. My family spent an hour picking them. I stayed in the car and watched. I didn't want to pick them in the forties and I didn't want to pick them in the eighties either. I sure liked eating them however—both times. My mother punished me nevertheless for not picking the blue berries by not letting me have any of her blue berry jams she made that year. My wife on the other hand let me eat as many as I wanted. I suppose there is a difference in love between mothers and wives—or is it simply that times had changed.

There was no swimming pool in Wells but there was a swimming hole next to the softball diamond which was located between Highway 26 (leading into town) and the Jack-O-Clubs Lake that most of us kids played in. Willow River wasn't very wide and at this juncture it was quite narrow but it was deep in parts and it was at a narrow bend in the river where we would swim. We couldn't really swim in it because it wasn't large enough to get a half decent stroke in so we more or less jumped in it or pushed each other into it.

Our eyes would always end up being red after playing in the

swimming hole because of the sodium cyanide that escaped to the river from the gold processing plants of both mines. When the gold was to be removed from the ore, the ore was mixed with sodium cyanide. The gold and the cyanide reacted to form a compound from which the gold was recovered by electrolysis. By the time the cyanide solution wound its way down the mountain to the creek, it was pretty well diluted but not enough not to redden our eyes that would then remain red for days on end. That's why we were always forbidden to swim in the creek but then who obeyed their mothers in those days. My mother always knew when we were swimming in the creek by the redness of our eyes. You can imagine how diluted the cyanide was considering the fact that an ingestion of less than a fraction of an ounce of cyanide will bring on instant death. It was used in gas chambers in some of the prisons in the USA.

There was one part of the river that we really enjoyed playing in. It was the wooden flume near the swimming hole which ran about two blocks in length to the lake. It was about ten feet (3.04 metres) wide and the walls were about six feet (1.8 metres) in height. The water was about two feet (61 centimetres) deep. It ran quite quickly through the flume so we would get wide boards and lay on them and float down the flume and into the lake at a very fast clip.

One summer, a number of us kids went hiking up Island Mountain and we found a large detonator box in what looked like a quarry. The large spark we created when we pushed down the plunger fascinated us. We were very disappointed when Ronnie Mast's father who was a miner insisted that we give it to him. He said it belong to the Island Mountain Mine.

It was the summer of 1942 that a religious group came into town to show us kids how to see the 'light' so to speak. Every morning, a bunch of us would go to some small hall on the south side of Pooley Street in which we would play games (that got us there) and be told stories (that kept us there) and then we would be given talks about Jesus and so forth. I remember on the last day, they asked us to kneel beside them and pray. They said that we could leave any time we wanted. They said that they would remain behind until the last kid got up off his knees and left. I was the last kid to leave. I stayed there kneeling with my arms across the seat of the bench with my head resting on them for an hour and a half with our two religious teachers kneeling on both sides of me. They were very impressed. I on the other hand, had fallen asleep. They may have suspected this after one of them later tapped me on the shoulder and whispered in my ear, "Would you like to pray longer, Danny?" and I responded with, "Where am I?"

It was during the summer of 1942 that the Canadian army sent a contingent of soldiers up to Wells to conduct maneuvers at playing at attacking a small town. It was great fun. The soldiers found us kids to be pests however considering the fact that we were always pointing to other soldiers who were attempting to hide behind buildings and houses.

Although the summer of 1942 was great fun for all of us in Wells, it was obviously not so in other parts of the world.

I doubt that any of us kids in Wells would have enjoyed ourselves fully that summer, or any other time of the year had we known then what was happening to the children in conquered Europe and in Asia. It was only after the war that we then became aware of the atrocities committed by the Germans and the Japanese. I look back at that period of time and realize just how fortunate we in the free countries were during those frightful and terrible war years in Europe, Africa, the Pacific and in Asia.

On July 7, 1942, Japan had entered its sixth year of war with China and on July 21st, Japanese troops landed on New Guinea in Southeast Asia.

On that same day, Reich Minister Heinrick Himmler (he was 42 years of age then) had meetings with SS doctors and ordered them to conduct sterilization experiments with Gypsy and Jewish women at Auschwitz and to conduct subzero freezing experiments with male prisoners at the camp. It was a cruel irony that of the freezing experiments, where the men were immersed into tanks of freezing water, it was later learned from those experiments that if airmen and sailors ended up in the cold seas of the Northern Atlantic, they would survive longer if the back of their heads were kept away from the water. Hence, life jackets were constructed in such a manner that the heads of the airmen and sailors were thrust forward so that the backs of their heads were kept out of the cold water. Many lives were saved this way. It's one of those ironies in life that so many lives were saved at the cruel expense of the suffering and lives of other human beings.

On July 22nd, the Germans began a roundup of Jewish children in the Warsaw Ghetto for transportation to the east which in effect, was directly to the gas chambers in the Treblinka Extermination Camp. Every day, thousands of children herded into box cars at the rail yards could be heard crying, "Mama, mama" or "Save us!" such cries tormenting their parents who had to stay behind. The parents had no idea that their children were on their way to the camp to be gassed.

On August 7th, the Americans landed on Japanese held Guadalcanal, one of the islands in the Solomon chain. Although the 19,000 marines only met token resistance, it was the first successful attack by the Americans on Japanese-held territory.

In August 1942, one of the War's colossal blunders took place. I am referring to the infamous Dieppe fiasco. This raid against the Germans on the French coast was conceived six months earlier. The purpose was to seize an enemy port to determine the enemy's readiness to defend it. The purpose was ridiculous because no plans had yet been made for an invasion against Fortress Europe and by the time the 1944 invasion did take place, the enemy's defensive tactics radically changed. And when the Anglo/Canadian raid did take place, it was discovered too late that the attack was dogged by disaster right from the start.

First, the element of surprise was lost when the landing craft had to fight with a small German convoy in the English Channel. The Germans sent radio messages to their comrades on shore of the impending attack. By five in the morning, the Canadians were landing on a steep pebble beach backed by steep cliffs and overlooked by the

Germans. The beach became a slaughterhouse. Another group of Canadians landed on the wrong side of the Scie River from their target. When they tried to cross the river, many were cut down by enemy fire. With the headlands on both sides of Dieppe still in German hands so it follows that the raid was bound to fail. The Canadians and the British soldiers were in the wrong end of a turkey shoot. Fifteen of the 29 tanks manned by Canadians reached the esplanade of Dieppe but no further. The Germans had earlier built concrete barriers across all the streets. One would have thought that a little pre-raid intelligence in that area would have brought that important tidbit of information to the attention of the planners of the raid.

In the end, 500 Canadians died and 900 surrendered before they too would be slaughtered. In all, the losses on the Allied side were 1027 dead and 2340 captured. Vice Admiral Lord Louis Mountbatten had been put in charge and notwithstanding the defeat, he later said, "For every soldier who died at Dieppe, ten were saved on D-day." Prime Minister Churchill said in his book, *The Hinge of Fate*, "It was a costly but not unfruitful reconnaissance-in-force. It shed revealing light on many shortcomings in our outlook." I suppose something can be learned from every failure and what was learned that fateful day was—do your homework first.

What was unknown at the time was the role King George the VI had intended he play in the Dieppe raid. He sent a note to Churchill stating that he wished to go on board one of the naval ships sailing towards Dieppe to give moral support for the soldiers. Churchill was aghast. He immediately sent the King a reply stating that if the King wanted to go to Dieppe, then so should the prime minister. King George then realized the foolishness of his own gesture and withdrew his offer.

An event occurred around this time in Vancouver B.C. that absolutely bears retelling. It is so funny that even writing it down is so much fun. On September 13th, 1942, the province of British Columbia was bracing itself for an attack from the Japanese navy. Of course looking back at it now, the suggestion was preposterous but nevertheless, the naval 12-pounder gun placed at a small fort in Stanley Park was aimed out to sea to sink any Japanese warship that might be coming over the horizon. Twelve-pounder? Give me a break! It's akin to shooting bears with a 22. calibre rifle. Well, on that particular day, a fish-packer approached Burrard Inlet and didn't radio in as to who it was (as what was required then) so a blank shell was fired ahead of her bow to stop her. As it turned out, the waves were a bit choppy and the shell hit a wave and then bounced on the second and the third and so forth until it passed the fish-packer and hit the *Fort Rae*, a 9,600-ton freighter. The shell went through her bulkhead above the waterline and then changed course slightly and went out of the opposite bulkhead just below the waterline. The captain of the ship didn't even know that his ship had even been hit by the 12-pounder or even that water was leaking in one of his holds until he was well inside Burrard Inlet. He beached his ship lest she sink right in the Inlet. Of course there was an inquiry but all was forgiven. The Department of Defence paid for the repairs. Naturally attempts were made to hush up the story but it circulated around Vancouver faster than the 12-pounder headed across the opening of the Inlet.

By September 21st, a great many Europeans had been executed by the Germans of which by that time, only 30,000 had been killed in concentration camps. I use the word, 'only' simply because millions more died in concentration camps as the years passed by. So in fact, as many as 117,373 persons were shot or hanged for alleged offences against the German occupying forces since Germany marched on Poland. Of course, no one knew then that as the war years progressed, as many as 55 million persons would die during those years as victims of the war. The loss in life would be comparable to a disease wiping out the entire populations of Iceland, Finland, Belgium, Denmark, Austria and Canada during a four-year period of time beginning in 1991.

Due to partisan activity around the village Kortelisy, in the Ukraine, its entire population of 2,892 men, women and children were put to death by SS and SD execution squads helped by local pro-German Ukrainian police on September 2, 1942. The village was then razed and burned to the ground, the fires of which blazed for four days. All over Ukraine as many as 459 villages were destroyed with all or part of their population massacred. In the Volhynia province 97 villages suffered the same fate and in the Zhitomir province 32 villages were destroyed. Of those villages razed, there were at least 27 villages in which every man, woman and child were killed and their houses completely destroyed. Most of the SS and SD units operating in the Ukraine consisted of locally recruited pro-German Ukrainians, Lithuanians, Estonians and White Russians. In all of central Russia there were only two regiments of German security police so most of the atrocities in that area were committed against the Ukrainians were by their home-grown thugs.

In Germany, the Nazis ordered six classes of people to wear patches on their clothes in which five of the patches were triangular in shape. The sixth was the yellow Star of David that was to be worn by all Jews. The five triangles were of varying colours—pink for homosexuals, red for politicals, light blue for pacifists, green for criminals, deep blue for anti-socials. (whatever that meant—probably rabblerousers)

On October 1st, the Japanese freighter, *Lisbon Mauri* was carrying 1,860 British and Canadian POWs that had been captured in Hong Kong when she was unfortunately torpedoed by an American submarine. The Japanese guards battened down the hatches of the sinking ship so that the prisoners would drown when the ship sank. Many of the prisoners were able to break open the hatches and escape into the water only to be met by machine gun fire by Japanese machine gunners on Japanese craft nearby. All told, 840 prisoners died as a result of that Japanese atrocity.

On October 18th, Hitler issued a secret order called *The Top Secret Commando Order* which stated, "From now on, all enemies on so-called commando missions in Europe or Africa even if they are in uniform, whether armed or unarmed, in battle or in flight, are to be slaughtered to the last man." General Jodl, passing on Hitler's orders—not unlike the messenger boy that he was, instructed the armed forces to make sure that such written orders didn't fall into enemy hands—of which, copies of the order finally did—which invariably brought about Jodl's own death in 1946 by hanging as a war criminal.

On October 25th, the Allies bombed Milan, Italy and the following day, the Americans bombed Hong Kong and Canton, China.

On the 27th, my ninth birthday, I was listening to a BBC news short wave broadcast in which the listeners were told that the *USS Hornet*, an American aircraft carrier was sunk about a thousand miles east of Guadalcanal by Japanese planes. With the aircraft *Enterprise* severely damaged, this left the American forces without a single aircraft carrier in the south Pacific theatre of war. On that same day in Germany, a 17- year-old German boy was executed for doing exactly what I was doing—listening to the BBC news radio broadcast on a short wave radio.

On the 29th, the Germans massacred 16,000 Jews in Pinsk, USSR and in Poland, Further, they gassed 64,000 Jews and gypsies at the Belzec extermination camp and 82,000 Jews and gypsies at the Treblinka extermination camp.

The war in Africa had not gone that well for the Allies up to the end of October. The Germans were half way into Egypt and they had created an effective barrier that ran north and south from the Mediterranean to the 'Quattara Depression' 60 kilometers (40 miles) south to prevent the British from attacking them from the east. The British could not attack Rommel from the rear by first going through the Depression in the south so they had to fight him head on. But that meant going through a German minefield that was 2 to 5 miles (3.2 km to 8 km) wide and in which was buried half a million mines, each of which could disable a tank. Throughout this area was barbed wire and booby traps. The area was aptly called, "The Devil's Gardens". There was no other way of resolving the situation but to promenade through the Gardens.

On the night of October 23rd a thousand British artillery guns bombarded the Gardens every three minutes, moving up 90 meters each time. The ground shook like the taught skin of a kettledrum.

Rommel retreated to the west with only 30 tanks, the British following closely behind with 600 tanks. The battle became forever known as the 'Battle of El Alamein'. The battle on November 3rd was costly but despite the casualties, the British prevailed under the leadership of General Montgomery. Canadians were not involved in this particular battle although there were Canadian airmen in Egypt. In fact, one out of every four airmen flying British aircraft were Canadians including my father. From the Battle of El Alamein onward in time, the outcome of the desert war in Africa was favourable to the Allies.

A funny story began circulating amongst the men of the American Armed Forces. It concerned the American General, Mark Clark. It seems that on November 5th, he slipped into Algeria for a clandestine meeting with Vichy/French leaders in an attempt to get them to side with the Allies. When he was returning to a submarine via a canvas dingy, it capsized after being struck by a large wave. The General swore he heard one of the men yell out, "Never mind the General. Get the paddles."

Only four days after their victory at El Alamein, the Allies struck the blow that invariably squeezed the Germans and Italians out of North Africa. It involved what was to be at that time, the largest amphibious invasion force the world had ever known. More than 500 ships ranging from converted cargo vessels to once luxurious passenger liners had been pressed into service to carry 107,000 men and thousands of tons of weapons and supplies and to land them on the shores of Morocco and Algeria. Code-named, *Operation Torch* it was the first Anglo/American operation of the war.

With the Anglo/American forces attacking the Vichy/French in the west, and the British forces attacking the German/Italian forces from the east, the Axis armies would be caught in between and be squeezed out of North Africa like pus is squeezed from a boil.

On November 8th, Algiers was the first objective to fall but not without a setback. As the American warships neared the harbour in the darkness of night, searchlights from the shore lit up the ships and two American destroyers were hit. One had to retreat and the other was sunk. The beach landings were more successful and by early afternoon, American tanks and armoured cars raced towards Algiers and by mid-afternoon, the city surrendered.

On the same day, a fierce naval battle took place at Casablanca as American warships fought the Vichi/French naval contingent still in the harbour however, eight direct hits from the 15-inch guns of the American battleship Massachusetts which was 12 miles (19 km) offshore and repeated aerial attacks, crippled the 35,000 tonne French battleship Jean Bart and put her out of action. By the time the other American warships finished with the other French ships, the French naval force was entirely annihilated.

General Patton who was in charge of the landings found confusion on the beaches. Obviously, nothing like this had ever been attempted before and equipment which should have been off loaded was still on board the landing craft. Despite the confusion, Patton got it all together and was ready for the attack on Casablanca. Just minutes before the city was to be shelled from the America warships, and bombed by the American planes, the city capitulated on November 10th with a loss of only 1000 French. The Vichy government of Madagascar had also yielded to the Allies three days earlier.

Hitler was furious. On November 11th, he ordered his army to invade Vichy France. This needs an explanation. As mentioned earlier, on June 10th, 1940 to be specific, the French government abandoned Paris to the German invading army but some of the members of the French parliament managed to flee to a small town to the south called Vichy. There, under the leadership of retired First World War veteran, Marshal Petain, the "Vichy" government was set up. The Germans agreed to let the Vichy government control two-fifths of France, the south and the centre, and all of its holdings in North Africa and elsewhere around the world. In return, the Vichy government cooperated to some degree with the Germans who then governed the northern and western part of France. Pierre Laval became the prime minister of Vichy France and ruled that part of France as a dictatorship.

When the Vichy French forces in Morocco and Algiers capitulated in November 1942, Hitler asked Vichy leader, Marshal Petain for permission to land German troops in Tunisia. Petain refused and Hitler used this opportunity to take control of all of France—which he did within 24 hours.

Up to November 9th, Canada had maintained relations with the Vichy government. Canadian Prime Minister King maintained all along that that part of France was unoccupied by the Germans and as such, there was to some degree, a semblance of freedom within the territories controlled by the Vichy government. He also felt that by giving the Vichy government recognition, it paved the way for the North African invasion. Canada withdrew its recognition of the Vichy government as did the United States 24 hours earlier as anticipation of it falling to the Germans, which of course it did two days later.

For my readers to appreciate the Soviet fighting abilities in the war, one only has to think of the 'Battle of Stalingrad'. This Russian city, now called Volgograd, is situated in the southwestern part of Russia. It was and still is a large industrial city with the bulk of the city located on the west bank of the Volga River.

During the Second World War, it was the plan of the Germans to seize Stalingrad in order to cut the vital supply artery of the Volga River at its westernmost part which was close to the Don River that ran south to the Black Sea. Fully realizing the importance of thwarting the German aims, the Russian commanders and their soldiers (many of them women) fought the German invaders ferociously. German bombs and artillery fire leveled the city to the extent that there were very few buildings still standing and even those had been severely damaged. The Germans reached the center of that vast city but they were never able to cross the Volga. The battles raged from its initial German inception on August 23, 1942 and continued on for the rest of the year. The shelling of enemy soldiers by both sides created so much smoke that it was at times hard to distinguish night from day. Often the fighting was so intense and with the battle lines fluctuating so often, both sides were often inadvertently shelling their own soldiers.

By the time November had come upon them, the entire city was nothing but rubble. But by the middle of November, as many as a million Russian soldiers, supported with 13,000 heavy guns, 900 tanks and 1100 aircraft, were poised for the Russian counter attack against the Germans which came about on the 19th. The Germans by way of contrast had little if any hope of reinforcement from Germany. The Russians attacked from the north and the south and surrounded the 250,000 Germans and their Romanian Allies in a giant pincher movement. Gradually the pinchers closed in on the German and Romanian soldiers who by now were also enduring the hardships of the cold Russian winter. On the 23rd of November, Hitler ordered Gereral Paulus commanding the Germans and Romanians to fight on with his promise, "I will do everything in my power to supply it (Paulus' Sixth Army) adequately and disengage it when the time is right." To supply the needs of the Sixth Army would require the use of all the transport planes the German Luftwaffe possessed and that wasn't at all possible. Slowly, the Germans and Romanians were gradually running out of ammunition and to make matters worse, their food rations had been cut to starvation levels.

By November 27th, the only part of France not under occupation by the Germans was the city of Toulon which was 30 miles (48 km) southeast of Marseille and the French fleet based there. As the Germans approached the city, there was concern to everyone, Allies and Axis alike as to what was going to happen to the French fleet. The Germans had mined the harbour and the British wanted the French fleet so bad that Churchill stated that he would walk on his hands and knees for a mile to talk the French into turning their fleet over to the Allied cause. Rather than fight their way out of the harbour, the French scuttled their ships. Two battleships, one battle cruiser, seven cruisers and 29 destroyers sank to the bottom of the harbour. The Allies were bitterly disappointed but they didn't suffer the disappointment like the Germans who had to stand on the shores of the harbour and watch their hopes of obtaining the French fleet, just as the fleet was sinking under the waves in front of them.

When the Germans invaded Vichy France, they arrested Petain and permitted Laval, the Vichy prime minister to resign. The French admiral, Dalan, whose headquarters was in Algiers, broadcasted to the world that he was now the leader of the French Government, if not defacto, at least in spirit because all of France was now under the heel of the German jackboot.

Up to now, everything was going for the Germans, the Italians and the Japanese. But at this juncture of the war, the Axis powers had reached the limits of their expansions. From now on, with few exceptions, the Allies would begin closing in on them, forcing them to retreat to their own homelands where the Allied bombing would devastate their homes, shops and industries and kill their families.

The Soviets began the next phase of their offensive against the Italian Eighth Army and that army was almost shattered. Hitler had given him permission to retreat from the Soviet advance but he was too late—Paulus was running out of fuel. The Soviet advances were rapid and they were retaking their cities. As well as their advance on the Stalingrad fronts, they were on the move in the Caucasus, forcing the Germans to retreat from that area.

By now, a good part of North Africa was also falling into the hands of the Allies and Madagascar had fallen to the Free French.

The Japanese were not faring that well either. They were still fighting the Americans in Guadalcanal at the beginning of December 1942. Because the Americans had control of much of Guadalcanal, the Americans were able to utilize their airbase on that island and from that airbase, the American planes flying out of Guadalcanal attacked the Japanese base at Rabaul. On the last day of 1942, the Japanese finally evacuated Guadalcanal and by now, the British had finally got a good foothold in Burma. The squeeze against the Japanese was beginning to be felt by them all the way to Tokyo.

Chapter Twenty-Two

Anyone living in the USA or Canada in 1942 was well aware of the war situation either through radio or *Movietone* or the newspapers but most people tried to put it out of their minds except when they thought of their loved ones fighting 'over there'. There was so much going on and so much to do, that it wasn't all that hard to put the war out of our minds. One of the things we were not aware of in North America until after the war was what was happening to German citizens who were considered mentally ill. In 1942, a total of 3,166 civilian prisoners from Dachau and Mauthausen were transported to Harthein, situated near Linz in Austria, (which is just over the German border) and then put to death by gassing when they arrived. They were classified as 'unfit to work'. The Schloss prison in Hartheim was the only prison from which there were no survivors. Used in the SS Euthanasia Programme, around 10,000 mentally retarded and crippled children were murdered there. Their bodies were then cremated and the ashes spread over the waters of the Danube and Traun rivers. Five such establishments were set up in Germany, including the infamous Hadamar Psychiatric Clinic. Since the Programme began in 1939, a total of 70,273 mentally retarded people were murdered in these centres. A total of 772 children from Vienna were put to death and their brains preserved in glass jars. Around 80 persons were employed at Hartheim encouraged by extra pay and a good alcohol allowance. The director of the programme was a psychiatrist, Dr.Rudolf Lonauer, of Linz, He was arrested by the Allies but he committed suicide by poison in May, 1945 before he could be tried. Today, the Schloss has been converted into flats housing 22 families. The only reminder of the terrible events that took place here is a large plaque on the wall of the entrance hall.

As I mentioned in the previous paragraph, euthanasia was being practiced earlier in Germany. In the spring of 1939, the 'Reich Committee for Scientific Research of Hereditary and Severe Constitutional Diseases' was set up. Headed by SS-Obergruppenführer Philipp Bouhler, it operated out of his headquarters at 4 Tiergartenstrasse in Berlin, hence its code name T-4. From all over Germany, deformed children, incurably sick and mentally retarded patients were transported from their hospitals and institutions to the euthanasia killing centres of which there were six (Bernburg, Brandenburg, Grafeneck, Hadamar, Hartheim and Sonnenstein). At these centres the patients were put to death individually, usually by injection. I suppose this was the beginnings of execution by injection which came into vogue in the United States in that latter part of the Twentieth century. Later, to speed up the process, cyanide gas, known as Zyklon B, was used. The first centre to be so equipped was Brandenburg in late 1939. The procedure was for groups of twenty or thirty to be ushered into a room camouflaged as a shower room into which gas piping had been laid. The equipment to operate the gas was located outside and operated by the doctor on duty. When the euthanasia programme wound down in late 1941, the gassing equipment in these centres was dismantled and transferred to the concentration camps of Belize, Majdenek and Treblinka in Poland in preparation for the forthcoming 'Final Solution' of the Jewish question.

Alas, Canada and the United States also mistreated their citizens who were mentally ill back in the thirties and forties of the Twentieth century. In one of the States and also in the province of Saskatchewan, mentally retarded children were sterilized against their wishes but at least they weren't murdered.

Radio came out with some new programs which included, *Suspense* which was a damn good thriller-type program, guaranteed to keep your ears glued to the radio. *People Are Funny* produced Art Linkletter, a Canadian who had moved to the States, was about strange things people would do for money, such as the couple who spent their entire honeymoon in a pitch black cave in Missouri. I once visited that cave and learned that that couple didn't know until they got there that the lights would be turned off and they would have only a flashlight to see them through their honeymoon. I strongly suspect that when they emerged and got their money, their honeymoon really began.

The regular radio shows were still a great hit. They were, *Fibber McGee and Molly* and the *Jack Benny Show* was always good for a laugh because he always appeared as an amateur violinist (he was extremely talented as a violinist) and was not a tightwad as he pretended to be as he was also extremely generous with his money. The *Aldrich Family* which always opened with a woman calling out, "HENRY! Henry Aldrich. You come here this instant!" was a laugh also. There were great movies that came out that year—all black and white of course. They were; *Casablanca* with Humphrey Bogart—about the French Vichy in that part of Africa; *Wake Island* with Brian Donlevy and William Bendix—about the last days of Wake Island before the Japanese overran it; *In Which We Serve* with Noel Coward and John Mills—about life on board a British destroyer. The musical, *Yankee Doodle Dandy* with James Cagney (who up to then had been playing gangster roles) was a great success as was *Random Harvest* with Ronald Coleman and Greer Garson was popular to those working on their farms.

The box office stars were; Abbot and Costello (incidentally, it was this particular year that Costello came out with "Hey Abbott. I'm a ba-a-a-d boy."); Clark Gable—still a heart throb to the women; Gary Cooper—the quiet man every man wanted to be like; Mickey Rooney—who still passed as a kid; Bob Hope—who was not only doing the "road shows" such as *Road to Morocco* with Bing Crosby and Dorothy Lamour, but was entertaining the troops at the front; Gene Autry who was a hit with the kids because he was their idea of a hero in the days of the west—can you believe this? He really did ride a white horse; Betty Grable—because of her legs which resulted in her pinup pictures being a great hit with the men in the armed forces; (her legs were insured for a million dollars by Lloyds) and Spencer Tracy who always appeared at the latter part of his movies as a man who was smarter than when he first appeared in the movies.

Some of the hit songs that came out in 1942 were; *Praise the Lord and Pass the Ammunition, Rosie, the Riveter*—which was dedicated to the women who worked in the factories or were building ships; *When the Lights Go On Again* which was dedicated to those people in London suffering from the Blitz. It's funny when you think of it. When the Northeastern seaboard of North America had blackouts in 1965 and 2003, not once did I hear any radio station play that song. Another popular tune was *We'll Meet Again* for those men and women who were separated in war. *This is the Army, Mr. Jones* which was a very catchy tune which told conscripts that life in the army wasn't what they thought it was going to be—it was worse. There were some non-war related songs that made the hit parade also, such as *A String of Pearls* by Glen Miller (who died in the war when an American plane accidentally dropped a bomb on his plane when his small plane was flying south over the English Channel) Another popular song was *I Got a Gal in Kalamazoo* performed by Glen Miller. (As an interesting aside, there really is a city by that name in Michigan. I bought a book on poetry in that city while I was getting evidence of adultery in a sex camp nearby when I was a private investigator in the mid 1970s) There was *That Old Black Magic* by Cole Porter; *Don't Sit under the Apple Tree* sung by the Andrew Sisters; *White Christmas* sung by Bing Crosby which probably became the most popular Christmas song of all time and of course. (More on that later) For comic relief, Spike Jones' *Der Fueher's Face* who had a funny way via strange sounds of telling you what should be dropped on Hitler's face. We will never know if Spike Jones knew that Hitler really did have a strange fetish—being shit on by prostitutes but the song certainly was apropos.

The United States became the world music centre for great conductors and composers, such as Bruno Walter, George Szell, Bela

Bartok, Darius Milhaud, Ernest Toch and Arnold Schoenberg. The famous Russian composer Shostakovitch managed to get his *Symphony No 7* through enemy lines to Toscanini, the famous conductor who performed the work with the NBC Symphony Orchestra.

There were a number of scientific breakthroughs in 1942 that bears telling, they being; the first safe self-sustaining nuclear chain reaction was accomplished in Chicago. This was the beginning the end for Japan's war of course although at this time, no one new where this discovery was going to lead; napalm, a jelly-like mixture of gasoline and palm oils that sticks to everything and everyone it touches was created at Harvard University; bazookas, shoulder-held rockets used as anti-tank weapons was developed; radar came into operational use; and a jet- propelled plane was developed by Bell Aircraft.

Non-war discoveries were created, such as Demerol, a synthetic morphine-like substance to cut pain was developed and for the first time, tubeless tires were successfully tested. Of course, none of us in Wells were aware of all these breakthroughs as I said earlier, the town was more or less a closed community and we kept pretty much to our selves. It wasn't until much later that we all benefited to some degree from these discoveries.

Our first Fire Hall was on Saunders Avenue in Wells and was built in the early 1930's. It burned down in the summer of 1943. The fire broke out on an early Thursday morning and completely destroyed the fire hall and the fire engine and all the fire fighting equipment that were inside the building. By the time the volunteer firefighters got to the fire, it was too late to save the fire hall and everything in it including a new 1942 Ford sedan belonging to the fire chief, Mr. Bev Adams. That's a tough lesson for fire chiefs storing their personal vehicles in their fire halls, especially when their fire halls are made of wood and are unmanned.

During one of that summer's mornings, some friends and I poked around in the basement of the burned-out fire hall and we found a bottle with some liquid in it. We found other containers with liquids in them also. I took them to the middle of the street and began pretending that I was a chemist. As soon as had I poured the contents of one of the containers into the bottle with the liquid, there was a chain reaction and I heard a swooshing sound and flames shot out of the neck of the bottle. As to be expected, we all ran in all directions. To this day, I have never learned what was in those two bottles. If I had, perhaps I would have discovered a new explosive substance and won the Nobel prize for chemistry. Of course, I could have been burned to death if the bottles were larger and then I could have got the posthumous prize for stupidity.

The Wells Fire Brigade attended quite a few fires in our town, mainly due to the fact that most houses had wood burning stoves, and during the winter months, there were many chimney fires. One winter night, my brother and I kept putting wood in the pot-bellied stove in our first house and we didn't notice that the stove pipe was getting red hot. My mother and uncle were heading to our place and saw in the distance, many sparks coming out of the chimney. They got to our place just in time before real fire damage ensued.

Another fire truck was finally purchased for the town although I can't remember where it was stored. I do remember however one Saturday afternoon when the new fire truck stopped on Dawson Street, a half block east of our house and the volunteer firemen were practicing with the fire hose. A number of the town's men sat on a fence nearby and that of course was an open invitation to get swept off the fence like ducks with a grand sweep of the fire hose by their fire fighters who all had sardonic smiles on their faces just before they were doing it. Those sitting on the fence should have guessed what was coming. The sardonic smiles of their fellow firefighters were a definite warning.

War had come to the Canadian Atlantic coast to some degree. Two German U-boats had slipped up the St. Lawrence River. That terrified the Canadian government and as a knee-jerk response, the government sealed off the River thereby trapping ocean-going vessels that had been in the Great Lakes, for the remainder of the war.

In 1943, Hollywood made a film called, *Guadalcanal Diary* staring

Preston Foster, Lloyd Nolan, William Bendix, Richard Conte and Anthony Quinn. It was a hot-off-the-wire account of what was really going on in the war in the Pacific. After seeing it, I began to realize that people really died in war. It was a real tear jerker. It was shown in Wells during several summer evenings in 1943 but it wasn't until the following morning (Saturday) after having seen the aforementioned movie the previous evening that its impact finally hit me. I was lying in bed listening to the birds singing while the bright morning sun was shining through my window behind me and I was thinking about all the fun I would have that day playing with my friends in the forests. Gradually I began thinking about those soldiers who died on Guadalcanal and who would never see the sun or hear the birds or play with their friends again. I couldn't stop crying for over an hour. After that, I began paying more attention to what was being said about the war. I think it was a turning point in my life when I began realizing that there was more to life than what was going on in Wells—I was emphasizing with others. It took a Hollywood movie to bring to my attention that all was not well in the world and that people did suffer and die in war.

I don't remember much of going back to school in September 1943 except that my teacher was a Mrs. Sullivan. She was the teacher for grade three and four. The grade three students sat in the three rows closest to the hallway and grade four students sat in the three rows closest to the windows. As I mentioned earlier, It was difficult trying to pay attention to our grade four studies when she was talking to the grade three students.

We didn't have ball point pens those days so we did all our writing with straight nib pens. Each desk had a small inkwell on the right upper part of the desk and we all had a supply of blotters about the size of a ten-dollar bill. How I hated using those pens. When the nib scratched against the grain of the paper—the paper wasn't as smooth as it is today, the ink would fly from the nib and splatter onto the paper and our writings. If we made a mistake, there was no rubbing it out with an ink eraser or using liquid whiteout. The procedure was merely to cross the mistake out. I had a lot of crossed-out markings on my pages, making the pages look like mysterious hieroglyphic markings not unlike that which one might find on the muddy floor in a chicken coop if you get my drift.

I remember how frustrating it was to put my hand up to answer a question when I knew the answer and the teacher chose to hear it from another student. I would always exclaim, "I knew that!" My teacher finally put an end to that when she said to me in front of the class, "Danny. You don't need to tell us that you know the answer. We can presume that when you raise your hand, you know the answer. I don't want to hear any further statements from you such as, 'I know that' if I don't choose you to answer the question." The class laughed. What the teacher said to me was quite right of course. I knew that.

Secret codes have been with us since time immemorial but one of Germany's top secret Cipher Machine E coding and decoding machines (called the Enigma by the Allies) was created by a German who bought the patent from a Dutchman. It was the cross between a portable typewriter and a cash register. It had adjustable rotors for enciphering the letters typed by the operator into an almost infinite variety of different letters. Virtually every German unit used the machines and at least 100,000 were made during the war. Such a machine was in the possession of the British and the Poles had discovered a method of how to break the code. The details were taken to London and turned over to the head of SIS (Secret Intelligence Service) on August 16, 1939, just before the beginning of the war.

Within hours of receiving the vital information pertaining to the workings of the machine, the British cryptanalysts began working on finding the way to deciphering the German code. The German's changed the key three times a day during the war, thereby making the task of breaking the codes even that much harder. And to make matters worse, nothing could be learned until at least 60 messages using the same key had been intercepted. One of the problems the Germans had to contend with was that the Enigma sent its signals out by radio rather than by telephone since its army units were always on the move. For this reason, their coded messages were able to be intercepted by hundreds of volunteer radio enthusiasts in England and elsewhere who picked up the messages on their ham sets and relayed them to the cryptanalysts stationed in Benchely Park, a country house 80 km (49 miles) northwest of London.

The British cryptanalysts finally broke the code and were able to interpret the hundreds of thousands of German coded messages raging from routine situation reports, request for supplies, mobilization orders and even complete battle plans. Throughout the war, the Germans never guessed or for that matter, even suspected that the Allies were listening in on their secret codes hourly. The British overall operation was called 'Ultra'.

There were a few times when the 'cat' was almost let out of the bag. One of those times occurred on September 11, 1942 when the Germans with documents captured a Royal Navy gunboat and charts detailing German convey movements. If the Germans had been on the ball, they would have put it all together and realized that their codes had been compromised. But they didn't realize the connection between the British documents and charts and the German convey movements and thus, the secret of the existence of 'Ultra' remained secret for the rest of the war.

On the 30th of October, two sailors entered a scuttled German U-boat and managed to locate the U-boat's Enigma cipher, which the people at Benchley Park needed so badly since, they hadn't cracked that particular code in over a year. Just as the two men handed over the long sought after prize to their comrades standing of the deck of the U-boat, the submarine began to sink quickly dragging the two sailors to their deaths. It shouldn't come as a surprise to anyone that many years later, Hollywood produced a movie in which it was the Americans who recovered the U-boat's Enigma cipher. Of course, it was fiction.

The winter of 1942/43 was the worst in the war in the Atlantic. Free to operate more or less unmolested from the Bay of Biscay in France, German submarine strength at sea rose from 91 to 212.

Canadian ships in 1942 had only been credited with four kills on the Canadian side of the Atlantic. During the winter of 42, they had none. In November of 1942, as many as 112 Allied ships were lost during the crossings. That was almost twice the number of replacements Allied shipyards were producing. In February 1943, as many as 63 were lost and in March, another 108. There were many reasons for these losses at this time. The Allies had temporarily lost the German naval code but one of the reasons included the fact that the Canadian's ships were not really prepared for combat with submarines. Further, the RCAF had no long-range aircraft to go beyond the western edges of the 'black pit' causing the crew of the U-boats to attack with relative impunity.

However, in May 1943, the tide turned. Of 130 U-boats in the Atlantic, 41 were lost, one of them commanded by the son of German Admiral Kark Doenitz, the man who was the head of Hitler's navy. The Germans then developed the acoustic torpedo which homed in on the propeller noise of the Allied ships. One such victim was the Canadian warship, *HCMS St. Croix* with a loss of all hands except one. The Allies more or less solved that problem by dragging behind their ships, devices which made more noise than their ship's propellers. The acoustic torpedoes homed in the noisy devices trailing behind the war ships.

The Royal Canadian Air Force grew slowly. By the end of 1941, only 500 Canadian pilots flew Canadian aircraft. Ten more squadrons however were formed in 1942 and in 1943, another four more were formed and in 1944, another three. An agreement had been announced for a British Commonwealth Air Training Plan to be centered in Canada. This project alone trained more than 131,000 aircrew personnel for the Commonwealth. Canada contributed 72,800 pilots, navigators, aerial gunners and bombardiers, and flight engineers. These Canadians saw service in almost every theater of war. The Royal Canadian Navy was increased from fewer than a dozen vessels to more than 400 by the end of the war. It became the third largest navy in the world, with only Great Britain and the

United States having more ships than Canada. The RCAF had 48 squadrons overseas and another 40 in Canada by war's end. They served primarily as an anti-submarine and convoy protection in the North Atlantic. Some of the units were deployed from time to time as far away as the Mediterranean and the Pacific.

When you think of it, we needed this many squadrons in the earlier part of the war. It may have helped shorten it. Probably, the pompous penny-pinching Canadian politicians didn't fully appreciate the need for so many aircraft until the war was coming to an end.

It was during this year when I was a ten-year-old that I wrote an essay as a project on the prospects of there being no need for runways in airports. I said that the wings of planes would have pivotal wings that would face upwards with their propellers acting like the blades of a helicopter until the aircraft was several hundred feet off the ground and then the wings and the engines would face forward and the aircraft would fulfill its normal function. Everybody laughed when I read my essay in class. Even the teacher said it was nonsense and gave me a failing mark for my efforts. Many years later, the British created the Harrier warplane that pivoted its jet engines so that the blast was downward, thereby holding the plane in a fixed position as it rose upwards until it was ready to be moved into a forward position. On May 7th, 1965, Canada tested its CL-84 Dynavert aircraft built by Canadair—a two engine plane that pivoted its wings and engines to an upward position so that it could take off from a standing position without the use of a runway. Unfortunately, there weren't any buyers so the CL-84 was scrapped not unlike the Canadian Avro which was also scrapped earlier. A newer model, the CL-246, which seated 48 passengers was also scrapped because they didn't have any buyers. Thirty-four years later, the Americans developed the Vertical-lift V-22 Osprey as America's newest military workhorse. Its two-engine aircraft pivots its wings and engines upward to lift off in a vertical position before moving them into a forward position for a normal flight. No one's laughing anymore.

One day, my uncle took me and my brother to Barkerville which is 8 kilometres (5 miles) from Wells. Barkerville, like Wells is located in a forested sub-alpine environment in the mountains 89 kilometres (55 miles) east of Quesnel.

The town of Barkerville sprung up overnight in 1862. The town was named after a prospector. In 1862, Englishman Billy Barker found gold on Williams Creek, a discovery that started a rush of fortune seekers from all over the world. His discovery made him and his partners rich. His claim would eventually yield 37,500 ounces (1,065 kg/2,350 lb) of gold. Barker had made $500,000 from his claim alone. In today's money (2008) his claim would have been worth over $35 million dollars. Lots of other miners rushed to look for claims as good as Barker's, and the town of Barkerville was born. During the 1860s Barkerville was the gold capital of the world. Miners searching gold bearing streams were followed by store keepers, barbers, school teachers, and post masters. Barkerville became the largest city west of Chicago and north of San Francisco. In addition to the usual saloons and dance halls it boasted a dramatic society, public library and poet laureate.

The town became the largest mining town to be built in the Cariboo. At its peak during 1863-1864, the town held about ten thousand residents, almost half of whom were miners working claims in the area.

Most of the trees in nearby hills were cut down for lumber to build the houses, shops, and mine shafts, and the resulting flash floods soon made the town very muddy. The houses and shops were raised on posts so as to battle the mud, and wooden plank sidewalks were built. This is how one frequent visitor described Barkerville:

"It was as lively a mining town as has ever existed in any gold-producing country the world has yet seen, not even excepting the famed and more modern Dawson City, product of the Klondike excitement. It had the usual gaming rooms, dance halls, saloons, etc., that figure in every camp, but it also possessed a host of sound legitimate businesses."

Barkerville was the main community for doing business in the gold rush-era of the Cariboo. The Cariboo Wagon Road, started at Yale in 1862 and reached Barkerville in 1864.

Barkerville had a strong Chinese community. 'Chinatown' consisted mainly of small shacks warmed by wood stoves; there was also a laundry and at least one gambling den. The Chinese men and a few women and children were used to farming, so they raised pigs and chickens and grew vegetables in their backyards. Mining wasn't the only work done by the Chinese; other occupations included doctor, herbalist, lodging-house keeper and storekeeper. There was the Wake Up Jake restaurant and Lung Duck Tong restaurant, a hotel, rooming houses, a bakery, a barbershop run by Wellington Moses, a Hudson's Bay Company office, several Chinese shops, a few doctor's offices, St. Saviour's Anglican Church, and a bowling alley. The printing press for the Cariboo Sentinel was in Barkerville; this newspaper was an important source of news throughout the Cariboo.

There were several active Chinese organizations loosely based on clan and birthplace, including the Chee Kung Tong, the Tsang Shang District Association, and Oylin Fangkou. These organizations existed to help their members when they were sick or in distress, provide friendship and entertainment, and to help people communicate with their families in China.

The Chinese community was so well organized, it was able to stage two Chinese operas in Barkerville in 1872. The Chinese also participated in the activities of the larger community for example, in 1869 they erected an arch at the entrance of Chinatown to welcome visiting Governor Musgrave, and prepared a speech "to offer you a cordial welcome, and to assure you of our loyalty and devotion to the Government of Her Most Gracious Majesty, the Queen."

By 1865 when the Royal Engineers completed the Cariboo Waggon Road, a man named Barnard had saved enough money to buy a stage coach and open an office in Barkerville. Barnard's Express took out freight, gold and passengers. Second in size only to Wells Fargo, it became the longest, most successful stage coach run in North America and a model for other operators. Barnard established a series of mile houses with fresh teams at each stop, one of the first in North America to do so. In time those stopping places grew into towns. 70 Mile, 100 Mile commemorate Barnard's planning. In addition to stage coaches, Barnard ran wagon trains. Up to 25 mules would haul 4 or 4 heavy freight wagons.

There were thieves and scoundrels along the Cariboo Road but they had no success with the Express. In one robbery attempt the thieves got the crate of gold off the wagon but the safe was so heavy they couldn't carry it away. Nor could they open it. They were forced to abandon it. Whereupon the driver came back and picked it up.

Passengers who wanted to go to Yale, (approximately 200 kilometers east of Vancouver) would leave Barkerville on Saturday and, barring accidents, arrive in Yale four days later after having traveled 300 miles. (482 kilometres) The fare, one way, was $80.00.

When gold output in Barkerville decreased, hydraulic machines replaced individual miners. Determined Chinese miners painstakingly panned out gold overlooked before. Eventually, except for a few determined residents, most people moved away. Barkerville declined into a wistful settlement of dilapidated houses and rusting machinery. By 1900 it was all but abandoned.

The town of Barkerville burned down in 1868, in what became known as 'The Barkerville Fire'. Barkerville started rebuilding the day after the first fire, but already the goldrush was dwindling and the town never regained its former glory.

The town of Barkerville stood abandoned for more than 70 years. In 1957, the British Columbia provincial government took over Barkerville and started the long process of restoring and reconstructing it into an historic site. It's a lot less muddy, dusty and dangerous nowadays than the original town, but the Barkerville of the twenty-first century replicates as much as possible the settlement of 1861. Over 120 buildings have been restored or reconstructed. Barkerville is the largest historic site in western North America. Popular special events are staged each summer and thousands upon thousands of vacationers go there every year.

Evidence of mining is everywhere. Above the buildings a system of flumes on stilts crosses the street carrying water from the mountain side. The dull constant squeak of huge Cornish wheels pumping water from mine shafts fills the warm August air. Mounds of mine tailings in every direction make it seem as if half the earth in the valley has been sifted for gold. Visitors can buy a (root) beer in a saloon, attend Evensong at St. Saviour's church, try their luck at gold-panning, observe a trial before Judge Begbie, saviour sour-dough biscuits and walk back in time as they follow 'Miss Wilson' along main street, entertained by her pithy comments on the settlers foibles. Around 200,000 tourists visit that town every year.

There were approximately 200 people living in Barkerville before we moved to Wells. But after the war began, most had moved out of that small village. During those years, Barkerville was not really a place people visited as it was just a ghost town then with ram shackled buildings in various states of disrepair. Since my uncle was the school bus driver, he would pick up the two Kelly kids (Russell and his sister) living in Barkerville for school and then return them to Barkerville after school. The two Kelly kids must have had a lot of fun playing in a town which much of it was abandoned. Talk about opportunities to play hide and seek. He also drove Jasen 'Barry' Curtis home. He lived a short distance west of Barkerville. Now that I have had a chance to reflect back to those days, I am wondering why my uncle drove that gas guzzler to and from Barkerville twice a day for just three kids. A small car would have sufficed. Perhaps it was an insurance thing.

The Kelly's father was a placer miner and he had a placer mining operation on a hill behind the town.

Placer mining (pronounced 'plass-er') refers to mining the precious metal deposits (particularly gold) found in alluvial gold deposits—deposits of sand and gravel in modern or ancient stream beds. The gold, having been moved by stream flow from an original source such as a vein, is typically only a minuscule portion of the total deposit. The containing material may be too loose to safely mine by tunneling, hence, it is placer-mined. Where water under pressure is available, the water is used to mine, move, and separate the precious material from the earth.

I was fascinated at what I saw. There was a fairly large stream on the mountain and it was funneled into a wooden sluice which was further on, then funneled into a metal pipe and finally into a small cannon-sized nozzle in which the water shot out of the nozzle of the large water cannon and blasted earth and rocks a hundred feet away. The earth and rocks were washed down the gorge towards a sluice box with barriers along the bottom to trap the heavier gold particles as the water washed them and the other material along the box. The blast of water was so strong, it had been said that one could support a boulder weighing a ton, in the air from one such water cannon.

I visited Barkerville again sometime the following year while living in Wells when Mrs. Berlin (my music teacher) and her husband (the minister of the Anglican Church in Wells) conducted a small church service in the only church in Barkerville. Built of local pine that has been burnished to a dark gray by the years, the church stands like a frontier cathedral at the head of Main Street. The Rev. James Reynard, from England, built the church in 1868 soon after most the buildings in Barkerville were destroyed by a fire. He built it almost single-handedly. But just five years after St. Saviour's was consecrated, Reynard was dead, at age 45, worn out by ridicule from the miners, cruel Cariboo winters and lack of money. It was and still is called St. Saviour's Church Anglican Church. When I first saw its walls were papered with old newspapers going back almost a century in order to keep the church warm in the winter months. I and the other members of the Berlin's Anglican Church's choir in Wells sang in that small church in Barkerville on that second occasion I was in that historic town.

Those were the only two times I ever visited Barkerville while we lived in Wells. I later visited it in 1984 when I took my family to Wells for a visit.

We moved into our second house in Wells around 1943. It was a three-bedroom house, two-story house situated right at the base of Island Mountain on Bartlett Avenue, a short distance from the junction of Dawson Street and Hard Scrabble Road. All three of us had our own bedrooms.

It was about that time that my uncle and aunt and their two children moved to Wynndel, B.C., a small town near the south end of Kootenay Lake and a short distance from the state of Idaho. The new principal who took over from my uncle bought a house about 30 meters (100 feet) from us and he used to let me come over on occasion and listen to his radio. That was the first time I heard a radio that had a knob to increase the radio's base.

We had our own victory garden at the new house in the front yard. Dale grew lettuce, I grew radishes and our mother grew carrots. Of course growing these veggies was purely academic since my mother could purchase them quite easily at the store but it was fun. What was really fun was the attempt of my brother and I to dam the stream a short distance from our house that resulted in Bartlett Avenue being flooded. Well, it wasn't really flooded but a lot of water flowed down the road which didn't make the users of the road happy because it turned the road into mud.

For some reason which I can't remember, I told some girls that my mother was going to start a Brownies club in Wells. She was upset when she heard I was saying that. Within a month, the rumor spread all over town and as a direct result, she was asked to begin Brownies which she did and later she also started Girl Guides and they gathered in the vacant house next to us two nights of each week. I on the other hand, had previously joined cubs and became a sixer. (patrol leader) This was the first time that I became a leader instead of just a follower.

The people in Wells, and I strongly suspect people elsewhere were beginning to believe that 1943 might be a better year all around as we were coming to the end of 1942. I remember feeling all aglow as I would listen *I'm Dreaming of a White Christmas* sung by Bing Crosby being played often on our neighbour's radio throughout the Christmas season. Irving Berlin wrote this song for the Astaire-Crosby movie

Holiday Inn. Irving had his doubts, but when Bing first heard the song in 1941 he reassured Berlin that he had another winner. The term "Winner" turned out to be a gross understatement. Bing recorded the song for Decca with the John Scott Trotter orchestra May 29, 1942, in the middle of World War II. No doubt the separation brought on by the War heightened the impact and success of this simple song. Before the year's end, *White Christmas* topped the charts, where it stayed for 11 weeks. It topped the charts again in 1945 for two weeks, and again in 1947 for a week. Bing recorded *White Christmas* again for Decca on March 19, 1947, with John Scott Trotter's Orchestra. It seems the original masters had been worn out in all the pressings. *White Christmas* was Bing Crosbie's largest selling recording and the largest selling Christmas single of all time—more than 30 million copies sold. *White Christmas* also won the Academy Award for the best song of the year.

Christmas in Wells was a great experience for every one of us living in that small town in 1942. There we were, huddled under the falling snow and so far from the war and so deep in the wilderness of the Cariboo Mountains with its townspeople thinking only of peace and tranquility and doing so to the music of *I'm Dreaming of a White Christmas*. Considering the fact that our Christmas seasons in Wells were always white with snow, the song had real significance to us.

As in the previous year, my mother took my brother and I up the street to her sister's place for Christmas Eve where we sang Christmas carols and for the turkey dinner the next day. On Boxing Day, Santa visited all of us kids again at the Community Centre.

It was this Christmas season that I began thinking that maybe the war would come to an end and my father would return home. I didn't really know him that much as my father but I needed a father and my uncle just wasn't filling the bill—this is not to say however that he didn't make the attempt.

Fathers play an important role in the upbringing of children but unfortunately, a great many children are brought up by their mothers alone. For example, in 1960, approximately 10 million children in the United States alone didn't live with their fathers. By the end of the twentieth century, the number was nearly 25 million. More than one-third of these children did not see their fathers at all during the course of a year. And, the trend is getting worse. By some estimates, 60 percent of children born in the 1990s will spend a significant portion of their childhood in a home without a father.

Experts agree that the lack of a father in the home has a negative impact on children. Research shows that nearly 75 percent of children in single-parent homes will experience poverty before they are 11 years old, compared with only 20 percent of children in two-parent families. Violent criminals are overwhelmingly males who grew up without fathers.

In contrast, the presence of two committed, involved parents contributes directly to better school performance, reduced substance abuse, less crime and delinquency, fewer emotional and other behavioral problems, less risk of abuse or neglect, and lower risk of teen suicide. The research is clear: fathers factor significantly in the lives of their children. There is simply no substitute for the love, involvement, and commitment of a responsible father. Dads play indispensable roles that cannot be measured in dollars and cents: nurturer, mentor, disciplinarian, moral instructor, and skills coach, among other roles.

When I was in grade five, Mrs. Barbara Alpen was my teacher. One of her eyes was crossed and because she wore corrective glasses, I could never be sure if she was looking at me or someone else. She wasn't pleased with my work so one day, she said to me, "Danny. I want you to pick up your things and follow me." She took me into Mrs. Sullivan's class. I asked her why and she replied, "Because I think you are not ready for grade five therefore you will have to do grade four again." I was absolutely devastated and embarrassed to boot. My mother wasn't too pleased either. I think she was informed of this change before I was because she didn't appear surprised when I told her what had happened. Disappointed, yes but not surprised.

Barry Curtis was in my grade four class and he was the best artist I ever saw for a kid of his age. What he could do with coloured chalk on a blackboard astounded everyone. There wasn't any teacher at school that could draw like this kid did so I have to presume that he was born as a gifted artist. He later became a very well respected artist but I didn't see just how good he was until I visited Wells in 1984. He was still living in Wells, that is, a few miles west of Wells on Highway 26. Some of his works were found as huge murals on the sides of buildings in Quesnel and his paintings and sketches of the Gold Rush days in Barkerville have been sold to a great many people around the world. I am fortunate enough to possess two of them which he personally signed for me. His murals in Quesnel have been retouched lest they fade away but several of his murals have been left to Wells.

Barry Curtis was born in a house a mile or so west of Barkerville. After he was an adult, his house was transferred to Barkerville so that it could become part of the houses in that historic site. When I saw him in 1984, he was sporting a thick beard and he told me that he acted as a guide on certain days in Barkerville when tourists would visit the site. He was quite amused at the surprise on the tourist's faces when he would point to a window on the second floor of his old home and say in a voice sounding like an old timer. "That's where I was born, many years ago." I strongly suspect that many of these tourists believed he was in Barkerville during the Gold Rush days especially when he told them that Barkerville had been a ghost town for almost a hundred years. The way he talked to them, one would think he was well over a hundred and fifty years old. Unfortunately, that talented artist died in his home one day when he was in his sixties during the latter years of the Twentieth century.

Needless to say, repeating grade four was a breeze. But when the final report cards were given out, I discovered that Mrs. Sullivan had failed me. I was totally aghast. It was beyond any reason at all. When my school friends asked me if I passed, I lied and told them I had passed into grade five—again. I even told my brother that I had passed. Of course, I knew that eventually I would have to show my mother my report card and she would know the truth and that after a while, everyone would know. I didn't return home until about four in the afternoon and of course I knew that the first thing my mother would say after showing her my report card would be that I wouldn't be spending two weeks at Bowron Lake with her and my brother.

I had no sooner got home when my mother hugged me and said, "You poor boy. Why didn't you come home earlier? You didn't have to bear that burden alone." I replied, "I'm sorry, Mommy. I don't know how I could have failed grade four. It was so easy." She looked at me and said, "Danny. You didn't fail grade four. You passed into grade five." I stood there stunned. She continued, "Mrs. Sullivan came here to apologize to you for making a mistake on your report card. She meant to say in your report card that you passed into grade five." Actually, Mrs. Sullivan had written in my report card that I had passed into grade four. That's why I was confused and I interpreted it to mean that I had to do grade four again. Needless to say, I was ecstatic and as promised by my mother, I spent two wonderful weeks at Bowron Lake that summer.

A somewhat similar error took place in Albany, New York in the fall of 2000 when 189 law students were told that they failed. It was discovered that in fact they had passed and the error was the result of a computer glitch. Previously in 1980, sixty law students were told that they too failed and it was discovered on that occasion that a computer glitch had made the error.

In that incident, if a student hadn't asked the school to manually check his score, the glitch wouldn't have been discovered. Aren't computers wonderful? In seconds, it can make mistakes that would take humans days to make.

My mother talked me into joining the choir of the United Church but I was only in the choir for a couple of months when my piano teacher, Mrs. Berlin who was the church organist of the Anglican Church (her husband was the minister) asked me to join their boy's choir. I agreed.

Chapter Twenty-Three

Truly one of the most remarkable uprisings in world history is that of the Warsaw Ghetto. The area intended for the Ghetto was described as "prohibited closed territory" and building of the encircling wall was commenced.

Everyday life in this separated district—although very restricted by the lack of living space and ability to move around the city, still existed. There are active educational courses, lectures of various kinds and concerts, Entertainment venues, small cafes where people met and discussed the current situation and night clubs, etc. were still open.

The building of the encircling wall was eventually commenced. However, the population was prohibited from using the term "Ghetto" under penalty of imprisonment. The official German name was *Seuchegefahrgebiet*, or district threatened by typhoid. The fencing-off was accomplished by means of the 3 metre-high (over nine feet) brick wall, stretching over more than 17 kilometres (10.5 miles) The bricks for this crippling wall came from buildings demolished or damaged during military activities in 1939. Broken glass from thick bottles has been cemented into the top of the wall. In addition the wall has been topped with barbed wire entanglements in some places. Elsewhere entanglements have been fitted into wooden frames placed on both sides of the wall—the Aryan as well as the Jewish side, so that no one could even approach it.

As time moved on, food became scarce. However, some of the children managed to find ways of getting passed the wall and retrieving food that had been left at the base of the walls on the other side by sympathetic Poles. Everyday life in this separated district—although very restricted by the lack of living space and ability to move around the city, still existed.

The Jewish Council had been ordered to strip the corpses of Jews found dead in the ghetto prior to burial and to take the bodies over the connecting bridge to the sports field. Identifications of their remains were not permitted.

After a while, the Germans began rounding up Jews and taking them to delivery points. They were told that they would be taken to a better ghetto somewhere else. They didn't know that they were being taken to an extermination camp—at least, not in the beginning anyway.

One day the Assistant Chief of the Jewish Division of the Gestapo, Karl Brandt, together with his assistant functionary, Mende, and an accompanying SS officer, paid a visit to the children at 'Centos'. Two days after the visit a column of SS vehicles arrived. The building was surrounded and all the children, together with the whole staff, were taken to the Umschlagplatz. (collection point or reloading point in the Warsaw Ghetto was where the Jews were taken to by the SS for deportation to the Treblinka extermination camp) There they were loaded onto cattle trucks and taken to Treblinka—exactly as was done with the children from Dr. J. Korczak's orphanage. Such was the action of the Nazis who had previously agreed to spare those children. Already the children in all orphanages, boarding schools, homes for the abandoned had been murderously liquidated in Treblinka.

As time went on, more Jews were being transferred to Treblinka. After that last expulsion it may have seemed that the ghetto was completely deserted, but this was not so. There still remained a mass of people hidden deep underground in places hard to reach. And so far the Germans had not been able to track down these places. The remaining Jews were living a different kind of life in the ghetto by then.

The Staff of ZOB (Jewish Combat Organization) when finally being apprised of the fate of the transferees published an appeal to the Jewish population not to go voluntarily—or, rather, involuntarily from fear to certain death. They were told that they must not give in passively. The Jewish organization decided to mount armed resistance against the Nazis. It was up to everyone to defend themselves, barricading their hideaways and cellars with whatever came to hand. The tract told the remaining Jews to fight and fight to the last Jew. The young fighters in particular considered that it was more important how and for what one died. And so they decided, in the name of the whole of society that they would die with honour, weapons in hand.

They constructed special shelters and bunkers. They had stocks of weapons bought by the ZOB command and brought from the Aryan side through canals and tunnels. They produced whatever weapons they could under present conditions, on the spot. For example; production of incendiary anti-tank bottles were filled with a mixture of kerosene, petrol and sulphuric acid. After carefully corking, a strip of paper soaked in an explosive solution was glued to the outside. When the bottle was thrown and the glass shattered, the internal content of the bottle came in contact with the explosive solution on the outside and a violent explosion and fire resulted. More sophisticated explosive devices were also produced using a plastic explosive manufactured from materials supplied to them.

Between the 15th and 17th of January the morning street round-ups intensified on the Aryan side. These were carried out at the Rozycki bazaar (Praga, Targowa, Zabkowska, Brzeska Streets); Kierbiedz and Poniatowski bridges; Zelazna Brama and Towarowa. People were dragged out of their homes and shops. Then the same thing happened each afternoon at Krakowskie Przedmiescie and Nowy Swiat. Thus the Pawiak prison and other prisons filled up again. The Germans were catching everyone, young and old - men and women alike. The people who were there (and there were very many) ran, panic-stricken, in all directions hiding in cellars, lofts and in the workshops. Only some of them had 'life numbers'. Some of the braver ones wanted to escape from Schultz's blocks back to the ghetto. Unfortunately, the whole area was surrounded by SS-men and escape was extremely difficult.

One of the ironies of this uprising in the ghetto was when one of its leaders, a man called Holodenko was killed outside his shelter when his knocking for admittance could not be heard above the noise and chaos resulting from the firing of guns and the throwing of hand grenades by the Germans. The previous day he had himself issued an order not to let anyone in after the doorway of a hideout had been closed.

In Schultz's workshops, footsteps resounded on staircases. People, beaten with riding crops, brutally grabbed by the neck or hair, kicked by soldiers' boots, fell on top of one another. Great panic resulted from this. Outside in the courtyard was a very large group of poor, ill-treated, frightened people. Most of those who did not have 'life numbers' were immediately transported to the Umschlagplatz. A rescue team from ZOB went there because a man named Szymek Kac had received a sum of money and authorization to rescue whomever he could.

Great tension was created among the people remaining in hideaways and speculating as to whom Szymek would succeed in rescuing from the square of death. The action in town and also at Schultz and Toebbens continued. Many people were still hidden in cellars. And so, from that moment, their resistance began and thus began the famous Jewish uprising in the Warsaw Ghetto.

Initial resistance was based on the fact that most of the inhabitants of the blocks had not left their homes despite orders from the Germans. The SS-men roamed through homes and killed everyone they met on the spot. Also, some of the braver ones were trying to escape from among those being driven to the Umschlagplatz. Quite a few succeeded, but German bullets found many others. Determined resistance took the form of blocking and barricading homes despite German orders to leave.

The first shots from the Jews against the Germans on Mila Street signaled the beginning of the Battle of the Ghetto. The ghetto fighters had grenades and weapons. On Miska Street the Jewish fighters set a building on fire, killing many SS-men. German ambulances collected a number of injured Germans in the workshop district.

The German police began to attack in earnest. Groups of Jewish fighters mounted a determined resistance at 30, Gesia Street on the corner of Zamenhof and Niska, and on the corner of Dzika and Niska, where they defended themselves with grenades. Those who had pistols and rifles were firing them at the Germans. Others, without firearms, defended themselves using what they had such as iron bars, picks, shovels, staves and even brooms from the broom works. Others poured urine and feces from buckets onto the heads of the SS-men. The Germans sustained considerable losses.

Meanwhile at the Umschlagplatz, once more another selection for death at Treblenka was made. Some of the very richest Jews managed to bribe their way out for very large sums, thus prolonging their lives. The drunken Latvian, M. Szmerling, a functionary of the Jewish police and Karl Brandt, were both greedily grasping the wealth of naive Jews.

Two military organisations operated within the ghetto: ZZW (Jewish Military Union) under the command of 'Marian' (Col. Mordechaj Anielewicz) and ZOB commanded by engineer Michal Klepfisz. Towards the end of April a group of ZOB members under the direction of Hersze Berlinski dressed as policemen and removed several hundred thousand zlotys from the Judenrat treasury.

The Nazis removed everyone from the hospital in the ghetto, doctors, nurses, the whole health department and all their patients. The only ones left in the surgical ward were those immobilized in plaster. The Germans walked by their beds and shot every last one of them in turn. The SS-men also transported the whole central lock-up, including the Gypsies. They were shot on the spot at the Umschlagplatz when they refused to enter the cattle trucks. Following such executions in this square, they forced Jews waiting their turn to wash away the blood. They did not even exclude the old veteran, crippled General Sunerling, whom they managed to drag out from a hideout.

In a mad rage for their resistance, Karl Brandt smashed with his gun butt or shot people brought there from Schultz's workshops. With his barbaric hands he tore women's hair from their heads, kicking and trampling them with his military boots. Afterwards exhausted, maltreated, tormented people were pushed into the waiting cattle trucks. Despite a 20 degree frost, the special team 'Werterfassung' forcibly stripped these people of footwear, coats, jackets and sweaters. Meanwhile, the Germans dissolved the Judenrat and the manufacturing enterprises. They conducted another selection of the ghetto police. It is difficult to describe these macabre scenes unless one has seen them and I have not.

On the third night of the uprising, many Jews were gathered in tight groups in their hide-aways. News spread by word of mouth that the end would come the following day but on the fourth day of action, their resistance grew even stronger. By organizing this active, armed resistance, their pioneering combat effort became a historical document about survival against all odds. On the night of 18-19th February the fighters set fire to a multi-million furniture store which burnt down to the ground. The furniture was ready to be sent to the Reich. Smiles appeared on our faces for the first time since the most recent tragedies. Mosze and Szmulek went mad with delight that the Nazis would not get this furniture. On February 21st another group from the same organization, ZZW, killed five Gestapo collaborators at the brush manufacturing workshops in Swietojerska St. The following day ZOB fighters killed the well-known Gestapo agent, Dr. Alfred Nossig, at his home at 42 Muranowska Street.

On the 4th of March at Brühl Palace, governor Fisher's residence, a postal package exploded, wounding two Germans. On the 6th of March a group of ZZW fighters set fire to German warehouses at 31 Nalewki Street. Also near the Umschlagplatz, ZOB fighters set fire to brush-making machinery which the Germans were preparing to remove.

There was an air raid alarm for two consecutive nights, March 8th and 9th, for the whole of Warsaw. This was repeated on March 14/15. All the people who had still survived and existed in the ghetto were filled with fresh hope.

The ghetto fighters attacked Ukrainian Werkschutz, a group who had been terrorising people in the workshop, robbing and pillaging whatever they could and too often, killing them. Thus, in revenge, the fighters disarmed and executed them. But SS-men immediately renewed their murderous action in retaliation and the streets were covered with corpses once again. The fighters didn't give up. They attacked individual Germans on Muranowska and Leszno streets. The younger fighters grasped their training lessons quickly and managed to fight against the Germans extremely well. under the command of the Ghetto's older fighters.

There was another air raid alarm for Warsaw on the 17th of March. In retaliation for the activities of the fighters, the SS-men continued killing hundreds of people in their homes and on the streets; mostly in the Mila Street area where the combatants' headquarters was located.

There were more air raid alarms for the whole of Warsaw on the night of 24-25th March and on the following days. Unfortunately nothing had improved in the ghetto and nothing has changed on the Aryan sideas there were still more intensive round-ups and arrests.

On March 27th, before curfew, an attack was carried out on the Aryan side on a transport carrying prisoners from the Pawiak in an attempt to free them. Germans suffered big losses near the Arsenal. but the Nazis immediately retaliated in revenge by murdering prisoners in the prison yard at the Pawiak—both Jews and Poles.

On April 18th—Palm Sunday, the Germans brought in reinforcing detachments of 'Askaris', who surrounded the whole of the ghetto. I should explain here that the Askaris were native soldiers (Muslims) in former German colonies. In SS parlance, "Askaris" were volunteers in auxiliary service to the SS, recruited from the indigenous population of conquered territories in Eastern Europe. They were mostly Lithuanians, Latvians, White Russians and Ukrainians, trained in SS-ausbildungslager at Trawniki, near Lublin. Not the best of soldiers in the opinion of the Germans. But at this time the most important thing for the SS was the fact that they were great anti-Semites. In addition, most of them were criminals and Russian deserters and as such ideally suitable to be included in the liquidation of the ghetto. This was the sort of murderer the Jewish combatants had to fight. The Jewish combatants on the other hand had no suitable battle experience. There had been no time for proper training.

When the Jewish headquarters received first reports of impending liquidating action on the night of 18th/19th of April, all fighters and Scouts were ordered to take up hidden positions at various points in the district. All stood faithfully on guard until dawn.

The Germans commenced their liquidation action by liquidating in the first instance the Jewish police at the Pawiak prison. They were brutally shot by SS-men. They were running across Dzielna Street opposite the entrance gates of the prison, with their hands held up high. Then on orders from an SS officer, they all were shot on the spot one by one by the SS men's pistols.

When the execution was finished, kerosene was poured over the stack of bodies (this was done by the Ukrainians) and they were set alight. The prison building which still held some prisoners was left intact.

A few hours later cars loaded with SS-men, as well as tanks and armoured cars, crowded into the depths of Nalewki. The Jewish fighters allowed them to get closer and closer. At last the order was given and from the upper storeys of houses very accurate machine gun fire rained down on them causing confusion and panic among the Germans. On the corners of Nalewki and Gasia, and also Mila and Zamenhofa, the fighters fired upon tanks and armoured cars. Many bottles and grenades were thrown at them.

As the battle became more fierce, hand grenades ('eggs', as the boys called them at one time) came into use, together with homemade bombs that were launched out of launchers made out of drainage pipes. The Germans on the other hand hit the Jews with the full force of their artillery along with the participation of their storm troopers.

There was great joy for the Jews at one point. A tank which had been on fire twice was finally immobilized. Also the same fate applied to a German armoured car. The Germans suffered considerable casualties, although the Jews had considerable losses too. The SS-men finally retreated and withdrew from the ghetto, but not for long.

In the afternoon, the Germans launched an action to destroy the fighters on Smoczna, Gesia and Lubecki with the SS-men attacking in increased strength. This renewed attempt to terrify the defenders did not succeed either, although the Jews were certainly aware that their defence against the onslaught of the Germans would eventually be beyond any hope of achieving lasting success.

The fighters could accomplish of their successes due to the creation of the bunkers prepared at, among others, Muranowski Square, Franciszkanska-Nalewki, Dzika-Gesia, Niska, Swietojerska, etc. However, the SS-men increased the strength of their attack. Despite stubborn resistance by the Jewish fighters, the SS-men took some of their defence positions in the end. Despite that, they had not taken a single Jewish fighter alive.

Those that weren't killed in the battle escaped from the bunkers and withdrew to the canals and then descending into the great labyrinth of underground passages. Unfortunately, many Jewish fighters were killed in the tunnels because the Germans flooded some canals with water and poured creosote down others lighting the creosote so that it would burn those still in the tunnels. Despite that, most of the fighters got through to their defensive positions. And although the battle lasted more than twelve hours, the Germans did not achieve the goal they had set for themselves. They had been unable to penetrate into the depths of the fighting central ghetto. Late in the evening, the firing on both sides ceased in the ghetto. The Germans withdrew their units.

That night, the Jewish combatants headquarters received a report from beyond the wall that during their armed struggle with the Germans, the first shots had been fired on the Aryan side on Bonifraterska Street between Konwiktorska and Franciszkanska streets. The report stated that a pioneer diversion unit of the Armia

Krajowa had tried to blow up the ghetto wall opposite Sapierzynska Street. In the battle of uneven forces the lives of some Armia Krajowa troops were sacrificed, although several SS-men also fell.

In the meantime, the Germans issued an ultimatum to the Jewish fighters to lay down their arms. As to be expected, this was ignored.

The German commander, General Jurgen Stroop arrived at 7a.m. to conduct further action to liquidate the ghetto. He struck immediately at the fighters' resistance position at Zamenhofa Street. Coming under severe fire from the fighters, he withdrew with his German staff beyond the ghetto boundaries, establishing himself at Zlota Street. In dogged battles with the fighters, the SS-men took the house at 29, Zamenhofa Street and others at Gesia and Nalewki streets thus forcing the fighters to withdraw from the roofs of these houses and to go down into cellars and bunkers. Other ZOB and ZZW fighters put up a determined resistance at Muranowski Square and on Muranowska Street. The fighting was terribly fierce. In spite of everything, the Jewish fighters had raised two flags on Muranowska Street—a Polish one (white and red) and a Jewish one (white and blue).

Fierce fighting also continued on the workshop premises of Schultz and Toebbens at Leszno, Nowolipie, Nowolipki and Smocza streets. These blocks were some of the most important points of the Jewish resistance. The Germans used flame-throwers there in order to take one house after another. Any of the people hiding here who were taken alive were shot to death by the SS-men on the spot. Others were driven to the Umschlagplatz for transport to the extermination camps.

On Wednesday, 23rd April, 1943, the Jewish fighters defended themselves with uncommon ferocity by throwing grenades and incendiary bottles and with machine guns. Many took their revenge, leaping from place to place, throwing grenades at the enemy with efficient accuracy. Other fighters, mined the area. In the heat of this battle it was difficult to see the fighting combatants through the smoke from the fires.

During that day's battle with the enemy, the Jewish fighters did not confine themselves only to defence, but instead they attacked the SS-men. A fierce, life-or-death battle was fought. Wounded men fall, yet continue firing despite their wounds. They fought to the death. Girls from Hashomer Hacair (Girl Guides) also took part in this action. Small, organized groups of girl-fighters, calm and self-possessed, often had to fire holding the calibre .08 pistol with both hands. Throughout the day, the SS-men suffered enormous losses in men and equipment.

By Thursday, 24th April, 1943, the battle thus far had opened a great new page in the history of rebellion against odds. The Germans had not been able to overcome by force the heroic defense of the ghetto. Fierce battles continued at Leszno, Nowolipie, Nowolipki and Smoczna streets.

The Germans had introduced a new method of fighting the ghetto combatants by burning down house after house. They even burnt those blocks where their own workshops and factory installations were located. They blew up any buildings which had remained standing. In their hideouts, the Jews ran in all directions as if they had lost their senses. On seeing this the SS-men reacted at once, shooting the Jews in flight like ducks at a hunt. The surviving Jews didn't know what to do with themselves, where to go, where to hide in order to preserve their lives. Some who had weapons, shot at the Germans and were killed. Others, however, sought escape in a different way. They sang their religious songs or cursed Hitler and died on their own volition by jumping into the flames. Among them women—some with children, including men who had survived the battle until then.

The weapons used so far by the Germans against the ghetto were not enough by then. General Jürgen Stroop, not only introduced the latest weapons into the battle with the Jewish fighters, but he then brought in aircraft for aerial bombardment. There was really nowhere for the Jews to hide.

German sappers blew up every point of resistance of the fighters—their defence positions, links, passage-ways. Using flame-throwers, they smoked the fighters out, screaming and moaning from the torment of severe burns and dying. In order not to fall into the hands of the SS, some of them committed suicide in the flaming bunkers.

Many underground bunkers still remained with fighters in them. Dust, terrible stench and so much suffocating smoke that it was dark even in broad daylight, brought to the defenders a real *Dante's Inferno* on Earth. And it was even harder for the Jews to believe the monstrous fact that it was really happening. They were all at the end of their strength.

Between them, Jewish fighters and Poles from the Aryan side, secured the sewers under the ghetto and these were guarded by Jewish fighters to prevent the Germans from flooding them. Any SS-men who ventured into them were met by gun fire. Smoke bombs thrown into the sewers by the Germans and the pouring in of creosote into them did not give them the results they had hoped for.

On Good Friday, 23rd April, 1943, for Jews, the Sabbath—day of rest. The fires and the clouds of smoke made it difficult to breathe. The rampaging fire flushed some groups of fighters from the positions they occupied. There were sparks and smoke driven on the wind, clouds of dust from toppling buildings, flying feathers, the smell of burnt bodies and materials, the thunder of canon and grenades as well as other firearms, also bomb-laden airplanes overhead.

Despite two hours' respite, hell broke loose again. The battle moved beyond the ghetto walls to houses occupied by Poles where the reserves and ammunition of the Jewish Uprising Command were located. The battle was terribly fierce but the Germans only succeeded in taking a few people.

Because of the flames encroaching on the defender's positions, they split into smaller groups, but it was often difficult to maintain contact between them. They held up bravely despite everything, exerting every effort to endure, not to surrender.

Holy Saturday, 24th of April 1943, was another Sabbath day for the Jews. For more than ten hours there has been silence from the German side. But after that ten-hour respite, the SS-men again attacked the ghetto strongly from all sides. Flame-throwers and airplanes above continued their additional destruction. Incendiary and explosive bombs fell on the defending Jew's positions.

This time, the German attack took all the Jewish fighters by surprise. Exhausted by yesterday's battles with the enemy, not all of them were at their appointed posts. Because of that, the SS-men uncovered many additional hide-outs and fortifications of the Jewish fighters. This time the Jews suffered great losses. About twenty-eight bunkers were discovered by the enemy. Also a lot of arms and ammunition, a mass of preserves and other food, and even valuables and money fell into enemy hands.

When, however, a few SS units attacked the bunkers of the Headquarters of ZOB on Mila and Zamenhofa Streets, a battle broke out which was worse than ferocious. It was a total slaughter.

Among the fire and smoke of battle, no one noticed when one of the young defenders leapt out of a bunker near a German tank with a bottle of kerosene in his hand. He wanted to hit the tank which was attacking his fellow defenders, in the right place so as to immobilize or liquidate it. Unfortunately, he had not noticed the approach of SS reinforcements from another direction. He was mowed down by automatic fire before he was able to throw the bottle, which did explode in the immediate vicinity of the SS. Some of the SS-men nearby were killed and others were wounded but the tank remain untouched. At that moment a German cursed: "Du schwein! Du bandite Jude!" ("You swine. You Jewish bandit.") I suppose he was upset by having lost several of his comrades to an enemy so young.

Looking from the direction of the next burning house, another of the fighters who had perhaps had seen the German tank deliberately running over the dead youth who had tried to throw the kerosene bottle at it, leaped out and hurled a bottle and a grenade at the tank which then burst into flames incinerating in its interior the German who had deliberately crushed the dead body of his previous attacker.

In the evening the Germans attacked another part of the ghetto where Wehrmacht weapons workshops were located. SS-men surrounded the whole block, completely cutting off the escape route of Jewish fighters who were there. Most of the fighters put up a determined armed resistance. The battle lasted more than ten hours. The Jewish fighters defended themselves fiercely, inflicting great losses on the enemy.

Here again the SS-men increased the number of flame-throwers. The streets and courtyards of houses were lit up as if it was day. Choking smoke and flames everywhere. Not in isolation, but whole oceans of flames. Falling beams, balconies and whole walls buried bodies as in a terrible cemetery. Many having no more ammunition and wanting to avoid death at the hands of the SS-men yet seeing no chance of surviving; jumped from the flaming walls into the body-strewn cemetery below, thus committing suicide. It was a horrific sight to see how they fell with their clothes in flames, their dirty faces, sooty from the flames, twisted in unbelievable agony.

The Nazis set fire to their 'Werterfassung' stores at Niska Street where they assembled the possessions of murdered Jews.

On Easter Sunday April 25th, 1943, was greeted with the red glow of fires, explosions and black smoke. That which the Germans could not accomplish was now being done for them by the fires which they started. The remaining surviving fighters could only see what was in front of them or behind them, or by their side, a great sea of flames.

By this time, the fires had closed off entire districts. The ring of flames was closing in even more. There was confusion among the remaining Jewish fighters. At certain times, there was such a bedlam of interchanged firing that in the noise and smoke the exhausted fighters became disoriented, not knowing which side was shooting. The aerial bombardment of the ghetto and of the thinned-out fighters within it continued. And despite that, they, with their last remaining strength but with great passion, continued to fight on.

Burning houses and walls fell with a great noise. There was a lack of air with only black, biting smoke and searing heat burning into their eyes, choking, cutting off their breath. The heat, radiating from burning walls, red-hot bricks and even concrete and marble stairs were crumbling under the heat.

On the second day of Easter, April 26th, 1943, SS-men attacked blocks on Niska Street one after another. The battle, equally hellish as that on Easter Sunday, lasted until eleven o'clock at night. And everything was the same again—the dragging out of Jewish fighters from the bunkers—some, full of fight to the last, screaming curses at the SS-men. Others were threatening, or singing the Polish national anthem or Jewish psalms, just before falling dead at the feet of the Germans.

During the last days of April and the beginning of May, the Hallmann's carpentry workshops on Nowolipki and Nowolipie streets and many bunkers were taken by the SS-men. But not all. And so special groups of SS-men and sappers penetrated further into the deserted districts of the ghetto, carefully seeking out the hidden fighters. The defenders now survived only as individuals. Others died miserably, yet heroically, dragged out by the Germans, yet still resisting and defending themselves fiercely, none of them surviving. To fight further was beyond the strength of anyone. Other groups of fighters barricaded themselves. Some at Nos. 5, 7 and 18, Mila Street and others at Wolynska, Szczesliwa, Niska streets and at Zamenhof and Nowolipki streets, all waiting for death at the hands of the Germans.

At the beginning of May, the bunker at 18, Mila Street, (the former nightclub, 'Arizona') was finally taken. This was the headquarters of the High Command of the Jewish Combat Organization. It was one of the larger bunkers and had several entrances and connections with the canal network and the whole labyrinth of tunnels built by the Jewish fighters. The battles for this bunker were long, fierce and very hard. Located there were: 'Marian', Commandant of the ZOB and leader of the Uprising; his great friend Ari Wilner (pseudonym 'Jurek'), a Scout; also fighters from Dror, Bund and Akiba. Defending themselves to within the last minute of their lives, they all chose to end their lives, not at the hands of the SS, but instead by their own.

On another day, the Germans took the next bunker at 30

Franciszkanska Street after a fierce, 3-day battle. Because the enemy used smoke candles and gases here some of the fighters who had hidden here entered a sewer. They waited there for over 48 hours in terrible conditions and with the foul odour normally found in sewers. They emerged safely onto the corner of Prosta and Twarda streets in broad daylight. Trucks from the Underground on the Aryan side drove up immediately and picked up these worn out, exhausted, but infinitely heroic Jewish fighters. They were taken to join the partisans in the forests. In this way, the whole of that group survived.

On the other hand, in a bunker at 29 Ogrodowa Street which was discovered by the Gestapo, another group of fighters perished on the spot. They had previously been led out from the ghetto through another sewer by the Underground on the Aryan side. Unfortunately, not all managed to save themselves. The bunker of Szymek Kac, one of the leaders of the ZOB, was located at 36 Siwetojerska Street, many Jewish fighters were lost in this bunker.

The Evangelical Hospital was located on the corner of Karmelicka and Mylna streets. When the ghetto was created the walls of this hospital were adjacent to the ghetto wall. Only one exit remained on the Aryan side. On the other hand, the Germans ordered all windows facing the ghetto to be bricked up.

This hospital had been very active in giving practical help to the Jewish population. It was one of the more important places where Jews were transferred to the Aryan side. As the result of continuing 'uprising' battles in the ghetto, the Germans set fire to the hospital—not, however, before the hospital managed to evacuate all its patients and staff.

On the night of 12/13th of May, there was another air raid on Warsaw. At first, hearing the bombardment on the Aryan side of Warsaw, all those still fighting fiercely were happy, being convinced that help for them had arrived. Despite the air raid, the battle to the death in the ghetto went on uninterrupted.

One group of about 26 persons aged between 16 and 19 (including many young fighters from the former organization, Hechaluc) got through to the bunker at Nowolipi Street. A collection of fighters from various groups, not all of them knew each other. But that did not mean very much. The important thing was their unity —to fight to the end, to the last bullet.

On the 13th of May, many Jewish fighters were captured alive by the Germans. All those taken alive were made to strip naked in front of giggling SS rabble standing with machine guns in their hands, ready to shoot. And the naked fighters; men and women were then made to run the gauntlet of SS-men armed to the teeth. Whenever the arms of any of the fighters became numb and dropped slightly, a bullet instantly put an end to them. Those who were still alive who had endured that torment and degradation, received additional indescribable tortures. Then, a slight pressure on a trigger and a whole series of bullets struck this handful of victims and another heap of flesh existed where a moment previously they had been Jewish fighters. Looking at it now, they would have been better off fighting to the death than be slaughtered like this in humiliation.

One by one the Germans kept dragging the fighters out their bunkers. One of the captured women still had a single 'egg' (grenade) in her skirt. When she saw the SS dragging a Jewish fighter from the bunker, tearing at his legs and arms, she threw the grenade and as she and the others ran away, she heard the explosion and then the screaming and moaning of the SS as they lay dying on the road. She lived for many years to savour that moment.

General Jurgen Stroop, the SS commander sent in to quell the Warsaw Ghetto uprising succeeded in his task but it cost him many men. In his report (which was a book bound in human skin) he explained to Hitler how he leveled the entire ghetto until there wasn't a wall standing. What he didn't tell Hitler in his book however was that his men found very few of the Jewish fighter's pistols and rifles. Hitler would not have been pleased if he had learned that thousands of SS soldiers couldn't quell a rebellion conducted by only hundreds of Jews with very few weapons to fight with. As I said earlier, after the war, Stroop was later executed in Warsaw as a war criminal.

The Warsaw Uprising will go down in history of one of the most outstanding of all uprisings, not just for the bravery of the Jewish fighters, but also for their audacity.

Chapter Twenty-Four

In 1943, it cost a person only $6 a day to stay at a resort in Maine and $29 a week to stay at a dude ranch in New York State. A two gallon fish tank could be had for only 49 cents. This was the year when good war movies came out such as *Five Graves to Cairo*, *Air Force*, *Guadalcanal Diary*, and *Watch on the Rhine*. There were also some other good movies produced that year such as, *The Ox-Bow Incident*, *For Whom The Bells Tolls*, *Madam Curie* and *The Song of Bernadette*.

This was the year that older teenage males began wearing the zoot suit. It had extremely wide shoulders, peaked lapels and (get this) high waisted trousers ballooning at the knees. A very large and heavy chain looped out of the right pocket extending to the wearer's knees. These fools then wore bright coloured stripped shirts and wide band hats. I later saw a couple of recruits show up at Cornwallis in these ridiculous clothes when we arrived at that navy base in 1951. Did they ever get ribbed. Women were wearing suits everywhere. Lounging teenage girls wore rolled-up jeans and sloppy shirttails.

The movie star, Leslie Howard who starred in the movie, *Gone With The Wind*, died, along with 16 others, in an airline crash between Lisbon and England. It was strongly suspected then as now that his plane was shot down by the Luftwaffe because he was at that time, a British Spy and the Germans knew it.

Uncle Bens, converted rice came into being. Butter was rationed at 4 ounces per week, cheese, 4 pounds (1.8 kilograms) a week, and the sale of sliced bread was banned. It is beyond me as to why that ban came about.

Long distance calls were restricted to five minutes. Cabs were obligated to take more than one passenger. It was not uncommon for three and four different persons to share a cab. To keep the employees at work happy, music began being piped in. It was called, Muzak.

Slumber parties began coming about for teenagers and hanging about the soda shop on Saturday nights was in vogue. Of course beach parties were popular at night. Dance steps such as the fox trot, the polka, rhumba, samba, the litterbug and of course that good old standby, the waltz, were very popular. It was during this year, that the opening three notes of Beethoven's Fifth Symphony, (dot dot dot dash which stands for the letter V) became the Victory theme of the Allies which was played nightly over Europe by the British Broadcasting Corporation (BBC).

"We men like War. We like the excitement of it, its thrill, its glamour, its freedom from restraint. We like its opportunities for socially approved violence. We like its security and its relief from the monotony of civilian toil. We like its reward for bravery, its opportunity for travel, its companionship of men in a man's world, its intoxicating novelty. And we like taking chances with death." *unquote*

I don't know if the Canadian who made that remark did it with tongue in cheek or whether it was the sentiments of Canadian soldiers, airmen and sailors who survived the war without a scratch, but it was inappropriate in any case. Ask any sailor or Allied merchantman crossing the North Atlantic in 1943 if he liked war, if the sinking of his ship in the deadly numbing waters of the sea was a relief from the monotony of civilian toil or if being severely burned was a novelty worth experiencing or if he liked taking chances with death with his fellow dying and screaming mates as they slipped under the surface of the icy cold sea. Ask him if the aforementioned statement really applied to him and the other seamen who shared the horrors of war together.

It didn't matter whether the Allied convoys assembled in Boston, New York or Halifax, they all ended up passing close to Newfoundland

and then headed east, sailing above the rotting hull of the Titanic so many thousands of feet below them on the ocean floor and into the dangerous waters of the North Atlantic. Waiting for them were the German U-boats moving about like marauding schools of sharks. And when the sharks attacked, a cargo ship would sink in minutes, an oil-laden tanker would explode and slip beneath the waves and the convoy would steam on at the speed of its slowest member so that no convoy would leave a ship behind to fend for itself. Losses were horrendous and it wasn't unusual to have a convoy of thirty ships leave the Atlantic Seaboard and finally arrive at the shores of the British Isles with only half that number.

The Germans submariners at the beginning of the War would pick up the stricken seamen from the sea and give them coffee and then put them back into their lifeboats but by the time 1943 came around, the submariners were machine gunning the seamen as they floundered in the water. Perhaps the Germans at this period of the war liked the 'opportunities for socially approved violence'. It was the worst kind of war and from late 1939 until late 1943 the 'Battle of the Atlantic' was being won by the German submariners. Of course, thousands of German submariners were also dying and this may have accounted for their cruelty in the latter part of the war.

Canada's corvettes played an important role in the 'Battle of the Atlantic'. By the war's end, Canada had built 122 of these 'sheep dogs'. The corvette was only 57.9 meters (190 feet) in length and 10 meters (30 feet) in beam. It's speed was at most only 16 knots which was too slow as the subs could outrun them) and it carried one four-inch (10.16 cm) gun, two machine guns and a fairly large stock of depth charges. One of its worst features was that it had the bad habit of rolling in the waves. (I served on a Canadian River Class navy frigate (*Antigonish*) in the 1950s as a helmsman so I can attest to that.).

One sailor told of his experience on board a Canadian corvette *Six War Years 1939-1935* when he said in part;

"Life on a corvette was pretty grim. One crossing, Derry—Londonderry to St. Johns, (It would take 15 to 20 days on an average) the weather was terrible. We took a terrible beating from the sea. We lost all the port wing of our bridge. All the lifeboats, all the life rafts—one wave and they were all lifted right off the deck and swept away. The seas were so heavy that the depth charges broke loose with as many as 20 rolling around, each being filled with 396 pounds (179.6 kg) of high explosives." *unquote* (Author's Note: They probably wouldn't have exploded because they hadn't been preset but anyone on the deck struck by one could be severely injured or even crushed to death) Another seaman serving on a corvette said in the same book; "Remember the advertising in the magazines. They never told us about the stink, the B.O. There were 30 of us in our quarters." (Author's Note: A corvette was built for a crew of 50 but more could sail in her.) "The smell got worse and worse as we crossed the Atlantic. The navy ruled, no showers on ships at sea. The ship was a floating pigpen of stink. Even the food absorbed the smell." *unquote* I should add that so did one's clothes. When I was in the navy, the main smell that permeated the ships was the smell of fuel oil. The only place you couldn't smell it was the cook's galley and the sick bay because of the odour from the food and medicine masked it respectively.

The worst part of sailing in these ships and any other ships that were in the convoys was being torpedoed. Joseph Schull wrote in *The Far Distant Ships* (A book about the Canadian Navy during the war) about one of the ships that was torpedoed. He said; "The seaman's mess decks were fiercely ablaze and the foretop of the ship had to be cleared. Smoke and flame compelled evacuation of the bridge. Inflammable materials in the paint shop forward of the mess decks added to the flames. Salt water pouring through the jagged gash in the ship's port side ignited calcium flares, which fed choking fumes into the inferno. As the forward magazine was flooded, the fore part for some 60 feet (18.2 meters) back from the bow began to bend, then a great section of the smashed hull broke off and sank." *unquote*

That ship being described was the Canadian River Class destroyer *Saguenay* and was the first of many Canadian warships to be torpedoed. That one made it to port with a loss of 23 men but many others didn't survive.

Believe it or not, some of the original corvettes were initially armed with only a wooded 4 inch gun (to frighten the enemy) and her load of depth charges. One such ship, the *Wind Flower* after it was finally given a real gun, but the crew never got to use it in a fire fight. The ship was accidentally rammed by a freighter in a heavy fog. Her boilers burst, spreading scalding steam over the wounded. She sank with a loss of 60 men. One merchant ship sank with a loss of 122 men including her skipper, Captain C.A. Rutherford who gave his life belt to one of his crew.

If the crews weren't killed in the explosions from the torpedoes or the ensuing fire and smoke, they died in the freezing water because no one could survive in the numbing water more than five minutes.

It was the deaths of so many Canadian and other Allied seamen in the 'Battle of the Atlantic' that makes the statement, "...we like taking chances with death." so obscene. Notwithstanding the horror of sailing in the North Atlantic in those years, there was a certain sense of humour that was shared with these men. The crests on these corvettes were descriptive of what their thoughts were. The *Moose Jaw* displayed a fire-belching moose chasing Hitler, the *Calgary* displayed a cowboy riding a bucking corvette, and the *Galt* displayed a corvette spanking a submarine. During a hurricane when the corvettes were rolling over almost on their sides, one captain radioed another with the words, "Can see down your funnel. Your fires are burning brightly." Another captain who discovered to his horror another ship closing in on the rear of his own, radioed, "If you touch my rear, I'll scream."

In 1953, I was one of the four helmsmen on the Canadian navy frigate, *Antigonish.* (slightly larger than a corvette) One day while steering the ship through a great storm, the ship was heading everywhere except where it was supposed to go. The Captain yelled down to the wheelhouse, "Batchelor. I don't mind you writing your name on the ocean with my ship but did you have to go back and cross the T?" When I was steering our ship through that violent storm in the North Pacific, the waves were two stories in height and when a wave weighing several hundred tons would smash into our rudder as it rose out of the sea, the hydraulic system would reverse itself and the wheel in the wheel house would spin like a circular buzz saw. Of course I knew better than to hang onto the wheel when such a wave smashed into our rudder. Had I tried to steer the ship at that moment, the wheel would have flung me into the bulkhead and I would have become part of the new paint job. More on my experiences as helmsman on that frigate in a later volume of my memoirs.

These Corvetts ships were designed primarily to remedy what were considered defects in their design, such as a lack of range, speed, and sea-keeping ability. In order to do this, the basic Corvette hull was widened and lengthened, and was given twin screws. This resulted in a faster ship with twice the range. Other than the war-built destroyers, these ships were the only ones to see service after the war in any great numbers, as 21 were converted into PRESTONIAN class frigates in the 1950s, and served until the mid-1960s. Many of these ships served in foreign navies after the Second World War.

Designed in Britain, the first frigates were named after British rivers, hence the description, 'River Class'. When Canada ordered frigates, they used the same design, so like the corvette, they kept the designation decreed by the British. In the naming of frigates however, the Canadians were a little more imaginative than the British, but not much. Canadian frigates were also named after rivers but later they were being named after towns, cities, glaciers, unique landmarks, Indian Chiefs, etc. Examples included *Beacon Hill*, *Kirkland Lake*, *Swansea*, *Waskesiu*, *Poundmaker*, *Comox*, and the *Antigonish*, just to name some of them.

As a young boy, I really didn't know about the 'Battle of the Atlantic' but I became more aware in early 1943 of the dangers of going to sea in wartime when I saw the movie, *In Which We Serve* (a 1942 British film) which describes life aboard a British destroyer serving in the North Atlantic during the Second World War) I cried all through the scenes which showed the men dying at their battle stations. Another movie I cried at was called the *The Sullivans*, an

American film which came out in 1944. It was the true story of five American brothers who served on an American warship. The brothers (Albert, Francis, George, Joseph, and Madison) served together as shipmates aboard the cruiser *U.S.S. Juneau* after requesting special permission from the Secretary of the Navy. The *Juneau* was sunk on November 13, 1942, off the island of Guadalcanal by Japanese submarine *I-26*. Of the crew of over 600 sailors, only 11 survived. The death of the five brothers caused Congress to enact a law, commonly referred to as the *Sullivan Act*, that prohibited more than one member of a family from serving in a particular combat zone at the same time. Even after hearing rumours of the death of her five sons, Mrs. Sullivan continued to support the war effort as evidenced by a letter she wrote to the Bureau of Naval Personnel. Franklin D. Roosevelt sent a personal letter to Mrs. Sullivan expressing his and the nation's sorrow. For wartime America, the Sullivan brothers became the ultimate symbol of heroic sacrifice.

During January 12-14th, 1943, two of the Allied leaders, Roosevelt of the United States, and Churchill of Great Britain, and their staffs, met at the Hotel Anfa, 4 miles (6.4 km) outside of Casablanca in Morocco in the first of a series of wartime summit conferences.

The British shelved their objections to new Pacific operations and the Americans agreed to participate in the invasion of Sicily.

Unfortunately, President Roosevelt made a blunder in Casablanca which invariably prolonged the war with the Axis powers in Europe. He proclaimed that any surrender on the part of Germany would have to be unconditional. To the Germans, that would mean a shameful surrender in which they would have no say in the terms of their surrender. By ruling out any terms of surrender for a defeated Germany, it weakened any opposition within Germany that existed at that time against Hitler. Gobbels, the Nazi propaganda chief pounced on this blunder with glee. He convinced the German people that the Allies were intent on the complete destruction of Germany and that because of that intention, the German people would have to fight to the very end otherwise, as a nation, they would exist no more. A similar blunder occurred with Japan in 1945. More on that later.

It was at Casablanca that American General Dwight Eisenhower (later to be elected president of the United States) was appointed as the supreme commander of the Anglo-American armed forces in North Africa. This didn't go well with some of his generals because of their doubts in Eisenhower's ability to win the North African campaign. Fortunately, he had three British deputies who supported him, Admiral Cunningham, General Alexander and Air Marshal Tedder.

The war in Russia had been going bad for the Russian people at the beginning but by January 1943, the Soviets were on the offensive.

At Stalingrad, the German Sixth Army was suffering terribly. The inadequate attempts to ferry in supplies by air was costly to the Germans. One only had to look at the route to Stalingrad from the west. It was littered with wrecked German transport aircraft.

In terms of manpower, the Germans were considerably superior in training and experience but the Soviet soldiers were better clothed and fed and that can make a great difference, especially in the middle of winter. Napoleon learned that hard lesson in Russia in the century before. Further, the Soviets had adequate ammunition, something that the Germans were running out of because of the difficulty in getting the supplies to the front lines of the beleaguered German army.

By January 10th, the Soviets moved in to retake Stalingrad and after a fierce barrage of rockets and artillery fire, the Germans were on the retreat. By the 25th, the various Soviet attacking armies met in the middle of Stalingrad and the Germans were pinned down to two small pockets of resistance.

By February 2nd, the last of the German troops surrendered. This was a terrible blow to the German esteem because up to now, the German people were still convinced that their armies were invincible, albeit there had been some great failures in North Africa. The Germans could live with those failures because they rationalized that their Italian Allies were inferior to them and also inferior to the British and Americans (which they were) and as such, they were of no help to the German army in North Africa. But to lose to the Russians was something else. The Germans sincerely believed that the Russians were inferior even to the Italians and to lose to the Russians up to now had been unthinkable.

Being sent to the Russian Front was in effect, being sent to one's death. In fact, many a German soldier and officer in North Africa and in the western part of Europe was threatened to be sent to the Russian Front as a means of punishment. The rumours of the horror of that Front filtered through the ranks of the German armies elsewhere to the extent that the mere thought of going there sent shudders up the spines of the Germans soldiers.

The German hierarchy can be totally blamed for the Russian fiasco. When the German armies attacked the Soviet Union, it was Hitler's belief that the war with the Soviet Union would be over in a short time. But as the first winter approached, he had neglected to see that winter clothing was sent to the front. By the time the winter of 1942 arrived, a great many of his Russian Front armies were inadequately clothed. By the time the second winter had reached the German armies at the Russian Front, they were better clothed but nothing really protected them from the iron grasp of the sub zero-temperature winds blowing across the Russian steppes. Many men froze in their fox holes and in the mornings, vapour puffs hardened like crystal on the side flaps of their caps and across their beards of those who survived the deadly freezing night. To free the ice from their weapons, they had to urinate on them.

Field Marshal Paulis surrendered his troops to the Russians. Hitler was galled. He screamed that Paulis should have killed himself rather than be taken alive. He said the entire German Sixth Army (what was left of it) should have killed themselves. He said in an outburst, "The soldiers should have formed a square and aimed their rifles at each other's heads and annihilated one another at a single command. When you consider that a woman who has her pride, goes out, shuts herself in her room, and immediately shoots herself just because someone has made a few insulting remarks." *unquote*

I can't help but wonder if the death of his niece prompted that remark. She was staying with him just prior to the war. After spending too many nights while being submitted to Hitler's weird sex, she too had lost her pride and she went into her room and shot herself.

From the defeat at Stalingrad, the war with the Soviet Union was a continuous retreat for the Germans and that retreat eventually took the fleeing Germans, with the Soviets close behind them, right into the heart of downtown Berlin itself.

It was too bad for Hitler that he didn't recognize earlier in his war with the Soviet Union the poignant fact of warfare that was recognized in the words of Suma Yokichiro, the Japanese Ambassador in Spain in March 1943 when the ambassador said; "It will be the same old story. The beginning of the hostilities in the spring, a big push in the summer and a nightmare in the winter." *unquote*

German Field Marshal Erwin Rommel was considered by friend and foe alike as one of the ablest commanders in the war. The British referred to him as the 'Desert Fox' as his cunning matched that of a fox. He made the acquaintance of Hitler as commander of the Fuehrer personal bodyguard during the entry into the Sudetenland during the Polish campaign of 1939. His request for command of an armoured command was granted and his 7th Panzer Division entered into the fray in the invasion of Belgium

By the time January of 1943 had arrived, Rommel's African Korps was short of munitions and fuel. Because of the onslaught of the Soviet forces in the east, much of the materiel needed for the North African Front was sidetracked to the Eastern Front.

The desert fox was also facing some pretty formidable hounds, such as Britain's Field Marshal Montgomery, and Field Marshal Alexander (later to become Canada's Governor General after the war) and coupled with America's General Eisenhower (not a tactician of note, but definitely a man who could muster the other generals together) and another great American soldier, and a great tactician, General Bradley, the desert fox was soon to be forced to flee them before the hounds got to him and tore him to pieces but the question on his mind was, where could he flee to with the hounds in front and back of him? There was the desert to the south but that would have been fatal and the Mediterranean would no longer available to him if Tunis fell to the Allies.

The Italians were of no great help to him now any more than they were when he first began fighting in North Africa. Back in the safety of Rome, Mussolini continued losing touch with the realities of the war. His armies were no longer the conquering forces that had swept over the poorly armed and untrained Ethiopian and Libyan natives in years past, his soldiers were now facing highly trained and highly mechanized armies who were led by men who were exceptional tacticians in war. The Italians must have sensed this and once that feeling of failure and inevitable defeat flows through your blood, it's difficult to stand up and face the enemy who you believe with all your heart is far superior in numbers and in ability than you are.

By January 23rd, 1943 the British had entered Tripoli. They had pushed Rommel over a thousand miles westward from the western gates of Cairo to beyond the shores of Tripoli. Not only did the desert fox have the British hounds biting at his heels, he would soon be facing the American hounds ready to nip at his nose head on.

Field Marshal Alexander was handsome and debonair and always immaculate in dress. He was born in 1891 and served in the First World War as an Irish Guards officer. In 1940, he commanded the 1st Infantry, supervised the last evacuation of Dunkirk then took over command of the southern forces in England when the German invasion was imminent. After a brief stint in Burma as commander in chief, he was then sent to North Africa as commander of the British forces there. From there, he went on to become the Supreme Allied Commander in the Mediterranean. On April 29th, 1945, he accepted the German surrender in Italy. After the war, he was created a viscount—his father was an Irish peer—and in 1945, he was appointed Canada's 17th Governor General and he took office on April 18, 1946 and served as Canada's Governor General until 1952. He then became Churchill's defence Minister until 1954 after which he then retired. He died in 1969. I saw him when he was visiting various cities in Canada as Governor General. He was visiting Nelson, British Columbia at that time. He was in his field Marshal's uniform and was being accompanied by his wife, Margaret. I was standing along the main pathway running through Lakeside Park in Nelson when he and his wife passed by me within a few feet. Everyone just stood there in awe and applauded as the two walked by me. Some Canadian veterans who had served under him in the Second World War (some wearing their uniforms for the occasion) snapped sharply to attention and saluted him. I can't remember the month but I remember it being sometime during the summer months of 1949—the same month the waters of the western arm of the Kootenay Lake flooded a great part of the park.

During the early winter months of 1942/43, there had been a lull in the fighting in North Africa and one of the reasons was because of the terrible weather. Despite the common belief that North Africa is always sunny, the weather during the winter months is often rainy and violent storms lash the hills and torrential rains flood the roads. The muck is so thick that it will suck the boots right off of one's feet. Tanks floundered and mules had to be used to carry supplies to the front. Despite the lull, the infantrymen would go out at night on patrol and during the day, spend much of their time scraping the muck off their uniforms and cleaning their weapons. The Germans continuously shelled the enemy infantrymen who had great difficulty in digging foxholes in the muck or alternatively in the rock. They just gritted their teeth and cringed as each shell burst amongst them, sending deadly shards of steel towards them—some which passed through the unprotected soldiers, others whistling past them within inches. It was all reminiscent of trench warfare in the First World War.

Eisenhower decided that it was better to spend the rest of the winter preparing for a spring offensive than try fighting through all that muck so the war in North Africa more or less came to a lull. By early January however, Montgomery was deep into Tunisia.

Rommel on the other hand decided that he would attack the Americans to the west in hopes of preventing them from reaching

Tunis, the capital of Tunisia and the closest seaport to Sicily where he was getting his reinforcements and supplies. He realized that if the Allies took Tunis—the British from the east and the Americans from the west—he would be cut off from his supply line coming from Sicily and the African Korps would be history.

In Western Tunisia, the Allies had formed a front along a barren mountain range called the Eastern Dorsal. It's a mountain range that runs north-south for almost 320 km (200 miles) from Dupont du Fahs to Gafsa and is split by narrow passes. The British held the northern sector, the French held the centre and the Americans held the southern end.

In one of the battles that ranged in the southern area between the Germans and the Americans, the Americans led by Major General Frendall, a general who was not cut out for command, suffered horrendous casualties. Of the 2500 men he sent into the hills to fight the German tanks and Stutka dive bombers, only 300 managed to fight their way out. The remaining 2200 were either killed or captured. The Americans ran in full flight towards the safety of the Western Dorsal mountains with the Germans in close pursuit.

Major General Frendall was a failure as a commander and worst yet, he was quarrelsome and didn't get along with other Allied commanders. That's the trouble with some persons who are inept as leaders—you can't tell them anything without getting into some kind of confrontation with them. What amazes me is that Eisenhower kept him on so long but when he did an inspection of Frendall's lines, he discovered that his men were spaced too thinly and Frendall was sitting in his headquarters 130 kilometers (80 miles) to the rear. Ike finally decided to sack him (the first American General to be sacked in the Second World War) and Frendall was sent back to the United States to head a training command. It makes you wonder if the prerequisite to being the head of a training centre is primarily to be sacked as an incompetent front line general. I ask that rhetorical question because when I was the head swim instructor and senior swim coach at the Vernon Army Cadet Camp many years later, our camp was commanded by Brigadier General Kitching. He too, like Frendall, had lost a great many tanks in a fight with the Germans during the Second World War and nearly got sacked for it. However in all fairness to him, I think he was a better commander than Frendall was. Of course not all generals who took over training commands were failures at war. General Anderson of the American Army was successful in North Africa and was sent home to take command of a training command.

Time and space doesn't permit me to go into great depth into the war in North African Tunisia. The fate of the German forces in North Africa would be decided upon in that area and nowhere else. On May 12th, 1943, that formidable army, the Afrika Korps, passed out of existence. Fortunately for Rommel, he didn't suffer the indignity of being captured. On March 9th, Rommel flew out of Tunisia to personally explain to Hitler why his Afrika Korps was in dire need of materiel and men. Hitler didn't return him to North Africa nor did he heed Rommel and that is why Hitler lost North Africa to the Allies. Winston Churchill best summed up the victory in North Africa when in his book *The Hinge of Fate* he wrote; "No one could doubt the magnitude of the victory of Tunis. It held its own with Stalingrad. Nearly a quarter of a million prisoners were taken. Very heavy loss of life had been inflicted on the enemy. One third of their supply ships had been sunk."

It was at this juncture of the Second World War that people thought of Winston Churchill's words when he said in an earlier speech at Mansion House in London on November 10th, 1942 at the time when Egypt was saved; "Now this is not the end. It is not even the beginning of the end but perhaps, the end of the beginning."
unquote

It definitely was the turning point of the war in Europe and North Africa. Germany and its Axis partner, Italy had gone as far as they could go and like a balloon being deprived of its air, the sphere of it's expansion was closing in on itself.

British intelligence allowed two World War II double-agents

nicknamed 'Mutt' and 'Jeff' to place and ignite bombs in Britain to maintain their cover, according to wartime documents from the domestic agency MI5 released years later. The previously classified papers, released by the Public Records Office, show that a power station and a food store were bombed to convince the Germans that the two agents they believed were theirs were operating effectively. In reality, the agents had been captured and "turned" by MI5, the papers showed. The papers were part of the biggest release of documents of its kind ever staged by the Public Records Office, Britain's national archive.

The double-agents fed the Germans false information, including that Britain was planning to invade Norway. "It should be recognized that friends as well as enemies must be completely deceived," the MI5 documents said. There were no casualties in the bombings. The agents involved were identified as Norwegians Helge Moee and Tor Glad, who flew part of the way to Britain, then completed the journey in a rubber dinghy, arriving in Scotland. Having being turned by MI5, the documents stated: "It was obvious that if the case were to be kept going a faked act of sabotage would have to be committed and the decision was therefore reluctantly made to attempt an explosion in a food store." *unquote*

A bomb was placed in a food store, with security officials on duty to warn people away. Another target was a power station in Bury St. Edmunds in eastern England. A bomb was placed near the generator, but in an area where serious damage was not likely. The Germans were pleased with the work and falsely claimed in a radio broadcast that the device killed 150. By the end of 1943, MI5 believed that 'Mutt' and 'Jeff' had been compromised and their work was ended. As an interesting aside, other released documents showed the MI5 kept tabs on British fascist leader Oswald Mosley, British Communist Party head Harry Pollitt and American writer and fascist sympathizer and poet, Ezra Pound. It investigated Clare Sheridan, a cousin of British wartime leader Winston Churchill, who published anti-British propaganda from Turkey but later claimed she was employed by the British to watch over a leading Soviet activist based in Istanbul. MI5 also kept files on St. John Philby, the eccentric father of Harold 'Kim'Philby, the infamous Soviet mole who infiltrated British intelligence during the Cold War.

Up to now, we in Wells had not seen any signs of the Canadian Army in winter and had only seen a few flashbacks in newsreels of the Canucks in action. But sometime in the month of January or perhaps it was February 1943, on one cold day, we heard a distant roaring sound—one that was unfamiliar to our ears. As it got louder, many people began heading down Pooley Street towards the lake to see what it was. The noise was coming from that direction on the road leading to Quesnel. In the distance where the road runs past the western reaches of the Jack-O-Clubs Lake, all we could see was a flurry of snow, not unlike an avalanche heading towards town. As we ran down the road to meet this flurry of snow, our hearts beat wildly because we had no idea what it was. Admittedly, there were a few in town who knew what was coming but they kept it to themselves. Even when we finally saw what was coming, we still didn't know what it was.

What it was of course was a large number of enclosed tracked troop carriers and their tracks threw up the snow in a fury and the noise from their engines were not unlike the engines of large power boats. As they rushed past us, blinding us in their wake, drowning out our questions to each other, we stood there in bewilderment and awe.

The soldiers ignored us and continued on into a staging area in the tailings area of our town. We ran after them and when we arrived in their staging area, the soldiers wouldn't let us approach them. They did tell us however that we would see the vehicles in action later the next day.

When I think of that now, I sometimes wonder how it was that we were so overwhelmed at such a sight and by the sounds of these vehicles but upon reflection, I am mindful of the fact that in Wells, we were a protected community and the occasional small truck and car was about the only thing that many up there had ever seen in that town before other than the large snow plow that flung snow onto the fronts of our houses.

For the next couple of days, (it might have been a week) we had plenty of opportunity to watch the Canadian soldiers do their maneuvers in those 'monsters' that our parents told us to stay away from but in which we crept up close to when they drove past us in a high speed of thirty miles an hour. It wasn't every day we kids got to flirt with death with such monsters, especially monsters that scared us half to death. A complaint by their commanding officer to my uncle Harold put an end to our carefree and dangerous games. He came into each of our school rooms and lectured us on the dangers of being crushed to death under the tracks of these huge vehicles. He didn't need to lecture us on the inherent dangers. Why did he think we risked our lives so foolishly? Was it because doing anything else was akin to knitting by the fireside?

Soon they were all gone and we never saw them again. I suppose the onslaught they suffered from us kids throwing snowballs at them was enough to prepare them for what they might be having thrown at them during the rest of the war. Sadly, in all probability, some of the soldiers didn't survive the war.

In North America where the screams of the dying were unheard, the civilians, for the most part, actively participated towards the war effort. Civilians knew that they played a vital part in the struggle and it was a great moral booster for them to know that one's effort in building a large gun, a plane, tank or ship and even helping in the manufacture of small arms ammunition was part and parcel to fighting the war also. And the impact of the home front on which the war efforts were tremendous is easy to appreciate when one considers that over two-thirds of the world's iron and steel industry, coal deposits and oil productions were under the control of the Allied powers. Our countries had the manpower at home to send all these natural resources to the front in the form of war machines. In fact, there really wasn't anything civilians did that didn't in some manner or other, contribute to the war effort unless he or she was a hobo or an invalid.

Mothers, included my own, contributed money in the name of

their children who were going to school. Each week, most if not all of the mothers of their school-aged children would give their children 25 cents (which was a lot of money in those days) to purchase 'War Saving Stamps' and we would give our teachers the money and the school would purchase the 'War Savings Bonds' in our names. The schools would choose a particular project and specifically ask that the monies received be applied to that particular project. The schools I went to in Toronto and the one in Wells during the war each picked a fighter plane. We were told how much of our money was being put towards the building of a fighter plane. However as I grew older, I strongly suspected that all our money went into that great war chest in Ottawa and was spent in any manner the Department of National Defence chose to spend it. Later in the 1950s and 1960s, the long-term bonds matured and we children whose parents had given us the weekly 25 cents for the purchase of War Saving stamps, began reaping in the benefits. I received several hundred dollars in the 1950s and another couple of hundred dollars in the 1960s. Money in those years was worth considerably more in the forties than it was in the 50s and 60s but even in the 50s and 60s, it was worth considerably more than it is today. When I eventually received my rewards for 'my' contribution to the war effort, they arrived as well-needed supplements to my otherwise skimpy income.

It was Napoleon who said that the army marches on its belly and by that of course he meant that the army had to be fed but everyone realized of course that even the people at home had to be fed also. This meant that because a great deal of food was being grown to feed the men and women of the armed forces, those staying home would have to do their share of providing food for themselves.

People everywhere, especially in Britain, Canada and the USA, were encouraged to grow victory gardens in their back and front yards so that they wouldn't have to purchase as much of the food in the market that was better destined towards the fighting men overseas. As such, my mother and my aunt had their victory gardens in Wells also. Of course we had the property to grow food on; that is we had front and back lawns. But many of the people in the cities had no lawns at all and they were forced to grow their victory gardens in their flower boxes. Some would grow radishes and other small vegetables that don't need a lot of earth.

There were a lot of signs up encouraging people to grow their own vegetables. In the cities many people were actually growing their gardens right on the boulevards and in vacant lots.

There was a shortage of farm workers during the war years and many German prisoners of war, interned Japanese, conscientious objectors and senior citizens would go work on the farms. In British Columbia, and Saskatchewan, the Doukabours, (men, women and children) would work in their own fields. That sect didn't have to send their men off to war to fight or send their children to school because of a deal made with the government of Canada many years earlier when the Doukabours came to Canada from Russia. In the preserving of fruit which was becoming very popular at this time, my mother would often make her preserved fruit, jellies and jams in preserving jars.

Elmer Davis, the Director of War Information in the United States quoted a statement from the American Secretary of Agriculture who said "Food will win the war and the right to peace". Elmer Davis then said, "As the war pace quickens we are all beginning to realize how true and how all important that slogan is." He went on to say that, "Food is a weapon in all wars but in this one, more than usual. We are using our food supplies as a weapon positively so distributing it so that the American army and navy and the American people will be well nourished. Yes, and so that the armies of our Allies will be kept strong too." *unquote*

Commissioner McNutt of War Manpower in the United States who was in charge of supplying manpower for the armed forces said, "No nation at war, particularly a democracy, can suspend everything on the home front while it fights on the battle front. We must grow food, we must process that food, put it into containers, transport it to the point of consumption and do the thousand and one thing needed to keep our home economy functioning. We could not possibly do away with all civilian activity even if one were foolish enough to wish it. Food like bullets and planes and tanks is ammunition. Men and women who worked to produce, process and to distribute that food was putting weapons in the hands of our fighting men as surely as the men and women who were producing the guns." *unquote*

There were sacrifices made. For example, Krafts Foods which makes the well-known Kraft's cheese sent an announcement out saying that for many years the Kraft gift assortment of cheese and salad products had been a favourite Christmas gift among thousands of members of the company, their friends, relatives and business associates. Because so many of the foods which were included in the assortment were needed to meet the needs of the American armed forces and its Allies overseas and because of the rationing of cheese products, Kraft said it would no longer be possible or practical to make the usual offer. The firm said in part; "We are sure that your knowledge of the urgent need for these basic foods and your pride in the part they are playing in the war will prompt your quick understanding." *unquote*

During those years, I was between eight, and twelve so I really didn't appreciate the significance of this constant talk about the shortage of food because as you may recall from my earlier comments about food in Wells, we were never without food but nevertheless, my mother permitted my brother and me to have our own gardens and I always liked radishes so I grew radishes and he always liked lettuce so he grew lettuce and my mom liked carrots and she was growing carrots so we all had our own gardens which were in our back yard at our second house in Wells.

Earlier in this book, I also wrote about Canadians (and that went for Americans and everyone else) saving scrap metal. In the United States alone there were 12,000 community recycling programs underway and more than 21,000 salvage committees were created for the war effort. There were scrap drives going on throughout the war and often signs would be put up telling us to put our scrap on the curb on such and such a day. Every category of citizens from young children to older folk, male and female, collected or gave up personal items or things for their homes for the war effort. I saw a picture once saying 'Lets help slap the Jap right off the map with our scrap.'

Many communities were prepared to give up their valuable antiques such as antique fire engines which would be applied towards the war effort. And on a number of occasions many war artifacts, which today would be considered important or historically valuable, were consumed by these intensive scrap drives, such as World War One Howitzers which would sit on the grounds of state and provincial capital buildings and city halls etc. Naturally, bronze statutes and memorials stayed where they were. Aluminum played an important role during the war. In the United States alone, 1.7 million tons of aluminum tins were discarded but one million tons of that were eventually recovered to be applied towards the war effort. Nowadays, it is not unusual to see large scrap yards where automobiles are stored so that parts can be taken from them. During the war years however, these cars would be taken away to be melted down.

As to be expected, rubber was hard to get since rubber plantations in the Far East by then was under the control of the Japanese Empire. As a result of the rubber shortage, often vehicles would be ridden on tires that would be worn bald. When I say bald, I mean some of the surfaces of those worn tires would make the scalp of the bald Hollywood actor, the late Yul Bryner, look like he had undergone a hair transplant with a long-haired Persian cat. No new rubber tires were being sold to anyone as all rubber was being provided for the armed forces instead. So if you had your four tires and a spare, you had to take good care of them because that's all you would have during the war years. In Wells and everywhere else in the surrounding areas, the roads were not paved so the tires wore down very quickly. Hence by the time 1943 had come about, almost everyone had baldies for tires.

In the United States, many people carried with them gas masks. Even schools kids would sometimes carry gas masks. That's because there was a fear that the Germans were going to someday invade United States and bring with them the gas weapons that they had used in the First World War. Of course it turned out that there was no need for the gas masks.

During the war years, it was a common practice to have the high school students join cadets and drill in school basements. Most of the large cities in the United States and in Great Britain had home guards to protect them from the German or Japanese invaders who might attack them. They were skilled in marksmanship with their deadly shotguns and rifles. They were called Guardian Angels. As we all know, Guardian Angels of today are the volunteer young people who travel around the streets protecting other people from thugs.

There were a lot of comic books and magazines available to children during the war that were telling us all about the war. Of course, they were in black and white. The coloured comics came out soon after the war had ended.

As children in Canada and the United States, we were mercifully spared the misery and fear of bombings, so most memories of that time were not as traumatic as those of the children of France, Belgium, England and other countries in Europe and in Asia. As children, we did not have the experience common to adults and while our mothers and fathers knew that a lot of the news was a product of wishful thinking, we as children accepted every shred of grandiose Allied propaganda as if it were absolutely true and not even subject to question.

Of course foremost in the propaganda war were the movies. In any Saturday afternoon, one would find all the neighbour kids at the theatres ready to scream and yell at deeds of the dirty Nazis or the Japs. We simply didn't scream at pictures of Italian soldiers because there didn't appear to be any pictures of them being shown. The 'courageous' Yankees without fail brought forth victory while the miserable Germans or Japanese were forced to crawl about in humiliation. Of course it wasn't until after the war that we learned that the fighting wasn't quite like that at all.

Everyone who was a child during World War II will remember the virtual disappearance of metal toys of course. A nation at war had little time devoted to children's playthings and it was rare indeed for a youngster in 1941 through 1945 to see metal toys for sale. Of course one thing that we had in North America was plenty of wood so a lot of our toys were made out of wood. Some manufacturers even went so far as to try to produce wooden scooters for kids. I had one like that when I was a child in Toronto. Rubber was like gold, so we seldom saw anything made of rubber other than the tires of our parent's cars so any toy requiring the use of rubber was nonexistent. The Lionel model trains were casualties of war-time as they didn't appear on toy shelves again until late 1945 since they were all made of metal. I don't remember any toys made of plastic during the war years.

We would get books of course. A lot of the books that were given to us were usually about the war, such as the book *Flying Fortress* by Barry Blake or we would get models of soldiers or sailors or a painting set that would depict scenes of war and there would be colouring books always showing scenes of war, either scenes of fighters in the air or tanks on the ground or ships at sea. There was some concern amongst parents and including school teachers that children would get too involved in the war effort and this might create emotional problems later. If it did, I never recognized the problems in myself or in my peers.

Campaigns were launched to encourage youngsters to collect paper, tin foil, scrap metal, to buy defense stamps, to make model airplanes, to join the junior Red Cross or other newly created clubs and most of those activities appeared to be good and sound although it wasn't really known for certain since insufficient observation had been made of their effects on various youngsters.

One of the things to be done was to define exactly the purpose and possible outcome of these new activities that the children were getting involved in. Knowing precisely why they wanted youngsters to engage in various war activities would have helped the parents to understand why certain boys and girls either lost interest or had little to begin with. Some of the dangers that were inherent in these new activities were, for example if the activity lost its meaning and became boring to children and at the same time the children were alternatively motivated by external and artificial means to continue it, they would perhaps become antagonistic and demoralized. If children are encouraged to engage in too many activities of that kind they may become over stimulated with the result that additional war tensions would be produced. If too much pressure was brought on the youngsters to engage in these tasks, they might break under the strain and the competitive element as a motivating force involving hazards. Competition as a sole motive is unhealthy to begin with and creates another new type of pressure. For example, children might steal money from one another to buy defense stamps as an illustration of this point. Under some circumstances youngsters were urged by adults to participate in war activities as one way for adults to work off their own war jitters. There appeared to be a great deal of this emotional exploitation of children during those years. Children's war activities in some cases were encouraged by adults in the interests of their own self promotion and aggrandizement and this constituted another kind of exploitation of youth in war time. Children were often called upon to help collect paper. In terms of military use there were over 2,800 items including draft cards, containers for food rations, protective bands for bombs, targets, shell and cartridge boxes and many other products used by scrap paper.

By April 1942 supplies collected by various methods completely overstocked the market however by late 1943 supply was exhausted again and another nationwide drive for scrap was conducted. Facing another paper shortage in 1945, General Eisenhower himself sponsored a nationwide drive. The Boy Scouts in the United States alone collected over 720,000 tons of paper. He was so impressed he had a medal created celebrating the scouts endevours. It was called the General Eisenhower Waste Paper Medal and was awarded by the War Production Board to boy scouts who collected at least 1,000 pounds of waste paper each during the General Eisenhower waste paper campaign and during this campaign which ran in March and April of 1945, as many as 299,936 Boy Scouts in the United States earned this award.

Speaking of Boy Scouts, it is interesting to note that in the United

State, the day after the bombing of Pearl Harbour, the President of the Boy Scouts, Walter Head and the Chief Scout Executive, James West immediately sent a telegram to President Roosevelt reconfirming help from the 1,500,000 active boys and men of the Boy Scouts but actually the Boy Scouts were active before America's involvement in the war, by distributing defense bomb posters and collecting scrap metal. Contributions by the Boy Scouts to the war effort would fill many pages. They were responsible for selling almost two billion dollars worth of war bonds and stamps, they participated in scrap metal, rubber and paper collecting, they also collected milk weed floss which was needed to replace the unobtainable k-pop for life jackets. They collected books, musical instruments and razors for the troops, clothing for citizens in Europe. In many areas, Scouts served as fire watchers and helped with fire prevention campaigns. Thousands of Scouts worked hundreds of thousands of hours raising and harvesting food. Three hundred thousand Scouts served as dispatch bearers distributing posters, war information and participating in various civilian defense programs. In addition, over a hundred thousand model airplanes were built by the boys in Scouting for use by the military to train in aircraft recognition. Scouts helped with U.S.O, the National Housing Agency, veterans hospitals, the Red Cross, the American Legion, the YMCA, foreign relief agencies and many community organizations. Their total contribution to the war effort was incalculable but that also applied to some degree in Canada but not to such a degree because obviously there were not that many Scouts in Canada compared to what was in the United States. I remember at the time, I was not in Scouts. I was in Cubs and although we did have Scouts in Wells at that time, I was not aware of what they were doing since I didn't attend any of their functions.

In Canada, we have Girl Guides but in the United States they were called Girl Scouts and in December 1941, the Girl Scouts in the United States were prepared. Program efforts were focused on skills involving community service, senior Girl Scouts explored wartime applications of food preparation and preservation of food, nutrition, child care, shelter, clothing, recreation, transportation and communication. They attended safety workshops, operated bicycle courier service, and promoted the sale of war bonds and stamps and during the war years, Girl Scouts launched three new specialized projects geared to assist the war effort such as hospital aid, child care and occupational therapy. Beginning in 1942, thousands of Girl Scouts in the United States worked on tens of thousands of farms throughout the war as part of the Farm Aid Project and during the summer and harvest months, girls were busy weeding, cultivating, spraying, picking and haying as well as feeding livestock, repairing small tools and canning. By the end of 1944, Girl Scouts in the United States had numbered as many as 1,006,644. I don't remember Girl Guides in Wells doing anything like this as there wasn't the same need as there was in others area of Canada and the United States.

Throughout the war, railroads provided about 97 percent of the transportation for military personnel traveling on duty, carried over 90 percent of all the military freight. In the 1940s, most of the nations railroads were converting to diesel locomotives. The war brought a vast strain to the railroads and every locomotive, whether steam, electric or diesel was pressed into service. Railroads were the life blood of Canada's vast industrial arsenal. Almost everything from the basic raw material to the finished product was moved by rail. Other forms of transportation was also used to capacity but only railroads could transport large bulky items over long distances. We did not have at that time the cross-Canada Highway so we had to rely on the railroads.

The railroads, like almost every other American or Canadian resource were used beyond their capacity. Material for the manufacture of new rolling stock was in short supply and the manpower drain deprived the railroads of many experienced men. After numerous problems, the U.S. government declared the railroads essential for war production and much of the metal that had to be used for the war effort was applied for building trains. In the United States more than 2,500 troop trains a month operated in the United States. As many as 100,000 troops rode in troop trains on any given day. This was the greatest mass movement of people that ever occurred in the United States and of course, it put a great strain on the railroads as well as reducing considerably the civilian traffic for the duration of the war. The railroad firms committed one out of four of their coaches and half of all the Pullman sleeping cars for troop transport. Not only were troops moved by train but movements of more than 12 hours duration were usually made in Pullman sleeping cars. Pullman carried 60 percent of all the troops which meant that approximately 30,000 men a night slept in a sleeper which were loaded every two minutes and forty eight seconds in 1944. This was possible only because the railroads had two thousand sleeping cars in storage at the start of the war.

Until 1943 the United States government had banned all new railroad passenger-car construction because of the shortage of steel and aluminum but with the unprecedented demand for sleepers, 1200 new troop sleepers were ordered from the Pullman Standard Company and 400 troop kitchen cars were also ordered. The train terminals on both coasts both in Canada and the United States were clogged with troops going to the battlefields of Europe, Africa, Asia and the Pacific.

War materiel and food stuff were unloaded at the ports for transfer to liberty ships which would carry them to the armies and to the Allies as part of the 'Land Lease Program'. Without the thousands of men and women who ran the nation's railroads, whether from an office, a station or on the trains, and who worked long hours in all kinds of weather, the materiel and troops would not have reached their final destinations.

There were constant reminders to the general public not to take the train unless they absolutely had too. Because the locomotives were in constant use all the time, they made it a policy in the United States that when an engine came in after a thousand-mile run, an crowd of attendants overhauled it. Prior to the war, the overhauling would take about eight hours but during the war it would only take only fifteen minutes. Hauling freight during the war, the American trains hauled a million and a quarter tons of freight a mile every minute. Over eight hundred thousand barrels of oil was moved across the country every day.

Airlines had unprecedented growth during the 1930s, with new all-metal passenger planes flying passengers from coast to coast. Even before the war, the American and Canadian airlines were already devoting many of their seats to military passengers. But once the war started, several of the major airlines were virtually turned into an arm of the military machine. For example, Pan American Airways which pioneered over water routes to Europe and the Orient with their flying boats, was put into immediate service on routes to Australia and across the Atlantic to Africa, the near East and India. American United North West Airlines were fast pressed into service flying around the world and to the distant outposts of Alaska. Many of the Airline pilots donned military uniforms and began to train other military men as pilots. Domestically, the airlines were much in the same position as the railroads with the military taking most of the seats and transporting critical war materiel both at home and abroad.

The total war of 1939 through 1945 was industrial as well as military. In the words of a popular song of 1942, "Its the girl that makes the thing, that holds the oil, that oils the ring, that works the thing-a-mabob that's going to win the war." who were behind the men who fought World War II.

Life in the fighting nations was organized to supply the arms and ammunition, transportation, clothing, fuel and food that were needed to keep the war machine running. The war spread far beyond the front lines and for many countries it became total war. The aim was to destroy the enemy utterly and this effort involved mobilizing the country's entire workforce and national resources. Inevitably, this meant that the civilian populations became legitimate targets for the enemy and civilian moral at the home front was as important as moral on the front line.

A great deal of women with Allies and Axis alike, were working in the factories and in most factories, it was the women who represented the majority of the factory workers during World War II. Of course in the Axis countries, many of the women were slaves but in the Allied countries, the women offered to work in the factories. Many did so for the extra income, many did so in revenge for the lost of a loved one and many simply did it to get a job. But whatever their motives were, they did the job and did it well.

There was a poster distributed all over the United States which showed a beautiful buxom young woman in short pants with a riveting machine in her right hand. She was Rosina Bonavita, later known as Rose Will Munroe, and the poster called her *Rosie the Riveter*. She worked as a riveter building B-29 and B-24 bombers at the Willow Run Aircraft Factory in Ypsillanti, Michigan. She also starred in a promotional film about women helping out in the war effort. Her role became synonymous with thousands upon thousands of women who took defence industry jobs which prior to the war, were held primarily by men. After the war, most of the 'Rosies' in the Allied countries returned to home life, office work or sales work and even Rosina kept working, driving a cab, running a beauty shop and starting a construction firm. She died at age 77 on June 2, 1997 in Clarksville, Indiana.

More that twenty million factory workers in Britain, Canada, the U.S. Australia, New Zealand, Rhodesia, and South Africa, one third of them women and mostly working at least sixty hours a week built over 700 war ships, thousands of merchant ships, 135,000 aircraft and more than 160,000 tanks and other armored vehicles by 1945. More than half of Britain's wartime industrial production was devoted to arms.

In such a struggle, the countries that organized efficiently their greatest manpower and industry output had the advantage. After 1941 the Allies were stronger than their opponents in both these areas. The population of Germany was 79 million, Japan 73 million, and Italy 45 million and as such, were far less even with the occupied nations added than that of the U.S.A. 132 million, Britain 48 million and the USSR 193 million not to mention the other Commonwealth countries like Canada. The Allies also had controlled through ownership, political rule or agreement, over two-thirds of the world's iron and steel industry, coal deposits and oil productions. One could add to these figures when you consider the populations of the other Allied countries including China which out-populated them all. So long as they organized their populations and economies well and use their forces effectively, victory for the Allies would be simply a matter of time. In other words, the Axis powers were out gunned and out manned by 3 to 1 so it was inevitable that as time progressed, the Axis powers would invariably be brought to their knees.

War for the civilians in Britain was vastly different than that of North America. There were many British families whose men-folk were too old or too young for the forces or did essential work in reserved occupations. For them, unless the bombs started falling, war was mainly a matter of tedious duty at the local air raid station or fire watching and occasional spells in the shelter or under the dining table when the air raid sirens sounded and the bombers were too close to run outside to hide in the shelters.

In the British Isles, the adults did what they could to shield the British children from the true terror and horror of the war. The childish optimism and love of excitement did the rest. For many children in Britain the war consisted of model spitfires and hurricanes and finds of shrapnel, or placing coloured flags on a map showing the progress of the war. (We had pins in maps in our classroom in Wells also) It was also as much fun making rude noised by blowing into their slobbery rubbery gas masks.

Loosing your dad, your uncle, a brother, fiancé, husband or son was shattering and almost everyone knew a family that had suffered so. The impacts of the loss only came later because the long separation that made these figures fictional. Reality lay in the dashes to the school basement or the smelly shelter or the grimy cold cellar when the air raid sirens began wailing their warnings.

Deep scars still linger in many adults from their experiences during the evacuations because of the uncertainty that when they returned to their homes, there would be any homes left to return to. City children bewildered and ill-prepared for the air raids, were sent to faraway homes, many as far away as Canada. The culture shock hit both ways. Hosts told of heads full of lice and bed wetting and constant crying resulting from the unhappiness and anxiety and children suffered from home sickness boredom and fear of open spaces.

So badly did things go for the children and their hosts that when the air raids did not come after the Blitz, two thirds of the evacuees returned home by Christmas. Three later evacuation schemes ended much the same way.

The 'Battle of Britain' is the official name given for that period in the war when the German Luftwaffe (air force) attempted to knock out the British Royal Air Force in preparation for the German invasion of the British Isles. It covers the area of time between July 10th and October 31st 1940. We read about it in our comics and books and watched the old black and white movies showing the exploits of the British airmen. We knew all the names of the participating aircraft and their performances. Hurricane fighting planes with their rugged, eight Browning .303 machine-guns, were able to take lots of punishment. The German Heinkel 111 which was slow and lumbering with its pitifully small bomb load was easy to shoot down. The Messerschmitt 109 on the other hand was fast and dangerous especially its cannon, but hampered by a very short range that reduced its loiter time over London to just a few minutes; and of course the Spitfire which everyone agreed was the most beautiful aircraft that had ever flown successfully brought the German planes down. We knew the names of the aces, Douglas Bader, (the pilot with no legs) Robert Stamford-Tuck, and the German, Adolf Galland. In our playground games we rushed around with our arms outspread, shouting rat-at-tat and nobody wanted to be a Messerschmitt. Everyone wanted to be a Spitfire or Hurricane for we instinctively knew that in the 'Battle of Britain' they were flown by the good guys.

By an accident of birth, those of us too young to join the armed forces were privileged to play games that reflected a historical and moral watershed. Some historians talk of crucial battles where the right man in the right place at the right time can alter the course of history. Others say that the forces of history are inexorable and mere mortals can barely hope to influence, much less deflect or halt them.

The 'Battle of Britain' is very close to evidence for the former view. In the summer of 1940, the ascendant star of German Nazism flush from a string of astonishing victories and seemingly invincible, clashed with the power of a declining British Empire, disillusioned by the carnage of the Great War (World War I) and beginning to feel the first pangs of doubt that perhaps their imperial mission was not a mission at all but just a monstrous self-indulgence that had outlived its time. Britain stood alone without allies save the far-flung dominions - those hands across the seas that had served her so self- sacrificing in the previous world war. A Nazi invasion was imminent and the shattered remnants of the equipment-less British Expeditionary Forces recently pulled from the beaches of Dunkirk, knew they would have little chance if Hitler's legions got ashore on the south coast of England.

As ever the Royal Navy was Britain's first and last line of defence, but things had changed since Napoleon had glowered with envious eye across the Channel. The German navy was too small to hope to control that narrow strip of water long enough for an invasion fleet to cross in the face of determined Royal Naval resistance. The Luftwaffe, however, could. To destroy the Royal Navy, the Luftwaffe had to secure command of the air and that meant the neutralizing of RAF Fighter Command and in particular 11 Group that protected the airspace over southern England.

On paper it seemed not too difficult. In an age when aircraft were still called machines, the Germans had far more than Britain did. More important than the machines were the men to fly them and the RAF was critically short of fighter pilots. They had little more than 800 of them. Young men, many who were university educated with their stereotypical image shows them as having flamboyant moustaches and a penchant for silk scarves. They embodied that spirit of individual enthusiasm that had seen Britons, first as pirates, then as merchants finally as soldiers bring many foreign lands under the aegis of the British Empire. Now it was up to the pilots of the RAF to save their homeland from destruction and in this their country's greatest hour of need they were not found wanting. They weren't just Britons of course. There were Australians, Canadians, New Zealanders, South Africans, Frenchmen, Poles, Czechs and Americans; the latter showing that even if the United States is hamstrung by political considerations, some of her sons at least will know where and when democracy has to be defended and will honour their homeland by doing so.

Britain had one great advantage, radar. Invented by a Scotsman, James Watson Watt, it was still rudimentary and often unreliable but it allowed Fighter Command to have a good idea of where German attacks were heading and how strong they were. It allowed the RAF to keep its planes on the ground until they were needed and then later the fighter controllers would vector them directly towards the attackers. It was a less than perfect system but it was the best in the world at that time, and it worked. The Germans tried to destroy the radar masts and the forward airfields of 11th Group. They did great damage to them but the radar chain nevertheless stayed intact and the airfields kept operating. Stukas, used in the first attacks were so badly shot up by the opposing Spitfires and Hurricanes that the Germans withdrew them and they never saw service over England again. It became a battle of attrition and not just in the air. The unsung heroes of Fighter Command were the ground crews who got the planes into the air, lived through the attacks on the airfields, came out and filled in the craters on the runways and were waiting for their own fighter plane when they came back thirsty for fuel and hungry for more ammunition.

Attacking the airfields was strategically and tactically the correct thing for the Germans to do. Soon 11th Group was close to collapse. There were not enough pilots, not enough ground crew, never enough sleep and too many enemy planes.

On one of those bombing raids, a German bomber being pursued by a British fighter jettisoned its bomb load over London. Churchill ordered retaliatory raids on German cities and an incensed Adolf Hitler ordered the Luftwaffe to switch its attacks to London and level the British capital. This gave the embattled 11th Group airfields a desperately needed breather. It also brought the fighters of 10 Group, based further north, into play and forced the Messerschmitts to go into combat at the extreme end of their range, something they had never been intended to do.

As Londoners bore the brunt of the German bombs, the RAF regrouped and eventually repulsed the airborne assailants. As the summer drifted into autumn the tide and weather patterns changed and soon invasion was no longer a practical possibility. Hitler started to look eastwards for fresh conquests. The Luftwaffe had been given a bloody nose and never again launched an air offensive on anything like a similar scale. The RAF had been hurt but not broken. As the war progressed it grew in size and power and its bomber arm carried the war deep into the heart of Germany with greater devastation than anything ever visited on British cities. As an interesting aside, Jonnie Johnson, aged 85, who died in his home in Buxton, England on February 1, 2001, was ranked as the Royal Air Force 's top gun with 38 confirmed kills, most of which occurred during the Blitz.

Winston Churchill said it best when praising the British Royal Air Force. He said in Parliament; "Never in the history of human conflict, have so many owed so much for the efforts of so few." Of course, he paraphrased that comment from another source that went back a century or so and I in turned paraphrased Churchill in 1985 when I was addressing a UN crime conference in Milan in 1985 and was praising the people who developed my proposed bill of rights for young offenders. I said, "Never in the history of juvenile justice will so many owe so much for the efforts of so few." Hey, if Churchill can paraphrase a great quote, why can't I do the same?

Rationing in England was a strain relieved a little by the inventiveness of mothers who concocted fatless cakes, and created miracles with rabbit and fish and relied on bread and margarine drippings to satisfy appetites. The diet was accepted as the norm by children who had few memories of prewar indulging.

Holidays at home in England were the high spots of the summer with local fairs and shows replacing trips to beaches that by then had been covered with tank traps or mines. What did the seaside matter when a talent competition was going on in a marquee in the park? Above all, one lived with the thrilling possibility of discovering a spy and played out fantasies with false beards, codes and invisible inks. The grand dreams were fed by family trips to the movies.

The worst plight facing the two and a half million wives in the area of England whose husbands were in the forces was that too many of them lived on the poverty line. A mother of two whose husband was an ordinary serviceman, struggled for most of the war to live on seven shillings or equivalent to $1.40 a week from her husband's service pay plus $5.00 a week government allowance. For a lucky few, their employer made up the income to its prewar level. Others did piecework at home or went out to work.

When the bombing raids came, the horrors proved even worse than imagined. Eastenders in the early days of the Blitz fled in thousands to the surrounding country side as well they might. As an interesting aside, when a bomb crashed through the roof of Buckingham Palace, Queen Elizabeth, later the Queen Mother, proudly said that she now understood the plight of the Eastenders. There were no gardens in which to put 'Anderson shelters' and it was still forbidden then to use the underground railway stations as shelters so all they had were street shelters which were brick shoe boxes to hold twenty people with concrete roofs which tended to fall in when the bombs exploded nearby. The most successful shelter in any such densely populated urban areas, which was designed at the instigation of a later Home Secretary, Herbert Morrison and issued from spring 1941, was called the 'Morrison shelter'. It comprised of a low steel cage for use indoors like the Anderson shelter was and it cost about $28.00 for those able to purchase it but it was free to many who could not afford to purchase it.

Many official preparations were wide of the mark. Millions of cardboard coffins were made to receive the legions of expected dead but shelter for bombed out homeless was woefully inadequate. It consists of mostly of so called rest centres, schools and church halls where shocked, exhausted people were meant to stay for only a night. Many had nowhere else to go and some stayed for weeks in the centres which became intolerably overcrowded. Large numbers of Eastenders in London made a home in such places as the Tilbury shelter, an underground goods yard which accommodated 16,000 people in horribly unsanitary conditions. Another 18,000 camped in a network of ancient tunnels in the chalk south east of the capital. Other Londoners invaded the forbidden underground stations. London authorities yielded as the blitz stepped up and supplied bunks, lavatories and some canteen facilities. The safety of the underground was variable for some stations were only a few meters beneath the street. Bellham for example received a direct hit on the evening of October 15th, 1940 and as a result, 64 people died. As the weeks passed, people in London and elsewhere learned to live with the bombing and even managed to extract a few rye jokes from it. The shop with some shattered windows might bare the sign 'More open than usual' while the common lapel badge read "Don't tell me, I've got a bomb story too". Children roamed the streets after raids collecting shrapnel. After restless nights in a shelter, people still had to go to work the next day exhausted but glad to still be alive.

Things were not doing well in Germany either. An early sign of the strain the war would impose upon the Germans came in the bitter winter of 1939/40 when most of the railways rolling stock was given over to the Wehrmacht severely restricting supplies of domestic coal in the winter of 1941/42. Germans were also experiencing their first food crisis. Abundant crops of un-rationed potatoes had bulked up their diet from the start of the war but the lack of farm workers (called up for the attack on the Soviet Union) and freight cars now used to supply the eastern front combined with a cold snap proved disastrous. Howard K. Smith an American reporter based in Berlin observed

"People's faces are pale, unhealthy, white as flour except for red rings around their eyes. The uninformed millions get no vitamins, work in shops and factories ten and twelve hours a day."

The push eastward appeared at first to be a massive rerun of the campaigns in the West. The law decreed that from the announcement of victories, radios and cafes, restaurants and other public places would be turned up. Waiters stopped serving, customers paused in their eating as trumpets and drums heralded the latest triumph.

As the advance on Russia slowed down, the public mood began to change. Large numbers of wounded appeared in German cities when the casualty list grew. Convalescents did not go home but were bundled off to distant nursing homes and recreation centres so that the general populace would not see what the war was doing to their loved ones and friends. Death notices in the newspapers were restricted to only a handful in each issue. An unheard of but rather decent ruling allowed grieving women to marry men killed in action to give any unborn children a family name and provide the mothers with a war widows' pension.

Shortages began to hurt. New clothing and footwear went entirely to the Wehrmacht. Children, air raid victims and refugees from the East had first claim on dwindling existing stocks. Improvisation became the order of the day. When cotton thread ran out, women darned their clothes with string dyed with shoe polish.

In Germany in June 1941, bread and meat rations were cut. In April 1942, fats were cut, potatoes were rationed and the daily diet deteriorated sharply. In October 1942 rations were increased again and troops coming home on leave were given further packages containing tin goods to take home to their families. Meat was cut once more in May 1943 but later, the supply of meat increased temporarily the following year as herds of stock were driven into Germany from the occupied countries. A barter economy grew and vigorous black market forging passports, work books, ration cards and other documents was a lucrative black market business.

The real impact of the war came upon Germany in 1942. Anglo/

Americans strategic bombing attacks brought the front line to Germany's cities in 1942. The RAF area bombing beginning with Essen, Duisberg, Dusseldorf, and Cologne. No longer had German war industry been the Allies' target. As a result of the bomber command directive from England, the moral of the enemy civil population and in particular the moral of the industrial workers, life in the early phase of the bombing became governed by cable radio a device attached to the family wireless set which was kept switched on. This cable radio radios usually gave off a steady tick-tock which was abruptly changed to a sharp ping-pong when any enemy bombers approached. An announcer periodically gave the position number and type of bombers and the expected target. When Hamburg was bombed in the summer of 1943, as many as 44,600 civilians and eight hundred service men were killed and German leaders feared that the will to work on in armament manufacture would crumble. In two thirds of the cities, 1.2 million population, most of them being non workers were evacuated. Berlin also took a terrible hammering. About half of the German capital's 1.6 million dwellings were damaged and every third house was either completely destroyed or uninhabitable. To anyone walking the streets of Berlin and the other German cities where there had been bombings, the distinctive smell of burning and the sweet fatty smell of the buried corpses not yet dug out of the ruins was everywhere. And yet, the cities clung to a semblance of normality even with the Red Army at the gates of Berlin in 1945. Twelve thousand policemen remained on duty, postmen delivered the mail, garbage was collected, the Berlin Philharmonic neared the end of its season, flower sellers applied their trade in the streets. Every morning, about thousands of Berliners negotiated through the rubble-choked streets to man the sixty five percent of factories that were still working.

Nevertheless, the war distorted Berlin's society. War casualties, the call-up for men and women for the armed services and the evacuation of a million citizens cut the population by one third. Two out of three residents were female and the males were nearly all under eighteen or over sixty. This pattern was repeated across Germany. Gaps in vital services were filled by the Hitler Youth. Seven hundred thousand of them were messengers, telephone operators, hospital orderlies, fire fighters, and anti aircraft gunners. When sixteen-year-old youths were called up on January 26th, 1943, the league of German girls filled their posts.

In 1943, Nazi leaders made a belated attempt to get the entire country behind the war effort. Six million workers were by then, producing consumer goods and 1.5 million women were maids and cooks. On February 18, 1943 after the defeat at Stalingrad, propaganda minister, Joseph Gobbels announced total war measures in a speech at Berlin's sport stadium—measures that took 5 months to enforce by which time they were too late.

All males between sixteen and sixty five were registered for compulsory labour. Hitler youths aged 10-15 were drafted to help farmers and collect rags. Even ordinary criminals were put to work for the war effort. Factories that managed—even after a great publicity effort and offers of extra rations—to pull in only 900 thousand women to help the war effort. Most would have preferred office jobs but these had already been filled by the wives of Nazi officials.

The bombing of Hamburg was a terrible experience for the citizens in that huge German city. A series of 33 major attacks on that city and others between July and November 1943 involved 17,000 bomber sorties. (one sortie—one plane) It opened with the great raid on July 24th by 791 bombers which included 374 Lancashire and thanks to the new navigational aids, clear weather and good marking, a vast number of incendiary and explosive bombs hit the center of Hamburg. Thanks also to a new radar distracting device called 'Window', only twelve bombers were lost. Moreover the 8th U.S. AAF joined in the attack on July 24th and 26th and Mosquitos which themselves could carry a bomb load of 4,000 pounds, kept the city's defenses busy on those two nights. On the night of the 27th, 787 British bombers renewed their devastating attack and only 17 were lost. On the 29th, 777 bombers hit the city again, although with less accuracy while British losses rose to 33 as the Germans began to adjust themselves to the effect of

Window. Bad weather prevented the fourth attack on August 2nd from being a successful one.

In summary however, the city suffered terrible devastation and the bomber command losses, although rising each time, averaged only 2.8 percent. The second night of the attack on Hamburg which used high explosives and incendiary bombs alternatively caused the first man-made firestorm which affected an area of 22 square kilometers (13.6 square miles). It rendered helpless the city's firefighting force and altogether it is estimated that the raids reduced half the city to rubble and nearly two thirds of what remained of the population had to be evacuated. Although the raids were aimed primarily at the civilian population, 580 industrial and war production firms were destroyed or damaged and the British bombing survey unit concluded that the loss of war production was equivalent to the city's normal output of the previous 1.8 months.

Firestorms were sometimes created by the intensive bombing raids in the built up areas of Hamburg. It was a natural process for a fire to draw in air to consume its oxygen but when many buildings were ablaze during a heavy raid, great heat was generated and the convection the fires caused by sucking in air, disseminating sparks and burning debris which started other fires around the surrounding areas thereby increased the size of the firestorm in the center of the city. The more fires, the greater the heat and the greater the convection until, in a matter of minutes, all the fires coalesced into one massive 22 square kilometer inferno which created hurricane-force winds coming from every direction—winds as much as 150 miles (241 km) per hour with temperatures in excess of 1,000 degrees centigrade (1,832 degress Fahrenheit). People who ventured into the streets to escape the fires within the buildings, were sucked up as if by a unseen vacuum cleaner and carried into the air towards the turning and twisting vortex of the firestorm to be suffocated and finally burned to a crisp before their charred bodies were dropped to the ground many blocks away, their bones to be finally turned to ashes as they were consumed by the fires raging on the ground.

The bombing was part of operation *Gomorrah* which killed over 46,000 civilians but only 800 military personnel. Thirteen percent of all German deaths due to bombing during world war II occurred during this attack on Hamburg. It's ironic when you think about. During the German Blitz over England, which occurred over a four-month period, 60,595 British civilians died from the bombings and ensuing fires but in Hamburg, two-thirds of that many civilians died in that four-day period the city was under attack from the air.

I remember when I was in my twenties reading an article in a magazine about the bombing of Hamburg. I was appalled at the suffering the people in that city had to endure. Thousands went to the water to escape the heat and to put out the fires that were burning on the surface of their own bodies, fires caused by the incendiaries of unquenchable fire, which, when the victims emerged from the water, would continue to burn through their flesh and bones Many gave up hope of ever putting out the fires on their bodies and chose instead to drown themselves—not an easy thing to do, no matter how desirable it would have been under those circumstances.

The main purpose of the raid on Hamburg was to instill terror in the minds of the German citizens and that it did. However, when you think about it, killing the German civilians really didn't shorten the war. They were not in a position to influence Hitler at all. When the end was approaching him, he condemned all the citizens of Germany so in effect, these civilians died for nothing.

What is really ironic about the bombing raids is that if the German bomber who initially dropped his bomb load on London (without authority I might add) hadn't done so, then the Britons wouldn't have bombed Berlin and if they didn't bomb Berlin, London wouldn't have suffered from the blitz and neither would Hamburg and other German cities been subsequently obliterated.

The Germans had taken Yugoslavia and their Allies in that country were the Croatian Ustashi Army. On April 28th, 1941 (18 days after the formation of the Ustashi 'Independent State of Croatia'), for instance, Ustashi storm troopers encircled the villages of Gudovac,

Tuke Brezovac, Klokocevac and Bolac, in the district of Bjelovar, and arrested 250 peasants. Having them led all to a field, the Ustashi ordered them to dig their own graves. This done, their hands were tied behind their backs and then they were all pushed into their graves and buried alive. On April 28th, 1941, army units of the Ustashi surrounded the villages of Gudovac and Brezovica and killed 234 inhabitants who were of Serbian nationalty. In the village of Blagaj, 520 men, women and children were murdered by being struck over the head. In the Koprivnica Forest near Livno, around 300 citizens were subjected to the most unspeakable acts of brutality before being killed. Hands and legs were cut off, eyes gouged out, (now we know where all the eyeballs in the basket in the office of the Ustashi leader, Dr Ante Pavelic came from) heads of small children were severed and thrown onto their mothers laps, women's breasts were severed. The well known industrialist and philantrophropist Serb Milos Teslic, who was 26 years old then and was from from Sisak, was cruelly tortured and murdered by Ustashi. His legs were broken, ears cut off, eyes gouged out, chest stabbed and finally his heart was extracted through a big hole made in his chest. As the withnesses were testifying the present Ustashi were telling later the heart of the tortured Milos was still beating on the palm of an Ustashi.

In the Livno area alone, the Ustashi killed 1,243 Serbs including 370 children. In the Risova Greda Forest, over 800 Serbs were killed and their bodies hurled into ravines. The Ustashi commander, General Dragutin Rumler, filed a report stating that so far, around 10,000 Serbs, Jews and Gyspies had been killed. The German occupation forces at that time turned a blind eye to the slaughter, after all, the Ustashi were doing what the Nazi Gestapo and S.D. units had come here to do—that is, execute them.

By far the worst crime committed by the Ustashi was the murder of children from the Mount Kozara region. The Serb children were separated from their parents and taken to various interment camps set up by the Ustashi. In the camp at Sisak, 6,693 children were housed in filthy conditions and soon as many as 1,600 died. At the camp at Jastrebarko, 3,336 children were housed in the same pitiful condition. Soon after their arrival the local cemetery caretaker had buried 768 boys and girls. In Plot 142 in the Mirogoj Cemetery in Zagreb lie the remains of 862 children who had died after being rescued by the Red Cross. Fifty years after this tragedy, a final count was made. The crimes committed by the Ustashi troops in 1941 and 1942 took the lives of 11,194 children, 6,302 boys and 4,874 girls. The average age of these children was 6.5 years. The Nazis, who for a time were posted in Croatia, were so horrified at the Ustashi atrocities that they set up special commission to investigate them. The Orthodox Church of Serbia, in fact, appealed directly to the Nazi General Dukelman to intervene and stop the Ustashi horrors. The Germans and the Italians managed to restrain the Ustashi while they were under their supervision. When the Nazis left Croatia, however, the Ustashi multiplied their atrocities, un-repremanded by their Government since the latter's policy was one of the total elimination of the Orthodox Serbian population via forcible conversions, expulsion, or straightforward massacre. This crime of Genocide, committed by the pro-German Catholic Croatians on the Orthodox Serbian population during World War Two is something the outside world knew little about until some time after the war had ended.

Unfortunately, there were still German commanders who continued to massacre innocent people, even their own allies. Almost unknown outside of Italy, there was another massacre which ranks with Katyn Massacre as one of the darkest episodes of the war.

The Gestapo's most cold blooded act of butchery was the murder of 50 RAF officers who escaped from the POW camp, Stalag Luft III at Sagan in Silesia in March 1944. Hundreds of officers had a hand in the building of a tunnel, 28 feet down below one of the huts. It ran for 360 feet, passing under the wire at a depth of 20 feet. The breakout on March 24th 1944, saw the escape of 79 men before the tunnel was discovered. The last three men out gave themselves up to the guards in the hope that they could delay the search for the rest.

Hitler issued a personal order that fifty escapees were to be shot on recapture. Within weeks, all had been recaptured, except three who eventually managed to reach England. After their capture, the 50 officers were confined to various jails near where the arrests took place. Early in the morning they were taken out of their cells and in groups of two or three, were bundled into cars in company with their guards, and driven out into the country. On the autobahn, near a forest, the car would stop and the prisoners were allowed out to relieve themselves. While performing this natural function, the guards would sneak up behind them and shoot them in the neck. Their bodies were then taken to the nearest crematorium. When the urns containing the ashes of the murdered officers began arriving at Stalag Luft III, the enormity of the massacre was revealed. Most urns had the officers name, date cremated and place-names such as Gorlitz, Brux, Breslau, Liegnitz, Kiel, Munich, Saarbrucken and Danzig. Most urns had the dates, 29th, 30th and 31st March 1944. Official Gestapo files noted that the officers were 'shot while trying to escape'.

After the war, the RAF Special Investigation Branch began its search for the culprits. It took over three years to bring the murderers to justice. Of the 72 killers traced, 21 were executed, 17 imprisoned, 11 committed suicide, the rest died, disappeared or were acquitted.

On the Greek island of Cefalonia, the Italian 'Acqui Division' was stationed. Consisting of 11,500 enlisted men and 525 officers it was commanded by 52 year old General Antonio Gandin. When the Badoglio government announced on September 8, 1943, that Italian troops should cease hostilities against the Allies, there was much wine and merriment on Cefalonia. However, their German counterparts on the island maintained a stony silence and soon began harassing their Italian comrades, calling them 'traitors'. The German 11th Battalion of Jager-Regiment 98 of the 1st. Gebirgs-Division, commanded by Major Harald von Hirschfeld, arrived on the island and soon Stukas were bombing the Italian positions. The fighting soon developed into a wholesale massacre when the Gebirgsjager troops began shooting their Italian prisoners in groups of four beginning with General Gandin. By the time the shooting ended, 4,750 Italian soldiers lay dead.

But that was not the end for the Acqui Division, some 4,000 survivors were shipped off to Germany for forced labour. In the Mediterranean a few of the ships hit mines and sank taking around 3,000 to their deaths. The final death toll in this tragic episode was 9,646 men and 390 officers. Major Hirschfeld was later killed during the fighting in Warsaw in 1945 after he was promoted to General. There was a good movie made about this event on the island of Cefalonia starring Nicolas Cage. It was called, *Captain Corelli's Mandolin*.

A few kilometres north of Cuneo in Italy, lies the town of Boves. After September 8th, 1943, it became an active centre of the Italian underground because of the stationing of many stragglers from the now disbanded Regio Esercito (Royal Italian Army). These partisans were led by Bartolomeo Giuliano, Ezio Aceto and Ignazio Vian. After repeated requests to surrender, the partisans refused in spite of leaflets being dropped by the SS. On the 17th of September, the German commander, SS Major Joachim Peiper, truly one of the worst Nazi killers in the war, ordered two 88 mm gun crews to shell the town. The partisans again refused to surrender. Two German soldiers were then sent forward as decoys to be captured by the partisans. Hoping they would be killed, it would give Peiper the pretext for a slaughter. The parish priest, Father Giuseppe Bernardi and the industrialist, Alessandro Vassallo, were ordered to meet with the partisans and to persuade them to release the two soldiers. The priest asked Peiper "Will you spare the town?" Peiper gave his word and the two prisoners were released. But the blood-thirsty SS then proceeded to burn all the houses in the town after which Father Bernardi and Vassallo were put into a car to do an inspection of the devastated town. "They must admire the spectacle." said Peiper. After the inspection, Father Bernardi and his companion, Vassallo, were sprinkled with petrol and set alight. Both were burned to death. Forty-three other inhabitants of Boves were killed that day and 350 houses destroyed. Next day, a column of armoured vehicles went up the road that led to the partisan base. A lucky shot from their only 75 mm gun destroyed the leading armoured car. After an intense fire-fight the SS retreated with heavy losses. One of the partisan leaders, Ignazio Vian, was later captured by the SS and hanged in Turin. On the wall of his cell he had written in his own blood the words 'Better Die Rather Than Betray'.

Peiper finally met justice in an unusual way. He was arrested after the war and he with 42 other defendants, was sentenced to death by hanging on the 16th of July 1946.

Eventually, the sentences of the Malmedy defendants were commuted to life imprisonment and then to time served. Peiper himself was released from prison on parole at the end of December 1956, after serving 11 and a half years.

On the 17th of January 1957 he began work at Porsche in Stuttgart in its technical division. He would later represent the company at car exhibitions. He was later put in charge of auto exports to the United States but his wartime criminal conviction prevented him from obtaining a visa for travel to the United States. This would not allow him to maintain this new position. Peiper then became a car sales trainer. Residing in France since 1972 he had a quiet and discreet life. However, he continued to use his given name. Upon recieving death threats, Peiper sent his family back to Germany. He himself stayed in Traves. During the night of the 13/14th of July 1976, a gunfight took place at Peiper's house, in which Peiper was shot several times and his house was set on fire. In the ruins, Peiper's charred corpse was later found with a bullet in the chest.

When the island of Kos in the Aegean fell to the German forces, a total of 1,388 British and 3,145 Italian troops were taken prisoner. Italy had signed an armistice on September 8th and the Italian troops were now fighting on the British side. On September 11th, Hitler gave the order to execute all Italian officers who were captured. The officer in charge of the Italian troops was Colonel Felice Leggio. On October 4th, 1943, he, and 101 of his officers, were marched to a salt pan just east of the town of Kos and there, shot in groups of ten. They were buried in mass graves. When Kos was returned to Greece after the war, the bodies were dug up and transported back to Italy for burial in the Military Cemetery at Bari.

Due to partisan activity around the town of Kalavryta in southern Greece, a unit of the German army 'Kampfgruppe Ebersberger', surrounded the town on the morning of Monday, the 13th of December 1943. All the inhabitants were herded into the local school. Females and young boys were separated from the men and youths, the latter being marched to a hollow in a nearby hillside. There the soldiers took up positions behind machine-guns. Below, they witnessed the town being set on fire. Just after 2:00 p.m., a red flare was fired from the town. This was the signal for the soldiers to start firing on the men and youths who were huddled in the hollow. At 2:34 p.m., the firing stopped and the soldiers marched away. Behind them lay the bodies of 696 men and youths, the entire male population of Kalavryta. There were 13 survivors of the massacre, the town itself almost totally destroyed with only eight houses out of nearly five hundred left standing. It was not until late afternoon that the women and young children were released to face the enormity of the tragedy. Their husbands, sons, brothers, fathers, grandfathers, cousins and uncles were all dead.

On September 5th, 1944, a unit of Belgian Marquis attacked a German unit, killing three soldiers. Two days later the American troops arrived in the area and the Germans retreated. Three months later, during the Ardennes offensive, the village of Banda was retaken. On Christmas Eve, a unit of the German SD (Sicherheitsdienst) set about arresting all men in the village. They were questioned about the events of September 5th, then lined up in front of the local cafe. One by one, they were led to an open door and as they entered a shot rang out. An SD man, positioned just inside the door, fired point blank into the victim's neck, and with a kick sent the body hurtling into the open cellar. After twenty had been killed this way, it was the turn of 21-year-old Leon Praile who decided to make a run for it. With bullets flying around him, he escaped into the woods. Meantime the executions continued until all 34 men had been killed. On January 10th, 1945, the village of Bande was liberated by British troops and the massacre was discovered. A Belgian War Crimes Court was set up in December 1944. One man, a German speaking Swiss national by the name of Ernst Haldiman, was identified as being a member of the execution squad. He had joined the SS in France on November 15th, 1942 and in 1944 his unit was integrated with other SD units, into No 8 SS Commando for Special Duties. Haldiman was picked up in Switzerland after the war and brought to trial before a Swiss Army Court. On April 28,1948, he was sentenced to twenty years in prison. He was released on parole on June 27, 1960, the only member of the SS Commandos that has been brought to trial.

By 1943, the Red Army was stronger than before. It had the best tanks up to then—the T-34s. It also had the strongest artillery in the world and it also had the Katyusha rocket launcher. Stalin's most trusted military advisor, General Zhukov, suggested to Stalin that the Red Army should wage a war of attrition, that is, remain where they are and let the Germans butt their heads against impossible odds.

Hitler decided to put his army on the eastern front to the test. They would make one more offensive which he described as one that "will shine like a beacon around the world." When the Germans were finally ready to begin the offensive, the Soviets had already had time to be prepared and when they counter attacked, Hitler's beacon began to dim. He realized that there was no hope of winning the war with the Soviet Union so he moved his troops to Italy to fend off the American attacks at Anzio. Of course, this move made it easier for the Red Army to moved closer towards Germany in the west.

It was Operation *Zitadelle* to the Germans and it was fought in July 1943, following the turning point of the War earlier in the year, at Stalingrad. If the latter battle marked the end of the high tide for the Axis, then Kursk marked the ebbing of the tide that would not stop until Germany itself lay in ruins.

To both sides, the Russian line of defence around Kursk which was 200 kilometres (124 miles) wide and 150 kilometres (93 miles) deep was the single most obvious target for the Germans to attack in 1943. To the Germans it provided the perfect target to repeat the successes of 1941 and 1942, encircling vast Soviet armies and destroying them in the process. For Hitler, it was once again the thought that the Soviets could not possibly suffer another catastrophe on that scale.

Stalin had already wisely relinquished his control over the Red Army to Marshal Georgi Zhukov—a similar control Hitler was never willing to give up over his German Army.

The Soviets considered the situation, weighed up the probable German attack routes and prepared themselves accordingly. Even if their spy ring helped out with information, it was hardly needed. They had time: after the spring 'rasputitsa' (thaw—whole place turned to mud) had brought a halt to the fighting, they had until July to build their defences and to re-build their forces. Hitler's insistence on waiting for his 'super-weapons' kept delaying the assault from the planned date in May, until the 5th of July.

This time he had been waiting for the long-awaited answer to the T-34 the PanzerKapmfWagen V—the 'Panther' - and the latest creation from his favourite designer, Dr Ferdinand Porsche. The Panther was destined to be a great tank, but in July 1943 it was still suffering teething troubles, the entire stock having been issued once and recalled for rebuilding, and now re-issued to Panther Abseiling 51 and 52, totaling 200 Panthers attached to the Wehrmacht's elite 'Großdeutschland' Panzer Grenadier Division. Dr Porsche's offering was the 'Elefant'—a beast of a tank destroyer, porting an 88 mm gun in a fixed mounting.

In all this time, the Soviets had dug in deeply on both forward areas of their defence. The immediate battle area contained up to seven defensive lines, with dug-in anti-tank strong points, anti-tank ditches and millions of mines.

The Soviets were also prepared in real depth for the first time. A new Front was set up (the Steppe Front) based 100 km behind them, including the full weight of Pavel Rotmistrov's 5th Guards Tank Army. All the units were brought back up above full strength. Their main problem was that they had large numbers of new, relatively inexperienced troops in the line.

When the German offensive finally broke on the 5th of July, the

Soviets were waiting. The German assault started, as always, in the early hours, with assault groups moving up on the Soviet outpost lines in the North and South in the moonless night, paving the way for the main assault. The Soviets had warning of even the exact hour of the attack from a German deserter and subsequently unleashed a massive bombardment on all the German assembly areas they could find. The German attack faltered for a moment, but the main assault went in around 07:00 local time. The Luftwaffe tried once more to catch the Soviet Air Force on the ground and to annihilate them but they failed in their attempt.

In the North, the German 9th Army stormed into the prepared Soviet positions. The 5th of July dawned with ferocious combat, tank-to-tank, gun-to-gun and most of all, hand-to-hand. The following days would be no differently. The German 9th Army slammed headlong into the Soviet positions for days, throwing more men and machines into the battle each day, until they exhausted themselves against the Soviet defences. The Soviets had prepared well and not only did they hold the lines, but they went over to the offensive themselves on the 12th, throwing the Germans back in complete disarray.

In the South, the Soviets faced the remaining cream of the German military machine, the 48th Panzer Corps and the 2nd SS Panzer Corps. The latter contained the first three SS Panzer Grenadier Divisions—LiebStandarte Adolf Hitler, Totenkopf and Das Reich. The SS formed the spearhead in the South and they managed to grind forward day-by-day, while the 48th Panzer Corps tried to keep pace on their left and 3rd Panzer Corps was held up on their right. The much-vaunted Panthers, attached to GroßDeutschland in 48th Panzer Corps were breaking down, catching fire, bogging in marshes and succumbing to minefields.

By the 12th, the SS felt they could finally break through, turning north-east to punch through the Soviet lines at Prokhorovka, a small land-bridge between the Psel and the Don rivers, leading to open country beyond. But, they hadn't reckoned with the Soviet 5th Guards Tank Army, which had moved up two days earlier. The Soviets met the SS head-on. This day has gone down in history as the 'largest tank battle ever fought'. In reality, LiebStandarte Adolf Hitler met the 18th and 29th Tank Corps (of the 5th Guards Tank Army) head on outside Prokhorovka which included 150 SS tanks (including a handful of Tigers and about 15 captured T-34s) running into 400+ Soviet tanks—many of which were light tanks. Hundreds of Russian T-34s scurried around the German's heavier Panther and Tiger tanks and went after them like vultures going after carrion. They fired round after round into the sides of the larger tanks until the Germans realized that they were being overwhelmed and they left the scene of the battle as fast as they could, leaving many of their burning tanks and dead comrades behind. The Soviet losses for the day were; even in those days of 'Perestroika' was in excess of 200 tanks. The German losses were light. But the SS were stopped by the sheer force of the blow. They were exhausted and could not get the offensive moving again in the following days.

With the Soviets successfully moving to the offensive in the North, and the invasion of Sicily a couple of days later; the German offensive was finished. The Soviets took heavy losses but the German offensive had been stopped dead in its' tracks. This would be the last time they even tried such an attack on this scale in the East. For the Germans, the only hope after this was to try and stem the 'Red Tide' and for the Soviets, it was their time to start wreaking their revenge on the German invaders.

As the Germans pulled back, they adopted a scorched earth policy, razing everything around them to the ground so that the Red Army soldiers would have nothing of any use to them on hand when they arrived. Though they destroyed factories and railway lines, they couldn't destroy all the food. In early November 1943, the Red Army retook Kiev and threw the German soldiers back toward the Dnieper line. (Approximately 280 miles (450 km) west of Moscow.

The Dnieper River is the fourth longest river in Europe (after the Volga, the Danube, and the Ural) and it is in Eastern Europe. With its many tributaries, the river drains much of Belarus and the Ukraine.

It originates in the low Valday Hills west of Moscow in Russia and flows about 1,400 miles (2,250 kilometers) to the Black Sea through a heavily industrialized region. The Dnieper flows in great curves across the vast Russian plain and drains an area of about 195,000 square miles (505,000 square kilometers). Before reaching Kiev, it is joined by the Pripyat, or Pripet, River. At Kiev it meets another tributary, the Desna. Leaving Kiev, it spreads to 1 mile (1.6 kilometers) in width. The center of the river's basin consists of broad lowlands. Its mouth is a swampy delta on a long inlet called Dnieper Liman. It was the area west of this river that the Germans had withdrawn to.

Chapter Twenty-Five

The Russians had captured a number of Germans whom they considered as war criminals. In the city of Krasnodar, the Russians held a war crimes trial. Charged were Germans accused of killing 7,000 victims by placing them in 'murder vans' in which the victims would be herded into and while being driven to burial locations, the victims died on the way when they inhaled exhaust fumes fed into the large airtight compartment in each of the vans. This was the first war crimes trial held during the Second World War. Needless to say, those found guilty were executed by the Russians. In the mid sixties, I wrote a play about a group of Jews being murdered this way. The play was later published by a magazine in Etobicoke.

After the Allies had retaken North Africa, it was decided at the Casablanca conference in January 1943 by the leaders of the Allies that the reentry into Europe would be best undertaken by going through the soft under belly of Europe, that is, Italy. But it was also decided that before attacking Italy, the Allies would have to attack Sicily.

The Italian garrison of Sicily consisted of only four field divisions and six static coast defense divisions that were poor in equipment and moral. The 'Hermann Goering Pancer Division' was sent to Sicily near the end of June, 1943 but Mussolini would not allow the Division to be constituted as a corps under a German commander. That Division and another were placed under the Italian army commander for the island and distributed in five groups along the 150 mile diameter of the island as mobile reserves. Hitler was becoming more dubious about providing help to Mussolini. On the one hand, he suspected that the Italians would overthrow Mussolini and make peace, a suspicion that was soon borne out by later events. For that reason, he hesitated to push more German divisions in too deeply that they might be cut off if their Italian Allies collapsed or changed sides. On the other hand, he came to think that Mussolini, the Italian command and Kesselring the German general were mistaken in their view that the Allies' next move from Africa would be a jump into Sicily. On that point Hitler was proved wrong. Hitler thought that the Allies were more likely to land in Sardinia than in Sicily. Sardinia would provide an easy stepping stone into Corsica and a well placed springboard for a jump onto either the French or Italian mainlands. At the same time, an Allied landing in Greece was expected and Hitler wished to have reserves kept back so that they could be rushed in that direction if the attack was upon Greece.

This brings to mind that fascinating 1955 movie *The Man Who Never Was* staring Clifton Webb. It was based on an actual event that took place during this period of time. Obviously the Allies wanted to confuse Hitler as to exactly where the next attack was going to be. An ingenious deception was devised by a section of the British Intelligence Service. This was so well worked out that the heads of the German Intelligence Service were convinced of its genuineness. The British Intelligence Service was able to get a hold of a body of a man who had just died from phenomena. Copies of important documents were placed inside a British Officer's uniform which was put on the body and it was dumped into the sea near the Spanish coast. Invariably the body washed to shore. Besides identity papers and personal correspondence, the documents including a private letter—of which the dead man had been the bearer—written by Lieutenant General Sir Archibald Nye, the vice chief of the imperial general staff, to General Alexander. This letter referred to recent official telegrams about forthcoming operations and its supplementary comments indicating that the Allies were intending to land in Sardinia and Greece while using a cover plan to convince the enemy that Sicily was their real objective. These letters ended up in the possession of the German Ambassador to Spain and from there the information was passed on to Hitler.

It made quite an impression on Hitler and he ordered the first Panzer Division to be sent from France to Greece to support the three German infantry divisions and the Italian 11th army there while the newly formed 90th Panzer Grenadier Division reinforced the four Italian divisions in Sardinia. Further reinforcement of that island was hindered by the difficulty of supply since most of the piers in the few harbours of that island had been destroyed by bombing. But as an additional insurance, Hitler moved General Students 11th Air Corps (of two parachute divisions) down to the south of France ready to deliver an airborne counter attack against an allied landing in Sardinia.

In July 1943, the first big seaborne assault on a coast held by the enemy took place on the island of Sicily. Its worth noting that the assault landing by eight divisions simultaneously was larger in scale even than that which took place in Normandy eleven months later. Some 150 thousand troops were landed on the first day and the next two days and the ultimate total was 478 thousand which comprised of 250 thousand British and 228 thousand American along with a contingent of Canadians. The British landings were made along a 40-mile stretch of coast at the south east corner of the island and the Americans along a 40-mile stretch of the south coast with a twenty-mile interval between the British left and the American right wing. A Naval side of the operation was planned and conducted under the direction of Admiral Sir Andrew Cunningham. It involved a complex pattern of moves leading up to a landing by night yet went through from start to finish with a wonderful smoothness that did great credit to the planners and those that carried out the plan. As an amphibious operation, it worked much better than *Operation Torch*, the landings in French North Africa the previous November from which much had been learned.

Right from the beginnings of the assaults on Sicily, the Italian soldiers did not have their heart in that fight. The Italians' weariness was more than physical. Most of them were tired of the war and not many had shared Mussolini's belligerent enthusiasm. Moreover, many of the defenders were mostly Sicilian. The Axis leaders thought that the Sicilians would fight hard against the invaders. The idea behind that kind of thinking being that they would be more inclined to live up to their fighting reputation when defending their own homes. But this assumption did not take into account of their long manifest dislike of the Germans or of their practically minded realization the harder they fought, the less would be left of their homes. Their reluctance to resist was deepened when daylight came on July 10th when they could see the tremendous array of ships filling the sea to the horizon and the continual flow of landing craft with reinforcements to back up the assault waves that poured ashore in the early hours of the invasion. The beach defences were quickly overrun and the anguish that many of the assault troops had suffered from sea sickness was amply offset by the slightness of their casualties from the enemy's fire on arriving ashore. The first stage of the invasion was summed up by General Alexander in two sentences. The Italian coastal divisions whose value had never been rated very high, disintregated almost without firing a shot and the field divisions when they were met were also driven like chaff before the wind. Mass surrenders were frequent. Thus from the first day onward, almost the whole burden of the defence fell on the shoulders of the two German divisions subsequently reinforced by two more.

 The British landings had met as little opposition as the American landings while progress was aided by the absence of any early counter-attack and although there were troubles and delays in the unloading process, this went rather well on the whole than on the western beaches which were more exposed. Air raids were more frequent after the first day. The air cover provided was also better so that shipping losses were almost as small on the American sectors. Indeed to those who had seen the earlier years of the war in the Mediterranean, it seemed as Admiral Cunningham remarked, almost magical that great fleets of ships could remain anchored on the enemy's coast with only such slight losses from the air attack as were incurred'.

The British forces had cleared the whole south eastern part of the island in the first three days, then General Montgomery decided to make a great effort to break through into the plain of Catania from the Lentini area and ordered a major attack for the night of July 13th. The key problem was to capture the Primasole bridge over the river Simeto a few miles south of Catalina.

Hitler and Mussolini met in Northern Italy on July 19th. For five hours, Hitler harangued his guest and told him in no uncertain words to put some backbone into his army. He promised Mussolini that he would give him reinforcements if he would show some initiative. All Mussolini did was pick at his food. He knew that his career as dictator of all he had conquered was slowly slipping away from his grasp.

This is a good time to speak briefly about Mussolini's fall from power. Although Mussolini was a dictator, he was answerable to the grand council of the fascist party and more importantly, to King Victor Emanuel III who had the support of the army high command.

On the evening of July 24th, 1943, Mussolini had a meeting with the fascist grand council and it was the first meeting they had had since 1939 and during that meeting, the council voted to return supreme power to the king. Mussolini had expected the king to let him deal with the crisis but Victor Emanuel had already agreed with Marshall Badoglio, a former lukewarm supporter of Mussolini, that Mussolini was to be stripped of his power. The next day, Mussolini, Italy's fascist dictator for 21 years, went to the Villa Savoia in Rome where the king was staying to tell the king of the vote of no confidence passed on him the previous night by the fascist grand council and after a brief talk and a handshake from the courteous king, Mussolini left the door of the villa and walked to his limousine where he was then approached by the military police armed with submachine guns and hustled into an ambulance and taken to the Podgodgora Barracks.

Badoglio formed a new government without one fascist member in it and started negotiating with the Allies. The Italians wanted to surrender and change sides but the Allies were loathed to fight alongside such recent enemies. Eventually on September 3rd, the

Italians did agree to an unconditional surrender with Victor Emanuel remaining as the constitutional monarch but the surrender was not announced until September 8th when the Allied invasion of Italy would be too far advanced for the Germans to respond effectively. Hitler was so angry at Badoglio that he seriously considered sending in an assasination team to kill him.

Meanwhile, the main British forces, after 3 days of stiff fighting in recapturing the bridge and reopening the way into the plain of Catania, had their attempt to press on northward, blocked by increasing strong resistance from the German reserves now concentrating to cover this direct east coast route of Messina 60 miles distance where the north east corner of Sicily lies closest to the toe of Italy.

The difficulty the Allies had in trying to capture the German forces in the north east part of Sicily, was aided by the shape as the ruggedness of north eastern Sicily—a triangle of mountainous country. While the German ground forces favoured that kind of terrain for defense purposes, each step backwards brought a shortening of the front so that fewer defenders were needed. The Allied armies became increasingly cramped in deploying their full superiority of force. The ably organized withdrawal across the straits by the Germans was carried out for the main part in the course of six days and seven nights without suffering any serious interception or loss from the Allied air or sea forces. Nearly forty thousand German troops and over 60 thousand Italian troops were safely evacuated although the Italians left behind all except some 200 of their vehicles the Germans brought away nearly 10,000 vehicles as well as 47 tanks, 94 guns and 17,000 tons of supplies and equipment.

American General George Patton committed a serious blunder. While visiting an army hospital in Sant Agata, Sicily, on August 10th, he asked a soldier why he was there. The soldier said he was suffering from shell shock—an ailment in war that was not too well recognized then. The general began slapping the soldier on his head with his gloves, all the time screaming, "Shut up that Goddamned crying. I won't have brave men here who have been shot seeing a yellow bastard crying. You are going back to the front lines and you may get shot and killed but you are going to fight. If you don't, I'll stand you up against a wall and have a firing squad kill you on purpose." Then the general reached for his pistol and yelled, "I ought to shoot you myself, you Goddamned whimpering coward!" When General Eisenhower learned of this, he was livid. He wanted to send Patton back to the States in disgrace but cooler minds suggested that Patton be temporarily relieved of his command. He ordered Patton to apologize in front of his men. He did. He also personally apologized to the man he had smacked when he learned that the soldier had been suffering from malaria at the time he was smacked by the general. Patton was a brave soldier and great tactician but he was also a buffoon.

About 6:30 a.m., on August 17th, the leading American patrol entered Messina and not long afterward, a British party appeared to be greeted with cries from General Patton's forces, "Where have you tourists been?" The success of this well planned getaway on the part of the Germans gave a rather hollow sound to what Alexander said that day in reporting the completing of the campaign to the Prime Minister Churchill. He said, "By ten am this morning August 17th, 1943, the last German soldier was flung out of Sicily. It can be assumed that all Italian forces in Sicily are gone. On July 10th they have been destroyed though a few battered units may have escaped to the mainland." *unquote*

So far as can be concluded from the records, the number of German troops in Sicily was a little over 60 thousand and the Italian troops 195 thousand. Of the German troops 5,500 were captured while 13,500 wounded were evacuated to Italy during the withdrawal. The British estimate of Germans and Italians killed was 24 thousand. The British losses were 2,721 killed, 2,183 missing and 7,939 wounded, a total of 12,843. The American losses 2,811 killed, 686 missing and 6,471 wounded, a total of 9,968. Thus in all, the Allied losses amounted to approximately 22,800. It was not a very heavy cost for the great political and strategic results of the campaign—which in the end, caused Mussolini's downfall and Italy's surrender but the bag of

Germans could have been larger with consequence smoothing of the path beyond if the Allies had made fuller use of amphibious moves in the area of the Strait of Messina. That was Admiral Cunningham's view and in his dispatch he pointedly remarked that, 'After the opening days of the assault, the small LSTs were kept standing by for the purpose and landing crafts were available on call'.

There were doubtless sound military reasons for making no use of this what to me appeared priceless asset of sea power and flexibility of maneuver but it is worth consideration for future battles whether much time and costly fighting could not be saved by even minor flank moves which must necessarily be unsettling to the enemy.

The Allied high command had not attempted a landing in Calabria, the toe of Italy behind the back of his forces from Sicily to block their withdrawal across the straits of Messina. Cunningham had been anxiously expecting such a move throughout this Sicilian campaign while having forces available to support it. In his view a secondary attack on Calabrul escape of the four German divisions engaged there, Kesselring had only two German divisions to cover the whole of southern Italy.

We have the advantage of hindsight but we now know that by permitting the German and Italian forces to escape to Italy across the strait of Messina, it was a colossal blunder on the Allies' part. They could have prevented this and the capture of the German and Italians would have shortened the war. Instead, they lived to fight another day and that they did which the Allies discovered when they later attacked Italy a short time later. More stupidity brought about by generals.

There is an old French proverb that says 'nothing succeeds like success' but the obverse is also true in that 'nothing succeeds like failure'. Religious and political movements, with their reigning authority crushed, have frequently been revived and come out on top in the long run after their leaders gained the halo of martyrdom. A crucified Christ became more potent than the living one. Conquering generals have been eclipsed by the conquered. That is shown by the immortal fame of Hannibal, Napoleon, Robert E. Lee and Rommel.

The failure to gain immediate success has at times turned out very advantageously by helping towards fuller success in making final success more sure. This happened for example in the invasion of Italy itself. After the swift capture of Sicily and the downfall of Mussolini, the second and shorter jump into Italy looked comparatively easy.

In every army, there are those who would commit atrocities against their fellow human beings. It is not criminal to shoot the enemy in the heat of battle. It isn't even criminal to accidentally shoot the enemy when his movements are suspect. But to shoot the enemy when he is unarmed and has surrendered, is something else.

Many massacres of prisoners of war were committed by the American 45th 'ThunderbirdDivision' during the invasion of Sicily in 1943. At Comise airfield, a truck load of German prisoners were machine-gunned as they climbed down on to the tarmac, prior to be air-lifted out. Later the same day, 60 Italian prisoners were cut down the same way. On July 14th, thirty six prisoners were gunned down near Gela by their guard, US Sergeant Barry West. At Buttera airfield, US Captain Jerry Compton, lined up his 43 prisoners against a wall and machine-gunned them to death. West and Compton were both arrested and convicted of murder. They were then sent to the front where both were later killed in action. I can't help but wonder if they were 'executed' at the front by shots from behind them. On April 29th, 1945, units of the 45th liberated the concentration camp of Dachau where more atrocities were committed by members of some of these units. What follows is what happened at that camp when soldiers of the 45th arrived at that camp.

When the war was in its final days, the Dachau Concentration Camp, near Munich, was liberated by US forces on the 29th of April, 1945. First to enter the camp and confront the horror within was Private First Class John Degro, the lead scout of I Company, 3rd Battalion, 157 Infantry Regiment, 45th Division of the 7th Army. Prior to entering the camp, the troops had come upon a train of thirty nine cattle trucks parked just outside the camp. The train had come from Auschwitz in Poland after a journey of thirty days. The trucks were filled with the corpses of 2,310 Hungarian and Polish Jews who had died from hunger and thirst. Enraged, the Americans rounded up most of the SS guard complement of 560 men, hundreds of whom had already deserted. Included in the round-up was a detachment from the 5th SS Panzer 'Viking Division' sent to Dachau earlier to maintain security and replace those who had deserted. Guarded by angry GIs, they were lined up against a wall to await the appearance of their commander, SS Obersturmfüher Heindrich Skodzensky. When he appeared, dressed immaculately with polished boots, and giving the military salute, which was ignored by the US company commander, Lt.William Jackson ordered "Line this piece of shit up with the rest of 'em over there." The GIs lost control and began shouting "Kill em, kill em." Filled with murderous rage and with tears streaming down his face, one of the GIs of the 15th Infantry Regiment, US 45th Division, opened fire with his machine-gun. After three bursts of raking fire by him and his fellow GIs, a total of 122 SS men lay dead or dying along the base of the wall. A few of the camp inmates, dressed in the familiar striped clothing and armed with .45 caliber pistols, then walked along the line of dead and dying guards and administered the coup de grace to those still alive. Forty other guards were killed by revengeful inmates, some having their arms and legs torn from their torsos.

At another site near the SS hospital, 346 German guards were machine gunned to death on the orders of 1st Lt. Bushyhead, the executive Officer of I Company, 3rd Battalion. Altogether, a total of 520 persons, acting as camp guards, and including many Hungarians in German uniforms, recently returned from the Eastern Front, were also executed that day. The sad fact is that many of these guards were new arrivals at the camp and were not the real culprits, the truly guilty had already fled.

I can understand the inmates wreaking their vengence on the dying SS guards but there is no justification on the part of the Americans to have done this.

On the same day that the Dachau Concentration Camp was discovered, a massacre took place in the little hamlet of Webling, about ten kilometres from the camp. A Waffen-SS unit had arrived at the hamlet, which consisted of about half a dozen farm houses and barns, to take up defensive positions in trenches dug around the farms. Their orders were to delay the advance of the American tanks and infantry of the 7th US Army which was approaching Dachau. The farms, mostly run by women with the help of French POWs, came under fire on the morning of 29th of April causing all inhabitants to rush for the cellars. One soldier of the US 222nd Infantry Regiment of the 42nd 'Rainbow Division', was killed as they entered the hamlet under fire from the Waffen-SS unit. The first German to emerge from the cellar was the owner of the farm, Herr Furtmayer. He was promptly shot dead. Informed by the French POWs that only civilians were in hiding, the GIs proceeded to round up the men of the SS unit. First to surrender was an officer, Freiherr von Truchsess, heading a detachment of seventeen men. The officer was immediately struck with a trenching tool splitting his head open. The other seventeen were lined up in the farmyard and shot. On a slight rise behind the hamlet, another group of eight SS were shot. Their bodies were found lying in a straight line with their weapons and ammunition belts neatly laid on the ground. This would suggest that the men were shot after they surrendered. Altogether, one SS officer and forty one men lay dead as the infantry regiment proceeded on their way to Dachau. Next day the local people, with the help of the French POWs, buried the bodies in a field to be later exhumed by the German War Graves Commission and returned to their families.

Hitler was well aware of course of the changes that were taking place in his part of the world. The political demand for unconditional surrender formulated by President Roosevelt and Prime Minister Churchill at the Casablanca conference had been made.

The new Italian government under Marshall Badoglio was naturally anxious to see if more favourable conditions could be obtained in negotiations with the Allied governments but found that it was difficult to get in touch with them. The British and American ministers at the Vatican were an obvious channel and easily accessible but proved useless owing to an extraordinary double case of official shortsightedness as Badoglio's account reveals. He said in his memoirs;

"The British minister informed us that unfortunately his secret code was very old and almost certainly known to the Germans and that he could not advise us to use it for a secret communication to his government."

The American charge d'affaires advised that he had not got a secret code so the Italians had to wait until mid August before they found a plausible pretext for sending an envoy to a visit to Portugal where he could meet British and American representatives. Even then, this round about way of negotiation entailed further delay in settling the matter.

Hitler wasted no time in taking steps to counter the likelihood that new Italian government would seek peace and abandon its alliance with Germany. On that date, he assembled his troops in the Alps and prepared for a possible entry into Italy. Fearing that the Italians might make a sudden move to block the alpine passes with the help of Allied parachute troops, Field Marshall Rommel gave orders on July 30th for the leading Germans to cross across the frontier and occupy the alpine passes. The Italians protested and for a moment threatened to resist the passage but hesitated to open fire and precipitate a conflict with their former Allies. The German infiltration was then extended on the pretext of relieving the Italians of the burden of defending the northern part of their country so that they could reinforce the south where it was manifest that the Allies were likely to land at any moment. Strategically this argument was so reasonable that the Italian chiefs could hardly reject it without showing their own intentions to change sides so by the beginning of September, German divisions under Rommel were established inside Italy's alpine frontier wall as a potential support or reinforcement to Kesselring's forces in the south.

At that same time, the Italian representatives secretly signed the armistice treaty with the Allies but it was agreed that the facts should be kept quite until the Allies made their second and principal landing which was planned to take place on the shin of Italy at Salerno, thirty miles (48.2 km) south of Naples.

On September 3rd 1943, the Allied invasion of Italy was opened by Montgomery's British 8th Army by crossing the narrow straits of Messina from Sicily and landing on the toe of Italy. The Canadians were seconded to the 8th and were also involved in that attack. Field Marshall Montgomery had very little difficulty attacking the toe of Italy.

The assault landing was mounted with Montgomery's habitual carefulness and thoroughness. Nearly six hundred long-range guns were assembled under the command of the 30th Corps where from the Sicilian shore; they provided an overwhelming barrage to cover the crossing of the straits and landings on the beaches near Reggio which were carried out by General Miles Dempsy's 13th Corps. The process of assembling this massive artillery delayed the assault for days from the intended date. The bombardment was further increased however by the fire from 120 navel guns.

During the previous days, intelligence reports showed that the Germans had left not more than two infantry battalions at the toe of Italy and even these were posted over ten miles back from the beaches to cover the roads leading up the peninsula. This makes me wonder why there was a tremendous waste of ammunition, firing on beaches which had been abandoned by now.

At 4:30 a.m., on September 3rd, two Canadian divisions employed an assault on the Italian beaches with the British 8th Army and the first Canadian landed on empty beaches devoid even of mines and barbed wire. The Canadians did record however that the stiffest resistance of the day came from a puma which escaped from the zoological gardens in the city of Reggio di Calabria and was seemingly taking a fancy to the Brigadier Commander. No casualties were suffered among the assaulting infantry. By evening, the toe of the peninsula had been occupied to the depth of more than five miles without meeting resistance. Three German stragglers and 3,000 Italian soldiers had been picked up as prisoners. The Italian prisoners readily volunteered to help unload the British landing craft. No serious resistance was met in the days that followed as the invaders pushed up the toe and there were only brief contacts with enemy rear guards but numerous demolitions which the Germans skillfully executed in withdrawing imposed repeated checks on the 8th Army's advance. By September 6th, the fourth day, it was barely 30 miles beyond the beaches where it had landed and it did not reach the toe joint, the narrowest part of the peninsula until the 10th. That was less than one third of the distance to Salerno.

The city of Reggio vies with Crotone for the distinction of being the ugliest city in the province of Calabria. Totally rebuilt after the 1908 earthquake, the city with narrow streets and drab buildings has little distinctive characteristics and some say with tongue in cheek that the two ferries linking Reggio to Messina in Sicily are the best sights in downtown Reggio. It's doubtful that the Allied soldiers were very anxious to hang about too long in that city. Unfortunately while there, they wouldn't have even had the time to swim at the sandy beaches nearby which were to the east at the underside of the toe of Italy.

By September 8th, the 5th Division of the British 8th Army had reached the town of Pizzo situated on the shores of the Tyrrhenian Sea, approximately 85 kilometers (53 miles) up the west coast from Reggio

Immediately before midnight on September 8th, the Anglo/American 5th Army under General Mark Clarke began to disembark in the gulf of Salerno a few hours after the BBC had broadcast the official announcement of Italy's capitulation. The Italian leaders had not been expecting the landing to come so soon and they were warned about the delivery of the broadcast only late in the afternoon. Badoglio complained with some justification. He said he was caught unready to cooperate before his preparations were complete but the Italian state of unreadiness and trepidation had already become so evident to General Maxwell Taylor who had been sent to Rome secretly by General Ike Eisenhower that the airborne descent on Rome had been canceled after Eisenhower had received that morning, a warning message from Taylor that the prospects of success were poor. It was then too late to revert to the original plan of dropping Ridgeway's troops along the Volturno river on the north side of Naples to block enemy reinforcements from moving southward towards Salerno.

The invaders reached the shores at Salerno at 3:30 in the morning of the 9th of September and that was done after the BBC had broadcast the official announcement of Italy's capitulation the previous evening. The broadcast of the Italian capitulation also took the Germans by surprise but their action in Rome was prompt and decisive despite the simultaneous emergency in the south produced by the landing at Salarno. The outcome might have been different if Italian action had matched Italian acting which had gone a long way to conceal intentions and lull Kesselring's suspicions during the preceding days. Field Marshall Kesselring signaled to all subordinate commands the code word axis the pre arranged signal which meant that Italy had quit at the axis and that appropriate action must be taken to disarm the Italians immediately. Subordinate commands applied a mixture of persuasion and force according to the situation and their own disposition. In the Rome area where the potential odds against them were heavy, General Student used shock tactics. He said later, "I made an attempt to seize the Italian General headquarters by dropping on it from the air but this was only partially successful." While 30 generals and 150 other officers were captured in one part of the headquarters, another part held out. The Chief of the general staff got away after Badoglio and the king escaped the night before. Instead of trying to overcome General Students couple of divisions the Italian commanders hastened to withdraw out of reach falling back eastward to Tivoli with their forces and leaving their capital in the hands of the Germans. That also cleared the way for negotiations at which Kesselring applied a more gentle form of persuasion proposing that if the Italian troops laid down their arms they should be allowed to go back to their homes immediately. That offer was contrary to Hitler's order that all Italians soldiers should made prisoners but it proved more effective at less cost of life in time to do it Kesselring's way.

The attack on the beaches of Salerno was preceded by intense bombardment from the large U.S. naval warships standing off shore. The troops wading ashore expected to be unopposed but instead, they were almost forced back into the sea and they would have been if it weren't for the fact that the German forces were to weak to do just that. To begin with, the Allied forces were spread far too thin along the coastal shores. When the landings were completed, it didn't help the Allied cause that their tanks and large army trucks coming ashore would never be able to navigate through the Old Town narrow streets of Salerno which go as far back as the Middle Ages.

On the same day as the invasion of Salerno, the first airborne Division of the 8th army was attacking Taranto (named after the Tarantula spiders that inhabit that area of Italy) which is at the heel of Italy.

The days that followed the Allied landing at Salerno were a period of intense strain on the Germans and all the more nerve-wracking through lack of information as to what was happening there. It was fortunate for the Germans that the main Allied landing came in the area that they had expected, where Kesselring could most conveniently concentrate his scanty forces to meet it. The British 8th army's advance up the toe of Italy also came about according to expectations but was too far away from Salerno to bring immediate danger to the German forces in the area of Salerno. Kesselring benefited much from the Allied commanders reluctance to venture outside the limits of air cover and in his calculations he was able to rely on their consistency in observing such conventional limitations. As a result, the Allied landings at Salerno, optimistically styled *Operation Avalanche*, suffered from that costly mistake on the part of Montgomery. Indeed General Mark Clarke later spoke of it as a near disaster. On September 10th, the American 46th Division finally captured Salerno but the Germans were well reinforced by now and they began beating the Allies in some areas of the coast, almost back to the beaches. Only by a narrow margin did the landing force hold off the German counter attack and avoid being driven back into the sea.

By the 14th, the 1stCanadian Division with the 13th British Corps arrived at the city of Corigliano Calabro, which is situated just behind the ball of the foot of Italy on the east side of the Gulf of Taranto after having proceeded along the bottom of the foot of Italy for almost a week and during that trek, passing by the beautiful sandy beaches along the route.

Hitler had considered Salerno as the centre of gravity. Kesselring's two other divisions were held in reserve near Rome ready to seize control of the capital and keep open the tense army line of retreat in the event of battalion treachery. The six divisions of the south comprised those divisions newly arrived in Italy, the 16th and 26th Panzer and the four divisions which had escaped from Sicily. Two of these four were depleted by having to leave much or their ordinance. The Herman Goering and the 15th Panzer Grenadier had been brought back to the Naples area to refit and the first parachute went to Apulia while the 29th 'Panzer Grenadier' to be left in the toe of Italy facing Montgomery. To help keep him in check, the 26th Panzer group which had arrived without any tanks was temporarily sent to Calabria. The 16th 'Panzer Division', the best armed of the batch was posted to cover the Gulf of Salerno, the most likely sector for a large landing. There, they could be quickly reinforced there by other divisions if necessary. Even so, it comprised only of one tank battalion and four infantry battalions although it was strong in artillery. That was nevertheless a slender force to meet the armada which was sailing toward the gulf of Salerno. Some seven hundred ships and landing crafts carrying some 55,000 troops for the initial landing and a further 115,000 for the follow-up.

The soldiers of Mark Clarke's army reached the beaches in the area of Salerno at 3:30 am on September 8th. There was heavy fire from the German divisions on the immediate area of Salerno. By the 15th of the month, the American and British finally made a foothold in that part of Italy. And there was a lull on the 15th while the Germans were reorganizing their shell and bomb battered units for a fresh effort with the aid of some reinforcements.

The American and British navies had certainly contributed a great deal toward the onslaught against the German forces. Naval gun fire had fired 15-inch shells dozens of miles inland which had a shattering effect both physically and morally on the German defenders. The Germans fired their new fx 1400 radio guided gliding bombs and got one of them into one of the warships which was disabled as a result. They had previously fired one of those radio guided gliding bombs into the Italian flagship *Roma* which was attempting to join the Allied navies. It is evident that once the German effort to control the invaders back into the sea had been curbed, the German withdrawal from Salerno became inevitable. For although Kesselring had striven to exploit the opportunity allowed by what he termed Montgomery's 'very cautious advance', it was clear that he could not hang onto this stretch of the mid-Italian west coast when the British army arrived on the scene. The British troops heading northward would inevitably outflank his position by advancing towards him after emerging from the narrow Calabrian Peninsula. Kesselring had far too few troops to cover such a widening front.

Mark Clarke's 5th Army had been slowly pushing forward from Salerno up the west coast and trying to force the withdrawal of the German 10th Army. The first stage was the stickiest as the German right wing hung on stubbornly to the hill barrier north of Salerno to cover the withdrawal of the left wing as it wheeled back from the southerly coastal stretch. Nearly a week passed after the beginning of that German withdrawal before the British 10th Corps on September 23rd, developed a successful offensive to force a passage from Salerno to Naples.

The 5th Army had taken three weeks since the landing at Salerno to reach Naples, its initial objective at the cost of nearly 12,000 casualties—7,000 British and 5,000 American. That was the penalty paid for choosing a too obvious line of attack in place of landing at the sacrifice of surprise on the ground at the Salerno sector was just within the limit of air cover. Another week passed before the 5th Army closed up to the line of the Volturno River to which the Germans had withdrawn. Muddy roads and sodden ground put a brake on the advances of the Allies. Rainy weather had set in during the first week of October, one month earlier than expected. Bad weather combined with the demolition of materiel by the Germans delayed the 5th Army's attack for a further 3 weeks until November 5th and then the Germans resistance proved so tough that after 10 days of struggling, with little progress except on the coastal flank, Mark Clarke was forced to pull back his weary troops and reorganize them for a stronger effort. The new push was not ready for launching until the first week of December. The 5th army losses by mid November had risen to 22,000 of which nearly 12,000 were Americans, the remainder being British.

During these long pauses in the battle of Italy, Hitler's view changed in a way that was of a far reaching effect. Encouraged by the slowness of the Allied advance from Salerno, he had come to feel that it might not be necessary to withdraw his forces to northern Italy and on October 4th, he issued a directive that the line was to be held while promising Kesselring that three divisions from Rommel's Army Group B in northern Italy would be sent to help him in holding on south of Rome as long as possible. Hitler was becoming more inclined to favour Kesselring's case for a prolonged stand but it was not until November 21st, that Hitler definitely committed himself to this course of action by putting all the German forces in Italy under Kesselring's command. Rommel's Army Group was dissolved, and its remaining troops were now at Kesselring's disposal. Even so, Kesselring still had to keep part of his forces in the north to guard and control that large area of Italy while four of his best divisions, three of them armoured, were sent to Russia and replaced by three depleted ones which needed to recuperate. By then, all of the German forces in Italy under Kesselring's command were now called Army Group C.

Meanwhile, the inmates at the Sohibor extermination camp were fighting a war of their own. The camp was in Poland and comprised primarily of Jews. They were armed with a few guns and hand-grenades stolen from the German barracks. The mutiny started in the afternoon of October 14th during an inspection of the prisoner's huts. The six hundred inmates who rose up against their guards were mainly women working in the tailor's workshop. Two hundred were shot by the guards and others died in the minefield surrounding the camp. Somewhere between 100 to 300 successfully escaped. The figure however was never really established.

On October 23rd, Jewish women were inside the room where they were undressing before being gassed in the gas chamber at Auschwitz-Bikenau in Poland. They had a small and short-lived revolt of their own. The pistol of SS Sergeant -Major Schillinger (a renown sadistic guard) was seized by one of the women who then shot him dead. The other woman mauled two other guards with their bare hands, scalping one and tearing off the nose of another. They escaped death from the gas chamber. The commandant of the camp, Rudolph Hoese was nearby and he had the women brought out the changing room, one by one where they were taken to another room after which they were immediately shot to death.

I didn't know until after the turn of the Twenty-First Century that at Auschwitz, the Jewish women and girls weren't raped because the SS men could be hanged for it. However, I don't think the feelings of the Jews was what made raping the women a capital offence. It was the fact that the Nazis considered Jews as subhuman and raping anything that was not human, such as animals was a capital offence.

On October 19th, arrangements were made between German and England for the exchange of seriously injured POWs and on October 25th, 3,694 repatriated POWs and British civilian internees arrived in England on two liners. On October 31st, the wonder drug, Penicillin began being distributed to the hospitals caring for the Allied wounded. It saved a great many lives. On November 6th, the Russian soldiers re-took their city of Kiev, the capital of the Ukraine. The battle only lasted three days. The Russians had virtually wiped out 7,000 German paratroopers dropped across the Dnieper River. The Soviets were making great advances against the Germans by now. They had 5,600 tanks compared with the German's 2,600. They had 90,000 heavy artillery against the German's 54,000. They had 8,800 against the German's 3,000. And the Russians could field 6,5 million men against Germany's 4.3 million. With odds like this, it isn't surprising that the Germans were being pushed back to their own homeland by the Russians.

Hitler by now had lost all faith in Marshall Petain as the ruler of Vichy, France so he was fired and arrested on Hitler's orders. About that same time, Churchill and Roosevelt flew to Tehran to meet Stalin. Churchill said that he wanted victory at all costs, Roosevelt said that he was looking for a post war world fashioned in the American image (which his successor, President Truman succeeded in doing when the Americans conquered Japan) however, Stalin played his cards close to his vest and didn't disclose what his intentions were.

Meanwhile, British RAF Lancashire were continuing to make its raids on Berlin, killing thousands of Berliners and making many more thousands homeless. Up to the end of November, 1943, the Allies had dropped in that year, as much as 12 thousand tons of bombs on Berlin. The city by now was almost in complete ruins. And still Hitler wasn't getting the message.

Chapter Twenty-Six

On January 22, 1944, Allied troops landed at Anzio, just 30 miles (48 km) south of Rome on the western shores of Italy. The Germans were caught by surprise and as a result, the Allies landed 36,000 troops before the Germans could do anything about it. Unfortunately, Major General Lucas, an American general in charge of the operation stopped his troops from going too far into the hinterland until his tanks were unloaded from the ships and as a result, the Allies lost the initiative to gain the advantage over the Germans. As a result of the German subsequent counter attack, the Allies remained there under siege for several months. A blunder on the part of 'No-Guts Lucas'. He was relieved of his command because of being overly cautious. In earlier times, he would have been shot for cowardice.

Perhaps this is a good time to introduce my readers to Heinrich Himmler. He was born in Munich on October 7th, 1900. His father was the son of a police president, a former tutor to the princes of the Bavarian court, and a headmaster by profession. Himmler originally intended to be a farmer and in fact acquired a degree in agronomy. He fought in World War I at the every end, and afterwards drifted into one of the many right wing soldier's organizations that were so prevalent at the time. It is here that he came into contact with Hitler. He took part in the Hitler Putsch (the attempt to overthrow the government) of 1923 as a standard-bearer. He married Margret Boden in 1926.

In 1929, Hitler appointed him head of the SS, which at that time numbered about 300 men and served mainly as a bodyguard for Hitler. A superb organizer, he had already expanded the SS to 50,000 men by 1933. He was 33 years of age when I was born that year.

By 1936, he had consolidated police power in Germany and was named Chief of the German police on June 17th of that year. With all organs of the police, especially the Gestapo (secret state police), now under his control, his power was virtually without limit other than he was answerable to Hitler only. In addition to his other responsibilities, he was also responsible for the security services (Sicherheitsdienst) and the concentration camps, which up to that time housed prisoners of the state.

Himmler's men staged the phony border incident that Hitler used to justify the invasion of Poland at the outbreak of World War II. As the war went on, the armored portions of the SS (the Waffen SS) began to rival the Armed Forces for power in the military field, culminating in Himmler's being named Minister of the Interior in 1943 and chief of the Replacement Army in 1944. Right up to the end, he was one of Hitler's most loyal men. Hitler called him "der treue Heinrich" (loyal Heinrich). At the end of the war, he didn' think Himmler was so loyal by then.

When it came time for Hitler to order the annihilation of the Jews, who better to select to carry it out than the man who was at once his most loyal follower and also in control of the apparatus necessary for its execution? And that is what Hitler did. The precise date is not known, but what is known is that Himmler obeyed the order he received with his customary thoroughness and efficiency. Interestingly enough, for a man who has been demonized as the incarnation of evil, Himmler makes it clear in several speeches that he was not particularly antisemitic. He simply blindly obeyed, displaying almost more amorality than immorality.

Whatever misgivings Himmler may have had, he carried out his orders with an efficiency and a zeal that at once astonished and repelled many who knew him. The first murders were carried out by Einsatzgruppen by shooting. As deadly as these shootings were, a more 'efficient' method had to be found, one that would accelerate the killing and would at the same time spare the SS men the necessity to murder women and children in cold blood. He made this decision when he witnessed the shooting of some Jews and one, a middle aged woman nearly fell on him after she was shot. He threw up after seeing that shooting. He decided to use poison gases (hydrocyanic acid and carbon monoxide) in both stationary and mobile gas chambers in Poland. It is estimated that around 6 million Jews were killed during the 'Final Solution', along with as many as another 6 million non-Jews.

At the end of the war, Himmler made attempts to negotiate peace through the World Jewish Congress. Attempting to flee in disguise in May 1945, he was captured by British forces and he finally admitted his identity. When a doctor was ordered to search him to ensure he did not have poison secreted on his person, he bit down on a cyanide capsule hidden in his mouth and was dead in a few minutes. Like Hitler, he chose suicide as his way to exit the world. He died at forty-four years of age. He was only in power for eleven years.

The following is from a speech given by Heinrich Himmler to about 100 SS Group Leaders in Posen, occupied Poland on October 4th 1943. As you read what he had to say, you will see the evil in his mind.

"One principle must be absolute for the SS man: we must be honest, decent, loyal and friendly to members of our blood and to no one else. What happens to the Russians, what happens to the Czechs, is a matter of utter indifference to me. Such good blood of our own kind as there may be among the nations we shall acquire for ourselves, if necessary by taking away the children and bringing them up among us. Whether the other races live in comfort or perish of hunger interests me only in so far as we need them as slaves for our culture; apart from that it does not interest me. Whether or not 10,000 Russian women collapse from exhaustion while digging a tank ditch interests me only in so far as the tank ditch is completed for Germany. We shall never be rough or heartless where it is not necessary; that is clear. We Germans, who are the only people in the world who have a decent attitude to animals, will also adopt a decent attitude to these human animals but it is a crime against our own blood to worry about them and to bring them ideals. I shall speak to you here with all frankness of a very serious subject. We shall now discuss it absolutely openly among ourselves, nevertheless we shall never speak of it in public. I mean the evacuation of the Jews, the extermination of the Jewish race. It is one of those things which is easy to say. 'The Jewish race is to be exterminated. That's clear, it's part of our program, elimination of the Jews, extermination, right, we'll do it. And then they all come along, the eighty million good Germans, and each one has his decent Jew. Of course the others are swine, but this one is a first-class Jew. Of all those who talk like this, not one has watched, not one has stood up to it. Most of you know what it means to see a hundred corpses lying together, five hundred, or a thousand. To have gone through this and yet apart from a few exceptions, examples of human weakness to have remained decent fellows, this is what has made us hard. This is a glorious page in our history that has never been written and shall never be written." *unquote*

This speech gives you some idea of how far a man will sink in human depravity when you realize that he knows that he is answerable to no one but another who is equally depraved. Let me describe some of the depravity of the German soldiers.

On March 23, 1944, (the 25th anniversary of the day Mussolini formed his Fascist Party) the 11th Company of the 3rd Battalion of the S.S. Polizei Regiment 'Bozen', consisting of 156 men, were on their regular daily march through the streets of Rome to the Macao Barracks, when they became the target of the Italian underground movement. The police company had reached the narrow Via (street) Rasella when the bomb, placed in a road sweepers cart, exploded. Twenty six SS policemen were killed instantly and sixty others wounded, two more died later. Some civilians were also killed. The German Commandant of Rome, General Kurt Malzer, drunk and shrieking for revenge, ordered the arrest of all who lived on the street. Some 200 civilians were rounded up and turned over temporarily to the Italian authorities. Hitler, on hearing of the bombing, immediately ordered that 30 Italians were to be shot for every policeman killed. This number was later reduced to 10 hostages for every policeman killed. Within twenty four hours, 335 people were loaded onto lorries and driven to a network of caves on the Via Ardeatina discovered by the Germans earlier and where the disbanded Italian army had hidden barrels of petrol and some vehicles. At 3.30 p.m. the executions started, each victim ordered to kneel and was then shot in the back of the head. They fell on the bodies of those shot before them. By 8 p.m., it was all over.

Following Germany's surrender, SS Obersturmbannfuhrer Kappler was tried for murder in a Rome Court, found guilty, and sentenced to 99 years in prison (Italy had abolished the death penalty). For years he was alone and abandoned while his wife (who had been a German nurse and was allowed to marry Kappler in 1972) appealed to the Italian government for leniency. Kappler suffered from stomach cancer, and his weight dropped radically until he was less than 100 pounds. Her appeal was for naught. In a brilliantly choreographed ploy, Frau Kappler visited her husband. She had brought some fresh clothes to him in a large suitcase. When she left the prison, guards joked about the large satchel. What they did not realize, on this night in 1976, was that inside the bag was Herbert Kappler, already in the final stages of cancer. His wife got him out and away from the prison and former colleagues of his from the SS helped smuggle him back into Germany.

The Italians made a token protest and request to Germany for his extradition, but nobody took that seriously. Herbert Kappler was greeted at a German airport by supporters and comrades. Seven months later he was dead—a free man at last.

On March 7th, 1998, former Nazi SS officers Erich Priebke and Karl Hass were sentenced to life in prison for their roles in the massacre of the 335 Italian men and boys. Priebke and Hass admitted they participated in the massacre at the Ardeatine Caves outside of Rome in 1944. Italians were outraged in 1996 when a lower court set Priebke free. That decision was later tossed out, and, in July 1997 another military court sentenced Priebke to 15 years for the massacre. Later it reduced his sentence to just five years due to mitigating circumstances. They even appealed that, hence they were sentenced again to life in prison. Ironically, it was their appeals of the earlier sentences to the higher court that led to the 1998 decision to lengthen their prison terms to life.

Priebke maintained that he executed the prisoners on orders from Nazi leader Adolf Hitler and would have been killed if he had refused. At his trial he said, "Executing the order was horrendous, a personal tragedy. If I could have avoided that horror, I would have." *unquote* But prosecutor Guiseppe Rosin told the court that Priebke and Hass deserved a life sentence because the killings were carried out with premeditation and cruelty.

In 1974, I visited the caves just outside of the southern part of Rome and which are a short distance from the famous catacombs. It gives you an eerie feeling walking through the caves. It will bring tears to your eyes as you picture in your mind the victims kneeling where those before them had been slain only minutes before, they knowing that they too, would be shot in the back of their heads. The pictures of the victims are on each of the sarcophagi. Some of the victims were only young teenagers.

Near Lille, On April 2nd, 1944, the 12th SS Panzer Division 'Hitler Jugend' set out on 24 rail trucks for Normandy to cover the coast in anticipation of an Allied landing. The convoy, under the command of SS Obersturmfuhrer Walter Hauck, was approaching the small railway station of Ascq near the town of Lille when a violent explosion blew the line apart. Stopping the train, it was found that two flat trucks had been derailed, holding up the whole convoy. Hauck, in a foul mood, ordered his men to search and arrest all male members of the houses on both sides of the track. They were assembled together and marched down the track about 300 yards (274 meters) where each man was shot in the back of the head. Altogether 70 men were shot beside the railway line and another 16 killed in the village itself.

After an investigation by the Gestapo, six more men were arrested and charged with planting the bomb. They were all executed by firing squad. When the war ended, a search for the perpetrators was set in motion. Most of the SS men were found in Allied POW camps in Europe and in England. In all, nine SS men stood trial in a French Military Court at Lille. All were sentenced to death, including Hauck. The sentences were later commuted to a period of imprisonment and Walter Hauck was released in July, 1957. Does his release represent justice in France? Was Walter Hauck one of the 'decent fellows' that Himmler spoke about in his speech? In the local cemetery at Ascq, two rows of identical tombstones, and a large plaque engraved with the names of all victims, stand in silent testimony to the tragic events of April 2nd, 1944—stark proof that their murderers were not decent fellows.

On June 9, 1944, the SS murdered 98 men in the town of Tulle in central France. This was in response to activities by the local resistance groups who had attacked and taken over the town. When the 2nd SS Division 'Das Reich' took over the town they found 40 dead bodies of the German 111./95 Security Regiment garrison troops near the school, their bodies badly mutilated. Other bodies were found around the town, bringing the total German dead in Tulle to sixty-four. Next day, the reprisals began. All males in the town were gathered together and 130 suspects were selected for execution. A number were released because of their youth and the remaining 98 were executed by the Pioneer platoon of SS-Panzer Aufklarungs Abteilung. Their bodies were hanged on lampposts and from balconies along the main streets of the town in the hope that the hanging bodies would deter future attacks by the Maquis. (French Resistance) More would have been hanged had not the SS ran out of rope. Instead, they rounded up 101 civilians and deported them to Germany for slave labour.

As this same SS Panzer Division marched towards the Normandy invasion area, arrived at the nearby town of Oradour-sur-Glane in Central France on June 10th, 1944. They were still angry at the French after having so many encounters with the local Marquis so they surrounded the village and ordered all inhabitants to parade in the market square. Once there, they were told by the Nazi commandant they were suspected of hiding explosives and as a result there would be a search and a check of identity papers. The entire population was then locked up.

Women and children were separated and locked in the local church. The men and older boys were herded in groups into local garages and barns and then shot and then their bodies were covered with straw and set on fire. The 452 women and children in the church were then killed by grenades lobbed in through the windows. The church was then set on fire after a series of explosions. Incredibly, one woman escaped by jumping through a window. Five men managed to escape also

The world heard of the massacre nine years later when some of those responsible were brought to trial. In 1953 a French Military Court established that 642 people (245 women, 207 children and 190 men) had perished. Three days after the massacre, a Catholic Bishop found the charred bodies of fifteen children in a heap behind the burned out altar inside the church. During the trial, one of the Germans testified that he remembered seeing one of the women in the church standing at the window as if waving at someone and while she stood there, her flesh was melting off of her face. The commander of the SS troops at Oradour was SS Sturmbannfuhrer Otto Diekmann. (His last name may have been Kahn as I got the information of this massacre from two different sources) He was later killed in action in the Normandy battle area. Twenty others members of his company were sentenced to death but later their sentences were commuted to terms of imprisonment. All were released by 1959. These murderers only spent six years for committing these unspeakable crimes. Today, the village of Oradour-sur-Glane stands in ruins, just as the SS left it as a silent monument to Nazi atrocities.

The sleepy French village of Izieu lies overlooking the Rhone River between Lyon and Chambery in central France. A number of refugee Jewish children, most of them orphans, were being sheltered in a home in the hope that the Nazi Gestapo would not find them. Supervised by seven adults, they felt safe and secure. However, on the morning of April 6th, 1944, as they settled down to breakfast, a car and two military trucks drove up in front of the home. The Gestapo, led by the regional head, Klaus Barbie, entered the home and forcibly removed the forty four children and their seven supervisors, throwing the crying and terrified children on to the trucks like sacks of potatoes. All were transported to the collection center at Drancy outside Paris where they were put on the first available train to 'points east'. Miron Zlatin, and two of the oldest children ended up in Tallin in Estonia where they were all shot. The others found themselves in the notorious concentration camp of Auschwitz. Of the forty-four children, aged between five and seventeen kidnapped from Izieu, not a single one survived the war. Of the supervisors there was one sole survivor, twenty-seven year old Lea Feldblum. It is a tragic fact that patriotic French citizens willingly helped the Gestapo in their search for these Jewish children. On July 3rd, 1987, Klaus Barbie was finally arrested, tried in a French court and sentenced to life imprisonment. He died of cancer in prison on September 25, 1991. The former children's home in Izieu is now a memorial-museum, opened on April 4th, 1994 by the then President of the French Republic, Francios Mitterrand.

In the small village of Frayssinet just south of Tulle, in central France, on May 21st, 1944, members of the underground shot and killed a German officer. For this crime, 15 hostages were taken and executed. These hostages were all young males from one child families. This, in the twisted minds of the SS, was to prevent any further family line of descent. Outside the entrance to the local church in Frayassinet stands a small monument mounted with a stone cross, and a plaque bearing the names of all the 15 young victims.

After the Italians surrendered on September 8th, 1943, Fascist and German troops continued their harassment of these unfortunate mountain people. As an example, about twenty kilometres (12.4 miles) south of Bologna is the massif of Monte Sole, part of the Apennine range. Around this area are dozens of small villages and towns,

Marzabotto, Sperticano, Cerpiano, San Martino, Creda and Casaglia to name but a few. Many Italians, forming themselves into small partisan groups, augmented by deserters from the Italian and German armies (ex Russian POWs) their strength grew to around 1,200 men. Calling themselves the Stella Rossa (Red Star) they confined their activities to sniping, derailing freight trains and the occasional ambush. In their efforts to subdue the Stella Rossa, the German SS often raided small villages and shot hostages. This only increased the determination of the partisans to commit more attacks on the enemy and for the Germans to shoot more hostages.

As the British and Americans fought their way north, the SS formed up for a mass attack on Monte Sole. At dawn on Friday, 29th September 1944, the SS attacked. At Creda, the SS surrounded a barn where a group of partisans were hiding. All the men, women and children of Creda, were assembled in the barn and after their valuables and money was confiscated, they were machine-gunned, grenades and incendiary bombs were thrown in and the group, about ninety, were left to burn. This scene was repeated at every tiny village and farmlet as the SS units continued their march. Soon, hundreds of fires could be seen on and around Monte Sole, each one a funeral pyre. During the three days of the Rastrellamento (September 29th to Oct 1st) a total of around 1,830 men, women and children, were brutally murdered by the SS. When the SS murder squads moved on, the killing continued as relatives of the victims, searching for the bodies of their loved ones, stepped on the deadly mines laid by the SS. Their commander, one-armed SS Major Walter Reder, an Austrian national, was later arrested by the Americans in Salzburg and handed over to the British who in turn passed him over to the Italians. In 1951, in an Italian military court in Bologna, Walter Reder was sentenced to life imprisonment at hard labour in the military prison at Gaeta.

In February 1944, Admiral Nimitz's forces advanced more than 2,000 miles from Hawaii to seize Kwajalein atoll and Eniwetok in the Marshall Islands. The next advance was some 1,200 miles to the Marianas. By mid-August Saipan, Tinian, and Guam had fallen to the Allies. New, long-range Super fortress planes (B-29s) were used to bomb Japan. Plans were made to seize the Philippines as a base for the invasion of Japan. Operation Reckless brought the Americans to Hollandia, at 800 km of their nearest base, was made on April 22nd. MacArthur surprised the Japanese. He then conquered Aitape August 5th and Sansapor July 30th.

The British with Admiral Somerville, attacked Sabang in Sumatra on April 19th. With the carrier *Illustrious*, the two escort carriers *Begum* and *Shah* and the battleships *Renown*, *Valiant* and *Queen Elizabeth*, Somerville closed in to 160 km (99 miles) off the coast of Sabang before launching its airplanes that took off guard the enemy. After conquering the Gilberts, the American admiral, Nimitz moved on to the Marshall Island. He chose to go around the well defended islands and land at Kwajalein. He landed on February 7th without too many losses. At the same time he launched attacks with his carriers on Eniwetok and Turk in the Carolines Islands. The Americans took control of Eniwetok on February 21st and still attacked the other Carolines Islands to let the Japanese think that these islands were their next targets.

Before going to the Marianas, the 5th fleet of American admiral Spruance went to Truk to make a sudden attack: As many as 200 Japanese airplanes and 137, 000 tons of ships were destroyed. American admiral Mitscher came back in February to finish the base by using the new technology of 'radar' to direct his planes in the night. By disabling Truk, Mitscher isolated completely Rabaul with its garrison of 50 000 soldiers.

June 15th, Spruance 's fleet appeared near Saipan, the largest island of the Marianas. The Americans passed over the Carolines and attacked Saipan which fell July 13th. By then, the Americans were only 2000 km (1242 miles) from Japan and were thus able to launch bomber raids on Tokyo. The Japanese had meanwhile already prepared a plan to fight back for the fall of Saipan: the combined fleet of 9 carriers, 5 battleships, 41 cruisers and destroyers and 473 airplanes on the carriers with another hundred on the land; all advanced to push back the Americans. But American submarines and planes sank 3 Japanese carriers and destroyed 411 Japanese aircraft so that the Japanese had no real aerial support. After that, the Americans were free to take Guam and Tinian and so re-conquer the Marianas.

On July 24th, 1944, the three most important Americans dealing with the Pacific War were, Roosevelt, MacArthur and Nimitz. They met at Hawaii to decide which of the following actions were to be taken. Nimitz wanted to go around the Philippines and fight the Japanese east of those islands, whereas MacArthur, and Roosevelt wanted to retake the Philippines first so that they don't have 350,000 Japanese soldiers behind them. It was decided that the two military leaders each would progress towards Mindanao (island in the South Philippines) from their respective positions—Nimitz from Saipan and MacArthur from New-Guinea. At last. MacArthur would be able to keep his word to the Philipinos. "I shall return."

Raoul Wallenberg's story begins in March of 1944, right after the German army invaded Hungary. Adolph Hitler, because of his extreme hatred of Jews, had ordered hundreds of thousands of Hungarian Jews to be deported to concentration camps and certain death. Between May 14 and July 18, 1944, more than 400,000 people from Budapest were packed into freight trains and shipped to a concentration camp in southern Poland.

When Wallenberg arrived from Sweden as a diplomat, there were only about 200,000 Jews left in Budapest. By this time, authorities were aware of the horrible acts being committed by Hitler's Nazis in concentration camps all across Europe.

Wallenberg's 'mission' (as it was known within the Swedish Government) was to do "everything in his power to ensure that the principals of humanity and justice were respected." His first task was to design a Swedish protective pass to help the Jews at greatest risk. It is reported that Wallenberg would even climb aboard boxcars filled with people and handout scores of protective passes then jump from the train and demand that those with Swedish 'protection' be allowed off the trains. However, it was clear that he could not issue enough passes to protect all the people who were in danger. So he helped establish international 'safe houses' where individuals were protected from deportation. By November of 1944, through the efforts of Wallenberg and others, there were 72 buildings in Budapest assigned to house Jews.

After the Russians had captured Budapest, Wallenberg was requested to go to the Soviet army headquarters. He had been warned about the great risk he was taking by going there. The Russians did not share the same views about his 'mission'. They also suspected Wallenberg of being an American spy and were skeptical of his contact with Germans. Yet Wallenberg found it necessary to explain his rescue mission to the Soviets and earn their support. On January 17th, 1945, Wallenberg and his driver left Budapest by car with a Soviet motorcycle escort to meet with Soviet officers in eastern Hungary. Neither Wallenberg nor his driver has ever been seen in public again.

The Soviets claim that Wallenberg died of a heart attack in prison on July 17th, 1947. Yet there have been many reliable reports that he was seen alive well into the 1970's. His fate is a mystery even today. Raoul Wallenberg was 34 years old when he was captured. If he were still alive in 2003, he would have been the same age as my mother when she died at the age of ninety during that year. Indeed, it is a sad irony that the man who freed so many had become a lifelong prisoner himself.

There have been many tributes to this great man. In 1996, The U.S. Postal Service unveiled a stamp honoring Wallenberg. At that time, Representative Thomas Lantos, the only survivor of a Nazi concentration camp ever elected to Congress, said, "In this age devoid of heroes, Wallenberg is the archetype of a hero – one who risked his life day in and day out, to save the lives of tens of thousands of people he did not know, whose religion he did not share." *unquote*

In April 8th, 1944, Soviet troops began an offensive to liberate the Crimea. Located in southern Ukraine, the Crimean peninsula juts into the Black Sea and connects to the mainland by a narrow strip of land at Perekop. Dry steppes cover more than two-thirds of the peninsula, and the Crimean mountains in the south rise up to 1,500 m. (5,000 ft.) before they drop down sharply to the Black Sea. The southern coast, protected by the mountains, has a mild climate. The Arabat Spit, which is a sand bar (110 km long) that extends northeast from the Kerch peninsula, separates the marshy Sivash Sea from the Sea of Azov. The Crimea covers an area of 27,000 square kilometers.

On May 9th, 1944, the Soviet troops recaptured Sevastopol, the major city in the Crimea. By the 10th, the German forces (half German and the other half Rumanian) were being pushed out of the Crimea. As many as 30,000 enemy troops surrendered to the Soviets on the 10th. By the 12th, the Crimea was in the hands of the Soviets.

For a final effort against the Gustav Line, Field Marshal Alexander decided to shift most of the 8th Army, now commanded by Major General Sir Oliver Leese, from the Adriatic flank of the peninsula to the west, where it was to strengthen the 5th Army's pressure around Monte Cassino and on the approaches to the valley of the Liri (headstream of the Garigliano). The combined attack, which was started in the night of May 11/12, 1944, succeeded in breaching the German defenses at a number of points between Cassino and the coast. Thanks to this victory, the Americans could push forward up the coast, while the British entered the valley and outflanked Monte Cassino.

The fortified town called Monte Cassino which is situated at the foot of a steep hill called Monastery Hill of which the 6th-century Benedictine abbey was located. From January until March of 1943, the Allies tried to capture the hill. The Germans had previously promised the Vatican that they would not enter the huge structure. Now comes one of those strange ironies in the war. The Germans had kept their word but General Freyberg, a New Zealand commander (another fool in the war) convinced Field Marshal Alexander that the only way to capture the hill was to bomb the abbey. Now anyone that has any knowledge of warfare knows that it is harder to attack the enemy in ruins than if structures are left unharmed and the American general,

Mark Clark realized this and counseled against bombing the abbey but it was bombed anyway. Guess what? There were no Germans in the abbey when it was being bombed. Weren't they fortunate indeed? The many Italian citizens of the area who sought refuge in the Abbey were not so fortunate. When the bombing ceased a few days later, the abbey was in ruins and the Germans realizing the opportunities available to them by defending the ruins, took advantage of the bombing of the Abbey and entered the abbey's ruins and took up defensive positions there. It was the Poles that finally took the abbey at a terrible cost. Isn't it interesting to note that all blunders in wars are brought about by the fools who hold the rank of generals and above.

Five days later, the Allies' force at Anzio struck out against the investing Germans (whose strength had been diminished in order to reinforce the Gustav Line); and by May 26 it had achieved a breakthrough. When the 8th Army's Canadian Corps penetrated the last German defenses in the Liri Valley, the whole Gustav Line began to collapse.

On June 5th, 1944, the Allies marched into Rome. In August of 1943, the new leader of Italy had ordered that Rome was to be considered an 'open city' thus sparing the 'Eternal City' from the ravages of war that had destroyed so many other historical cities in Europe so the entry was more or less uncontested when Field Marshal Kesselring forces retreated 150 miles (241 km) north of Rome to a location near the city of Pisa close to the western shores of Italy.

Mussolini had been held in custody by Italian police officers after his downfall but on September 12th, 1944, he was rescued by hand-picked German paratroopers who landed on a hillside in northern Italy and snatched him from his captors who were holding him at the Campo Imperiale Hotel. The leader of the paratroopers was a SS Captain Otto Skorzeny who later wrote a book about his exploits during the war. On September 18th, Mussolini, with the backing of Hitler, announced that he was going to form a new fascist regime at the city of Gargnano on Lake Garda in northern Italy. (I visited that lake in 1985. It's a beautiful lake surrounded by low mountains).

Born in 1868, Miklós Horthy was the regent of Hungary between 1920 and 1944. He was the military leader of the 'White Terror' of 1919, a counterrevolutionary campaign against the socialist regime of Béla Kun. After the occupying Romanians were evacuated, Horthy became regent of Hungary on March 1st, 1920. Foreign and domestic policies between the wars were motivated by a fervent desire to recover territories the country had lost in the Trianon settlement of 1920.

Although Horthy authorized a series of harsh anti-Jewish laws, he resisted Hitler's pressure to ban Jews from all economic activities, to gather Jews into ghettos or to deport Jews to camps.

After German forces occupied Hungary in March, 1944, Horthy nominated a pro-German government that was given total control of anti-Jewish measures. On July 7th, after half a million Jews had been deported and under pressure from Allied countries such as Sweden and the United States, Horthy ordered that the deportation of Jews stop.

When Horthy attempted a separate armistice for Hungary on October 15th, 1944, he was ousted and replaced by Ferenc Szálasi. After the war, the allies allowed Horthy to go to Portugal. He died in 1957. Szalasi wasn't so fortunate as Horthy. Szálasi was the leader of the Hungarian fascist Arrow Cross party. On October 15th, 1944, he replaced Horthy as head of state with the help of the Germans. Szálasi's brutal and murderous regime lasted until the end of the war. When the war ended, he was captured by the Americans and extradited to Hungary. Found guilty of war crimes and crimes against the people, he was executed on March 12th, 1946 by the Hungarian people.

Chapter Twenty-Seven

My father wasn't in the active war very long. He left Canada for England on December 10th of 1942 and then left England for the Suez on February 27th 1944 and served in the Middle East and flew 28 sorties with the 148th Squadron. On his 28th sortie, his plane crashed and he suffered a slight spinal injury.

He returned to England as a sergeant and flight engineer. He was hospitalized because of his back injury. He was then sent back to Canada on June 27th, 1944 and although he was officially discharged from the air force on December 19th 1944, he was permitted to return home earlier. All told, he served four years and three months in the RCAF. He would have normally had to finish out the war but because of his injuries, he was released earlier.

Sometime during the summer of 1944, my father wrote my mother and told her that he would arrive in Wells on a particular day. For three days in a row, we waited for him at the bus stop at the Esso gas station on Pooley Street. The bus really wasn't a bus of course. It was a rundown limousine that could carry eight passengers. In any case, he finally arrived on the third day. Needless to say, we were all excited—that is, my brother and I. On the other hand, my mother was not feeling the same way that my brother and I did. I didn't learn until many years later why she wasn't that excited at the prospects of my father coming to Wells to live with us.

My mother sent me an audio tape in the 1980s in which she talked about her life from 1932 to 1946. She said in the tape that my father almost didn't come to Wells after the war. In one of those strange coincidences that occur every once in a while, my Aunt Althea, happened to be getting off the boat in Squamish (the small town at the northern tip of Howe Sound which is 54 km (33.5 miles) north of Vancouver) to catch the PGE train heading north towards Wells and she saw my father getting off of the train that had traveled south from the direction of Wells to meet the boat in Squamish. He told my aunt that he had been heading towards Wells but had changed his mind and was going back to Toronto. I never learned just how far north towards Wells he had gone on the train before he decided not to proceed to Wells. My aunt talked him into getting back on the train and going to Wells and before he got on the train with my aunt, she sent a telegram to my mother in Wells, telling her that she had a hard time trying to talk my father into going to Wells but he promised that he would go there. All the time my brother and I were waiting for him at the limo stop in Wells, we had no idea that his original plan was not to come to Wells and see his family. It is beyond my understanding as to why a man who had been away from his family for so long, would cross Canada and perhaps be only a short distance from them and then turn around and head back to where he started out from. But then, that was the kind of creep he was so I guess I shouldn't be surprised. In any case, he finally arrived and naturally, I was excited. He called me Gail (my brother's name at that time) because the last time he saw me, I was a bit bigger than my brother when he saw me in Lethbridge years earlier. Dale was seven by then and I was ten so I could see why he was confused.

    We were still living in our second home on Burnett Avenue at the base of Island Mountain at that time. Within days, through the efforts of my mother who was friends with the wife of the mine's superintendent, he got a job as an assistant electrician in the Island Mountain Mine that was about a kilometer from our house. That mine and two other mines in the area finally closed down in 1967 although there were prospectors still out there searching for more gold long after we all left Wells.

One day, my mother and father were talking at the table and I heard them discussing one of the strangest things I have ever heard. As mentioned earlier, while my father was in Egypt, his bomber crashed in the desert. When he began crawling out of the plane, he heard a voice behind him and turned to face whoever was calling him. Then he passed out and woke up in a hospital in Cairo. My mother's face went white. She ran into their bedroom and pulled out her diary. She brought it to the kitchen and began reading from it. When she finished reading from three pages, even my face went white. It seems that she had a dream that his plane crashed and that she was inside the plane when he began crawling from it. She called him and he turned around and faced her. Then she woke up. She had this same dream three nights in a row. What was incredible was that she began having these dreams three nights before his plane actually crashed.

I learned of another strange event similar to that of my parents from a black lady I met in the 1970s. She was living in Toronto when she had a dream one night that her aunt had died and she was visiting her aunt in the funeral home nearby. This part of the dream didn't seem strange to her because she knew her aunt was near death anyhow and plans had been made ahead of time to have her taken to that particular funeral home after she died. What was strange however was that she also dreamed that when she visited the funeral home that night, it was lit up only by candles and not electric lights. When she showed up the following night to visit her aunt at the funeral home, it was lit up only by candles. Apparently, that afternoon and night (November 9, 1965) the 'Great Blackout' touched some 30 million people over an area of 80 thousand square miles from eastern Ontario through New York State and much of New England for periods ranging from a few minutes to 13 hours.

One day in July 2000, a neighbour of mine told me of a dream he had in which he dreamed of an event which came about the next day. His dream was that he was applying for a job and when he entered the building, he found himself inside a cave and that he was interviewed by a thin bald Irishman. The next day, he entered the building of the company he was to go into for the job interview and the foyer of the building was undergoing renovations and he entered through a tent-like area which had no lights in it. After he got off the elevator, he was greeted by his interviewer who was a thin Irishman with very little hair on his head.

He told me of another dream he had in which he dreamed of his mother lying on a gurney in the hallway of a hospital with her belly ballooning up. Several months later, his mother was in the hospital lying on a gurney in a hallway, waiting to be wheeled into an operating room where a fibroid tumor the size of a grapefruit was to be removed.

How my mother and the black lady and my neighbour foresaw these happenings in their dreams before they occurred is beyond any explanation I can give you. However it does raise the specter that possibly, everything of our future is already pre-ordained to happen and that these three people had precognitive powers and what they saw in their dreams was a look into what was actually going to happen in the future and what in fact did happen in the future.

I don't know if I have precognitive powers but I remember one morning in July 2000 at 7:00 I was dreaming that I was getting dressed to go see my wife who in my dream had died earlier and was resting in a funeral home and my friends were assisting me putting on a shirt. I immediately woke up and my wife who was getting dressed at that time then told me that she would be late for supper as she was going to a funeral home with a friend who lost a loved one. I am more inclined to believe that probably what happened in this instance is that my wife was thinking of the funeral home and I picked up her thoughts as radio frequencies while I was dreaming.

Now one could say that what happened that morning was pure coincidence. But if so, what are the odds of two people thinking about funerals at the same time? For example, the human mind processes approximately 70,000 different thoughts in a 24-hour period. Between us, we had processed 140,000 thoughts in a 24-hour period. The odds of us thinking of funerals at the same time are 490 million to one and when you think of all the same things we could have been thinking about, the odds are increased by countless billions.

Apparently, this phenomenon about radio frequencies emanating form human brains is recognized by scientists as being very common between couples. Often both are thinking of phoning the other at work or at home at the same time, irrespective of the distances between them. Our brains have electrical current in them so it follows that there is truth in that old saying that minds often think alike because radio signals are sent out and picked up by humans. As impossible as this may appear to us, one has to consider what other alternative answer is there to consider. I can't think of any other possibility and I have ruled out co-incidence as that is far too remote.

The famous inventor, Nikola Telsa who invented the rotating magnetic field which is the basis of alternating current, believed that we as human beings had high frequency radio waves in our brains and that with those to whom we are close; we could be tuned into one another on the same frequency. On the night his mother died, he was asleep a great many miles away and he dreamed that he saw her as an angel in a cloud. The next morning, he learned that his mother had died.

One day my mother dreamed that my maternal grandmother was walking down the beach next to my mother's home in Hawaii. My mother got up and walked to the window and called out to my grandmother. My stepfather awoke and called out to my mother. She suddenly became wide awake and she told my stepfather that she dreamed that her mother was walking away from her on the beach. She said that she thought her mother had died. My uncle called my mother the next morning to tell my mother that their mother had died several hours earlier. My grandmother died in St. Catherine's, Ontario, many thousands of miles away at the same time that my mother had her dream.

When my maternal aunt's husband, Harold was in a hospital in Vancouver, my mother and aunt visited him. Just after the visit, they were getting out of the elevator and my mother turned to her sister and said, "Althea. You had better return to Harold. I think he's dying." They returned to his room and Harold had died just seconds before they arrived.

After my Aunt Althea had visited my wife and me in Toronto for a few days, I drove her to the airport. As I and my wife were heading home, I had the distinct feeling that someone was asking me to return to the airport. I immediately returned and looked for my aunt. I found her. She was waiting in a long line. It was the wrong line. I took her to the right one. Later she told me that she kept wishing I was there with her because she wasn't sure if she was in the right line.

When our oldest daughter, Sarah was about four months old, I was driving to work one day and about ten minutes later, I thought I heard my wife, Ayako calling out to me. But that was impossible but mindful of my belief that my father had called out to my mother when he was Egypt years earlier (albeit three days before his plane crashed) I turned about and headed back home. I no sooner arrived at my front door when I saw Ayako carrying Sarah in her arms. Apparently Sarah had fallen down the stairs and was unconscious. I immediately drove them to the hospital. Ayako later told me that while she was at the bottom of the stairs trying to bring Sarah around, she kept wishing I was there with her.

One of my clients told me an interesting story in December 2001 about he and his twin sister. He was living in Toronto and she was living in Lebanon. At 4:00 p.m., in the afternoon of one day in March 1995, he was in his bathtub when all of a sudden, he felt himself slipping under the water for no reason and before his girlfriend could come in and rescue him, he went unconscious. She pulled him out of the water and he survived the mishap. As soon as he got out of the bathtub, his phone rang and his mother in Lebanon was on the phone telling him that his twin sister had just been hit by a car and was taken to the hospital unconscious. What is equally strange about this event is that their father had decided to take a different route home that day and he arrived on the same street that his daughter was crossing and when his daughter was hit by another car, she flew into the air and landed directly in front of her father's car. She like her twin brother, also survived the mishap.

If Nikola Telsa had lived long enough, no doubt he would have discovered how this all comes about.

Emanuel Swedenborg, (1666—1772) the great eighteenth-century mathematician and scientist apparently developed in his later years, a supernormal perceptive gift. At six-o'clock one evening, while dining with friends in the town of Gothenburg, Swedenborg suddenly got excited and stated that a dangerous fire had broken out in his native city of Stockholm some three hundred miles (483 km) away. A little later he told his guests that the fire had burned the home of one of his neighbours and was threatening to consume his own home. A bit later in the evening, he told his guests that the fired had been checked three doors from his home. Two days later, his statements were confirmed.

Swedenborg's case is only one among hundreds of similar instances recorded in history and in the biographies of the great, the near-great and the obscure. At some times in their lives, Mark Twain, Abraham Lincoln, Saint-Saens, to name a few, had, according to their biographers or by their own accounts, strange sudden visions of events taking place far away or near, or events that took place or events about to take place later in their lives. I believe that this is not an unusual phenomena but a common occurrence among human beings.

A study conducted in the year 2002, showed that 40 percent of Canadians that were asked, believe that that some people have special abilities to predict the future.

Having my father back home at first seemed to me and my brother a happy experience for us because it was the first time in our two lives that our father had actually lived with us for an extended period of time. Of course my mother was really not sure if he was going to desert us again so she may have felt uneasy during the months that followed after he arrived in Wells.

However, he still had his job at the mine and he seemed happy with that job and he had become friends with a number of the men working in the Island Mountain Mine.

Little did I know during June of 1944, that in the summer of the following year, my father would not only desert us again (and this time permanently) but he would also do something to me that no father should ever do to his child. My life as a child was going to change for the worse by the time the end of 1945 arrived. I will tell my readers how that came about in Volume Two of *Whistling in the Face of Robbers*.